Religion

& Science

Religion & Science

History, Method, Dialogue

Edited by W. Mark Richardson

and Wesley J. Wildman

ROUTLEDGE

NEW YORK & LONDON

Published in 1996 by

Routledge
29 West 35th Street
New York, NY 10001

Published in Great Britain in 1996 by

Routledge
11 New Fetter Lane
London EC4P 4EE

Printed in the United States of America
Design and typography: Jack Donner

Library of Congress Cataloging-in-Publication Data

Religion and science : history, method, dialogue
edited by W. Mark Richardson and Wesley J. Wildman
p.   cm.
Includes bibliographical references.
ISBN 0-415-91666-6 (cloth: alk. paper)
ISBN 0-415-91667-4 (pbk.: alk. paper)

1. Religion and science. 2. Religion and science — History.
3. Religion and science — Methodology.

I. Richardson, W. Mark, 1949–
II. Wildman, Wesley J., 1961–

BL240.2.R43 1996
261.5'5—dc 20   95–47045
CIP

CONTENTS

PART II: METHOD

Introduction   84

ROUND I

ROUND II

PART III: DIALOGUE

FOREWORD

IAN G. BARBOUR

This volume provides an unusual opportunity to see in action some of the most
creative examples of the dialogue that is
occurring between scientists and theologians
today. Many of the leading participants in this
interdisciplinary dialogue in the English-speaking
world are represented here. While each of the essays
could stand on its own as a contribution to the emerging field
of "science and religion," a unique feature of the book is the way the authors have
responded to each other. The volume has overall coherence and unity despite the diversity of viewpoints included. The editors have written a general introduction as well as
introductions to each section to help the reader in following the issues that are raised.

The first part gives valuable historical background. In place of the myth of a protracted "warfare between science and religion" (won by science, according to the myth),
it portrays a far more complex history in which the divisions cut across disciplines, with
both scientists and theologians expressing a variety of viewpoints. Among other developments, these chapters trace theological responses to Newtonian physics, natural theology and the secularization of knowledge in the Enlightenment, and the diversity of
reactions to Darwin's theory of evolution. This section also includes an analysis of the
cultural context of the current discussion and an interesting reflection on the directions
in which it may develop in the future.

The second part examines the methods of inquiry used in the sciences and those
used in theology—and the similarities and differences between them. Some of the
authors stress the similarities and the common structures of rationality in the justification of beliefs in both fields. Others are more impressed by the differences and
describe the distinctive role of religious experience and religious communities. These
chapters draw from recent work in the philosophy of science and the philosophy of religion, such as the claim that a scientific theory (or a religious belief) is not tested individually against data, but is assessed as part of a network of theories (or beliefs) and
assumptions tested together. The authors reply to each other in a "second round" of
shorter essays. Much of the value of this broad discussion of methodology lies in its
applicability to the specific case studies which follow.

The six case studies of Part III, constituting more than half the book, are its most original feature. In each case a presentation by a scientist is paired with a response by a theologian (though several of the theologians also hold degrees in science). The relationship between particular scientific theories and particular theological doctrines is explored: the Big Bang and creation; chaos theory and divine action; information theory and revelation; and molecular biology and human freedom, for instance. There are significant differences in interpretation between the authors and among the case studies. The diverse kinds of relationships discussed in the historical and methodological chapters appear here in these dialogues about current scientific theories and their theological implications.

The book will be appreciated by scientists and theologians, clergy and laypeople, professors and students, and others interested in these crucial issues. It will be useful in courses in science and religion at the advanced undergraduate level or in graduate studies. The credibility of religion has indeed been questioned in an age of science, but it has also been strongly defended. The quest for coherence will not allow us to keep science and religion in watertight compartments. Most (though not all) of these authors hold that new discoveries in science call for the reformulation of some traditional doctrines—about creation, providence, and human nature, for example. They also believe that science raises many questions which it is not itself able to answer—about ultimate origins, ethics, and the meaning of human life, for instance. Science gives us increasing power over the environment, and even the ability to alter human genes, but it does not guarantee that we will use that power wisely as we face an uncertain future on an endangered planet.

Earlier versions of six of the essays in this volume were presented at a conference celebrating the tenth anniversary of the Center for Theology and the Natural Sciences (CTNS) in Berkeley, California; the other essays were subsequently commissioned to make a more comprehensive volume. The center is an affiliate of the Graduate Theological Union, a graduate school and consortium of nine Protestant and Catholic seminaries adjacent to the Berkeley campus of the University of California. Under the leadership of its founder and director, Professor Robert John Russell, CTNS has given courses for seminary and Ph.D. students, and has sponsored conferences, public lectures, and publications reaching a wider audience. The room in which many CTNS conferences have been held offers a spectacular view of the Golden Gate Bridge across the bay—a fitting symbol of the pioneering work in bridge-building dialogue so well represented in this volume.

GENERAL INTRODUCTION

This book is about one of the most fascinating and important features of human
intellectual geography: the landmasses of
natural science and religion, and the little-
explored region between them. Formerly
thought to be so far apart as to be unbridgeable,
or so near as to make a bridge between them unnecessary, science and religion now appear to be two
families of activity with a most intriguing relationship. A large
number of scholars are systematically exploring this relationship and facilitating the
movement of intellectual traffic back and forth between the two regions. This book
aims to introduce the complex and exciting interdisciplinary venture of religion and
science to the reader with some background in religion, natural science, or both. It
also seeks to contribute to that venture in a number of ways.

The bulk of this introduction is concerned with discussing religion and science in
terms of the metaphor of "building bridges," and then arguing that this form of inquiry
so understood is called into existence and motivated by a multifaceted mandate. This
argument expresses the editors' view of the nature and importance of the hybrid discipline of religion and science.

Throughout the introductions of this book, "theology" is used to refer to the "intellectual wing" of religion, that part of religion that is concerned with the articulation and justification of religious beliefs. This is a more general enterprise than just Christian
theology or Jewish theology, though in practice most theological work is done within the
context of a particular tradition. Some of the contributors treat their theological subjects
from the point of view of specific religious tradition, usually Christianity. Some of the topics covered are also oriented to particular traditions (such as the third and fourth case
studies of Part III), though others are more widely applicable. Being aware of the scope
each author intends for "theology" or "religion" will aid understanding. The editors use
"religion" more or less broadly and "theology" more or less narrowly in their introductions.

I. BUILDING BRIDGES BETWEEN RELIGION AND SCIENCE

Intellectual work at the junction of religion and science resists simple characterizations.
It seems odd to call it a "field" or a "discipline" since its subject matter does not have the

requisite distinctiveness. Moreover, "area of inquiry," though accurate enough, is too vague to generate any insights into what it is, or into its relations to theology, to science, to philosophy, or to any other "area of inquiry."

The actual work done at the intersection of religious and scientific concerns is highly varied, covering what Ian Barbour has described as dialogue over boundary issues and methodological parallels, as well as the construction of natural theologies, theologies of nature, and entire worldviews in which theological and scientific insights are systematically integrated. Added to this, one might use theology or religion to advance a critique of scientific culture. For example, Christian liberation theologies of the Third World, a variety of Jewish religious intellectuals, and eco-feminists of various religions examine the relationships among scientific knowledge, technology, and socioeconomic power. Furthermore, the interface between religion and science can be and is considered from ethical, historical, or hermeneutical perspectives, among others. And the mode in which these explorations are carried on varies from rigorously systematic to vaguely suggestive, from spiritually enlightening to ethically motivating, from multi-scholar research programs to individual ventures.

In view of this diversity, it is obvious that a book of this type requires a center of gravity. This volume focuses above all on the way religion and science contribute to our knowledge of the world, and so on the relationship between *theology* and science. This involves turning to the past for insight (as in Part I), exploring the ways scientific and theological knowledge claims are similar and different (as in Part II), and trying to mount dialogues between specific scientific and theological themes (as in Part III).

The plurality of approaches to studying the relationship between religion and science warns against hastily drawn or oversimplified definitions of the specialization devoted to that task. What we are calling "theology and science" is far from being the whole of the specialization of religion and science, but it has its own importance and value. The intrinsic importance and wider cultural ramifications of "theology and science" can be appreciated through a discussion of its conception and central tasks in terms of the image of "building bridges."

"Building bridges" serves as a generalized, metaphorical description of much of the dialogue that takes places in theology and science. The metaphor expresses the fact that there is a breach evident at the surface between theology and the sciences in our present cultural context. There will be no intellectual traffic without active *construction*. All of the elaborate engineering detail that goes into bridge building aptly expresses the sometimes technical and painstaking labors associated with making connections and free traffic possible between these aspects of our culture.

Perhaps the most important virtue of the metaphor is its suggestion of pillars penetrating the deep waters and connecting the bridge to solid bedrock below. The stability, the very possibility, of a bridge depends on there being solid, albeit invisible, bedrock underlying and connecting the landmasses to be bridged. So it is with the interdisciplinary activity of theology and science: it presupposes and makes evident in an illuminating way what theology and science have in common, and does so at a time when their differences are more obvious to many than their similarities.

The metaphor is not without its liabilities, but even these are illuminating. It would be misleading, for example, if the bridge metaphor were thought to imply that theology and science were independent, well-defined, tightly focused activities, remaining conveniently stationary as the bridge builders do their work to connect them with a definitive bridge. On the contrary, theology and the sciences are internally complex and dynamic enterprises whose subject matter boundaries shift. Between such interesting and variegated intellectual activities it is appropriate to think of there being as many bridges as there are tasks to be pursued; or else a single bridge with an indefinite number of supports, corresponding with the many supporting moves to be made in order to connect these fields; or else one or more bridges with a large number of entry points for traffic on both sides, as theology and science are both families of related intellectual enterprises, offering a number of starting points for interdisciplinary considerations.

Our metaphor would also be misleading if the bridge were to suggest the permanency of our accomplishments at the interface of theology and science. If we are properly modest about our constructions we will recognize their historical, contingent nature, and we will anticipate change no less in the bridge than in the states of theology and science themselves. We may want our bridges and highways to stay put, but we can expect the theology-science enterprise to shift and turn from time to time. Sometimes the changes will be minor. But we cannot preclude the possibility that some changes will be more substantial and structural.

The "building bridges" image would also mislead if too much were made of the fact that the materials and apparatus used in bridge building are quite unlike the natural base at each end. On the contrary, the intellectual connections drawn between science and theology are not artificially imposed "add-ons," but intrinsic to the disciplines being linked. For example, science and theology alike contain metaphysical assumptions, operate according to certain methods, possess characteristic epistemological principles and constraints, and produce warrants for beliefs of particular kinds. The connections between them are "built" of the very same stuff.

II. THE MANDATE FOR THEOLOGY AND SCIENCE

On the basis of this discussion, it is possible to pose, and suggest an answer to, the question of the purpose of "theology and science." Why go to the trouble of building bridges? Why is the interdisciplinary traffic made possible by such bridges worth the effort? One crucial answer—and it seems to us to be the most important answer—is that bridge building between theology and science is a form of inquiry into the nature and function of human understanding, and so the world we inhabit. Therefore, the metaphorical bedrock invisible beneath the deep water spanned by the bridge is more than what theology and science have in common; it is what human beings are, and what the world is. After all, it is human beings who engage in theological and scientific activities, and it is the world, the ultimate "dialogue partner," that corrects and improves our theological and scientific beliefs about it.

If human rationality is mysterious, then surely the contrast between scientific and theological work is an instance of this mystery—a rather vivid one, in fact. Mysteries are to be enjoyed and celebrated, of course, but they also invite investigation and the attempt at explanation, at least by those predisposed to such a response. The interdisciplinary venture of theology and science, it seems to us, is inspired by a vision of a unified conception of human rationality and of the world, a vision in which the spiritual and the intellectual impulses of humanity are harmonized in an ethically, socially, and environmentally healthy way. This, then, is a mandate for the interdisciplinary venture.

Something like this vision motivates most of the theologians, philosophers, poets, ethicists, and scientists who work at the interface of science and theology. They are in general agreement on the two tasks that are implied in the vision, one primarily theoretical and one practical. On the one hand, they are seeking to gain clarity about human rationality and the world in which it functions. On the other hand, they wish to understand and solve the practical problems that arise in the absence of coherent relations among our many rational activities.

For some people this mandate is discharged through inspiring poetry and suggestive allusions, through almost worshipful reticence and illuminating illustrations. For the contributors to this volume, and for the Center for Theology and the Natural Sciences, whose tenth birthday this volume celebrates, this mandate is chiefly fulfilled through painstaking analysis of theological and scientific procedures and results; systematic comparisons and contrasts of theological and scientific content; elaborate models of the interaction between the two families of disciplines, tested rigorously and adjusted with impressive ingenuity; and the tracing out of implications not only for theology and science themselves, but also for philosophy, ethics, spirituality, ecology, social policy, historiography, and still other domains of inquiry.

The mandate for the interdisciplinary science-theology study is implicit in its hybrid nature. By comparison with the autonomous character of theological and scientific activity individually, the hybrid character of the theology-science specialization is plain to see. For example, it does not possess a distinctive subject matter nor a specific method, as do autonomous disciplines. Rather, like interreligious dialogue, it consists in *tasks*: to facilitate mutual understanding, to foster the exchange of substantive and relevant information between the two disciplines, to generate insight both for the philosophical construction of conceptions of human rationality and for guiding practical decisions. This orientation to tasks, rather than a characteristic set of objects or methods, suggests a contingent, transitory form of inquiry that typifies neither theology nor the natural sciences. Such an interdisciplinary form of inquiry is brought into existence deliberately by its advocates because a perceived need mandates it.

This mandate arises in different ways for each of the autonomous disciplines that contribute researchers, insights, and content to the theology-science enterprise. First, from a philosophical point of view, there exists a demand for consistent theories of knowledge and of reality across all human rational activities, because these activities have shared rational principles. Methods and goals may vary as the contours of subject matter demand, and conceptions of what is valuable or useful may likewise differ. But intersubjective structures of meaning in the form of language and practices, methods and rules, exist in every kind of rational human activity. When these activities are as diverse as systematic religious reflection, natural scientific investigation, and practical decision making, some kind of spelling out of the rational commonalities is called for. Some see the beginnings of an explanation of this commonality in the unity of the human biological organism, while others look to sociohistorical and constructive explanations stimulated by the structure of the similarities themselves. In any case, bringing together two diverse disciplines with rich and entangled histories is a good place to begin the investigation.

Second, theology within the Western traditions for the most part demands the integration of understandings of the world that emerge from the religious-theological and natural-scientific spheres. One of the core beliefs of these traditions bears directly on the interdisciplinary theology-science project. The unity of God, as the single source of all creation, implies that the quest for coherence in our various descriptions of reality is not only reasonable but necessary. Implicit in the Jewish, Christian, and Islamic understandings of God and creation is the contingency and intelligibility of the universe, and a respect for the human capacity to "know," at least in part. The very content of this theological claim leads to an investment in the success of interdisciplinary dialogue.

To say this, of course, rules out certain conceptions of theology that deny any factual element in theological statements. Theological statements do not *merely* express emotional states, though they certainly do that. Nor are they *merely* coded exhortations for eliciting religious or moral attitudes, though they do serve that purpose also. Most who undertake the theology-science enterprise are committed to the view that, along with their expressive, exhortative, aesthetic, and moral dimensions, theological statements usually have a fact-asserting, representative element; they make claims about reality that may be true or false. In some cases, empirical evidence may be brought to bear as a test of theological truth claims. In other cases, the truth claims are inherently beyond the reach of empirical testing, being more akin to traditional metaphysical propositions. But in all cases familiar theoretical ideals, such as intelligibility, consistency, coherence, applicability, adequacy, fruitfulness, and aesthetic value, function as criteria for excellence in attempts to present theological statements in a coordinated way.

The process of systematically articulating theological propositions has always had to satisfy these criteria in two overlapping arenas. Consider the ideals of adequacy and intelligibility, for instance. Theological propositions must adequately convey the beliefs of members within the particular religious community. But beyond the confines of the tradition, those same theological propositions must be intelligible, and they must be adequate to knowledge about reality autonomously gained. Of course, the two arenas overlap because members of religious communities also belong to a wider context of life. However, there is a real distinction to be maintained here. The need to give rational and practical expression to religious convictions (for example, the unity and goodness of creation) will appear very differently from an internal religious perspective and from the point of view of contemporary physical cosmology. For instance, the rational articulation of the Christian and Jewish conviction of divine providential activity is one thing when thought of as having to warrant such religious activities as worship, prayer, and social action, and quite another when asserted in the context of a deterministic metaphysic in the natural sciences. The criteria of adequacy and intelligibility are demanding, therefore, and meeting them is greatly aided by interdisciplinary studies connecting theology to other spheres of discourse.

It is the existence of truth claims in theological discourse—notwithstanding the presence there of other modes of speech and levels of meaning—which requires that theology account for its claims in a wider cultural milieu. Since this demand arises *within* theology, rather than being imposed upon it from without, the call to be accountable for theological truth claims cannot be evaded on theological grounds. For instance, in an age when the world's cultures interact more than ever, traditionally exclusive theological claims are having to justify themselves in the face of religious pluralism. Dealing honestly and effectively with this issue, and others like it, has become a matter of credibility for theology in the contemporary world, and credibility in these matters is a *theological* interest. This indicates the scope and origin of the theological requirement to account for its truth claims in a broad, intersubjective context. The mandate to engage the content and method of the natural sciences is an instance of this more general requirement.

Third, natural scientists bring with them their own mandate for working at the junction of their discipline with theology. Owing to the more constrained method of the natural sciences, which has no obvious concern with comprehensiveness in the way that philosophy and theology do, it is difficult to see how this mandate could arise from anything except the personal interest of scientists. For instance, the geneticist with some personal religious commitment desiring to coordinate his or her religious and scientific beliefs about human nature might get involved in the science-theology dialogue to satisfy this personal aim.

However, there is one sense in which this mandate can be seen to arise from within the bounds of the autonomous natural sciences themselves. If the accounts given by some philosophers of science are correct about the constructed character of scientific theories, then there is reason to ascribe responsibility to the scientific community *specifically as scientists* (rather than generally as humanitarians) for the constructions they choose to explore and defend. This responsibility takes the scientist—again, *as* scientist—beyond fidelity to experimental results to consider ethical, metaphysical, and theological concerns that may underlie his or her theorizing. In any event, scientists of all areas within the natural sciences join in the work of the theology-science specialization with a desire for a unified conception of reality, and in some cases this is motivated by ethical and theological concerns about the development of scientific theories.

Finally, we may note the impact of the many practical crises facing humanity. Some of the more significant of these crises are the direct result of an imbalance in human competencies: while we have developed enormously powerful technologies for all manner of applications, we lack the powers of foresight and will to use them responsibly and with appropriate concern for other species, for future human generations, or even for the survival of our own generation. While problems of nuclear and biomedical technologies, and environmental and social degradation, are enormously complex, and solutions to them are not at all clear, they highlight a need to integrate the critical and spiritual-religious impulses of our species. Identifying problems and refining technologies are not enough; we must face squarely the values that justify our apportioning of intellectual and monetary resources, and the motives that lie behind public policies and behaviors. This may seem abstract in view of the urgency of the practical problems, but this integration is inescapable if we are to meet new and present challenges. The interaction of theology and the natural sciences is one obvious place to turn for a case study of the tension between human critical and spiritual-religious instincts.

III. THE POSSIBILITY OF FULFILLING THE MANDATE FOR THEOLOGY AND SCIENCE

In all of these ways, the interdisciplinary venture of theology and science is clearly and powerfully mandated. However, the weight of this confluence of concerns might cause us to ask whether the fulfilling of the mandate is even possible. Can the theology-science specialization contribute to a unified conception of human rational and practical activity? Can it show such a conception to be resilient and fruitful when tested against the history and substance of the interaction between theology and science? Can practical crises be more effectively addressed with the aid of such an interdisciplinary venture?

There is no shortage of skeptics who look askance at an interdisciplinary project with such goals. Some reject theology as a legitimate discipline at all, not finding there the same kind of definite procedures characterizing scientific activity. Others are so firmly committed to a view of theology and science as separated and incommensurable disciplines that the effort to relate them seems wasted. Still others repudiate the view of theological language usually presupposed in the interdisciplinary effort, namely, partly representative, fact-asserting discourse. And yet others believe all attempts to construct a unified conception of human rationality are in principle, like all totalizing projects, more misleading than enlightening. These implied criticisms are not easy to dismiss, but neither do they constitute knock-down arguments against the interdisciplinary attempt. If the theology-science venture produces stable and illuminating results, that is the only rebuttal needed.

This pragmatic reply to the skeptics is appropriate, simply in view of the outstanding work accomplished in the theology-science specialization in recent decades. However, there are several perspectives from which the interdisciplinary project of theology and science appears to be well positioned to secure the results it seeks.

First, the ground has been cleared for productive interaction by the advance of scientific knowledge itself, especially in areas such as general relativity and cosmology; quantum mechanics; chaos, complexity, and nonlinear dynamics; evolutionary and molecular biology, and sociobiology; and the neurosciences. Ironically, these advances have made some scientific areas more amenable to theology at precisely those points where, formerly, they had been antagonists. Although possibly temporary congeniality can never be the premise for a hybrid discipline, it cannot be denied that consonance (and not just the familiar dissonance in details) between scientific theory and established theological positions is encouraging.

Second, a clearer understanding of similarities and differences between theological and scientific method is gradually emerging. Philosophers of science have furnished a more subtle and complex account of the method by which scientific communities assign warrant to, and select among, their hypotheses. Similarly, theologians have begun to pinpoint some continuities with the scientific method thus reconstrued. At root, this is probably because they are both forms of inquiry and, as intimated already, human inquiry may have some general features that can be expected to appear in any particular instance of it. In any event, with these well articulated similarities in the background, theologians are becoming more confident in affirming those differences that distinguish theology from the natural scientific ideal of progressive knowledge. This is a marked improvement over the former posture of utter separation based on the impression of irreconcilable methodological differences. Though much more needs to be done in this direction, the future of inquiry into human rationality within the science-religion specialization looks more promising than it has for many years.

Third, we are gradually seeing how exposure of theologians to scientific material and scientists to theological modes of reflection fosters greater understanding of the familiar discipline as well as the unfamiliar one. This applies both to historical studies of interaction in the past and to substantive interactions in the present. Interreligious dialogue has shown us that one of the greatest fruits of interdisciplinary work is enriched understanding, and not merely a more peaceful coexistence. This increased level of familiarity is hopeful, since partial successes in practice eventually can lead to systematic intellectual expression.

Fourth, a widespread sense of urgency among academics and the general public alike calls for intellectual resources to be applied to practical interests. This is powerful motivation to press onward toward the fulfillment of the mandate for the theology-science specialization, as well as an indirect reason to expect some success.

The future holds the evidence for whether the theology-science venture is really capable of fulfilling its bold aims. Conceivably, the interdisciplinary project might cease because its goals prove too difficult to reach, or dissolve because the goals are largely met. Alternatively, the interdisciplinary venture might continue on indefinitely as a distinct field, developing methods and identifying a distinctive subject matter. It is not easy to predict its fate. At present, however, the awkwardness of the dialogue, and assumptions of culture at large, make it abundantly evident that an independent forum, almost on the scale and complexity of a small field of study itself, is essential. And hope for at least some success seems appropriate.

IV. STRUCTURE AND PURPOSE OF THIS VOLUME

This volume is intended primarily as an introduction to the interdisciplinary theology-science venture, and has been designed with a class in religion and science at the advanced undergraduate or graduate level in mind. Additionally, however, the essays in this volume advance research on a number of frontiers. It is a measure in some ways of the youthful state of the religion-science specialization that both elements can be included in the same design.

The various sections of the book correspond to three major kinds of inquiry that are undertaken in the theology-science specialization: historical studies, methodological analyses, and substantive dialogue. As we have said, other kinds of inquiry are omitted in deference to the need to maintain a clear focus.

The essays of Part I are historical in character, the notable partial exception being the prospective reflection of Holmes Rolston, III. However, even this forward-looking essay is based on a clear understanding of historical context. Each paper presents important aspects of the history of the relation between theology and science in various periods from the European Enlightenment onward.

There is considerable controversy and an ongoing lack of consensus in the area of comparative methodology of theology and science. Accordingly, Part II has been constructed as a two-round discussion involving four perspectives. Each perspective is clearly set forth in the first round, then most of the participants react to each other's positions in the second. The introduction to this part of the volume includes a brief critical appraisal of the debate, with the aim of securing some degree of clarity about similarities and differences between theological and scientific method.

Part III is a set of six case studies demonstrating different types of constructive interaction between science and theology. In addition to their obvious research value, we believe that the case studies as a whole illustrate for students of theology and science a variety of ways that interdisciplinary work may be carried out. There is no single model in all six case studies for the constructive task, neither do we claim to have represented all possibilities. The set of case studies not only illustrates a high level of informed creativity and openness to new perspectives in the study of theology and science, but also is particularly useful as a family of partial tests of adequacy for the methodological constructions of Part II. One might also compare these efforts with the modes of interaction discussed in the historical essays of Part I.

The book concludes with suggestions for further reading that highlight many of the major books and papers of the last few decades in religion and science. There will be found abundant suggestions for readings to supplement those provided here. There are also suggestions of books to move the reader beyond the "theology and science" constraints of this volume into other approaches within the gamut of the study of religion and science.

V. ACKNOWLEDGMENTS

There are many people to thank for the inspiration and production of this book. First and foremost, we must recognize the Center for Theology and the Natural Sciences (CTNS), an affiliate of the Graduate Theological Union in Berkeley, California. Founded and directed by Professor Robert John Russell, CTNS continues to be among the world's leaders in advancing the dialogue and interaction between theology and the natural sciences. Since its beginnings in 1982, CTNS has significantly affected the shape of this kind of interdisciplinary research. Its work has inspired this volume, which exists in part as a celebration of that first decade of work and service. Although the structure and purpose of *Religion and Science* stands on its own, early versions of a few of the essays contained in it were presented at a conference celebrating the tenth anniversary of the Center. Furthermore, CTNS has provided valuable administrative support, for which our thanks go to Robin Ficklin-Alred, Bonnie Johnston, and Karen Cheatham.

We also thank the many essayists in this volume. They represent one of the most talented and accomplished collections of scholars one could find for a volume such as this. They have contributed because of their commitment to the field, and because of their appreciation for the leadership of CTNS. Many of them have had an increasingly important impact on theological education in recent years through their participation in the theology-science venture, including the establishment of organizations with purposes allied with those of CTNS.

Among contributors to this volume we want to single out Ian Barbour. His *Issues in Science and Religion* helped rekindle the theology and science discussion shortly after the middle of the twentieth century, and he helps keep the fire going even now. We appreciate his kindness in agreeing to write the Foreword for the volume.

We are grateful for the generous support of the Templeton Foundation, whose Fellowship grant made much of the contribution of W.M.R. possible. Boston University's ongoing support of the work of W.J.W. is likewise appreciated.

Marlie Wasserman at Routledge has been a powerhouse of enthusiasm from the first moment she encountered this volume, and we are thankful for her expertise and advice. The staff at Routledge, especially Karen Deaver, has been most professional in the production of the volume.

Finally, we wish to thank Brenda Richardson and Suzanne Wildman, our wives, who have faithfully supported our endeavors. Editing a volume of this sort complicates an academic life that is already more than a "nine-to-five" proposition, and their patient companionship is appreciated.

History

INTRODUCTION

Theologian James Wm. McClendon used to tell his graduate students, "A scholar who knows the work of only one philosopher is prepared to be ideological. But a student who knows the work of two begins to be a critical thinker." There is a message here for those who study the interface between religious and scientific reflection: knowing the history of the theology-science relationship—the patterns that endure as well as the unique adaptations to changing circumstances—provides an indispensable perspective for understanding current activity in this interdisciplinary field. Thus, this volume opens with historical essays that examine the science-religion relationship from the Enlightenment forward, even into the twenty-first century.

Together, these essays sketch out the developing relationship between religion and science in the modern period. It is impossible to cover this history comprehensively with just a few essays, however, for there are too many key names, dates, and places to discuss, and too many important stories to tell. Because of this, the first three essayists in this part of the volume have focused their contributions by concentrating on one characteristic story in the periods they consider, and arguing for an interpretation of that story that illumines the relationship between religion and science in a concentrated way. The final essay in this part, while providing an overview of this relationship in its current form, programmatically calls for a more ethically responsible and religiously informed future approach to technology, environment, and human life.

I. THE COMPLEXITY OF THE HISTORICAL RELATIONSHIP BETWEEN THEOLOGY AND SCIENCE

Important as the history of relations between theology and science may be, it is certainly not simple. Indeed, a theme which runs through all of the essays of this section is that the science-theology relation from the Enlightenment forward is notable for its complexity, and that some accounts of it have oversimplified the story in significant ways. For example, many earlier histories (both popular and professional) have cast the relationship largely in terms of competition and conflict; accordingly, they tell the story of a steady retreat and narrowing of theology and its domain in the face of growing strength and influence of science. This rather blunt interpretative idea may have yielded some insight, but today historians find there are subtleties lost, deep intellectual connections between theology and science minimized, and variations of expression within each era unaccounted for under this thesis.

There are several aspects to this complexity including, first, the contingency and unpredictability of history in general. We can rarely if ever identify explanatory principles for a given era or across multiple eras without serious qualifications. We can note trends, usually in retrospect, but anomalies always remain to complicate even the very best employments of the ways theology and science have related to each other. The problem is an order of magnitude more difficult when it is the near future and not the past we seek to understand. Rolston demonstrates a keen awareness of this as he considers the form theology and science may take in the twenty-first century.

Second, as Wildman suggests, there may be both deep- and surface-level features to be named in the history of theology and science. For example, underlying the often divided consciousness in twentieth-century Westerners on matters of science and religion, Wildman argues, is a more fundamental crisis of human rationality that affects many of the culture's institutions. If he is right, a critical history of the science-theology relationship will probably be useful for gaining an understanding of this deep structural problem.

II. THE STRUCTURE OF THE HISTORICAL RELATIONSHIP
BETWEEN THEOLOGY AND SCIENCE

In spite of the complex relationship between theology and science, the essayists of Part I attempt to discern patterns and tendencies that persist through the eras they examine. Brooke, for example, highlights modernity's striking intensification of the search for universal and rational grounds of justification and truth. The successes of science in the seventeenth century (most notably in Newtonian physics) turned the wider intellectual culture, including theologians, toward science as the intellectual standard-bearer. In response, especially in the Enlightenment, some theologians tended to downplay the particulars of religious experience, and overconfidently identified natural philosophy as the basis for theological apologetics, often straining ineffectively against philosophical atheism. Today the tension between universal principles of reason and the particularities of immediate personal experience takes a different form, but is no less challenging.

The critical historical examinations of the essayists also disclose major intellectual transition points in the modern era which have deeply affected the science-theology relationship. Perhaps most obvious are the theoretical transformations in the sciences themselves: in cosmology, microphysics, molecular biology, and the new sciences of ecology and chaos theory. Changes in these areas have not been quickly integrated into theological frameworks. Nor have theological responses been uniform. Yet these changes are forcing theologians to rethink the nature of theology itself: its method, its objects, and its relation to other descriptive and explanatory frameworks for interpreting the world.

Another transition that affected the relationship between theology and science was the "turn to the subject"—in which interpretation of all kinds became more *self*-conscious—and the sharpening of historical consciousness during the eighteenth and nineteenth centuries. These developments offered new possibilities and posed new problems for theology, ranging from the nature of theological language to the connections between theological and scientific procedures and results.

In a third example of transition, Wildman notes a shift after World War I toward a more searching, self-critical instinct, and a resulting suspicion of many common assumptions held in Western intellectual culture. This self-critical shift should be interpreted, Wildman argues, as an extension and correction of the critical instincts stimulated so intensively in the Enlightenment. In the relations between science and religion, this self-critical mood expresses itself in suspicion of the pretensions to all-competence of the scientific method, and reaffirmation of a role for other modes of interpreting and shaping the world.

The historians of this volume have achieved an impressive synthesis of critical objectivity and sympathetic understanding of past sources. In addition, they share with contemporary philosophers of history an appreciation for the inevitable self-involvement—the influence of one's own outlooks, judgments, values—in the doing of critical histories. The aim of this openly intersubjective process is precisely to achieve a more accurate assessment of one's understanding of the past, and a more honest involvement with one's own world of thought and action.

III. THE ESSAYS IN PART I

John Hedley Brooke's rendering of the history of science and theology in the seventeenth and eighteenth centuries challenges the assumption that theology steadily and invariably shrank from the bright light of the new epistemology and method of science. There are too many factors not captured by this picture, including the quality of the Enlightenment itself. Says Brooke, "We can no longer speak of archetypal Enlightenment mentalities or goals."

Nevertheless, a recurrent theme of this era is the quest for a religious creed that could withstand rational assaults while marginalizing sectarianism in religion. In attempting to manage this delicate balance, much theology tended to depend heavily on natural philosophy in the face of the success of Enlightenment science in the form of Newtonian classical mechanics. This, however, was not a successful strategy. Brooke cites Michael Buckley, author of *At the Origins of Modern Atheism*, who sees the attempt to understand "a personal God principally in terms of impersonal nature" as one of the chief reasons for the rise of modern atheism. Brooke views this same phenomenon as a most costly strategic misfire of ecclesial theology in the modern era.

In addition to the power of science in Enlightenment culture, philosophers of the era were challenging traditional epistemological foundations and establishing new ones. This led to the development of a polarity between theological adaptations to the Enlightenment's enthusiasm for an ahistorical, universal ideal of human rationality (sponsored by the success of science), on the one hand, and theology's need to acknowledge the force of particular and personal religious experience, on the other hand. This tension persists in new forms in Western culture today.

In an essay on the nineteenth century, Claude Welch finds a new turn related to the above theme. He claims that the most significant development in the nineteenth century was the movement from the Enlightenment's quest for a universal objectivity toward a science of critical history, which began the path toward relativizing cultures and their ideas. Deeply connected with this awakening of historical science was a sharper awareness of the role of human subjectivity in cultural life, epistemology, ethics, and religion. This connection was focused in the empirical studies of the origins of Christianity and its problematic relation to the faith and values of the believer. However, it also directly impacted the relationship between theology and science. It offered a way forward for theology but simultaneously threatened to "emasculate" theological language by showing it to be a set of historically and culturally conditioned expressions of the religious self-consciousness. This is the point at which historical and natural sciences combine their influence to cause a reevaluation of the nature of theology.

On another theme regarding the nineteenth century, Welch recalls the popular myth of "warfare" between theology and science, as exemplified in the histories of John William Draper and Andrew Dickson White, in order to show the distinction between factual and symbolic "histories." He argues that the symbolic warfare myth, as portrayed in these histories, reveals more about the particular contexts of White and Draper than it does about the larger dynamism between theology and science in the nineteenth century.

The issue that made this warfare image seem most apt was, of course, the publication of Charles Darwin's *Origin of Species*, which also marked a shift toward much greater interest in the biological sciences. Welch emphasizes the variety of theological responses to Darwin's groundbreaking evolutionary thesis, in contrast to the popular assumption that theology found itself uniformly in conflict with Darwin. Again, we find an emphasis on the complexity of the theology-science relationship.

In an important respect Wesley J. Wildman's essay reinforces and examines the consequences of the developments depicted in the first two essays. Wildman sees the twentieth century as harvesting the effects of critical objectivity turned inward on the subject of knowing. The fruits—intellectual and moral doubt, a loss of intellectual confidence and consistency, fragmentation—have been widely evident in the institutions of Western culture. Under this interpretive scheme, the conflicted science and theology relationship is seen to be indicative of a deeper cultural crisis, one evolving out of failure of human beings to coordinate and unify the spiritual, ethical, intellectual, and social aspects of their being.

In the end, Wildman puts a hopeful face on his own profoundly disturbing portrayal of the twentieth-century West. He sees the tendency toward a divided human consciousness, and the unrelenting work of self-criticism and deconstruction, as a necessary prelude to, though not a sufficient condition for, a more integrated vision of rationality that recognizes all of the dimensions of human beings. The relation between theology and science witnessed in this century both symbolizes and facilitates the passage toward a more adequate, practical, and vital human understanding of self and world. Wildman argues that this is one of the important justifications for attending to the integration of theology and science.

Holmes Rolston, III, offers a unique essay on the future of theology and science in the twenty-first century in light of his rich understanding of the modern era. His claim is that science and theology, both indispensable human institutions, need each other. Theology is the reservoir of meaning that pushes science, in its quest for theoretical explanation, toward questions of ultimacy and value: "religion can keep science deep." Science keeps religion from sinking into fantastic assumptions that would ensure its marginalization and impotence in the wider culture. Fortunately, as he sees it, developments in twentieth-century science offer hope of a more congenial relation with Western religious traditions. However, learning from the past, we must be cautious of linking theological assertions too closely with current theory in the sciences.

Rolston sees moral and practical questions as paramount in the next century. The power of science will need to be steered by larger natural and cultural wisdom and values. The traditionally prophetic voice of religion will need to be reinvigorated. But rather than stressing the virtue of a newly constructed vision of human rationality for this purpose, Rolston simply and emphatically declares the ethical and practical imperative for a convergence between science and religion if we are going to survive as a species. The partnership of theologian and scientist is not optional.

SCIENCE AND THEOLOGY IN THE ENLIGHTENMENT

I. INTRODUCTION: NATURAL PHILOSOPHY AND DIVINE PROVIDENCE

JOHN HEDLEY BROOKE

The implications of scientific advance for Christian theology are often reduced to a plausible but simplistic formula: as natural phenomena, formerly explained by the will of a deity, were increasingly understood in mechanistic terms, increasingly brought within the domain of natural laws, so the belief in an active, caring Providence was eroded until the God of Abraham, Isaac, and Jacob became nothing more than a remote clockmaker. On this view, the relationship between Enlightenment philosophy and the so-called "scientific revolution" of the seventeenth century is straightforward. Eighteenth-century freethinkers simply drew out the implications of Newtonian science, rejoicing in what human reason had achieved, celebrating the power of new empirical methods, questioning (in the spirit of John Locke) whether there was any privileged route to knowledge either through intuition or revelation. It is a view often substantiated by reference to Voltaire, as keen to popularize Newton's science as he was to denounce the "priestcraft" of the Catholic clergy. And Voltaire was certainly not alone in preferring the rational deity of the Newtonian universe to the whimsical, interfering deity of the Old Testament who, on Voltaire's satirical reading, was so bereft of moral sensibility that he had commanded the prophet Ezekiel to eat his barley bread cooked with shit.[1]

That there are continuities between seventeenth-century science and the rationalist philosophies of the Enlightenment no one could deny. Scholars of the calibre of Ernst Cassirer[2] and Peter Gay[3] have detected a new tone of thought, new and more stringent criteria for making truth claims, reflecting the great achievements of Galileo and Newton in the physical sciences and the rationalist epistemology of Descartes. I shall, however, begin with some conclusions from recent scholarship that point to richer, more complex sets of relations between what one might be tempted to call a scientific mentality and attitudes towards religious belief. High on any list would be the growing recognition that the concept of a "scientific revolution" in seventeenth-century Europe cannot properly capture the enormous diversification of scientific practice that can be detected during the period that separated Newton from Copernicus.[4] Well-worn formulas, to the effect that the "revolution" had consisted in the rejection of Aristotelian philosophy, or in the substitution of Baconian empirical methods for book-learning, or in the displacement of organic by mechanistic images of nature, have become increasingly threadbare as they have failed to capture the fine texture of seventeenth-century debates. A major "discovery" such as that of William Harvey on the circulation of the blood was made by an avowed Aristotelian, interested in finding "final causes" (such as the purpose of valves in the system), not in rejecting them. The mathematical methods employed by Galileo for the analysis of moving bodies have been shown to have much in common with those taught by the Jesuit scholars of his day. And that great symbol of a mechanized universe, Isaac Newton, was arguably less of a mechanist than Descartes, whose speculative cosmology bore the brunt of Newton's attack in Book II of his *Principia* (1687). Whereas Descartes had presumed to explain why the planets orbit the sun in the same direction and roughly the same plane (a consequence, he argued, of their being carried round in a vortex of subtle matter), Newton simply ascribed the arrangement to the aesthetic considerations that had weighed with God at Creation. Any suggestion that what was revolutionary in seventeenth-century thought was the complete separation of science from theology[5] would be disqualified by Newton himself, who once wrote that the study of natural philosophy included a consideration of divine attributes and of God's relationship with the world. Newton's immersion in the study of Biblical prophecy shows that he was as concerned with the role of Providence in human history as in nature. There was certainly no simple continuity between Newton and Voltaire, the former describing the God of the Old Testament as a God with dominion, a God to be feared; the latter, in clandestine literature, making Him a figure of fun.

It has long been recognized that natural philosophers such as Robert Boyle and Isaac Newton saw the study of nature as a religious duty. A knowledge of God's power and wisdom could be inferred from the intelligence seemingly displayed in the designs of nature. Newton affirmed that the natural sciences had prospered only in monotheistic cultures, and recent work has shown the stamp of his Unitarian religion on his construction of nature.[6] He denied that the gravitational force was an inherent, defining property of matter, for that would be tantamount to materialism. He believed the *universality* of his laws was grounded in the omnipresence of a single divine Will, and he asserted that space was to be conceived as if it were the sensorium of a God who immediately perceived everything. In the depth of his biblical study, Newton may not be representative of late seventeenth-century natural philosophers, but if he is made to symbolize new canons of scientific rationality, then it cannot be said that the scientific revolution saw a separation of science from theology. If such a separation is seen as a prerequisite of the secularization of knowledge, then that secularization had not yet taken place. But the concept of secularization may itself be too blunt to do justice to the subtle interplay between statements about nature and statements about God. The dangers of the word may be apparent from the fact that the historian who has gone furthest in denying any ultimate separation of science from religion during the seventeenth century has nevertheless used it to describe an unprecedented *fusion* of natural philosophy and theology. In a powerful reinterpretation, Amos Funkenstein has argued that theology began to be secularized precisely because God's attributes were increasingly described through the categories of natural philosophy and by scholars who were not members of the clergy.[7] Newton's philosophy of nature would again illustrate the point, because the concept of God's omnipresence was given new meaning through his discussion of space, whilst the concept of divine Providence was filled with new content as Newton discussed God's control of comets, which in turn helped to stabilize the solar system. In a letter to Thomas Burnet, Newton insisted that where there were natural causes to hand, God would use them to effect His purposes—a view that Burnet clearly shared, for in his own book on the *Sacred Theory of the Earth* (1684) he explained how Noah's flood had come about through the release of subterranean water when the earth's crust cracked. Far from detracting from divine Providence, Burnet saw in the synchronization of this event with the moral decay described in Genesis a powerful supportive argument.

The important lesson is that in late seventeenth-century natural philosophy it was possible to describe the same events in terms both of natural (or "secondary") causes and of divine Providence. It was not a question of either/or, as it became for later polemicists. The fact that mechanistic and providentialist interpretations could coexist reflects an even deeper level on which the quest for scientific understanding had been integrated with theological concerns. For Newton, as for Boyle and Descartes, there were *laws* of nature only because there had been a Legislator. That simple equation with which we began—that laws of nature impinged on the scope of divine activity—is simplistic precisely because to a Christian theist these laws merely expressed the way God normally chose to act. Boyle and Newton might imply that such laws obtained for long periods without alteration, but they were equally explicit in saying that God was free to change them—as free, if not more so, to direct events in nature as we are to control the movement of our limbs. It was part of the rhetoric of Newton's own philosophy that God had been free to create whatsoever world He had wished, that the law of gravitation might have been other than an inverse square law, that the planets might have been propelled in other paths. It was a powerful rhetoric against opponents, such as Leibniz, who appeared to argue that the world must conform to some prior canons of rationality if it is to be the best of all possible worlds. For several of Newton's defenders, the whole point of an empirically based method would be negated if one could know in advance how God *must* have made the world. Again this undermines the simple equation with which we began, for Newton's philosophy of nature did not evacuate the meaning of references to a divine will. Rather it sought to give them content by comparing nature, as disclosed through Newton's analysis, with nature as it might have been had the deity freely chosen otherwise.[8]

It would clearly be unwise to assess the bearing of science on theology during the Enlightenment by assuming as "given" some timeless model of their relationship.

Polarities that later became part of popular culture had not yet been articulated or might leave few traces when they were. During the seventeenth century the provinces of "science" and "religion" had been *differentiated* in many ways that facilitated innovative inquiry; but the study of nature largely remained a study of the book of God's works, complementing that of His words.[9] There is, however, a critical consequence of such a perspective: it tends to magnify rather than diminish the importance of the eighteenth century in creating those polarities which later began to seem more natural—between nature and supernature, science and magic, reason and superstition, laws and miracles, proof and faith. If Funkenstein is correct in stressing the unprecedented fusion of science and theology in seventeenth-century natural philosophy, there is the fascinating corollary that the God now more sharply defined by His discernible activities in nature became a more immediately identifiable target for those wishing to destroy Him. As we shall see, the God *known* through science would prove most vulnerable to being *overthrown* in the name of science.

II. THE UTILITY OF THE NATURAL SCIENCES

In his *Dictionary of Chemistry* (1789), the entrepreneur James Keir reported that a new spirit was abroad: "the diffusion of a general knowledge, and of a taste for science, over all the classes of men, in every nation of Europe." An exaggeration, no doubt, but between 1660 and the closing decade of the eighteenth century, the scientific world established itself, with more than seventy official scientific societies (and almost as many private ones) in urban centers as far removed as St. Petersburg and Philadelphia. Within their membership were men who saw in the sciences a vehicle of social and intellectual liberation, who believed that the solutions to human problems lay with human effort rather than through the protection of the churches. Historians have detected a growing aversion at that time among natural philosophers, especially those in France, to talk of divine intervention. Other shifts in sensibility also seem characteristic of cultural developments in eighteenth century Europe—a greater reluctance, for example, to ascribe illness to divine retribution; and, towards the end of the century, the opening of new vistas on Earth history which specifically challenged a conventional reading of Genesis—that the Earth and the human race were of the same age. To interpret such developments within a rubric of "science versus religion" would, however, be unsatisfactory—not least because, among religious dissenters such as the Unitarian minister Joseph Priestley, science and true religion were fighting on the same side against the superstition and arbitrary political power which they saw vested in the established churches. Moreover, the sciences were popularized for many reasons having nothing to do with attacks on religion. In some cases they were perceived as supportive, not destructive of Christianity. Conversely, the motivation of those who attacked the established churches, and particularly the Catholic Church in France, often stemmed from social or political grievance.

It would therefore be a mistake to imagine that the sciences were valued in the eighteenth century only, or even principally, as an antidote to "priestcraft." As propagandists for science found new social contexts in which to assert its utility, it was practical utility, in the sense of solving technical problems, that usually came to the fore. A classic example would be the determination of longitude at sea. One of Newton's popularizers, William Whiston, was instrumental in petitioning the British Parliament in 1714 to offer incentives for a viable solution. Another, John Theophilus Desaguliers, placed before the Royal Society the benefits to be gained from mechanical inventions: his centrifugal bellows, eight feet in diameter, would, he hoped, clear the air in a ship's hold, in sick rooms or in noxious gasses dispersed from mines. A recent commentator has observed that Channel Row in London, where he gave his lecture courses, must have been a "jungle of instruments and machines."[10] The Royal Society was itself approached in the 1770s when the British government wished to know whether a blunt or pointed lightning conductor would be the more effective. By opening new avenues for patronage, the scientific societies often provided a forum in which a rhetoric of utility could yield new dividends. The chemist William Cullen addressed himself to problems in agriculture, bleaching, and salt purification to please aristocratic patrons with whom he conversed at the Philosophical Society of Edinburgh. In England, the Lunar Society of Birmingham gave Joseph Priestley access to the wealth of entrepreneurs, such as Matthew Boulton, James Watt, and Josiah Wedgwood. In return he would offer advice on the effects of different gases in the steam engine or analyze clay samples for Wedgwood's pottery.[11]

The concept of utility carried broader meanings, however, than the solution of technical problems. In a town such as Manchester, at the heart of Britain's industrial revolution, those who gathered at the Literary and Philosophical Society (founded 1781) justified their allegiance to science with many arguments. The promise of technical application was one, but so was the value of science as polite knowledge, a means of cultural expression particularly congenial to the medical membership. Science was also promoted as rational entertainment, suitable for the youth of a burgeoning town who might otherwise be seduced by tavern or brothel. A "relish for manly science" was considered by one member of the Manchester society, Thomas Barnes, to be second only to religion in cultivating business acumen.[12]

Scientific knowledge could be prized for its supposed objectivity, in salutary contrast to the warring factions of political or religious parties. A dispassionate quest for objective knowledge was proclaimed a virtue in its own right, as by Fontenelle, secretary of the Paris Academy of Science, whose eulogies of deceased members invariably praised their selfless commitment to human welfare. In a statement which shows how commitment to scientific research could almost become a surrogate religion, he claimed that physics became a kind of theology when properly pursued. In the Manchester society, science was commended as a profession and an integral part of a reforming ideology that placed higher value on intellectual attainment than noble birth or inherited wealth.

This picture would still be incomplete without reference to another kind of utility, a theological utility that stemmed from the disclosure of seemingly intelligent designs in the fabric of nature. Whether one referred to the exquisite, microscopic structures in living organisms that had so captivated Robert Boyle, the marvellous migratory instincts of birds that so impressed John Ray, or the elegant laws of nature that governed the Newtonian universe, there was a profound sense in which the sciences could reinforce arguments for design, thereby proving their utility against skeptical and atheistic philosophies that were commonly seen as subversive of a stable society.[13] Boyle himself had this in mind when he had declared that one could only be an atheist if one had *not* studied nature. He had also left money to sponsor annual sermons that would prove the Christian religion "against notorious infidels, viz. Atheists, Theists, Pagans, Jews, and Mahometans," but without descending to controversies among Christians themselves. In the first of these "Boyle lectures," and with the approval of Newton himself, the Cambridge scholar Richard Bentley established precise links between science and natural theology[14] by showing that the ordered motion of the planets could never have arisen through chance. Such infusion of natural theology with the latest science was to be a prominent feature of religious apologetics for much of the eighteenth century and, in the English-speaking world, an integral part of scientific culture until well into the nineteenth. Charles Darwin would later concede how very difficult it had been to emancipate himself from the belief that every detail of organic structure must serve a purpose. Because arguments for design constituted the main bridges between science and theology during this long period, their significance deserves special attention.[15]

III. THE AMBIVALENCE OF NATURAL THEOLOGY

In broad terms it is not difficult to explain why design arguments came to prominence in the apologetic literature of the Enlightenment. They were a convenient resource in the promotion of science, as when the great Swedish taxonomist Linnaeus gave his endeavors a theological justification:

> If the maker has furnished this globe, like a museum, with the most admirable proofs of his wisdom and power; if this splendid theatre would be adorned in vain without a spectator; and if Man the most perfect of all his works is alone capable of considering the wonderful economy of the whole; it follows that Man is made for the purpose of studying the Creator's works that he may observe in them the evident marks of divine wisdom.[16]

For those seeking a Biblical justification, there was always Romans 1:20, which seemed to imply that one could know enough of God through rational reflection on creation to be without excuse at the Day of Judgment. Design arguments had featured in the earlier rhetoric of Fellows of the Royal Society, who, if they were advocates of the new "mechanical philosophy," found it necessary not only to remove the stigma of atheism with which the atomic theories of antiquity were encumbered, but also to dissociate themselves from the materialism of Thomas Hobbes, who had extended the limits of mechanism to embrace a corporeal soul. Arguments for an intelligent designer could help to assuage suspicion and even promised some hope of consensus after political turmoil. It seemed reasonable to hope that everyone might agree on the evidence for a Creator, where finer points of doctrine were divisive. Among the pious it was hoped that rational arguments might convict hedonists and libertines of their errors. In almost every period there have been those who, like the Anglican bishop and mathematician, John Wilkins, have claimed they are living in a "degenerate age . . . miserably over-run with skepticism and infidelity." The fundamental requirement, Wilkins had written in 1675, was to "establish the great principles of religion, the being of God, and a future state; by showing how firm and solid a foundation they have in the nature and reason of mankind." This is revealing, because it shows how natural theology meant more than merely constructing arguments from the physical world. Wilkins had spoken of natural religion, meaning that it could be grounded in the natural faculties of men and especially their natural reason. That Wilkins had been both a Fellow of the Royal Society and a bishop suggests a further reason why natural theology was to enjoy such longevity in Britain. It helped to unify the interests of those steeped in both scientific and theological literature. It is no coincidence that the fashion for constructing design arguments did not seriously decline until the middle of the nineteenth century, when a new generation of scientific "professionals" effectively marginalized the clerical amateurs.[17] In the 1830s, when the British Association for the Advancement of Science was founded, clerics would constitute some thirty percent of its membership. In the period 1831 to 1865, no fewer than forty-one Anglican clergymen would preside over its various sections. Between 1866 and 1900, the number would fall to three. Appeals to the disclosures of science to generate a sense of religious awe were therefore integral to a sociocultural tradition which found its classic expression in William Paley's *Natural Theology* (1802). In Paley's celebrated argument, a world that resembled a watch had to have a maker with intelligence and personality. The human eye was so remarkable an instrument that it was as certain that it had been designed for vision as it was that the telescope had been made for assisting it.

To these general considerations one must add the political motivation that often lay behind the construction of natural theologies. To show that one form of government rather than another is the more "natural" is, after all, one of the most basic political devices. Some of Newton's popularizers observed that a constitutional monarchy in which a sovereign's power was moderated by Parliament bore a happy resemblance to the rule of a God whose power, according to Newtonian philosophy, was mediated through natural laws. Newton's emphasis on an active Providence in nature had also meant that low Church clergy who wished to justify the displacement of James II from the throne in the Glorious Revolution could appeal to a providential mandate that, in their view, took priority over the more conservative principle of the divine right of kings.[18]

The history of natural theology constitutes a challenge because there are no neat generalizations concerning its political dimensions. An obvious complication is that design arguments grounded in the natural sciences could be employed by pious Christians of every denomination, but also by their rationalist critics. Christians found them useful in their dialogues with unbelief, securing independent proof of a God, who they believed, had also revealed Himself in Christ. Yet the so-called Deists, vilified by Christians for their attacks on revelation, also had reasons for promoting the design arguments. The more that could be known of God through rational inference, the less, perhaps, was it necessary to refer to revelation at all. Among such freethinkers, the essence of true religion was often distilled into an ethical system ostensibly based on our "natural" sense of right and wrong. The creed of this "natural religion" was succinctly formulated by Voltaire:

> When reason, freed from its chains, will teach the people that there is only one God, that this God is the universal father of all men, who are brothers; that these brothers must be good and just to one another, and that they must practise all the virtues; that God, being good and just must reward virtue and punish crimes; surely, my brethren, men will be better for it and less superstitious.[19]

Such a creed appealed to the notorious republican Tom Paine who, in his *Age of Reason* (1794–1807) expressed the Deists' case with great aplomb. Whereas the Bible had been written by people, nature was the handiwork of God. Whereas the Bible had suffered corruption through copying and translation, nature had an indestructible perfection. Whereas the Bible portrays a passionate God, changeable and vindictive, nature shows Him immutable and benevolent. The biblical revelation had come late and been vouchsafed to one nation only. The revelation in nature had been always, and universally, available. In the Bible, God communicated with men through magic; in nature it was through their ordinary senses. Paine's triumphant conclusion was that theology was merely the study of human opinions concerning God, whereas science was the study of the divine laws governing nature.

The fact that Paine, no less than Paley, was confident that nature displays the handiwork of God can be confusing, but what it shows is that the bridges built between the sciences and theology by eighteenth-century thinkers often look the same when, in terms of political reality, they led to quite different programs of conservatism or reform. Consequently, to examine the bridges alone is not sufficient to give one an understanding of where such thinkers were heading. Each must be examined in context and with proper regard for their intentions.

IV. THE VULNERABILITY OF NATURAL THEOLOGY

It is easy to overlook the genuine sense of awe once experienced by those probing nature's secrets. Even the scales of a fish could be objects of great beauty when seen through a microscope. Appeals to the quality of divine craftsmanship even played a role in the liberation of natural philosophy from a lingering scholasticism. Reformist clergy in Spain, for example, pointed out that learned treatises on the nutritive and locomotive faculties of living things did little to generate an image of the Creator. Experimental philosophy, by contrast, had opened up a microscopic world that spoke volumes. According to the Benedictine monk Feijoo, when a dog's heart had been brought to his cell, his fellow monks agreed that "we had never seen or contemplated anything which gave such a clear idea of the power and wisdom of the supreme Craftsman."[20] It should not be surprising, then, that design arguments found favor among the pious. In an ongoing dialectic with unbelief, they supplied reasons for faith when that faith was being attacked as unreasonable. The New England divine Jonathan Edwards was moved by a spider's web but also by what he learned of comets from Newton's devotees. Edwards noted that " 'tis wisely ordered that when they are nearest the sun, where they are among the planets, and where their orbits come nearest together, they move swiftest and stay but a little while; which renders 'em less liable to be disturbed in their motions." Typically the argument was that, unless things had been arranged as they are, they would have been decidedly worse. Noting that "the wisdom of God appears in placing of the planets at a greater or lesser distance from the sun, according to their density," Edwards observed that "the water of our seas, if removed to the distance of Saturn from the sun, would remain perpetually frozen; and if as near the sun as Mercury, would constantly boil."[21]

We smile at the unsophistication, but the concern that church historians have often expressed is that such writing tends to celebrate God the Creator, God the Craftsman, God the Architect, God the Mathematician, at the expense of God the Redeemer. In other words, in meeting their rationalist critics on their own ground, Christian apologists were almost unwittingly sacrificing what was distinctive in their understanding of God. Writers such as Edwards, and Joseph Butler in England, would stress that there were dimensions of the gospel that could be gleaned only from revelation. But there certainly was a tendency in some Enlightenment theology to diminish the significance of Christ's redemptive mission. Long before Newtonian science gave new evidence of design, Pascal had warned that those who sought God apart from Christ, who went no further than nature, would fall into atheism or deism. To base arguments for a personal God on impersonal forces would lead to a bankrupt religion, because to neglect the person of Christ in dialogue with atheists was to neglect the one mediator between God and humanity. It is ironic that attempts to establish God's existence should encourage atheism, but there is a sense in which Pascal's prophecy came true. It is an old adage, attributed to the eighteenth-century freethinker Anthony Collins, that it would never have occurred to anyone to doubt God's existence if theologians had not tried so hard to prove it.

The thesis that physico-theology was damaging to Christian theology has recently been cast in persuasive form by Michael J. Buckley.[22] In his view, Newtonian popularizers such as Richard Bentley, William Whiston, and Samuel Clarke *were* engaged in the paradoxical enterprise of proving a personal God from impersonal nature. If they claimed their God could be known only through evidence of design in nature, they were digging His grave as well as their own. A Christian apologia reduced to the argument from design was easy prey to the alternative metaphysics of Lucretius: was not the appearance of design surely illusory, reflecting the simple fact that defective combinations of matter had not survived?

Buckley's argument is that atheism takes its meaning from the particular form of theism it rejects. So to understand the origins of modern atheism it is no good looking at the history of atheism. It is essential to examine the history of theism. Only then can we find the kind of theism to which modern atheism was an appropriate response. And he finds it in the theism of the Boyle lecturers. He notes how one of the central figures of the French Enlightenment, Denis Diderot, appears to have accepted their reasoning in his *Pensées Philosophiques* (1746), only to reject it in his *Lettre sur les Aveugles* (1749). The key point is that in the *Pensées* Diderot had already said that a physico-theology provided the *only* road to God. With the collapse of that road there was simply nothing left.

Further investigation is necessary to determine whether Christian apologists had been so reductive as to imply that there was only the one route by which God might be apprehended. It is possible that their critics, such as Diderot and Hume, found it convenient to pin such a belief upon them. Nevertheless, the stark polarity between a physico-theology and the refutation it invited did have an echo in contemporary literature. This was Pierre Maupertuis in his *Essai de Cosmologie* (1756):

> All the philosophers of our time belong to two sects. One group wishes to subjugate nature to a purely material order and to exclude all intelligent principles from it. . . . The others, on the contrary, make constant use of final causes to discover . . . the views of the Creator, penetrating his intent in the smallest of phenomena. According to the first group, the universe could do without God. . . . According to the latter, the tiniest parts of the universe constitute repeated demonstrations [of his Being]. His Power, Wisdom and Goodness are painted on the wings of butterflies and in every spider's web.[23]

It is not, then, surprising that atheism should have emerged in Paris, if the case for a Christian theism was suspended from a spider's web.

The physico-theology of the Enlightenment attracts critical comment for the additional reason that it was logically flawed. In their well-known critiques, both Hume and Kant showed how the argument from design assumed the existence of a Creator, the very point it was designed to prove. Through the character of Philo in his posthumous *Dialogues Concerning Natural Religion* (1779), Hume voiced a series of telling objections. Even if the world does resemble a machine, or some other human artifact, this would not itself prove the existence of a single transcendent Mind, because many minds can be involved in the design and construction of a man-made machine.

Stressing the fragility of analogical argument, Hume observed that the order and purpose in nature, which theologians captured with their mechanical analogues, could just as easily be predicated of an animal or vegetable. And if the world, as Philo suggested, resembles an animal or vegetable more than a watch or knitting loom, the cause of the world might be an egg or superseed rather than a prescient Creator. If there were other worlds with which this might be compared, then it might be possible to say whether this is more like a machine than another, but faced with the singularity of our universe, any inferences drawn on the basis of analogy are bound to be precarious. Hume also insisted that a cause must always be proportioned to its effects, and that it was therefore hopeless trying to elicit the infinite attributes of a transcendent deity from the patterns of a finite world. That there was so much pain and grief in the world could, on the basis of the same reasoning as that of the apologists, suggest a malevolent Mind. Although Philo conceded that the world might bear some remote resemblance to a work of human intelligence, the analogy was too weak to have any bearing on how we should lead our lives. Hume's skepticism, as has often been observed, amounted to atheism for all practical purposes. Although engaged on a different philosophical exercise, Kant, in common with Hume, argued that it was impossible in *reason* to find a justification for any dispensation in a future life different from that experienced in this. To make the world morally coherent, it was necessary, according to Kant, to *postulate* a rational and moral Being who, as Creator and sustainer of the world, has the necessary power to make happiness proportional to virtue. But this was very far from claiming that the objective existence of such a Being could be rationally demonstrated. Kant's important conclusion was that all theodicies, all attempts to rationalize suffering, were misguided. The only authentic stance in the face of adversity was that of Job, who had refused to accept the rationalizations of his friends.[24]

Consequently, if the bridges built by physico-theologians eventually collapsed, it was not simply that they were undermined by science. It was rather that a greater burden had been placed on the sciences than they could support. By the end of the eighteenth century this was becoming increasingly transparent, as new developments, especially in the historical sciences, threw into doubt some of the presuppositions on which natural theology had depended. An obvious example would be the recognition of extinction in the fossil record, demonstrating that the world had not been static and fixed. Other important contrasts can be drawn between the late seventeenth and late eighteenth centuries, indicative of what might be called a secularization of knowledge.

V. THE SECULARIZATION OF KNOWLEDGE

During the eighteenth century there certainly were transformations within natural philosophy that created new opportunities for critics of religious orthodoxy. There were such changes in matter theory, in celestial mechanics, in the earth and life sciences.

One hundred years separated the chemistry of Joseph Priestley from that of Robert Boyle. But what a transformation occurred in that period! For Boyle, matter was corpuscular but had no inherent powers. It owed its motion ultimately to God. In Boyle's universe there was also room for spirits and for things above reason. With Priestley, however, the matter/spirit distinction collapses. Powers previously ascribed to spirit agencies were now lodged in matter itself. In fact, chemistry provided a metaphor for a material cosmos. With controlled experiments on different airs (gasses), Priestley argued that the vocabulary of chemists need no longer refer to spirits. Correspondingly, he argued that the term "spirit" should also be expunged from the vocabulary of theologians. Christianity, he believed, had been corrupted by Platonism. Whereas Boyle could say that he had received "pregnant hints" from a greater Chemist than he, Priestley dismissed the idea of divine influence on the human mind as vulgar superstition.

One hundred years separated Newton and Laplace. The contrast between them has become archetypal for the exclusion of God from the universe. Contradicting Descartes, Newton had insisted that an orderly solar system could not have emerged through natural causes alone. There had been the intervention of that Being who, like Newton himself, was "very well skilled in mechanics and geometry." And in Newton we find those reformations of the solar system which, whether directly or indirectly, were under divine supervision: the loss of planetary speed through friction and the loss of matter from the sun through evaporation had to be corrected. In Laplace we find a self-correcting solar system and a nebular hypothesis that allowed the system to *emerge* from a rotating, cooling, contracting, solar atmosphere. A God known through Newton's science was, in the name of science, reduced to a dispensable hypothesis.

One hundred years separated the *Sacred Theory of the Earth* of Thomas Burnet from the *Theory of the Earth* (1795) of James Hutton. During that period the word *sacred* was lost. In Burnet, the Earth's physical history had a direction, reflecting biblical phases. Noah's flood, for example, had had permanent effects on the earth's surface. There was a mechanistic explanation for the flood, but the mechanism had been exquisitely timed to reflect a divine initiative in the face of human depravity. In the controversial system of the Scotsman, James Hutton, the Earth's physical history did not have a sense of direction. We find repeated cycles of mountain building and erosion. And we also find those famous words: no vestige of a beginning, nor prospect of an end. As for Providence, Hutton saw wisdom in his physical system, but the synchronization between physical catastrophe and divine punishment had gone.

One hundred years separated Lamarck's theories of organic transformation from the published work of John Ray. There was no mention of the deity in the title of Lamarck's works; but Ray had chosen for his, *Of the Wisdom of God as Manifested in the Works of Creation*. By the works of creation Ray explained that he meant "the works, created by God at first, and by Him conserved to this day in the same state and condition in which they were at first made." There was no space here for extinction or the emergence of new forms. Perplexed by strange fossils, Ray had simply suggested that their living counterparts were yet to be discovered. The contrast with Lamarck is striking. Although the French naturalist was almost as loath to admit extinction, organic forms were now described as products of nature rather than as God's unchangeable creatures. In Ray, the immaculate adaptation of an organism to its environment was evidence of design. For Lamarck, those powers of adaptation resided in the organism itself. Whereas Ray had no need to extend the age of the Earth, by the time Lamarck was writing, his patron Buffon had already placed the appearance of the human race relatively late in what he called the "dark abyss" of time.

To describe such transformations as a secularization, or perhaps profanation, of knowledge would seem perfectly appropriate. And it would be easy to show how each met with clerical resistance. Whether such changes in the character of science should be described as *agents* of secularization is, however, a rather different question.

VI. SCIENCE AS AN AGENT OF SECULARIZATION

The large-scale transformations we have just considered give the impression that the meaning attributed to novel science is always unilateral—on the side of liberation against intellectual dogma. But when the controversies surrounding scientific innovation are studied at ground level, all sorts of complications arise. To discern the secularization of knowledge in eighteenth-century transformations is not the same as locating in the sciences the motor of secularization. Four considerations justify this distinction:

(1) The immediate response to reports of scientific innovation do not usually support a simple polarity between the sacred and the secular.
(2) Conclusions seen by some religious thinkers as subversive of their authority are often welcomed by others, or modified in an attempt to make them harmless.
(3) In many of the conflicts in which both scientific and theological interests were at stake, the science was merely giving substance to, or illuminating, preexisting conflicts between different metaphysical positions.
(4) Particular styles of science may reflect secular attitudes that have already come about through quite distinct social and economic forces.

I have discussed these complications in more detail elsewhere,[25] but a brief illustration can be given of each. An instructive example of how the polarity between the sacred and the secular can collapse is provided by responses to John Needham's claims for the spontaneous generation of microorganisms from an infusion of rotten corn. His data, according to Voltaire, were proving a delight to materialists anxious to show that matter could organize itself. Operating with a simple polarity, we might expect Voltaire to welcome them. But no. He dismissed Needham's results as the work of an Irish Jesuit who was merely faking a miracle. He could vent his anticlerical feelings more freely by attacking the results than by accepting them—a little uncharitably perhaps, given that Needham, an English Catholic, was neither Irish nor Jesuit.

Again, when Buffon made the heretical suggestion that the Earth might have originated in the collision between a comet and the sun, Voltaire, far from warming to a liberating idea, complained that it reminded him of the Greek fable in which Minerva had emerged from the brain of Jupiter. It was too conjectural. Buffon was dismissed for having tried to create a world with the stroke of his pen. Attacks on what were termed "hypotheses" and "physical romances" came *both* from obtuse champions of tradition and from those who rejected a type of science too removed from experience. For the latter, Buffon's science did not constitute a secularization of knowledge—for it was not yet knowledge.

The response to Laplace in Britain and America illustrates the second complication: the diversity of meanings that can be attributed to a particular piece of science. In Britain there was discomfort at the thought that Laplace had deliberately excluded teleological considerations. But since he had started with the assumption that planets revolving in the same direction and almost the same plane could not be the result of chance, it was actually quite easy to turn his reasoning into an argument for design. What for Laplace was an antithesis between chance and mechanism could easily be translated into an antithesis between chance and design.[26] Faced with Laplace's rejection of divine intervention in the maintenance of the solar system, the Cambridge philosopher William Whewell simply argued that a system in which the machinery could stabilize itself was evidence of more sophisticated engineering than one requiring frequent attention.

The third complication can be illustrated by reference to one of the most beguiling questions in popular scientific literature: Is there intelligent life on other worlds? As Michael Crowe has shown, there were theological arguments both for and against, and scientific arguments both for and against.[27] In such circumstances it becomes impossible to make science the agent of secularization. All one can say is that new scientific data may actuate or illuminate a debate, the metaphysical parameters of which already exist. For example, the question whether there are superfluous features of creation was usually at the heart of the plurality-of-worlds debate. What was the purpose of those manifold suns, if not to shine on other worlds? How easily might an atheist exploit a universe in which, by some lucky fluke, life had appeared on one planet only! And yet, to admit other worlds was to raise awkward questions about the spiritual state of their inhabitants, which Tom Paine used to attack the Christian revelation. There were uncomfortable decisions, but no straightforward coordination between a scientific and a secular position. In his *Astro-theology* of 1715, the Boyle lecturer William Derham rejoiced that Christians had been liberated from an infantile anthropocentric view of the universe. Later commentators, including John Wesley and William Whewell, would feel less comfortable with a pluralist position. It could so easily compromise the uniqueness of the Incarnation. On the issue of extraterrestrial intelligence, the scientific data remained, and still remain, indeterminate, but the basic choices had existed in some form since antiquity.

In the fourth complication resides the crucial question whether particular styles of science already reflect changing cultural values—rather than cause them. A glance at the deist literature of the late seventeenth and early eighteenth century shows that freethinkers in Britain, such as John Toland, Anthony Collins, and Matthew Tindal, did their best to capitalize on a new scientific understanding of the world. But they could only do so by re-interpreting it in ways that suited them. Toland even drew attention to this fact by saying that Newton's science did not have to be interpreted as Newton had done. Inclining towards pantheism, Toland wanted matter to contain its own inherent powers—the very proposition Newton had denied with reference to his gravitational force. There was, in other words, a cultural contest between Christian theists and their detractors for the correct interpretation of a scientific concept. It is not that the concept had some inherent secularizing force. If the science constructed by Laplace towards the end of the eighteenth century is considered, there is a strong case for saying that it reflected the secular values associated with French intellectual life preceding and at the time of the Revolution. According to Roger Hahn, the exclusion of God from celestial mechanics occasioned little surprise in Paris. Indeed, during the preceding twenty years or so, the deity had already been so excluded even *before* the mathematics required it.[28] There had even been professors at the College de Navarre in Paris who, as early as 1781, had deemed it bad *theology* to invoke divine activity as a solution to physical problems.[29]

VII. SOME CRITIQUES OF CHRISTIAN THEOLOGY

In shaping attitudes towards Christian theology there were, arguably, more potent forces than the natural sciences. There was, for example, nothing like religious intolerance for spawning intolerance of religion. Throughout his life Voltaire sympathized with those persecuted for their religious beliefs. In 1762, a Huguenot merchant was tortured and executed in the Catholic city of Toulouse for allegedly murdering his son, who wished to become a Catholic. Voltaire was convinced that the evidence pointed to suicide and that the wretched father had been victim of religious prejudice. Three years of campaigning, in which Voltaire played a prominent role, finally forced the government to rescind the verdict. Much of the venom that went into Enlightenment attacks on established Christianity was produced by a sense of political injustice. Thomas Jefferson was deeply impressed by the extent of religious intolerance he encountered during his European travels, especially in German lands. In his diary he recorded the oppression of Protestants by the ruling Catholics in Köln, noting the converse persecution of Catholics by Protestants in Frankfurt.[30] Jefferson was to have much in common with Joseph Priestley, who campaigned for the toleration of Catholics as well as Protestant dissenters in late eighteeenth-century England. But prejudices ran very deep and, by including Catholics in a scheme of universal toleration, Priestley offended many of his fellow dissenters, who felt their own case was being jeopardized.[31]

In waging war against the privileges of the established churches, the task of ridiculing Christian dogmatism was made easier by reference to other cultures. The argument could take many forms. How were the unregenerate of distant lands to be judged when they had had no opportunity to learn of Christ's redemptive mission? The notion that Christian teaching was a prerequisite of a civilized polity was difficult to sustain in the light of reports from China. Among the more barbarous nations, as David Hume put it, miracles abounded. In fact every religious tradition seemed to have its own miracles, thereby calling all into doubt. In his *Christianity as Old as the Creation* (1730), sometimes called the "Bible of the Deists," Matthew Tindal's arguments against revelation were almost all grounded in forms of cultural relativism. There were simply too many contending claims for special revelation for any one to be authentic. His argument against the Christian miracles was not that they were impossible because they contradicted scientific laws, but that they were rendered nugatory by the existence of comparable marvels in every tradition. Indeed an ingenious method of undermining the Christian religion, whilst appearing to uphold it, was to pretend that the claims of Christianity were better authenticated than those of other religions, whilst actually showing that they were susceptible to the same exposure.[32]

Critics of Christianity would also focus on the ethical demands of a faith that seemed to require the suppression of natural instincts or to inhibit the fulfillment of human potential. In Edinburgh, Hume complained of the futility of the monkish virtues when what was required was a civic morality in which men and women would take pride in working for the good of their town and nation. In Paris, Diderot drew an attractive contrast between the guiltless sexuality of the Tahitians and the sexual repression of Catholic clergy. In shaping secular attitudes there were more accessible forms of rhetoric than those drawing on the sciences. A telling example, from the clandestine literature of eighteenth-century France, would be the tirade of the heretical priest Jean Meslier, who considered it pointless to ask who made matter and set it in motion. That question merely prompted another: Who made the being who had supposedly done the job? And what was to be gained by speaking of a perfect being when it would have to be held responsible for evil as well as good? Atheists, he insisted, were just as capable as others of practicing virtue. Religions in general were fabrications fostered by ruling elites. The Old Testament notion of a favored people he considered morally repugnant. Christian morality, too, was indefensible, because it encouraged the acceptance of suffering, submission to one's foes, acquiescence in the face of tyranny—just such tyranny as had been practiced by the kings of France, their police, censors, and tax gatherers. Theologians habitually and horribly explained away injustice and deformity as the will of an all-wise being. Their doctrine that the wrongs of this world would be righted in the next was equally distasteful. It enlisted a fraudulent immortal soul and encouraged apathy towards social reform.[33]

Such a rhetoric, however extreme it appeared to those who would be most hurt by it, could stand by itself without needing support from the natural sciences. Studies of those who lost their faith in nineteenth-century Britain have similarly shown that one may greatly exaggerate the relevance of scientific innovation.[34] Much of this essay has been written with the intention of showing that greater subtlety is required in discussions of the relations between science and theology, because the disciplinary boundaries and concerns of later generations might not have been those that most animated their predecessors. The very enterprise of abstracting the "science" and the "theology" of earlier generations with a view to seeing how they were related can lead to artificial results. There is, however, a degree of consensus among historians that one of the most striking features of eighteenth-century philosophy was the emergence of the human sciences and that they, arguably more than the natural sciences, effected a kind of secularization even where this was unintentional. To regard human beings no longer as pilgrims, as immortal souls in need of salvation, but as objects of study, whose minds, habits, and beliefs might even be explained in social terms, was one of the most profound shifts associated with the Enlightenment.[35]

There is no space here to discuss the new theories proposed for the workings of the human mind, many of which referred to the association of ideas as a principal mechanism and some of which, as in David Hartley's *Observations on Man* (1749), offered material explanations for how particular ideas came to be associated. Hartley spoke of patterns of vibration in a medullary ether that could be, as it were, reactivated with the appropriate stimulus. It would be incorrect to imply that there were atheistic intentions behind such schema. Hartley saw no threat to human immortality from such an explanatory program and nor did his great admirer, Priestley, for whom belief in the resurrection of the dead remained the only ultimate guarantee of social control.[36] Nevertheless it was obviously possible to place a more subversive interpretation on materialist accounts of the mind, especially where they were perceived to undermine free will.

If developments in the human sciences could have unintentional but nevertheless insidious effects on perceptions of human sanctity, it has to be said that the effects were sometimes intentional. In arguing that human personality was shaped not by innate reason but by social experience, Hume created further analytical tools for a critique of Christian theology and the pretensions of those who defended it. We have already had occasion to note his critique of the argument for design. Potentially more devastating was his *Natural History of Religion*, a work composed about 1750 but left unpublished. In this, Hume rejected the contention of both Deists and divines that monotheism was the "natural" religion of mankind. The origins of religious practices were to be found neither in the exercise of natural reason nor in the contemplation of the natural order, but in fear, ignorance, and attempts to placate local deities. The original religions of the world, Hume suggested, were polytheistic, as the contrary events of human life were ascribed to limited and imperfect deities. Nor was the historical movement from polytheism to monotheism the product of rational refinement. Men had either supposed that, in the distribution of power among the gods, their nation was subject to the jurisdiction of their particular deity or, projecting earthly models heavenward, had come to represent one god as the "prince or supreme magistrate of the rest." And it was again through fear of this supreme god that his praises were sung. Monotheism had been reached not by reason but by the "adulation and fears of the most vulgar superstition." Once the attributes of the deity had been extrapolated to infinity, he had become so remote and incomprehensible a figure that mediators had been invented which, like the Virgin Mary, had become more accessible objects of devotion. When this process was overdone, a reaction towards a purer theism would again set in. Hume applied this scenario to every religion, observing in them all a tendency towards fanaticism. Monotheistic religions, more than polytheistic, had been guilty of intolerance. The cynicism in his suggestion that the prospect of an afterlife had too feeble a grip on human minds to influence behavior proved difficult to refute.

VIII. CONCLUSION: THEN AND NOW

There are few more discomfiting experiences for believers than to be told why they hold a particular set of beliefs, to be given social or historical reasons that have not been part of their consciousness. Hume's account was damaging in this respect. But it was even more so because Hume was denying that monotheism was either the most natural or the most rational form of belief. In this respect he undermined one of the Enlightenment's most cherished projects. One of the main lessons of historical scholarship is that we can no longer speak of archetypal Enlightenment mentalities or goals. There was striking variation from one European nation to another, and in different contexts the bridges between science and theology were differently constructed.[37] A sense of opposition between the two was more keenly felt in France than in England. The quest for a religious creed that could withstand rational assault and which marginalized sectarian interests was, however, a recurrent one. It is typified perhaps by Thomas Jefferson and his educational preferences.

In the twentieth century we have become used to the idea of local rationalities that are context-dependent. For Jefferson and many of his contemporaries, this would have been an alien notion. The hope was to achieve a kind of universality by abstracting human rationality from communities of interest that might limit or distort its conclusions. From a tradition-free, confessionally neutral starting point, universally compelling reasons were sought to accept the existence of God, the immortality of the soul, and the authority of the moral law. For Jefferson such a rational religion was appropriate for public consumption. Confessional religion, in its many sectarian forms, was to be privatized—not even studied according to the statutes of his University of Virginia. Only the rational nucleus, allegedly common to all the sects and embracing the proofs of God's existence, was deemed worthy of public consideration.[38]

In retrospect, the belief that there was a rational core that could be abstracted from all religions and that would eventually triumph as the best and most "natural" religion seems strangely optimistic. It has been seen as parochial in that it reflected the strains (in both senses) of Protestant Christianity. It was vulnerable to the kind of critique we have just seen in Hume. Insofar as it drew on scientific theory to inform the "proofs" of God's existence, it placed on the sciences a burden they would eventually be unable to carry. Rational theologies were apt to create a rather arid spirituality, in reaction to which the evangelical religion of a John Wesley could offer a more personal and emotionally supportive experience. In early nineteenth century Britain, the poet Coleridge complained that he was weary of the word *evidence*, weary of reference to "evidences of Christianity." Make a man feel the need of it, was his advice. Even within the small scientific community of the early nineteenth century, there were reactions against the physico-theology of a mechanistic universe. Coleridge's young chemical friend, Humphry Davy, spoke of a religious experience in which "Every thing seemed alive, and myself part of the series of visible impressions; I should have felt pain in tearing a leaf from one of the trees."[39]

In our own day the pendulum has swung again in such a direction, with ecological concerns informing organic theologies of nature. It has been observed, however, that something of the Jeffersonian view still survives in the academic study of religion, at least where the philosophy of religion is conceived as having as a primary goal the elucidation of what is common to the major religions of the world. In the increasingly pluralistic societies of the Western world, and with the resurgence of fundamentalist and nationalist movements elsewhere, a clarification of their differences is arguably a more urgent desideratum.

NOTES

1. Voltaire, "Sermon of the Fifty," in Peter Gay, ed., *Deism: An Anthology* (Princeton: Van Nostrand, 1968), pp. 152–153.

2. Ernst Cassirer, *The Philosophy of the Enlightenment*, trans. Fritz, C.A. Koelln, and James P. Pettegrove (Princeton: Princeton University Press, 1951).

3. Peter Gay, *The Enlightenment, An Interpretation*, 2 vols. (New York: Alfred P. Knopf, 1966-9).

4. David C. Lindberg and Robert S. Westman, eds., *Reappraisals of the Scientific Revolution* (New York and Cambridge: Cambridge University Press, 1990).

5. The inadequacies of this "separation" thesis are explored more fully in John Hedley Brooke, *Science and Religion: Some Historical Perspectives* (New York and Cambridge: Cambridge University Press, 1991), ch. 2.

6. Richard S. Westfall, *Never at Rest: A Biography of Isaac Newton* (New York and Cambridge: Cambridge University Press, 1984); James E. Force, "The Newtonians and Deism," in James E. Force and Richard H. Popkin, eds., *Essays on the Context, Nature and Influence of Isaac Newton's Theology* (Dordrecht; Boston: Kluwer Academic Publishers, 1990), ch. 4; Brooke, *Science and Religion*, pp. 135–151.

7. Amos Funkenstein, *Theology and the Scientific Imagination from the Middle Ages to the Seventeenth Century* (Princeton: Princeton University Press, 1986).

8. John Hedley Brooke, "Natural Law in the Natural Sciences: The Origins of Modern Atheism?" *Science and Christian Belief* 4 (1992), pp. 83–103.

9. *Science and Religion*, ch. 2.

10. Larry Stewart, *The Rise of Public Science: Rhetoric, Technology and Natural Philosophy in Newtonian Britain, 1660–1750* (New York and Cambridge: Cambridge University Press, 1992), p. 225.

11. Jan Golinski, *Science as Public Culture: Chemistry and Enlightenment in Britain, 1760–1820* (New York and Cambridge: Cambridge University Press, 1992), chs. 2 and 3.

12. Arnold Thackray, "Natural Knowledge in Cultural Context: The Manchester Model," *American Historical Review* 79 (1974), pp. 672–709.

13. Neal C. Gillespie, "Natural History, Natural Theology and Social Order: John Ray and the 'Newtonian Ideology'," *Journal of the History of Biology* 20 (1987), pp. 1–49.

14. John Gascoigne, "From Bentley to the Victorians: The Rise and Fall of British Newtonian Natural Theology," *Science in Context* 2 (1988), pp. 219–256.

15. The discussion that follows is largely based on the more extensive treatment in *Science and Religion*, chs. 5 and 6, where fuller documentation is given.

16. C. Linnaeus, *Reflections on the Study of Nature* (1754), trans. J.E. Smith (1786), quoted in D.C. Goodman, *Buffon's Natural History* (Milton Keynes: Open University Press, 1980), p. 18.

17. Frank M. Turner, "The Victorian Conflict Between Science and Religion: A Professional Dimension," *Isis* 69 (1978), pp. 356–376.

18. Margaret C. Jacob, *The Newtonians and the English Revolution, 1689–1720* (Ithaca, N.Y.: Cornell University Press, 1976); John Gascoigne, *Cambridge in the Age of the Enlightenment: Science, Religion and Politics from the Restoration to the French Revolution* (New York and Cambridge: Cambridge University Press, 1989); and compare Stewart, *Public Science*, pp. 143–182.

19. "Sermon of the Fifty," pp. 152–153.

20. David C. Goodman, "Science and the Clergy in the Spanish Enlightenment," *History of Science* 21 (1983), pp. 111–140.

21. Jonathan Edwards, *Scientific and Philosophical Writings,* ed. Wallace E. Anderson (New Haven: Yale University Press, 1980), p. 309.

22. Michael J. Buckley SJ, *At the Origins of Modern Atheism* (New Haven: Yale University Press, 1987).

23. Quoted by Roger Hahn, "Laplace and the Mechanistic Universe," in David C. Lindberg and Ronald L. Numbers, *God and Nature: Historical Essays on the Encounter between Christianity and Science* (Berkeley: University of California, 1986), pp. 256–276, on p. 265.

24. John L. Mackie, *The Miracle of Theism: Arguments For and Against the Existence of God* (Oxford: Clarendon Press; New York: Oxford University Press, 1982); Michel Despland, *Kant on History and Religion* (Montreal: McGill-Queen's University Press, 1973); F.E. England, *Kant's Conception of God: A Critical Exposition of its Metaphysical Development* (New York: Dial Press, 1930; reprint ed., 1968), pp. 143–168.

25. John Hedley Brooke, "Science and the Secularization of Knowledge: Perspectives on Some Eighteenth Century Transformations," *Nuncius* 4 (1989), pp. 43–65; Brooke, *Science and Religion*, ch. 5.

26. Ronald L. Numbers, *Creation by Natural Law: Laplace's Nebular Hypothesis in American*

Thought (Seattle: University of Washington Press, 1977); John Hedley Brooke, "Indications of a Creator: Whewell as Apologist and Priest," in Menachem Fisch and Simon Schaffer, eds., *William Whewell: A Composite Portrait* (Oxford: Clarendon Press; New York: Oxford University Press, 1991), pp. 149–173.

27. Michael J. Crowe, *The Extra-terrestrial Life Debate 1750–1900: The Idea of a Plurality of Worlds from Kant to Lowell* (New York and Cambridge: Cambridge University Press, 1986).

28. Hahn, "Laplace," in Lindberg and Numbers, *God and Nature*, p. 272.

29. L.W.B. Brockliss, *French Higher Education in the Seventeenth and Eighteenth Centuries: A Cultural History* (Oxford: Clarendon Press; New York: Oxford University Press, 1987).

30. James McGrath Morris and Persephone Weene, eds., *Thomas Jefferson's European Travel Diaries* (Ithaca, N.Y.: Cornell University Press, 1987), pp. 115, 119.

31. Martin Fitzpatrick, "Toleration and Truth," *Enlightenment and Dissent* 1 (1982), pp. 3–31.

32. David Berman, "Disclaimers as Offence Mechanisms in Charles Blount and John Toland," in Michael Hunter and David Wootton, eds., *Atheism from the Reformation to the Enlightenment* (Oxford: Clarendon Press; New York: Oxford University Press, 1992), pp. 255–272.

33. John Stephenson Spink, *French Free Thought from Gassendi to Voltaire* (London: University of London Press, 1960), pp. 277–278.

34. Susan Budd, *Varieties of Unbelief: Atheists and Agnostics in English Society 1850–1960* (London: Heinemann Educational Books; New York: Holmes and Meier Publishers, 1977).

35. Roger Smith, "The Language of Human Nature," in James G. Buickerwood, Christopher Fox, and Roy Porter, eds., *Inventing Human Science* (Berkeley: University of California Press, 1995).

36. John Hedley Brooke, "'A Sower Went Forth': Joseph Priestley and the Ministry of Reform," in A. Truman Schwarz and John G. McEvoy, eds., *Motion Toward Perfection: The Achievement of Joseph Priestley* (Boston: Skinner House Books, Unitarian Universalist Association, 1990), pp. 21–56.

37. Roy Porter and Mikulas Teich, eds., *The Enlightenment in National Context* (New York and Cambridge: Cambridge University Press, 1981); Thomas L. Hankins, *Science and the Enlightenment* (New York and Cambridge: Cambridge University Press, 1985); George S. Rousseau and Roy Porter, eds., *The Ferment of Knowledge: Studies in the Historiography of Eighteenth-Century Science* (New York and Cambridge: Cambridge University Press, 1980).

38. John P. Clayton, "Thomas Jefferson and the Study of Religion," an Inaugural Lecture, University of Lancaster, November 18, 1992.

39. Quoted by David M. Knight, *Humphry Davy: Science and Power* (Cambridge, US and Oxford: Basil Blackwell, 1992), p. 36.

I. THE WARFARE MYTH

For any viable present discussion of the relations between theology and the sciences, it is essential to understand the profound changes in the theological scene that have occurred since the beginning of the nineteenth century. All too often in the contemporary discussion, both by scientists and by theologians, attention is focused sharply on the impact of new scientific views; the equally dramatic theological changes have been ignored or misunderstood. My concern here is, therefore, to direct attention to aspects of the nineteenth-century story, though with a few suggestions of implications for the present.[1]

To start in the simplest terms, it is necessary to dispell some common myths about a presumed "split" between theology and science—and I use the term "myth" here in the popular or vulgar sense of an imaginary story that is untrue. One such myth is the so-called "warfare" between science and theology/religion, which allegedly took place (or was intensified, though it certainly did not originate) in the nineteenth century.

This conflict language comes in part from the titles of two widely known books of the latter years of the century. One was the *History of the Conflict Between Religion and Science*, by John William Draper, professor of physiology at New York University (written in 1873, published in 1874, and translated into French, German, Italian, Spanish, Polish, Russian, Portuguese, and Serbian—and put on the Vatican's Index in 1876).[2] The other was *A History of the Warfare of Science with Theology in Christendom*, by Andrew Dickson White, for many years president of Cornell University—a work that originated in a lecture and small book of the 1870s (entitled, respectively, "The Battlefields of Science" and *The Warfare of Science*) and gradually expanded into two large volumes by 1896.[3] Particularly because of the hypostatization of "science" and "religion" which these two books represented and encouraged (especially Draper's book), a more careful look is worthwhile.

Both of these works seem clearly to have had their origin as responses to Pope Pius IX's *Syllabus of Errors* of 1864, which concluded by listing the 80th "error" of supposing that the Pope ought to reconcile himself "with progress, with liberalism, and with modern civilization." And both books turn out to be bitter attacks on *institutional*

Christianity much more than serious discussions of substantive issues.

In Draper's case, the animus is directed almost exclusively toward the Roman Catholic Church. He largely exempts Protestantism (and the Greek churches as well) from the criticism, since he thinks Protestantism has never allied itself with the civil power, as Catholicism has regularly done in its attempt to maintain an imperious and domineering position. And he professes support for "religion," affirming that "modern Science is the legitimate sister—indeed it is the twin-sister—of the Reformation."[4] His concluding contention is that

> Institutions that organize impostures and spread delusions must show what right they have to exist. Faith must render an account of herself to Reason. Mysteries must give place to facts. . . . There must be absolute freedom for thought. The ecclesiastic must learn to keep himself within the domain he has chosen, and cease to tyrannize over the philosopher, who, conscious of his own strength and the purity of his motives [*sic!*], will bear such interference no longer.[5]

Enough about Draper, whose language here represents the kind of "balloon dualism" (Owen Chadwick's image[6]) by which he represents the whole history of science and institutional religion. (Draper, incidentally, had been privately ridiculed by scientists at the famous 1860 Oxford meeting of the British Association, where Wilberforce and Huxley had their debate over the *Origin of Species*.) White, though often haphazard in his long account, written over decades in the midst of his presidency and some periods of government service, and published periodically as "New Chapters in the Warfare of Science" in *Popular Science Monthly*, was from the outset much concerned to distinguish *religion* from *theology*. Though he is never clear about what he means by religion, the attack is always against the "theologians," and he considers himself a friend to religion. For example:

> In all modern history, interference with science in the supposed interest of religion, no matter how contentious such interference may have been, has resulted in the direst evils both to religion and to science, and invariably; and, on the other hand, all untrammelled scientific investigation, no matter how dangerous to religion some of its stages may have seemed for the time to be, has invariably resulted in the highest good both of religion and of science.[7]

In other words, it is the recalcitrant "theologians" who have been the problem.

It also needs to be noted that for both Draper and White, especially White, the development of biblical criticism gets more attention than does evolutionary theory. White does begin with a discussion of the latter,[8] concluding that despite the "final effort of theology," evolution is established and "science has given us conceptions far more noble, and opened the way to an argument from design infinitely more beautiful than any ever developed by theology."[9] But the longer, concluding chapter of Volume II is devoted to higher criticism, which has opened "treasures of thought which have been inaccessible to theologians for two thousand years," and has led to "the conception of a vast community in which the fatherhood of God overarches all, and the brotherhood of man permeates all," so that the Bible is no longer an oracle or a fetish, but a revelation of the ascent of man and of the "eternal law of righteousness—the one upward path for individuals and nations."[10] This is "a most fruitful fact, which religion and science may accept as a source of strength to both."[11]

Now, this is language remarkably similar to what many liberal theologians were saying in response to evolutionary theory and to biblical criticism. Draper and White do complain, with much detail and validity, about the obstacles that institutional Christianity so often placed in the way of free scientific inquiry. But the popular legend epitomized by the titles of their books is no more than legend. The story of theological response to Darwin is infinitely more complex, as I have tried to show in my own history of Protestant thought in the nineteenth century,[12] and this is even more fully documented in James R. Moore's masterful work *The Post-Darwinian Controversies*, which demolishes the metaphor of warfare as an historical interpretation for the British and American theological scene.[13] Most recently, Frederick Gregory in *Nature Lost?*[14] has shown how, in nineteenth-century German theology as well, there were quite varying responses to Darwin, ranging from the enthusiastic embrace of David Friedrich Strauss in his 1872 *The Old Faith and the New*, through the mediating efforts of Rudolf Schmid, to the conservative Lutheran Otto Zöckler of Greifswald (who, Gregory argues, "wrote earlier and more about theology and Darwinism than any other theologian in Europe, England, or America"[15]). Reactions to *Origin of Species* among the theologians, especially Protestant but also Roman Catholic,[16] were in fact just about as varied as among scientists, as Thomas F. Glick has amply demonstrated.[17] To be sure, major accommodations in theology were made in response to both evolutionary theory and biblical criticism (and I agree with White that the latter was actually much more important—more of this later). But the image of "warfare" has almost nothing to do with the actual history of theology or of science in the nineteenth century (though it may be relevant to the fundamentalist controversies of the 1920s, symbolized by the Scopes trial, and to the ridiculous attempts at "creation science" in recent years).

If we want real instances of warfare, we would do better to think of Comte's positivism, or of the emergence of a radical materialistic monism particularly in Germany in the 1850s, for instance, in Ludwig Büchner of Tübingen, in Jacob Maleschott of Heidelberg ("no thought without phosphorus"—his book led Feuerbach to coin his famous epigram "Der Mensch ist, was er isst"), and in Karl Vogt, who came from Giessen, was driven out of Germany as a revolutionary after 1848, and settled in Geneva as "professor of geology, hater of clergymen and fierce advocate of a materialist philosophy."[18] These latter three especially seized upon Darwin to further an anti-Christian

agenda they had already developed. And this antagonism was even more widely popularized by Ernst Haeckel, who undertook in the 1860s to convert Germany to
Darwinism, and whose *Riddle of the Universe* (1900) became a symbol almost as important as Darwin's book. Haeckel was apparently a serious scientist, but had only the
most superficial knowledge of Christianity. Yet in his hands Darwinism could become a
symbol of antireligion for reasons that had little to do with evolution, as among the
Social Democrats in Germany who hailed Haeckel and Büchner and claimed to find in
Darwinism the scientific justification for materialism and socialism. Here the logic was
simple. Religion was opposed to the aspirations of the workers. "Darwinism" disproved
religion. Therefore Darwinism supported socialism.

II. WHAT WAS REALLY GOING ON?

Now what was really going on theologically in the nineteenth century in relation to scientific development? As I have suggested, the relationships in detail were very complex. But, as also suggested, the century was marked by a continuing process of
theological accommodation (with, of course, a good deal of grudging change) to new
scientific conceptions, notably in geology and in biology, with some reference to cosmology (if that is a scientific venture), but little to physics or chemistry. As Loren
Eiseley describes it, first the world became "natural" as a result of the work of Newton,
Laplace, and Hutton, especially by acceptance of the latter's axiom that "the understanding of present forces is the key to the past."[19] Then, on the basis of the fossil
record and notably in Charles Lyell's uniformitarian geology, death became "natural,"
not as the mass destructions cited by the "catastrophists" but as the manifold and continuing extinction of whole species. And in Darwin, life became "natural," that is, in
the natural explanation of the development of species. (Eiseley's concluding question
is "how natural is natural?")

   Now all these changes were (gradually, to be sure) incorporated into the theological
vision. Some theologians, of course, resisted at every point, largely on the basis of a received tradition of biblical authority, even inerrancy. But many welcomed the changes
as providing a more glorious way of understanding the ways of God in the world. As
Aubrey Moore put it in the 1889 manifesto of liberal Anglo-Catholicism, *Lux Mundi*,
writing on the importance of evolution:

> The one absolutely impossible conception of God, in the present day, is that which repre-
> sents Him as an occasional Visitor. Science has pushed the deist's God farther and farther
> away, and at the moment when it seemed as if He would be thrust out altogether,
> Darwinism appeared, and, under the guise of a foe, did the work of a friend. It has con-
> ferred upon philosophy and religion an inestimable benefit, by showing us that we must
> choose between alternatives. Either God is everywhere present in nature, or He is
> nowhere. . . . It seems as if, in the providence of God, the mission of modern science was

to bring home to our unmetaphysical ways of thinking the great truth of the Divine immanence in creation, which is not less essential to the Christian idea of God than to a philosophical view of nature.[20]

And evolutionary ideas (usually vague ideas, reflecting Spencer more than Darwin) were widely taken up by theologians as explanations of the history of religion and of culture as a whole.

Granted, then, the defensiveness and resistance of many churchly types, the really interesting theologies of the nineteenth century, among which I include the varieties of liberal Protestant theology, the "mediating" theologies in Germany of the post-Schleiermacher tradition (for instance, in Isaak Dorner and Richard Rothe), the powerful stream of idealism in late nineteenth-century philosophy of religion in Britain, and the beginnings of liberal Catholicism, were fully committed to positive mediation between the "gospel" and modern thought, to building bridges in the modern world, including bridges between theology and science. This was true even of Albrecht Ritschl, so often cited for his supposed sharp distinction between religious knowing, in which value judgments are intrinsic, and scientific or theoretical knowing, in which value judgments are only concomitant. Yet, for Ritschl, both kinds of knowing are "interested," both are attempts to understand the world, and he can even say that the religious view of the world is philosophically and theoretically more adequate than a scientific view, so that knowledge of the universe is "consummated" in the Christian idea of God.

For such bridge-building or mediating kinds of theology, this endeavor meant a liberal spirit of open-mindedness, of tolerance and humility, of devotion to truth wherever it might be found. It called specifically for profound respect for science and the scientific method, which was recognized as being rooted in the same Enlightenment spirit of criticism that had to characterize religious thinking. It usually involved an emphasis on the principle of continuity and (generally) a confidence in the future of humankind. And it often meant a tentativeness or skepticism about the possibility of achieving valid theoretical knowledge of ultimate reality, with a growing sense of the ambiguity or figurative nature of religious language (for example, in S.T. Coleridge, F.D. Maurice, and Horace Bushnell). And I do not think such developments can be fairly described as rearguard actions in any sort of general retreat.

What, then, did the popularity (or notoriety) of Draper and White really represent? These were not wicked men. Draper was guilty of incredibly sweeping generalizations and even caricature, but he had a serious complaint about the hostility of institutional religion to anything new. And White genuinely believed he was supporting true religious values against the obscurantism of "theologians." The work of Draper and White, to say nothing of Haeckel and Huxley, caught the popular mind of the late nineteenth century, not because of the intrinsic soundness of their arguments, but because of the real growing secularization of the European (and American) mind in the nineteenth century, which Owen Chadwick has so beautifully described in his book of that title.

Never mind whether religion and science were really in conflict; they were increasingly *thought* to be in conflict.[21]

Why that could be thought may be partly explained by the fact that the nineteenth century was indeed marked by widespread (one could almost say wholesale) abandonment of many cherished religious notions. As early as Schleiermacher's *Glaubenslehre* (1821), it was proposed that the doctrine of creation has no particular interest in a point of origination, that the idea of the Fall has no reference to an event in early history, and that the term "miracle" does not refer to any intrusion into natural sequence but is rather the religious name for an event of disclosure. And by the time of Isaak Dorner in mid-century, the idea of the immutability of God was being profoundly reinterpreted.

At a more popular level, the preoccupation with an afterlife was countered by the emergence of the "secular societies," which, though never large, reflected a much broader concern with *this world* than the next, and promoted the disentanglement of "morality" from theology. Church attendance, notably in Britain and Europe, declined dramatically. Anticlericalism was rife and came to mean not just opposition to the priestly profession as such, which was after all an old story, but an attack on all ecclesiastical power, especially churchly power allied with political authority (a complaint that Draper and White well represent). There was deep alienation, even apart from Marxist circles, of the urban workers from institutional religion. Victorian Britain was almost as much characterized by doubt as by faith and "morality."[22] And though the notorious lack of reliable detailed information on popular beliefs makes it difficult to speak with confidence, it seems that there were wide-ranging changes in religious belief at the popular as well as at more sophisticated levels. Belief in the infallibility of scripture was being deeply eroded in the latter half of the century, as it had been destroyed by biblical criticism in Germany. The process was marked in England by Coleridge's *Confessions of an Inquiring Spirit* (1840) and by George Eliot's translations of both Strauss's *Life of Jesus* (1846) and Feuerbach's *Essence of Christianity* (1854), though it did not really burst into the open in Britain until the 1860 publication of the controversial collection of ideas in *Essays and Reviews*. One bit of evidence for this erosion is the intensity of the insistence on biblical infallibility in pre–World War I protofundamentalism in America. In the popular press in Britain in the 1860s—and this *has* been studied (for instance, in Alvar Ellegard's *Darwin and the General Reader*[23])—Darwin's theory was hardly referred to except in relation to religion and as a stick with which to beat the Bible.

The fear of hell, and even the idea of hell, was greatly weakened, and by the 1850s many working-class as well as middle-class people were turning to spiritism and other vague conceptions of an afterlife in contrast to the "barbarous" idea of a God who condemned to eternal punishment. From early in the century, the Christian doctrines most objectionable to the secularists, as to unitarians, universalists, and liberals generally, had been the ideas of eternal punishment, hell and damnation for unbelievers, and substitutionary atonement. And by the late nineteenth century, the question could be whether there was any future life at all.

Further, one can clearly observe a pervasive decline in the sense of Providence, except possibly in the American idea of Manifest Destiny. Owen Chadwick nicely illustrates the change by noting the radical difference in tone between the reactions to the sinking of the *Titanic* in 1912 and H.P. Liddon's sermon of 1870 following the destruction by storm of the British warship *HMS Captain.* Liddon's response was a theodicy which, while unable to state the particular meaning of the tragedy within the purposes of a God who made the laws of nature and numbers the hairs of every head, still focused on affirming that the event was within the scope of eternal Providence. In the reactions to the *Titanic* disaster, the religious atmosphere and theological language were still there, but the focus had shifted to a judgment on human pride in its exaltation of science and materialism, and God was set at a distance from the detail of a catastrophe which should be blamed on human error in design.[24] To such we may add the growing change, in relation to illness, from prayers for divine healing to reliance on the ministrations of physicians.

I have said earlier that the central problem, theologically, of science and religion was focused not on geology or even biology, and certainly not physics or cosmology, but on "scientific" historical criticism, especially as applied to the Bible. In the late nineteenth and early twentieth centuries, no theologian argued more vigorously than Wilhelm Herrmann (an early disciple of Albrecht Ritschl and one of the most powerful teachers of the day) that science could do nothing to disprove or affirm the validity of faith. In particular, he was talking about scientific historical critical (*historisch*) judgments about Jesus. At best, scientific historiography could have the positive value of destroying false props for faith (for example, in biblical infallibility and in church dogma). But the inadequacy of scientific history to lay hold of objective reality for Christian faith is part and parcel of its belonging to the sphere of scientific objectivity; it falls in the general category of knowledge of the world, from which faith is to be sharply distinguished. It can make only tentative judgments, whereas faith requires certainty. No alliance (or mediation), therefore, can be made between the thoughts of faith and science. The effort of the "ruling theology" at such alliance, Herrmann asserted, is something "from which only a worldly, grasping church could gain anything." But:

> It is just as clear to the believer as it is to those who are acquainted with science, that science has no part or lot in the content of these thoughts [of faith]. . . . In these thoughts the believer breaks down every bridge between his own conviction and all that science can acknowledge to be real, simply because these thoughts have grown out of the faith awakened by God's historical revelation.[25]

In short, science and theology have nothing to say to each other. Each is wholly independent of the other.

Now here indeed is an example of a real split between science and theology—and behind it lies Ritschl's insistence on the distinction between spirit and nature, which was an attempt to save personality from extinction by a "scientific" worldview that had no room for it. But Herrmann was an extreme case, and we ought to think of his kind of antithesis as a local phenomenon, even though it may have continued (in a different way) in the dialectical theology of the 1920s (for example, Barth and Bultmann, who were both students of Herrmann), or in sharp distinctions of "internal" from "external" history, or in certain existentialist traditions. That sort of radical distinction was certainly not characteristic of British or American liberalism generally, nor of the British idealist thinkers. For them, as well as for Schleiermacher and Ritschl, for the whole mediating tradition, and for the conservatives of nearly every stripe, religious faith involved genuine cognition of a sort that could not be simply opposed to the "theoretical" knowledge of philosophy or science.

What really happened theologically in the nineteenth century, of which Herrmann may be partly an expression, though an atypical one, is a profoundly new view of the nature, limitations, and possibilities of religious truth, which came to be established in the nineteenth century—following, and partly because of, the work of Immanuel Kant. I have earlier called this an epochal demythologizing of theology which emerged in Schleiermacher and Hegel.[26] This has frequently been described as the anthropological turn, or as I prefer to call it, a Socratic turn to the self, away from the objectivism of both the Enlightenment and scholasticism toward "a subjective view of the religious object"; that is, toward a recognition that any significant speech about God has to be talk in which the self is concerned, talk about God as the object of devotion, or of utter dependence, or of passionate concern and fidelity.

In this insistence, the thinkers of the nineteenth century were in part continuing (or recovering) a basic theme of Luther and Calvin, of pietism and of Pascal: that God and faith belong together, that God is to be described only as apprehended in faith. But Schleiermacher's proposal to develop theological statements as implications of the religious self-consciousness, and Coleridge's conception of a Reason that at its highest is an act of will, a venturing forth and throwing of oneself into the act of apprehension, also represented a new way of bringing the believing self into the theological program. Consciousness of the truth becomes peculiarly one with self-consciousness. The religious subject—in point of view, in cognitive limitations, in "interest," in willing and choosing—has to be self-consciously and systematically recognized as ineradicably present in that with which Christian theological reflection begins. This theme is the foundation for a striking community of interest and effort in the whole course of theology in the nineteenth century, and it qualifies the concerns for "subjectivity" as clearly distinct from those of the Reformation or of pietism or of rationalism. Consequently the idea of "revelation" had to be fundamentally reinterpreted, and the former kind of confidence its truths was reinterpreted.

The self's involvement in theological assertions was expressed in many other ways in the nineteenth century: in F.D. Maurice's insistence on the partiality of every apprehension of the headship of Christ; in Horace Bushnell's theory of religious language; in Albrecht Ritschl's idea that religious knowledge consists strictly in "judgments of value"; in William James's account of the will to believe; in the Erlangen School's effort to develop and confirm the theology of the Lutheran confessions from the "deep inner grounds and life roots" of Christian experience; in Isaak Dorner's effort to show the coincidence of the interests of piety and speculative science; in John Henry Newman's "illative sense"; and of course (most strikingly) in Søren Kierkegaard's idea of truth as subjectivity. This is not to say, of course, that all these views are the same, or even that they are all consistent with one another, but just that in their varying ways they testify to a new recognition of the place the believing subject occupies in the sphere of religious truth.

To change the image radically, what we have in the nineteenth century, from Schleiermacher and Hegel on, is both a massive effort at mediation or synthesis, a uniting of theology and science, of religion and culture, and at the same time a demythologizing within theology, whereby theological assertions take on new kinds of meaning. And as part of that transformation we must also reckon the development of a new historical consciousness, which I have referred to only indirectly in connection with the biblical-critical problem—but which emerged as a parallel and related theme culminating in the work of Ernst Troeltsch at the end of the century and continued, even in the dialectical theology, in a widespread focusing on the problem of hermeneutics (even to the point of the identification of theology and hermeneutics).

Now, to what extent does this imply a "split" between theology and science—as if these were utterly discrete and independent enterprises? That too would be a myth that needs to be dispelled. Surely we are required to make distinctions. Theological statements cannot be taken as *simply* the same kinds of assertions as the statements of geology or physics or biology. And the failure to recognize any distinction is doubtless one of the reasons why the notion of a warfare between science and religion could be entertained, either by opponents of religion or by defenders of the "faith." But to recognize the peculiar nature of religious affirmations is not to say that they have no relation to scientific kinds of assertions. One might, perhaps, understand Schleiermacher's call for an "eternal covenant between the living Christian faith and an independent and freely working science, a covenant by the terms of which science is not hindered and faith not excluded"—as he put it in a letter to Dr. Lücke in 1829[27]—as an opening to complete independence of the two enterprises. But that would not be true to Schleiermacher, for whom also Christian theology had to be "public" theology, one whose warrants could be made clear and whose statements would be intelligible outside the believing community, thus not unrelated to the whole range of scholarship and organized knowledge, that is, to *Wissenschaft*.[28] And, with few exceptions, the subsequent course of nineteenth century theology reflected the continuing search for a positive relation of theological and scientific judgments, both of which involved cognitive claims.

III. IMPLICATIONS FOR THE PRESENT

Now, if my analysis of the theological development of the nineteenth century in any way approximates correctness, certain consequences follow for twentieth-century discussions of the question of theology and science.

First, recall that the most important problem for science and theology in the nineteenth century, from the standpoint of theology, was not the relation to physics or geology or chemistry or even biology, though geology (especially with respect to the age of the world) and biology were certainly of great significance, but to "historical science," which demolished the old confidence in scripture, and to the new "sciences" of psychology and sociology. At the outset, then, one must raise the question whether one can meaningfully talk simply about "theology and science," or whether one should not always talk about the relations of theology (or more properly theolog*ies*) and the scien*ces*, including the human sciences.

Second, the gains of the nineteenth century must not be lost by unconscious relapse into theological models that may once have been viable but are no longer so, any more than is Newtonian physics. We can see how much of the putative conflict, or other relations, of science and theology in earlier times rested on the assumption that religious affirmations are descriptive/explanatory statements of precisely the same order as scientific judgments or theories. But the problem remains. Nancey Murphy's essay in Part II of this volume, with its emphasis on logical relations between scientific and theological assertions, seems to perpetuate that kind of mistake by regarding theological statements as cognitive in more or less the same way as scientific statements are. Many of the fascinating and otherwise excellent contributions to the case studies of Part III do not escape it either. But whatever may be said about the tentativeness and nonobjective character of scientific judgments, it is now clear that God cannot be referred to in precisely the same sort of language that refers to the "world." God is not objectifiable in the same way. This is not to say that faith has no "cognitive" content, but that since the nineteenth century the "knowledge" that is in faith has to be reconceived.

We might, of course, take a wholly instrumentalist view of theological language, which, as described by Janet Soskice, "provides a useful, even uniquely useful, system of symbols which is action-guiding for the believer, but which is not to be taken as making reference to a cosmos-transcending being in the traditional sense."[29] And this would then parallel a kind of social constructivism in science that holds that scientific theories are less discovered within the world, than imposed upon it, being socially useful constructions of our own making.

But such a move would not in fact be a necessary or proper outcome of the new understandings of religious language that emerged in the nineteenth century. Some form of realism, albeit critical realism, was always implicit in those emphases. And this is in accord with our common usage, in which statements about God or the world are understood to be genuinely referential in character, that is, statements about reality.

Ludwig Wittgenstein's notion of "seeing as," as in his famous illustration of the "duck/rabbit," would seem more appropriate. There is an object of reference, but *how* its reality is seen depends much on the perspective of the viewer, thus scientific and theological views differ because, in the one case, certain kinds of values for the observer are deliberately and systematically excluded, whereas in the other case (theological assertions), human values and interests are consciously factored into the judgments. Some such view would seem consonant with the emphasis on the metaphoric and analogical processes in the essay in Part II of this volume by Mary Gerhart and Allan Russell. And it is not altogether unlike Albrecht Ritschl's distinction between those enterprises in which value judgments are only concomitant (for instance, science) and those in which value judgments are intrinsic (for instance, theology).

It follows that any attempt to move back and forth between scientific and theological kinds of statements depends utterly on clarity about the character and the warrants for the kind of statements being made. In particular, from the theologian's standpoint, any attempt to derive certain notions (for example, about creation, or time and eternity) from theology, and offer them as informative for the scientist's ideas of creation and time, is extremely hazardous and can even become comical in execution. Prior to any such efforts, the whole basis and status of such theological ideas must be reconsidered from the ground up. Even if one wants to emphasize strongly that scientific pictures are also models or metaphors or symbols, essentially involving the role of the observer, the question of comparability with religious symbols cannot be dealt with meaningfully without thoroughgoing analysis of the ways in which theological statements are models or metaphors or symbols. Without this, the conversation is in great danger of being simply out of step with what is really going on in theology, and of unreflectively adopting models of theology that no longer correspond to the realities (and confusions) of how theology is to be done.

Thus it would seem that the prior question for any attempt to relate "scientific" and "theological" ventures is essentially one of appropriate methodologies or ground rules, in the sense of understanding the *kinds* of statements that are involved, in particular the richness of theological language that includes moral, volitional, and even aesthetic elements that are systematically excluded in scientific judgments. It is not clear in much of the contemporary discussion of science and theology that such methodological questions have been treated on either side with the depth needed for meaningful conversation to take place.

NOTES

1. In the historical analysis here, I have drawn frequently on material much more fully developed in my *Protestant Thought in the Nineteenth Century, Vol. I, 1799-1870*, and especially *Vol. II, 1870–1914* (New Haven: Yale University Press, 1972, 1985).
2. John William Draper, *History of the Conflict Between Religion and Science* (London and New York: D. Appleton and Company, 1874).

3. Andrew Dickson White, *A History of the Warfare of Science with Theology in Christendom* (London and New York: D. Appleton and Company, 1896).

4. *Conflict*, p. 353.

5. *Conflict*, p. 367.

6. Owen Chadwick, *The Secularization of the European Mind in the Nineteenth Century* (New York and Cambridge: Cambridge University Press, 1975).

7. *Warfare*, Vol. 1, p. viii.

8. *Warfare*, Vol. I, pp. 1-88.

9. *Warfare*, Vol. I, p. 86.

10. *Warfare*, Vol. II, p. 395.

11. *Warfare*, Vol. II, p. 396.

12. *Protestant Thought*, Vol. II, ch. 6.

13. James R. Moore, *The Post-Darwinian Controversies: A Study of the Protestant Struggle to Come to Terms with Darwin in Great Britain and America, 1870–1900* (New York and Cambridge: Cambridge University Press, 1979).

14. Frederick Gregory, *Nature Lost? Natural Science and the German Theological Traditions of the Nineteenth Century* (Cambridge: Harvard University Press, 1992).

15. *Nature Lost?* p. 112.

16. See, for example, John Root's dissertation on *Catholics and Science in Mid-Victorian England* (Bloomington, Indiana: Indiana University, 1974).

17. Thomas F. Glick, ed., *The Comparative Reception of Darwinism* (Austin, Texas: University of Texas Press, 1972; reprinted Chicago: Chicago University Press, 1988).

18. *Secularization*, p. 165.

19. Loren Eiseley, *The Firmament of Time* (New York: Atheneum, 1960), p. 26.

20. Aubrey Moore, "The Problem of Pain" in Charles Gore, ed., *Lux Mundi: A Series of Studies in the Religion of the Incarnation* (New York: Young, 1890), p. 82.

21. This argument is made in Wesley Wildman's paper in Part I of this volume.

22. See Walter E. Houghton, *The Victorian Frame of Mind, 1830–1870* (New Haven: Yale University Press, 1957).

23. Alvar Ellegard, *Darwin and the General Reader: The Reception of Darwin's Theory of Evolution in the British Periodical Press, 1859–1872* (1958; reprinted Chicago: University of Chicago Press, 1990).

24. See *Secularization*, pp. 259–263.

25. Wilhelm Herrmann, *The Communion of the Christian With God*, ed. Robert T. Voelkel (Philadelphia: Fortress Press, 1971; *Lives of Jesus Series* reprint of 1906 2nd trans. ed. of the 1903 4th German ed.), p. 354.

26. *Protestant Thought*, Vol. I, p. 61.

27. Friedrich D. E. Schleiermacher, *On the Glaubenslehre: Two Letters to Dr. Lücke*, trans. James O. Duke and Francis Fiorenza (Atlanta: Scholars Press, 1981).

28. See *Protestant Thought*, Vol. I, pp. 62–64.

29. Robert John Russell, William R. Stoeger SJ, George V. Coyne SJ, eds., *Physics, Philosophy, and Theology: A Common Quest for Understanding* (Vatican City State: Vatican Observatory, 1988), p. 175.

THE QUEST FOR HARMONY

AN INTERPRETATION OF CONTEMPORARY THEOLOGY AND SCIENCE

WESLEY J. WILDMAN

A discussion of science and religion in the contemporary period could justifiably present a historical narrative of the major scientific advancements and theological movements in the twentieth century along with the key developments in the rapidly growing specialization of religion and science. This approach would illumine the origins of the specialization as well as the events that have shaped it—and surely the emergence of a systematic, international dialogue among scientists, philosophers, and theologians is the biggest story of the twentieth century as far as religion and science is concerned.

Another approach is to examine the relationship between the contemporary study of science and religion, and its Western cultural environment. Historical narrative is less important in this approach, while interpretation and argument are more prominent. However, such an analysis promises desirable insights into the potential importance of the specialization of religion and science. This is the approach taken in this essay.

Presenting the relationship between the contemporary study of science and religion and its Western milieu inevitably involves a certain amount of cultural analysis. There are dangers in all attempts to characterize such an amorphous reality as a culture, some obvious, and others less so. Yet the significance of the interaction between science and religion is *broadly rooted* in the contemporary situation, and this point can be conveyed only by accepting the confusions and perils of cultural analysis and venturing some general judgments about the Western cultural context.

Accordingly, the first part of this paper offers a sweeping glance at those features of contemporary Western culture that are most pertinent to the emergence and modification of what can be called its "critical spirit." The second part aims to relate science, religion, and the study of their interaction to this cultural analysis, in a bidirectional way. On the one hand, a broad cultural perspective illumines the significance of the relationship between science and religion, and so confirms the importance of its systematic study. On the other, the relationship between science and religion is richly informative about contemporary Western culture.

The relationship between science and religion is fascinating partly because it compactly expresses a kind of schizophrenic anxiety within the contemporary West generally: *How can we think and act scientifically and theologically, critically and worshipfully, technologically and ethically at the same time?* This phenomenon has been noticed and discussed many times. I am not especially attached to the term "schizophrenia" for describing it, but the analogy has some advantages. In clinical psychology, schizophrenia tends to mean dissociation from reality. In its popular sense, however, it suggests a split personality, in which the dissociation is internal rather than external—what psychologists might call multiple personality disorder. The two are not completely independent, since dissociation from reality is often the result of an attempt to avoid awareness of an internal tension or split, and vice versa. I will use "schizophrenia" as an analogy drawing on both meanings. Analogized by an internal personality split is the tension commonly experienced in the West between critical and spiritual impulses within human life. The image of dissociation from reality corresponds in the analogy to the failure to perceive accurately the nature of human life that follows from discomfort with its simultaneously present spiritual and critical moments. This failure of perception is expressed, for instance, in anthropologies and metaphysics that fail (or refuse) to build both these moments into their explication of human nature and of the world in which it has arisen.

A concrete, homey illustration of this tension might be helpful. It is well expressed at several points in the movie *The Last of His Tribe*, produced in 1992 by Home Box Office Entertainment. The following exchange from that film succeeded in conveying the relative spiritual numbness cultivated in at least some minds given over to criticism and systematic observation. The person lacking spiritual mobility and resourcefulness in the encounter is an otherwise generous and thoughtful anthropologist, but the same tendency can be found in theologians and natural scientists, and perhaps even the general way of being of the West. Alfred Kroeber, the anthropologist, convinces the last of the Yahi tribe—dubbed Ishi by Kroeber—to lead him and some colleagues to the lands of the Yahi. There, before his old hut, Ishi recalls the wiping out of his people, and tries to reach his awkward, disengaged companion:

ISHI: Put your hands on the earth. *(Uncomfortably, anxious to take this moment with due seriousness, Kroeber joins Ishi on his knees in the dirt.)*

ISHI: Do you feel her breathing?

KROEBER *(embarrassed, uncertain)*: Ah . . . yes. . . .

ISHI: Do you hear her singing?

KROEBER: I . . . I don't know . . . I think so. . . .

ISHI: What does she sing? *(Kroeber is silent.)*

ISHI *(suddenly)*: Sing it.

KROEBER *(unable to maintain his cooperative facade)*: I . . . ah . . . I can't.

ISHI *(louder)*: Sing it!

KROEBER *(now totally out of his depth)*: Ishi, I can't.

ISHI *(after a pause, with heartbreaking energy)*: Ishi, last Yahi. *(Ishi grasps the soil in tightly clenched fists, weeps, and begins to sing mournfully.)*

Contemporary Western culture's uneasiness with combining the critical and spiritual aspects of life is Kroeber's discomfort writ large. It is an awkwardness deeply connected with the historical origins and working assumptions of that culture.

The primary argument to be made here is that the interaction between science and religion within the modern West exhibits the same awkward tension that strains the culture as a whole. The science-religion relationship is by no means the only manifestation of this awkward cultural confusion. There are signs of it whenever religious or ethical or artistic impulses collide with critical or analytical or controlling ones. As a result, the *systematic study* of science and religion is not unique in its importance. Exploiting the analogy again, every schizophrenic symptom is a window of understanding onto the underlying tension, and in many cases also an opportunity for easing it. The interaction of science and religion, however, presents the tension between the religious and critical tendencies of human life with interesting directness, because of the contrast between the *spiritual and critical tendencies of human rationality* immediately evident there.

I. THE CONTEMPORARY SITUATION

The Soul of the Modern West: Criticism

Modernity happened to Western civilization. It is one name given to the series of spectacular transformations of life that are the very stuff of any interpretation of our contemporary situation: from feudal economic systems, to free-market, industrialized economies; from political power concentrated in the hands of a few, to vast democratic institutions that encourage wide distribution of information and responsibility; from natural science as primarily classification and description, to an internationally coordinated quest for progressive, experimentally supported theories that enable prediction and control; from candles and ox-drawn plows, to a panoply of technological marvels that have transformed the average standard of living and the way we relate to the world around us; from widespread superstition and credulity that lent itself to exploitation by a few and preserved ignorance of social and psychological realities, to an equally widespread spirit of criticism that has given birth to free speech and the free press, to social and political institutions with a rudimentary capacity to criticize and correct themselves, and to the systematic study of human psychology, religion, and social life.

Modernity, however, has proved to be both boon and bane. These transformations are so powerful and pervasive that it is scarcely possible to escape their influence, no matter where in the world one lives; the modern West seems to sweep all before it, or under it, capturing or breaking the imagination of many people in other cultures, and transforming life for better or worse. To many non-Western cultures less geared to expansion and consumption, this is a matter of great concern, for they find themselves changing rapidly under the influence of the West, but with little internal capacity to assess, assimilate, control, or resist what is happening.

The ambivalence of modernity is also evident from an internal Western point of view. For instance, in spite of the collapse of the Soviet Union's centrally planned economy, the future of capitalistic, free-market economies is far from secure: they are stubbornly geared into practices that are undermining the moral and natural resources necessary to their own continuation, and they threaten as a result to contribute to the decline of many Western societies into turmoil and the whole planet into an ecological catastrophe. Likewise, Western democratic political institutions are too often struggling in vain to offer needed leadership to their constituents because, in the final analysis, they are failing to cultivate and protect social institutions such as family, education, and religion that are essential to maintaining the healthy tone of political life.

These more objective, institutional signs of ambivalence are accompanied by more vague and subjective ones in the conceptual life of Western culture. Perhaps most important among these is widespread overreliance on our analytical and controlling expertise, to the point that our feeling for nature, for community, for history, and for spirituality has been dramatically weakened. Most of us in the West no longer confuse myth and history, but neither do we know how to reappropriate our demythologized stories. We seem to know a great deal about how we human beings and the world work, but we are often at a loss to know how to affirm meaning for our existence in that supposedly "well-understood" world, unless it is by means of regression to that naïveté so seductively packaged in religious fundamentalism and political fanaticism of the right and left.

Modernity is in some respects the prodigal child of the West, an increasingly uncontrollable nexus of forces that is threatening to fly free from its creative source. The grave question is unanswered as to whether this Western cultural prodigal will return home. Finding a positive answer to that question is one of the most urgent global challenges, not withstanding its Western provenance. Most major social, economic, and political concerns feed into it, and the continuation of much life on the planet depends upon solving it.

This is the threatening practical context within which science and religion interact with each other. Both science and religion, in their distinctive ways, must come to terms with this clutch of crises, and they must find ways of attacking them together.[1] A promising starting point for such common work is the awareness that the root cause of the problematic character of modern Western culture is a profound confusion, a schizophrenic uncertainty, about how to *be* in the world.

The Heart of the Contemporary West: Self-Criticism

As modern optimism has increasingly given way to dismay at the darker side of modernity tragically evident in the twentieth century, so modernity's critical spirit has been directed inward in a more sustained, penetrating way. That has made possible a more balanced view of the changes in Western life that distinguish the modern era from previous times: they have a creative, brilliant aspect, and a darker, perhaps suicidal one.

In everyday social life, this heightened self-critical mood has occasionally led to the angry or despairing rejection of everything Western and modern, as embodied in some of the more extreme Western religious sects and cults. It is also present to some extent in the support being found for non-Western religions among Westerners, in the flowering of environmentalist movements, and in the self-mortifying grief for, and romanticization of, cultures overwhelmed by Western expansion. Fundamentalist Christianity, which turns its back on criticism altogether, can be understood partly as a repudiation of the modern confidence in autonomous criticism, and so as an extreme and unstable form of self-critical correction. This spirit of cultural self-criticism appears in less grand ways, too, such as the increasingly popular quest for a simpler, more self-sustaining lifestyle. More generally, the news media report high levels of dissatisfaction with the disintegrating moral fabric of modern Western societies, and a widespread frustration about the apparent absence of practical solutions.

Moving from social context to the recent intellectual life of the culture, the turn of modernity's critical spirit against its own principles and achievements has found expression in equally diverse ways. The emergence of the deconstructionist "method" is one of the most notable of these. Echoing tendencies toward fragmentation and abstention from recognizable structures evident in twentieth century art and literature, deconstructionist philosophers renounced social and philosophical construction and turned their analytical skills to the task of uncovering the hidden agendas and structures of power in ideas, institutions, and cultural practices. The culture at large has also expressed widespread suspicion—verging on cynicism—about the possibility of social and intellectual creation that can be open to criticism and ready to discover its own negative social consequences.

A second intellectual expression of modernity's self-critical spirit is a penetrating reassessment of modern Western institutions, such as family, education, politics, and religion. In Western economics, the mood of reassessment is represented most recently by Daly's and Cobb's *For the Common Good*. While there have always been relatively ineffective external critiques of capitalism, *For the Common Good* is an instance of the increasingly powerful breed of *internal* critiques, advocating a capitalistic free market and the profit motive, at the same time as arguing for a transformation of the free market in the direction of sustainability. The novelty of Cobb's and Daly's argument turns on the observation that the capitalist market has a tendency to erode the very foundations upon which it stands. For instance, the market does not allow very effectively for inherent limitations in both natural resources and the ecosystem on which life depends. And the individualistic self-interest that drives the market tends to dissolve the community's moral virtues of honesty, freedom, initiative, and industriousness, without which virtues the market is weakened dramatically. Since the market cannot produce or even conserve these moral virtues, it is dependent upon social institutions to produce them.[2]

The recognition of the dependence of capitalistic economies upon both the ecosphere and community institutions is alive and well in other areas. For example, sociological works such as *The Good Society*, by Robert Bellah and his colleagues, lead the way in analyzing the deterioration of vital Western institutions, and in urging greater discussion of these issues as the first step to reversing the alarming consequences.[3] Noam Chomsky's *Necessary Illusions* is a recent representative of an emerging criticism of democracy itself—one of the recent criticisms from *within* to complement the long-standing critiques of it from without.[4]

If these forms of Western social and political self-criticism are in search of a more comprehensively unified and harmonious view of society, they are also determined not to continue the pattern of artificially securing such harmony by propounding theories that are overly abstracted from the concrete circumstances and organic interrelatedness of life. We cannot do good economics without taking account of the ecosphere and social institutions, and we cannot revitalize politics without also working on family, religion, and education.

In and through all of these examples, in both academia and the wider society, modernity expresses the willingness to criticize itself, to recognize the self-destructiveness of its consumptive and expansionist tendencies, and in turn to face the partial failure of its economic, social, political, and religious institutions—along with enjoying their imperfect success. This shift is encouraging, and the hopefulness for the future that it engenders shows up in lots of ways. Not surprisingly, the changing relationship between science and religion attests to it. If the unrestrained critical mood of early modernity made inconceivable anything except conflict between science and religion, or their rigid separation, the later, more self-critical phase of modernity has discovered a richer, more ambiguous relation between the two. In this new stage, there seems to be the possibility of reuniting the vast critical capacity of modernity with the habitually marginalized spiritual side of human life.

"Postmodernity" is the common catch phrase for this restructuring of the mentality of the West. As the name itself suggests, these changes are intimately related to modernity. This implies that postmodernity may best be understood as an essentially modern, self-critical rebound of modernity against itself, a necessary step toward a more consistent appropriation of the Enlightenment principle of independent criticism. Some writers prefer to interpret the widespread changes as indications of a new era, in much the same way that modernity is thought to be marked off from medieval European culture by the transformations mentioned earlier. In any event, since the social and ecological problems confronting humanity grow more severe with alarming rapidity, it can only be hoped that a "postmodern outlook" will be effective in helping the West to ease them.

There is a sense in which the willingness of the modern West to engage in this sort of penetrating self-criticism is disappointingly late in coming. Is it a sign that modernity, and with it the ancient stream of Western culture, is embracing greater maturity, albeit a maturity forced by the negative consequences of its own uncontrolled brilliance, its careless treatment of other cultures, its reckless careening into an untenable future? Or is it merely an enactment of the fact that the drive to survive is stronger than the drive to consume? If these mounting crises were to abate, would signs of the modern West's newfound maturity prove to have staying power? Though I lean toward discerning a tentative maturation in and through this self-criticism in the last century or so, the most basic observation of human nature—religiously expressed, for example, in the Jewish myth of the Garden of Eden, the Christian doctrine of original sin, and the Buddhist teaching about the universality of *dukkha* (suffering)—insists that such maturity is a fragile thing at best. Like all intangible cultural phenomena, its survival depends upon being institutionally embodied, and even then there can be no guarantees. Our families, religious communities, schools, economies, and the scientific and technological traditions must each in their own way build self-critical insights into their ordinary modes of operation. Religious insight has customarily been marginalized in this process. However, in the light of an adequate appraisal of the interconnectedness of human life—one less skewed by modernity's infatuation with objectivity and critical rationality—it is indispensable.

II. SCIENCE AND RELIGION

This is one description of a few important features of the contemporary Western world, and doubtless each reader would adjust what I have said at a number of points. This interpretation has emphasized the modern spirit of criticism—and its unsteady enhancement in the twentieth century as cultural self-criticism—as the driving force behind the social, economic, political, and religious motifs of the modern Western way of being in the world. With more space, I would want to comment on several other prominent strands of our contemporary cultural tapestry, including attitudes about the natural environment, a range of human justice issues, the rise of psychological and social sciences, and astonishing advances in the physical sciences. I would also discuss the prominence of historical relativism and cultural and religious pluralism.

No matter how complete the picture, however, the West clearly has developed a highly distinctive way of viewing the world. It is not set in concrete, and will change and change again. As Heidegger has reminded us, we human beings are the creatures who are always trying to understand ourselves, and whose self-understanding is constantly in a state of metamorphosis. This way of being in the world is therefore not the only way, and certainly not necessarily the best or most advanced. Nevertheless it is *our* thought-world, the world we actually inhabit, and consequently the arena for the interaction of science and religion. When we consider the science-religion relationship in this rich and problematic context, two lines of thought suggest themselves, and I gather my thoughts under two headings accordingly: this interaction is *informative*, and the systematic study of it is *important*.

The Interaction between Science and Religion is Informative

The contemporary form of the interaction between science and religion is informative about all of the modern West in one way. The nature of this interaction in the recent past, in conjunction with the way our culture has been inclined to represent this history to itself, is enlightening in a different way. I will start by looking to the past, and return to the current situation later.

The story of the conflict between science and Christian theology is a popular tale, told and retold even now in both schools and the media. A few strident intellectuals keep the embers of plausibility glowing beneath the story by urging the rational weakness of religious faith or of church theology. Though actual instances of explicit conflict are rare, there are enough contemporary examples—such as religious creationists, educators, and scientists having it out on daytime television talk shows—to sustain a popular confidence in the story's veracity. And what narrative unfolds in this popular, widely believed story? A tale about how Christian theologians have duped the West to protect their own sacred narratives: first, theology insisted that certain things were true of the world; next, science discovered that these beliefs were false; and then, theology resisted this new knowledge, until finally it was forced to give up its false claims about the world, one by one. The keys to this triumph of science over the pretensions of religion, so the story goes, are its impartial method and the corresponding certainty of its results. What chance did religion have? The dubious assertions of faith, stubbornly based on misinterpretations of beautiful biblical myths and legends, eventually had to bow to the objective and reliable assertions of the natural sciences.

It is quite a story. In many ways, however, it is dissociated from reality. In it, a profound tension within human rationality as this has developed in the West is grossly distorted by cartoonlike caricatures, to the point that the story conveys little useful information about anything that really happened. Instead, like the good legend it is, every ritual retelling of it merely expatiates the underlying tension.

The signs of this dissociation are abundant. Most obviously, many ordinary religious people, nowadays as a century ago, while intimidated by what the story portends for their faith in a general way, tend to be confused as to what the fuss is all about, since they personally have little trouble reconciling to their satisfaction most *specific* scientific discoveries with their faith. Of course, the practice of petitionary prayer is discernibly affected by suggestions from science about the world that make, for example, God's action in it harder to imagine. Moreover, it is not theologically adequate to deflect these suggestions—as many religious people do—by saying merely that "God creates through evolution," as if that settled the deeper issues of providence or divine action. But the fact that this response was and is so obvious to many indicates that the story of warfare is *exaggerated*. Most people simply did not and do not experience the impact of scientific discoveries upon religious belief as a conflict in which science vanquishes their faith.

Having said this, it is important to emphasize that there *were* real conflicts from time to time. However, another sign of dissociation is that examples of hostility are just not as abundant or as protracted as the story implies they ought to be. For instance, in the second half of the nineteenth century, the mutual antagonism was supposed to be at its height because of the publication of Charles Darwin's *Origin of Species* (1859). However, Claude Welch has pointed out, in his *Protestant Thought in the Nineteenth Century,*[5] the relative ease with which scientific discoveries were assimilated during this period. In the warfare story, the theological assumptions that God providentially directs the universe, that the Hebrew myths of creation describe actual events, and that human life is the pinnacle of creation, are presented as held with straightforward definiteness by theologians and religious believers alike, and then challenged with unexpected directness by discoveries in geology and biology, leading to protracted controversies. In reality, there has never been that much unanimity about anything in Christian, Jewish, or Muslim theology, let alone in religious groups. Moreover, a considerable readiness for a new way of seeing nature and history was in place because of the impact of historical criticism, Schelling's and Hegel's transformation of the philosophy of history, and work in natural history such as Charles Lyell's *Principles of Geology* (1830–1833) and Robert Chambers' *The Natural History of Creation* (1844), all of which prepared the way for the public and academic reception of such creative contributions as Darwin's.

There was controversy, of course, over Lyell and Darwin, as well as Hegel, Strauss, Feuerbach, Marx, Durkheim, and Freud. There ought to have been, since theological issues of great importance were at stake. But most folk merely observe controversy, and participate in it only on street corners or over the dinner table, where solutions are unsought, or easy to come by. Even in theological circles, any particular controversy was short-lived, and the scientific discoveries were assimilated with only slightly more difficulty than in casual amateur discussions. It is strange, and telling, that, in spite of little actual resistance from mainstream theology to those scientific discoveries, so much fuss is made about it now. Shakespeare comes to mind: "much ado about nothing," or "the lady doth protest too much, methinks." The *symbolic value* of the story is the reason it was and is so infamous, rather than its *fidelity to facts*.

This conclusion can be corroborated by noticing a third sign of dissociation. What were the big changes in theology that made the ready assimilation of scientific discoveries by theology possible? What were the new understandings of providence, anthropology, salvation, the church, and creation that resulted? Shockingly—though this is old news to students of the history of the relations between science and religion—there were hardly any large changes at the time. Eventually, of course, substantial theological changes occurred, but only in some areas, and there only partially. Many of the sharpest problems are still the subject of vast amounts of energy and time; some have barely been touched. It follows that the rapidity of assimilation itself was *not due to the discovery of substantially new theological solutions* to the challenges posed for theology. In fact, from that point of view, the fractiousness between science and religion in the nineteenth century and on into the twentieth should have been greater than it was. Shakespeare comes to mind again here, but in the guise of lines he never wrote: "the lady doth protest too little, methinks," or "hardly any ado about a whole lot." This facile assimilation is confirmation of the presence of a deeper, unresolved perplexity, the same profound problem that drives the exaggerations in the overhearty celebration of the warfare story, one whose arousal needs to be quieted as quickly as possible, even though there are no adequate theological solutions ready to hand.

The wrenching tension in our modern Western way of being in the world may be expressed in a variety of ways: in terms of rationality, we do not know how to think consistently about our world; in terms of ethics, we do not know how to act for the best; and in terms of the religious life—what used to be called piety—we do not know where our spiritual allegiance lies, or what we can finally trust. This tension is signified in the immensely sharpened form that modernity has brought to of all the classical theological problems: the problems of God and nature, faith and history, grace and freedom, eternity and time. The modern versions of some classical philosophical conundrums express it too: the problems of body and mind, freedom and determinism, absolute and relative, substance and process, society and individual.

Of course, thinking about these problems has been a pasttime of many different societies, so they appear to be deeply embedded in a human quest for understanding that is cross-cultural to some extent. In this sense, there is nothing novel about them. What is new in the modern West is the unsettling of older, *Western* solutions and the reframing of the problems in more definite terms, thanks to a habit of criticism, of organized curiosity. For centuries the West has been turning the tentative answers of both theology and philosophy over and over, examining and criticizing, searching and probing. In the Enlightenment, however, this curiosity exploded, and one after another of the most firmly established answers fell.

For constructive theology, three important examples of reigning solutions that lost their grip—though they are still not completely destroyed, even today—were a comfortable understanding of divine action, uncomplicated access to the historical person of Jesus of Nazareth; and an unquestioned acceptance of the preeminent status of human beings in the natural order. In every case, the curious, critical spirit of the Enlightenment marked a turning point.

(1) Newtonian mechanics, complemented by Voltaire's, Hume's, and other deistic philosophical attacks on miracle, forever changed the Christian doctrine of God. Quantum mechanics alters the details, but the comfortable solution of a God who miraculously intervenes in spite of the course of nature no longer seems possible.

(2) The rise of modern history, and with it literary and biblical criticism, permanently muddied the waters into which one formerly could gaze confidently, envisioning (partly through the convenience of reflection) the life and personality of Jesus. The internationally coordinated, interdisciplinary quest for the historical Jesus is but a refinement of the biblical-critical toolbox; inherent limitations in the presently available sources ensure that the Jesus of history will remain an enigma.

(3) The realization that our sun was one of uncountably many stars in an immense universe, together with the recognition of the universe's age and its chancy, evolutionary production of humanity, put an end to the possibility of an anthropocentric interpretation of creation. Once again, the anthropic principle changes the details in a fascinating way, but not the dislodging of the human species from center stage in the universe.

In all three cases, the formalizable edge of our critical curiosity—the natural sciences, historical criticism, and lately even the human sciences—has thrown down the gauntlet to the intangible, religious aspect of our natures: "Are you real? What is your status? Should you perish? Do you matter?" This challenge is deeply disturbing, and the history of science and religion in the modern era suggests an anxious West casting about for assurance that "everything is alright." Supposing that we hear nothing but the echo of our own voices in the newly demystified universe, we feel bereft, and so turn to, and become overly dependent on, our abilities to control and criticize. In the process, we have vastly overreached our capacity to take care of ourselves and our world, and are in imminent danger of destroying both human cultures and those other streams of life with which we share our planetary home. The challenge has become to rediscover how to feel at home in the universe now that we have become relatively good at interrogating and controlling it. This is a fundamentally religious problem and, as long as our modern self-understanding remains one-sidedly fixated upon our ability to control and criticize, the schizophrenia that grips us will continue to set the limits on our future options.

It is misleading to think of the natural sciences as causing these existential crises and their theological and philosophical correlates. Likewise, it is unhelpful to imagine that the historical or social sciences are to blame. That would be as absurd as supposing that there were a clear cut division between scientific and religious kinds of rational apparatus. This fantastic scenario posits the "critical, scientific" mentality rising independently from out of nowhere to challenge the "existential, religious" mentality, without harm to itself. But this is obviously unrealistic. Human rationality is united with every other aspect of human life in a biological, emotional, spiritual, practical unity. Scientific and theological modes of reflection are both aspects of the rich and finally unfathomable reality that is human rationality. This rational unity is in tension with itself, and it is this—rather than any projected, external conflict—which gives rise to the crises within the psyche of the modern West, and to the attendant misreading of reality and of human nature. The many modern theologies and natural sciences are all the production of the modern West's strained spirit, and the story of their exciting, conflicted relationship is an unusually telling symptom of this deeper tension.

If there were such a thing as cultural psychotherapy—and sociologists sometimes tend toward this in approaching their subject matter—the obviousness of the dissociation from reality on which the story of the warfare between science and religion trades would attract instant and intense attention. The same goes for the phenomenon of over-rapid assimilation. They are dead giveaways, simpleminded, half-sincere cover-ups of a deeply painful wound in the contemporary Western psyche, a wound that shows itself in many different ways having little to do with science and religion. From a "cultural-psychotherapeutic" viewpoint, three fascinating questions about this characterization of the modern Western mind suggest themselves, all reminiscent of Friedrich Nietzsche's concerns: How did this inner tension arise within the West? What does the possibility of its emergence mean about the nature of reality? Can we reasonably expect this situation to develop into a more unified, peaceful way of being in the world? Passing over the first two questions, we can assess the possibility of an optimistic prognosis by considering what is disclosed about the contemporary West in and through the currently flourishing study of the interaction between science and religion.

The study of science and religion has, by now, passed well beyond simple characterizations like "warfare" and "conflict." Facile assimilation, too, is seen for the pointless avoidance tactic that it is. So what does the current state of the relationship between science and religion disclose about the brilliant and dangerous schizophrenia of the modern West? Is the contemporary interaction between science and religion continuing to broadcast the confusion and anxiety of the modern West? With an important qualification, to which we will come presently, I think the answer is "yes."

There have been fairly dramatic advances in understanding the relationship between science and religion in the last couple of decades, thanks primarily to the emergence of a specialization devoted to the systematic study of this relationship. We are now conversant with consonance as well as dissonance between theological and scientific ideas. We have learned that religious convictions can and do play a role in the discovery, development, and judgment of scientific theories, even as religious theorizing is conditioned in related ways by natural science. We have discovered important similarities—unsurprising in view of the organic unity of human rational processes—in the way scientific theories and theological doctrines are constructed, the result of a richer appreciation of the complexities of scientific method, and of the rationality of theological construction. We have noticed that theology and science interact not only by means of metaphysical and philosophical suggestions—perhaps "buffering" propositions is an apt description—but by means of ethical, aesthetic, and religious ones too.

In numerous ways, therefore, our understanding of the interaction between science and religion has broadened and deepened, to the point that we wonder how anyone could ever have been satisfied with calling it "warfare." At least within the area of its study—though how far beyond its borders this insight extends is debatable—little need is felt to distort the fascinating story of science and religion into a symbolic scapegoat for our modern anxieties. It is what it is: the noble and ignoble mixed up together, scientists and theologians working side by side, sometimes rigidly and overcautiously, at other times with overconfident hubris. This signals a major improvement over the discussion of science and religion in earlier years, as well as over that discussion as it is carried on in many quarters outside the science-religion specialization even now.

It can be agreed, then, that the academic study of science and religion—I will strain normal usage and call it a "discipline"—is no longer trumpeting the modern crisis of spirit by means of promulgating a view of the interaction between the two that is dissociated from reality. However, this cultural crisis is still present. The difference from earlier years is that the discipline of science and religion tends to deal with it more openly, though involvement in details doubtless obscures awareness of this at times. For instance, building methodological bridges between science and theology amounts to trying to figure out how it can be that the same human beings, using the same rational capacity in the same existential context, can engage in activities that, on the face of things, appear to be so different. It is an attempt to understand the unity of our own rationality. Again, trying to understand how science interacts with individual theological *loci* is equivalent to grappling with our cultural schizophrenia under relatively controlled conditions, and trying to unify the disparate tendencies of our thought under a single, adequate, rational perspective. It follows that the contemporary discipline of science and religion still yields valuable information about the schizophrenic state of the modern Western mind, albeit in a more direct and hopefully healthy way than was the case formerly.

Now we come to the promised qualification, which may be a happy one. Religion is less apt these days to tremble at every new instance of a scientific discovery that sits awkwardly with theological ideas. Indeed, theology appears more resilient in the face of secular assertiveness generally. The cause of this change has superficial and more profound components. On the surface level, it is due in part to the fact that the material content of the natural sciences is in general significantly more amenable to theological concepts than seemed to be the case a century ago. We live in a more interesting, less rigid, more vague world than we once thought. Chaos theory, quantum mechanics and the reevaluation of causality it sparks, the cosmological anthropic principle, and the ever-deepening understanding of the role of chance in biological systems are but four outstanding developments of recent years. They suggest both consonance and dissonance with the religious dimension of our self-understanding, to be sure, but more importantly, they confirm the hope that religion does not need to panic whenever there seems to be a conflict between its beliefs and the provisional results of science. The scientific context for theologizing presumably will change in the future as it has changed in the past, and disciplined, creative minds can fruitfully relate religion and science in almost any circumstance. Unchecked pessimism in the science-religion relationship is as inappropriate as unrelieved optimism.[6]

But this is an unstable justification for religious self-confidence. At a deeper level, this growing confidence confirms what was discussed earlier: the modern West is self-critically beginning to tire of tormenting itself with its own acuity, and is starting to take its needs for meaning, happiness, and justice more seriously. It is more conceivable today than ever before that scientifically responsible theology might be willing to take a stand on something that seems to fly in the face of scientific consensus—on the basis, say, of recognizing the validity of human religious experience—and to wait to see what science turns up. This is the cash value of taking the emotional and spiritual aspects of human life more seriously. The often vague references to postmodernism are angling in at this transformation in character, which amounts to a shift toward having greater courage to seek out wholeness of life and thought. It seems, then, that interaction between science and religion remains informative about the conflicted nature of much of modern Western self-understanding, but that the beginnings of a new and potentially happier message are discernible.

The Discipline of Science and Religion is Important

The irony of this growing religious assertiveness is that it is building *in the absence of major theological breakthroughs*. This also applies to the relations between religious thought and both historical criticism and the human sciences. To make this point, I shall briefly summarize one issue in need of a breakthrough—the problem of divine action—arguing that very little of major significance has changed in the shape of this problem. I will conclude that the unprecedented level of systematic, interdisciplinary attention paid to such problems by the discipline of science and religion is of the utmost importance.

The idea of God as a causal agent in the world like any other has never been an acceptable understanding of divine action, for it fails to respect the transcendence of God. Something like it, however, proved itself workable from early medieval times. This traditional solution recognized the possibility of two means of divine agency: primary causation, understood by analogy with ordinary human causal agency, which means that God acts independently of any other causal agents; and secondary causation, understood by analogy with a monarch who acts through an officer of the crown, which means that God acts in and through human beings and nature. The idea of nature as regulated by laws did raise problems for this general view of divine action, as medieval contention over "first cause" arguments for the existence of God shows. But primary divine causation remained plausible, because the conception of "law of nature" was not strong enough either to make miracles seem problematic or to make identifying the causal nexus of God's interaction with nature a pressing issue. Even the person constitutionally predisposed to doubt reports of miracles could still affirm primary divine causation by means of a mystery-shrouded causal joint—the point at which God's action impacts the world. Such a skeptical person could also continue to think of divine action as a secondary cause, imagining that human causal agency is used to achieve divine purposes, for this does not require imagining that a divine act breaks the causal chain of events.

The traditional solution was sufficiently compelling to hold off its three major competitors, each with deep roots in the West, though other traditions show signs of them, too.

(1) The deistic account of divine action—presupposing a God who is responsible for the orderliness of the natural world but who does not act in it—is evident in early Greek philosophy, and preeminently in Aristotle.

(2) The pantheistic account can be traced back in the West to the Pythagoreans, who held that the world was infused with mathematical-musical harmonies—that it was, to use language not available to them, divine in and through its magnificent, mystical naturalness.

(3) The other major competitor to the traditional account can be traced to its embryonic Western beginnings in the legendary tension between Socrates and Protagoras the Sophist. Socrates' confidence in reason and suspicion of appearances was opposed by Protagoras, who was wary of the pretensions of reason and preferred the world of appearances. This classic expression of uncertainty about the extent to which reason or appearances can be trusted gave rise to the agnostic view that neither human freedom nor divine action in the world can finally be affirmed with certainty.

Deism, pantheism, and agnosticism, in these incipient forms or in their later developments, do not rule out the possibility of special divine action, which was needed by the major Western religions to make sense of special revelation, redemption, and petitionary prayer. Thus the traditional solution remained persuasive for a long time.

This satisfactory view of divine action became unmanageable with the simultaneous rise of naturalistic, historical consciousness and Newtonian mechanics, with its correspondingly rigid "laws of nature" such as universal causality. Universal causality made divine primary causation of all kinds problematic, and naturalistic, historical sensibilities were on average disinclined to believe in divine action through natural-law-suspending miracles. The apparent loss of a viable understanding of God as a primary causal agent—and the awkwardly heavy dependence on divine acts as secondary causes that resulted—led to the powerful resurgence of the traditional alternatives.

(1) The most obvious response—though problematic for traditional Jewish, Christian, and Muslim theology—was that of the Enlightenment Deists, who revived the argument from design on the basis of a world set in motion by a loving, clockmaker God who was forever after a patient observer. The modern Deists thus denied both primary and secondary causation, after the act of creation.

(2) Spinoza, Schelling, and Hegel were famous sophisticated representatives of ancient pantheism, and they made a massive virtue of secondary causation, with God acting in and through everything, but the possibility of envisaging divine intentions was seriously obscured.

(3) Kant took the traditional agnostic solution to its radically hopeful terminus: being the creatures we are, we have no option but to perceive the world as a closed causal network, yet our knowledge is only of experience caused by things in a world presumed to be out there, and not of the things in themselves, of which we have neither experience

nor theoretical knowledge. This wedge so forcefully driven between experience and reality allowed Kant to affirm simultaneously rigid causality (as our own inevitable contribution to experience), and the freedom of human will and the activity of God (as hypotheses necessary to account for our moral life and our ability to act at all).

Each of these three modern expressions of the classical alternative solutions was variously attacked or conditionally affirmed by theologians, in a rather messy process of trying to figure out what to say about divine action now that the traditional solution had lost much of its plausibility. But none of the theological appropriations of these alternatives was particularly amenable to the traditional Western idea of a transcendent-immanent God. This left mainstream theology at best in an awkward holding pattern. Of course, secondary divine causation in principle cannot be ruled out by any scientific discovery, but partly because of that, it is a desperately weak thesis when thought to exhaust divine action. Thus mainstream theology tended to deal with the problem of divine action by positing a mechanism for divine primary causation that either permanently transcended human understanding or awaited clearer articulation. This strategy may have been convenient and common, but it was really just avoiding the problem in its sharpest form, presumably in the hope that a persuasive, more traditional account of the action of God would be forthcoming. The consequences for spirituality of this lack of clarity are well known. Prayer remains meaningful to most, but often because the ancient, theologically deficient, anthropomorphic, mythical view of God's action lives on. Rare is the Jew, Christian, or Muslim who has felt the problem of divine action and does not thereafter pray with shaken confidence in God's responsiveness to their concerns.

Now we must ask whether anything has changed in this story of competition among the four basic Western accounts of divine action, besides the partial collapse of the traditional view. Have philosophical analyses like those of Austin Farrer and others achieved a new view of divine action? Far from it; they are simply clear about the problem, as when Farrer argues that the subjective discernment of divine acts does not illuminate the mode of divine action, which necessarily remains shrouded. Has anything been added by the interpretation of divine action as a subjective discernment of ordinary events as "special," within the constant field of providential divine activity? On the contrary, not only does it leave unclear the mode of God's everyday sustaining action, this subjectivizing view has given away any sense of positive, special, divine action independent of human recognition of it, making a confused virtue of collapsing divine action into secondary causes. Have theologies using Alfred North Whitehead's philosophy of organism advanced the problem? By no means, for process theology purchases a solution to the pantheistic problem of not being able to speak concretely about divine intentions at the cost of supposing that God and the universe are coeternally locked in a process of mutual co-determination. This is an intriguing theological strategy, but it baptizes as a Christian (Jewish, Muslim) view what formerly was considered a competitor, so it must be thought of not as a breakthrough, but as a revolutionary correction. Like the other views, it also has its own conceptual problems.

Process metaphysics (the modern representative of the pantheistic approach), deism in its post-Enlightenment form (common among contemporary religious scientists), and the ingenious Kantian development of traditional agnosticism (common among modern theologians) together constitute the three partially viable, partially problematic modern competitors to the traditional theistic account of divine action. After all this time, therefore, though many of the details have changed, the theological problem of divine action retains much the same shape and sharpness as it has had for 2,500 years, except that the most audacious account of all—the traditional Jewish-Christian-Muslim insistence that God acts in history and nature—has become quite obscure. The same is true for most other theological problems newly framed by scientific discoveries.

The recognition of the notable failure of modern religious thought to produce compelling and widely accepted explications of many of its classical affirmations is the first reason why the discipline of science and religion is *important*. This is the area in which fertile discussions occur that are beginning to overcome the widespread neglect of the natural sciences by religious thinkers. For example, it is in the sphere of science and religion that process philosophers, classical theists from several religions, philosophers of action, quantum physicists, chaos theorists, and philosophers of science struggle together to figure out whether there is anything helpful in the changing details of the problem of divine action. It is there that process philosophers, deists, and Kantian agnostics press their claims to be the most adequate inheritors of the traditional theological understanding of divine action. And it is the specialization of science and religion that has produced and criticized the major reconstructions of the traditional solutions, including John Polkinghorne's use of chaos theory, Robert Russell's nuanced construal of quantum indeterminacy as the epistemically impenetrable locus of divine primary causation, and Arthur Peacocke's modeling of divine primary causation after the human mind's top-down control over the body.[7] All of these views face serious problems, but each promises to revive the traditional account, and only in the discipline of science and religion do resources exist to explore them with the scientific and theological thoroughness required.

Producing tolerably acceptable solutions to theological problems *matters*, and believability hinges on taking what we know about the world as seriously as we can. Only by paying attention to the natural sciences with the same degree of care that is brought to scriptures, the history of religious teaching, or the nature of religious experience can persuasive, realistic, durable solutions be generated. Of course, this same requirement applies to aspects of modern self-understanding besides the natural sciences, especially historical criticism, social psychology, literature and the arts, comparative religions, and cultural anthropology. Understandably, but tragically, much contemporary religious thought is in a "divide-and-survive" mode, effectively disguising its intellectual inadequacy beneath a horde of relatively self-contained, narrowly focused, and individually important special interests. Work at the interface of science and religion is one way in which religious thought can become less defensive and more adequate. It is not the only way, but it is a relatively effective one.

This leads to the second way in which the discipline of science and religion is important: it is a good way to *educate* ourselves about ourselves. There can be no question that deeper self-knowledge is needed. Without a clearer understanding of contemporary Western culture, we probably cannot achieve a markedly greater sense of personal and social integration, Western religious institutions will continue to have little of transforming relevance to say to their contexts, and we certainly cannot seriously hope to avert the catastrophes relentlessly pressing in upon our societies and ecosystem. This statement does not imply that every Westerner must gain a sophisticated appreciation of the contemporary situation if these benefits are to be attained. Nor does it imply that the discipline of science and religion is indispensable. It does mean, however, that a critical mass of people must break through to clearer insights and to consensus on key issues. The discipline of science and religion is an important long-term factor in cultivating this kind of consensus. Its special contribution is to join forces with other intellectual and educational efforts in helping people to understand that religious and spiritual interests are complementary to critical, scientific ones, and not contradictory. To be sure, such intellectual and educational work is of limited value, for practical problems are best solved by action. However, effective, stable action requires hard-won clarity of thought and educational strategies with a vision to match. The impact on practical issues of education in the discipline of theology and science is indirect, to be sure, but powerful in the long term.

There are three educational tasks for the discipline of theology and science. First, the academic community needs a clear appreciation of the richness of human rationality and its fundamental unity in spite of the powerful tension that racks it. The muting of religious, affective dimensions of human life in the name of the critical, scientific dimensions is absurd. Though it is less common than it once was, this attitude is still far too prevalent among academics. The discipline of science and religion is in a good position to offer a correction to this extreme tendency. Similarly, the discipline is well equipped to bring about some reforms in mainstream academic theology, by easing it over its discomfort with and withdrawal from natural science. Other reforming forces must continue to do the same for other fields of human knowledge.

The second educational task involves religious groups and the schools that train their leadership. Religious believers need to understand why prayer seems more pointless than it did to their great-grandparents, why eternal life is more difficult to affirm, and why it feels harder and perhaps irresponsible to trust the future of the earth to divine providence. These are three of the many signs that ordinary believers are deeply affected by the schizophrenic tendencies of their modern Western context. Indeed, as I noted above, an argument can be made that the rise of fundamentalism in the West (and maybe elsewhere, too) owes something to a generalized awareness of the conflicted character of Western life and thought. The discipline of science and religion has much to offer at this point, both by making its results intelligible to religious believers, and by cultivating an awareness of science and religion in religious educational settings. Once again, other forces must achieve parallel goals for other aspects of contemporary knowledge.

Without such an educational effort in seminaries and other venues for the training of religious leaders, how can graduated priests and rabbis possibly give an account of their personal faith—a faith historically responsible, in spite of the existential reality for some of their parishioners that the modern, scientific view of the world makes the traditional stories about Moses, Jesus, and the Qur'an seem like fairy tales; a faith hopeful, in spite of the difficulty of believing in life everlasting when consciousness is biological in origin; a faith relevant, in spite of the comic implausibility of traditionally absolute conceptions of redemption and revelation in the light of the vast stretches of time and space that envelop us; a faith scripturally rooted, in spite of the fact that the supernaturalism of the Bible and the Qur'an clashes with our scientific view of the world as a closed causal network with no room for miracle? How can such under-equipped leaders possibly help their scientist followers who feel driven to separate their faith from their scientific research, because they can find no natural way to relate the two? How can they hope to bring the richness of scientific wonder and discovery to bear in their preaching and teaching, without gross ignorance or ridiculous naïveté? The sad fact is that religious leaders simply will not be able to do this, unless they voluntarily seek the training they lack. Thankfully, some are slightly better equipped to deal with the theological aporias induced by other aspects of the contemporary thought-world. But a theologically informed response to the scientific nature of our era lags behind.

The third educational task is less specific. The general public needs to be encouraged to take their religious impulses seriously, instead of cultivating insensitivity toward them. Of course, religious experience and interest have not declined significantly as secularization has grown. But mainline church and synagogue attendance, which involves intellectual assent through participation in a theologically self-conscious community, has with variations dropped sharply throughout the West. At this point, the discipline of science and religion joins numerous other forces and groups with the same goal. Educational strategies are hard to develop in this context, and the effects of any concrete attempt tend to be diffuse and difficult to assess. The effort is important, however, for it is one way in which the mood of a culture—or at least an interested subculture—is changed, hopefully to the point that organized religion can recover a more significant, positive role in the maintenance and transformation of our social and political institutions.

This in turn leads to the final sense in which the discipline of science and religion is important: exploration of this area can actually help *to bring about reconciliation* of the underlying tension to which it attests. We are no longer speaking here merely of education of religious believers or the general public, nor of some reforms in the academic community, but of assuaging one of the fundamental intellectual and practical crises of our era. It is in this sense that the contemporary science-religion specialization is a *quest for harmony*, for a unified, consistent understanding of human nature and the world in which it has arisen.

At first sight, this appears to be an inappropriately grandiose goal. However, while decidedly grandiose, it is far from being unrealistic. Though the schizophrenia of the modern West is ubiquitous in its intellectual and practical life, there are few areas as well equipped to explore the possibilities of reconciliation as the systematic study of science and religion. As I have tried to show, this fitness is due in large part to the inescapable lucidity with which this interaction discloses the simultaneously fractured and exciting character of the modern Western world. Successes in this area readily feed back into easing the uncomfortable, driving tension that gnaws beneath the surface of modern Western life. To be sure, major successes have been rare. But we live in dangerous times, now that the future of Western civilization and the fate of the planet lie in human hands. Intellectual adventures are not the only way forward, but there is a handful of academic enterprises, each of which is indispensable to the quest for harmony in human self-understanding, and vital for negotiating a daunting future. I have argued that the specialization of science and religion is one of them.

NOTES

1. The "Joint Appeal by Religion and Science for the Environment" (Washington, May, 1992) and other similar events are the results of a solid consensus among religious leaders and scientists about the need to avert looming ecological catastrophes. A recent article in *Parade* (an insert in many weekend U.S. newspapers, including the *Oakland Tribune*) of March 1, 1992, pp. 10 ff, by Carl Sagan, entitled "To Avert a Common Danger: Religion and Science, Old Antagonists, Forge a New Alliance," gives an account of this cooperative approach.

2. Herman E. Daly and John B. Cobb, Jr., *For the Common Good: Redirecting the Economy Toward Community, the Environment, and a Sustainable Future* (Boston: Beacon Press, 1989). See esp. ch. 2, pp. 49–52.

3. Robert N. Bellah, Richard Madsen, William M. Sullivan, Ann Swidler, and Steven M. Tipton, *The Good Society* (New York: Alfred A. Knopf, 1991).

4. Noam Chomsky, *Necessary Illusions: Thought Control in Democratic Societies* (Boston: South End Press, 1989).

5. Claude Welch, *Protestant Thought in the Nineteenth Century*, 2 vols. (New Haven: Yale University Press, 1972, 1985). Welch's paper for this volume extends this argument. A similar point is made in relation to the period of the European Enlightenment by John Hedley Brooke in his paper for this volume.

6. For an interesting example of balancing the promise of consonance and the threat of dissonance, see Robert John Russell's essay in Part III of this volume.

7. See Robert John Russell, "Theistic Evolution," *CTNS Bulletin* XV.2 (Spring, 1995). Also see the articles by Polkinghorne and Peacocke later in this volume.

SCIENCE, RELIGION, AND THE FUTURE

HOLMES ROLSTON, III

Without the gift of prophecy, looking into the future is hazardous. The sun will rise tomorrow because it rose yesterday and the day before. Induction is reasonably reliable if one is predicting simple systems. But induction is notoriously problematic, both for logical and empirical reasons, especially if one is dealing with complex systems. If one predicts on the basis of past and present, one will be right much, even most of the time, but wrong at the times of critical innovation, the most important times of all, when the future is unlike the past.

The future develops what is already seeded into the present. An acorn, planted, reliably yields an oak. But the oak may be struck by lightning, depending on the luck of the weather, or cut, depending on national forest policy. The present century has taught us how historical contingency mixes with dependability and rationality. The one thing certain is that there will be surprises, the more so in more complicated systems. It is easier to predict eclipses a century hence than to predict tomorrow's headlines. To a considerable extent, therefore, the future is open.

We have been living through a century of change in our ideas about how determinacy and contingency, design and chance, order and chaos fit together to make up the world. These changes shape religion in its account of both science and nature. It now looks as though that reshaping will continue. There are no laws, plus initial conditions, by which we can predict the new millennium; but there are stories that will be told. Science deals with causes; religion deals with meanings; we can be sure that both causes and meanings will be ingredients perennially interwoven in the fabric of history. And, dramatically, we write the next chapters of the story.

Anticipating the future relations between science and theology, we can only extrapolate and wonder. In this century, we human beings have come to know who we are and where we are in ways unprecedented in all past millennia. We know the size, age, and extent of our universe; we know the deep evolutionary history of our planet, and ourselves as part of this story. These facts of science have required integration into our classical religious worldviews; and this blending of theory and principle in science and religion will continue. In this century, we human beings have gained, through science and technology, more power than ever before to affect, for better or worse, our own well-being, that of the human and natural worlds, and even planetary history. The fate of the Earth, the fate of all who dwell thereon, depends, in the next century, on the responsible use of that power. Everything depends on how we join science, ethics, and religion in practice.

I. WHERE ARE WE? SCIENCE AND RELIGION IN THEORY AND PRINCIPLE

Ian Barbour has summarized four ways of relating science and religion: conflict, independence, dialogue, and integration.[1] It is difficult to conceive of two subject areas whose relations would not lie somewhere within these broad categories. Barbour finds examples of all four present and past; and, one assumes, there will be examples of all four for the indefinite future. Perhaps their frequency ratios will shift, less conflict and more integration, or vice versa. Perhaps the shifting frequency ratios will vary with the discipline. At present, for instance, there is more dialogue and integration in physics, ample conflict and considerable independence between biology and religion. Whether that trend will continue depends partly on discoveries as yet unknown in physics, astronomy, and molecular and evolutionary biology.

Astrophysics and nuclear physics are describing a universe "fine-tuned" for life, although physics has also found a universe with indeterminacy at its most fundamental levels. Meanwhile evolutionary and molecular biology seem to be discovering that the history of life is a random walk with much struggle and chance, although they have also found that, on this seemingly random walk, over millennia, order is built up a negentropic slope, attaining in Earth's natural history the most complex and highly ordered phenomena known in the universe, such as ecosystems, organisms, and—most of all—the human mind.

Cosmology: The Origin of the Universe

Theology has as its principal focus persons in their relationships to God and neighbor, and we will below be amply concerned about science and technology as they in practice help or hinder such relations. Such practice requires a worldview giving persons a sense of who and where they are, an orientation to undergird their sense of what they ought to do. In the monotheistic West, God created the world; that is the first article of the Christian creed, preceding the second article, about Christ and redemption, and the third, about life in the community of the Spirit. In the second half of our century, a remarkable dialogue between theology and astrophysics about this creation has become possible.

The possibility of a natural theology, frowned upon earlier in the century by most theologians, has even been taken up by some physicists. Many, perhaps even most, today think that physics, especially cosmology, is compatible with some kind of monotheism. Victor Weisskopf is explicit:

The origin of the universe can be talked about not only in scientific terms, but also in poetic and spiritual language, an approach that is complementary to the scientific one. Indeed, the Judeo-Christian tradition describes the beginning of the world in a way that is surprisingly similar to the scientific model.[2]

A big surprise in recent decades has been the anthropic principle in cosmology. The universe (this universe at least) originated twenty billion years ago in a "Big Bang" and has since been expanding. From the primal burst of energy, elementary particles formed, and afterward hydrogen, the simplest element, which serves as fuel for the stars, where all the heavier atoms were forged. The heavier elements were collected to form, in our case, the solar system and planet Earth. Recent physics interrelates two levels; astronomical phenomena such as the formation of galaxies, stars, and planets depend critically on microphysical phenomena, such as the charges on particles and their energy transformations. In turn, the mid-range scales, where the known complexity mostly lies (in ecosystems or human brains), depend on the interacting microscopic and astronomical ranges.

It now seems that the universe has been "fine-tuned" from the start for the subsequent construction of stars, planets, life, and mind. A plausible interpretation is divine design. Theologians and philosophers have often been wary of design arguments, remembering William Paley, his fine-tuned watch, and the many telling criticisms of such arguments. Nevertheless the physical world is resembling a fine-tuned watch again, and now many quantitative calculations support the argument. Astrophysicists and microphysicists have joined to discover that, in the explosion that produced our universe, what seem to be widely varied facts really cannot vary widely, indeed that many of them can hardly vary at all, and still have the universe develop life and mind. We find a single blast (the Big Bang) fine-tuned to produce a world that produces us, when any of a thousand other imaginable blasts would have yielded nothing.

Theologians and scientists alike can find it perfectly intelligible to draw conclusions from a fine-tuned universe, though monotheist conclusions are not the only ones that can be drawn. Indeed, "conclusions" is probably not the word we want here; little is really concluded as we face the next century. Trying to keep more modesty in the insight, we are careful to say only that monotheism is "consistent with" or "complementary to" physical cosmology, but not a hard conclusion commanded by it. Freeman Dyson puts it this way:

> I conclude from the existence of these accidents of physics and astronomy that the universe is an unexpectedly hospitable place for living creatures to make their home in. Being a scientist, trained in the habits of thought and language of the twentieth century rather than the eighteenth, I do not claim that the architecture of the universe proves the existence of God. I claim only that the architecture of the universe is consistent with the hypothesis that mind plays an essential role in its functioning.[3]

The issue seems to be: How friendly is too friendly a relationship between physics and theology? For those with good historical memories, there is a dilemma. The religion that is married to science today is a widow tomorrow, while the religion that is divorced from science today leaves no offspring tomorrow. Within recent memory there were two seriously competing cosmologies: the steady state theory, discarded since the mid-1960s, and the now-favored Big Bang theory. Suppose that the steady state had proved true? Would theology have been the worse? The steady state theory posited the continuous but infrequent *ex nihilo* insertion of subatomic particles throughout the universe, and thus no absolute beginning. That theory too still required the assembly of the light elements, then the stars, galaxies, the heavier elements within the stars, then planets, then people—hardly any less creation for the lack of an initial one. Nothing in Christianity implies the detail of the Big Bang theory; many other cosmologies are compatible with Christian faith in creation. The Big Bang model might prove wrong and the now novel plasma cosmology might replace it.[4] Then the search for consonance would have to start all over.

Meanwhile it is difficult to envision any cosmology that does not require creation of the complex out of the simple, more out of less, something somehow out of nothing. It is difficult to imagine that all of the remarkable phenomena that work together to make our universe possible will disappear, even though the proportions that we ascribe to contingency and to necessity may change. It is difficult to imagine a universe much less staggering, dramatic, and mysterious, for all its rationality. No doubt there will be surprises in cosmology in the next century, but it would be even more surprising if these were wholly uncongenial to theology.

BIOLOGY: THE NATURAL HISTORY OF LIFE

Creation refers in part to the genesis of life on Earth over the last five billion years. Like physics, biology has developed on two scales: the microscopically small and big-scale history. Molecular biology, discovering DNA, has decoded the "secret of life" (once ascribed to the Spirit of God). Evolutionary history has located the secret of life in natural selection operating over incremental variations across enormous time spans. As with physics, the two levels have been theoretically interrelated. The genetic level supplies variations, does the coding of life, and constructs molecular proteins. Organisms cope at their native-range levels, inhabiting ecosystems. Across deep evolutionary time, species are selected and transformed as they track changing environments.

This process is not fine-tuned. To the contrary, evolutionary history can seem tinkering and makeshift. The genetic variations bubble up without regard to the needs of the organism, and the evolutionary selective forces select for survival without regard to advance. Many evolutionary theorists insist that nothing in natural selection theory guarantees progress.

Here the cause of relating science to religion has been taken up adversely by some biologists, as with Richard Dawkins and his *Blind Watchmaker*.[5] Stephen Jay Gould insists, "We are the accidental result of an unplanned process."[6] Jacques Monod exclaims, "Chance *alone* is at the source of every innovation, of all creation in the biosphere."[7] Outspokenly monotheist biologists are as rare as those who think physics is compatible with monotheism are common. Typically, biologists seem to insist that if, from the perspective of science, they find what looks like contingency, then God is eliminated.

But there are also biologists who emphasize the richness in biology: the fecund Earth, the vital creative processes continuing over time, the ascent of life from the simple to the complex, the production of more out of less over long millennia. Biologists can doubt creation, but none can doubt genesis. In fact, the earthly genesis is as impressive as anything in astronomy, because the life genesis requires a coding and a coping, factors wholly novel to anything previously encountered in physics or chemistry. Indeed, we can get from equally eminent scientists (though they are still not outspoken monotheists) a quite opposite reaction: the claim that life is the destiny of these earthly chemicals.

During the chemical evolution of life, when predecessors of DNA and RNA appear, bearing the possibility of genetic coding and information, they are conserved, writes Melvin Calvin, a biochemist, "not by accident but because of the peculiar chemistries of the various bases and amino acids. . . . There is a kind of selectivity intrinsic in the structures."[8] The evolution of life, so far from being random, is "a logical consequence"[9] of natural principles. "This universe breeds life inevitably," concludes George Wald, an evolutionary biochemist.[10]

Michael Polanyi, a philosopher of science, finds that "there is a cumulative trend of changes tending towards higher levels of organization, among which the deepening of sentience and the rise of thought are the most conspicuous. . . . From a seed of submicroscopic living particles—and from inanimate beginnings lying beyond these—we see emerging a race of sentient, responsible and creative beings. The spontaneous rise of such incomparably higher forms of being testifies directly to the operations of an orderly innovating principle."[11]

Also it begins to become clear that the genes, once thought to operate blindly and at random, are a rather sophisticated problem solving device, conserving the successes of the past so as to search the nearby living space for novel innovations, without which life can neither survive nor develop. A kind of genetic engineering has been going on for several billion years, long before the biochemists began recently to undertake this in their laboratories.[12] Rather surprisingly, computer scientists, at the forefront of cognitive science, have discovered that analogues of genetic problem solving can be effectively used in advanced computing.[13]

Meanwhile, looking backward, we discover a primitive planetary environment in which the formation of living things had a high probability, that is, a pregnant Earth. And looking forward to the next century, it is difficult to imagine that our evolutionary natural history will come to seem any less startlingly fecund and prolific. The dialogue between biology and religion will increasingly try to figure out whether in the genesis of these riches we need interference by a supernatural agency or the recognition of a marvelous endowment of matter with a propensity toward life. Do we need something to superintend the possibilities? There will not be much doubt that there has been a marvelous natural history, but there will be dialogue, debate, conflict over whether and how the story needs an Author. My prediction is that the watchmaker-design approach to the Creator, though it may remain appropriate in physics, will not prove the appropriate model for biology, where more autonomy and self-creativity must be combined with the divine will for life, a divine parenting entwined with spontaneous creative process.

Order and Disorder

The scientific question can be put this way: What is the mixture of order and disorder in the world? The theological question then becomes: Can we detect God in, within, and under the order established, maintained, sustained over against the disorder? When we envision an orderly innovating principle, the randomizing element begins to look different. It does not need to be taken away, at least not all of it, but it can remain as openness and possibility. In both biology and physics, there is a world of infinite possibilities, one in which there is a superposition of possible mutation states over actual ones, but also one where many of the possibilities become briefly actual, real mutants, and then a fractional few stay actual (survive).

In the surviving organism, there is a locally autonomous center of order. The individual organism is fine-tuned at the molecular level to nurse its way through the quantum states by electron transport, proton pumping, selective ion permeability, DNA encoding, and the like. The organism, via its genetic information and biochemistries, participates in forming the course of the microevents that constitute its passage through the world. The organism is responsible, in part, for the microevents, and not the other way round. The microscopic indeterminism provides a looseness through which the organism can steer itself by taking advantage of the fluctuations at the microlevels.

But what about the larger system in which these autonomous organisms come to be? What is the origin of this ongoing biological order? The swarms of organisms are edited, so that from many options the well-adapted survive, and this results, at least in the top trophic rungs of the ecological pyramids, in advancing evolutionary creativity. There is an editing on the basis of fitness, which stretches on into advancement. Here we are going to emphasize not the shuffling but the overall sorting. What most needs to be explained is not the disorder, but the negentropic ascent. Biology must posit some constructive forces that give a slope to evolution.

Since life is evidently a highly ordered event, and since presently living organisms in ecosystems on Earth, human beings included, are the most complex things known in the universe, and since there has been the phenomenal evolution of increasing order over the millennia of natural history, we will have to ask natural selection theory to give what account it can of this composition of order, and press it to do enough explanatory work. We will welcome its causal chains; but, if there is too frequent an appeal to contingency, we will begin to worry that the most striking feature of all, the ascent of life, becomes an anomaly, that is, something which cannot be predicted, derived, or given adequate account of, out of the theoretical model.

It is not that the theoretical model fails altogether to permit and explain what has happened. But it explains only in a weak sense. The story is of chemical evolution, the survival of the fittest, genetic evolution, and so on. But there is not yet enough explanation in the strong sense. We have mostly possibility explanations, seldom necessity explanations, never the assurance that what did happen had to happen. We are given a phenomenal tale of more and more later on out of less and less earlier on. As events move from quarks to protons, from amino acids to protozoans, to trilobites, to dinosaurs, to persons, from spinning electrons to sentient animals, from suffering beasts to sinful persons, the tale gets taller and taller.

It is not just the necessities, nor the contingencies, but the prolife mixing of the two that impresses us. It is not just the atomic or astronomical physics, found universally, but the middle-range earthly system, found rarely, that is so remarkable in its zest for complexity. My prediction is that, in the century to come, science will reveal this order achieved on Earth to be even more remarkable still, and that biological science will continue both to support and to underdetermine it. That will keep an active dialogue between biology and theology about the ultimate source of this creative ordering of our world.

Outspoken biologists may continue to chant, "chance, chance, chance," finding only that across all these millennia. What in fact has resulted is *order*—increasing in complexity and sophistication, millennia after millennia; and all these incantations of chance do not exorcise the evident order that accumulates. The astounding drive that really needs explanation is what transforms chance into order, as the creatures emerge and exploit the opportunities in their environment, and are themselves transcended by later-coming, more highly ordered, more dazzling forms and dynamic processes. In that sense, though biologists in the next century will likely continue an emphasis on contingency, there will be other biologists who, along with the theologians, continue to insist on "saving the appearances" with theories that not only yield but explain what has evidently appeared in the course of natural history. If such a theory is found in bioscience, it may prove congenial to theology. If it cannot be found there, theologians will find it in their metaphysics, for they will need a metaphysics adequate to occurrent reality. With genius enough, we might some day achieve an integration.

Information, Cognition, and History
Beginning with chemical evolution, where complex living forms are constructed from simple building blocks of amino acids, and continuing onward after a coding evolves in

DNA and RNA to transmit discoveries over generations, we have the steady negentropic climb based on increasing information. Marjorie Grene says:

> What makes the DNA do its work is not its chemistry but the order of the bases along the DNA chain. It is this order which is a code to be read out by the developing organism. The laws of physics and chemistry hold, as reductivists rightly insist, universally; they are entirely unaffected by the particular linear sequence that characterizes the triplet code. Any order is possible physico-chemically; therefore physics and chemistry cannot specify which order will in fact succeed in functioning as a code.[14]

That order represents something more than physics and chemistry; it is superimposed information. Therein lies the secret of life.

The organism has to flow through the quantum states, but the organism selects the quantum states that achieve for it an informed flow-through. The information within the organism enables it to act as a preference sieve through the quantum states—by interaction sometimes causing quantum events, sometimes catching individual chance events that serve its program—and thereby the organism maintains its life course. The organism as a whole is program-laden, a whole that executes its lifestyle in dependence on this looseness in its parts. On the basis of this information, there is a kind of downward causation which complements an upward causation, and both feed on the openness, if also the order, in the atomic substructures. The genetic coding informs the electronic states of the constituent atoms.

In biology there is a shift from simple systems, like those in physics and chemistry, to complex ones, structured and informed by the information content within them, information that is discovered and accumulates over time. There we shift from a lawlike science to a historically cumulative one in which, in once-upon-a-time, cumulating stages, photosynthesis is discovered. So is the Kreb's cycle, and backbones, and eyes, and hiding, and thinking. Many, perhaps most, biologists doubt whether there are any absolute laws in biology in the physicist's sense: universal laws that can be formalized in equations and applied across the universe. In biology there are only trends, where discoveries are developed and unfolded, until new discoveries launch variant trends. Protein molecules and the genetic codes are earthbound; matter and energy are necessary but, after that, their composition is as historical as it is material and energetic.

Biofunction runs right down to the molecular level, and life is coded to the genes. So it can seem that life has been reduced to molecules in their coded motion. But what determines the codings on these genes? They have been selected for—not at the microscopic level but at the level of organisms in ecosystems. The needs, the environmental niche of the organism determines what genotype is selected and maintained. So the shape of the activity, the molecular conformations, the information at the molecular level are thrown back up to the macroscopic level. The coding at the molecular level is for coping at the ecosystemic level. And the coping is carried on over the millennia, developing historically. The information stored in the molecular shapes and codings is a story about what is going on in the whole organism at the middle-range level—something like a book with its small print that contains a story of the big world. Molecular and organismic biology tracks big-scale evolutionary biology.

The ecosystem determines the biochemistry as much as the other way round. The shape that the microscopic molecules take is controlled "from above," as information discovered about how to make a way through the macroscopic, terrestrial-range world is stored in the molecules. Sometimes it is hard to say which level is prior and which is subordinate; perhaps it is better to say that we find storied achievements at multiple levels. There is connectedness between the levels through and through. Everywhere there is the interplay of order and disorder, with historically discovered information vital for sustaining and increasing order.

Late in this story, and rather surprisingly, human beings arrive. One can first think that their enlarging brains are to be expected, since intelligence conveys obvious survival advantage. But then again, that is not so obvious, since all the other five million or so presently existing species survive well enough without advanced intelligence, as did all the other five billion or so species that have come and gone over the millennia. In only one of these myriads of species does a transmissible culture develop; and in this one it develops explosively, with radical innovations. There is only one line that leads to persons, but in that line at least the steady growth of cranial capacity makes it difficult to think that intelligence is not being selected for. "No organ in the history of life has grown faster."[15] With this growth, natural selection passed over into something else. Nature transcended itself in culture, with radical new chapters in the ongoing story of the evolution of information, cognition, and history. The world moved into a future quite unlike its past.

Information in wild nature travels intergenerationally on genes;[16] information in culture travels neurally, as persons are educated into transmissible cultures. In nature, the coping skills are coded on chromosomes. In culture, the skills are coded in craftsman's traditions, religious rituals, or technology manuals. Information acquired during an organism's lifetime is not transmitted genetically; the essence of culture is acquired information transmitted to the next generation. Information transfer in culture can be several orders of magnitude faster than and can overleap genetic lines. A human being develops typically in some one of ten thousand cultures, and each heritage is historically conditioned, perpetuated by language, conventionally established, using symbols with locally effective meanings.

The novelty is not simply that human beings are more versatile in their spontaneous natural environments. Deliberately rebuilt environments replace spontaneous wild ones. Animals are adapted to their niches; human beings adapt their ecosystems to their needs. The determinants of animal and plant behavior, much less the determinants of climate or nutrient recycling, are never anthropological, political, economic, technological, scientific, philosophical, ethical, or religious. Natural selection pressures are relaxed in culture; in all but the most primitive cultures human beings teach each other how to make clothes, thresh wheat, make fires, bake bread. Human beings help each other out compassionately with medicine, charity, affirmative action, or Head Start programs. Human beings hold elections and plan their affairs; they teach their religion to their children. They worry about justice and love.

Two of the notable cultural achievements are science and religion, and both are products of this historical development, which, though it requires the prior achievements in biology, breaks through to radically new levels. Both science and religion not only seek to explain the historically developing worlds they study; each is itself caught up in this history, each needs to explain itself and the other as part of the cognitive story on Earth.

Agency: God's Action in the World

Where is God in such a story? The character of answer here has been shifting; and in the coming decades, I predict, this will further shift in the direction of detecting God within the cybernetic processes. God forms by informing the world, bringing order out of disorder.

In earlier years, one would have cast this as the problem of the natural and the supernatural. As scientific understanding has deepened, the signs of God's active agency in nature have become equivocal. Science gives causal explanations where none was available before, and these have become increasingly detailed with advancing scientific information. God acts—so it once was claimed—in the causal gaps. But the gaps have become fewer and smaller, with progressively less place for God to intervene. God also acts, we are reminded, using natural causes; but if the causal network is unbroken, there is no place for the local agency of God. There is no place for a supernatural God, intervening in nature. So, over the years, monotheism has been steadily pushed toward deism, with a God who, once upon a time, started up the causal nexus, since unbroken.

At the same time, scientific causal explanations, impressive though they are, have not proved to be all that complete, especially in the complex biological world, to say nothing of the even more complex cultural world. Complete causal chains are traced a few steps rearward, but after that they become sketchy, loose, statistical, probabilistic. They involve genes, where, on the one hand, patterns are conserved over millennia, and, on the other, novelties appear in every generation. Present-day cytochrome c molecules, pervasively present in fauna and flora, follow (we believe) in causal chains going back billions of years to early ancestors. Yet myriads of differences have steadily arisen in the billions of other functional and structural biological molecules, which have mutated dramatically over the epochs of natural history. Mutated DNA codes for variant proteins, which are selected for their novel coping capacities, resulted in trilobites, dinosaurs, and human beings.

Many, most, or—by some accounts—even all of the interesting events here are contingent, put down to such explanations (or nonexplanations) as "genetic drift" or "random mutations." Disorder everywhere punctuates the order, contingency permeates the certainty. With this discovery, the theological problem has become an opposite one, not too much but too little causation, since the events that matter are said to be fortuitous. Scientific explanation underdetermines events. Are these gaps returning? Is there yet a place for God in the story?

The events that do take place, in addition to their contingent element, at once are marvelously impressive and yet also have a certain provisional and even makeshift quality. They are both wonderful and wandering. Also, they continue to have the elements of struggle and of suffering, the "nature red in tooth and claw" that has troubled theology since Darwin and before. Yet again, as always, there is the counterpoint: nature is also a prolific scene of genesis of life, a system of life support, into which the species are selected as fit adaptations.

The discovery that information is a critical determinant of history has thrown the causal/contingency debate into a new light, and this promises to redefine the mode of God's agency in the world. The world is composed of matter and energy, with the two united in relativity theory—so physics and chemistry have insisted. But the earthly world, biology now insists, is composed by information that superintends the uses of matter and energy. That vital information is carried on the genes. What makes the critical difference is not the matter, not the energy, necessary though these are; what makes the critical difference is the information breakthrough.

Afterwards, as before, there are no causal gaps from the viewpoint of physicist or chemist, but there is something more: novel information that makes possible the achievement of increasing order, maintained out of the disorder. The same energy budget can be put to very different historical uses, depending on the information in the system. Motoo Kimura estimates that the evolution of higher organisms has accumulated genetic information from the Cambrian to the present at an average rate of 0.29 bits per generation.[17] Thus there is spun the negentropic story of life. If in natural history we define "progress as increase in the ability to gather and process information about the environment,"[18] then, again and again, evolution produces phenomena that rise above the former levels with breakthroughs in achievement and power. The secret of that information, from the perspective of biology, is the genetic process.

Is that all that there is to be said? Yes, by biologists, perhaps; but no, say the theologians who detect God in, with, and under this dramatic informing of the life story. Loren Eiseley straddles the two fields: "I would say that if 'dead' matter has reared up this curious landscape of fiddling crickets, song sparrows, and wondering men, it must be plain even to the most devoted materialist that the matter of which he speaks contains amazing, if not dreadful powers, and may not impossibly be . . . 'but one mask of many worn by the Great Face behind'."[19] "Nature is one vast miracle transcending the reality of night and nothingness."[20]

Ernst Mayr, one of the most knowledgeable biologists of our century, and no particular friend of orthodox religion, says, "Virtually all biologists are religious, in the deeper sense of this word, even though it may be a religion without revelation. . . . The unknown and maybe unknowable instills in us a sense of humility and awe."[21] We sense something sublime, something that takes us to the limits of our understanding and mysteriously beyond. Science studies the phenomena; but the phenomena prove increasingly phenomenal. The secular world proves to be spectacular stuff. Perhaps we have lost our confidence in the supernatural, only to find it replaced by increasing confidence that nature is super, superb, mysteriously animated, and enspirited.

We might say that nature has actualized its potential. The molecular self-assembling that issues in evolutionary natural history is a sort of self-actualizing. But neither is it a complete explanation of these phenomena to find that they are natural, until we have asked whether nature is its own self-sufficient explanation. If not, we may find ourselves asking whether the phenomena of natural history are a response to the brooding winds of the Spirit moving over the face of these earthly waters. The phenomena could be revealing the noumena.

The miraculous is not the punctuation of natural order with supernatural intent, God sneaking into the causal gaps. The miraculous is the more-out-of-less that the coupling of natural order with disorder generates, with nature wonderfully, surprisingly, regularly breaking through to new formations because there is new information emergent in the life codings. These achievements are, if you like, fully natural—they are not unnatural; they do not violate nature. But they also are new achievements of discovery and power. Something higher is reached, and in that sense there is something "super" to the precedents, something superimposed, supervening on what went before; there is more where once there was less, something "super" to the previously natural.

There is creativity, genesis, about which these biologists find it difficult not to be religious, whether they are monotheists or not; and monotheists can detect here the divine superintendence without violating the natural processes. There is autonomy in the natural processes; the creatures are what they are in their own self-actualizing, yet surprisingly, too, there is an informing of them that lifts them to new emergents of performance. Sometimes, when we find what looks like contingency, God is not so much eliminated as called for, and especially so if the cumulative contingencies, coupled with the marvelous endowments and possibilities of matter, issue in a superb story. If we define a miracle as a wondrous event without sufficient natural causes, as far as is known, then there remains miracle here, and we hardly yet find that, under bioscience, the secret of life stands explained, certainly not explained away. Man and woman arising via all the intermediate steps (trilobites, dinosaurs, primates) from the maternal Earth is not less impressive, rather more so, than Aphrodite arising from the formless seas.

Without denying that the secret of life lies in the DNA, theists may also say that the secret of life lies in the breath of YHWH animating and informing the dust, conserving life in the midst of its perpetual perishing, and lifting it to self-transcendence. This cannot be "fine-tuned" without violating the creaturely autonomy, but must be finely detected in the vitalities that, over the millennia, spin such a story on this home planet. Our account of natural history cannot be by way of implication, whether deductive or inductive. There is no covering law (such as natural selection), plus initial conditions (such as trilobites), from which one can deduce primates. Nor is there any induction (expecting the future to be like the past) by which one can expect trilobites later from procaryotes earlier, or dinosaurs still later by extrapolating along a statistical regression line (a progression line!) drawn from procaryotes to trilobites. There are no human beings invisibly present (as an acorn secretly contains an oak) in the primitive eucaryotes, to unfold in a lawlike way. All we can do is tell the epic story—eucaryotes, trilobites, dinosaurs, primates, persons who are scientists, ethicists, sinners, and saints—and the drama may prove enough to justify it.

Where is God in the story? God is the historian, the author who informs the action, slipping information into the world, making the improbable probable, converting contingency into destiny. Along these lines, the dialogue between biology and theology faces a promising future. No doubt there will be surprises in biology in the next century, but it would be even more surprising if these discounted the critical role that information plays in both molecular and evolutionary biology, and also surprising if this increasingly cognitive account of biology were wholly uncongenial to theology.

When those in the nineteenth century tried to relate physics and theology, they sometimes failed because the theology was inadequate. The present conflict is also, in part, because classical theology is inadequate. But the nineteenth century reconcilers had more than a theological problem; in the twentieth century we learned that the physics then was not ready either. Perhaps today the biology is not ready. Is there any unity in historical biology, any "arrow of evolutionary time"? John Maynard Smith, one of the most eminent theoretical biologists, frankly says, "I do not think that biology has at present anything very profound to say about this."[22] The full story in natural history remains to be told. When it is, I predict that it will be more congenial with theology, provided that theology, too, is sufficiently resilient. We do not expect biology [B] to imply God [G]: If B, then G. Nor God to imply biology: If G, then B. But we hardly have an unequivocally plausible account yet of their consonance.

Such an account of God's agency, made for the biological sciences, is readily consistent with an account made for the human culture, where again God is the one who informs the history, though now, as we have noted, the transfer of information is no longer merely genetic, because critical determinants are ideological. The drama shifts to forming and reforming human intelligence, with its dramatic possibilities for good and evil in the building of cultures, more or less humane, more or less godly. This intelligence has to be coupled with goodwill. God appears now, not so much as manipulator of the causal processes, as inspiration for meaningful human existence. In the subjectivity of existential presence, in *Existenz*, the coding is not so much in the genes as in religious codes, in the scriptures and creeds that have been so pivotal in our transmissible culture. Now too the information breakthroughs, the revelations, are moral, appropriately for this moral species, *Homo sapiens*, whose members are called to live together wisely—as their specific epithet claims. This takes us from theory to practice.

II. WHAT OUGHT WE TO DO? SCIENCE AND RELIGION IN ETHICS AND PRACTICE

Science, Conscience, and Values

Science increasingly finds itself facing the philosophical truth that, for all our advances in culture, scientific and modern though these may be, the value problems remain as acute as ever. In 1993, George Brown, Jr., Democrat from California, the influential chair in the United States Congress of the Science, Space, and Technology Committee, addressed the annual American Academy of Science and Technology Policy Colloquium:

> Global leadership in science and technology has not translated into leadership in infant health, life expectancy, rates of literacy, equality of opportunity, productivity of workers, or efficiency of resource consumption. Neither has it overcome failing education systems, decaying cities, environmental degradation, unaffordable health care, and the largest national debt in history. . . . Basic human needs—elemental needs—are intrinsically different from other material needs because they can be satisfied. Other needs appear to be insatiable, as the consumption patterns of the United States clearly demonstrate. . . . Once basic human needs are met, satisfaction with our lives cannot be said to depend on the amount of things we acquire, use, and consume. . . . More technology-based economic growth is not necessary to satisfy humanity's elemental needs, nor does more growth quench our thirst for consumption. In terms of the social contract, we justify more growth because it is supposedly the most efficient way to spread economic opportunity and social well-being. I am suggesting that this reasoning is simplistic and often specious.[23]

The soaring consumption in a consumer society is a doubtful blessing. Surveys in our modern age—an age that can even proudly proclaim itself to be heading into the postmodern age—do not reveal any increasing happiness or sense of well-being.[24] We are putting science in the service of satisfying desires on an ever-accelerating tread-mill, without being sufficiently critical of those desires; and, unsurprisingly for the theologians, we find science an uncertain savior. The problem is an information gap again; science tells us how to get what we want, and yet does not provide the information, much less the resolution and goodwill, necessary for high-quality living, for what, in Christianity, has been called the abundant life. Science is a means, but not an end for either conscience or values.

JUSTICE FOR ALL

Not only has a science-based technology failed to solve the deeper problems of developed nations, but a larger problem looms globally. There are about five billion persons in the world. Approximately one-fifth, those in the developed nations, produce and consume about four-fifths of the material goods that a science-based industry provides; about four-fifths of the world divide the remaining one-fifth of the wealth, and about half of these live in poverty.[25] There are more poor persons today than ever before; there will be yet more in decades ahead. For every person added to the population of the developed nations, twenty individuals are added in the less developed ones. For every dollar of economic growth per person in the one, twenty dollars accrue to each individual in the other. Of the ninety million new people on Earth this year, eighty-five million will appear in the Third World, the countries least able to support them. Meanwhile, the five million new people in the industrial countries will put as much strain on the natural resources and cause as much environmental degradation as the eighty-five million new poor.

There are three problems: overpopulation, overconsumption, and underdistribution. The reasons for these outcomes are complex, but whatever justifications one finds for this maldistribution of wealth, the outcome hardly seems either just or loving. There is a first tendency to say that the problem is that too many of the Earth's peoples are unblessed by the fruits of science and technology; what we need is to teach everyone how to produce up to Western standards. The distribution pattern reflects achievement; what the other nations need to do is to imitate this.

But one soon sees that we simply cannot have five billion persons—projected to be twelve billion persons in the next century—all consuming at the escalating, all-American rates that Congressman Brown finds so insatiable, even if we could distribute the world's produce equitably. Teaching everyone how to be an escalating consumer is absurd. That ought not to be the next chapter in the story we are writing. Worse, that illusory promise only hides how much the existing distribution patterns reflect exploitation, callousness, self-aggrandizement, and greed. The poor regularly come off poorly when they bargain with the rich; and wealth that originates as impressive achievement can further accumulate through exploitation. Much, even most, of the answer has to lie in sharing as well as producing, if there is to be an ethic of either justice or love.

To solve this problem, science is necessary, since providing for human needs in the next century without science and technology is unthinkable, but science is not sufficient without conscience that shapes the uses to which science is put, informing policy. Science and religion must face together the impending disaster of today's trends projected cumulatively into tomorrow: population explosion, dwindling food supply, climate change, soil erosion and drought, deforestation, desertification, declining reserves of fossil fuels and other natural resources, toxic wastes, the growing gap between concentrated wealth and increasing poverty, and the militarism, nationalism, and industrialism that seek to keep the systems of exploitation in place. Few problems or none loom more foreboding on the horizon than these, and I predict that these value problems are likely to become more acute than ever in the coming century.

Religion has been the classical informer of conscience, and still remains a powerful force in moral life. Ethics can be autonomous—independent of religion—but such ethical systems have not yet proved themselves capable of shaping cultural reformations over generations. Here the religious ideologies do persist over changing science. It is much safer to predict that the Golden Rule will be an imperative in ethics a century hence than it is to predict that cosmology will continue to affirm a Big Bang with an inflationary period in the first few nanoseconds. It is also, alas, much safer to predict that the seven deadly sins will still be present a century hence, with human life needing to be redeemed from these sins, than that biologists will be emphasizing the contingency in natural history over against a tendency for increased complexity over evolutionary time. Whether the Golden Rule or covetousness will have done more to shape the future is not safe to predict; that outcome depends, in significant part, on the extent of the dialogue between science and religion.

A critic may demur that science has been productive and beneficial enough, spectacularly so, and that it is too much to expect science to redeem humanity from all its failures. Yes, but these failures, rather than faulting science or scientists, do reveal what science is incompetent to do. They reveal science as a human institution. They reveal not so much what science should do, but what religion must do, complementing science. Religion continues to occupy this critical role, along with the other humanities, for science has the same need for evaluation as do all other human activities, including religion. A century hence, we will still be needing God's agency in the world, informing and inspiring the courses of history to make and keep life human.

The same critic may next object that religion is no more competent than science to deal with these immense problems of good and evil. That also may be true, though religion has always claimed whatever successes it has had in the midst of another claim about a perpetual human brokenness. Saints there sometimes are; frequently there are persons struggling to be redeemed from evil, with limited successes; and always there is original sin—order and disorder again, but now at the moral levels. Religion knows that human beings are warped by ambiguity, by the evil that besets their loftiest aspirations toward the good. When human beings emerge out of natural history into culture, we emerge into, and fall into, a process that contains the seeds of its own destruction. We rise to a vision of the good that has evil as its shadow side. We rise to the possibility of being children of God, in love, justice, and freedom, at the same time as we fall into being demonic, in arrogance, in lust, in bondage to sin.

Both scientific rationality and would-be morality, unredeemed from self-love, will prove dysfunctional. This is the value crisis again, taken to a new level. The prophetic genius of Israel is epitomized in the admonition "to do justice, and to love kindness, and to walk humbly with your God."[26] That loving of God and neighbor is a basic human commandment, likely to remain the secret of whatever abundant life is attained in the centuries hence. Science in the service of concupiscent human nature is likely to prove tragic, as much in the twenty-first century as in the twentieth.

Caring for Others

There is a rising and revealing critique of science, one that is likely to prove still more forceful in the decades ahead. Science presents itself as detached and objective, capable of describing the world as it is in itself. That first seems plausible; indeed it is somewhat plausible. After all, the claims of physics about the Big Bang and the expanding universe, or those of biology about evolutionary history, are claims about what once took place on Earth, long before human beings arrived. The genetic coding in the DNA and the protein synthesis by which organisms are produced and maintained, the food chains in ecosystems, the adapted fitness of organisms, their capacities for coping as they make a way through the world—all these seem to be descriptive claims. Science seems to have its independent authority warranting these claims.

But look more deeply. Science is the quest for knowledge, and knowledge is power. Even pure science is driven by a desire to understand, and that, *ipso facto*, is a desire to conquer, seldom pure. The fundamental posture of science is one of analysis, the discovery of laws and generalizations, theory with implications, prediction, testability, repeatability. One wants better probes, better techniques, higher-resolution detectors, more computing power. This always invites control; but more than that, this very approach to nature is driven by the desire to control. The underlying premise of all scientific logic is mastery; and with that insight, the claims to detachment, objectivity, and independence take on a different color. Allegedly objective science is inevitably bent, sooner or later, into the service of technology, and such scientific knowledge coupled with technological power is neither detached nor objective. Willy-nilly, such information will be put to use for some better or worse ends. Thus relativity theory is used to make nuclear weapons; the human genome, mapped, invites first medical therapy and later genetic engineering. Such utility is not simply an outcome of science, it underruns its worldview.

The unavoidable question is: What do scientists care about? What do those to whom their science becomes available care about? This is the value question again, now probing the logic of science and worried about its zest for mastery, fearful lest this become a lust for mastery. This sees not only the outcome but the presumption of science in the escalating consumerism of the First World and in the disproportionately distributed wealth between First and Third Worlds, or, as we will increasingly say, between North and South. These are symptoms of a fundamentally misplaced caring. Science is the product of white Western men, lament the feminists, out to dominate nature, and ready enough to colonize elsewhere and harvest whatever resources they can wherever they can, to build machines of industry and of war, to dominate other peoples and races, having long since dominated their own women.[27]

The scientist, to be sure, when moving from pure to applied science, pretends to care; the benefits of science in the service of human beings are preached incessantly. No doubt such benefits are often realizable; but it is equally certain that science without critical caring for others has produced the present crisis. And caring for others—loving one's neighbor—is the central claim in religious ethics. Science is not religion. Religion cannot suggest the content of any science, but religion can notice the forms into which such content is being poured; it can also defend a content of its own. One can do science without adverting to theology, but one cannot live by science alone. Indeed, science cannot teach us what we most need to know—that about which we should most care. In that sense, science is not independent. There is an information gap, this time not in the causal chains of science, but in the very logic of science itself. More computing power is not likely to give us the information we need here. There are no algorithms for good and evil. All this suggests that the dialogue between science and religion is likely to continue. There will be a humane future only if we can integrate the two.

Saving the Earth

Science and religion have their differences of outlook and interpretation; and we earlier said that dialogue between the two has of late been more problematic in biology than in physics. We hoped for more congenial relations in the future, as biological theory is further developed. But we are already seeing one comprehensive area where, primarily in practice and not without implications for a concept of nature, science and religion are increasingly partners. That is in concern for biological conservation, for the well-being of the biosphere. Though biologists are often uncertain whether life arrived on Earth by divine intention, they are almost unanimous in their respect for life, and seek biological conservation on an endangered planet. That concern for saving the Earth is certain to increase, with considerable promise for dialogue between theology and biology.

Biology is earthbound, so far as we know. This is the only home planet, the only planet with an ecology, on which there has been an evolutionary natural history. And what are we to anticipate for the future of this quite special planet? Earlier, future salvation might have been couched largely as the question of heaven, or as the hope for an *eschaton* launched by divine intervention; and the question might have been whether science permits such heaven and hope. Those questions are still relevant. But the question of salvation has become earthy. Nature and the future of nature, and the future of human cultures in entwined destiny with natural systems—that is increasingly not only a scientific but also a religious assignment. Our escalating human desires, coupled in this century with more power than ever before to transform the Earth, have put nature at risk.

For perhaps two hundred thousand years, the human brain and hand have produced cultures superposed on natural systems—cultures broken and failed enough in the midst of their glories. Meanwhile, diverse combinations of nature and culture have worked well enough for nature to continue over many millennia. But no more. As we face the next century, our modern cultures threaten the stability, beauty, and integrity of Earth, and thereby of the cultures superposed on Earth. In the same century when we gained the vision of one world, symbolized by photographs of Earth from space, we also came to fear the shadow of none, first as a nuclear threat, now the threat of environmental tragedy, an outcome more probable than ever was the nuclear threat (which itself still looms). As a result of human failings, nature is at more peril today than at any time in the last two and a half billion years. The sun will rise tomorrow, because it rose yesterday and the day before; but nature may no longer be there. Unless in the next millennium, indeed in the next century, we can regulate and control the escalating human devastation of our planet, we may face the end of nature as it has hitherto been known.

Several billion years worth of creative toil, several million species of teeming life, have now been handed over to the care of this late-coming species in which mind has flowered and morals have emerged. Science has revealed to us this glorious natural history; and religion invites us to be stewards of it. That could be a glorious future story. But the sole moral and allegedly wise species has so far been able to do little more than use this science to convert whatever we can into resources for our own self-interested and escalating consumption, and we have done even that with great inequity between persons. There is something perverse about an ethic, practiced sometimes in the name of religion, sometimes in the name of science, and often both, that regards the welfare of only one of Earth's several million species as an object and beneficiary of duty.

Justice and love—those are thought to belong to an interhuman ethics. But when we ask about appropriate caring, the boundaries enlarge to the whole community of life on Earth. Care for human beings we must, and religions have been an inspiration for that appropriate care. But caring only for human beings will increasingly be replaced by caring for human beings as residents in a larger biotic community. Our responsibility to Earth might be thought the most remote of our responsibilities; it seems so grandiose and vague beside our concrete responsibilities to our children or next-door neighbors. But not so: it is the most fundamental, the most comprehensive of our responsibilities. The next five hundred years of science and technology cannot be like the last five hundred years, indeed the next century cannot be like the last. And, though recent and novel on global scales, the future imperative recalls the first commandment: to till the garden earth and keep it.

This is the Earth in which we live and move and have our being, and we owe this Earth system the highest allegiance of which we are capable, under God, in whom also we live and move and have our being. Biologists, again, may not share the monotheism, but they are coming to share the concern for the Earth. When they do, the mentality of dominance in science, about which we have worried, can itself become regenerated, and science put in the service of responsible care for this only home planet. Scientists, as much as anyone else, theologians included, wish for a sustainable harmony between human beings and this very special planet. That bodes well for increasingly congenial relations between biology and theology.

III. WHERE ARE WE GOING? SCIENCE AND RELIGION IN THE FUTURE

My projections, then, are that astrophysical cosmology will remain reasonably congenial with theology and that, on Earth, the dialogue between religion and biology will grow more subtle, with an increasing understanding of the relationship between order and disorder and of the historical character of the evolutionary genesis, with information transmission and breakthrough a critical determinant of that history. The agency of God may be to fine-tune the astrophysics and the microphysics, an aboriginal creative forming, but the agency of God is to superintend by informing an earthbound, autonomous biology, where possibilities become actual in a perennial struggling through to something higher.

The radical differences between nature and culture, if not already evident, will become yet more evident as the speed of cultural innovation increases. In the more recent centuries, and in the most recent decades of this century, information has accumulated and traveled in culture at logarithmically increasing speeds. The pace of the story steps up, and now, as we turn from the long evolutionary and cultural past to face the future, there is a certain feeling that the pace of the action is accelerating, both with excitement and danger. The computer revolution exemplifies this, with its dramatic capacities for extending human computational power, for information storage and processing, for long-distance communication and networking. Discoveries in physics and chemistry let us in on how the world was made. Discoveries in the biosciences—mapping, for instance, the human genome, with the further possibilities of genetic engineering—offer us the possibility of remaking the world. We human beings are also agents, powerful agents.

We seem to have reached a turning point in the long, accumulating story of cognition actualizing itself. We are now coming around to oversee the world and to face the prospect of our own self-engineering, to the genesis of a higher-level ordering of the world in the midst of its threatening disorder. Increasingly we are like gods. But we need the wisdom of God, and that programs poorly on computers, and is not found in physics, chemistry, or biology textbooks. There is an information gap about good and evil.

So my projection is also that ethically and axiologically there lie crises ahead, not for the lack of science but for the lack of wisdom, a wisdom that only religion in the broad sense can supply—worldviews that orient us philosophically and that can redeem our human nature from its perennial failings. The need for justice, for love, for caring will remain undiminished, and science will need conscience in the next century more than ever before. What on Earth are we doing? There is no figuring that out without both science and religion; there is no doing it right without integration of the two.

Science seeks to understand the world, and that understanding, we have hoped and feared, is in order to change it. We certainly must recognize the underlying agenda of science in the context of larger social and psychological forces. But pure understanding is one of the glories of being human, and science and religion in integrated understanding are godly indeed. Here, too much emphasis on the pragmatic utility of science is increasingly likely to obscure the most genuine reason for doing it, which lies in the joy of, and human need for inquiry into the nature of things. At this point science does need religion to keep science humane, not only in the pragmatic sense but in the principled and deeply metaphysical sense of keeping science meaningful. Among the humanities, religion pushes science toward questions of ultimacy, as well as of value, and it can keep science from being blinkered, or, more elegantly put, religion can keep science deep. That is why there now is, and always will be, room after science for religious conviction.

NOTES

1. Ian G. Barbour, *Religion in an Age of Science* (San Francisco: Harper and Row, 1990).

2. Victor F. Weisskopf, "The Origin of the Universe," *American Scientist* 71 (1983), pp. 473–480, citation on p. 480.

3. Freeman Dyson, *Disturbing the Universe* (New York: Harper and Row, 1979), p. 251.

4. John Noble Wilford, "Novel Theory Challenges the Big Bang," *The New York Times*, February 28, 1989, pp. C1, C11.

5. Richard Dawkins, *The Blind Watchmaker* (New York: W. W. Norton, 1986).

6. Stephen Jay Gould, "Extemporaneous Comments on Evolutionary Hope and Realities," in Charles L. Hamrum, ed., *Darwin's Legacy*, Nobel Conference XVIII (San Francisco: Harper and Row, 1983), pp. 95–103, citation on p. 102.

7. Jacques Monod, *Chance and Necessity* (New York: Random House, 1972), p. 112.

8. Melvin Calvin, "Chemical Evolution," *American Scientist* 63 (1975), pp. 169–177, citation on p. 176.

9. "Chemical Evolution," p. 169.

10. George Wald, "Fitness in the Universe: Choices and Necessities," in J. Oro, *et al.*, eds., *Cosmochemical Evolution and the Origins of Life* (Dordrecht, Netherlands: D. Reidel Publishing Co., 1974), pp. 7–27, citation on p. 9.

11. Michael Polanyi, *Personal Knowledge* (New York: Harper and Row, 1964), pp. 384–387.

12. John H. Campbell, "Evolving Concepts of Multigene Families," *Isozymes: Current Topics in Biological and Medical Research*, vol. 10: *Genetics and Evolution* (1983), pp. 401–417.

13. John H. Holland, *Adaptation in Natural and Artificial Systems* (Ann Arbor: University of Michigan Press, 1975); D. Whitley, T. Starkweather, and C. Bogart, "Genetic Algorithms and Neural Networks: Optimizing Connections and Connectivity," *Parallel Computing* 14 (1990), pp. 347–361.

14. Marjorie Grene, "Reducibility: Another Side Issue?" in Marjorie Grene, ed., *Interpretations of Life and Mind* (New York: Humanities Press, 1971), p. 18.

15. E.O. Wilson, *On Human Nature* (Cambridge: Harvard University Press, 1978), p. 87.

16. Some higher animals learn limited behaviors from parents and conspecifics, but animals do not form transmissible cultures.

17. Motoo Kimura, "Natural Selection as the Process of Accumulating Genetic Information in Adaptive Evolution," *Genetical Research* 2 (1961), pp. 127–140.

18. Francisco Ayala, "The Concept of Biological Progress," in Francisco Jose Ayala and

Theodosius Dobzhansky, eds., *Studies in the Philosophy of Biology* (New York: Macmillan, 1974), p. 350.

19. Loren Eiseley, *The Immense Journey* (New York: Vintage Books, 1957), p. 210.

20. Loren Eiseley, *The Firmament of Time* (New York: Atheneum, 1960), p. 171.

21. Ernst Mayr, *The Growth of Biological Thought* (Cambridge: Harvard University Press, Belnap Press, 1982), p. 81.

22. John Maynard Smith, *On Evolution* (Edinburgh: University Press, 1972), p. 98.

23. Cited in *Science*, May 7, 1993, p. 735.

24. Alan Durning, *How Much Is Enough?* (New York: W. W. Norton, 1992), especially ch. 3, "The Dubious Rewards of Consumption."

25. World Development Report 1991 (Oxford University Press).

26. Micah, 6:8.

27. Rosemary Radford Ruether, *Gaia and God: An Ecofeminist Theology of Earth Healing* (San Francisco: HarperSanFrancisco, 1992).

Method

INTRODUCTION

The question of the similarities and differences between theological and scientific activity is an old one. Part of the history of this question has been retold in Part I. At times it has seemed as if theology and science had nothing in common at all. At other times they have been regarded as only partially distinguishable aspects of a single kind of intellectual inquiry.

I. REVISITING AN OLD PROBLEM

Since the rise of the natural sciences in their modern form, and throughout the modern period, this fundamental problem has been shaped by two looming considerations. On the one hand, the natural sciences have proved to be extremely successful in a general way. They have been able to build on previously established results, to make accurate predictions about how the natural world would behave in experiments, and to produce beautiful and fruitful explanations of all manner of natural phenomena. On the other hand, there is an ongoing crisis about the status of religious knowledge. This crisis affects everything from the interpretation of mystical and ordinary religious experiences to assessing the truth of assertions that have traditionally been held to be divinely revealed knowledge.

The contrast between theology and science established by these considerations has long been the obvious starting point for investigating their relations, and the numerous characterizations of it need not be recapitulated here. What is important to note is that theologians and scientists alike have interpreted this basic situation differently. Some have judged the apparent differences between theological and scientific activity to be entirely appropriate and have sought to construe the two spheres as independent of one another. This has been the tactic of those who disclaim there is such a thing as religious *knowledge* as well as those who, more moderately, see religious knowledge as established on a basis different from knowledge about the natural world. On this view, it was possible to regard theology as "scientific" only in the sense of ordered exposition and elucidation of a deposit of revealed truth, unknowable in detail apart from its being divinely revealed.

Others, again both scientists and theologians, have deplored the apparent chasm between theology and science, and have sought to understand theology as "scientific," in some sense resembling the way that the natural sciences are scientific. These thinkers tend to believe that all human knowledge is obtained and articulated in fundamentally similar ways because of the rational unity of the human beings who do the discovering, and they are convinced that a scientific theology would be methodologically continuous and substantively consonant with natural science.

These two postures taken toward the apparent differences between theology and the natural sciences have helped to make the debate over similarities and differences between theology and science an intense one in the modern period. But the current version of this debate is conditioned by several, highly important, new elements.

First, from the philosophical study of the history and methods of science, we have a better understanding of the complex, social nature of scientific activity, and we have a more nuanced appreciation for the processes of generation and justification of scientific knowledge. These new understandings have reinforced (and actually largely stimulated) the widespread conviction that foundationalist epistemology is a poor model for explaining the workings of the natural sciences. According to foundationalist epistemology, sound arguments are based on indubitable premises and lead logically to assured conclusions. Foundationalist approaches differ in specifying various ways of discovering these unquestionable, foundational premises (through sense data or rational intellection, for example) but all foundational epistemologies affirm an indubitable foundation of some kind.

Suspicion of foundationalist epistemology, especially as a model for scientific activity, appears in the philosophy of science and epistemology of Charles Sanders Peirce and subsequently in John Dewey's writings, and is surely one of the most important contributions of the United States to world philosophy. The view can be traced through Willard Van Orman Quine and beyond in epistemology, and through Imre Lakatos and beyond in the philosophy of science. The consequence for understanding the relations between theology and science is dramatic and well-known: scientific and religious knowledge, and in fact all kinds of human knowledge, are of essentially the same kind. The old foundationalist scenario was especially problematic for theology because it has had a tortured history since the Enlightenment of vainly struggling to explain how its premises were indubitable. So the failure of this scenario as the basis of the scientific method was welcome relief for those theologians haunted by the obvious difficulties of scientific or rational theology.

It now appears that, in science and theology alike, the nature of creative intellectual work is to form hypotheses that are sufficiently well-defined to allow the deduction of testable consequences. Controlled experimentation is the most efficient form of testing, but other avenues of hypothesis-correction exist and come into play in everything from literary criticism to metaphysics, from social ethics to theology. In all forms of inquiry, then, rationality of procedure consists in arguing from relatively secure (but necessarily fallible) knowledge to less secure knowledge, the tentative securing of which would serve to broaden the stock of knowledge and to deepen one's understanding of knowledge already in hand. Thus, while differences remain due to subject matter, natural science and theology now appear to have a great deal in common methodologically.

Second, the material content of several natural sciences has made it evident that, quite apart from the colorful and strange realm of mystical experiences, the natural world is a more mysterious place than early modernity had realized. From the foundations of quantum physics to the cosmic anthropic principle, and in the interplay of contingency and necessity in the biological sciences, the same message is heard by those trying to understand the relation between theology and the natural sciences: the natural world is not a simple, closed network of causal relations, and explaining its wonders is a task to which philosophical and theological understandings may make relevant contributions.

There are other, less crucial influences shaping the current form of the problem of the theology-science relation, but these two are the most prominent. In this atmosphere of seeing theology and science as essentially two instances of a single kind of inquiry, much systematic religious reflection is once again fascinated with the possibilities of understanding itself as "scientific." There are as a result many works articulating continuities between the processes of scientific and religious knowing. But contemporary Western religious reflection is also the recipient of a nineteenth-century heritage that has insisted on the complex, relational, existentially rooted mode by which religious knowledge emerges and is preserved in communities.

Thus, a sharp awareness of difference remains between scientific and religious language, one so strong that, relative to mainstream theology, the science-theology dialogue can sometimes seem painfully out of step, an esoteric specialization dominated by one-sided preoccupation with the cognitive aspects of religious language to the exclusion of its expressive and prescriptive dimensions. This is an indication that differences as well as similarities must be respected and explained in any account of the relation between natural science and theology. It should also not be forgotten that contemporary theological activity is an extremely diverse family of projects, guided by apparently conflicting methodologies and assumptions. The relation between science and theology cannot be the same in the case of all of these theological projects.

These, then, are some of the leading considerations giving shape to the current version of the problem of the relation between theology and the natural sciences. In this situation, it is possible to discern a number of basic similarities and differences to which any account of the relation between Christian theologies and the sciences must do justice. A selection of these is presented here as an introduction to the debate that follows.

II. SIMILARITIES

1. *Cognitive content.* Scientific and theological statements both have cognitive content, in the sense that they are capable of being true or false, however truth is to be understood. Theological statements, along with their undisputed expressive and exhortative aspects, have a propositional, cognitive component. Scientific statements are better known for their cognitive content, but perhaps in some contexts have other aspects as well. Scientific practice makes a virtue of emphasizing cognitive content exclusively over other possible aspects of scientific statements. Such an exclusive emphasis is natural, given the subject matter of science, which lends itself to fairly exhausitive characterization in propositional, cognitive terms. By contrast, the subject matter of theology is more diffuse and, according to many theologians, partially transcends human reason. This makes focusing exclusively on the cognitive content of theological statements a rather dubious, perhaps misleading, thing to do. With care, however, it can be done.

2. *Participation in the structures of human rationality.* Whether or not the nonfoundationalist view of human rationality described above is accepted as the most adequate account of the human quest for knowledge, both theological and natural scientific activities are understood to be rational operations of some kind. Both draw upon the imagination, creativity, and extant knowledge of their participants to produce arguments and to test assertions where possible against what is experienced and already accepted as known.

3. *Being impacted by the one world.* Critical realism is the post-Kantian name for the belief in a reality that causes human experience, exists independently of our experiencing it, and can be understood only in an indirect, mediated way. This is the most common philosophical basis for both theological and scientific discourse. But whether or not this (rather general) metaphysical-epistemological position is held, it is nevertheless the case that theology and science both intend to speak with tolerable accuracy about reality beyond the confines of human mentality.

III. DIFFERENCES

1. *Different epistemic heritages and warrants.* Scientific and theological propositions, as we noted above, can be regarded for some purposes solely in their cognitive aspects. It is possible, therefore, to obtain theological and scientific propositions that have literally identical subjects (say, "The universe is created by God" and "The universe is the result of processes characterized by such-and-such physical laws"). At least in some cases, however, scientific and theological knowledge, even about the same things, is obtained in different ways.

As a poignant example, nineteenth-century theologian Friedrich Schleiermacher regarded statements about God and the world as expressions derived from more fundamental statements about religious self-consciousness. On this view, "The universe is created by God" is the result of a complex process—within a community possessing a shared history—of theological reflection on the human experience of what has variously been called unconditional dependency, human finitude, or creatureliness. This epistemic heritage—the *way* it comes to be known—is directly relevant to what may be claimed in regard to the reliability of the theological statement, precisely to the extent that the way we come to believe something (heritage) is used to justify the belief (warrant). For example, if we are not to move glibly from the experience of "creatureliness" to the metaphysical-theological affirmation that God created the world, then it is vital to be assured that we have a viable, indeed the best, interpretation of the experience of "creatureliness."

For many theological assertions, epistemic heritage and warrant are tightly knit. By contrast, in the natural sciences the discovery of an hypothesis and the process of its justification are almost always entirely separable. A scientific hypothesis may be concocted in any way at all, and many are conditioned by unarticulated cultural and personal factors, including religious ones. However, if the hypothesis explains and produces testable consequences, its warrant will stand sufficiently independent of its epistemic heritage to secure a public dimension for it. Correlative to this difference between theology and science is another that is relevant to the warrants for theological and scientific truth claims: scientific communities have an extremely efficient method for establishing widespread agreement, precisely because of the separability of the context of discovery and the process of justification, whereas religious communities find agreement much more difficult to achieve on almost everything.

2. *Ethical and existential applicability.* Theological statements are usually more readily applicable to existential concerns and ethical issues because of the complex epistemic heritage just described. In fact, theology has traditionally made a virtue of the tight-knit connection between the existential and ethical situation of the theologian and the content of his or her theology, and the theological task has often been defined as properly discharged only when this interconnection is explicitly thematized. By contrast, scientific propositions are less obviously relevant to ethical questions and existential matters. This kind of relevance is generated in a subsequent move, one not intrinsic to the scientific method itself, narrowly understood.

3. *Data.* A process of inquiry is scientific in the strongest sense when the data and method are of the right sort to allow tests that differentiate between competing theories, in the sense of eventually marking one off as more adequate than the others in such a way as to win assent from the relevant community of inquirers. Many factors can interfere with inquiry of this particularly efficient sort. For example, when sufficient relevant data are not available, speculative hypotheses about such data as exist do not lead to testable deductions. Under such conditions, coherence and other criteria are still available for testing explanatory theories, but controlled experiments are no longer possible. The natural sciences work with the kinds of data that enable experimentation to distinguish competing theories, though some areas—such as interpretations of quantum mechanics and making sense of the fossil record—are problematic. However, in most areas, theological data appear not to be of the sort that can differentiate the most adequate speculative hypotheses from among the multitude of competing hypotheses. Put differently, direct experimental testing of theological theories (doctrines) is virtually impossible, and indirect testing is difficult to control and interpret, and notoriously unable to compel widespread assent in the community of theological inquirers.

IV. THE PAPERS IN PART II

The aim of Part II is to bring into the open key issues for understanding the differences and similarities between theology and science, some of the most important of which have just been described. To that end, four authors or teams of authors holding interestingly different views of the relations between theology and science engage in a two-round debate. In the first round of the debate, the four positions are laid down. In the second round, some of the authors respond briefly to the other contributions, differentiating their positions from each other. This approach enables the reader to enter more deeply into the issues than would otherwise be possible.

The papers of Nicholas Wolterstorff and Nancey Murphy are especially relevant to discerning methodological continuities between theology and natural science. In "Theology and Science: Listening to Each Other," Wolterstorff argues that we should think about science in terms of the triple distinction between data, theory, and control beliefs. By control beliefs in scientific activity, Wolterstorff means convictions about what sorts of theories count as acceptable. In situations lacking equilibrium among these three components of the process of scientific theory weighing, equilibrium is restored either by adjusting an interpretation of the data, by modifying or discarding a theory, or by altering a control belief. Wolterstorff points out that this same cognitive structure is found in other disciplines, such as ethics, and argues that it offers a good model for the way religious communities deal with their canonical scriptures. Wolterstorff contends that, with such profound cognitive structures in common, it is not plausible to construe theology and science as non-overlapping disciplines, either in terms of methodology or subject matter. On the contrary, conflicts are to be expected, and it is understandable that control beliefs demarcate the arena for many of the most profound conflicts between science and religion.

Murphy's aim in "Postmodern Apologetics, or Why Theologians *Must* Pay Attention to Science" is to show that relating theology to science is a crucial element of the apologetic task facing Christian theology at the present time. Murphy's understanding of the "apologetic task" is determined by her advocacy of nonfoundationalist epistemology: we ought to seek not indubitable foundations for Christian knowledge, but arguments that connect Christian beliefs into the rest of the web of beliefs. This approach highlights the spontaneous aspect of the theology-science relation, in which imagination, ingenuity, and readiness to improvise are paramount. To the question of what kinds of relations between theology and science we should look for, therefore, Murphy naturally answers "Any kind we can get!" Using some of the case studies in Part III as examples, Murphy articulates a number of different kinds of relations between theological and scientific propositions, including direct implication, mutual implication of philosophical theories, hypothetico-deductive connections, operation of control beliefs, and complex combinations of these kinds of relations. Whether all of these logical relations are equally useful for justifying Christian beliefs, however, is debatable.

The widespread popular conviction that science and religion are fundamentally different kinds of human activity has its correlates among views of the relation between theology and natural science: they are distinct language games; they deal with separated spheres of reality; the statements of natural science are cognitive whereas theological statements are expressive and exhortative; or theology is the exposition of existentially potent, communally mediated, divinely revealed truth, and natural science is a matter of discovery and evidence. As we have seen, there is something to this conviction of difference between theology and natural science, even if it is not to be explained along any of these lines. In the wake of an antagonistic history, however, most scholarly energy that has engaged the problem in a sustained way has tried to unmask the formerly obscured similarities between the two spheres of activity. Yet it is clear that articulating what is similar between the two activities is only part of the task of understanding their relation. The two collaborative papers in Part II seek to do justice to the differences between theology and natural science, as well as their similarities.

In "Mathematics, Empirical Science, and Religion," theologian Mary Gerhart and physicist Allan Melvin Russell argue that the relation between theology and natural science is analogous to that between natural science and mathematics, in two ways. First, unlike empirical science, mathematics systematically prescinds from statements about the world in order to proceed freely within the domain of demonstrable consistency with postulates that characterize a mathematical system. Analogously, empirical science, unlike theology, prescinds from making empathic allowance for the experience of human beings in order to preserve the possibility of publicly and efficiently verifying and correcting scientific assertions. Second, mathematical advances expand the realm of "computable or otherwise analyzable relations" in a way that opens up new possibilities for scientific description of the world. Analogously, advances in scientific knowledge set the limits on what theology can assert, determine the context within which theological assertions must be formulated, and establish partial criteria for the believability of theological assertions. Gerhart's and Russell's exposition of this analogy helpfully articulates important differences between natural science and theology.

In "Rationality and Christian Self-Conceptions," Philip Clayton and Steven Knapp endeavor to situate the question of the relation between theology and science within a broadly anthropological perspective. It is only such a broad-ranging inquiry, they contend, that can exhibit the logical distinctiveness of what it is to have a Christian self-conception, which in turn is the necessary preliminary step to understanding the interaction between theology and anything else (including natural science). The assumption that a person engaging in theological activity possesses a Christian self-conception—axiomatic for Schleiermacher, Barth, Tillich, Rahner, and many other modern theologians—is frequently not granted by contemporary theologians. Nevertheless, insofar as theological reflection about the Christian tradition is regarded as intimately tied to a Christian self-conception, Clayton's and Knapp's approach is as helpfully clarifying as it is adventurously general. They argue that "Christianity can be equated neither with scientific hypotheses nor with a set of individual values. Instead, a religious self-conception, at least of the Christian variety, is an interesting *tertium quid* that evinces important similarities to, and differences from, the kinds of self-conception someone has to have in order to engage in formal scientific inquiry on the one hand, or ordinary practical deliberation on the other."

The second round of the debate helpfully illuminates these positions. Yet it is clear that divergences remain. Three of the most contentious of these can be noted here in the form of questions.

1. *How is Christian theology to be understood?* The diversity of theological activity is not affirmed clearly enough in this debate, with the result that the contributors may unwittingly leave the impression that theology is a unified intellectual enterprise with just one method. Even so, it possible to ask whether Christian beliefs are in any sense the result of a process of inquiry. It seems that some Christian beliefs are—what Clayton and Knapp call theoretical Christian beliefs—but the sense in which they are explanations and what they are supposed to explain are contested issues that need further clarification.

2. *When are Christians entitled to hold their beliefs?* It seems that establishing connections between Christian beliefs and the rest of our "web of beliefs" constitutes at least a weak form of entitlement. However, it is not obviously the case that any logical connection whatever is an evidential relation that justifies Christian beliefs. Thus, the various senses in which logical relations between Christian beliefs and the wider web of beliefs function as justifications for Christian beliefs need to be distinguished and compared. Clarification is also needed on the question of the extent to which actively seeking critical feedback from beyond the boundaries of the Christian community is an *essential* criterion for entitlement. Furthermore, clarification is needed on how much weight must be given to the continuity of Christian beliefs with Christian tradition when such beliefs conflict with wider cultural judgments about what is possible in the world. Such clarity is necessary, for example, in decisions about when the scientific worldview should be assumed by theology, and when it should be resisted on the basis

of traditional convictions. Incorporating the function of traditions within a nonfoundationalist interpretation of entitled belief is a topic of intense reflection within philosophy and ethics at present, and promises clarification on each of the issues bearing
on entitlement to hold Christian beliefs.

3. *How is the apologetic task of Christianity in relation to science to be understood?*
Some theologians, of course, deny that there is any task of this sort to be pursued.
Some believe apologetics to be a matter of arguing for traditional religious beliefs while
critiquing any aspects of the scientific worldview incompatible with them. Others
understand the apologetic requirement to be a matter of making sure that Christian
theology remains in step with scientific insight, with the understanding that such
coherence is indirect confirmation of Christians' entitlement to hold their beliefs. Still
others hold that apologetics is a matter of expressing Christian beliefs so as to render
them discussible in a broad variety of communal contexts, which is as efficient a way
as exists of justifying them. The diversity of approaches to apologetics may to some
extent be an indication of the variety of theological projects that Christians undertake,
but clarification of this contentious point is also needed.

ROUND

I

THEOLOGY AND SCIENCE

LISTENING TO EACH OTHER

NICHOLAS WOLTERSTORFF

I. MODERNITY AS DISENCHANTMENT, AND THE PLACE OF RELIGION

The most powerful and profound interpretation of modernity remains that of Max Weber. Weber's thesis was that the essence of modernity lies, first, in the emergence of differentiated action spheres in the domain of society and differentiated value spheres in the domain of culture, and then, second, in the spread of rationalization within these spheres. Specifically, in the social domain, economy, state, and law get differentiated from each other—with the economy becoming capitalistic under the pressure of rationalization, the state becoming bureaucratic, and law becoming codified and formalized. In the cultural domain, the cognitive, expressive, and ethical spheres become differentiated from each other. Rationalization in the cognitive sphere takes the form of science and technology; in the expressive sphere, the form of autonomous art; and in the ethical sphere, the form of an ethic of generalized principles.

The emergence and perpetuation of these differentiated spheres in society and culture calls for a certain personality type—namely, the methodical type. The characteristically modern person is the one who discards both tradition and affect as determiners of action, and instead engages in rational calculation of means and rational appraisal of values before acting. The expressive sphere provides a bit of relief; though the arts are themselves rationalized in the modern world, they provide at the same time some room for self-expression.

Given this picture, the question that Weber asked himself over and over was this: "What led to such an extraordinary development?" The clue that he followed in developing his answer was the fact, or what he took to be the fact, that to participate in modernity one must treat the world as *disenchanted*—literally, as *demagicalized*. Weber used "disenchantment" broadly. We who participate in modernity do not think of the trees and the streams as containing mysterious powers; hence we have no reluctance to cut down the trees and dam the streams. But more generally, we who participate in modernity regard the cosmos as devoid of meaning. Rather than finding meaning in contemplating the world, we regard the world as at our disposal.

And how did this disenchantment come about? Once upon a time, said Weber, in the days of primitive religion, humanity lived in an "enchanted garden"—a magical garden. It was the dynamics of rationalization working on those primitive religions, especially in the attempt to explain unjust suffering, which led to the emergence of the world religions; and the world religions all represent a process of disenchantment. We have all left the magic garden. Of course the different world religions represent structurally different solutions to the problem of theodicy. Some, the theocentric ones, sharply separate divinity from the cosmos; others, the cosmocentric ones, locate divinity within the cosmos. Secondly, some are *world-rejecting,* whereas others are *world-affirming.* And lastly, some are centered on a disciplined, ascetic attempt to reshape the world, whereas others are centered on a mystical flight from the world. Christianity (along with Judaism and Islam) is theocentric, world-rejecting, and ascetic; and it is exactly that structure which bears within it the most potential for radical disenchantment of the world.

What Weber thus explains is the emergence of a *necessary* condition for modernization, namely, disenchantment. That leaves us looking for the sufficient condition; as I interpret Weber, he never does provide us with that.

Now for my purposes and interests here, what is striking about the Weberian account of the nature and origins of modernity is that religion is treated as just disappearing from the scene. This grand sweep, from the enchanted gardens of primitive religion, to the progressively disenchanting world religions, to the disenchanted world of our differentiated modernized societies and cultures, represents the disappearance of religion from the human scene. Or more accurately, Weber locates religion in the modern world in the remnants of the irrational; religion does not have a cultural sphere of its own where it can follow out its own "logic," as do science, art, and ethics. Other sociologists, thinking along generally Weberian lines, have located religion within the expressive sphere of modern life, along with art and phenomena such as sex and recreation.

The truth, however, is that religion has not disappeared from those various differentiated spheres which Weber identified. It has not disappeared from the economic sphere; most emphatically it has not disappeared from the political sphere. And there is a multitude of indications that religion has also not disappeared from the cognitive sphere. I think we all have the feeling, when coming up against the grand sweep of Weber's theory, that there is a great deal of profound truth in it; yet, once we step out of its aura to look at the facts, it becomes clear that it has not got things quite right. We need a new model.

I am not competent to produce such a model; nor, if I were, would this be the place to present it. Rather, with these remarks as context, I want to look at the place of religion (and theology) in what Weber would identify as the *cognitive sphere.* My thesis will be that Weber was reflecting the Enlightenment understanding of science and its relation to religion—an understanding which has come crashing down in the last quarter century.

II. THE BREAKDOWN OF FOUNDATIONALISM IN SCIENCE

The Enlightenment practice and understanding of the newly emergent natural sciences represented a significant break with the practice and understanding of the antecedents of these in the High Sciences (*scientiae*) of the Middle Ages. After much debate on the matter, hypotheses began to occupy a central place in the new science; they were rigorously excluded from medieval *scientia*. Predictions became an important part of the new science; though the medievals naturally wanted predictions, they did not look to the *scientiae* to provide them. The new science was, from the very beginning, praised and pursued for its technological potentials; medieval *scientia* was regarded as more relevant to the life of contemplation than to the pursuits of the technologist. The Enlightenment theorists gradually came to see their science as eliciting the contingent causal structure of nature; the medievals were after essences in their *scientia*. Probability, in our modern sense of that term, was granted a place in the new science; though the nominalists of the *via moderna* allowed probability in *scientia*, they did not mean by "probability" quite what we mean by it; and in any case, they were innovators on this point—Aquinas allowed only demonstrative inferences in *scientia*.

However, amidst all these differences there were also fundamental points of continuity between the Enlightenment understanding of the new natural sciences and the medieval understanding of High Science, or *scientia*; and for our purposes it is at least as important to discern those continuities as to note the discontinuities. A fundamental feature of the intellectual life of medieval Europe was the appeal to the textual tradition for the settling of quandaries on a large range of issues which we would now identify as ethical, theological, philosophical, and natural scientific. The medievals did not, however, regard such an appeal as yielding science—*scientia*. If it is *scientia* one wishes to construct, one must begin from what is evident, either to oneself or to someone else, and then proceed to construct deductive arguments. *Scientia*, properly understood, is the conclusions of such demonstrative arguments; and its most salient characteristic is its certainty.

Enlightenment thinkers, such as John Locke, perpetuated these convictions. In the construction of science we must have nothing to do with tradition, unless, of course, we have confirmed the veracity of the tradition in question; "to the things themselves," said Locke, and what he meant to suggest was: not to what people say about the things. Locke furthermore agrees that we must begin with that of which we are certain. And he vigorously insists on what the medievals never so much as questioned—that in the practice of science, truth and the avoidance of falsehood are to be our sole concern. The possession by some theories of attractive features which are truth-irrelevant must play no role whatsoever in our decision as to whether to accept those theories.

One additional continuity must be singled out: we who engage in science are to do so just *qua human beings*. Before entering the halls of science, we are to shed all our particularities—our particular social locations, our particular genders, our particular religions, our particular races, our particular nationalities—and enter those halls with just our humanity. Of course we always to a greater or lesser extent fail in this stripping-off; but then it is the responsibility of our peers to call to our attention where our religion, our gender, our social position, our race, our nationality, is influencing our science. As science has traditionally been understood in the West, such phrases as "feminist sociology" and "Muslim aesthetics" and "Christian philosophy" and "Marxist biology" are oxymorons—either that, or they point to some horrid amalgams that, whatever else they may be, are not science.

By no means did Locke and the bulk of eighteenth-century theorists regard this paradigm of science as dictating atheism in the cognitive sphere. Quite to the contrary: Locke offered a cosmological argument for the existence of God, and most eighteenth-century thinkers thought that an argument from design could be given for God's existence. And as to so-called revealed religion: Locke thought that good probabilistic arguments could be given for the conclusion that the New Testament is a record and report of divine revelation—indeed, an *infallible* record and report. It was especially the rise of evolutionary theory at the end of the nineteenth century that shattered this confidence in an evidentially grounded natural theology, just as the rise of historical biblical criticism shattered the confidence in an evidentially grounded revealed religion.

This foundationalist picture of science, though it probably still inhabits the prefaces to high school science textbooks, has all but disappeared from that part of the academy which is acquainted with developments in philosophy of science over the past twenty-five years. When I went to graduate school, philosophy of science still consisted of trying to show that science, in spite of appearances, really does have the Lockean structure; it was seen as being the business of philosophy of science to lay bare that hidden structure. The significance of Thomas Kuhn's book, *The Structure of Scientific Revolutions*, was that Kuhn, backed up by an intimate knowledge of the history of physics, claimed that there was no hidden Lockean structure to reveal. Kuhn was apparently content to think of "normal science" as having roughly a Lockean structure; he contended that "revolutionary science" certainly does not. Most people nowadays, if they are willing to work with the normal/revolutionary distinction, would say that normal science also does not have a Lockean foundationalist structure. We live in a new day.

My aim in a little book that I published in 1976, called *Reason within the Bounds of Religion*, was to illuminate the relation of religion to science when science is understood as nonfoundationalist in character. I tried to speak as generally as possible, so that my discussion would include not just what we normally think of as covered by the English word "science," but the academic disciplines generally. Instead of following the customary practice of working simply with the distinction between data and theory, I recommended that we work with the triple distinction between data, theory, and what I called *control beliefs*. I had the usual thing in mind when I spoke of "data" and "theory"; and as to control beliefs, what I had in mind is the fact that always, when engaging in science, we operate with certain convictions as to *the sorts* of theories that we will find acceptable. Control beliefs are of many different sorts. Sometimes they take the form of methodological convictions; a huge dispute raged in the seventeenth and eighteenth centuries over whether hypotheses were acceptable in science. Sometimes they take the form of ontological convictions. And so on. The picture I offered was that, insofar as the theorist is engaged in what I called *theory weighing*, he or she tries to find a theory that both fits the data and satisfies the control beliefs.

Though I observed that to some extent the data/theory/control belief distinction is relative to a given episode of theory weighing—what is taken for granted on one occasion for the purpose of "weighing" may be the very thing "weighed" on another occasion—I did not focus as sharply as I might have on what happens in cases of perceived conflict between what we take or are disposed to take as data, what we take or are disposed to take as theory, and what we take or are disposed to take as control beliefs. The answer is that we try to eliminate the conflict and achieve equilibrium by making a revision in one of the three—preferring that complex of data, theory, and control belief which seems to us to have the most likelihood as a whole of being true. To achieve that end, we sometimes revise or discard the theory; sometimes we alter our convictions about the data; and sometimes we alter our control beliefs. Truly deep alterations in science will characteristically be of this last sort. And I suggested that most of the deep conflicts between science and religion occur at the control-belief level.

III. PARALLEL DEVELOPMENTS IN OTHER DISCIPLINES

This last point must be developed further for my purposes here. But before I do that, let me observe that I find it fascinating that essentially this same paradigm emerged independently at roughly the same time in two other areas of philosophy. In his *Theory of Justice,* John Rawls introduced the notion of wide reflective equilibrium to explain the method that he thought appropriate for ethics. The method was carefully elaborated and discussed in a 1979 article by Norman Daniels entitled "Wide Reflective Equilibrium and Theory Acceptance in Ethics." Let me allow Daniels to describe the method in his own words:

> The method of wide reflective equilibrium is an attempt to produce coherence in an ordered triple of sets of beliefs held by a particular person, namely, (a) a set of considered moral judgments, (b) a set of moral principles, and (c) a set of relevant background theories. We begin by collecting the person's initial moral judgments and filter them to include only those of which he is relatively confident and which have been made under conditions conducive to avoiding errors of judgment. . . . We then propose alternative set of moral principles that have varying degrees of "fit" with the moral judgments. We do *not* simply settle for the best fit of principles with judgments, however, which would give us only a *narrow* equilibrium. Instead, we advance philosophical arguments intended to bring out

the relative strengths and weaknesses of the alternative sets of principles (or competing moral conceptions). . . . assume that some particular set of arguments wins and that the moral agent is persuaded that some set of principles is more acceptable than the other. . . . We can imagine the agent working back and forth, making adjustments to his considered judgments, his moral principles, and his background theories. In this way he arrives at an equilibrium point that consists of the ordered triple (a), (b), (c).[1]

Though a few of the details are different, obviously the picture here is the same as the one I have developed.

Again, essentially the same model is to be found in Mary Hesse's essay, "Models of Theory-Change," first published in 1973.[2] We can think of science, says Hesse, as a "learning device"—as a "learning machine." The machine has a *receptor*, whereby it receives empirical input from the environment. It has a *formulator*, whereby it describes that input in sentences. It has a *theorizer*, whereby it formulates theories designed to fit and explain the data. And it has a *predictor*, whereby it draws out empirically observable consequences of the theories.

These are the functions of the learning machine that is science. And now two things must be said about the way in which the machine carries out those functions. First, in its theorizing the machine tries to satisfy certain "coherence conditions," as Hesse calls them. "For example," she says, "we may be interested in finding universal law-like generalizations within the observation sentences, or our desire for an economical and coherent system of laws and theories may involve more elaborate considerations, such as requirements of symmetry, simplicity, analogy, conformity with certain *a priori* conditions or metaphysical postulates."[3] And secondly, "the machine permits internal feedback loops for the adjustment of theory to observation sentences, as well as the usual external loop which allows comparison of predictive output and empirical input. The internal feedback loops make a direct comparison of the current best theory with the observation sentences. . . ."[4] So what happens if there is what Hesse calls a "mismatch"? Sometimes we conclude that the receptor mechanism was malfunctioning; sometimes we get the formulator mechanism to describe the data differently; sometimes we get the theorizer to yield a different theory. But sometimes, "usually as a last resort," we modify the coherence conditions

in the light of success and failure of the sequence of best theories in accounting for the available observation sentences, and in making successful predictions. There seem to be a number of examples of this kind of modification in the history of science: abandonment of the postulate of circular motions of the heavenly bodies; rejection of the notion that some theoretical postulates such as Euclidean geometry or universal determinism, can be known *a priori*; adoption and later rejection of the mechanical philosophy as a necessary condition of scientific explanation; the postulate of reducibility of organic processes to physicochemical theories. Such varieties of coherence conditions in fact constitute the main subject matter of philosophical dispute regarding science, and it will now be my contention that the more usual disputes between different accounts of the structure of science are almost vacuous except insofar as they reflect different views about the nature of the coherence conditions.[5]

In summary, what we find in all three of these discussions is a picture of the theoretical enterprise as typically involving something that can be called data, something that can be called theory, and something that can be called theory constraints. If the focus of our attention is on the weighing of theory, then what has to be said is that the theorizer tries to find a theory that fits the data and satisfies the constraints. If the focus of our attention is instead on situations in which there is perceived conflict among data, theory, and theory constraints, then what has to be said is that the theorizer tries to achieve equilibrium by juggling prospective revisions in data, in theory, and in theory constraint, until finally he or she arrives at a complex which seems likely to be true and on balance to possess more of what he or she judges to be the relevant cognitive/doxastic merits than any other alternative that comes to mind.

IV. APPLYING THE MODEL TO RELIGIOUS COMMUNITIES

Let us now move from science to religion; more specifically, to religious communities, such as the Christian community, which have a canonical scripture. In how such communities live with their scriptures there is a closely similar structure at work. To see this, imagine a religious community that has certain texts which it regards as canonical; and then suppose that in this community there is widespread agreement on the benefits desired from the use of those canonical texts, in particular, from interpreting them; the community enjoys near consensus on what might be called *canonical benefits*. For example, it is characteristic of religious communities to want and expect of their canonical texts that they will provide access to a certain domain of truth, and that when used in certain ways they will prove religiously edifying. Suppose secondly that, from among all the senses that are or might be associated with those texts, there is widespread consensus in the community as to which of those it will concern itself with; of the various senses of the text, there is in the community an established sense. Suppose thirdly that there is an established practice of interpreting that sense which yields results (that is, interpretations) on which there is widespread agreement. The practice may yield fresh interpretations in the hands of some practitioners; but when it does, consensus emerges about the cogency of those fresh interpretations. Suppose fourthly that there is also an established practice of appropriating those interpretations which yields results (that is, applications) on which there is widespread agreement. (This too is not to be viewed as incompatible with novelty of results.) And suppose, lastly, that there is widespread agreement that those applications of those interpretations of those senses yield the desired and expected canonical benefits.

Now suppose that someone presents to the community an argument to the effect that, contrary to what members of the community had supposed, the outcome of the chain moving from text to established sense to result of established practice of interpretation to result of established practice of application does not possess or yield the canonical benefits which the community desires and expects from that chain. Perhaps this person argues that the propositional content of one of the standard interpretations playing a key role in the community's appropriation is false. One option for the community is to reject the conclusion of that argument. But if it accepts the conclusion, then perforce it has introduced cognitive dissonance into its life, and some revision is called for if equilibrium is to be restored.

One option, abstractly speaking, is for the community in some way or other to alter the canon so as to remove the offense. Someone might propose, for example, that the Letter of James be deleted from the Christian canon; or that a different, nonoffending version of the text causing the problems be adopted. There are not many significant issues for which the latter of these proves to be a live option; and the former seldom gains consensus. Ordinarily the person who argues for deleting texts from the canon is treated as a heretic and deleted from the community!

Another option is for the community to alter its views concerning canonical benefits. The community has always supposed, let us say, that this sense of this text when properly interpreted and properly applied yields access not only to certain fundamental truths about God but also to certain fundamental truths about the origins of the cosmos. The tension will be resolved if the community changes its mind about the latter desired and expected benefit, and rests content with using the text to find out about God. It is obvious that religious communities do change their expectations concerning the benefits from appropriating their canonical texts, often under exactly the sort of pressure indicated. Galileo's proposal for recovering equilibrium was along these lines; the authority of scripture, said Galileo, should not be understood as extending to what it may say about the structure of the cosmos.

But sometimes, depending on the character of the original objection, the alterations required for relieving the pressure by changing expectations concerning canonical benefits would be so radical that other options look more attractive: release that sense from being the established sense; or alter the practice of interpreting that sense, so that a different interpretation acquires consensus; or alter the practice of appropriation, so that a different application acquires consensus. The goal, once again, is to arrive at an equilibrium which the community regards as likely to be true, and as possessing more cognitive/doxastic merits than any other that comes to mind.

V. CONCLUSION

And now to put things together. I have proposed a model for understanding what goes on within a theoretical discipline, and a closely similar model for understanding what goes on within the Christian community as it struggles to live with its canonical scriptures. I now propose that we use this same model for understanding how the Christian community struggles to live with its canonical scriptures, on the one hand, and with the methods and results of the theoretical disciplines, on the other.

One course to take at this point would be that of formulating in an abstract and fully general manner the equilibrium model as it applies to this highly complex situation. I judge that some important benefits would be achieved by doing that; I rather doubt, however, that for our purposes here they would be sufficient to repay the effort. I think the model is already sufficiently clear by now to enable us to conduct our discussion. So let me instead content myself with emphasizing three important points which have so far not come to the fore.

First, as I see things, the Christian faith is such and the theoretical disciplines are such that we must expect conflict—disequilibrium—to emerge repeatedly. Sometimes the conflict is the result of a particular part of science having been developed using theory constraints quite alien to Christianity. For example, a friend of mine who works in world religions says he finds that almost all contemporary anthropology assumes that religion is irrational and epiphenomenal. But that is not always how conflict arises; sometimes it arises from the work of scholars pursuing their work in fidelity to the Christian gospel. There have been a number of attempts over the last couple of centuries to delineate religion, on the one hand, and science, on the other, in such a way that between religion and science "properly" understood there can be no conflict. Perceived conflicts are always the result of either a wrongheaded view of religion or a wrongheaded view of science—or both. Religion and science are just "into different things." But rather than this being the settled truth of the matter, it is to be seen as just one proposal, and an extremely radical one at that, for the recovery of equilibrium. My own view is that, on the best equilibrated view of the matter, religion and science—and in particular, Christianity and Western theorizing—overlap in their concerns. I am gratified to see that this is also the assumption underlying the very interesting papers by the scientists contributing to the case studies in Part III of this book.

The second point I wish to emphasize is that, in the ongoing struggle of those of us who are both Christians and theorists to bring our faith and our science into satisfactory equilibrium, the revisions required can go either way. Sometimes the best strategy is to revise something in our complex of Christian belief; but sometimes the best strategy is, on the contrary, to revise something in what science presents to us. For a variety of reasons, there is a deep tendency in most contemporary members of the academy in the West to assume that, in case of conflict between science and religion, religion has to give. But why should that be? Suppose that part of what it means to affirm the authority of scripture is to say that scripture gives us our best access to certain realms of truth. Then to say that always, in cases of conflict between religion and science, religion has to give, is to imply either that scripture does not have such authority, or that theorizing somehow never speaks about that realm of truth to which scripture gives us our best access. On what seems to me the best equilibrated view of the matter, neither of these implications is correct.

Lastly, it is my impression that rather often in the social sciences and humanities, when we probe the roots of a conflict between Christian conviction and the results of theorizing, we find that the theorists in question are working with theory constraints which are alien to Christian conviction. When that is so, then the debate has to be conducted at that point. Theorizing in general is far indeed from being a religiously neutral endeavor. We human beings do not and cannot leave our religions in the narthex as we enter the halls of science. Rather than working with that old model of stripping off all our particularities before we can properly engage in science, we shall have to work with the new model of persons with different particularities engaging in the dialogue of theorizing, hoping for consensus as the outcome, rather than insisting on it as the beginning—but acknowledging with sad candor that often that hope is not attained.

We are presented with the challenge of working out a picture of cosmos and self that brings contemporary science into equilibrium with Christian belief—or so at least I would describe the challenge presented. Rather than trying to meet it, I have talked methodology. I have argued for a genuine, two-way dialogue between theology and science, between Christian conviction, on the one hand, and the results of theorizing, on the other.

NOTES

1, Norman Daniels, "Wide Reflective Equilibrium and Theory Acceptance in Ethics," *Journal of Philosophy* (1979), pp. 258–259.

2. Mary Hesse, "Models of Theory-Change," reprinted in *Revolutions and Reconstructions in the Philosophy of Science* (Bloomington: Indiana University Press, 1980).

3. "Models," p. 126.

4. "Models," p. 127.

5. "Models," p. 128.

POSTMODERN APOLOGETICS

OR WHY THEOLOGIANS *MUST* PAY ATTENTION TO SCIENCE

NANCEY MURPHY

I. INTRODUCTION

My title includes the old-fashioned word "apologetics"—a word that, for a time, nearly disappeared from polite circles of theological discussion. It may, however, be making a come-back.[1] I teach an apologetics course at Fuller Seminary—not because I had to adopt one that was already in the catalogue when I came, but rather because the intellectual world has changed in recent years, and it has now become an intriguing problem to rethink the entire enterprise. Modern apologetics has, rightly, I think, been judged hopeless or misguided. But what about a postmodern apologetic? Relating theology to science just might be the single most important apologetic task in our postmodern era.

To explain this thesis I shall take the following steps: first, I will explain what I take to be (genuinely) postmodern philosophy; second, I will describe the central apologetic problem within that context; and, third, I will relate what I have been saying to recent work on the relation of science and theology.

II. POSTMODERN THOUGHT

Several groups of scholars are competing to define the term "postmodern." It is a word we seem to *need*: there is a growing recognition that the ways of thinking developed in the modern period have reached their limits, have been effectively criticized from within, and need to be replaced. We have as yet no more descriptive term for what comes next than to say that it is that which follows the modern—the postmodern.

The best-known claimants for the term are probably the deconstructionists in literary criticism and their followers in other disciplines as diverse as law and theology. David Griffin and his school want the term to describe their process approach to reality. In addition, James McClendon and I have tried to claim the term to describe revolutionary changes in philosophy that account for the distinctiveness of self-proclaimed postmodern or "postliberal" theologians such as George Lindbeck and Ronald

Thiemann. According to our definition, some of the above turn out to be postmodern; some merely extreme (and strident) moderns.[2]

However history settles the issue of terminology, no one will be able to deny that there have been ground-shaking changes in Anglo-American philosophy, whose reverberations cannot fail to be felt in theology, textual criticism, theological ethics and elsewhere.

So what are these changes? While there has been a thorough rethinking of ethics and of philosophy of language, both of which are equally important, I shall concentrate here on changes in epistemology—theory of knowledge. I will describe the change first of all as a change of metaphors. For moderns, knowledge was a building. Thus, two concerns predominated in epistemology: the first was to find a suitably solid foundation for one's beliefs. The primary requirement for foundational beliefs was that they be indubitable—otherwise the "foundation" itself could be called into question, and it would turn out that one was trying to begin construction in midair. The second concern was the manner of construction from there on up. Descartes's foundation was his *cogito* (and a mixed bag of other ideas he found himself unable to doubt, such as the metaphysical principle that there must be at least as much reality in the cause as in the effect); the means of construction was demonstrative reasoning. For Locke, the foundation was ideas derived from sense perception; and Hume then pointed out that deductive reasoning—the only solid mode of construction— could not be used on a foundation of that sort.

These notions about knowledge had their effect on theology in due course. The only two options for theological foundations seemed to be scripture or some form of self-authenticating religious experience. (When it comes to foundationalist theologians, fundamentalists are the best of the lot because, if one is to use scripture in this way at all, the epistemological doctrine calling for *indubitable* foundations demands a theological doctrine of *inerrancy*.)

Modern epistemology had consequences for apologetics, too, of course. The modern strategy called for finding some way to attach to the "bottom" of the Christian belief system some small number of additional premises that would be unquestioned by non-Christians and would in turn warrant the entire system of thought. And so, for instance, Locke's strategy was to use miracles and fulfilled prophecies as a "deeper layer" of support for the claim that the Bible was the revealed word of God. Much later, E.J. Carnell, my predecessor at Fuller, presented as "the axiom of a decent society that in all matters where a good man is competent to judge, his word should be accepted unless sufficient reasons are found for rejecting it." Jesus was unquestionably a good man and it follows that the whole of his teaching is to be trusted.[3]

If we liken knowledge to a building, the picture these apologists present is of a massive structure teetering on a few thin supports. No wonder most have abandoned the entire enterprise. The quest for an unquestionable foundation has turned out to be quixotic.

```
┌─────────────────────┐
│      Theology       │
├─────────────────────┤
│     Revelation      │
└─┬─────────────────┬─┘
  │                 │
  │                 │
 ┌┘                 └┐
```

The new metaphor for knowledge—the "web" of belief—was suggested by Willard Quine. I like Quine's sparse prose, and so I will let him speak for himself:

> The totality of our so-called knowledge or beliefs, from the most casual matters of geography and history to the profoundest laws of atomic physics or even of pure mathematics and logic, is a man-made fabric which impinges on experience only along the edges. Or, to change the figure, total science is like a field of force whose boundary conditions are experience. A conflict with experience at the periphery occasions re-adjustments in the interior of the field. Truth values have to be redistributed over some of our statements. Re-evaluation of some statements entails re-evaluation of others, because of their logical interconnections—the logical laws being in turn simply certain further statements of the system. . . . But the total field is so underdetermined by its boundary conditions, experience, that there is much latitude of choice as to what statements to re-evaluate in the light of any single contrary experience. No particular experiences are linked with any particular statements in the interior of the field, except indirectly through considerations of equilibrium affecting the field as a whole.[4]

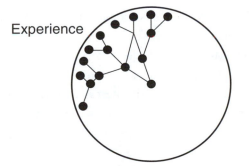

Experience

Apart from the picture, Quine's "holist" theory of knowledge differs in several important respects from foundationalism. First, there are no indubitable (unrevisable) beliefs. There were two different categories of beliefs that moderns tried to use this way—deliverances of sense perception and quasi-metaphysical deliverances of "reason." For Quine there are no *sharp* distinctions among types of belief, but there are degrees of differences in how far a belief is from the experiential boundary. It turns out that beliefs nearest the edge and beliefs furthest from the edge are both resistant to change. Those near the interior (where metaphysical assumptions would go) are resistant to change because they are so thoroughly interconnected with the rest of the content of the web. Beliefs near the edge are resistant to change because they are closely associated with experiences—unless, of course, new and surprising experiences come along. But when they do, there are always numerous ways to restore consistency. We may, for instance revise theory (a kind of belief located toward the interior) in light of new and surprising data; or we might instead use the entrenched theory to argue that something must have been wrong with the experiment. So there is no special category of beliefs that serve as an unquestioned starting point for justifying all the rest.

This relates to a second important difference from foundationalist epistemology. For foundationalists, reasoning (construction) goes in only one direction—up from the foundation. For holists there is no preferred direction. We may, as suggested above, use data from the edge to argue against a theory; we might instead use that theory to argue in the opposite direction—for the rejection of the data. One belief within the web may be supported by the fact that it *follows* from a set of premises. But each of the premises may also be justified by the fact that we need to *presuppose* it to support a conclusion we do not want to reject.

The kinds of connections among beliefs in the web are many: strict logical implication, weaker probabilistic arguments, arguments "forward" to further conclusions; arguments "backwards" to presuppositions. In general, what "holism" means is that each belief is supported by its ties to its neighboring beliefs, and ultimately, to the whole; the criterion of truth is coherence.

Ronald Thiemann is probably the best example of a theologian whose methodology reflects holist epistemology. He says that:

> nonfoundational or holist justification is not a matter of devising a universal theoretical defense of Christian language-as-such or of discerning the causal relation between our concepts and their external referents. Holist justification consists, rather, in seeking the relation between a disputed belief and the web of interrelated beliefs within which it rests. Holism understands justification as a process of rational persuasion. "We convince someone of something by appealing to beliefs he already holds and by combining these to induce further beliefs in him, step by step, until the belief we wanted finally to inculcate in him is inculcated."[5]

III. THE POSTMODERN APOLOGETIC PROBLEM

Modern thinkers' thorn in the flesh was skepticism. If a foundation could not be found, or if construction failed, there could be no knowledge. For postmoderns, the constant threat is relativism. It shows up in comments on Thomas Kuhn's philosophy of science, where he is accused of presenting an irrationalist account of science. It shows up in responses to Alasdair MacIntyre's ethics, where he is accused of sanctioning moral relativism. It shows up in literary and textual criticism, in claims that there are as many meanings of a text as there are interpreters.

One way of raising the worry is this: Quine seems to have given us only a web-dependent, web-relative definition of truth. We can judge the truth of one belief (or of a relatively small set of beliefs) by its consistency with the rest. But we want the answer to a bigger problem: we picture *our* web of beliefs, bounded by *our* experiences. We picture alongside it other communities' webs and other worlds of experience. So how do we know that our web is true, rather than some other competing, perhaps equally coherent web. There they all are before us. We must choose. On what basis can we justify the choice of *this* web rather than that one?

Wittgenstein warns us not to be misled by mental pictures. Was not the picture of knowledge as a building the source of much misbegotten philosophical flailing about? Is the picture of competing webs likewise misleading? Quine would answer "yes." We never stand outside our total knowledge system—there *is* no such place to stand. So alongside the picture of the web, we need another corrective picture. Quine suggests that, with regard to our knowledge, we are on a ship at sea. We cannot rebuild the whole thing at once—we can only make small repairs here and there, keeping the rest intact in order to keep ourselves afloat. Or—to extend the metaphor a bit—we cannot walk on water; we cannot jump ship to examine it from the outside and compare it to all the other ships at sea. We cannot judge them all from the outside on the basis of some universal standards.

To put this point in plain language, it is impossible to call all of one's beliefs into question at once. This may be a psychological truth—doubting *everything* is one road to madness. But more important, it is an epistemological truth. Particular beliefs may *reasonably* be doubted only with good reason (an informative tautology?). To have good reasons is to assume certain propositions to be true. So, for example, Descartes's most thoroughgoing doubt was based on his argument from dreams. But he did not notice that he had to assume a great deal about human sleep experiences to make the argument work. Furthermore, he had to make assumptions about *language*. To raise doubts, he had to use a common language, assume constancy of meaning. Along with language comes a number of assumptions about reality that are built into the use of the words. And so in his argument for the existence of God, he traded upon the fact that within his linguistic community it was a part of the meaning of "cause" that a cause must have at least as much reality as its effect.

So the idea that we must somehow justify the whole of our web of beliefs is either a holdover from foundationalist thinking or else an illusion created by a mental picture. We cannot do so, and therefore we need not do so.

Now, when Quine speaks of knowledge, he means to include science, primarily, and logic, and everyday knowledge of the physical world. I do not think he means to include religious belief or theology. But for Christians this is a significant part of our web, of our worldview. The problem for Christian apologetics is that the antirelativist arguments alluded to above do not work here. We know that it *is* possible to call the whole of Christian belief into question without disturbing much of the rest of the web since we live our lives in the company of those who have done so. Our agnostic and atheistic friends seem to get along quite well with Christianity excised from their worldviews. It also seems possible to replace Christianity with some other set of religious beliefs, leaving the rest intact.

So it appears that, even if it is not possible or necessary to justify the Western scientific worldview, it *is* necessary to justify the inclusion of Christianity within that web of beliefs.[6] But is it possible, and if so, how? Answering the "how" question is easy if we accept the postmodern account of knowledge. As with any other belief or subset of beliefs, justification consists in seeking relations between the disputed beliefs and parts of the web that we have no good reason to doubt.

This brings me to my main point: the two predominant views in the modern period on the relation between theology and science (the two-worlds view and the conflict model) have each in its own way served to insulate theology from science—the very part of the web that, as a whole, is least likely to be called into question. *The* apologetic task for the present is to attempt to repair the damage done by these two misguided views of the relation. This means rebuilding logical connections between Christianity and science in order to show that Christianity is not merely an optional addition to Western thought.

In practical terms, this means that scholarship by the likes of the contributors to this book, and courses like the ones they teach, fulfill to a great extent the role old-fashioned apologetics courses did in other times. Research and teaching at the intersection of theology and the natural sciences are not optional additions to the theological curriculum.

IV. IS IT POSSIBLE?

I raised the question earlier whether it is possible in postmodern terms to justify the inclusion of Christian theology within the Western scientific worldview. The best evidence for possibility, of course, is actuality. So in this section I want to reflect on some of the connections we can see between theology and science. This will not be an exhaustive list of the areas where fruitful work has been done. Rather, I shall select examples from recent writings—including the case studies in Part III of this book—that illustrate the variety of ways theology and science can be related. In the process, I want to show that one question that has been debated in theology-and-science circles can now be settled—namely, the question of the *kind* of relations we should look for between theology and science; for example, should theology and science be merely consonant, or should we look for evidential relations between the two? Should they relate directly or via a philosophical bridge? The answer is: we should seek any kind of relation we can get! In effect, with a holist epistemological model, any logical relation between a theological belief and another part of the web *is* an evidential relation.

Direct Implication

The simplest relation between theology and science is direct implication, and we find an example of this in William Stoeger's discussion of quantum cosmologies in the first case study of Part III. There he points out that the universe may not have had a *beginning* in the ordinary sense of the word. The direct consequence for theology, if one of these cosmologies is eventually confirmed, is that there could have been no *creation event*. This means that certain avenues of thought in explicating the doctrine of creation would be closed. Many have assumed that the doctrine of creation is a doctrine about the beginning of things and about the temporal finitude of the universe; others have emphasized instead that it is a doctrine about the dependence of all things on God. The acceptance of a quantum cosmology would rule out any interpretation of creation as a doctrine about the temporal beginning of the universe, and would necessarily shift attention to the metaphysical question of *ultimate* origins. Using S to mean science and T theology, I will represent this type of relation as:

$$S \longrightarrow T$$

Mutual Implication of Philosophical Theories

In a conference on quantum cosmology and time, Robert Russell presented an argument that exemplifies another type of relation between theology and science.[7] Russell's claim was that if one of these cosmological theories is accepted, it follows that we need a much more complex view of the nature of time than has previously been supposed. Russell's paper argued that some theological views (Barth's in particular) already involve a suitably rich concept of time, arising out of consideration of God's relation to temporality. So here the relation between theology and science is not direct. Rather, a particular view in science and a particular view in theology each shape a philosophical theory (about the nature of time), and these philosophical positions turn out to be the same or highly congruent. Using P, $P1$, and $P2$ to mean philosophical positions, I will represent this relation as follows:

I have come to think that this is a very common sort of relation in the field of theology and science. That this is the case is not surprising if we consider the place of philosophy in a holist view of knowledge.

One of the main motivations for Quine's holist theory of knowledge was his objection to the view that knowledge could be distinguished into two types: analytic and synthetic, or conceptual and empirical. This was one of the "two dogmas of empiricism" that he dismantled in his landmark article by that name. Philosophy, of course, was supposed to belong on the analytic or conceptual side of this distinction. A major tenet of holist epistemology is that philosophical knowledge is different from scientific knowledge only in degree—that is, only as a matter of its relative distance from experience. In metaphorical terms, it falls near the center of the web.

What we are doing here, in this exploration of a holist account of the relations between science and theology, is asking where theology fits in the web of beliefs, and how it is interwoven with scientific beliefs. It makes a great deal of sense, with this picture in mind, to expect that a scientific theory and a theological theory, each located about midway between the edge and the center, would turn out to be connected to certain central (philosophical) beliefs. So placing this relation in its context in the web, using the earlier notation, we get:

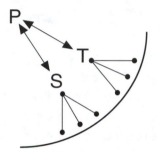

Another example of theology and science each implying a more central philosophical position is found in Stoeger's reference to the impact of quantum physics on epistemology. The fact that, at the quantum level, observation of a system inevitably interacts with and changes the system shows that the modern ideal of objectivity is inherently unattainable. Stoeger says that the repercussions on theology have been and are serious. I would prefer to put the matter differently. Theologians have been aware for much longer than scientists of the interactive character of knowledge. For example, the interpretation of a text never occurs in a vacuum; its meaning is partially constituted by the linguistic context in which it is read. It is fascinating to see the congruence between epistemological conclusions drawn from current philosophy of science on one side, and textual criticism on the other.

Hypothetico-Deductive Relations

I want to look now at another of the scientific areas that has important points of contact with theology. From Stoeger's paper of Part III below, we learn that our universe seems peculiarly hospitable towards life and consciousness. This is because of what is sometimes called the fine-tuning of the laws of nature. That is, calculations show that a number of factors at the beginning or very early in the history of the universe had to be adjusted with remarkable precision in order for the universe to evolve in such a way that it could support life. One factor is the mass of the universe. In addition, there are the four basic forces: gravitation, electromagnetism, and the strong and weak nuclear forces. There are the ratios of the masses and charges of various subatomic particles, and a few other factors besides. If any of these numbers had been much different than it is the universe would not have turned out to be a place in which life of any sort could exist. Life requires a universe with a sufficient time span. It requires the existence of elements heavier than the gasses that constituted it in the beginning. It requires stars and planets. In countless ways things could have gone wrong, leaving it an uninhabited waste.

Cosmologists began noting these strange "coincidences" in the 1950s. By now several books have appeared with page after page of such conclusions.[8] What are we to make of these results? Scientists have proposed several sorts of answers. One is to say that it is very remarkable indeed that, from among all the possible universes, the one that exists happens to be suitable for life, but this is simply a matter of chance. Others believe the best explanation is that there are vastly many universes, either preceding and following this one, or contemporaneous with it, but beyond the range of our observation. All have different basic numbers. By random variation, then, one can expect one or more universes to have values suited for carbon-based life, and of course only such a universe would contain observers to wonder at its being so.

The chance hypothesis is really not an explanation; it is better understood as a claim that there can be no explanation. The assorted many-universes hypotheses are as yet unconfirmed scientifically, and may not in fact be scientific at all. It is not unreasonable, then, to suggest that science may have reached the very edge of its competence—there may never be a scientific answer to the puzzling question of why the universe turned out, against such tremendous odds, to be life-supporting.

I have argued that the fine-tuning of the universe opens up possibilities for a new sort of design argument.[9] The logical relation involved in this argument is what philosophers of science call hypothetico-deductive reasoning. A hypothesis (usually the existence of an unobservable entity, process, or relationship) is supported or confirmed by the fact that it is the best explanation we can give of an observed phenomenon. That is, if the hypothesis is true, then the existence of the observed phenomenon follows deductively. So the argument here is that if God exists (the hypothesis) then, given that God intended there to be intelligent life in the universe, and that certain physical conditions are necessary for life, it follows that those physical conditions will be fulfilled. Using the notation from above, I will represent this relation as follows:

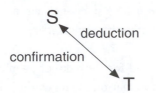

Conclusions from Combining Science and Theology

I want to draw a further conclusion from the fine-tuning of the universe, but first I need to revert to Quinian holism. I have already spoken of Quine's demolition of the analytic-synthetic distinction. Another modern dogma has been the distinction between facts and values, or between what is and what ought to be. Quine's holism erases this distinction as well. I cannot make the argument for this here, but will simply assume it, since I want to suggest briefly some ethical consequences that follow from combining the Christian (or Jewish or Islamic) doctrine of creation with the cosmology discussed in Stoeger's paper and again here with regard to fine-tuning.

Christians for many years have thought of the natural world as a stage for human life and history. As such, it was seen to have little intrinsic value to God. There was no strong theological tendency to counter those who took biblical language about dominion as license to exploit and destroy the environment. The cosmology we have just examined, however, highlights the interconnectedness of human life with its natural environment. We are the result of an unimaginably complex, finely-tuned, fifteen-billion-year process. A better analogy than that of actors on a stage to represent our relation to the natural world is to think of ourselves as fruit on a tree. Without the tree, without a healthy tree, we could not be here. Carl Sagan, for all his limitations as a theologian, makes the point nicely in saying that we are made of stardust. Immersion in the world of science, especially contemporary cosmology and astronomy, produces a sense of reverence for the natural world that may be a more effective deterrent to exploitation than any prudential calculations of dire future consequences.

But there is a second motive for environmental consciousness built into a theistic interpretation of contemporary cosmology. Let us think what the process of creation tells us about the character of the Creator: the immense time span speaks of the Creator's patience. True, a thousand years is as a day for God, but we still have to recognize a vast difference between the instantaneous creation that Christians assumed for many years, and the slow, painstaking process that current cosmology suggests.

The point I wish to emphasize here is the great respect God seems to show for the integrity of the entities and processes that have been created. Diogenes Allen emphasizes that creation involves God's self-limitation—a withholding of divine power so that other things, things genuinely distinct from God, can exist.

> When God creates, it means that he allows something to exist which is not himself. This requires an act of profound renunciation. He chooses out of love to permit something else to exist, something created to be itself and to exist by virtue of its own interest and value. God renounces his status as the only existent—he pulls himself back, so to speak, in order to give his creation room to exist for its own sake.[10]

This voluntary restraint, exercised for the sake of people *and things* out of respect for their reality, is grace. "The very creation of the world is an act of such grace."[11]

The view that God withholds power to allow for free *human* actions is common-place. It has long been recognized that God wants no coerced responses to divine initiatives. But (following Allen) I suggest that we must extend this view of divine self-limitation, speaking not only of free *will,* but (as John Polkinghorne does) of free *processes,* going right back to the very beginning of creation. God brings the universe into being with its inbuilt laws, initial conditions, and potentialities, and allows the entities and processes, as they unfold, to become (in Philip Hefner's terms) "created co-creators." God values and respects the integrity of each new order of being as it emerges.

There are obvious implications for our attitudes toward the natural world: a corresponding respect for nature with its intricate patterns and balances. If *E* signifies ethical attitudes, then this relation can be represented as follows:

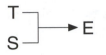

Control Beliefs

I want to turn now to the previous work of a participant with me in the present debate, Nicholas Wolterstorff. In his book, *Reason Within the Bounds of Religion,* he argued for a method of relating theology and science that I believe has received too little attention in the theology and science discussion.

A crucial term in Wolterstorff's book is that of a "control belief." Scientific theories are never determined solely by the facts. This logical gap between theory and data indicates that the weighing of theories must involve other considerations. Wolterstorff suggests that one of these other considerations is beliefs as to what constitutes an acceptable *sort* of theory of the matter under consideration.

> We can call these *control* beliefs. They include beliefs about the requisite logical or aesthetic structure of a theory, beliefs about the entities to whose existence a theory may correctly commit us, and the like. Control beliefs function in two ways. Because we hold them we are led to *reject* . . . certain sorts of theories—some because they are inconsistent with those beliefs; others because, though consistent with our control beliefs, they do not comport well with those beliefs. On the other hand control beliefs also lead us to *devise* theories. We want theories that are consistent with our control beliefs.[12]

Wolterstorff points out that control beliefs can be derived from either theological or philosophical positions. His examples show that some have had a positive effect in science, and some have inhibited its progress. For example, Descartes allowed his philosophical control belief that there can be no action at a distance to prevent him from accepting Newton's theory of gravitation. Ernst Mach held a philosophical control belief that prohibited theories postulating nonsensory entities. This led him to reject many theories of his day but also to begin to reconstruct physics on a new basis.

These two examples illustrate the effects of philosophical control beliefs on the progress of science. Our interest is in the relations between science and theology, and so our concern here is with theological control beliefs and their function in science.[13] David Griffin presented a paper to the Pacific Coast Theological Society in 1993 that provides a nice example of a theological control belief that functioned positively in the history of science.[14] He argued that Newton's view of matter as inert represented a choice not only against the Aristotelian worldview, but also against a neo-Platonic, spiritualist tradition, and that his motives were in large part theological: the spiritualist tradition did not maintain a suitable distinction between the Creator and the creature; it gave away some of God's power to the material world.

So here we have an example (although an outdated one) in which theology has implications for science—not directly, but via presuppositions about what matter must be like, and consequently about the kind of theories one ought to pursue in science. In the notation already introduced, perhaps this relation can be represented as follows:

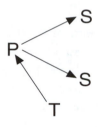

I want to turn the tables, now, and consider an extension of Wolterstorff's thought—namely, the possibility that science provides control beliefs for theologians. Ironically, the worldview that Newton did so much to establish (with the best of theological motives) has turned out to be extremely inhospitable to theology. It is a worldview of rigidly determined natural processes, wherein it is difficult to make sense of God's continuing involvement. I believe that much of modern theology has been shaped by a control belief based on this deterministic worldview: theological theories cannot postulate supernatural interference in the natural order. Rudolf Bultmann is probably the clearest example here, but we find the same control functioning in Langdon Gilkey's critique of biblical theology, in Maurice Wiles's discussion of God's action in the world, and countless other theologians.

A number of contributors to this volume are participants in a series of conferences on God's action in the world in light of assorted developments in contemporary science. The first was on quantum cosmologies and fine-tuning; the second was on chaos. The general topic of God's action was chosen because, in our view, modern science had made this issue problematic; thus, it would be possible to have a major impact on theology by showing how science had changed in this regard, and by asking what these changes entailed for God's action. Another way to put it is that we believe the modern control belief regarding God's action must be revised in light of more recent developments in science.

So far it appears to me that Arthur Peacocke's work represents the best revision in this way of the scientific worldview and its relation to God.[15] For Peacocke, the sciences can be organized into a hierarchy so that higher sciences study higher orders of complexity or broader and more inclusive systems. The modern worldview typically affirms such an organization. However, the modern worldview is reductionistic, and causation is always from the bottom up. That is, all entities at higher levels are ultimately composed of the simplest entities at the level of physics, and thus the laws of physics ultimately govern all higher-level processes.

However, this reductionistic view of causation has turned out to be inadequate; processes at one level of the hierarchy can often be explained completely only by invoking causal factors from both below and above. The environment (the more complex and therefore higher system) has a causal impact on the entities within it; and so one cannot predict the entity's behavior merely be analyzing its parts.

Thus, Peacocke argues that we must make room in our worldview for "top-down" causation. In addition, he points out, the most complex system—the top of the hierarchy—is the system of God in relation to the entire universe. Consequently God's action in the world can be conceived of as an instance of top-down causation. Peacocke holds a panentheist view of God: God transcends the world, yet the world is also *in* God, who influences it in a manner similar to the influence of any environment on the entities it contains.

So we have in Peacocke's work the beginning of a new vision of God's relation to the universe, derived from science, and from which new control beliefs for theology can be developed. No longer will theological theorizing be restricted by the view that limits God's action to creation in the beginning or irrational sorts of interventions in natural processes. It is difficult to imagine, at this point, the extent to which theology might be changed by means of this indirect interaction with science. Returning to our notation, I suppose the relation here could be represented as:

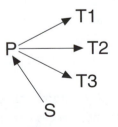

Complex Interactions

Another kind of relation appears in David Cole's contribution to the fifth case study of Part III. The issues of predestination and free will are complex, and I am going to begin with the simpler issue of determinism.

Throughout Christian history, Christians have experienced the gospel and the Spirit of God as liberators—liberation from fate or the stars; liberation from bondage to the material order. So there are two questions about human freedom: (1) Considered purely from the natural point of view (apart from the action of God), are human beings free, determined, or somewhere in between? The Pelagian controversy had to do with this issue—Pelagius saying we had a measure of freedom that we could use to extricate ourselves from sin; Augustine arguing for complete bondage to sin. (2) The second question is about the impact of God's grace, or the Spirit, or the gospel in our lives. One way of answering the question is to emphasize Christian liberty. But, paradoxically, Augustine and his followers have spoken of the liberating power of God's grace, which gives us the ability to choose the good, in ways that make it sound like a new version of determinism. God chooses those who will be gifted with freedom from sin; therefore God determines that some will be saved (or lost).

Cole's paper on genetic determinism versus the self-determining effects of memory could be interpreted as a contribution to question one: Considered apart from God, are our actions free or determined? His conclusion: our actions are not entirely free, but not strictly determined by genetics either. Framing the issue this way, we have another instance of theology and science related via a philosophical position—the view that human beings possess limited free will.

I think there is a better theological use to be made of Cole's discussion, however. I have just discussed Peacocke's theory of top-down causation, and the opportunities it presents for understanding God's action. Let us look at the matter this way. The human person can be considered from the perspective of a number of levels in the hierarchy of the sciences. The genetic level is one of these; the neurological level another; and the conscious or intelligent level a third. With the top-down view of causation, the most reasonable way to understand divine influence in human life is at the level of human consciousness—or in more traditional language, by means of the *word*. From the very beginning in Christian thought, there has been an appreciation for the liberating effects of God's revelation, coupled with a view of human behavior as determined in one way or another from below. Cole's account of how consciousness interacts with genetic determination can be used to describe at least a part of the *modus operandi* of the counterdeterministic influence of God's action. God's message affects human consciousness which, in top-down fashion, interacts with and mitigates bottom-up causal factors.

So we have here a fairly complex interaction between theology and science. Numerous results from several different sciences have suggested the hierarchical ordering of reality according to levels of complexity and the notion of top-down causation (theses belonging to the realm of philosophy). Theology contributes a top level to this hierarchy, along with the belief that human life is open (at the top, we might say) to divine influences. And finally, Cole's scientific analysis contributes to our understanding, in concrete terms, of how these divine influences are possible without violating the laws of nature. (I'm not going to try to diagram this one).

V. CONCLUSION

Let me sum up. I began by introducing a postmodern, holist theory of knowledge, and argued that Christian apologists must adopt a new strategy in its light: they must proceed not by attempting to find indubitable premises from which Christian beliefs follow, but rather by showing that the Christian belief system is well connected to the rest of the web. I then proceeded to describe some of the connections that have been drawn by a variety of people, including contributors to this volume. Still others could have been mentioned, but these provided a nice illustration of the variety of kinds of connections that are possible: direct implication of theological conclusion from scientific theories; mutual implication of a philosophical position by both theology and science; ethical implications drawn from a union of theological and scientific theories; arguments from science to a theological conclusion via hypothetico-deductive reasoning; control beliefs for scientific theories drawn from theology; control beliefs for theological theories drawn from science; and, finally, complex combinations of such relations. (Note that in light of this epistemological model, there is no reason that scientific conclusions cannot be suggested and weakly supported by theological theories.)

I want to end by noting that Ian Barbour has argued for caution in making the sorts of connections between science and theology that I have described and advocated here. The worry is that science changes—and often changes rather rapidly. Insofar as theology is justified by ties to science, it is setting itself up for rejection when the science changes. I have two replies: certainly theologians must not jump the gun and use scientific ideas that are still highly speculative. When we speak of the web of beliefs, we must not think of it as the beliefs of one or several individuals, but rather of the community. Only conclusions that are widely accepted by the relevant experts merit inclusion.

But, second, it is unnecessary and inappropriate to be any more defensive about theological theories than any other kind. Theology ought to be expected to change along with the rest of our dim and faltering knowledge. The web model helps here. Theology does not rest in any case on a scientific foundation such that a change in science brings the whole tumbling down. Each theological belief is tied to a number of other beliefs— some theological, some experiential, and (ideally) some scientific. When one support is lost, or when an inconsistency arises, there will always be a number of ways to revise and repair the web. So the task of relating theology to science will never be finished—it is bound to be an ongoing job, and there will surely be disappointments, but has not that been the lot of theologians and apologists from the beginning?

NOTES

1. See for example, William Placher, Unapologetic Theology: A Christian Voice in a Pluralistic Conversation (Louisville: Westminster/John Knox Press, 1989); Paul Griffiths, *An Apology for Apologetics: A Study in the Logic of Interreligious Dialogue* (Maryknoll: Orbis Books, 1991);

William Werpehowsky, "Ad Hoc Apologetics," in *Journal of Religion* 66 (July, 1986), pp. 282–301.

2. James Wm. McClendon, Jr. and Nancey Murphy, "Distinguishing Modern and Postmodern Theologies," *Modern Theology*, April, 1989.

3. E.J. Carnell, *The Case for Orthodox Theology* (Philadelphia: Westminster Press, 1959), p. 82.

4. Willard V.O. Quine, "Two Dogmas of Empiricism," in *From a Logical Point of View: 9 Logico-Philosophical Essays* (Cambridge: Harvard University Press, 1953), pp. 42–43; the essay was originally published in 1951.

5. Ronald Thiemann, Revelation and Theology (Notre Dame: University of Notre Dame Press, 1985), pp. 75–76. The last sentence is a quotation from Quine and J.S. Ullian, *The Web of Belief* (New York: Random House, 1970), p. 127.

6. My main point of disagreement with postmodern theologians such as Lindbeck and Thiemann is their conclusion that Christianity needs no such justification.

7. Presentation by Robert John Russell, Castel Gandolfo, Vatican City State, September 22–27, 1991.

8. Two prominent books are J. Barrow and F. Tipler, *The Anthropic Cosmological Principle* (Oxford: Clarendon Press; New York: Oxford University Press, 1986); and John Leslie, *Universes* (London and New York: Routledge and Kegan Paul, 1989).

9. See my "Evidence of Design in the Fine-Tuning of the Universe," in Robert John Russell, Nancey Murphy, and C.J. Isham, eds., *Quantum Cosmology and the Laws of Nature: Scientific Perspectives on Divine Action* (Vatican City State: Vatican Observatory, and Berkeley: The Center for Theology and the Natural Sciences, 1993), pp. 407–435.

10. Diogenes Allen, *The Traces of God in a Frequently Hostile World* (Cambridge, Massachusetts: Cowley, 1981), p. 35.

11. Traces of God, p. 36.

12. Nicholas Wolterstorff, *Reason Within the Bounds of Religion,* 2nd enlarged ed. (Grand Rapids: Eerdmans, 1984), pp. 67–68.

13. Wolterstorff gives an example of a theological control belief that functioned negatively, but none that functioned positively.

14. David Ray Griffin, "Theology and the Rise of Modern Science," paper presented at the Spring Meeting of the Pacific Coast Theological Society, April, 1993, in Berkeley, CA. See also Eugene Klaaren, *Religious Origins of Modern Science* (Grand Rapids: Eerdmans, 1977).

15. See especially, *Creation and the World of Science* (Oxford: Clarendon Press, 1979), and *Theology for a Scientific Age: Being and Becoming Natural and Divine* (Oxford: Basil Blackwell, 1990; expanded ed., 1993).

MATHEMATICS, EMPIRICAL SCIENCE, AND RELIGION

I. INTRODUCTION

MARY GERHART AND ALLAN MELVIN RUSSELL

As a theologian and a physicist who have collaborated for a number of years, we know the value of interdisciplinary cooperation between Christian theology and natural science. In particular we have found that such collaboration makes possible a deeper understanding of what it means to claim to know something in either science or theology than, we believe, can be achieved within the confines of either discipline alone. The understanding to which we refer derives not from the traditional epistemology of either medieval scholasticism or Cartesian dualism, but from an improved insight into the epistemological dynamic itself, what we have come to call knowledge-in-process. Accordingly, this paper focuses on the process relations that obtain between pure mathematics and natural science on the one hand, and natural science and Christian theology on the other.

While it is clear that new ways of seeing the world suggested by scientific advances have *some* implications for theology, the precise nature of those implications is far from obvious. The empirical sciences have control of human rationality, in the sense that they are, today, the arbiters of what constitutes the reasonable. However, for philosophy and theology, the speculative sciences, the situation is like that imagined by Richard Wilbur in his poem "Mind" (1956)—the situation is like a bat flying in a dark cave, contriving to avoid crashing into the wall, not needing to explore, knowing what is there. Wilbur describes a kind of cognitive change—what we call metaphoric process—with the lines, "And in the very happiest intellection / A graceful error may correct the cave."

In this paper we argue that the natural sciences influence Christian theology not so much by causing necessary changes in doctrine, but by reforming the world of meanings within which human beings explore the limits of human understanding. This process is analogous to the enlarging of the realm of the analytical that occurs in the interaction between pure mathematics and the natural sciences. The structure of our argument is an analogy in the classical form:

A : B :: B : C

which we read as "A is to B as B is to C." A-is-to-B is the relationship between Christian theology and the natural sciences. That relationship is understood as analogous to the B-is-to-C relationship that obtains between the natural sciences and mathematics:

Theology : Science :: Science : Mathematics

We argue as well for what might be called a conservation of epistemological sufficiency, in which a move from one discipline to another involves a sacrifice of one aspect of thought in order to gain another.

We intend to clarify the distinction between the synthetic epistemology of empirical science on the one hand, and the noetic epistemology of theology on the other, by borrowing and extending the argument of one of Carl Hempel's papers on mathematics and the natural sciences. Although these three realms of human thought—mathematics, science, and religion—have the practices of human reflective thought in common, they differ one from another in the nature of their subjects and objectives.

We begin the analogy by examining mathematics from the formalist perspective and ask how mathematics and the natural sciences are related.

II. THE RELATIONSHIP OF NATURAL SCIENCE TO MATHEMATICS (B IS TO C)

In 1945 Carl Hempel published an article entitled "Geometry and Empirical Science" (hereafter GES).[1] In December of the same year he published a paper entitled "On the Nature of Mathematical Truth" (hereafter NMT).[2] These papers, which have been widely reprinted, demonstrated the distinction between the analytical epistemology of mathematics on the one hand, and the synthetic epistemology of empirical science on the other.

Hempel begins GES with a memorable sentence:

> The most distinctive characteristic which differentiates mathematics from the various branches of empirical science, and which accounts for its fame as the queen of the sciences, is no doubt the peculiar certainty and necessity of its results.

It is the certainty of mathematical results—which Hempel characterizes as "peculiar"—that we wish to emphasize. NMT, the second paper, begins with the sentence:

> It is the basic principle of scientific enquiry that no proposition and no theory is to be accepted without adequate grounds. In empirical science, which includes both the natural and the social sciences, the grounds for the acceptance of a theory consist in the agreement of the predictions based on the theory with empirical evidence obtained either by experiment or by systematic observation.

While the certain truth of a mathematical statement is grounded on principles of validation—on the deductive relationship between that statement and an axiom previously established as a cornerstone of the particular mathematical system under consideration—the merely probable truth of a scientific statement is grounded on principles of verification—on the agreement between the scientific statement and empirical evidence derived from experiment and observation.

Thus formal mathematics achieves its certainty at the cost of sterility—a worldly meaninglessness—while natural science achieves a required worldly relevance by giving up certainty. Hempel expresses this situation in GES by quoting Albert Einstein to the effect that: "As far as the laws of mathematics refer to reality, they are not certain, and as far as they are certain, they do not refer to reality."

So much for formal epistemological comparisons. What about the functional relations between mathematics and empirical science? What implications are there for physics, say, when a new mathematical structure is discovered? Most likely, depending on the branch of mathematics involved, there are no implications at all. The physicist sees new mathematics as a region in which to prospect when in need, just as Einstein did when he needed an analytic geometric structure for his general theory of relativity. He found and made use of Riemann's geometry, a development in fundamental mathematics made fifty years earlier.

A more general statement might be that new mathematics expands the realm of computable or otherwise analyzable relations, and that some of these relations may, at some time, turn out to be of value to physics. As you can see, there is a certain parasitic quality here, especially from the point of view of mathematics.

Having described the B-is-to-C relationship between natural science and mathematics, we now turn to the A-is-to-B half of our analogy, and construct the parallel relationship we see between Christian theology and natural science.

III. RELATION OF CHRISTIAN THEOLOGY TO NATURAL SCIENCE (A IS TO B)

For the purposes of this paper, we define theology as philosophical reflection upon explicitly or implicitly religious experience and language. Experience here refers to consciousness of a subject in relation to images, actions, events, texts, and language.[3]

The dominant referent for theology would seem to be human experience, as reported in texts and in living traditions, both past and present. By human experience we do not mean, as one does in the natural sciences, the reports of observations or measurements: we mean instead, the lived experiences of human-being. Such experiences are notoriously absent from the data of the natural sciences.

It is a parallel between the lack of "worldliness" in mathematics and the lack of the experience of human-being in the natural sciences that stimulates the analogy we argue for here. Just as the mind must give up the certainty of mathematics if it is to address the world of natural science, so must the mind give up an aspect of the natural sciences if it is to address the world with the empathy for human-being that is required by theology. What is it that the mind must leave behind in order to include the experience of human-being?

We think that the theological mind must forego that truth, both probable and predictive, that is established through empirical verification. Theological propositions are not constructed as falsifiable assertions. The mathematical certainty that empirical science gives up when it addresses quantitative measurements of the world—measurements that are necessarily imprecise—corresponds, in our analogy, to theology's abandoning the requirement of quantitative verification through measurement, incorporating, instead, verification by assent. Since theology is based on lived experience, and since consciousness of the self has no equivalent in science, but is the ground of the lived experience of human-being, it is fitting and necessary that such a shift in the source of verification be made.

The development of human beings, however, is determined by interaction between genetic constitution, on the one hand, and environment, on the other. Through evolution, human beings change over history as genes and environments change. Individual human beings change as well through reflective thought. And when the last human being to verify a theological proposition dies, the theological truth of that proposition dies. The natural sciences also change, but not in this way. The laws of physics, according to the theory of relativity, are time- and space-invariant. Which is not to say that the laws never change—they change as our understandings of the world change—but the laws, as we understand them at any time, apply and have always and will always apply to all worlds and all peoples—whether or not any of these people understand any of these laws. In making its turn toward the human and away from measures of the world, theology turns away also from this time and space independence of scientific understandings. Theology is not apologetic for doing so, just as the natural sciences do not apologize for their lack of certainty.

What then can be said of the dynamic relations, the knowledge-in-process, that obtains between the natural sciences and theology? E.L. Mascall said that " ... present day science leaves a good deal more elbow-room than the science of yesterday left for theological speculation."[4] But there is a good deal more going on here than a mere increase in elbowroom. There is a fundamental challenge to reconstruct the possible. We find—analogous to the expansion of the realm of the computable and analyzable, achieved by mathematics and seen as hunting ground by the natural sciences—an often dramatic change in what is accepted as reasonable and believable, a reconstructed world of meanings—a world of meanings shared by theological reflection—that is the fruit of research in the natural sciences. This process of cognitive reconstruction, we have argued, is best understood as metaphoric process.

If it is the case, then, that, in order to be able to make intelligible claims about God and freedom and immortality (Kant's triad), theology must give up both mathematical certitude and empirical atemporality, how does this process play itself out? For example, is it reasonable to expect that there should be a direct and immediate relationship between natural science and Christian theology?

IV. NATURAL SCIENCE AND DOCTRINE IN CHRISTIAN THEOLOGY

Of all the differentiated tasks in the field of theology, that of doctrine is the most visible. The task of doctrine is to make those minimal statements that express a historical consensus in a tradition. Doctrines (in science as well as in theology) originate as formal historical answers to questions. Perhaps inevitably, doctrine comes to be invoked apart from the questions in which it originates. As it becomes familiar and communicable, doctrine may seem to be a timeless truth from which all ambiguity and ground for conversation and argument have been removed. Today we expect that clarification and correction are necessary to the growth and development of doctrine. Although we may expect such clarification and correction of theology to come from the sciences, as a matter of historical record the most important twentieth-century revisions of doctrine—for example, the doctrine of God/ess—have not come directly as a result of empirical discoveries in either natural or social science.

Moreover, doctrine is only one genre in Christian theology. In theology, historical answers to questions (before and after being formulated as doctrine) are expressed in a variety of other genres, such as poetry, fiction, biography and autobiography, dialogues, creeds, and oaths. Doctrine and apocalyptic, for example, are two major genres in early Christianity, and, according to David Tracy, both are better understood as playing corrective, rather than constitutive, roles in interpreting New Testament texts. In his view, apocalyptic emphasizes the sense of present inadequacy before the event not yet realized, whereas doctrine relaxes (but does not eliminate) the tension between the everyday present and the extraordinary Christic event.[5] The plurality of genres in theology cautions us against literalizing Christian doctrine with too direct a relationship to natural science. Dostoyevsky was fond of saying that one could have as radical a doctrine of sin as one wanted, so long as one had an equally radical doctrine of grace. The problem remains: How to model the process of theological change in relation to changes in the natural sciences?

Factors such as those described above complicate any expectation we might have of moving directly from natural science to doctrine. There is a sense in which the central doctrines of Christianity are parallel to major theories in the natural sciences; both scientific theories and religious doctrines tend to persist in the face of contrary evidence. Belief in the face of contrary evidence in the natural sciences, though common, is often thought to be pathological. In theology, on the contrary, such belief, understood as faith, is a normal part of religious understanding. Indeed, the theological virtues of faith, hope, and love are premised on the *absence* as well as the presence of confirming evidence: faith is in that which is seen, but through a glass darkly; hope is for that which is anticipated, but has not been realized; and love is most remarkably love in its ability to persist somehow during times when love is not returned. If it is the case that direct and immediate consequences cannot be established between theory and empirical data on the one hand, nor between theological doctrine and lived experience on the other, then we should not expect there to be a direct and immediate relationship between Christian theology and the natural sciences.

But what other than a direct and immediate relationship between natural science and Christian theology is possible? In *Metaphoric Process* (1984), we described and distinguished between analogical and metaphoric processes—both of which are indirect and mediated.[6] Most developments in scientific and religious understanding have been analogical—they are a mapping of a knowledge structure (a known) from one field of meanings onto another (an unknown). By contrast, metaphoric process—the equation of two knowns—results in a distortion of a field of meanings, an epistemological change that gives rise to new understandings. Physics's proclamation that a particle is a wave or theology's claim that the human is divine[7] come to mind as examples.

How might recent developments in natural science impact Christian theology? Genetic determinism might be related by analogy to the doctrine of judgment. If we should think that theology lacks criteria for blame, for example, a knowledge of inherited behavioral characteristics might provide a template for such criteria. Second, the implied challenge to theology made by microbiological determinism is not in kind different from the question with which theology has always had to contend, namely: To what degree are we not responsible for our actions? However, it is not immediately clear that such a construction would constitute an improvement over the concepts of divine grace and forgiveness which come into play in the traditional world of meanings here. Contemporary understandings in physics and cosmology have relevance for contemporary theology through the changes these new understandings make in what we can believe, rather than being suggestive of specific changes in any doctrine—say, that of the divine creation of the world. While it seems to us that the doctrine of judgment might be understood as a live theological issue today, the doctrine of the divine creation of the world is not in the same category. Once beyond the questions of who created the world and why—questions which are no longer of concern to theology and never were of concern to natural science—we are left with the "how" questions, which continue to be important to physics but not to modern theology. We are reminded of the stunning impact of the Copernican metaphoric pronouncement that the sun, and not the earth, is the center of everything—an impact that has completely disappeared in the modern world. Indeed we are at pains, in trying to understand the treatment of Galileo Galilei, to know what the theological fuss was all about. Such, we think, is the case with any facts that clarify the details of creation.[8]

What science creates from the point of view of theology is a cognitive environment. The development of theology within that environment occurs by selection and not by instruction. In other words, we can find no direct and immediate relationship between scientific discoveries and theological development: we think it more likely that theological development is a creative and somewhat stochastic process, one that results in *some* speculations proving to be productive.

V. EXAMPLES OF INTERACTIONS BETWEEN SCIENCE AND THEOLOGY

Productive speculations have been described by E.L. Mascall in his *Christian Theology and Natural Science*. There he analyzes a variety of examples of what he calls the "conflict" between scientists and theologians. First he reminds us of two historical disagreements among scientists themselves, namely the arguments between geologists and physicists regarding the age of the solid earth: nineteenth-century physicists claimed it could not exceed one hundred million years, while geologists (and many biologists) claimed evidence for many billions of years; and the disagreement among physicists themselves whether light was to be understood as made up of particles or of waves. In the first instance, discoveries of natural radioactivity and the conversion of mass into energy made it possible for physicists to bring their theoretical understanding of the age of the earth into agreement with those of the geologists. In the second, the wave nature of atomic particles predicted by quantum mechanics, and demonstrated by G.P. Thomson and by Davisson and Germer in the first quarter of the twentieth century, extended the wave-particle duality beyond light to include matter as well, and drove physicists to revise their conceptions of what had constituted contradictory descriptions.

Consider how these disagreements within the natural sciences—the issue of the age of the earth, and the wave-particle duality— affect thinking in theology. Initially, the age of the earth might be thought to be the more theologically relevant of the two. However, a little reflection on the development of theological understanding as it has occurred over the past few hundred years makes it clear that the age of the earth is no longer a significant issue for theology, because the Genesis creation story is not understood today as it appears to have been in earlier times. Therefore, apparent contradictions are seen to be unimportant. Moreover, as we have just observed, the very concept of contradiction itself has undergone metamorphosis.

The second disagreement regarding the understanding of light as waves or particles, on the one hand, and the corresponding understanding of atoms as particles or waves, on the other—unlike the merely factual issue of the age of the earth—is an issue that has had profound implications for theology, because it challenges the grounds of our judgment of what constitutes a rational understanding of any kind. Theology must have standards for what is to be believed, as other fields of intellectual endeavor do, and the most profound impact that science is likely to have can be understood to be on the answer to the question: What is it possible for human beings to believe in the light of what natural science has learned is highly probable about the world?

The importance of the scope of what can be believed is not to be minimized. William James observed that "as a rule [human beings] believe as much as they can."[9] So any increase in our believable world of meanings will have repercussions even beyond theology. Arthur Kantrowitz, in a recent issue of *Physics Today*, notes that "the triumphs of Newtonian mechanics, its unification of terrestial and celestial mechanics, played a major role in establishing the faith of reason, the French Enlightenment and the realization of some of its ideals in America."[10] No one is likely to claim that Newton's *Principia Mathematica* had an immediate and direct effect on the status of freedom in America, but can anyone deny the changes that Newton's metaphor wrought in our world of meanings?

When we look back at controversy stirred up by Copernicus's assertion that the earth circles the sun or Newton's claim that the laws of the heavens are the same as the laws of the earth (a cognitive restructuring we call metaphoric), we can recall no immediate theological revisions, assuming there were any. And with that retrospective understanding, we should be wary of thinking that a new scientific paradigm could constitute a threat to any theological understanding. It is much more likely that a breakthrough in the natural sciences will cause a change in what is possible, in the same way that a breakthrough in pure mathematics can cause a change in what is analyzable.

VI. CONCLUSION

The greatest contributions of science and religion to human ways of thinking are those which become possible through the metaphoric process in both science and religion, a process that brings about a change in what is believable. It is frequently said that the universe is not only stranger than we imagine, but stranger than we can imagine. However, our ability to imagine continues to improve. Empirical science serves theology by increasing the scope of human awareness, by making possible a broader, more flexible, more imaginative human mind. If we contemplate the differences between what is believable today and what was believable five hundred years ago, we can see that the work of science is what makes it possible to believe more. What science proposes for us to believe today is far *less* credible than what religion required of us in the past.

Christian theology, however, has its own agenda, an agenda which is not a point-to-point mapping of the agenda of the natural sciences. And we have asserted that, just as the physicist prospects among the accomplishments of pure mathematics for the means to the achievement of the ends of science, so only the theologian is able to determine what changes in our world of meanings brought about by the many inventions and discoveries of the natural sciences can be of use in furthering the ends of theology. We merely wish to reaffirm the freedom of the theological quest for an understanding of the impact of the divine on the lives of human beings. Without that freedom, the theologian is limited to the same shiny pebbles on the beach that Newton claimed were the objects of his study. Without that freedom, the ocean of the human experience of the divine would constitute a horizon forever beyond us.

NOTES

1. Carl Hempel, "Geometry and Empirical Science," *American Mathematical Monthly* 52, pp. 7–17.

2. Carl Hempel, "On the Nature of Mathematical Truth," *American Mathematical Monthly* 52, pp. 543–556.

3. From this perspective, theology is neither inside nor outside explicitly religious traditions. Indeed, the margins of what is inside (i.e., explicitly religious) or outside (i.e., implicitly religious or secular) shift within the texts of many traditions.

4. E.L. Mascall, *Christian Theology and Natural Science: Some Questions on their Relations* (London: Archon Books, 1965), p. 29.

5. David Tracy, *The Analogical Imagination: Christian Theology and the Culture of Pluralism* (New York: Crossroad, 1981), p. 267.

6. Mary Gerhart and Allan M. Russell, *Metaphoric Process: The Creation of Scientific and Religious Understanding* (Fort Worth: Christian University Press, 1984).

7. One of the perennial religious metaphors results from classical theology's insistence that God is human. According to our model of metaphoric process, this claim is metaphoric in the sense that the field of meanings associated with being human (mortal, being born, being self-conscious, being reflective, worshipping an Other) is claimed to be equivalent to the field of meanings associated with being divine (being immortal, having no origin in time, being omniscient, being omnipotent, being self-sufficient, and formally having only internal relations). In other words, God/ess is no longer necessarily understood as omniscient, unchanging, and all-powerful, but is already understood in revisionary theology as eminently related to all, as becoming and being, as providing the space for human freedom to be realized.

8. Popular accounts of the relation between religion and science typically feature the search for such details. See, for example, Jeffrey Sheler and Joannie M. Schrof, "The Creation: Religion's Search for a Common Ground with Science," *U.S. News and World Report* 111 (December 23, 1992), pp. 56–64. See also the "Letters to the Editor" commenting on Sheler and Schrof in *U.S. News and World Report* 112 (January 13, 1992). For a theological account of the "silent, secret attraction" that the classical "proofs" for the existence of God (two of which address the issue of divine creation) continue to exercise in contemporary thought, and as well of the "challenge to thought" they provide, see Hans Küng, *Does God Exist? An Answer for Today* (New York: Doubleday, 1980), pp. 529–536.

9. William James, *Principles of Psychology* (Princeton: Princeton University Press, 1981; first published 1890).

10. Arthur Kantrowitz, "Physics in the 'Age of Diminished Expectations'," *Physics Today* 45 (March, 1992), pp. 61–62; quote is on p. 62.

RATIONALITY AND CHRISTIAN SELF-CONCEPTIONS

PHILIP CLAYTON AND STEVEN KNAPP

Christianity is neither a scientific hypothesis nor an existential stance toward the world.[1] But until we clarify *what* it is, we will not know how to proceed with the discussion between Christian theology and science. In particular, we will not yet be in a position to answer questions such as: What does it mean for Christian belief to be rational or irrational? *Is* it rational? How are Christian beliefs like or unlike scientific beliefs? How should we go about drawing implications for Christian theology from the results of natural science?

We suggest that the question of the rationality of Christian beliefs, and hence the religion-science discussion itself, is best approached by analyzing the question: What is it, in general, to be a rational agent, whether the agent in question is a scientist, a religious believer, or merely someone who deliberates rationally about ordinary human decisions? In this paper, we argue that Christianity can be equated neither with scientific hypotheses nor with a set of individual values. Instead, a religious self-conception, at least of the Christian variety, is an interesting *tertium quid* that evinces important similarities to, and differences from, the kinds of self-conception someone has to have in order to engage in formal scientific inquiry, on the one hand, or ordinary practical deliberation, on the other. Coming to understand the logical distinctiveness of a Christian self-conception is an important prerequisite for progress in the theology-science discussion.

In order to provide this basic account of Christian believing, we begin with a consideration of the role played by self-conceptions in ordinary human practice and move gradually toward religious and scientific self-conceptions. In the interests of brevity and clarity, we will formulate our position as a series of theses.

I

Religious self-conceptions can best be understood by analogy with ordinary practical self-conceptions (SCs).[2]

Consider the sort of reflection that any individual agent engages in when she wishes to make "the best decision for her," and to do so in a rational manner. Each deliberating agent, insofar as her deliberation is rational, must have some grasp, however min-imal, of the motivations that go with being the kind of person she takes herself to be. For in the first place it is necessary for me, if I wish to deliberate at all about my actions, to know what desires, wants, and other dispositions I seek to actualize. And insofar as I want my deliberation to be *rational*, I have to have some notion of how these dispositions make sense as belonging to a certain *kind* of person.

We are not arguing that every agent has to be rational, or even that every agent has an obligation to be concerned about rationality. It is not hard to show, however, that every agent who does have an interest in being rational needs to have a self-conception, that is, an image, however ill-defined, of the self she wants to be or become. After all, the basic issue in theories of practical rationality is the issue of what it is to perform an action rationally. This then raises the question: What are the minimal conditions for rea-soning about any action? Acting rationally means, at least, giving (or being able to give) a rationale for one's proposed or past actions. And a rationale is a reason that would be taken to be adequate in the right social—or, as we shall say, *intersubjective*—context. Now, in order that my reason for action be available (in principle) for assessment by a relevant community of other persons, it has to be possible to pose the question of whether the action I contemplate performing makes sense for *me* to do, that is, *given the kind of agent I am*. For only if I can represent (or imagine representing) my actions as the actions of a certain *kind* of agent, can I coherently engage (or imagine engaging) in a discussion with others about what it makes sense for *me* to do. No one, then, can deliberate rationally about her possible actions without relating those possible actions to one or more conceptions of the kind of agent she takes herself to be. It follows that every rational agent who wants to deliberate rationally is actually required to have (at least one) self-conception.[3]

The fact that there is a rational imperative to have a self-conception does not mean, however, that self-conceptions are *derived* from rationality. My obligation, if I want to make practical decisions that are rationally justified, is not to derive them all from a rational source, but, rather, to hold them open to critical feedback from others. An individual cannot rationally suppose that an action she performs (or contemplates per-forming) is the right one for someone like her to perform unless she thinks her evalu-ation of that action is confirmable, at least in principle, by what she takes to be the right critical community. Rationality presupposes intersubjective standards, and their application to oneself is rational only when subjected to the (actual or rightly imag-ined) test of intersubjective debate. And this requirement of critical feedback implicitly commits every rational agent to a certain minimal set of ethical values—namely, the set of values implied by the conditions of critical feedback itself. Take an example: if (Kantian) attempts to derive a universal ethics from rationality alone fail, then we may find ourselves unable to provide a rationally compelling argument against the prefer-ences of a racist, a corporate embezzler or, say, Jack the Ripper. Jack can ply his trade on the streets of London, secure in the knowledge that he is not directly betraying any universal rational obligation by aspiring to realize his criminal SC. Nonetheless, if he wants to pursue his SC rationally, he cannot disregard the requirement that he remain open to feedback from what he takes to be an appropriate community of critics. Even Jack will need his club at the end of the day, where he can report his day's accomplishments and verify his evaluation of their significance. Should his reports be dishonest (he actually spent the day helping orphans and widows in their distress), or should he fail to exclude his peers from his activities (he murders *all* persons upon sight), he cannot count as acting in a rational manner, since he is acting in ways that deprive him of the relevant means of determining whether his actions meet or fail to meet the standards set by his own character ideal.

What do these conclusions have to say about the nature of a Christian SC?

II

A Christian SC is different in structure from an ordinary practical SC inasmuch as it includes from the start theoretical *beliefs that are intrinsic to being Christian.*

To hold a Christian SC rationally is to hold certain beliefs about what being a (certain kind of) Christian entails (or forbids). The beliefs in question are normative: they are part of what it *means* for one to have the conception of oneself as being a Christian in the intersubjectively shared sense of the word.

III

To be more specific, for a SC to be Christian it must include certain beliefs that together constitute the minimal doxastic requirements *of the Christian SC.*

These beliefs seem to us to fall into three categories:

(1) minimally personalistic theism, or belief in a God-creator; the content of this belief can be specified by contrasting it with, for instance, atheism, polytheism, and pantheism;
(2) a minimal Christological belief, a belief that God has in some manner attested the unique authority of Jesus;
(3) a minimal ecclesiological belief, belief in the necessity of involvement with a community of other Christians.

Of course, most Christian communities have traditionally expected their members sooner or later to go beyond such minimal beliefs. Traditionally, the expectation has been that believers will proceed to a set of beliefs that accords ever more fully with the biblical doctrines and teachings of the church, such as belief in the Trinity, or in transubstantiation, or in a full Chalcedonian christology. But meeting such expectations is not usually taken (and need not be taken) as a prerequisite for any Christian belief whatsoever.

The same holds true for presently disputed beliefs: Does being Catholic require me to attend mass? Does it entail the belief that birth control is wrong? Or the belief that the study of physics helps me to understand the handiwork of God? Certainly such beliefs, however important they may be within the context of particular Christian traditions and communities, cannot be taken as requirements for a Christian SC simply as such.

IV

In general, the rationality of beliefs lies not in their source but in their being held open to subsequent testing.

This conclusion can be defended in light of the now widely accepted distinction between prerational and rational levels of belief and inquiry.[4] Just as a practical self-conception typically begins with a set of prerational motivations, a religious SC typically begins with a prerational set of traditional beliefs. It is not necessary to derive Christian truth claims directly from reason, nor to claim that they are fully rational from the start, any more than I must derive my desire to be a successful lawyer or a great tennis player directly from reason. Still, if I am to hold Christian beliefs in a rational manner, I must hold them open to feedback. That is, I must be willing, at least in principle, to enter into rational discussion of them, and to accept (and respond to) indications of how well they stand up to intersubjective criticism.

It follows that Christian theology starts from premises that may not yet be fully rational, but that seek full rationality. Theology, on our account, proceeds by applying rationally discussible procedures of inquiry to premises that are not themselves derived from intersubjective inquiry, and that in many cases are not, at least initially, capable of intersubjective confirmation.

This theory of rationality is best understood in terms of the "inference to the best explanation" model adapted from the philosophy of science.[5] On this view, many Christian beliefs are potential explanations: they tell why certain data that need to be explained are the way they are; they account for certain facts about human existence. When I believe them, I believe they do a better job of explaining the data than the other explanatory hypotheses of which I am aware. The task of rational discussion is to weigh competing explanations, whatever their respective sources, and to select the one or more that do the best job of explaining the data at hand. For example, Christians claim that theism provides a better explanation of human experience, ultimately including scientific knowledge itself, than naturalism does.

V

The Christian is therefore justified in introducing proposals into the arena of intersubjective discussion whose source lies in an alleged divine revelation.

We have seen that doxastic claims do not have to be justified *ab initio*, but only in terms of their subsequent explanatory success. Beliefs may thus originate from a source initially accessible only to a particular religious community. For instance, from the Christian scriptures, or the tradition for which they have been authoritative, or, in principle, from religious experience.

Further, the Christian breaks no epistemic obligations by believing some things that have not been verified through intersubjective testing. The epistemic requirement for rationality is merely that all beliefs be held open to criticism in principle and that those beliefs (or groups of beliefs) that are shown to be less adequate than their rivals be rejected. As we will see, this fact provides some important parameters for the way in which Christians should pursue discussion with the natural sciences.

VI

Inseparable from the minimal doxastic requirements of a Christian SC are certain minimal practical requirements.

Here again, as in the case of minimal doxastic requirements, there are normative requirements that belong necessarily to a Christian SC. The normativity even of a minimal Christian SC is not purely theoretical, since the minimal Christian beliefs themselves have implications for the agent's practical life; they are, in short, theoretical beliefs with direct practical entailments.

For example, if one Christian belief is that I ought to model my behavior on the life of Jesus Christ (if, for instance, this is rightly seen as a component of a minimal christology), then seeking to live in this way is one of the practical goals that is directly implied by my Christian SC. Some involvement with the church and/or concern about the church's fate is also implied. Even for the rather skeptical Christian (who meets the minimal doxastic requirements but does so with a significant degree of doubt[6]), the nature of that about which he is uncertain carries with it *some* necessity of practical involvement—if only, at first, the necessity that he take a lively interest in figuring out what the right practical entailments are!

We can clarify the practical side of Christian SCs by contrasting them with the SCs required by ordinary practical deliberation. The practical requirements of a Christian SC are derived directly from Christian theoretical beliefs, whereas, in the case of ordinary practical SCs, normative strictures arise only from the necessary conditions of openness to critical feedback concerning how well one is doing at actualizing one's own goals. For this reason, Christian SCs involve a greater and more immediate interest in theoretical investigations. Of course, Christian believers do not limit themselves to dispositions that can be derived from Christian theoretical beliefs, or even to dispositions defined by any Christian norms; Christian SCs generally also include practical and experiential elements that are neither theoretically nor practically required, but that reflect the individual and collective predilections—the psychological, spiritual, and aesthetic preferences and possibilities—that define the content of each particular form of Christian life.

VII

An appreciation of the specific nature of Christian SCs suggests that two widespread views of Christianity—roughly, the "conservative" and "liberal" views—are either mistaken or irrelevant to the theology-science discussion.

The "conservative" theological tradition has stressed the propositional content of Christianity. Its mistake lies not in the insistence that Christianity has irreducible doxastic requirements, but in the assumption that these requirements must be such as to entail from the start a full range of traditional beliefs, and even a certain kind of experience—for example, the experience that a being is present who listens to the thoughts one is now having. Distinctive Christian beliefs may eventually foster distinctively Christian types of experiences, but these experiences are not an immediate or automatic consequence of a Christian SC.

By contrast, the liberal tradition has treated Christianity as an ethical ideal, a stance toward life—radical-revolutionary or spiritual-otherworldly, depending on the theologian's preference—inspired by a particular historical story but not bound by it. This tradition is not mistaken in insisting that Christianity cannot be reduced to some normative propositional content. The problem, instead, lies in the claim that one can have the existential experience or the practical code of ethics independent of any specifically Christian beliefs (or after they have been dismissed as no longer rationally credible). Someone *could*, of course, define a Christian SC in terms devoid of theoretical content, offering an existential experience (say, the feeling of absolute dependence) or a moral code (requiring, for instance, compassionate regard for others) as sufficient; there is no way (and no reason) to police the application of the term "Christian." But it is hard to see why there would still be any point in making a case for such a SC as specifically Christian, let alone any point in worrying about the relation of Christianity, so defined, to natural science.[7]

VIII

The special relation between its doxastic and practical components distinguishes the Christian SC in important ways from the kind of SC entailed by inquiry in the natural sciences.

The core of scientific practice is one's set of beliefs or hypotheses and the accepted principles of inference (or criteria) by which they are judged. Likewise, as we have seen, Christianity includes some indispensable beliefs, such as claims about who God is and what God has done.

Of course, the scientist will also have a "scientific self-conception," a view of herself as a practicing scientist, which includes both normatively binding and nonnormative (person-relative) elements. On the normative side, scientific practice does include something like ethical theories: there are ways in which a scientist should proceed (for example, holding her theories open to criticism) and behaviors that are forbidden (lying about sources); these can even be formulated as ethical precepts ("scientists ought not to falsify their data"). Other features of the scientist's SC may be unique to her ("like my doctoral advisor, I prefer certain types of computer modeling techniques"; "the scientists I most admire run their labs in this way"). In both respects, a scientist's SC may be structurally similar to a religious or ordinary practical SC.

Nonetheless, scientific SCs play an essentially different role in science than Christian SCs do in Christianity. There are important differences between *being a Christian* and *being a biologist*—differences in source, in motivation, and in testability (see below). Perhaps most important for present purposes, the practical components of a scientist's SC *are not derived directly from her scientific theories themselves*. To the extent that a scientist reflects on her SC as a scientist, she does so in a manner analogous to the rational agent who reflects on how her conception of herself should guide her practical deliberation. Where a scientist's SC includes binding requirements on her, these are grounded in the need for intersubjective feedback and the careful evaluation of hypotheses, as in the case of the ordinary practical agent, and not in the specific conclusions of her discipline.

Apparently, then, we must distinguish rational inquiry in Christianity and in natural science in a crucial respect. Christianity is like science in that it begins with certain theoretical beliefs. It is unlike science in that these beliefs are intrinsically about how the Christian ought to act. The scientist, like the Christian, will hold a SC that contains elements above and beyond her theoretical beliefs. But whatever practical norms the scientist is required to adopt are derived from the necessity of intersubjective feedback and evaluation for doing science—just as the need for feedback gives rise to certain ethical norms that govern the practical reflection of any rational agent. In contrast both to science and to ordinary practical deliberation, what is practically binding for the Christian is inseparable from the theoretical content of her Christian beliefs.

IX

It is clear from the foregoing that the engagement of Christian theology with the natural sciences, and with other disciplines outside the confines of the Christian community itself, is unavoidable.

In fact, such an engagement is directly entailed by the need for intersubjective assessment of the Christian SC and its cognitive content. To hold a Christian SC rationally is precisely to seek critical feedback from the broader community on Christianity's doxastic claims and how well it does at maintaining them. Hence the rational pursuit of a Christian SC would seem to entail an ongoing interest in the outcome of rational discussion into the truth of Christian theoretical beliefs; and Christian hope itself, insofar as it is rational, must include a hope that such discussion will uphold the continuing rational attractiveness of Christian truth claims.

But the process cuts both ways. To put it bluntly, it is also possible that rational discussion will turn *against* Christian truth claims. We have seen that SCs do not have to be derived from reason alone, and hence that Christians have no rational obligation to believe only what results from scientific or philosophical debate. Still, to hold one's beliefs rationally is to hold them contingent on their seeming to remain the best explanations of the data in question. Should the debate indicate the preferability of naturalistic alternatives, or should it reveal inconsistencies in her system of beliefs, the Christian discussion participant must be prepared to acknowledge this outcome and to reflect on what it may entail.

X

Indeed, the most urgent task for Christian apologetics at the moment is to make Christian beliefs available to intersubjective assessment.

The apologetic task cannot be dropped. In light of what it means to hold a SC rationally, it is not enough for Christians merely to compare their beliefs with those of the broader community of inquiry—for example, by noting formal similarities between scientific and theological theories. (Such comparisons need not be rejected, but they are not sufficient for carrying out the project in question.)

In order to accomplish this task, we need to do more than merely show the coherence of Christian beliefs with other generally held beliefs. Coherence is, frankly, too low a standard, and too easily met: one can always adjust what needs adjusting, as some recent apologists have adjusted the terms of traditional theodicy to bring them into line with current accounts of natural process. Nonbelievers are perfectly happy with, because perfectly indifferent to, attempts to bring religious beliefs into line with the beliefs they already hold.

More urgent, and far more difficult, is the task of holding Christian proposals open to genuine criticism from others—indeed, of showing Christian beliefs to represent the better explanation of some body of data. Christian discussion with the sciences should thus include discussion of the overall case for Christianity, spelling out the various areas in which Christians are engaged in discourse concerning their rational credentials. (One cannot just apply the Trinity to cosmology without asking about the rational credentials of the doctrine of the Trinity itself.) Theological participants in the religion-science discussion must *also* continue to worry about the truth of Christian claims, since otherwise they may rest content with comparisons that only superficially resemble genuine critical assessment.

Accomplishing this task involves making religious beliefs available to intersubjective assessment—translating them into the terms, and connecting them with the kinds of evidence, that will make them genuinely discussible by a broad community of inquiry that comprises believers and nonbelievers alike. The need is for the religion-science discussion to become a "correspondent" discussion, that is, one in which there is a "correspondence" between successive theories, rather than the abandonment of one theory or approach for its opposite or contrary.[8] In order to maintain this sort of rational accessibility, Christian participants in the religion-science discussion must avoid immunizing techniques.[9] The likelihood of receiving genuine feedback is increased by the use of risky theological hypotheses (those with enough content that they *can* be shown to be false), by the careful presentation of one's claims and supporting arguments, and by the indication of how the success or failure of a given claim will affect other areas of one's system of beliefs. Proscribed would be, for example, claims that Christian beliefs are inaccessible to rational assessment, or that Christians possess principles of inference unique to them, or that theological models in the religion-science debate lack the requirement of scientific models to demonstrate their explanatory value.

XI

Various difficulties, however, have prevented the religion-science discussion from making the advances in intersubjective assessment to which Christians are rationally committed.

The distinctiveness of the Christian SC helps to explain why it is difficult to set up actual explanatory contests between cognitive claims from the diverse fields of religion and science. In many cases there will be no obvious way to devise such a contest, give the role of metaphysical and historical claims that are not immediately testable, and the differing levels and structures of discourse (including differing relations between theoretical and practical requirements—see Thesis VIII above) in the two fields. Consequently, although the goal is to determine rationally whether naturalistic or theistic accounts provide the better inference from (or explanation of) the data, discussion with the natural sciences has rarely progressed beyond a comparative discussion of the models in each field and the preparation of "translation manuals" between them.

In the typical case that figures in the religion-science discussion—for instance, the case of cosmological explanation—the comparison of theological doctrines with the results of scientific inquiry falls short of genuine critical competition. It may lead a theologian to favor certain traditional alternatives over others, or even to devise new theological theories. Thus a discovery by physicists that the universe appeared to lack a temporal origin would tend to favor a metaphysical over a temporal interpretation of divine creation.[10] But it would be a category mistake to view the theologian's claim about the ultimate origin of all things as an attempt to explain what the physical cosmologist tries to explain, namely, the origin of the observable universe.

In order better to understand why these difficulties arise, imagine the case of an ideally rational religion-science interchange. In this thought experiment, one would be trying to convert a theological proposal into something that could be assessed in a debate that includes non-Christian scientists and philosophers. At any given time, the discussion participants would include a (roughly) equal number of constructive theologians and scientists, with a balance among atheists, agnostics, and theists. The theologians would begin with the minimal doxastic beliefs of Christianity, and would formulate ever-larger portions of the Christian tradition in such a way that they would be available to intersubjective debate.

But there are problems besetting such a dialogue, even in its idealized form. For instance, why not expect scientists, at least in their capacity *as* scientists, simply to ignore supernaturalistic hypotheses on methodological grounds?[11] Wouldn't—shouldn't—a physicist always argue that the naturalistic account of a given phenomenon provides a better explanation than a theistic account? Would the debate ever lead scientists to abandon their naturalistic methodological assumptions as ungrounded? That is, would it ever make sense for an evolutionary biologist to conclude, "OK, you've got me there: *that* mutation had to be divinely inspired"?

The goal, we suggest, is that theological proposals be available to discussion and criticism in the way scientific proposals are available to discussion and criticism (or something like that way). This is not itself part of the religion-science discussion, but a necessary precondition (or accompaniment) of it. For example, in the review cited in Note 8, William Stoeger is able to argue that contemporary physical cosmology is subject to testing in a variety of areas, and that some positions (for instance, steady state theory) have been decisively rejected. If Christian theology is to be a rational discourse, must we not be able to say the same thing about at least some *theological* options? But it will not be possible to note such progress and to keep track of the options that have been tried and abandoned if we draw upon theological models at will, using them when and in the respects that they are helpful to us, and setting them conveniently aside at other times. It would thus be a mistake to take theological proposals for granted and then to compare them with scientific proposals to see where they match up with each other, except in cases where this process shows some prospect of yielding critical feedback regarding Christian truth claims themselves.

In fact, for reasons whose explanation falls outside the scope of the present paper, it seems to us that the only cases in which theological and naturalistic claims genuinely compete as rival explanations of the same phenomena are cases of alleged miracles, such as the Resurrection, where naturalistic and supernaturalistic explanations are genuinely incompatible. Otherwise, genuine competition is largely confined to the philosophical contest between naturalism and theism as rival explanations at the level of reality as a whole—a level that is, of course, beyond the reach of natural science.

XII

In conclusion, then, although comparative discussions of theological and scientific theories remain suggestive, they cannot be a substitute for the direct assessment of Christian beliefs themselves.

The rational demands of the Christian SC can only be met by a direct evaluation of Christian proposals themselves in the widest sense—that is, in the widest arena of discussion and in light of the broadest question: Are they true?

NOTES

1. We speak in this paper exclusively of Christianity. This is not, however, to privilege Christianity; rather, it expresses the conviction that Christians face some particular difficulties in the discussion with the sciences that Jews or Buddhists may well not have to worry about.

2. The following account of practical self-conceptions is excerpted from our article, "Ethics and Rationality," *American Philosophical Quarterly* 30 (1993), pp. 151–161.

3. We are not supposing that an agent ever begins with a fully formed SC, any more than we are supposing that an agent begins with a fully formed image of the relevant community of inquiry. Presumably an agent starts with motivations that point in the direction of various SCs and that provide hints as to the sort of inquirers whose opinions would be relevant to the rational assessment of each of those self-conceptions. Isolating one or more self-conceptions and defining the relevant community or communities is likely to be a long-term, if not indeed a lifelong, process.

4. It has also been the basic premise of discussions of scientific rationality since Karl Popper's 1935 *Logik der Forschung* (*The Logic of Scientific Discovery*) (London: Hutchinson, 1980). The most satisfactory statement of the position, we believe, is that of Imre Lakatos; see his "The Methodology of Scientific Research Programmes," in *Philosophical Papers*, Vol. 1, ed. John Worrall and Gregory Currie (Cambridge University Press, 1978). Recent applications of this theory of rationality to religion and theology include Philip Clayton, *Explanation from Physics to Theology: An Essay in Rationality and Religion* (New Haven: Yale University Press, 1989); Nancey Murphy, *Theology in the Age of Scientific Reasoning* (Ithaca: Cornell University Press, 1990); Michael Banner, *The Justification of Science and the Rationality of Religious Belief* (Oxford: Clarendon, 1990); and Wentzel van Huyssteen, *Theology and the Justification of Faith* (Grand Rapids: Eerdmans, 1989). For interchanges between these positions, see *Zygon* 27/2 (June 1992), pp. 221–234; *Zygon* 27/3 (September 1992); and the *CTNS Bulletin* 11/1 (Winter 1991), pp. 29ff.

5. Important recent presentations and defenses of this theory include Peter Lipton, *Inference to the Best Explanation* (London: Routledge and Kegan Paul, 1991), and Michael Banner's book, above.

6. Clayton has dubbed this type of person a *secular believer* and defended its compatibility with traditional religious belief in *Explanation from Physics to Theology,* ch. 5.

7. We are not suggesting that no one could ever have a reason to adopt a Christian SC that was defined exclusively in ethical or aesthetic terms. Indeed, it is easy to imagine an agent who might hold that the reduction of Christian claims to mere symbols of ethical attitudes or occasions of aesthetic experience is what makes them interesting—or even what makes them *tolerable*—for the first time. Consider, for instance, a feminist who decides to participate in the church for purely strategic reasons (because there are women there who need liberating from androcentric doctrines and patriarchal structures). All we can say about the *strategic* adoption of a Christian SC is that it can at best be a temporary measure; for as soon as the strategy succeeds (even if this takes a lifetime), the agent's Christian involvement ceases to matter. Or take the case of someone who goes to church out of a love of stained-glass windows; here again, we have no argument against this way of conceiving Christianity. The most we can say, in the present context, is that there is no interesting way to think about the relation of a Christianity defined in these terms to natural science.

8. The term is from A.G. Pacholczyk, *The Catastrophic Universe: An Essay in the Philosophy of Cosmology* (Tucson: Pachart, 1984); see the recent review by William R. Stoeger, SJ, in the

CTNS Bulletin 12/1 (Winter 1992): pp. 39–42. In Kuhnian terms, one should avoid the appearance (or the reality) of a series of radical paradigm shifts, where the newer paradigm is discontinuous with the previous. In more general terms, the ideal of rational progress presupposes that each new proposal will be rationally indicated by the previous ones, representing a progressive refinement of the starting position and one that is open to fewer and fewer counterexamples.

9. This may be said to have been the central thesis of Karl Popper's work in epistemology; see, e.g., *Conjectures and Refutations,* 4th ed. (London: Routledge and Kegan Paul, 1972) and *Objective Knowledge,* 2nd ed. (Oxford: Clarendon, 1979). Nothing in Lakatos's modifications of Popper calls this particular requirement into question.

10. See the paper by William R. Stoeger, SJ, "Key Developments in Physics Challenging Philosophy and Theology," in Case Study I, Part III of this volume.

11. Consider, for instance, the reasons mentioned by David L. Hull in his review of Phillip E. Johnson's attack on Darwin; *CTNS Bulletin* 12/1 (Winter 1992), pp. 31–33.

ROUND

II

ENTITLED CHRISTIAN BELIEF

NICHOLAS WOLTERSTORFF

A prominent theme in two of the papers from the first round of this exchange is that of *entitled Christian belief.* Rather than commenting on a variety of different topics from all of the first-round papers, I have decided to focus my reflections entirely on that one theme.

I. CLAYTON AND KNAPP ON ENTITLED BELIEF

Clayton and Knapp do not use the phrase "entitled Christian belief." Prominent in their paper are, instead, the words "rational" and "rationality." In philosophical discussion, I myself have adopted the policy of avoiding, if at all possible, the word "rational" and its cognates. The word has become so polymorphous as to have lost almost all utility. Clayton and Knapp themselves use it in a number of different senses. Nonetheless, it seems clear that most of the time they use "rational" as a synonym of "entitled." A rationally held belief is a belief which the person in question is entitled to hold; a rationally held self-conception is a self-conception which the person in question is entitled to hold; and so on. Rationality thus understood is a normative concept; specifically, it is the concept of being entitled to hold some belief.

Perhaps, though, Clayton and Knapp would not say of all cases of a person holding some belief entitledly that the person is holding it "rationally"; perhaps they would say this only of those cases in which *reasons* enter essentially into the conditions that account for the entitlement. That might be the import of their embrace of the distinction between "prerational and rational levels of belief and inquiry." They say that "Just as a practical self-conception typically begins with a set of prerational motivations, a religious [self-conception] typically begins with a prerational set of traditional beliefs. It is not necessary to derive Christian truth claims directly from reason or to claim that they are fully rational from the start. . . ."[1] Perhaps the thought here is that a truth claim which is not fully rational from the start may nonetheless be held entitledly from the start. Alternatively, perhaps the thought is that the concept of entitlement just lacks application to "prerational" beliefs.

In any case, my interest lies in what Clayton and Knapp offer as the criterion for entitlement (alternatively, for *rational* entitlement). The criterion is this: To hold "beliefs in a rational manner, I must hold them open to feedback. That is, I must be willing, at least in principle, to enter into rational discussion of them and to accept (and respond to) indications of how well they stand up to intersubjective criticism."[2] "The epistemic requirement for rationality is . . . that all beliefs (or groups of beliefs) that are shown to be less adequate than their rivals be rejected."[3] What exactly is it that is supposed to take place in the "rational discussion"? "The task of rational discussion," say Clayton and Knapp, "is to weigh competing explanations, whatever their respective sources, and to select the one or more that do the best job of explaining the data at hand."[4]

Christians are obligated to come to the position of holding their Christian beliefs "in a rational manner." Given what Clayton and Knapp see as the nature of "rational discussion," this implies that Christian beliefs are *explanations*. Clayton and Knapp themselves highlight this implication: "On this view, many Christian beliefs are potential explanations: they tell *why* certain data that need to be explained are the way they are; they *account for* certain facts about human existence. When I believe them, I believe they do a better job of explaining the data than the other explanatory hypotheses of which I am aware."[5] Clayton and Knapp do not explain what they have in mind by saying that *many*, rather than *all*, Christian beliefs, are potential explanations. But I surmise from the remainder of their article that, on their view, some Christian beliefs are *practical* beliefs, that is, beliefs pertaining to what may or should be done, or what would be good to do; and these are not explanations. Their full view appears to be, then, that all "theoretical" Christian beliefs, as they sometimes call them, have the character of explanations of data. And to hold such "beliefs rationally is to hold them contingent on their remaining the best explanations of the data in question."[6]

That last sentence puts the point in a rather more externalist fashion than Clayton and Knapp, as I understand them, mean it. The issue is not whether *in fact* they are the best explanations. The issue is whether the majority verdict of the relevant community is that they are the best explanation. Clayton and Knapp speak of the debate as *showing* Christian beliefs to represent the better explanation—showing, one presumes, to the majority of the relevant community. In any case, Clayton and Knapp insist that though "Christians have no rational obligation to believe *only* what results from scientific or philosophical debate," since self-conceptions "do not have to be derived from reason alone," nonetheless, to "hold a Christian [self-conception] rationally is precisely to seek critical feedback from the broader community on Christianity's doxastic claims and how well it does at maintaining them."[7]

The broader community to which Christians must submit their beliefs for appraisal, if they are to hold those beliefs rationally, is apparently the community of theoreticians in general. It will certainly not consist only of Christian theologians. It will include Christians who are scientists; and more broadly yet, it will include "non-Christian scientists and philosophers." The whole community of theoreticians—scientists and theologians, philosophers, and historians—will be invited to discuss with a view to assessing the *explanatory* beliefs of Christians. It is at precisely that point that the engagement of Christianity with natural science should be focused, say Clayton and Knapp. Often non-Christian members of the dialogic community will have alternative explanations of the data cited by Christians; thus contests will arise as to whose explanations are better. And sometimes scientists who are Christians will have alternative explanations to those cited by Christian theologians. Being entitled, or being *rationally* entitled, to continue in one's Christian belief depends on the outcome of such discussions.

What we have here is essentially an interesting variant on the classic Enlightenment understanding of the relation between Christianity and science. With all such understandings, including this one, I have my difficulties—more than I can mention here.

My fundamental difficulty lies in thinking of Christianity as an *explanation* of certain *data*, in conflict with alternative explanations of those same data. What are those data? A core element of Christian belief is that Jesus rose from the dead. Is one of the data in the region here that Jesus rose from the dead; and do Christians (and others) try to explain this datum? Or is there no such datum? Is it rather the case that the belief that Jesus rose from the dead is an *explanation* of something else which is the datum? What might that other datum be? The perceptions of Jesus by the disciples over some weeks, beginning three days after his burial? Is the doctrine of the Resurrection an explanation of that datum?

When Christians submit their explanatory beliefs to the assessment of the larger community, are they to gain prior consensus on data? If so, then of course this will not do as a datum, since many members of that larger community will not concede that the disciples perceived Jesus alive again some three days after his death.

To gain consensus on the data, presumably we shall have to retreat to some such things as *mental images*. But here we have to beware. The fact that we are not permitted to insert, into some discussion or other, that somebody perceived so-and-so, but only that he or she had such-and-such a mental image, does not prove that he or she did not perceive it—does not prove that perceptual beliefs are all explanations of mental states rather than reports of what actually happened.

My own conviction is that the disciples *perceived* Jesus alive again after his death; as it is my conviction that we human beings sometimes have *awareness* of God. Some reports of religious experience are indeed reports of states of consciousness; but some are reports of awareness of God. And sometimes beliefs about God which are not reports of awareness of God are nonetheless evoked in us immediately by one and another experience; they too are not explanations.

It would be possible for Clayton and Knapp to respond by conceding that they were mistaken in saying that Christian beliefs, other than the evaluative ones, are all explanatory in character, while insisting that they were nonetheless right in holding that entitlement to beliefs, or *rational* entitlement to them, depends on submitting them to the appraisal of the broader community and living with the outcome.

I myself think that, in one respect, this is too relaxed a view of entitlement. Clayton and Knapp say that the *source* of a belief does not enter into considerations of its (rational) entitlement; only how it stands up in the discussion. But sometimes we know very well, or ought to know, that the way we are forming our beliefs is not a reliable way; surely then source is relevant to entitlement. But let that pass. Suppose someone is persuaded that she has had an awareness of God—perhaps even that God has spoken to her. She now submits this to the "broader" community for its assessment. After a period of time, the verdict of the majority is rendered: she is mistaken, says the jury. She did not have an awareness of God; she only had certain subjective religious experiences. And of these, the Freudian explanation is the best.

I take it to be the view of Clayton and Knapp that if that is the verdict, then she is no longer entitled to her view. But why is that? Consider an analogue: all of the "objective" evidence available to the jury may point to Herbert having stolen the car. Yet I may have been walking by at 2:00 in the morning and distinctly saw Vincent driving off with it. Perhaps I ought to consider the evidence available to the jury so as to find out whether there is anything in that which would legitimately undermine my confidence. But it may well be that after doing so I am still fully entitled to my view—obligated even—no matter what the jury decides.

I do agree with the claim, or suggestion, of Clayton and Knapp that the Christian community is obligated to assess the import of whatever is seriously alleged against its beliefs. But it will have to assess the import *for itself*, and act accordingly. I fail to see any reason for supposing that, just because the verdict of the majority of the scholarly community goes against it, the Christian community is no longer entitled to its beliefs. The verdict which the non-Christian academic renders on Christian truth claims is neither some foundationally grounded, nor some generically human, verdict. It will be made within a framework of conviction containing a wide variety of contested items. I see no reason to think that the Christian is bound by such verdicts.

II. MURPHY ON ENTITLED BELIEF

Whereas Clayton and Knapp think that the Christianity/science dialogue should focus on the assessment by scientists and others of the explanatory claims of Christians, Nancey Murphy holds that those who are interested in both theology and science should explore whatever sorts of relations they can find between these two bodies of inquiry. I am with Professor Murphy on this issue. But I do not think finding such relations has quite the import that Professor Murphy thinks it has. Let me explain.

Central to Professor Murphy's discussion is her proposal that we replace the foundationalist account of knowledge and of justified belief with a "holist" account, and that, correspondingly, in our thinking about these matters we use Quine's image of a web of belief in place of the traditional picture of a building. She quotes a passage from Quine in which he explains something of what he has in mind by this metaphor.

But let us look closely at what exactly this metaphor is a metaphor for. Quine himself emphasizes two things. The web of belief "impinges on experience only along the edges." And though a "conflict with experience at the periphery" calls for redistribution of truth values over some of our statements, we always have considerable latitude as to how that redistribution will take place so as to attain "equilibrium." I myself think that redistribution of truth values is occasioned by a good many more things than what Quine would count as *experience*; apart from that, though, this picture seems to me generally correct. Against Quine, I do not think that it follows that there are no necessary truths; necessity is an ontological fact, revisability, an epistemological one. But it is true that, because of the "logical interconnections" of our beliefs, revising one belief typically requires revising others as well; and often one finds oneself confronted with live options for reachieving equilibrium.

I fail to see, however, that this tells us anything about knowledge. Presumably the idea behind calling it a "holistic account of knowledge" is that a belief is true just in case it belongs to an equilibrated web of beliefs. But suppose that you and I have virtually identical sets of beliefs; and that both of us experience something—the same thing—which we both recognize as calling for substantial revisions in our belief-webs. You revise in one way; I in another. At some points, then, there will be contradictions between our belief-webs. But then they cannot both be true; and so they cannot both constitute knowledge.

Though she does now and then speak of Quine as offering us a holistic picture of knowledge, Professor Murphy more often suggests that he offers us a holistic picture of *justified belief*—that is, of entitled belief. Specifically, as "with any other belief or subset of beliefs, justification consists in seeking relations between the disputed beliefs and parts of the web that we have no good reason to doubt."[8] Even without having in hand the details of this suggestion, however, I think we can see that it will not do. Suppose that someone comes to believe something on the basis of sloppy encyclopedia research—or even on the basis of sheer guesswork. The propositional content of the belief might fit very nicely into the person's whole web of beliefs—might even fit much better than the truth of the matter would fit! But surely the person would not be *entitled* to believe it. Quine's web metaphor focuses entirely on the logical interconnections among the propositional contents of a person's beliefs. But a conclusion that we drew earlier in our discussion of Clayton and Knapp is relevant here too: sometimes, at least the *source* of a belief—its mode of formation—is relevant to assessing its entitlement.

So I heartily endorse Professor Murphy's suggestion that we who are Christians should work to uncover and articulate whatever connections there may be between theology and science; and further, not just uncover and articulate connections between *extant* theology and *extant* science, but suggest and work out revisions in one or the other of these whenever we find revisions called for. In Professor Murphy's words, we must ask "where theology fits in the web of beliefs, and how it is interwoven with scientific beliefs."[9] I fail to see, though, that success in finding connections, or success in finding revisions which will recover equilibrium, does anything at all to *jus-*

tify Christian belief. A person who holds wildly eccentric religious beliefs will be able, given some imagination, to do the same. It's not true that "any logical relation between a theological belief and another part of the web is an evidential relation."[10]

NOTES

1. Clayton and Knapp, p. 134.
2. Clayton and Knapp, p. 134.
3. Clayton and Knapp, p. 135.
4. Clayton and Knapp, p. 134.
5. Clayton and Knapp, p. 134.
6. Clayton and Knapp, p. 138.
7. Clayton and Knapp, pp. 137, 138.
8. Murphy, p. 110.
9. Murphy, p. 112.
10. Murphy, p. 110, italics omitted.

ON THE NATURE
OF THEOLOGY

NANCEY MURPHY

I. INTRODUCTION

I shall begin my response by replying to the
paper by Mary Gerhart and Allan Melvin
Russell, since they present a view of theology
and its possible relations to science that is very
different from my own. The focus of my response will
be a discussion of the nature of theology and of theological
rationality. Having laid out my own view of theology, I shall turn to the paper by Philip
Clayton and Steven Knapp, with which I have a great deal more sympathy. My strategy
will be to indicate how *I* would have written their paper had it been my own. Finally, I
shall turn to Nicholas Wolterstorff's paper. Since I find myself in close agreement on
the issues he raises, I shall use his paper as a starting point for further reflection on
the parallels between theology and science.

II. GERHART AND RUSSELL ON THE NATURE OF THEOLOGY

Gerhart and Russell emphasize the differences between theology and the natural sciences. They use an interesting comparison to describe the character of theology: theology is to the empirical sciences as the sciences are to mathematics. In particular,
theology differs from empirical sciences in that it is incapable of the same sort of confirmation that is appropriate to the natural sciences.

My position on the character of theology is quite different. I have argued that theology differs only in degree from science—science can be confirmed by data that are
more precise than the data supporting theology. But to see the (actual or potential)
similarities between theological and scientific reasoning requires a more complicated
theory of scientific reasoning than Gerhart and Russell describe in their paper.[1]

The differences I have with the Gerhart-Russell position go much deeper, though,
than the disagreement over theories of confirmation. Gerhart and Russell state that
"[t]he dominant referent for theology would seem to be human experience, as
reported in texts and in living traditions, both past and present."[2] From my perspective, this description confuses two issues: what theology is *about* (that is, its "referent"), and the *source* of knowledge (that is, data) through which we obtain that

knowledge. I would say that while we do obtain theological knowledge through the "lived experiences of human-being,"[3] the referent of theology is God and God's relation to all that is.[4]

While I cannot provide adequate arguments here for the claim that theology is a science-like discipline whose object is God, I think I can show that the Gerhart-Russell view of the nature of theology actually requires a view much like my own in order to succeed. They speak of theology as working within the world of "meanings"—a term often used these days in accounts of theology. I must confess I have never been sure I understand what is meant by "meanings" in this context, but allow me to offer what I take to be an example.

In a recent paper, Holmes Rolston addressed the issue of suffering and death in the animal world.[5] Earlier, Christians interpreted this fact as a consequence of the Fall, but the study of biology has made it clear that the death of countless animals not only *did* precede the first human sin, but was a necessary condition for human beings to come on to the scene at all. "We really cannot envision a world, on any Earth more or less like our own, which can give birth to the myriad forms of life that have been generated here, without some things eating other things."[6]

Rolston's response to this "fact" of biology is to interpret animal pain and death in light of the cross and the Resurrection. The God we have come to know in the passion of Christ is the God who is constantly suffering in and with creation, but who is also constantly resurrecting life out of chaos, goodness out of evil:

> The secret of life is seen now to lie not so much in the heredity molecules, not so much in natural selection and the survival of the fittest. . . . The secret of life is that it is a passion play. Things perish in tragedy. The religions knew that full well, before biology arose to reconfirm it. But things perish with a passing over in which the sacrificed individual also flows in the river of life. Each of the suffering creatures is delivered over as an innocent sacrificed to preserve a line, a blood sacrifice perishing that others may live. We have a kind of "slaughter of the innocents," a nonmoral, naturalistic harbinger of the slaughter of the innocents at the birth of the Christ, all perhaps vignettes hinting of the innocent lamb slain from the foundation of the world. They share the labor of the divinity. In their lives, beautiful, tragic, and perpetually incomplete, they speak for God; they prophesy as they participate in the divine pathos. All have "borne our griefs and carried our sorrows." The abundant life that Jesus exemplifies and offers to his disciples is that of a sacrificial suffering through to something higher. There is something divine about the power to suffer through to something higher. The Spirit of God is the genius that makes alive, that redeems life from its evils. The cruciform creation is, in the end, deiform, godly, just because of this element of struggle, not in spite of it . . . God rescues from suffering, but the Judeo-Christian faith never teaches that God eschews suffering in the achievement of the divine purposes. To the contrary, seen in the paradigm of the cross, God too suffers, not less than his creatures, in order to gain for his creatures a more abundant life.[7]

So here Rolston is claiming that the death and Resurrection of Christ provide an ultimate paradigm for interpreting other instances of death and suffering, even those in
the animal world.

Is this an instance of theology doing what it is intended to do? I say, emphatically:
yes! Is it adequately described as the provision of *meaning*—an interpretation in light of
the experience of human-being that goes beyond the verifiable facts of science? Yes and
no. It does go beyond the scientific facts, but notice that the interpretation, the meaning bestowed on the biological state of affairs, is only available because of the historical
figure of Jesus, and the fact that he died by crucifixion, and that afterwards something
happened of so strange a nature that his disciples could only describe it metaphorically
as his "Resurrection." If it is not in some fairly straightforward sense *true* that the creator of this kingdom of beasts has raised Jesus from death, then what grounds have we
for Rolston's theological interpretation of animal death as sacrifice, as "sharing in the
labor of divinity"?

My point is simply that facts and meanings cannot be neatly separated. If theological meanings are not grounded in theological facts—facts about the character and acts
of God, in particular, then they are mere fairy tales, however comforting they may be.
Not the opiate of the masses, but the opiate of the intelligentsia.

Thus, I believe the correct view of theology is to say that while it serves the purpose
of giving meaning to our lives, this cannot be its defining feature. Instead, the central
business of theology must be an examination of the claims about God and God's relation to us that give substance to our interpretations of experience. It must be, in short,
the science of God. And its claims must be supported by means of arguments. These
arguments turn out to be very similar, in their form and complexity, to those used to
support scientific research programs.

I have described my own view of theology in contrast to that of Gerhart and Russell;
Clayton and Knapp present a similar contrast between "conservative" and "liberal"
views of theology. Conservative theologians emphasize the propositional content of
Christianity; liberals have treated Christianity as "an ethical ideal, a stance toward life,"
"inspired by a particular historical story but not bound by it."[8] What accounts for this
wide diversity in views about the nature of theology? Part of the answer is found in
Wolterstorff's account of modern thought—the parcelling out of human life and
thought into discrete spheres. This is not a complete account, however, since we still
want to know why religion and theology (for the liberal tradition) ended up in the
sphere of the ethical or the expressive, rather than the cognitive.

The answer I suggest is the following: the rise of modern science posed a threat to
theology, both in virtue of its content and of its method. The content of modern science conflicted with a theology worked out in terms of medieval cosmology. The scientific method represented the rejection of an epistemology based on authority. There
were at that time only two options: to ignore the advances of modernity, or to insulate
theology in one way or another from the threat from science.[9]

What we see in the views of Gerhart and Russell is an extension of the modern liberal tradition. What we see in the writings of Knapp, Clayton, and Wolterstorff (as well as in my own writings) is a variety of attempts to get beyond the dichotomy between liberal and conservative. These attempts have some hope for success because many of the assumptions of modernity regarding knowledge and language have been overturned. Another way of putting this is to say that we now have at our disposal new and more sophisticated philosophical tools to use in examining and explaining theological rationality.

This brings me to a point of agreement with Gerhart and Russell. They claim that science has an indirect effect on theology by "increasing the scope of human awareness, by making possible a broader, more flexible, more imaginative human mind."[10] One instance of the broader and more flexible thinking that I have in mind is the more sophisticated understanding of theoretical reasoning that the development of contemporary science has thrust upon us—a conception of reason that is, at long last, sophisticated enough to account for theological rationality as well.

A second broadening effect of recent science has been to require us to accept the fact that much of our knowledge is not only of the invisible, but even of the unimaginable. It used to be possible to criticize theologians for speaking of realities that could not be imagined; but the theologian can now answer the cosmologist or the physicist with a *tu quoque* (you also) argument.

III. CLAYTON AND KNAPP ON THEOLOGICAL RATIONALITY

Clayton and Knapp present an argument that closely parallels the one I have made above: I have argued that theology necessarily involves making truth claims about God in order to justify Christian interpretations of experience; Clayton and Knapp argue that while Christianity may be understood in terms of an existential experience or a moral code, a rational conception of oneself as a Christian requires commitment to at least a small number of beliefs about God, Christ, and the church. However, they side with the liberals against the conservative theological tradition by claiming that Christianity cannot be reduced to its propositional content.

I believe it would be helpful at this point to make as clear a distinction as we can between the Christian *religion* and Christian *theology*. The Christian religion is a complex phenomenon that involves beliefs, moral standards, worship, and other practices. Clayton and Knapp are correct that the Christian religion cannot be reduced to a set of beliefs; Gerhart and Russell are also correct in claiming that religion has much to do with providing a meaningful interpretation of human experience. Doing theology is a part of being a Christian, but not something all Christians have to do to be Christian. We might define Christian theology as the discovery, understanding, and justification of the convictions that are held by Christians or presupposed by their beliefs and practices.[11] Another way of putting it: theology is a second-order discipline that investigates the theories that must be true (or well supported) if the practices and beliefs of Christians are to make sense. While I do not think that it is helpful to compare the Christian religion with science, I do believe it makes sense to compare *doing* theology with *doing* science, and to relate the propositional content of theology to the content of science.

If I were to rewrite Clayton's and Knapp's paper, one alteration I would make throughout would be to consider the conditions for rational *theologizing*, rather than for religious belief.

A second change I would make would be not to ask about the requirements for an individual self-conception to be held rationally; instead I would concentrate on a community's or tradition's conception of what it is to be human, and what counts as the good life for a human being.

I will not, of course, rewrite the whole of the Clayton-Knapp paper, but merely sketch out how it would go with these two "transpositions": from the level of *individual religious* belief to the level of *communal theological* rationality. My hope is that their arguments will not only be preserved through this transformation, but will become even more compelling. My version goes as follows:

In order to answer questions within the realm of practical rationality, especially ethical questions, it is necessary to have a concept of the nature and purpose of human life. That is, each community, insofar as its deliberation is rational, must have some grasp, however minimal, of the purposes and goals that go with being the sort of beings they take themselves to be.[12] Religious traditions are one source of such conceptions.

The fact that there is a rational imperative to have a conception of human nature and of the human good does not mean, however, that such conceptions are derived from rationality. A community's obligation is, rather, to hold its tradition open to challenges from other traditions. Rationality presupposes some standards whereby competing traditions can be rationally evaluated.[13]

To be a part of a community, with its tradition and its traditional conception of the end of human life, includes certain intrinsic theoretical beliefs. For a conception of human nature to be a Christian conception, it must be related intrinsically to certain minimal doxastic requirements: belief in a Creator-God, belief in the unique authority of Jesus, and belief in the necessity of Christian community.[14]

Because traditions are justified not by their source but by their openness to the insights and criticisms from other traditions, Christians are justified in introducing proposals whose source lies in alleged divine revelation.

It is clear from the foregoing that the engagement of the Christian tradition with natural-scientific traditions is unavoidable. Indeed, the most urgent task for Christian apologetics at the moment is to make the Christian tradition available to assessment in light of other traditions.[15]

Let me stop my translation of Clayton and Knapp at this point, and turn to commentary. The point I wish to make is that questions of rationality have become doubly complex in our era. I raised the issue in my own paper for this volume: while holist epistemology offers new insights for answering questions about the rationality of individual beliefs, it raises new and more difficult questions about the rationality of entire webs or networks of beliefs. We may justify a single theological belief by showing that it is well connected with other beliefs that we have no good reason to call into question. But for Christians in a post-Christian world there seems always to be reason for calling the whole system into question.

The epistemological problem that emerges from this holist approach, and also from my translation from the level of individual believer to the beliefs of the whole community is this: What is the counterpart to Knapp's and Clayton's "intersubjective criticizability"? What are the criteria for criticizing and justifying entire traditions?

Readers familiar with recent works by Alasdair MacIntyre will recognize his influence in my transposition of Clayton's and Knapp's proposals, and it is MacIntyre, I believe, who offers the best account to date of what it takes to criticize or justify an entire tradition. In briefest summary, he claims that a tradition is *justified* or *vindicated* when its adherents have exposed it to dialectical questioning—that is, have raised questions and problems for it not only from its own point of view, but also from the points of view of its rival traditions—and have shown that it can be reformulated, in a way faithful to its formative texts, in order to solve those problems and answer those questions. Further, a tradition is shown *superior* to its rival if it can solve its rival's problems while the rival cannot solve its own.

This is a tall order. The only thing that makes it seem reasonable to demand such intellectual feats is the fact that MacIntyre himself has gone a long way toward reformulating and vindicating the Aristotelian-Thomist tradition in ethics.[16] It is obvious that no single scholar can complete the task that rationality seems to demand; if for no other reason, this fact alone would make it necessary to view theoretical rationality as a property of communities rather than of individual thinkers.

IV. WOLTERSTORFF'S CONTROL BELIEFS IN SCIENCE AND THEOLOGY

Wolterstorff has made an important comparison between science and religion. His original contribution to the understanding of science was to call attention to the role of control beliefs: beliefs about what counts as a suitable kind of theory for science. In his paper for this volume, he points out that religious communities have not only their canonical texts and interpretations of the texts, but also "canonical beliefs" about the kind of benefits the texts are to be expected to provide to the community. Science, in its quest for equilibrium (consistency) can and does make changes in all of its three kinds of beliefs; Christians, likewise, can make changes in beliefs about what texts are canonical, in their interpretations of the texts, and in their canonical beliefs.

Religion and science can influence one another when positions in one discipline suggest changes in the control or canonical beliefs of the other. Wolterstorff has mentioned one fateful instance of change in religion: the introduction of canonical beliefs that count any perceived conflict between canonical texts or interpretations as the result of a wrongheaded view of religion—religion and science are just "into different things."[17]

I would like to propose, as I did above in the discussion of the paper by Knapp and Clayton, that we "transpose" Wolterstorff's views from religion to theology. In this case, we see a closer parallel between theology and science than the one Wolterstorff has noted between religion and science. And we can translate his point about equilibrium-seeking between science and religion into the following: liberal theologians since Friedrich Schleiermacher can be taken to have introduced new control beliefs regarding the nature of theological theories—describing them as being in the first instance descriptions of human religious awareness, or expressions of values or meanings, or of moral commitments. I suggested above that these changes were motivated, at least in part, by a desire to avoid conflict with science.

I want to pursue, now, a few more similarities between theology and science. If we appropriate from Wolterstorff the idea of equilibrium among data, theories, and control beliefs, what parallels do we find in theology? It might be suggested that canonical texts play the same role in theology as data do in science. However, this raises an important question for theology: there seems to be no justification needed for taking scientific data *as* data, but it does seem to be necessary to justify taking the texts as data. Is such a justification necessary, and if so, how can it be provided? Two replies might be made. First, the issue is not so simple in science. The results of experiments, of observations made by means of complex measuring instruments, *do* need to be justified as appropriate data for the theory they are used to support. To take a simple example, one needs the kinetic theory to justify the use of a glass tube containing mercury or alcohol to measure a property called "temperature." In philosophy of science, the theories that justify the use of such measures are called theories of *instrumentation*. In theology, theories of *interpretation* play an analogous role—theories regarding the nature of the texts: records of religious experience, or records of salvation history, or products of divine dictation. These theories in turn have specific consequences for the ways it will be appropriate to use the texts for theological purposes. So the differences between science and theology are not as sharp as our original question suggested.

A second sort of reply to the question of why it is legitimate to begin with the canonical texts can be found in the writings of both David Kelsey and MacIntyre. Kelsey claims that to say the Christian scriptures are authoritative for Christian theology is analytic—this is just what it *means* to call texts "scripture."[18] MacIntyre adds that a tradition just *is* an ongoing argument about how best to interpret and apply its formative texts. All traditions have formative texts; traditions are constituted when succeeding generations apply them to new situations.

Thus I suggest a more complex view of theology than the one that arises immediately from Wolterstorff's account of the use of canonical texts. Christian theologians seek equilibrium among a number of factors: the texts, and theories of interpretation; theological theories, and theological control beliefs; current experience, and associated theories about appropriate kinds of experience and how it is to be related to the theological enterprise.

Consequently, texts are to be compared not so much to scientific data as they are to classic texts within a scientific tradition. Thomas Kuhn has, in fact, argued for the importance of classic textbooks in establishing a scientific paradigm.[19] So while there is certainly a difference between the Christian theologian's willingness to give up on the Christian scriptures and the scientist's willingness to change paradigms, this is a difference of degree, not a difference in kind.

V. CONCLUSION

I have directed this second-round contribution primarily to the issue of the nature of theology. It may be valuable, in concluding, to indicate why this topic is an appropriate one to pursue in a volume on the relations between theology and science. There have been two influential views of the relations between these two kinds of disciplines: one is the "two-worlds" or "two-languages" view, which insulates the disciplines from one another by emphasizing their differences. The other is the "conflict" model, which takes theology and science to be quite similar in kind, but finds them regularly at war with one another.

If dialogue between theology and science is to be possible, especially if it is to be a two-way conversation, it is important to show that the disciplines are similar enough to be able to speak to one another and learn from one another.

An interesting fact about the short history of the dialogue between theology and science is that it has caused a number of thinkers to reevaluate the status of theology as an intellectual discipline, whether or not this was the intention of the theologians who initiated the dialogue. The dialogue has gone a long way toward ending "the warfare of science with religion"; the reevaluation of the status of theology that it has prompted may go a long way toward softening the differences between conservative and liberal theologians. The latter is my fervent hope.

NOTES

1. See Murphy, *Theology in the Age of Scientific Reasoning* (Ithaca, NY: Cornell University Press, 1990).
2. Gerhart and Russell, p. 123.
3. Gerhart and Russell, p. 123.
4. I do not know how to reconcile the statements that the referent of theology is human experience, and that "when the last human being to verify a theological proposition dies, the

theological truth of that proposition dies" (Gerhart and Russell, p. 124) with the implication that theology intends to make intelligible claims about God, freedom, and immortality. This latter statement contradicts my account of Gerhart's and Russell's position, but the remainder of their paper seems consistent with my interpretation.

5. Holmes Rolston, "Does Nature Need to be Redeemed?" presented at the November, 1992 meeting of the Theology and Science group of the American Academy of Religion.

6. "Does Nature Need to be Redeemed?," p. 11.

7. "Does Nature Need to be Redeemed?," p. 19.

8. Clayton and Knapp, p. 136.

9. See *Theology in the Age of Scientific Reasoning*, ch. 1.

10. Gerhart and Russell, p. 128.

11. For a comparable view, see James Wm. McClendon, Jr. and James M. Smith, *Understanding Religious Convictions* (Notre Dame, IN: University of Notre Dame Press, 1975).

12. Clayton and Knapp, p. 131.

13. Clayton and Knapp, p. 132.

14. Clayton and Knapp, p. 133.

15. Clayton and Knapp, p. 138.

16. Two of MacIntyre's works have influenced this presentation. In *After Virtue* (Notre Dame: University of Notre Dame Press, 1981) he argues that the justification of ethical positions requires a concept of the human good that can best be supplied by a tradition, such as the Aristotelian or Christian traditions. In *Whose Justice? Which Rationality?* (Notre Dame: University of Notre Dame Press, 1988) he undertakes the justification of the Aristotelian tradition of the virtues, and both illustrates and defines the criteria for judging one tradition superior to another.

17. Wolterstorff, p. 103.

18. See David Kelsey, *The Uses of Scripture in Recent Theology* (Philadelphia: Fortress Press, 1975).

19. See Thomas Kuhn, *The Structure of Scientific Revolutions*, 2nd ed. (Chicago: University of Chicago Press, 1970).

IS HOLISTIC JUSTIFICATION ENOUGH?

I. INTRODUCTION

PHILIP CLAYTON AND STEVEN KNAPP

We find ourselves admiring, and even agreeing with, much of what is said by our colleagues in their contributions to Round I of this discussion. Mary Gerhart and Allan Melvin Russell in their paper, and Nancey Murphy in hers, do a fine job of locating numerous analogies and points of intersection between science and theology. As Gerhart and Russell point out, science constrains religious belief in the sense of establishing "what [it is] possible for human beings to believe in the light of what natural science has learned is highly probable about the world."[1] Also, they are certainly right that there is a continuum in the rigor of testability as one moves from mathematics through the natural sciences to theology: strict deduction, formal validity, and conclusive falsification characterize mathematical reasoning, whereas empirical testing, explicit predictions, and (at least partial) verification represent the distinctive strengths of natural scientific reasoning. By contrast, theological reasoning begins with "the lived experiences of human-being"[2]; its starting point is not (in the first place) empirical data but texts, symbols, and practices; and it must remain sensitive to the "world of meanings" of particular religious traditions. We disagree that theologians must as a result "forego" empirical truths,[3] if by this Gerhart and Russell mean that there are and can be *no* direct evidential or entailment relations between science and theology. Still, the methodological commonalities between the two fields, argued in recent works on Lakatos's philosophy of science, must not be allowed to obscure the distinctive features of testing in the case of theology.[4]

In his contribution, Nicholas Wolterstorff provides a clear summary, but also an interesting correction or at least extension, of his argument in his influential 1976 work *Reason within the Limits of Religion*[5]; we think in particular of his new focus on the way epistemic agents and communities handle conflicts that arise among the various kinds or levels of belief involved in what he calls "theory weighing." Wolterstorff convincingly shows how the restoration of epistemic "equilibrium" depends on reciprocal effects of "data," "theory," and "theory constraints"; the result is a holistic picture of epistemic stability and change that seems closely similar in many respects to the Quinian holistic picture presented by Murphy.

The similarity is not surprising, since Murphy and Wolterstorff both reject founda-tionalism, which Murphy, however, also associates with what she calls "modernism." Presumably, what Murphy calls "postmodernism" and what Wolterstorff would call "antifoundationalism" amount to essentially the same position.[6] So rather than devel-oping any further the terms of this particular agreement, we concentrate on two other issues: first, the contention that scientific and Christian beliefs are epistemically on a par, and second, the question of whether it is sufficient, if one wishes to increase the justification of theological beliefs, to establish coherential relations between theology and science. We then turn to a closer look at the "justifying" relations that Murphy pro-poses, before concluding with a brief explanation of what we take to be the most urgent apologetic task confronting Christian theology at the present time.

II. EPISTEMIC PARITY BETWEEN SCIENTIFIC AND CHRISTIAN BELIEFS?

Murphy and Wolterstorff agree in positing a certain reciprocal relation between scientific and religious inquiry; they also agree that Christianity and science, as Wolterstorff puts it, "overlap in their concerns."[7] But for Wolterstorff, the reciprocity or mutual influence of science and religion seems to amount to a kind of symmetry or parity. Hence he writes that:

> in the ongoing struggle of those of us who are both Christians and theorists to bring our faith and our science into satisfactory equilibrium, the revisions required can go either way. Sometimes the best strategy is to revise something in our complex of Christian belief; but sometimes the best strategy is, on the contrary, to revise something in what science presents to us.

And he therefore rejects what he sees as "a deep tendency in most contemporary mem-bers of the academy in the West to assume that, in case of conflict between science and religion, religion has to give."[8]

Murphy would seem to be one of the contemporary academics Wolterstorff has in mind; at least she seems to grant scientific belief an impressive epistemic (or at least doxastic) privilege that she withholds from Christian belief. Unlike Christian belief, what Murphy calls "the Western scientific worldview" is in an important sense indubitable; for her, the task is "to justify the inclusion of Christian theology within" it.[9] Now one might think that abandoning epistemological foundations would lead to sheer relativism; for if our sense of what is true depends only on the holistic interrelations of *our* beliefs, how can we justify a preference for *our* web of beliefs over someone else's web of beliefs? But, according to Murphy, the relativist mistakenly (indeed, incoherently) supposes that we can stand altogether outside our web of beliefs, in order to see how it compares to someone else's web. And we cannot; for "it is impossible to call all of one's beliefs into question at once."[10] What makes this impossible is the fact that the total set of beliefs one was questioning would have to include the very beliefs one was relying on in calling one's beliefs into question.

But this argument against relativism only works at the level of one's *total* web of beliefs; particular beliefs, and sets of belief that form only parts of one's total web, *can* be questioned without the futility or absurdity of trying to question all one's beliefs at once. Thus Christian belief is a significant part of a believer's web, but it is still only a part; so "it *is* possible to call the whole of Christian belief into question without disturbing much of the rest of the web"; and we know this is so, Murphy writes, "since we live our lives in the company of those who have done so."[11] Hence the crucial lack of parity between science and Christianity: it is "not possible or necessary," according to Murphy, "to justify the Western scientific worldview," but "it *is* necessary to justify the inclusion of Christianity within that web of beliefs." In this respect, Murphy explicitly sets herself apart from "postmodern theologians" such as Lindbeck and Thiemann,[12] and implicitly sets herself apart as well, it seems, from Wolterstorff.[13]

It is here, on the need for (nonfoundational) justification, that Murphy's position comes closest to ours. In "Rationality and Christian Self-Conceptions," we argue that critical feedback from others is necessary for holding a self-conception (SC) rationally. The goal, for the agent herself, is to acquire the sort of feedback that will determine whether the criteria that she takes to indicate success in her project actually do indicate such success—and, of course, whether she in fact meets those criteria. The question then becomes: What would constitute the right sort of feedback regarding the truth of a Christian SC? And how do we solicit it, that is, put ourselves in the epistemic position in which we might obtain it?

Where do the other authors come down on these questions? The dialogue and the "listening" that Wolterstorff envisions between science and theology are certainly not *in*consistent with our notion of religious self-conceptions. Still, there is no indication in his essay that Wolterstorff thinks, as we do, that to be at least interested in critical feedback from beyond the boundaries of the Christian community is an essential part of what is involved in rationally pursuing a Christian SC.

Murphy comes closer: for her, the dialogue with science is apparently more than optional, since, as we have noted, she stresses the necessity of justifying the inclusion of Christian beliefs within broader web beliefs that she identifies as the Western scientific worldview. In our terms, this would amount to saying that a Christian who wants to pursue her SC rationally cannot rest content with critical feedback from the Christian community itself, but is compelled to find out whether her beliefs can also be justified within the terms of the broader community or communities in which the Christian also participates. Nor is there any way to limit in advance the scope of such an inquiry.

III. ARE MURPHY'S JUSTIFICATORY RELATIONS ENOUGH?

Unfortunately, as we see the matter, Murphy's notion of what counts as "justification" is so broad—in our terms, her standards of confirming feedback are so generous—that, by the end of her essay, it is hard to see *why* she thinks justification is necessary after all. Consider, for instance, her summary of the various ways, explored in her essay, of connecting Christian beliefs to "the rest of the web." According to Murphy, these merely illustrate "the variety of kinds of connections that are possible"; others "could have been mentioned."[14] The crucial point is that she sees them as kinds of relation that help to "justify the inclusion of Christian theology within the Western scientific worldview"; and she sees them in this light because, "with a holist epistemological model, any logical relation between a theological belief and another part of the web *is* an evidential relation."[15] Here is Murphy's list of justificatory relations:

> direct implication of theological conclusion from scientific theories; mutual implication of a philosophical position by both theology and science; ethical implications drawn from a union of theological and scientific theories; arguments from science to a theological conclusion via hypothetico-deductive reasoning; control beliefs for scientific theories drawn from theology; control beliefs for theological theories drawn from science; and, finally, complex combinations of such relations.[16]

There is much that is interesting about these relations, each of which Murphy suggestively develops in the course of her paper. One of them—hypothetico-deductive reasoning, exemplified earlier in Murphy's essay by a new version of the argument from design—seems evidential in a quite familiar sense. After all, what better way to justify the inclusion of Christian theological beliefs in the Western scientific web than to show (if this is indeed possible) that a certain Christian belief does the best job of explaining some set of scientific data? Most of Murphy's connections, however, would seem to have little or nothing to do with justifying Christian beliefs themselves, no matter how holistically one construes the task of justification. Look again at the first kind of connection Murphy offers: "direct implication of theological conclusion from scientific theories." Her example[17] is the possibility that a new cosmological theory may force theology to abandon the notion of a specific creation event. But the fact that a scientific theory may cause a *revision* of Christian beliefs hardly shows that Christian beliefs are justified in the first place!

Or consider Murphy's second kind of connection, "mutual implication"; her example is a case where "a particular view in science and a particular view in theology each shape a philosophical theory (about the nature of time), and these philosophical positions turn out to be the same or highly congruent."[18] While this outcome may encourage a person who already holds Christian beliefs and scientific beliefs to endorse the philosophical theories to which their Christian and scientific beliefs both point, in what way does it add to the justification of that person's Christian beliefs, *or* her scientific ones? My trusting the *National Enquirer* and my trusting Carl Sagan may give me more reason to believe in extraterrestrial life than I would have if I trusted only one of them, but it is hard to see how this fortunate convergence would justify my trusting the *National Enquirer* (or my trusting Sagan).

We mentioned earlier that one of the kinds of connection Murphy discusses *does* seem to us to bear directly on the project of justifying Christian beliefs in the context of a broader community of inquiry, rather than merely linking them in one way or another to extra-Christian beliefs. Thus, as an example of "hypothetico-deductive reasoning," or what we would call *inference to the best explanation* (IBE),[19] Murphy asks what is the best way to account for the apparent fact that our universe is capable of sustaining life and consciousness, whereas a universe whose physical conditions differed only slightly from the ones that obtain in our universe would have been "an uninhabited waste."[20] If it is true that naturalism cannot explain this fact but theism can do so convincingly (and if it is true, as we ourselves happen to doubt, that the data in question actually needs the kind of explanation Murphy supposes it does), then the relative explanatory success of theism will indeed increase one's justification for including theistic beliefs within one's scientific worldview.

Another of Murphy's examples—Arthur Peacocke's theory of top-down causation[21]— strikes us as providing a somewhat more promising opportunity for testing Christian beliefs by means of IBE, although Murphy herself introduces it as an example not of IBE, but of the influence on theology of a scientific "control belief." Peacocke's theory, as Murphy develops it, suggests that human behavior will be better explained by an account that makes room for "counterdeterministic" influences (for instance, from human consciousness) than by an account that relies exclusively on causal factors, such as genetic determinants, that operate "from below." If it turns out that Peacocke's theory of causation does the better job of explaining human behavior, and if Peacocke's theory is (as it seems to be) more readily compatible with theism than with naturalism, then we will indeed have arrived at a case where Christian beliefs have been (partly) confirmed via feedback from a community of inquiry whose boundaries extend beyond those of the Christian community itself. But this is because the Christian beliefs in question will have been tested against the standards of the broader community (to which, as Murphy points out, *the Christian also belongs*)—not because they have merely been in some way "connected" or "related" to the broader community's beliefs.

IV. THE IMPORTANCE OF TESTING BELIEFS

We have not yet said exactly *why* we think IBE can increase one's justification, whereas the other kinds of relation mentioned by Murphy do not. The answer lies, once again, in a rational agent's need for feedback. An agent—*if* she wants to pursue her SC rationally—brings to the relevant discussion a belief for which she seeks confirming feedback, and she encounters a range of beliefs that apparently conflict with her own. Her question then becomes: How does my belief hold up in the face of its competitors? In our view, the best way to answer this question is to identify a common problem to which each of the various competing beliefs offers a possible solution. And in the case of religious and scientific beliefs, the goal would be to find an explanatory question that will provide an opportunity for comparing the competing beliefs by asking which offers the best explanation of some agreed-upon set of data. Hence it is the agent's own interest in testing her belief that ends up committing her to an IBE methodology—and to searching for the sort of evidence that may decide between explanatory options.

It seems then that scientific data *can* provide an opportunity for testing—and therefore, when the results are positive, for *justifying*—theological beliefs, but only if the notions of testing and justifying are understood in terms of the rational agent's need for intersubjective feedback. Rationality entails that one work to preserve the possibility of feedback. And this entails the attempt to structure a certain type of discussion, namely one characterized by the striving for feedback of either a confirming or a disconfirming sort. One cannot say in advance that such discussion is possible in any particular case, or that it is possible with everyone; one cannot even say how much prior agreement among the discussants will be needed, in any given case, to make a genuine test possible. For example, it may turn out *not* to be possible to glean any actual feedback from scientists (*qua* scientists) about the truth of the Christian doctrines of the Trinity or the Spirit. But it would be a mistake—a mistake, that is, from the point of view of each rational agent's own interests—to exclude the possibility of genuine testing by settling, in advance, for something less.

These reflections lead us in the end to a somewhat different sense from Murphy's or Wolterstorff's of what is the most urgent task, at the moment, of Christian apologetics. As we argued in our contribution, the Christian should not rest content with showing the coherence of her Christian beliefs with other parts of her web; coherence is, unfortunately, too low a standard, and too easily met. We can always adjust what needs adjusting, as Murphy shows[22] when she explains how Diogenes Allen adjusts the terms of traditional theodicy in a way that brings them into line with current accounts of natural process. Insofar as the Christian also belongs to broader communities of inquiry, including scientific ones, the more pressing question will be whether it is possible to make Christian beliefs available to intersubjective assessment; to translate them into the terms, and to connect them with the kinds of possible evidence, that will make them genuinely discussable by a broad community of inquiry that comprises believers and nonbelievers alike. And—this is the really hard part—we have to find a way of doing this without thinning out Christian beliefs to the point of breaking their connection with their historical origin; for especially in the case of *Christian* beliefs, that origin remains the primary source of any claim they have to capture something like the truth.

NOTES

1. Gerhart and Russell, p. 127.
2. Gerhart and Russell, p. 123.

3. Gerhart and Russell, p. 124.

4. The precise nature of this continuum, as one moves from natural science through economics and literary criticism to theology, has been developed in Philip Clayton, "Disciplining Relativism and Truth," *Zygon* 24/3 (September 1989), pp. 315–334. Science/theology parallels developed on the basis of Imre Lakatos's philosophy of science are defended in Clayton, *Explanation from Physics to Theology: An Essay in Rationality and Religion* (New Haven: Yale University Press, 1989) and Nancey Murphy, *Theology in the Age of Scientific Reasoning* (Ithaca: Cornell University Press, 1990).

5. Nicholas Wolterstorff, *Reason within the Limits of Religion* (Grand Rapids: Eerdmans, 1976).

6. This is, however, a somewhat idiosyncratic use of the term "postmodernism," which is widely employed in architecture, the social sciences, literary theory, and theology with a more specific technical meaning. See, e.g., Jean François Lyotard, *The Postmodern Condition: A Report on Knowledge* (Minneapolis: University of Minnesota Press, 1984) and Mark C. Taylor, *Erring: A Postmodern A/theology* (Chicago: University of Chicago Press, 1984), as well as the recent series of exchanges in *Zygon* concerning postmodern and neopragmatist approaches to religion/science, e.g., Vol. 27/4 (December 1992), pp. 455–459, and "On the 'Use' of Neopragmatism" in Vol. 28/3 (September 1993).

7. Wolterstorff, p. 103.

8. Wolterstorff, p. 103.

9. Murphy, p. 110.

10. Murphy, p. 109.

11. Murphy, p. 109.

12. Murphy, p. 110, n. 6.

13. Now, it does seem that there is a curious gap in Murphy's argument for this conclusion. Why would one identify someone's total web of beliefs, which cannot be questioned all at once, with what she calls, once again, "the Western scientific worldview"? Surely believers can convert (and have converted) from a belief in that worldview to something else; and in any case the Western scientific worldview cannot constitute the *whole* web for a believer whose web includes supernaturalistic beliefs, such as a belief in traditional Christian theism. So why is the Western scientific worldview not just another *part* of the web, and therefore subject to doubt like any other part?

14. Murphy, p. 119.

15. Murphy, p. 110.

16. Murphy, p. 119.

17. See Murphy, p. 110.

18. Murphy, p. 111.

19. An important recent defense of inference to the best explanation in theology has been given by Michael Banner, *The Justification of Science and the Rationality of Religious Belief* (Oxford: Clarendon Press; New York: Oxford University Press, 1990). The general theory is defended in Peter Lipton, *Inference to the Best Explanation* (London: Routledge and Kegan Paul, 1991), e.g., chs. 3–4. For an application to theology, see Clayton, "Inference to the Best Explanation," *Zygon* (1996).

20. Murphy, p. 113.

21. See Murphy, p. 117.

22. See Murphy, p. 114.

Dialogue

INTRODUCTION

This part of the volume consists of "case studies" that explore the complex interface between theoretical developments in the sciences and critical religious reflection (especially Western theological traditions). A summary for the nonspecialist of significant contemporary developments in a given field is always included in the first essay of each case study, and a constructive philosophical or theological argument is always advanced in the second.

Beyond this basic similarity, there is wide variation in approach among the case studies. The interaction involved in a case study may be one-way or two-way. The scientific material may be illustrative of a theological theme, it may furnish a key analogue for systematic reflection, or it may be evidential support for a theological belief. The critical-religious reflection may be broadly relevant to religious traditions, or it may be focused on a single tradition (usually Christian theology). The authors may claim that the science has implications that call for large-scale theological revision in theology, or they may issue a critique of reductionism in science where it is believed to foster inadequate interpretations. Finally, in some cases the authors worked together, and in other cases one author responded to the other.

A fuller description of each case study is provided below. However, before plunging into details, a few remarks on noteworthy features of these case studies as a group are in order.

First, these case studies show *diversity* in the ways that current theology interacts with science and the wider intellectual culture, reflecting the pluriform nature of theology today. Some of these essays are more historical, others more phenomenological, and still others more representational in their emphases. Even so, it is clear that six case studies could not possibly exhaust all of the constructive possibilities.

Second, by appropriating current scientific understanding of the natural world, the theological essays represent something new in theology today. Major change in our understanding of self and world puts revisionary pressure on theology no less than on other areas of intellectual culture, and the pace of change in the twentieth century has been staggering. These theological essays are usually new, sometimes tentative, attempts to articulate classical religious beliefs (especially but not exclusively of the

Christian tradition) in the contemporary setting, and in relation to developments in some of the sciences.

Third, these essays in varying degrees are sensitive to the philosophical and methodological issues discussed in Part II. Consequently, they exemplify a new openness in the relationship between contemporary science and theology that is far more conducive to constructive dialogue than could have been expected during the first half of this century. Behind this shift toward greater amicability lies a more unified understanding of the relationship between empirical evidence about the physical universe and theological belief. In theological terms, these essays express a tendency to collapse the "two-books" model of theological knowing (that is, the biblical book of special revelation and the universal book of nature) into a single authoritative tradition with many strands of input. Emphasis is placed on achieving *intelligibility* in the relations between theology and knowledge from all domains of human experience.

Finally, the case studies have been conducted according to a wide range of methodologies. In the first, second, and fifth case studies, the science essay was written first, after which a philosopher or theologian responded with a constructive contribution, interacting with the specific arguments of the scientific essay to greater or lesser degrees. In the first case study, two scientist-theologians with a long history of interaction with each other's thought produced the essays, whereas the second and fifth case studies bring together thinkers with no prior history of interaction. The third case study has three essays rather than two, each of which deals with the complex issue of quantum complementarity, one primarily from the point of view of a philosopher of science, another from the perspective of a scientist-theologian writing team, and a third from the position of a theologian-philosopher. Each of the contributors was already familiar with the previous work of the others, but the papers were written in the order reproduced here. In the fourth case study, two scientist-philosopher-theologians already familiar with each other's thought advance competing theological interpretations of Jesus Christ. In this case, a draft of the second essay was made available to the first contributor so that he could direct the case study in the direction of a debate. The sixth case study was based on an unusual model of cooperation and interaction, with both essays emerging during an extended period of discussion and mutual criticism, as the postscript to the case study indicates. This range of methods is interesting in itself, not least because it offers the attentive reader an opportunity partially to evaluate the value of the methodological positions delineated in Part II of this volume.

CASE STUDY I: COSMOLOGY AND CREATION

William R. Stoeger, SJ opens this study with an introduction to some of the profound changes in scientific cosmology in the last century. Stoeger notes that our most recent scientific pictures of the early universe (variations on the Big Bang model) give meaning to the idea of a "totality": everything in the physical universe derives from a common evolution from simple materials and laws.

One of the chief foci of his essay is the Hartle-Hawking quantum cosmology theory that the universe *is finite but has no beginning*. This initially very puzzling idea plays a central role in Robert John Russell's theological essay on creation.

Russell has two basic intentions in his essay. The first is to show how a theology of creation can find a path between independence from, and overidentification with, science. To achieve this, he tries to identify what "theological data" might be, and discusses the relation of such data to theological core hypotheses by means of a network of interacting beliefs. This understanding of theological reflection clarifies the function of scientific information in the theological context. Moreover, it gives theology a way to discriminate in more rational, less arbitrary, fashion among competing theological views.

Second, Russell illustrates the above by showing how one might relate the theological notion of creation as "ontological origination" to the Hartle-Hawking conception of "a finite universe with no beginning." In a discussion of fundamental features of both the theology of creation and scientific cosmology, Russell shows how one of theology's central concepts (namely, finitude) is informed and constrained by the Hartle-Hawking model. Russell is careful to point out that this process of informing and constraining of theology by science does not impugn the integrity of theology; its subject matter and tasks are distinctive and mark out theology as a discipline with independent standing among the various types of intellectual activity.

CASE STUDY II: CHAOS THEORY AND DIVINE ACTION

Karl Young introduces chaos theory, tracing the history of its development. According to Young, chaotic systems, based in classical mechanics, have two principal features: they are *deterministic* (the system functions according to rigid, deterministic laws, so that any state of the system is traceable to precise initial conditions), and they are *nonlinear* (the sum of two states of the system at times t_1 and t_2 is not generally the state of the system at time $t_1 + t_2$). Since chaotic systems are deterministic and explicable without any reference to a designer, Young doubts the weighty theological significance that some have placed on them. However, he does ask whether there might be a modest epistemological insight for theologians: Does the intrinsic unknowability of outcomes in chaotic processes indicate a potentially uncrossable line between human knowledge and (divine) omniscience? Young closes with a brief discussion of recent attempts to integrate quantum mechanics and chaos theory.

In his theological response, John Polkinghorne offers a bold interpretation of divine action in light of chaos theory. He brings to the theological task a distinguished background as a particle physicist, and a more recently developed interest in chaos. Leaning on the realist's dictum that "what we can or cannot know is a reliable guide to what is actually the case," Polkinghorne asserts that limits on human knowledge in the spheres of quantum mechanics and chaotic systems are evidence for genuine openness in nature. As a way of accounting for and responding to this openness, Polkinghorne defends a metaphysics guided by Christian faith but true to scientific insights about the world. In this respect, Polkinghorne turns the position of Young on its head, denying the assertion that chaos in nature presupposes metaphysical determinism, and making this the critical point for his theology.

The most controversial element of Polkinghorne's theological proposal is that God acts in particular, law-conforming ways in the natural world by means of the input of active information. Such information cannot in principle show up in experimentation, though it may be grasped by faith, and may count in one's interpretation of natural events and processes. Note that he does not say that the epistemic openness of chaotic systems *proves* that God has a place within creation to act in conformity with natural laws, and that God does in fact do so; rather, Polkinghorne's claim is that nature is such that *it is intelligible to believe* God acts within it to effect particular outcomes, and he then goes on to confess that he personally believes this is the case.

Polkinghorne's attempt to demystify the "causal joint" (the elusive nexus of divine interaction with the world) has captured the attention—both supportive and critical— of a number of theologians. Those who support his view appreciate two of its consequences: illumination of law-conforming divine action, and insight into the basis in nature of human freedom. Those who are most sharply critical interpret the move from epistemic limits on human knowledge to affirmation of openness in nature as a dramatic mistake, holding instead that chaos in nature supports (without finally proving) the thesis of metaphysical determinism, rather than that of metaphysical openness.

CASE STUDY III: QUANTUM COMPLEMENTARITY AND CHRISTOLOGY

Whereas the first two case studies dealt with the somewhat general Western religious themes of divine creation and divine action, the third focuses on a specific doctrine of Christian theology, namely, that Jesus Christ is truly human and truly divine. This doctrine, called the incarnation, is widely believed among Christians, though Christian theologians debate whether incarnation is intelligible and, if so, whether the person and work of Jesus Christ is unique in such as way as to signify absolute ontological status. While the unique applicability of incarnation to Jesus Christ is not debated in this case study, the question of the intelligibility of the Christological concept of being "truly divine and truly human" is treated in great detail.

Ever since quantum complementarity was discovered, advocates of the incarnation have tried to exploit wave-particle duality as an analogy for divine-human "duality." At the level of linguistic trope, likening the incarnation to quantum complementarity illumines neither; the analogy has no obvious metaphysical implications, and is merely suggestive in a vague way. Unfortunately, appeals to complementarity as a way to understand incarnation are often nothing more than uninteresting restatements of this analogy. This case study is set apart from these superficial attempts to connect quantum complementarity and incarnation by its attempt to discern a common metaphysical thread in both, one intimately linked with paradox. At this level of discussion, arguments for the intelligibility of the incarnation by means of an appeal to quantum complementarity and paradox in nature are serious, if difficult, instances of the interaction between theology and the natural sciences.

Edward MacKinnon begins the case study by exploring philosophical implications of Niels Bohr's interpretation of quantum mechanics. He places Bohr's concept of complementarity within the larger history of apparent contradictions in philosophy, drawing attention to the fact that reality cannot be conceived within the limits of our ordinary language and its network of concepts and meanings. The epistemic structure of complementarity in quantum physics—the application of concepts from mutually exclusive frameworks in order to understand different aspects of one reality—is one more instance of our inability to describe realities that are unique or otherwise outside the range of the conventional applications of our concepts. The typical example in quantum physics is wave-particle duality: genuinely contradictory assertions cannot simultaneously be true (that would be irrationalism), but the assertions that "electron is a particle" and "electron is a wave" are not contradictories but contraries, and jointly offer important insights into a reality too complex for the categories of ordinary language.

MacKinnon's thesis that ordinary language plays an indispensable role in our descriptions of reality is crucial. He argues that the language of classical physics is a specialized form of ordinary language which must be employed in understanding the quantum domain. For it to be used coherently toward this end, one must "develop incompatible extensions that play a complementary role in describing reality." MacKinnon's interpretation of complementarity is that it expresses epistemic limits, but in a helpfully precise, and not an irrational, way.

This raises the question of whether there is insight to be gained from juxtaposing Bohr's complementarity with the sometimes paradoxical formulations of religious reflection. James E. Loder and the late W. Jim Neidhardt coauthored an essay on this topic, with an eye especially toward the famous paradox of classical Christian theology that Jesus Christ is truly divine and truly human. Their task is a bold one, first, because the material is intrinsically complex (Christology, quantum physics, and dialectical logic applied to our thought about them); and, second, because the spotty history of attempts to theologize about complementarity does not immediately warm the informed reader to their project.

Without loss of clarity, however, the Loder-Neidhardt essay sets exacting standards for making epistemic comparisons between physics and theology, and is able, because of this focus, to throw light on the material: the relation between Christian faith and understanding, and its object. The nature of Christ, they claim, is beyond the reach of human reason and experience, so the theologian is led into conceptual paradox in describing him. However, the paradox embedded in the classical formulation of "truly divine, truly human" does not indicate irrationality; instead, much like the way complementarity functions in physics, it points to a higher order, unified reality.

Thus, the dialectical logic needed to explain classical formulations of Jesus Christ's form of being is far from being an oddity called for by an obscure theological formula. Rather, it is present in many different thinkers and fields: it appears not only in Bohr's thought, but also in the thought of theologian Karl Barth, as well in the writings of philosopher-theologian Søren Kierkegaard, who inspired both Bohr and Barth. The breadth of presence of this kind of thinking suggests both that reality really does require dialectical descriptions of this kind, and that theology and metaphysics may have much to offer the theoretical imagination of scientists.

Christopher B. Kaiser is a pioneer in constructive efforts to integrate insights from physics and theology in this area. Kaiser crisply states the fundamental issues covered in the two preceding essays, showing points of agreement and disagreement between them, and revealing an alliance with the Loder-Neidhardt perspective where it differs from MacKinnon's view. In the last section of his paper, Kaiser focuses on four issues that he thinks require further attention: (1) expanding on the thesis of theological impact on the scientific quest for explanation; (2) determining more exactly the conditions in human experience under which dialectical or bipolar reasoning arises; (3) reflecting on theological implications of the relation in science between measuring instruments and quantum objects; and (4) exploring the meaning of "asymmetry" in bipolar epistemic structures, as described in the Loder-Neidhardt essay.

CASE STUDY IV: INFORMATION THEORY AND REVELATION

The fourth case study continues the focus of the third case study on the specifically Christian doctrines of Jesus Christ (C hristology). Whereas the focus in the last essay was on the intelligibility of the concept of incarnation as "truly divine and truly human," the focus here is on revelation in Jesus Christ: the sense in which God can be thought to be present in, and to communicate through, the human person Jesus. The issue of how information is processed in biological systems is directly relevant to such questions, and this relevance is exploited in a number of recent works in Christian theology, including especially the writings of Arthur Peacocke and John Polkinghorne.

Though not in itself properly described as a science, information theory is a widely used mathematical-philosophical tool in many sciences today. Thus, this case study represents a three-way dialogue among religious reflection (on revelation and Christology), a natural science (biology), and a tool proving itself useful in many sciences, including biology (information theory). Scientists sometimes voice the objection that information theory ought not be applied beyond its original domain of applicability (primarily the biological sciences). Yet there seems to be nothing in principle blocking the attempt to use information theory to ensure that discussions about such topics as revelation are intelligible and plausible. That is the way information theory is used in the essays of this case study.

John C. Puddefoot presents an overview of the salient features of information theory. Information is divisible into three kinds, according to this theory: *counting* information, *meaning* information, and *shaping* information. Roughly speaking, the theory is about the ways in which the input of data into a natural system can affect the organization and behavior of that system by virtue of patterns of significance the receiving system finds in the data.

Puddefoot draws attention to the kinship between information theory and systems theory, as they are both based on the principle that "nothing is self-interpreting because meaning is distributed over systems." Information theory brings a nonreductive accent to disciplines such as biology by its insistence that the functions of genes and cells can be understood only in relation to each other.

Information theory, states Puddefoot, also sheds light on nature's dynamism, openness, and plasticity: a system must be flexible if it is to embody new information, and adapt to data that has not yet become intelligible or usable to it. He also discusses what is called the "K" factor, which is employed in formalizing the relationship between new information important for a system's organization, and entropy.

On the basis of his introduction to information theory, Puddefoot briefly gives an account of Jesus as fully human and as "Word" of God. This sets up a stimulating interaction with the next essay, by Arthur Peacocke, who closely follows Puddefoot's perspective on information theory but offers a different interpretation of its significance for christology. Peacocke sees revelation as divine "informing" of the natural world, and asserts that this happens most fully in Jesus Christ. He finds this outlook intelligible within the present scientific worldview. What and how God reveals in Christ is continuous with what we find in the world in general; yet it also is an emergent new expression of divine being and becoming.

Peacocke feels compelled to revise those aspects of classical christology which stress Christ's preexistence, his "two natures," or any articulation of the self-communication of God in Christ which interprets it as an event different in kind from what God is doing generally in the world (and herein lies Puddefoot's opposition). He prefers, instead, to think of Jesus as the fullest expression of a human potential that we share. Jesus Christ is not represented in the gospels as "a unique invasion of the personhood of an individual human being by an utterly transcendent God; but rather as the distinctive manifestation of a possibility always inherently there for human beings."

One important question to be asked in the wake of this debate is whether one of these christological interpretations is more consonant with the insights of information theory. Put differently, and more sharply: Is information theory sufficiently specific to select between competing theological visions of Jesus Christ, or must such decisions be settled on other grounds?

CASE STUDY V: MOLECULAR BIOLOGY AND HUMAN FREEDOM

With Case Studies Five and Six, the themes being treated are once again more generally relevant to Western religious traditions, though the Christian context is at times still used for the sake of concreteness. The fifth case study is concerned with the relation between molecular biology, with its vague suggestions of determinism, and religious reflection, which finds the notion of human freedom indispensable.

Individually and in their interaction, the two essayists urge that the human experience of freedom can neither be understood in isolation from molecular biology, nor adequately explained solely at the level of molecular biology. As in other case studies, we see here the importance of respecting the integrity and independence of the various natural sciences in their diverse relations to one another: we may readily acknowledge the validity of causal reductionism (for instance, neurophysiology is the causal basis for mental activity) without slipping into the much more aggressive position of ontological reductionism (for instance, explaining mental activity demands no new ontological categories beyond those already explicit in neurophysiology).

R. David Cole introduces three general features of the biology of the human organism: cell adaptation, cellular structures and functions, and plasticity in neurobiology. The common characteristic in each of these areas is that genetic information predetermines a range of possibilities, but actual expressions in each case are dependent on a plurality of factors within and external to the organism. Cole then reflects on the possible significance of this for our understanding of human freedom. He concludes that there is legitimacy to the idea of human free will, but that we must more clearly understand it within the limits of the human genetic constitution.

W. Mark Richardson attempts to show that the implications of scientific data of the kind Cole introduces can be made intelligible in the context of a theological understanding of "free will" only after it is interpreted within a mediating philosophical-theoretical framework. Richardson attempts to show the congeniality between what he calls theology's commitment to "commonsense psychology" and an emergent theory of mind-brain, on the one hand, and between emergence and Cole's account of neurobiology, on the other. In this way, biological insights can be employed both to sharpen our concept of free will, and to specify the nature of the limits on finite human freedom. Richardson also asserts that some current alternatives to emergent theories of mind, in particular eliminative materialism, cannot simultaneously satisfy the conditions set by the theology of free will and by neurobiology. He concludes with illustrations of ways that an emergent theory of mind informed by contemporary neuroscience might illuminate certain aspects of theological anthropology.

CASE STUDY VI: SOCIAL GENETICS AND RELIGIOUS ETHICS

The final case study is the only one of the six to draw the social sciences into dialogue with critical religious reflection. Sociobiology and evolutionary science together form the basis for a powerful explanation of the emergence of religious and ethical structures within societies, one that appears to offer an alternative to traditional religious self-understandings. Making a positive *religious* assessment of religion and ethics cannot casually ignore the existence of such a powerful explanation, but must take full account of it. This case study, the unusual cooperative procedure for which is described in its conclusion, presents both a sociobiological explanation of the origin and continuance of religious and ethical social structures, and a bold attempt to achieve a synthesis between this explanation and a positive religious assessment of those structures.

William Irons applies an evolutionary model to the understanding of human morality, based on the premise that human beings are "bundles of inclusive fitness maximizing mechanisms shaped by a history of natural selection." This sociobiological anthropology has advanced in recent years with the aid of game theory. Irons views his proposal as superior to E.O. Wilson's theory, as it explains cooperative behavior among individuals in non-kin situations, invoking sociocultural and not just individual survival criteria to do so. Nevertheless, the theory still shows the utility of certain social, non-kin cooperative behaviors according to the criterion of the survivability of individual genes. In this respect it does indeed build upon earlier sociobiological theory.

In an interpretive move strongly reminiscent of Durkheim's theory of religion, Irons holds that religion, in evolutionary-based morality, stabilizes and deepens, through symbol and ritual, the biological, cultural, and environmental forces that shape group behavior. Irons finds this basis for morality and religion preferable to a traditional theological basis in one crucial respect: the account of sociobiological anthropology can be evaluated on evidence, whereas traditional theological construals of morality and religion rest on incontestable "truth" claims which are immune from correction and verification.

Philip Hefner offers an intriguing theological response which he believes can take seriously the sociobiological model of Irons, yet go beyond it as an explanation of morality. One of the most important of Hefner's arguments involves a rejection of Irons's claim about the difference between religious and evolutionary bases of morality. Hefner insists that an understanding of the human person based on the evolutionary principle of natural selection is a regulative principle, in something like the Kantian sense, and thus has a theoretical function equivalent to the function of "God" in theological systems. Each operates as an axiomatic core for the building of theory and testing of data. Thus, Hefner believes that Iron's reasons for preferring an anthropological over a theological foundation for morality and religion are based on an unarticulated prejudice. Each is grounded in a metaphysical vision of the world and of human beings within it.

Hefner concludes that the Christian theological model is a more inclusive one for explaining cooperative and self-giving behaviors, for it is based on the largest possible construal of what nature is. However, utilizing a hierarchical perspective of scientific disciplines created by E.O. Wilson, Hefner argues that the Christian theological basis for morality does not cancel, but builds upon, the insights of evolutionary theory, allowing the latter to constrain the theological model, even though, ultimately, more can be explained on the theological basis. Hefner reinforces this last claim by citing the kinds of human behavior for which he believes his theory can account, but that Iron's theory cannot. At the conclusion of this case study, we have included a short paper, jointly written by Irons and Hefner, reflecting on the process they developed for interacting on this case study. We believe their work bears out the fruitfulness of process and we hope the readers will also find it useful.

CASE STUDY I

COSMOLOGY AND CREATION

KEY DEVELOPMENTS IN PHYSICS CHALLENGING PHILOSOPHY AND THEOLOGY

WILLIAM R. STOEGER, SJ

I. THE THREE CONSTELLATIONS OF SCIENTIFIC REVOLUTION

The explosion of knowledge about the world and its constitution emanating from physics, chemistry, and the other physical and natural sciences has left us all amazed and breathless. Key developments in these areas have radically altered our perspectives on our world, our universe, and who we are as part of it. It has, and is having, as a result, a decisive impact on philosophy and theology in the twentieth century—and will continue to do so. Though the general importance of these astoundingly successful discoveries and programs for philosophy and theology cannot be denied, it is often difficult to specify or describe in detail what particular developments in the physical and natural sciences have the most crucial impact and why.

There are three constellations of such developments that pose a crucial challenge and opportunity to philosophy and theology. They focus on physics and chemistry, but with a glance into the distance towards biology. They are:

(1) the relativity, cosmology, astronomy constellation;
(2) the quantum physics, atomic physics, nuclear physics, fundamental particle physics constellation; and
(3) the dynamical systems, chaos, nonequilibrium thermodynamics, physics of self-organization and of complex systems constellation.

There is also the important intersection, or overlap, between the first and second constellations—the impending marriage of General Relativity (gravitational physics) and quantum field theory in an adequate unified field theory, together with its consequences for cosmology, and then its implications for philosophy and theology.

In this paper, I shall briefly describe these three constellations and their present and potential impact on philosophy and theology. Then I shall concentrate on the relativity, cosmology, and astronomy constellation, and on its overlap with the quantum physics constellation, in more detail.

The Cosmology Constellation

The relativity, cosmology, and astronomy constellation, which I shall be treating at greater length later, focuses on physical reality at the largest scales, and thus upon the overall extraterrestrial context in which we find ourselves. We live on a planet orbiting one of a hundred billion stars that make up our spiral galaxy, which we call the Milky Way. Our planet is in one of the Milky Way's spiral arms, about fifty thousand light years from the galactic center. Our galaxy is one of thirty or so galaxies in what is called the Local Group—including the Large and Small Magellanic Clouds (which we can see only from the Southern Hemisphere) and Andromeda—those which are so close to ours that they are gravitationally bound to us. There are many other clusters of galaxies in the universe—and some of them consist of thousands of galaxies all bound together and orbiting one another, making our Local Group look very small and insignificant indeed. These clusters of galaxies are further arranged into superclusters that span on the order of one hundred to two hundred million light years. We belong to one such supercluster—called the Local Supercluster.

Relativity, cosmology, and astronomy deal not only with our position in space, but also with our position in time—our earth and sun are about 4.8 billion years old, and the universe is about thirteen to twenty billion years old, beginning with the Big Bang. Cosmology and astronomy together assure us that the universe has been evolving on all scales during that time—even the physical laws, like gravity and the nuclear forces which hold the nuclei of atoms together, have been evolving. There was an epoch in the very early universe, for instance, before which the nuclear forces were indistinguishable from the electromagnetic force. And even earlier, right after the Big Bang, physics was even simpler—gravity itself was indistinguishable from the nuclear forces and electro-magnetism. Of course, that means that space and time were also completely different then from now. We have no clear idea what physical reality was like in those first moments after the Big Bang, except that it was extremely hot and probably very homo-geneous. In fact, up until at least three hundred thousand years after the Big Bang, the universe was so hot that structure could not form. There were no stars or galaxies, no planets, no life. These important structures, or lumps, developed gradually only after the matter in the universe decoupled—was set free—from the radiation it contained.

Thus, this first constellation deals also with the mysterious realities of space and time, their connection with one another and with matter and energy. From the devel-opments of Special and General Relativity early in this century, our concepts of space and time have been almost completely altered. They are no longer absolute, nor can they be considered independently of the mass-energy they "contain."

These revolutionary ideas about the reality of space and time, the vastness of the universe compared to our infinitesimal location in space and time within it, and the universe's evolutionary character have transformed the perspectives from which we view ourselves, our world, and the ultimate realities for which we search. They have also altered our ideas and images of God and God's interaction with us and with our world. I shall discuss these and other consequences of the revolution in relativity and cosmology a little later. But now I wish to go on and briefly discuss the second area of revolution.

The Quantum Physics Constellation

The revolution associated with quantum physics, atomic and nuclear physics, elementary particle theory, and field theory is composed of many outstanding individual breakthroughs whose collective impact is overwhelming. This revolution does not immediately affect our knowledge and description of large scale structures—involving space and time, and the question of the beginning of it all—but rather the microscopic layering of physical reality and the explanation of the characteristics of the basic structure, diversity, and knowability of matter as we find it.

The fact that at microscopic levels there is an irreducible indeterminism, represented both by the Heisenberg uncertainty principle and the unlocalizability of unmeasured particle-waves, has proved to be philosophically challenging and continues to be controversial. Equally perplexing are other quantum phenomena, such as quantum correlations over spacelike intervals (the Bell inequalities); the Einstein-Rosen-Podolsky paradox; quantum tunnelling; the problem of decoherence and the transition from quantum to classical regimes, particularly in its applications to quantum cosmology; and the outstanding problem of an adequate understanding of the measurement process, particularly the collapse of the wave-packet. All of these problems together have seriously undermined traditional forms of realism—certainly all forms of naïve realism, and all but the weaker forms of critical realism.

Abner Shimony gives a very succinct summary of the radical innovations introduced by quantum mechanics.[1] They are:

(1) Objective chance—the chance character of outcomes is a property of the physical situation itself, not a consequence of the observer's ignorance. It presupposes objective indefiniteness.

(2) Objective indefiniteness—there are eventualities which do not have a definite truth or falsity, independent of the observer.

(3) Objective probability—there is a definite probability of finding an eventuality to be true, and definite probability of finding it to be false, depending only on the state of the system and on the eventuality itself, not on the knowledge or beliefs of the observer. This objective probability is embodied in the wave function, and connected with a notion of potentiality.

(4) Potentiality—eventualities are potential. There are procedures by which a given potentiality, initially indefinite, is actualized. "A quantum state is a network of potentialities."

(5) Entanglement—there can exist situations involving two (or more) states, say *a* and *b*, in which neither state *a* nor state *b* are actualized, but state *a* + *b* is.

(6) Quantum nonlocality—we observe correlated actualization of potentialities over spacelike intervals (intervals which cannot be connected by light signals), which implies that the important entities ("wholes") may be nonlocal (that is, their various components may be widely separated in space and time).

From these somewhat startling discoveries, it is now clear that we, as human knowers, do not have a purchase on physical reality *as it is in itself*. What we know about it, particularly at the quantum level, is inextricably convolved with *our* observation of it. Our knowledge is founded on the reality that is "out there," but we can never compare how *it is in itself* with how we observe it, because we have no independent handle on the former. These surprising and somewhat unsettling developments have served to underscore in a new way the limits to our knowledge about the physical reality we investigate, our essential distance from it, and the essentially evanescent and indeterminate characteristics it manifests at these submicroscopic levels. This has had, and continues to have, a profound impact on other types of knowledge, on our understanding of human knowledge itself, and on the character of physical reality in general. In particular, we come to realize that there are no "raw facts" and that, though we must spurn subjectivism, there is no human knowledge which is or can be completely "objective." It is always from some "point of view" or other, and there is always something essential contributed by the observer, who is indeed always a participant in what he or she observes. Though the coupling of observer and observed is often weak, fortunately for us and for our fields of endeavor, it is never completely negligible, rarely insignificant, and it is often stronger than we think.

Key philosophical questions arise with regard to the complex family of quantum phenomena themselves. These questions become ever more insistent when broader issues pertaining to the scope and character of human knowledge and the status of observed reality are broached. The repercussions on theology have been and are serious.

Apart from the peculiarities and counterintuitive characteristics of quantum phenomena themselves, there are perhaps the even more important consequences and applications of these fundamental principles to the microscopic structure of matter in all its forms and variety. Three examples can be mentioned.

(1) The realization that the structure of the atom depends on quantum mechanical principles has sponsored our understanding of and power over chemical processes, the laws of chemical bonding, and ultimately molecular folding, from the simple to the very complex. This includes now DNA, RNA, proteins, the processes by which they are produced and marshalled to maintain and control cells and multicellular organisms, and how those organisms reproduce and pass on that information genetically.

(2) Nuclear physics, at a more fundamental level than atomic physics, has produced a detailed understanding of atomic nuclei, of their stability and their instabilities, and of the processes whereby most varieties of nucleii are produced in stars.

(3) Fundamental particle physics has shed light on the structure of nuclear constituents and mass-energy at very high energies, and on the forces governing high energy interactions. This has led to a vision of the deep internal relationships between the three fundamental forces of electromagnetism, and the strong and weak nuclear interactions. Inclusion of the fourth, gravitation, must await the marriage of the quantum physics with General Relativity, which we shall touch upon later.

Just as cosmology and astronomy have served to show us who we are and where we are within the larger macroscopic context, so do these quantum-mechanically based disciplines of physics show us who we are and what we are in terms of both the hierarchical levels of constituents which make us up, and the processes and relationships which govern our development, existence, and eventual demise. We are, to be sure, more than those constituents, but we can never disown those constituents or pretend we are not subject to their strengths and weaknesses. They connect us to our universe, to other creatures and to one another. We share the same origin and, in one sense, we share the same fate. Philosophy, and particularly theology, must integrate these insights and facts into their reflections on human life, its origin and destiny, and the meaning and significance of physical reality. It is only through them that anything else can be known. We turn now to the third and final constellation of influential developments in the physical sciences.

The Complex Systems Constellation

The dynamical systems, order out of chaos, physics of self-organization, and complex systems constellation is of more recent vintage than the previous two, and returns us to the "real world"—the world with which we are familiar. If we look around us, we see that much of our environment, including ourselves, consists of highly complex systems manifesting complex behavior. Fortunately, a significant and important portion of this complex environment can be broken down into subsystems that can be modelled by the idealized systems, usually linear or in-equilibrium, which we all struggled to understand and control in our physics and chemistry classes. But what about the rest? There are obviously important constituents of our world that cannot be reduced to such simple models, systems whose complex functions and behavior, and very existence, defies understanding on the basis of traditional physics. The obvious example is something that is living—even a single cell. But there are many nonliving examples which manifest complex and ordered behavior, too—the turbulent flow of a fluid, the formation of an ice crystal, convection in a heated pot of water.

This constellation includes the behavior of dynamical systems; chaos; dissipative structures; nonlinear phenomena; systems operating far from equilibrium; systems manifesting self-organizing behavior, the ability to store and transmit information, and even the capacity to reproduce; systems that develop feedback loops; and so on. All these overlap in what is generally called the physics of complex systems. It is on the basis of work being done in these fields that important strides have been made, for instance, in understanding how living systems function and maintain themselves, and even how living molecular systems may have developed from nonliving ones. Though all the pieces have not yet been placed into the puzzle, most scientists think that it will be solved without invoking *Deus ex machina*. Understanding the origin of consciousness is an analogous quest to which developments within this constellation are making strong contributions. The implications for philosophy and theology are obvious and profound.

In physics the standard example of self-organizing behavior in a nonequilibrium system is convection. As water heats in a container from below and increases in temperature, it reaches a threshold at which bulk motions are initiated and an organized pattern of convection cells develops. In chemistry, the Belousov-Zhabotinski (BZ) reaction—in which the continual addition of reactants produces a nonlinear, nonequilibrium situation—leads to regular oscillations in the excesses of the different ions in the system, manifested by a periodic change in color, from red to blue, and back to red again. Examples like this are relatively common in chemistry and biochemistry, and provide the building blocks, so to speak, of the more intricate self-organizing behavior and information-storing and -transferring capabilities of living systems. In the BZ reaction, nonequilibrium and nonlinearity lead to self-organizing behavior and the breaking of time symmetry. In the case of convection, we have the breaking of spatial symmetry.

There are many other requirements for the development of living systems, which are so very complex, and yet exhibit remarkable homeostasis. We need very large molecules with vast information-storage capacities, and with the capability to replicate without losing that information—molecules like DNA and RNA. We also need molecules that are simultaneously information carriers and functionally highly specific—like proteins, which are made up of amino acids. These two classes of molecules are intimately inter-related and interdependent in carrying out their functions. How could such complicated biochemical systems have originated and developed? How could life have developed? A great deal of very detailed work has been done to show that many of the crucial steps in this drama are understandable and indeed probable without invoking something like direct divine intervention. Self-organizing processes like the BZ reaction are one essential ingredient.

As Bernd-Olaf Küppers has emphasized,[2] there are three separate phases involved in the evolution of life. There is, first of all, chemical evolution, during which the *noninstructed* synthesis of nucleic acids and proteins occurs. Second, there is molecular self-organization, during which there is *instructed* synthesis of nucleic acids, proteins, and their organization into self-reproducing genetic systems. Finally, there is biological evolution, in which complex multicellular systems develop from primitive genetic systems.

How did this second stage, molecular self-organization, happen? As I mentioned above, the origin of life in this epoch of molecular self-organization is physically explicable in detail on the basis of the known laws of physics and chemistry. The key elements in this transition from nonliving to living are:

(1) the laws of chemical reaction kinetics;

(2) molecular systems which are far from equilibrium (there is an injection of energy or material);

(3) nonlinearity—the reactions are autocatalytic or cocatalytic;

(4) a random element (mutation) which can provide novelty;

(5) enzymes like the polymerases that can control mutability and integrate and stabilize favorable mutations into the system;

(6) the origin and stabilization of the genetic code, by which the information in the nucleic acids in translated into functional proteins; and finally,

(7) systems which participate in cooperative development, or coevolution, providing a principle of selection and stabilization, the leading proposal for which is named the "catalytic hypercycle."[3]

Of the several live theoretical options about origins of life, all the leading contenders take as given the general aspects of complexity summarized above.

This very sketchy summary provides some idea of the work being done and the results being obtained in this fascinating study of the transition between nonliving structures and living ones. The basic message is that there is every indication that it can be accounted for on the basis of chemistry and physics. The origin of life is not basically a biological question; it is very much a question of physics and chemistry, perhaps the most important question with which physics and chemistry have ever dealt. Moreover, the implications for philosophy and theology are enormous. Now, however, we must return in more detail to the cosmology constellation.

II. RELATIVITY, ASTRONOMY, AND COSMOLOGY

There are several developments within this constellation that have in themselves been revolutionary, beginning with the fundamental results of Special Relativity: the constancy of the velocity of light and therefore the fixing of an upper limit on the speed with which information and energy may be transmitted; the equivalence of all inertial frames; the equivalence of mass and energy; the relativity of time, space, and velocity; and the independence of physics from coordinate systems and inertial frames. In some ways the findings of General Relativity—Einstein's revolutionary contribution to gravitational physics—are even more unsettling and fundamental, emphasizing the deep connections between space, time, and mass-energy, and demonstrating very clearly that space and time can no longer be considered absolute. Space is not a pre-existing container within which massive objects and electromagnetic radiation (light) move. And time not only is relative but also lacks uniqueness and is an internal and derivative feature of physical reality. Mass-energy generates space-time, but the structure of space-time constrains the behavior of distributions of mass-energy.

Since we are concerned to make connections with philosophy, and particularly with theology, it is important to say more about the status of time in General Relativity.[4] In Newtonian physics, time has an absolute, independent and universal status. In General Relativity, however, it is only space-time that possesses such a status—there is no fundamental or universal choice for the time variable. It is an internal property, so to speak, of the space-time manifold—certainly not something external to it. It can be defined in General Relativity only in terms of something else, for instance the volume of the universe, or of some large part of the universe. Finally, there are many ways of defining such a time parameter, and, generally speaking, none of them has a preferred status.[5] If we pick a four dimensional space-time, we can slice it into a stack of three-dimensional spatial surfaces in many different ways. In any such slicing, we can label each slice by a single real number which increases from one slice to the next, and plays the role of a time parameter. All the points on a slice are then simultaneous with respect to that definition of time. But, as I have just indicated, there are an infinite number of different ways of doing this. Thus, events that would be simultaneous relative to one definition of time will in general not be so relative to another. Furthermore, the properties of the spatial slices themselves defined by the time parameter choice will be very different from one another. For instance, one choice may give very smooth slices—density is constant—while another choice of slicing in the very same space-time will give very lumpy spatial slices.

Cosmology and astronomy employ Special and General Relativity as fundamental theories to provide their overall space-time framework, which includes such features as the expanding universe, with hotter, denser phases as we go back into its past; its fifteen-billion-year history since the Big Bang; its vastness; its hierarchical structuring into stars, clusters of stars, galaxies, cluster of galaxies, superclusters, and so on; its very early homogeneous phases when the mass-energy of the universe was (smoothly) distributed and disposed very differently from now; its fundamentally evolutionary character on every level; and the extreme states of matter and gravitational configurations we find in our universe today—black holes, neutrons stars, quasars, and so on. There was a time, about one hundred thousand years after the Big Bang, for instance, when there were no stars or galaxies, or planets—when the matter in the universe was a hot, homogeneous soup still strongly coupled to the radiation. The temperature then was about 10,000 degrees Kelvin. At that epoch, too, there were only hydrogen, helium, and few light metals; no carbon, oxygen, phosphorous, or iron had been formed. These elements, which are so essential to our being and our environment now, came into existence only quite a bit later through the nuclear manufacturing capabilities of the first stars.

If we go back to times earlier than one hundred thousand years after the Big Bang, the matter and the radiation is hotter and in even denser states. Roughly three minutes after the Big Bang, the temperature was at about six billion degrees, which is just the temperature at which hydrogen nuclei can fuse to helium and a small percentage of other light elements such as deuterium and lithium. This is the age of *nucleosynthesis*. This is the explanation of why we have more helium and deuterium in the universe than can be accounted for by stellar nucleosynthesis; these light elements existed almost from the very beginning.

At even earlier times, much less than a second after the Big Bang, the temperature and the density of the universe would have been above other key transition thresholds. There was a point, for instance, when it was too hot for there to be protons and neutrons, the components of atomic nuclei. There was only a sea of quarks, the underlying components of protons and neutrons. As the universe expanded and the temperature and density dropped to lower values, hadrons (specifically the baryons we call protons and neutrons) condensed out of this quark sea. This is often referred to as "the quark-hadron transition."

Quantum field specialists are convinced that at even higher temperatures our physical laws—the four distinct fundamental forces of gravity, electromagnetism, and the strong and weak nuclear interactions—were unified. There was a time and a temperature at which the electromagnetic and the weak nuclear interaction were subsumed into a single undifferentiated "electro-weak" force. And even earlier, there was a time and a temperature at which there was only gravity and what is called the GUT (Grand Unified Theory) interaction, which unifies the electro-weak and the strong nuclear force. Just after the Big Bang itself, it is likely that there was an epoch, called the Planck epoch, during which there was only one "superforce," which unified gravity with the GUT interaction. At that point, the gravitational theory we have been using, Einstein's General Relativity, as well as the model of the universe we have based upon it, breaks down. In fact, it is difficult, if not impossible, to identify space and time—or space-time—as we know them during this extremely early phase of the universe's emergence. A detailed quantum theory of gravity, and of space-time itself, is necessary to describe the physics and the geometry in this extreme situation.

From this brief description of the thermal history of the universe, we see clearly that it is radically an evolutionary universe. It developed from a phase when it was very hot, very dense, very homogeneous, and subject to a single physical interaction, through a succession of transitions as it expanded and cooled, by which it became progressively more differentiated and complex on every level. Eventually clusters of galaxies, stars, and planets formed, and on at least one of those there emerged living beings, and conscious knowing organisms of astounding complexity and capabilities. We also see that our observable universe is extremely old and extremely large—much older and larger than people in the centuries before us ever imagined.

What is the future of this universe of ours? Will it continue to expand? We do not yet know. It seems to be hovering just at the boundary between being open—expanding for-ever—and being closed—eventually ceasing to expand and then collapsing under its own "weight." Whether it expands forever, or eventually begins to collapse and reheat in the process depends on the amount of matter it contains. Is there enough mass-energy in the universe to close it? We are not sure. Strangely enough, the amount of mass-energy we see—luminous matter—in stars and galaxies is only about five percent of the critical amount needed to reverse the expansion. But there is abundant evidence that there is a great deal of "dark" matter—matter that we cannot see and can detect only through its gravitational influence. Only a small proportion of this dark or hidden matter can be in the form of baryons (protons or neutrons). The rest must be nonbaryonic—probably composed of what are generally referred to as WIMPs (weakly interacting massive parti-cles). So far we have no really good, known, particle candidate to fill this role of pro-viding for this remaining ninety-five percent of the matter of the universe which we know must be there.

The initial singularity at "t = 0"—which we sometimes refer to as the Big Bang—is a consequence of the cosmological models. The limit or "beginning" of the succession of hotter, denser phases of the universe—which is given by the classical (nonquantum) evolution equations of the standard Friedmann-Robertson-Walker (FRW) cosmological models based on General Relativity—is a point where the density and temperature become infinite. It is conventionally designated by the time "t = 0." Since the temper-ature and density given by the model are infinite at this "time," it is a singularity, which means that it is unlike other points, and is amenable to neither mathematical manipulations nor physical interpretation. That is why it is a limit of the cosmological model—the limit of the succession of hotter, denser phases that do have mathematical meaning, and can be physically interpreted and brought into correspondence with observable or experimentally verifiable phenomena. It is worth mentioning in passing that the initial singularity or Big Bang, for reasons I shall not go into here, could not have been just a single event or geometric point—rather it had to be a whole manifold, or three-dimensional spatial surface, of events or geometric points. It is also important to mention that the presence of an initial singularity is not peculiar to the highly sym-metric FRW models. The Hawking-Penrose singularity theorems[6] assure us that such a singularity will occur in practically all of our acceptable cosmological models.

On the face of it, the existence of this initial singularity seems to indicate that there was indeed a beginning in time—or rather a beginning of time—and that this begin-ning was a point, or rather a manifold of points, characterized by infinite density and infinite temperature. Certainly, as a limit to the hot, dense, early phases of the uni-verse, we cannot, within the model, go to phases or times antecedent to it. In fact, strictly speaking, we cannot examine the initial singularity itself in any complete or understandable way within the model. To that extent it stands outside the model, even though it is indicated by it. Thus, according to most researchers, this initial singular-ity signals a breakdown not only of the cosmological model itself, but also of the manifold model of space-time underlying it, necessitating the use of a quantized theory of gravity, and therefore of space and time. Whatever the ultimate significance of "t = 0," it can only be considered a "beginning" within the model itself—a limit, moreover, that falls outside the model in the sense that the model itself cannot adequately deal with it or interpret it. Not only can we not meaningfully specify an antecedent state to the Big Bang within the model; we cannot even meaningfully specify the Big Bang itself, for instance, as a real origination event or manifold of events, or as the origination of time.

As I have pointed out above, before the Big Bang is reached in the FRW models, there is an extremely high temperature at which the gravitational theory underlying General Relativity breaks down. At this point, a quantum theory of gravity and a quantum cosmology must take over. I shall discuss this in somewhat more detail in the next section. We do not yet have adequate theories of this sort, but the indications are that, when we do, the singularity will disappear, and we shall be left with a phase of the very early history of the universe completely dominated by quantum states, devoid of the categories of space and time with which we are familiar in General Relativity, and lacking a component which could be clearly interpreted as an origin or a beginning, except in a relative or accommodated sense. Thus, we can see that the Big Bang, however we describe it within the framework of cosmology, should not be considered as a beginning either of the universe or of time in any specific or definite sense, much less of creation in the theological sense of that word. Rather, it underscores the fact that our universe at one time was very, very different from now—and was once dominated by such extreme conditions that none of the categories we now rely upon to describe physical reality would not have been applicable, including those of space and time, matter and particle.

Our failure within physics and cosmology to deal with the origin of time and space, and absolute origins in general, should not blind us to the extraordinary significance of what space-time physics, cosmology, and astronomy have taught us. Even the discovery, so to speak, that there is a huge coherent entity we can call "the universe"—the totality of all that is observed or ultimately observable—is very significant and enormously influential. To find that this totality is more than a disparate random collection of objects with disparate and unconnected histories—and in fact, gives every indication of having both a common origin and an overall common thermal evolutionary history—is somewhat startling when you stop to think about it.[7] As Stanley Jaki has pointed out,[8] it brings the concept of the totality back into philosophy and theology, and gives it concrete form.

Each one of the developments we have mentioned corresponds to a revolutionary scientific discovery sponsoring new perspectives. And yet the accumulation of these developments into a single, interacting constellation of knowledge about the universe in which we live—its small-scale, intermediate-scale, and large-scale structure, its history, and its evolution—is more influential on our imagination and thinking than the simple sum of its components. Each development is like a single piece of a large and intricate jigsaw puzzle, which, when nearing completion, yields a beauty and a perspective and an insight into reality which could not have been imagined or anticipated on the basis of the individual pieces considered separately.

This constellation of cosmological developments essentially provides a new story of who we are, where we came from, where everything came from, where we may be going, and how we are connected or not connected with the rest of reality. This is a story of origins not in ultimate or theological terms, but in concrete and very startling scientific terms. It is by no means complete, but it is a powerful corrective to illusions of the past. We are from a physical point of view extremely fragile and small—and not at the center of the universe. The universe has no center. Our history is infinitesimal and, from a physical point of view, possibly insignificant, compared to that of the universe itself, or even of our galaxy. We are helpless in confrontation with cosmic and galactic forces and phenomena. Similarly, our destiny, from a purely physical point of view, seems very uncertain and ultimately bleak, whether the universe is open or closed. And yet this universe of ours seems peculiarly hospitable towards life and consciousness—oriented towards producing it. So much so that we fantasize in an educated way about other civilizations in other solar systems in our galaxy and in other galaxies. And there seems to be a wealth of possibility for that fantasy to be realized. The discovery of complex organic molecules in the cool, dark clouds of our own galaxy and in other galaxies, for example, points in this direction.

Obviously, philosophy and theology must take these new cosmic and human perspectives and possibilities seriously. How they are to do that is not something I shall deal with here. To the extent that they do not critically assimilate and confront these truths and perspectives, they will fail to articulate authentically and truthfully who we really are, what the world and the universe really is, and who God really is or is not. For God has expressed the divine nature in the reality we experience around us and experience in ourselves. True, we are more than what the sciences reveal us to be, and the universe itself is more than that, too, but that "more" cannot be adequately articulated or rediscovered without allowing this new knowledge to confront, purify, and enrich the philosophical and theological knowledge of the past, and the revelatory experiences of past and present.

In themselves the new astronomy and the new cosmology do not answer the question of ultimate origins—nor can they, when carefully analyzed. But they pose that question with new insistence, and cast long shadows on pretended answers that invoke special events of divine intervention in time and space. They also cast doubt on the importance and reality of an ultimate temporal origin for creation, and reinforce the importance of metaphysical origins, and of the veiled underlying sources of possibility and necessity. Finally, they concretely elaborate in intricate detail and overwhelming scope the ways in which God has continued God's creative activity through the physical, chemical, and biological regularities and processes established and maintained within reality.

III. UNIFICATION, QUANTUM GRAVITY, AND QUANTUM COSMOLOGY

In the past fifteen to twenty years, developments in the two constellations of cosmology and quantum physics have joined and begun to reinforce and modify one another. What I have already discussed in the previous section indicates this. Here I shall treat this mutual influence and interaction more specifically.

Relativity and cosmology typically deal with physical reality on the very largest scales, and treat the geometry and evolution of space-time through the gravitational interaction and its intimate relationship with mass-energy. Quantum physics and fundamental particle and field theory, in contrast, focus on physical reality on microscopic and submicroscopic scales, and particularly on the interactions mass and energy, in their different forms, exhibit at higher and higher energies through the electromagnetic, weak nuclear and strong nuclear interactions. Space-time is the context within which these take place, but is typically unaffected by them. Gravity is present, but is so weak that it is normally insignificant. Thus, the developments in these two constellations have proceeded independently from one another for many decades. The physics of the astronomical and cosmological was dominated by gravity, and the physics of the microscopic was dominated by the other three interactions. There was little need for unification or even dialogue between the two at a fundamental level.

As I have indicated above, however, there was the dawning realization, present even at the time of Einstein and his contemporaries, that ultimately the two realms must fit together in a unified scheme. There must be a way in which all four interactions can be understood and modelled within a single theory. Cosmological questions concerning the very early universe, particularly in light of the succession of hotter and denser epochs terminating in an initial singularity of infinite temperature and density, strongly encouraged such a view, as we have already seen. It became clear that there would have been situations just after the Big Bang in which the temperature of the universe was so high that gravity and space-time, as modelled by General Relativity, would break down, and would need to be replaced by quantum gravity and by a quantum space-time. In this extreme case, the physics of the very large would have to be radically unified with the physics of the very small. This also seems to imply, according to most physicists, that gravity as an interaction must be unified with the other three forces—electromagnetism, and the weak and strong nuclear interactions. However, this may turn out to be incorrect. A rather different theory of gravity and space-time at these extremely high temperatures and energies is certainly needed, but that does not necessarily imply that such superunification must follow.

So now there is the intense and fascinating quest for a unified theory of all basic physics—a single model that will describe and explain the four fundamental forces, including gravity; their relationship with one another at all energies, even the highest ones; and all of their consequences, including the particles that carry those forces (the bosons), those which are subject to them (the fermions), and the space-time within which their interactions occur. This almost certainly requires quantization of the gravitational field itself, and therefore, in some way, a quantum description of space and time along with mass-energy at extreme energies. If this is correct, then space and time are not continual in this primordial phase, but give way to some other more fundamental realities—very different from the space and time with which we are familiar. These quantum space-time realities, whatever they turn out to be, then yield or give birth to our space-time continuum once the temperature of the universe falls below 10^{32} degrees Kelvin.

The exciting work that is being done in this quest makes important use of symmetry groups and other related mathematical structures, out of which, so to speak, the physical particles and their mutual interactions derive. In the standard model of fundamental particle physics, extremely good agreement with experiment has been attained by describing the behavior of the electromagnetic, weak and strong nuclear interactions, and the particles they affect by a product, to put it technically, of the three symmetry groups $SU(3)$, $SU(2)$ and $U(1)$. Complete unification of these three interactions would be effected by subsuming this product into a single larger symmetry group, such as $SU(5)$ or $SU(10)$. An adequate unification has been achieved for the electromagnetic and weak nuclear interactions in the Salam-Weinberg electro-weak unification model. An adequate GUT theory would do this for all three of the nongravitational interactions.

A complementary idea intimately related to the role of symmetry and symmetry groups is that of spontaneous symmetry breaking. At very high energies or temperatures, physics is symmetric, and we have a large symmetry group describing it. As the universe cools below some threshold temperature, that large symmetry is broken, and physics loses some of its symmetry in a well-defined way, while still manifesting some residual symmetry. This loss of symmetry in such a transition may yield a newly differentiated interaction—for example, the splitting of the electro-weak force into separate electromagnetic and weak nuclear interactions, or the endowing of formerly massless particles with "rest mass." These ideas are being extended to gravity and space-time themselves, through programs like those of supergravity and superstrings. What is envisioned is incorporating all of known physics in a single, very large symmetry group, such as the exceptional group denoted E8, or actually two copies of this—E8 × E8—and then specifying how that enormously large symmetry group would be broken into a product of lower symmetry groups to yield gravity and the GUT interaction when the temperature slipped below the magical 10^{32} degrees Kelvin. This is one major component of the conceptual framework involved in this quest.

This dominance of symmetries (expressed by Lie groups and their representations) has brought with it a certain Platonic or neo-Platonic flavor to the musings of theorists and their followers. "In the beginning, there was E8 × E8." This may or may not be justified. But it is significant for philosophy and theology. This search has also been called the quest for a "Theory of Everything." Once that holy grail has been found, all else will have been explained. So maintain many physicists. This may be true at the level of physics, but it cannot be ultimately correct, even at the levels of chemistry and biology.

Cosmology forces the issue of the marriage between General Relativity and quantum field theory in a way no other branch of physics does. For, if this did not occur, then the initial singularity is essentially inevitable, or, more precisely, there would be no way of replacing this essentially uninterpretable limit of the standard model with a model that yields a consistent, meaningful, and interpretable characterization of physical reality at these extreme energies. That would be very difficult to accept at face value. It is with good reason, therefore, that most physicists see the predicted initial singularity as an indication of a regime within which the classical continuum model of space, time, and gravity does not apply, and needs to be replaced with a quantum description of gravity. Only a theory of quantum gravity can account for a regime with such high temperatures that space and time, as we know them, were still broken down into their quantum counterparts, and all four forces were subsumed into one superforce.

This, however, may mean that the universe never had a beginning in the usual sense of the word—because, if it did, there was "a time" at which time itself as we know it did not exist. In the previous section, we spoke of the internal, intrinsic, and uncertain character of time in General Relativity. Instead, there may have been some material quantum reality integrated with some quantized space-time reality, whatever that would have been, in which time as we know it was hidden, and from which it only gradually emerged. Time would then have a beginning and be finite in the past, but in its primordial "spatial" form, it might also be unbounded as well, and would have an origin which was different from that of created reality itself. To picture this, imagine the surface of a sphere. It is finite and unbounded, in the sense that there is neither beginning nor end (no edge) to its surface, and yet it does not have infinite extent or area. Time may turn out to be like this.

This is essentially what proposals like those of Hawking and Hartle (their no-boundary ground state proposal) and Vilenkin point towards.[9] As we approach the initial singularity, time becomes imaginary—that is, it becomes equivalent to a spatial dimension, and the singularity is never reached. The "timeless" spatial manifold at the "origin" of things would exist and be subject to certain primordial laws of physics, and we could, in a sense, speak of an origin of time from this "cosmic egg." But we would not be any nearer to describing or accounting for the ultimate origin of reality from physics—that is, furnishing an account of the origin of this timeless manifold, of the laws of physics which pertain to it, and of its explosion into the ordered physical reality with which we are familiar. Even from the perspective of physics, therefore, there may have never been a creation event, as such. This compels us to emphasize more strongly the metaphysical concept of ultimate origin, rather than the somewhat uncertain and unimportant idea of an ultimate temporal origin. Of course, using a temporal beginning as a symbol and a sign of metaphysical dependence is acceptable and even desirable, as long as we are cautious about its scientific, philosophical, and theological significance.

IV. THEOLOGICAL IMPLICATIONS

Here I shall merely summarize, without discussion, theological implications already indicated in passing or implicitly throughout the course of this discussion.

With regard to specific topics, we can point first, of course, to the implications of developments in the natural sciences for the doctrine of creation. The radically evolutionary character of the universe compels us to conclude that God is continuing to act creatively precisely through the regularities and processes in nature which we imperfectly describe and model in the natural sciences. New possibilities are actualized, new entities and organisms are "created," including ourselves, through the operation of these laws, as the universe expands, cools, and complexifies. With regard to "creation from nothing" and the issue of a temporal beginning to creation, contemporary cosmology and physical science, despite their scope and power, will probably never come close to accounting on their own terms for cosmic existence. As disciplines, they are not competent to bridge the tremendous gap between absolute nothingness (except God) and something created. Nor will they be able to explain or account for the laws of nature we discover in reality which endow it with order.

Similarly, because of the internal, derivative, and ambiguous character of time, it seems unlikely that cosmology and physics will ever determine whether or not the universe (created reality) had a beginning in time or existed from all eternity. The Big Bang as a relative, model-dependent limit to the hotter and denser phases of the universe as we travel back in time, is a powerful symbol of contingency and of ultimate origins, but, as we have seen, it cannot be accepted as an adequate description of that origin, nor as proof that it constituted a beginning in time, whatever that might mean. The derivative, internal nature that time manifests in General Relativity and in quantum gravity and quantum cosmology leaves us with the uneasy feeling that perhaps the notion of an absolute beginning of created reality in time is either meaningless or incorrect. However, this also seems to indicate that there may have been a primordial state of created reality prior to the emergence of time. If this is true, cosmology and physics may be indicating that there is a sense in which created reality is eternal. Putting these mind-bending possibilities to one side, we can still say, though, that cosmology and the physical sciences strongly demonstrate that all entities within the universe had a beginning in time, emerging from antecedent, less complicated, physical, chemical, or biological states.

The second specific issue stems from cosmology, and is reinforced by contemporary developments in the other natural sciences, particularly within the constellation of complexity, chaos, and the self-organization of matter: there is less and less support for any form of matter-spirit dualism, except for the radical dualism of God and not-God. This does not deny the spiritual but it does deny that the spiritual demands some separate principle. Matter and spirit must be different aspects of the same reality—spirit arises out of matter and is based somehow in matter. Related to this issue are the implications flowing from the sciences that, first, the entities that make up reality are all interconnected with one another on many different levels, sharing many of the same constraints and ordering principles, and many of the same constituents; and, second, the relationships that obtain among components in different entities are crucially important, and are in the most profound sense what constitutes them—they are constitutive relationships.

Finally, a third issue is that of God's action in the world, in physical reality. How we describe God's relationship with and action in the world must be tempered and partially determined by what we are discovering in the contemporary sciences. There is the familiar negative criterion of avoiding "the God of the gaps." But there is a positive resource here as well. The scope, the interconnectedness, and the intricacy of the laws of nature on so many levels—together with the radically evolutionary character of reality—express very strongly, though always imperfectly, some of the principal modes of divine action, and point tantalizingly to other, more profound, and pervasive modes which lie just beyond the horizons of our understanding and our inquisitive gaze.

However influential these three specific theological implications are or may be, they are less important than a more general theological implication. The physical sciences represented by these three constellations of revolutionary developments have, as I indicated at the beginning of this paper, radically modified our idea of the universe and of physical reality in general—its size, its complexity, its internal unity, its possibility, its past and its future, and the origins and interconnections of the entities and the organisms we find in it, including ourselves. It is also no longer a static universe, but an evolutionary one—in which even the laws of nature develop and evolve. Nothing in it is absolute or unchanging in the strict sense. Furthermore, these developments have significantly altered our view of ourselves as part of the universe and our view of ourselves as knowers in relation to the reality we seek to understand. In doing so, it has expanded the range of our capabilities and, at the same time, revealed previously unsuspected limitations and shortcomings. The myths, symbols, concepts, and categories that derive from these modifications are profoundly affecting both the way we live and the way we interpret our lives and our experience. Thus, they are also profoundly influencing our reflection on our experience of faith, and will continue to do so. Clearly, whether we are always aware of it or not, theology is and will continue to be deeply affected—one might also say determined—by this shifting intellectual and cultural milieu.

NOTES

1. Abner Shimony, "Conceptual Foundations of Quantum Mechanics," in Paul Davies, ed., *The New Physics* (Cambridge: Cambridge University Press, 1989), pp. 373-395.

2. See the first chapter of Bernd-Olaf Küppers, *Molecular Theory of Evolution*, 2nd ed. (Heidelberg: Springer-Verlag, 1983).

3. M. Eigen and P. Schuster, *The Hypercycle—A Principle of Natural Self-Organization*

(Heidelberg: Springer-Verlag, 1978).

4. For a more thorough treatment of this, see Chris J. Isham's articles, such as "Creation of the Universe as a Quantum Process," in R.J. Russell, W.R. Stoeger, and G.V. Coyne, eds., *Physics, Philosophy and Theology: A Common Quest for Understanding* (Vatican: Vatican Observatory, 1988), pp. 375–408; and "Quantum Theories of the Creation of the Universe," in R.J. Russell, N. Murphy, and C.J. Isham, eds., *The Quantum Creation of the Universe and the Origin of the Laws of Nature* (Vatican: Vatican Observatory; and Berkeley: CTNS, 1993).

5. In certain cases, for instance in Friedmann-Robertson-Walker space-times, which are isotropic and spatially homogeneous and used as the zeroth order approximation of our universe, a preferred or universal time parameter can be chosen.

6. See S.W. Hawking and G.F.R. Ellis, *The Large Scale Structure of Space-Time* (Cambridge: Cambridge University Press, 1973), pp. 256–275.

7. From an observational point of view, this conclusion is strongly supported by the existence, the blackbody character, and the near isotropy of the cosmic microwave background radiation, which we observe in all directions, and which left the cosmic plasma to propagate unimpeded toward us just 300,000 years after the Big Bang, when the universe was about 4,000° K, and protons and electrons had just combined to form neutral hydrogen atoms. Thus it is sort of an "afterglow" of the Big Bang. Such a conclusion is also supported by the systematic redshifting of distant galaxies we observe, which indicates that the universe is expanding as a single entity.

8. Stanley Jaki, emphasized in a talk at Steward Observatory, University of Arizona, April 1991, and elsewhere in his writings.

9. See C.J. Isham, "Creation of the Universe as a Quantum Process."

T = 0

IS IT THEOLOGICALLY SIGNIFICANT?[1]

ROBERT JOHN RUSSELL

In this paper I will attempt to respond theologically in some detail to the account of contemporary cosmology given here by William Stoeger.[2] To do so, I will first offer a brief account of the biblical sources for the doctrine of creation, and then outline in bare form several major historical developments of the doctrine from the Patristics to the watershed of the Enlightenment. I pick up the story again in the contemporary period to examine several positions on the relation between the theology of creation and scientific cosmology taken in response to this history. After this review, I defend an "interaction" model that will enable a bridge to be built between *creatio ex nihilo* and the "t = 0" in Big Bang cosmology through the philosophical categories of dependence and finitude. Finally, I will show how this philosophically mediated link between creation and cosmology can be modified so as to take account of quantum cosmology.

I. A BRIEF OVERVIEW OF THE HISTORY OF THE DOCTRINE OF CREATION

Biblical Sources

The Hebrew Bible (the Old Testament) characteristically affirms that "Help comes from the LORD, who made heaven and earth" (Ps. 121: 2), and offers a variety of images and narratives depicting the creation of the cosmos. No single account dominates; instead, the diversity is in itself a distinctive characteristic of biblical revelation. Here I will briefly touch on four sources, following the insightful analysis of Richard Clifford:[3] Psalms, Wisdom literature, Deutero-Isaiah, and Genesis 1–11. In several Psalms of communal lament (notably 44, 74, 77, 89), the poet calls upon God to prevent a present threat to Israel, and does so in the context of recounting God's creation of the world. Psalm 104 links the purpose of the creation of the world with the possibility of human life. In Psalms 19, 136, and 121, praise for God's redemption is linked with God's creation of the world.

Isaiah 40–55, written during the Babylonian captivity, prophesies a new creation of the people of Israel. A new exodus, this time from Babylon, and a return to Canaan (Zion) will mark the recreation of Israel as God's people (see especially, 43: 18–19). In a pivotal passage (44: 24) we find a clear connection between the LORD as redeemer and the LORD as creator. In dispute is whether creation theology is a later addition to Israel's faith that God saves, as Von Rad has argued,[4] or whether it permeates the historical development of Israel, as Westermann and Anderson believe.[5]

Proverbs 8: 22–31 offers one of the most profound visions of the creation of the world in Hebrew scripture. Here we are told that Wisdom was created as the first of God's acts, and that she was beside God during the creation of the foundations of the earth and all that is within. Clifford points out the anthropocentric tone of Proverbs, and the assumption that God's will can be seen in what is created. However, these features are in striking contrast with the creation account found in other parts of Hebrew Wisdom literature, such as Job, in which God's will and purpose surpass human understanding.

In the first eleven chapters of Genesis, we find the texts that have most dominated theological reflection on creation. In the Priestly account of the creation of the world (1: 1–2:3a), arguably the most important features are the Sabbath rest of God, together with the sevenfold assertion that creation is good. Still, the Priestly account raises a number of complex issues, including the original meaning of 1: 1, and the role it should play in the theological understanding of creation. Even the translation of the 1: 1 text is highly debated. Should we side with the traditional depiction of an absolute beginning (read as "In the beginning . . . "; compare Gen. 1: 1 with II Macc. 7: 28) or with more recent exegetes who interpret it to mean an ordering of a pre-existent chaos (read as "When God began to form. . .")? Does the creation story encourage us to view creation as something happening at the beginning or as an ongoing process, linked to salvation?

Questions surrounding the meaning of creation were important to the early Christian Church as it sought to understand its new experience of faith in God through its witness to Christ. Paul often links creation with redemption in the person of Jesus Christ, and other New Testament writers do the same (Col. 1: 16-17; I Cor. 8: 6; II Cor. 4: 3-4; Heb. 1: 2-3). The Synoptic Gospels continue to explore the relation between God's creation and providence (Mt. 7: 26; 7: 28-30; 8: 26; 10: 29; Lk. 15: 3), and the radical newness of God's act is underscored by the New Creation in Christ. The Gospel of John opens with a vision of the Word (the Greek *logos*) as God's active principle of creation, reflecting the formulation of Gen. 1: 1.

Given this extraordinarily complex textual landscape, how is biblical theology to render the diverse original witness to creation? How are systematic and philosophical theology to rekindle this witness for each age and culture? How are the fruits of these cultures—their truest knowledge, clearest reasoning, finest art and most compelling values—to be taken up and appropriated to this witness?

Themes in the Development of the Doctrine of Creation

These biblical images were gradually structured into a complex doctrine of creation consisting of several streams of thought that remained relatively stable from the Patristic period to the seventeenth century Enlightenment.[6] Sometimes the tradition is spoken of in terms of creation and preservation. At other times it is formulated in terms of *creatio ex nihilo* ("creation out of nothing") and *creatio continua* ("continuous creation"). A third model, depicting creation as divine emanation, has played a lesser role in the tradition as a whole. Part of the difficulty in interpreting the history of the doctrine of creation is dealing with the complex, changing and often ambiguous relations between these various terms. For the purposes of this essay, I will adopt the perspective afforded by Langdon Gilkey in his influential 1959 text, *Maker of Heaven and Earth*.

One stream in the creation tradition is *creatio ex nihilo*. According to Gilkey, *creatio ex nihilo* was born out of the early church's effort to reject, or at least absorb and attenuate, several prevailing theories of creation: metaphysical dualism, in which the world was an eternal divine substance equal and opposed to God; moral dualism, Zoroastrianism, and gnosticism, in each of which, in varying ways, the world was an evil power resisting a good God; emanationism, in which the world emerged from and was the body or substance of God (but see below for a qualified endorsement of emanationism in the tradition); and various monisms, including pantheism, in which the world was God.

Hence the *creatio ex nihilo* perspective first of all affirms that God alone is the source of all that is, and God's creative activity is free and unconditioned. In attempting to capture the most prevalent biblical conception of creation, *creatio ex nihilo* stands for the belief that God creates without preconditions. For example, the world was not merely shaped out of preexisting matter by the Demiurge while gazing into an ideal realm of transcendent forms, as Plato taught in the *Timaeus*. Neither the material of this world, nor the set of possible patterns it can assume (what we would now call the "laws of nature"), existed prior to God's creative act. Rather, these were created by God in the process of creating the world.

Creatio ex nihilo also affirms that the world is an autonomous and distinct reality because it was created by the free resolve and decree of God. As a creation by God, and not God's own self, the world is contingent, finite, temporal, and relative; only God is necessary, infinite, eternal, and absolute. The world's reality and goodness are entirely contingent upon God as ultimate reality, ultimate goodness, ultimate source.

There is an important connection between this thesis and the origins of modern empirical science. Since God creates freely, the world need not be at all, and it need not be the way it is. Hence for us to know the world, we must experiment; we cannot discover the way nature is by reason alone. Moreover, since the world is not divine, it is not sacrilegious to experiment with nature. Thus we both (morally) can and (epistemologically) must experiment with nature to gain knowledge. The method of empirical science embodies the view of nature framed in the doctrine of *creatio ex nihilo*.

The term *nihilo* means "nothing" or nonbeing. Though the history of this term is complex, a distinction between two meanings of nonbeing found in Greek metaphysics can help. Nonbeing understood as *ouk on* meant absolute or nondialectical nonbeing;

as *me on* it meant nonbeing as the relative negation of being, in dialectical relation to being. According to Ted Peters, *me on* "represents the quality of temporal passage that erodes what is now and makes way for what is yet to come. It is the power of not-yet-being." Whereas *creatio ex nihilo* works principally within the framework of *ouk on*, the absolute abyss of nothing out of which only God can create anything, such as an absolute beginning of time or the actual existence of the universe, there is also a role for the concept of *me on* in *creatio ex nihilo*. "Dialectical nonbeing is necessary [if we are] to think of divine creativity as continuing [in time]."[7]

A second stream in the creation tradition is that of an ongoing process of *creatio continua*. Not only does God give the world its actual existence, but God also acts as its creator moment by moment in time. Whereas *creatio ex nihilo* tended to emphasize God's transcendence with respect to the universe as a whole, *creatio continua* tended to shift attention to the immanence and participation of God in the processes of nature, history, and personal experience.

According to Pelikan,[8] it was the second century apologist, Theophilus of Antioch, who first clearly shifted the doctrine of creation away from its early emphasis on continuous creation and identified the central commitments of the doctrine of creation instead with *creatio ex nihilo*. The continuing creation tradition remained subordinated to *creatio ex nihilo* during the thirteenth to seventeenth centuries. Since then, continuous creation has resurfaced in the form of an "order out of chaos" motif, emphasizing the emergence of more complex structures and processes out of older, simpler ones.

In the more static cosmology that dominated Christianity until the rise of modern science, continuous creation meant primarily the preservation of the world in its given and fixed hierarchical structure. More recently, because of the change to a dynamic cosmology, language about *creatio continua* has largely replaced the term "preservation," since in this cosmology God is seen to act continuously in time as the source of novelty.

Today it remains an open question whether *creatio continua* is best viewed as a relatively separate model from, and even a replacement for, *creatio ex nihilo*, or as a subordinate but increasingly important part of *creatio ex nihilo*. It is also an open question whether *creatio continua*, though referring to the occurrence of the genuinely novel in time, still assumes that novelty is the product of mere recombination of the already-given (what Thomas Aquinas called "change"), or whether the genuinely novel points to God acting *ex nihilo* at each moment, as it were, to create something "radically" new. We will discuss later the views of several contemporary theologians on these topics.

Thirdly, it is important to note briefly the ambiguous role played by emanationism in the history of the doctrine of creation. Its roots lie in gnosticism and neo-Platonism, and it was frequently condemned or at least suppressed by Christian orthodoxy. Nevertheless it represents an important counterpoint to *creatio ex nihilo*.

Emanationism envisages spiritual beings and all of nature as originating in a necessary overflowing of a perfectly good and unitary principle into plurality and moral ambiguity, whereas *creatio ex nihilo* is rooted in the concept of creation as the result of God's absolute and free decree. The Reformed tradition, well-represented by theologian Karl Barth, has especially emphasized creation as divine decree. However, creation as a necessary emanation of the perfect divine nature is also represented in recent writings, including those of Paul Tillich and Jürgen Moltmann. It also has important links to the Jewish Kabbalistic and Christian mystical traditions.

Contributions to the Development of the Doctrine of Creation

While a detailed history of the doctrine of creation is obviously out of the question, three turning points in the history of the doctrine must be mentioned, since they are of lasting importance to theology and of particular relevance to this essay. These were brought about by Augustine, Aquinas, and Schleiermacher.

Augustine of Hippo, in the fourth century, made the most lasting mark of all the Patristics on the meaning of creation *ex nihilo*. In Book 11 of the *Confessions*, again in *The City of God*, and in his commentary on Genesis, Augustine argued that God did not create the world at a certain moment within a preexisting and everlasting span of time. Instead, God created time along with the world; time is a part of the created world, not something "prior" to the world in which the world is created.[9]

According to Etienne Gilson,[10] Augustine held this view about the creation of time because he saw himself forced to choose between the emanationist belief that God made the world out of the divine substance, and the *ex nihilo* belief that God made the world from nothing. Since the former presupposed a changing divine substance, which he saw as self-contradictory, Augustine chose the latter. We find a key text in the *Confessions* where Augustine prayerfully addresses God:

> Time itself was of your making. . . . Let them see, then, that there cannot possibly be time without creation. . . . Let them understand that before all time began you are the eternal Creator of all time, and that no time and no created thing is co-eternal with you, even if any created thing is outside time.[11]

This move also settled the problem of the apparent arbitrariness of God's choice about "when in time" to create, since if there were no "preexisting" time, no choice of a particular moment for the creation of the world was needed.

In the thirteenth century, the rediscovery of the writings of Aristotle once again opened the question of the origin of the world. According to Aristotle, the world was eternally, *without beginning*. Thomas Aquinas opposed Aristotle in this, arguing instead that the question of the age of the world could not be settled by appealing to reason alone. Aquinas also opposed the the view of Bonaventure and other contemporaries that the world could be *shown* to have a finite age. By contrast, Aquinas advanced two distinct but related assertions: (1) the created world is contingent, it is ontologically dependent for its very existence on God; and (2) the world has a finite past, a beginning of time. He defended the first assertion as the conclusion of a strictly philosophical argument that expressed the fundamental meaning of the doctrine of creation, and that would stand whether or not the world in fact had a beginning in time. The second, however, he considered strictly an article of faith, known by revelation alone.[12]

The traditional formulation of the doctrine of creation was profoundly altered by the whole complex of developments beginning with the Enlightenment and extending to the present intellectual climate at the close of the twentieth century. As Langdon Gilkey points out, three claims—God as the source of all that is, creatures as dependent on God for their being and goodness, and God's action in creating the world as free and purposeful—dominated the creation tradition, especially in the *ex nihilo* form, from the early Patristics (Irenaeus) to the Reformation leaders (Calvin, Luther, and others).[13] All this was to be challenged by the Enlightenment. The rise of critical philosophy (for instance, Hume and Kant), the primacy of efficient causation and mechanical explanation in science (for instance, Galileo and Newton), and the major transitions in the wider intellectual culture induced enormous changes in the content and method of theology. A snapshot of the doctrine of creation within this pattern of transformation is offered by one of the most influential contributors to the modern debates: Friedrich Schleiermacher.

The method of Schleiermacher's *Glaubenslehre* (second edition, 1830)[14] called for admitting only those doctrinal propositions which could be traced back to their basis in immediate religious self-consciousness.[15] Schleiermacher believed that the content of religious self-consciousness regarding creation is completely given by the proposition that "the totality of finite being exists only in dependence upon the Infinite." With the idea of dependence as the core, the distinction between creation (*creatio ex nihilo*) and preservation (*creatio continua*) virtually dissolved. Since Schleiermacher thought that the religious self-consciousness does not contain the idea of a "beginning of being," but only the idea of absolute dependence, he minimized the importance for dogmatics of a purported beginning of the world in time.[16]

Schleiermacher freely admitted that questions about the beginning of the world could be asked. In fact, he sided with Augustine about the origin of time with creation. But he argued that such questions were matters of speculation, not genuine piety, and so only of indirect interest to Christian faith. When language about creation "out of nothing" is used in Christian theology, we are to understand it strictly in terms of an exclusion of any matter or form existing independently of God's act of absolute origination. Beyond this, nothing more is meant by *ex nihilo*. It follows from this perspective that the Christian doctrine of creation is neutral toward scientific and speculative explanations as long as they remain compatible with the fundamental claim that the world is absolutely ontologically dependent on God.

Twentieth-century theology has been defined by the neo-Reformed rejection of Schleiermacher's liberal style of theology. This rejection is associated with the writings of Karl Barth, Emil Brunner, Reinhold Niebuhr, Dietrich Bonhoeffer, and others. However, when it comes to the doctrine of creation, there is surprising continuity between Schleiermacher and these writers. The distinction between ontological dependence and creation at the beginning of time, the central importance of the former and the essential irrelevance of the latter to *creatio ex nihilo*, and the basic independence of theology from science, all serve to characterize much of this century's theological convictions, even as they were important in Schleiermacher's thought.

There are obvious exceptions to this pattern, including the theologies of Karl Rahner, Jürgen Moltmann, and Wolfhart Pannenberg, all of whom are greatly influenced by science. There are also the process theologians, and such key figures as Pierre Teilhard de Chardin. Most important, however, is the new movement of "theology and science," which points toward a deep and mutual, if asymmetric, interaction between these disparate fields. Beginning with the pioneering work of Ian Barbour in the early 1960s and growing rapidly over the past three decades, we have witnessed a resurgence of interest in the question of the bearing of science and the philosophy of science on theology, theological method, and the philosophy of religion—and even of the influence of theology on science. In these discussions, the question of how to relate the doctrine of creation and scientific ideas about cosmic origins has been reopened and answered in a variety of ways. I turn next to an examination of these answers.

II. THREE WAYS TO RELATE CREATION AND COSMOLOGY

Augustine developed his interpretation of the doctrine of creation against the background of Manichaeism and neo-Platonism, Aquinas in relation to Aristotle's science, and Schleiermacher in dialogue with deism and Newtonian mechanics. In much the same way, the doctrine of creation in the latter part of the twentieth century has richly engaged Big Bang cosmology. Indeed, in Julian Hartt's succinct summary of five key issues at stake in the contemporary theological discussion of creation, the first is whether "Christian thought about creation (can) take seriously the notion of a world-originating divine act."[17] In particular, Hartt points to Big Bang cosmology as "stirring hopes for the successful revival—perhaps we ought to say resurrection—of the (traditional) view."[18]

Physicists, too, discern monumental significance in the possibility that the universe "came to be" at some finite time in the past, some ten to fifteen billion years ago. According to John Archibald Wheeler, the essential singularity, $t = 0$, poses the greatest crisis physics has ever faced.[19] What, then, is the scientific status of $t = 0$? Is there a singularity in nature, as it suggests, or will the "singularity problem" vanish when traditional Big Bang cosmology is replaced by a better model? What philosophical issues are involved here? And is there a way in which such a scientific claim, and the philosophical issues connected with it, can be brought into the theological conversation about divine creation, particularly about creation *ex nihilo*?[20] Answers to these questions, especially the last, are the primary criteria for distinguishing the following models of the relation between creation and cosmology, all of which are articulated today.

Direct Support

To many, the event at "t = 0" in Big Bang cosmology lends immediate support, even proof, to *creatio ex nihilo*. In June, 1978, *The New York Times* ran an article "Found by God?" by astronomer Robert Jastrow, the founder and director of NASA's Goddard Institute for Space Studies. He stated that theologians ought to be "delighted" that astronomical evidence "leads to a biblical view of Genesis." Jastrow concluded by describing the beleaguered scientist who, as in a bad dream, having scaled the highest peak of discovery, finds a "band of theologians . . . (who) have been sitting there for centuries."[21]

Similarly, when minute fluctuations in the microwave background radiation were discovered by researchers at the University of California, Berkeley, the event was heralded as having theological overtones. A long-standing problem for the Big Bang model was how to account for the development of massive clumps of matter, protogalaxies, in the very early universe if the previous era was dominated by an entirely uniform distribution of elementary particles and radiation. Asymmetries in the background radiation, discovered in the data from NASA's COBE satellite, suggested that protogalaxies could have arisen out of these pattern of fluctuations in the radiation. This provided additional evidence in favor of the Big Bang model. But did it prove a Genesis account of creation? Whatever their considered opinions might have been, several scientists involved with the research gave credence to such a view in the media. According to George Smoot, project leader, "What we have found is evidence for the birth of the universe. . . . It's like looking at God."[22] Results such as this have fueled organizations like *Reasons to Believe*, which have long sought to link scientific discoveries to a literal reading of scripture.[23]

Actually, neither Jastrow nor Hugh Ross, the head of *Reasons to Believe*, was the first to gain wide recognition for the claim that science can offer direct support for Christian theology. In 1951, in an allocution to the Pontifical Academy of Sciences in Rome that received broad publicity, Pope Pius XII claimed that science had now provided new grounds for belief in God. The "mighty beginning" of the universe discovered by astronomers could now help scientists "ascend to a creating Spirit."

There are theologians in the mainline Protestant tradition who take this position, motivated partly by the desire to give concrete empirical force to the idea of "dependence on God." For example, Ted Peters, in one of his earlier writings has stated:

> It simply makes sense these days to speak of t = 0, to conceive of a point at which the
> entire cosmos makes its appearance along with the spacetime continuum within which it

is observed and understood. . . . To reduce *creatio ex nihilo* to a vague commitment about the dependence of the world upon God—though accurate—does not help much. It simply moves the matter to a higher level of abstraction. We still need to ask: just what does it mean for the world to owe its existence to God?[24]

I find three problems with directly linking the theology of *creatio ex nihilo* to scientific cosmology in this way. First, from a scientific point of view, if (and it is inevitably a "when," as we shall see with research on quantum gravity) science moves beyond General Relativity, it may find a way to embed the description of *this* universe in a prior one. Here one thinks roughly in terms of an ever-oscillating universe, or a prior superspace, or any of a dozen other ideas. So it is an open question whether nature has the absolute singularity that Big Bang theory suggests. If it does not, then the direct connection between t = 0 and *creatio ex nihilo* will be lost.

Second, and more philosophically, as Stoeger points out, it is far from clear whether the "event" designated by t = 0 in Big Bang cosmology is really open to scientific investigation. If indeed there were a physical event such as t = 0 that was both uncaused and yet the cause of future events, it would fall outside the purview of scientific analysis.[25]

Third, and thinking now theologically, the identification of *ex nihilo* with t = 0 would seem to narrow the meaning of *ex nihilo* considerably, neglecting the ontological dependence of every moment of time on God's creative power, and tending towards a deistic interpretation of creation.

I agree with Peters and others who want to link *creatio ex nihilo* directly with t = 0 that it is a mistake to void theological assertions of all empirical content, but I think this must be accomplished without a direct and literal identification of creation and Big Bang's initial singularity. More recently, Peters has modified his earlier view, affirming that theology and science should be in "consonance."[26] I shall discuss this term below when I present an alternative approach to the direct support view.

Independence

In a widely distributed recent publication drafted by the American Scientific Association, *Teaching Science in a Climate of Controversy*, the approach taken on the issue of the possible significance of t = 0 is one that stresses the limits of science. The origin and source of the universe, why there is something rather than nothing, the status of its laws, and so on constitute "ultimate questions (that are) approached from a philosophical perspective, not a scientific one. . . . People need to understand that *science continually raises philosophical questions that go beyond the competence or purview of science.*"[27]

Some voices have been raised in support of an even stronger separation of theology and science. The account of the creation tradition given above was drawn from one of the clearest and most influential recent examples of the "two worlds" model in which science and religion are essentially independent, namely the groundbreaking text by Langdon Gilkey, *Maker of Heaven and Earth* (1959). Gilkey's interpretation of the problem of the origin of the world, though clearly indebted to the neo-Orthodoxy prevalent at that time, is highly compatible with that of Schleiermacher, and also draws on independence motifs in Aquinas.

Gilkey reminds us that the idea of an "'originating' activity of God" has always been a part of the Christian creation tradition. It has, however, taken two distinct forms which, for simplicity, I shall refer to with the previous discussions in mind as ontological dependence and creation at the beginning.[28] By ontological dependence, Gilkey means that in the very fact of its existence as such, and without regard for any qualification of that existence (for instance, age, mode of beginning, and so on), the world is absolutely dependent on God. As Gilkey puts it, " . . . God originates the *existence* of each creature out of nothing, whatever its position in the time scale." In contrast, by creation at the beginning, Gilkey means a narrative account or cosmogony about the coming-to-be of the world. "(I)t has meant 'originating' in the sense of founding and establishing at the beginning, starting the whole sequence of things at a first moment."[29] Gilkey cites Anthony Flew's contrast between the "scientific" sense of creation at the beginning of time and the "theological" sense of absolute ontological dependence on God. Presumably Gilkey endorses Flew's comment here that the scientific sense of creation is "simply irrelevant" to the theological sense of creation.

According to Gilkey, theologians routinely accepted creation in both senses as being true until the rise of modern science. Until then, the world could be thought of as created at the beginning of time and then preserved over the ages by God. Now, with a dynamic view of nature, we must think of creation as taking place "*in* time . . . (God is) continuously bringing forth new creations. . . . God's creation and preservation are. . .different aspects of the simultaneous activity of God, who continually . . . mold(s) the new as well as preserv(es) the old." Here Gilkey is reflecting both Schleiermacher's collapse of the distinction between creation and preservation, and the dominance in contemporary theology of the *creatio continua* tradition.

But Gilkey also points out a problem with the concept of an "absolute beginning" itself. Neither science nor theology could, in fact, include such a concept—science, because it would be forced to presume that the universe arose from *something*, and theology, because revelation cannot inform us of scientific facts. In support of his position, Gilkey cites Aquinas: only through revelation as propositional could we know that the world had an absolute beginning; philosophy on its own could never establish it.[30] Since Gilkey does not hold a propositional understanding of revelation like Aquinas, he is ready to abandon as mythical any empirical language about creation, and he expresses his theology of creation strictly in terms of ontological dependence. "The idea of a beginning to time has a great theological and cultural value; but . . . we have been forced to deny that there can be for theology any factual content to this idea."[31]

Stoeger's view of the relation between the doctrine of creation and Big Bang cosmology constitutes a second example of "independence." In his previous writings
Stoeger has given an extensive, challenging, and profound analysis of the philosophical problems underlying General Relativity, quantum gravity, and cosmology. In this
volume, Stoeger's commitment to an independence view emerges particularly in his
comments about t = 0, where he makes five distinct but related points:

(1) Technically, the initial singularity should not be thought of as a part of the early uni-
    verse, but as a *limiting case* which we approach as we move backwards in time. In the
    limit of t = 0, physical parameters such as temperature and density tend to infinity.[32]

(2) Because it is a limit to, and not an event within, spacetime, it "is amenable to neither
    mathematical manipulations nor physical interpretation." Although it may suggest a
    beginning of time, "we cannot examine the initial singularity itself in any complete or
    understandable way within the model. To that extent it stands outside the model,
    even though it is indicated by it."[33]

(3) From this Stoeger concludes that, at best, the suggestion of a beginning of time is
    only meaningful within the Big Bang model itself. This means that t = 0 cannot be
    used in metaphysics, nor in theology, to refer to "creation."

> In themselves the new astronomy and the new cosmology do not answer the
> question of ultimate origins. . . . But they pose that question with new insis-
> tence. . . . They also cast doubt on the importance and reality of an ultimate
> temporal origin for creation, and reinforce the importance of metaphysical
> origins, and of the veiled underlying sources of possibility and necessity.[34]

(4) On this basis, Stoeger asserts that cosmology and metaphysics are separated by an
    unbridgeable gap. Though cosmology may raise the question of ultimate origins, in
    principle it cannot answer it.

> With regard to "creation from nothing" and the issue of a temporal beginning
> to creation, contemporary cosmology and physical science . . . will probably
> never come close to accounting on their own terms for cosmic existence. As
> disciplines, they are not competent to bridge the tremendous gap between
> absolute nothingness (except God) and something created.[35]

(5) Finally, Stoeger reminds us that the problem of t = 0 in Big Bang cosmology may be
    overcome by science itself. The presence of this limit may signal not a physical sin-
    gularity in nature, but merely the breakdown of the Big Bang model, and the need to
    turn to quantum gravity for a cosmological theory which overcomes the problem of
    an initial singularity; I will have more to say about this presently.

In Stoeger's view, t = 0 might raise questions *for* metaphysics, but it cannot be
incorporated into the discussion *of* metaphysics, let alone theology, both because of

the unbridgeable relation between these fields and because $t = 0$ lies on the borderline even of scientific cosmology. Instead it functions to help move scientists from the existing theory of gravity (Einstein's General Relativity) towards its successor (quantum gravity).

I strongly agree with Stoeger that we need to do a great deal more research on the role, significance, and meaning of limit points and other technical problems in theoretical physics, lest we treat them superficially in metaphysics or theology. However, I am not convinced that his conclusion about the impossibility of discussing $t = 0$ within metaphysics and theology follows from the problematic status of $t = 0$ in physics. I am still less persuaded by his assertion that there is an unbridgeable gap between cosmology, on the one side, and metaphysics and theology, on the other. In fact, Stoeger does not actually develop an argument for why the gap is *unbridgeable*; he merely asserts it. Later, I hope to show that we do *not* need to view cosmology, metaphysics, and theology as completely separate domains of discourse. If my claim can be sustained—and here we encounter the entire question before us, namely, that of the relation between science, philosophy, and theology—then the limit, $t = 0$, and other complex and ambiguous concepts in science might well be given a broader interpretation.

Interaction

Naturally, theologians fit on a spectrum between the positions presented here. Taking the independence model as our starting point, for example, there are theologians such as Ian Barbour who sympathize with the primacy of ontological dependence in the meaning of *creatio ex nihilo*, but who nevertheless conclude that $t = 0$ may have a subsidiary role in the interpretation of *ex nihilo*. Barbour states, in *Religion in an Age of Science*:

> I do not think that major theological issues are at stake in the case of $t = 0$, as has often been assumed. If a single, unique Big Bang continues to be the most convincing scientific theory, the theist can indeed see it as an instant of divine origination. But I will suggest that this is not the main concern expressed in the religious notion of creation.[36]

Barbour and others recognize that scientific information about cosmic origins can provide interesting specifications of the doctrine of creation without ever having direct bearing on its fundamental meaning of ontological dependence.

It seems to me, however, that we can and must make still closer and more systematic connections between scientific cosmology and the doctrine of creation than the independence model allows, while also resisting the overclose connections of the direct support model. Thus, I turn to a description of a third model, interaction, which is gaining momentum in religion and science discussions today.

In an essay whose effects were to be extensive on the discussions of theology and cosmology, Ernan McMullin called for what he termed "consonance" as a middle ground between the positivistic restriction of knowledge to science alone, and the biblicistic attempt to construct science out of scripture. Science cannot be separated from theology, but we must "distrust the simpler pathways from one to the other." Instead the goal is consonance, in which a coherent worldview is constructed not only out of science and theology, but also out of history, politics, literature, and other human products. "This consonance ... is a tentative relation, constantly under scrutiny, in constant slight shift."[37] It is this "time dependent" and constructed character of McMullin's view of consonance that I find so very potent, and which enabled McMullin to place cosmology and creation theology into an evocative relation.

> ... if the universe began in time through the act of a Creator, from our vantage point it would look something like the Big Bang that cosmologists are now talking about. What one cannot say is, first, that the Christian doctrine of creation "supports" the Big Bang model, or second, that the Big Bang model "supports" the Christian doctrine of creation.[38]

In a number of writings since McMullin's essay,[39] I have sought to develop this notion, emphasizing the dialectic between consonance and "dissonance," and the value of both by drawing on the epistemological tension in "metaphor" analyzed by such writers as Paul Ricoeur, Ian Barbour, Janet Soskice, and Sallie McFague. This yields an understanding of the changing patterns of consonance and dissonance between elements of scientific and theological theories as they follow their developing internal trajectories. The term has also been picked up and given important interpretations by Ted Peters, Ian Barbour, Willem Drees, and others.[40]

More recently, I have sought to embed the general goal of consonance within a more tight-knit methodological structure patterned after the methodology of scientific research programs. I will explain this approach after offering, as one warrant for it, the problem we face if we follow the extremes of either direct support or independence.

Both of the extreme models treat ontological dependence and creation as alternatives, differing only in the choice regarding what is theologically important. Whereas advocates of independence abandon the "at the beginning" aspect of creation, the advocates of direct support reduce the ontological meaning of creation to its context of creation at the beginning. But if the critical issue in the *ex nihilo* tradition is ontological dependence, the radical dependence of finite being on God, then the latter move cannot be acceptable. Likewise, if the finitude of created time cannot be entirely abandoned, as the *ex nihilo* tradition suggests, then the independence position is also unacceptable.

Interestingly, it is Gilkey who sees the issue of t = 0 as critically important, since it forces us to confront a *foundational* problem which governs and characterizes *every* major doctrine in Christian theology—namely, the problematic theological status of factual claims in the context of assertions about ultimate or transcendent things. "This same dilemma dogs the heels of every major theological idea. Every doctrine of

Christian faith expresses the paradoxical relation between the transcendent God and the world of facts."[41]

Although I am critical of Gilkey's resolution of the problem,[42] we are indebted to him for his lucid insistence on its importance. If Gilkey is correct, as I believe he is in this regard, the epistemological problems surrounding t = 0 are well worth *our* pursuing because they are *inherent* to the theological agenda as such, and not a minor issue best forgotten. Indeed, they raise the fundamental and unavoidable problem of the rationality of theology in an age of scientific epistemology.

III. A METHOD FOR ENABLING INTERACTION

I believe we must challenge the crucial premise lying behind the problem, namely, having to choose between ontological dependence and creation at the beginning. Instead, I propose we embed language about the latter within the broader context of ontological dependence, thus giving a factual basis to which language about ontological dependence can be related, without literalization (Peters) *or* equivocation (Peacocke, Barbour, and Stoeger).

We can begin to do this by recalling an insight of Aquinas. I take his strategy in our context to be something like the following. On the one hand, if science supports an eternally old universe, as Aristotle argued, one can still maintain that the universe is the creation of God, since it can still be shown to be ontologically dependent in the philosophical sense by the mere fact of its existence *per se*. On the other hand, if science supports a universe with a finite age, as the Big Bang suggests, this can count as indirect empirical evidence in support of its being the creation of God, although other evidence might count against it, too. Ontological dependence is thus the *crucial*, but not the *exhaustive*, meaning of creation.

Next, I propose that we incorporate this position within a more complex theological methodology. To do so, I will draw on research first anticipated by Ian Barbour, and very recently developed in detail by both Nancey Murphy and Philip Clayton.[43] These scholars in various ways appropriate current research in philosophy of science into theological method, drawing particularly on the writings of Imre Lakatos.[44] According to Lakatos, a scientific research program consists in an abstract core hypothesis surrounded by a belt of auxiliary hypotheses, and beyond them the sea of empirical data. The auxiliary hypotheses give successively more specific empirical meaning to the core, linking it indirectly with the data, and thus allowing the program as a whole to be tested and potentially falsified. They also direct the progress of the program as it seeks to incorporate and explain new domains of data; they provide theories of instrumentation by which data are produced; and, by lying between the core and the data, they immunize the core from immediate falsification by anomalous data.

Lakatos also gives specific criteria by which a research program should be pursued as progressive or abandoned as degenerating, allowing for rational means to decide between competing research programs. The most important criterion is that a modification of an auxiliary hypothesis to account for an anomaly should also lead to a novel prediction, and that such predictions should frequently be verified. A theory that is inherently piecemeal, that does not lead to novel predictions, or whose novel predictions are consistently wrong, is clearly degenerating and should be abandoned.

So, for example, General Relativity consists of a core hypothesis (Einstein's field equations), an auxiliary belt relating it to astronomical and cosmological data (for instance, a model for a rotating neutron star or for magnitude-redshift data via the Big Bang model), theories of observation (for instance, how to allow for gravitational distortion in measuring the distance of cosmological objects), and a modification of the belt of hypotheses to account for anomalies (for instance, inclusion of the cosmological constant to explain problems in standard Big Bang cosmology, such as the matter/antimatter ratio or the horizon problem). Since the Big Bang model could account for novel facts which Hoyle's steady state theory could not, such as the background radiation and the ratio of hydrogen to helium in the universe, the latter was eventually abandoned in favor of the former.

Can reasoning such as this be employed fruitfully by theologians, as they seek to incorporate data from many domains (including cosmology) within their theological research program and, in the process, to suggest why one program and not its competitors is the more convincing?

As a first step in responding to this challenge, I propose we structure the doctrine of *creatio ex nihilo* and its relation to data in cosmology as follows: I suggest we place at the core of the theological research program the hypothesis, "*creatio ex nihilo* means ontological dependence." Next we deploy a series of auxiliary hypotheses which use *philosophical* categories to surround the core and relate it to relevant types of data, including those from cosmology. I propose as one such auxiliary hypothesis the claim: "ontological dependence entails finitude." By finitude, I mean the traditional Aristotelian concept of something with determinate status, measure, or boundary, as opposed to that which is unbounded, unlimited, endlessly extensible.[45] The function of this philosophical understanding of finitude is to prevent "ontological finitude" from being reduced to a univocal, empirical meaning. Keeping some distance in this way between the theological core and the data from science will, in turn, at least partially address the concerns voiced from the direction of the independence model by Gilkey, Peacocke, Barbour, and Stoeger.

Yet the concept of finitude need not be entirely restricted to an abstract, philosophical context. Instead it can be developed in a variety of ways to make increasing contact with physics and cosmology, and thus with an empirical meaning of origination. To do so we construct a second auxiliary hypothesis, "finitude includes temporal finitude," that is, that which is bounded in time. From this we construct a third auxiliary hypothesis: "temporal finitude includes past temporal finitude," that is, the property of a finite age. Now we are in a position to connect this series of hypotheses to Big Bang cosmology, in which the data of astrophysics, the theory of General Relativity, and other factors, assumptions, and simplifications lead to the conclusion that the universe has a finite age and an initial singularity, t = 0. In this way the concept of finitude can serve as a *philosophical bridge* between the core *theological* theory, "*creatio ex nihilo* means ontological dependence," and the *empirical* data for theology, here seen in terms of the origin of the universe at t = 0, thereby satisfying at least part of Peters's intent of making a connection (albeit *not* a direct one) between ontological dependence and empirical origination.

Through this process, I claim we can argue that the empirical origination described by t = 0 in Big Bang cosmology tends to confirm what is entailed by the theological core theory, "*creatio ex nihilo* means ontological dependence." In a sense, what we are looking for is a judgment call, not a logical proof—something to help us decide between a theistic and an atheistic explanation for the existence of the universe. To draw on a legal analogy, t = 0 serves as a *character witness* in a trial, but not as an *eyewitness* to creation theology.

Moreover, to the extent that Big Bang cosmology continues to gain scientific support, the confirmation of *ex nihilo* is indirectly strengthened as well. For example, recent evidence from the COBE satellite showing the existence of minute structure in the microwave background constitutes additional support for Big Bang cosmology, and thus *indirectly* it lends additional support for *creatio ex nihilo*.

I want to emphasize, though, that this method allows for disconfirmation as well as confirmation of the theological core, lest I appear to be setting up a "no-lose" scenario. Evidence against t = 0, such as offered in the 1950s and 1960s by Hoyle's steady state model, can be seen as counting against *ex nihilo*, or at least as neutralizing the indirect support of certain data for *creatio ex nihilo*. Recent developments in quantum gravity and quantum cosmology that undermine t = 0 offer other kinds of challenges to creation theology, given our strategy of finding ways to relate theology to the empirical context. Even the Big Bang model can be taken as offering disconfirming evidence if we can argue that its past can be characterized as infinite. For example, using temperature to define the age of the universe makes even the Big Bang universe infinitely old.[46] Yet ontological dependence could never be absolutely disproven by *any* empirical evidence, since the sheer existence of the universe is the foundational basis for the central philosophical argument for *ex nihilo*.

In concluding these methodological reflections, it ought to be mentioned that, although there are some theologians today who would deny altogether the fact-asserting value of theological language, most theologians do not go this far. The problem has more often been one of how to place theological utterances within the wider range of fact-asserting intellectual domains, whose objects are more definite and whose tasks are more circumscribed; and how to appreciate the subtlety and richness of theological activity that goes with the nature of its concerns. This problem has sometimes led to a difficulty in judging the relative merits of alternative theological perspectives, and even what counts as success and failure in theology.

The research program methodology of Lakatos, adapted for theology, has many advantages in this problematic context of debate about the nature of theological language. It takes account of the multifaceted nature of religious language while avoiding exclusive stress on its fact-asserting function. Yet it recognizes that the function of asserting facts is crucial in theological language, and on this basis insists that theological utterances have a public dimension, and must seek criticism and confirmation in a variety of intersubjective contexts. Finally, it allows for a relation between a core theological hypothesis and a wide range of data, including data from the sciences, while systematically showing *why* this relation cannot be direct.

IV. AN ILLUSTRATION OF THE STRENGTH OF THE METHOD: QUANTUM COSMOLOGY

The changing climate in cosmology calls for a shift in this discussion, even if briefly, to quantum gravity. Until now we have been focusing on the relationship between *creatio ex nihilo* and Big Bang cosmology with special attention to t = 0, and to finitude as a philosophical category that can relate these two worlds of discourse. We have seen that severe scientific and philosophical problems revolve around the status of t = 0. In particular, as Stoeger reminds us, Big Bang cosmology depends upon Special Relativity—and *its* assumptions are "classical" (that is, pre-quantum mechanical). Thus much attention is now being devoted to the goal of obtaining a quantum treatment of gravity. One of the goals being pursued *via* quantum gravity is a quantum cosmology that will be free of the initial singularity, t = 0. As such a goal is approached, what will happen to the theological research program I have sketched above? I will argue that this research program is able to incorporate a view of the cosmos sponsored by a quantum account of gravity—and that this flexibility is one of its strengths.

The Hartle-Hawking Proposal

There are a variety of approaches to quantum gravity (QG) and the cosmological models that emerge from it, that is, quantum cosmology (QC). Following Stoeger, I will focus here on the Hartle-Hawking model, and draw on several recent papers by Chris Isham, George Ellis, and Stoeger that the reader interested in more detail than can be provided below should consult.[47] Though these proposals are clearly *speculative*, I hope to show that their value for theology is relatively independent of their longevity in science.

Unlike other approaches to QG,[48] the Hartle-Hawking model does not assume a background space-time out of which the universe arises. However, it does assume a set of three-dimensional spaces out of which space-time can be constructed. It also presupposes the existence of the appropriate laws of physics, including quantum physics (in particular the Feynman path integral approach) and General Relativity, and it employs a mathematical trick (the introduction of complex numbers) to simplify calculations.[49]

One of the goals of QG/QC is to overcome the problem posed by the absolute singularity, t = 0, in Big Bang models. To tackle this, Hartle and Hawking looked for a *quantum* treatment of gravity using imaginary time (in the sense of complex numbers), and a state function approach to represent the universe. Their proposal is governed by the following stipulation: space-time must have only *one* boundary, the present, not two as in standard Big Bang cosmology (namely the present *and* t = 0). In particular, it *cannot* have a singular initial boundary whatsoever, including a temporal one such as t = 0. Hartle and Hawking succeeded in constructing just such a model. In their calculations, the universe has no "beginning," since there is *no* initial boundary. It simply has the "present" boundary (its current "size," to speak loosely) and a *finite* past history. It is this feature of their model which led Hawking to refer to the boundary condition as the "no-boundary" condition, and to the claim that, rather than being created, the universe "would just BE."[50]

Theological Appropriation of the "No-Boundary" Condition

The Hartle-Hawking proposal makes it evident that a self-consistent scientific conception of the universe can be constructed in which the universe has a finite age but no "beginning," that is, the finite past is unbounded.[51] This may be the most important aspect of the Hartle-Hawking proposal for theologians to consider.

My proposal grows out of my previous interpretation of the theological significance of t = 0. There t = 0 provides corroborating data for the theological claim of *ex nihilo* via the philosophical category of finitude. T = 0 expresses this finitude through the empirical claim that the universe is finite in the past, i.e., that it has a finite age. With the Hartle/Hawking model, this claim is maintained in a certain sense, even though the meaning and status of time is radically reconceived. With the Big Bang model, having a finite age was understood in terms of having a beginning. Now, with Hartle-Hawking, we discover the fascinating insight that there can be a finite age without a beginning, that is, that the universe can be finite in time without being bounded in time. I believe this teaches us theologically to recognize the former claim, the finitude of the past, and not the latter claim, having a beginning, as capturing the essential point of the bridge we have made between *creatio ex nihilo* and the empirical context of cosmology.

There is an added advantage here. Hawking's work can free us of an unnecessary constriction on the central meaning of creaturely finitude. In this way, Hawking's work will have been very helpful to the task of Christian theology, even if scientifically it represents a speculative and transitory stage in the pursuit of a fully developed theory of quantum gravity. While engaged in purely scientific research, Hawking's results have inadvertently illuminated a subtle distinction in the concept of finitude, which is highly pertinent to Christian theology. For this we ought to be grateful. I believe this sort of interaction between theological and scientific insights can be highly creative. Previous work has too often been limited to well-established conclusions in science in order not to base theological positions on changing scientific grounds. The present approach, however, is indifferent to the long-term status of the Hartle-Hawking model, since the survival within cosmology of the Hartle-Hawking proposal is irrelevant to the validity of the mathematical concept of an unbounded finitude. It is precisely this fact which allows theologians to ponder the significance of something as *controversial* as the Hartle-Hawking proposal with impunity, as they theologize about time and eternity.

We might go further. The possibility of an unbounded finite past suggests that theological issues about "the beginning" might best be excised from theological discussions about creation. Since Augustine we have known that the *ex nihilo* tradition prefers to think of the creation of time and not creation in (pre-existing) time. Nevertheless the theological and empirical status of the beginning of time has been a continuing problem for theologians down to the present. Indeed this was one of the reasons why Gilkey abandoned the connection between creation theology and scientific cosmology. More recently, Jürgen Moltmann has raised this question explicitly in *God in Creation*. He asks "Does *the beginning* of time belong in time or in eternity?" His response is concise and penetrating: "If it belongs within time, then there was time before time; if it belongs to eternity, time itself is eternal."[52]

With the concept of an unbounded finitude in mind, however, theologians need not accept Gilkey's solution of severing the connection between theology and cosmology. Instead, we can maintain the bridge between theology and cosmology, and simply leave aside questions about how to treat the "moment of creation" theologically, since it is an unnecessary element in the discussion of the "finite creation of the universe." We can think of the past universe as a set of events which have no past boundary, rather than a set of events with a boundary (t = 0). The universe is in this sense a *finite creation with no beginning*. Every event is on a par with every other event; since time is unbounded, each event has temporal neighbors past and future, and we need no longer focus on t = 0 in order to retain a sense of creation at the beginning in *creatio ex nihilo*.

The Creation of Time

I want to add two points of agreement with Hawking. First, in other proposals for quantum gravity, such as that of Roger Penrose, our universe arises as a quantum fluctuation in an ontologically prior superspace. Hawking rejects these proposals, but his rejection of a "time before time" is reminiscent of Augustine's argument about "creation of time." Hawking himself has noted this fact, as have a number of commentators, including Paul Davies, Chris Isham, and Willem Drees.[53] This leads to an intriguing question: Would current discussions of Trinitarian creation, as a critique of the Augustinian-Thomistic understanding of creation, offer further insights or conceptual parallels with the choices being made by scientists between competing models in QG/QC? Further pursuit of this relationship may prove illuminating.

Second, even in Hawking's proposal, the existence of the universe as such requires further explanation. For instance he himself raises the question: "What is it that breathes fire into the equations and makes a universe for them to describe?"[54] Stoeger, too, suggests that cosmology "poses the question," even if it cannot provide the answer to ultimate origins. I think this point highlights the fascinating way in which science raises "boundary questions," to use David Tracy's famous phrase, which open the door to theological exploration. Just how this exploration further involves cosmology is the key question we must continue to address in the future.

Finally, we might frame this point in terms of the "Lakatosian theological research program" advocated above. The Hartle-Hawking claim that the universe has no initial singularity would count as evidence against the theological claim that the universe has a finite past, if finitude is taken in its usual sense of requiring a boundary. Hence we are led to frame an additional auxiliary hypothesis, namely that the claim of a finite past can entail either a bounded or an unbounded past. This additional hypothesis allows us to include either the bounded finitude of Big Bang cosmology or the unbounded finitude of the Hartle-Hawking cosmology as confirming evidence of the core hypothesis, "*creatio ex nihilo* means ontological dependence."

However, for this to avoid being an *ad hoc* move, we want it to generate some novel predictions. This brings us to the edge of research today. My tentative thoughts point in two directions: What would it be like to continue with Hawking-style finitude in pondering human origins, the *imago dei*, continuity/uniqueness questions in Christology, resurrection, and the parousia? I must leave these as open questions, suggestive of the "novel predictions" motif in a Lakatosian theological research program.

V. CLOSING REFLECTION ON STOEGER'S THEOLOGICAL IMPLICATIONS

I want to conclude with some specific responses to the theological implications Stoeger mentions at the end of his essay.[55]

I certainly agree with Stoeger's judgment about the second and third issues he mentions, including the lack of support for a "matter-spirit dualism" and the need to avoid a "God of the gaps" interpretation of God's action in the world. Philosophically I find language about emergence helpful in steering between the alternatives of a thoroughgoing reductionistic materialism and a split ontology when dealing with the tremendously complex problems involved in the psychosomatic reality of the human person in its evolutionary context. Theologically, I find support for this anthropology both in Hebrew Scripture and New Testament, and in the history of the development of theological anthropology.

I also agree that theology should not view God as violating the very laws which God has created and which are required for the evolution and action of moral free agents. However, I have already suggested that quantum physics and, to a lesser extent, chaos theory open the possibility of reconceptualizing God's action in nature based upon what we know about nature. At most this would be a "distant cousin" to the kind of "gaps" arguments which Stoeger and I want to avoid, and its advantages and liabilities deserve at least a fair hearing.

I find myself questioning Stoeger's first set of theological implications. I agree that the laws of nature reflect God's action as creator, whether these laws are taken as prescriptive or descriptive. Stoeger himself has argued for the latter quite persuasively in previous work.[56] The real question is whether this exhausts the full meaning of continuing creation. Even if the laws are statistical, and life evolves through the interplay of law and chance, it is not clear that this gets us beyond what could be called "statistical deism." In my opinion, a more fully developed understanding of ongoing creation will come from an explicitly Trinitarian doctrine of God, for this framework inherently overcomes the God/world dilemma that pervades most discussions of God's action.[57]

I also agree with Stoeger that science may never determine whether the universe had a temporal beginning or, more generally, whether the universe is in fact contingent. What I want to stress more fully than Stoeger suggests here, at least, is the overlap between philosophy and science—and theology. For example, his discussion about the contingency of the universe is actually a combination of philosophical arguments that serve as essential presuppositions to the scientific method, and technical arguments that surface within the scientific theoretical framework. In addition, issues regarding the origin and contingency of the universe are intrinsic to theology's own methods and conceptual framework, specifically its doctrines of God and creation. Thus issues such as origin, contingency, and the evolution of complex phenomena in time represent the inherent overlap between theology, philosophy, and science, and can best be discussed through a trialogue amongst them. This eliminates the strict separation between them that tends to surface here and in other parts of Stoeger's essay, and I believe it more correctly represents the view Stoeger holds in general, as evidenced by his excellent essays on this topic already in the literature.

NOTES

1. This paper has some similarities with an earlier publication: "Finite Creation without a Beginning: The Doctrine of Creation in Relation to Big Bang and Quantum Cosmologies," in Robert Russell, Nancey Murphy and Chris Isham, eds., *Quantum Cosmology and the Laws of Nature: Scientific Perspectives on Divine Action* (Vatican City State: Vatican Observatory Publications, and Berkeley: Center for Theology and the Natural Sciences, 1993; hereafter *QCLN*). I also refer the reader to "Cosmology" in Donald W. Musser and Joseph L. Price, eds., *A New Handbook of Christian Theology* (Nashville: Abingdon Press, 1992), an introductory account of cosmology and its philosophical and theological implications.

2. Both in his paper for this volume and in his previous writings, Stoeger has produced a series of extraordinary introductions to issues in physics and cosmology. His writings on their philosophical implications are some of the finest in the field. See W.R. Stoeger, "Contemporary Cosmology and Its Implications for the Science-Religion Dialogue," in Robert J. Russell, William R. Stoeger, and George V. Coyne, eds., *Physics, Philosophy and Theology: A Common Quest for Understanding* (Vatican City State: Vatican Observatory Press, 1988); George F.R. Ellis and Stoeger, "Introduction to General Relativity and Cosmology," in *QCLN*; and Stoeger, "Contemporary Physics and the Ontological Status of the Laws of Nature," in *QCLN*.

3. R.J. Clifford, "Creation in the Hebrew Bible," in *Physics, Philosophy and Theology*, pp. 151–170.

4. Gerhard von Rad, *The Problem of the Hexateuch* (New York: McGraw-Hill, 1966), pp. 131–143.

5. Claus Westermann, *Creation* (Philadelphia: Fortree Press, 1974); Bernhard Anderson, ed., *Creation in the Old Testament* (Philadelphia: Fortress Press, 1984).

6. There are many reliable and insightful introductions to the history of the doctrine of creation. See for example Julian N. Hartt, "Creation and Providence," in Peter C. Hodgson and Robert H. King, *Christian Theology: An Introduction to its Traditions and Tasks*, 2nd ed. (Philadelphia: Fortress Press, 1985). Hartt refers to the classical doctrine of creation as the "theological consensus from Origen to Calvin." See also Langdon Gilkey, *Maker of Heaven and Earth: The Christian Doctrine of Creation in the Light of Modern Knowledge* (Garden City: Doubleday, 1959); Philip J. Hefner, "The Creation," in Carl E. Braaten and Robert W. Jenson, eds., *Christian Dogmatics* (Philadelphia: Fortress Press, 1984); Jaroslav Pelikan, "Creation and Causality in the History of Christian Thought," in Sol Tax and C. Callender, eds., *Issues in Evolution* (Chicago: University of Chicago Press, 1960), Vol. III, *Evolution after Darwin*, pp. 29–40; Jürgen Moltmann, *God in Creation: A New Theology of Creation and the Spirit of God* (New York: Harper & Row, 1985); and Robert C. Neville, *God the Creator: On the Transcendence and Presence of God* (Chicago: University of Chicago Press, 1968).

7. Ted Peters, "Cosmos as Creation," in Ted Peters, ed., *Cosmos as Creation: Theology and Science in Consonance* (Nashville: Abingdon Press, 1989), p. 77.

8. Pelikan, "Creation and Causality in the History of Christian Thought."

9. This view also appears in the writings of Philo of Alexandria, *On the Account of the World's Creation by Moses*, ch. 26.

10. Etienne Gilson, *The Christian Philosophy of Saint Augustine*, ET L.E.M. Lynch (New York: Random House, 1960), ch. 1.

11. St. Augustine, *Confessions*, Book XI, Sections 13–14, 30.

12. Thomas, *Summa Theologica*, Part I, Question 46, Article 2.

13. Gilkey, *Maker*, p. 43.

14. Friedrich Schleiermacher, *The Christian Faith*, trans. H.R. Mackintosh and J.S. Stewart (Edinburgh: T. & T. Clark, 1928).

15. *The Christian Faith*, ch II, pp. 94–128.

16. *The Christian Faith*, §§36–41, pp. 142–156.

17. "Creation and Providence," p. 162.

18. Hartt himself, in fact, sees little real hope here, citing the contrast of language and meaning in scientific and theological discussions about origins, and adopting what surely seems to be a "two worlds" approach.

19. Charles W. Misner, Kip S. Thorne, and John Archibald Wheeler, *Gravitation* (San Francisco: W. H. Freeman & Co., 1973), p. 1198.

20. For an intriguing foray into these questions by a leading scientist, see "Did God Create the Universe?" in Paul Davies, *God and the New Physics* (New York: Simon & Shuster, 1983).

21. Jastrow published this claim in his widely read *God and the Astronomers* (New York: W.W. Norton & Company, 1978); see p. 116.

22. In private conversations Smoot is much more circumspect about *any* theological implications of his findings (private communications).

23. See for example "Big Bang Ripples: Proof Positive for the Creation Event," tape available

from *Reasons to Believe* (P.O. Box 5978, Pasadena, CA. 91117); see also Hugh Ross, *Genesis One: A Scientific Perspective* (P.O. Box 5978, Pasadena, CA. 91117).

24. Ted Peters, "On Creating the Cosmos," in *Physics, Philosophy and Theology*, pp. 273–296; see p. 291.

25. Another way of saying this, drawing on epistemology, is the following: Science describes events which fall within a lawlike framework; t = 0 seems to be an event that cannot be described by science, precisely because there is no "prior" event with which it could be connected in a lawlike manner within the Big Bang model. See Stoeger, "Contemporary Cosmology and Its Implications for the Science-Religion Dialogue," in *Physics, Philosophy and Theology*, p. 240.

26. See Ted Peters, "Cosmos as Creation," pp. 78–85.

27. Whereas the authors do not explicitly advocate a particular position on the relations between theology and science, this remark clearly indicates a separation of intellectual domains that highly restricts the relationship.

28. In "Finite Creation without a Beginning," I called these terms "ontological origination" and "historical/empirical origination," respectively.

29. *Maker*, p. 310.

30. See *Maker*, pp. 313–314, where Gilkey cites Aquinas' *Summa Theologica*, Part I, Question 46, Article 2.

31. It should be clearly noted that in recent work Gilkey has abandoned the independence model for an interaction one. See, for example, *Nature, Reality, and the Sacred: The Nexus of Science and Religion* (Minneapolis: Fortress Press, 1993).

32. Stoeger, "Key Developments in Physics Challenging Philosophy and Theology," in this volume p. 192. Note that, unlike more conventional "infinities" which occur even in classical physics (such as the field strength of a monopole at its site), here even the space-time arena itself becomes singular.

33. Stoeger, p. 192.

34. Stoeger, p. 194.

35. Stoeger, p. 198.

36. *Religion in an Age of Science, The Gifford Lectures 1989–1991*, Vol. 1 (San Francisco: Harper and Row, 1990), p. 129.

37. Ernan McMullin, "How Should Cosmology Relate to Theology?" in A.R. Peacocke, ed., *The Sciences and Theology in the Twentieth Century* (Notre Dame: University of Notre Dame Press, 1981), p. 52.

38. "How Should Cosmology Relate to Theology?" p. 39.

39. Robert Russell, "Cosmology, Creation, and Contingency," in *Cosmos as Creation*; "Contemplation: A Scientific Context," in *Continuum*, Vol. 2 (Fall, 1990); "Theological Lessons from Cosmology," in *Cross Currents: Religion & Intellectual Life* (Fall, 1991); "Finite Creation without a Beginning: The Spiritual and Theological Significance of Stephen Hawking's Quantum Cosmology," in *The Way: Review of Contemporary Christian Spirituality* 32/4 (October 1992); and "Cosmology: Evidence for God or Partner for Theology?" in John Marks Templeton, ed., *Evidence of Purpose* (New York: Continuum, 1994).

40. Peters, "Cosmos as Creation"; Barbour, *Religion in an Age of Science*; Willem B. Drees, *Beyond the Big Bang, Quantum Cosmologies and God* (La Salle: Open Court, 1990), pp. 26–29.

41. *Maker*, pp. 315–316. See also, Gilkey, "Cosmology, Ontology, and the Travail of Biblical

Language," *The Journal of Religion* 41 (1961), pp. 194–205.

42. The strategy Gilkey adopted to resolve the problem was to view religious language about historical/empirical origins as myth, thus insulating it from scientific discourse. Does this strategy work? In my opinion it does not, since it marginalizes theology by insulating it from the cognitive claims and discoveries of secular inquiry. Moreover, I believe we now have an alternative. See *Maker of Heaven and Earth*, pp. 316 ff.

43. Ian G. Barbour, *Myths, Models and Paradigms: A Comparative Study in Science & Religion* (New York: Harper & Row, 1974), esp. chs. 6, 7; Nancey Murphy, *Theology in the Age of Scientific Reasoning* (Ithaca: Cornell University Press, 1990) and her paper in this volume; and Philip Clayton, *Explanation from Physics to Theology: An Essay in Rationality and Religion* (New Haven: Yale University Press, 1989).

44. See in particular, "Falsification and the Methodology of Scientific Research Programmes," in *The Methodology of Scientific Research Programmes: Philosophical Papers*, Vol. I, eds. John Worrall and Gregory Currie (Cambridge: Cambridge University Press, 1978), pp. 8–101.

45. I do not want to make this into a *definition* of finitude, since I want to argue that the distinction between the finite and the infinite need not include the concept of boundary. Since the work of Gregor Cantor, the notion of finitude has been extended to include unbounded finitude. We shall see the importance of this latter concept as it surfaces in the work of Hartle and Hawking below.

46. See "How Should Cosmology Relate to Theology?" p. 35.

47. C.J. Isham, "Creation as a Quantum Process," in *Physics, Philosophy and Theology*, and "Quantum Theories of the Creation of the Universe," in *QCLN*; G.F.R. Ellis and W.R. Stoeger, "Introduction to General Relativity and Cosmology," in *QCLN*.

48. See comments on Roger Penrose's work in papers by Isham, Happel, Grib, Russell, and Drees in *QCLN*. See also Drees, *Beyond the Big Bang*.

49. The use of complex numbers is commonplace in mathematical and applied physics. Complex numbers consist of so-called "real" and "imaginary" parts, the latter involving the square root of a negative number. They have nothing whatsoever to do with the meaning of "imaginary" in artistic, literary, or personal contexts.

50. Stephen Hawking, *A Brief History of Time: From the Big Bang to Black Holes* (Toronto: Bantam Books, 1988), p. 136.

51. I am using the term "unbounded" here as meaning "having no boundary." Mathematicians often use the term "unbounded" in a different sense. They might instead say that the Hartle-Hawking model involves four-manifolds that are past-bounded, but "open."

52. Moltmann, *God in Creation*, p. 116. Moltmann's response to this question, including his exchanges with Augustine and Barth, are good illustrations of his Trinitarian approach to creation.

53. See *QCLN*.

54. *A Brief History of Time*, p. 174.

55. Stoeger, pp. 198ff.

56. See "Contemporary Physics and the Ontological Status of the Laws of Nature," in *QCLN*.

57. Here I am relying on the work of such Trinitarian theologians as Karl Barth, Karl Rahner, Jürgen Moltmann, Catherine Mowry LaCugna, Wolfhart Pannenberg, Elizabeth Johnson, and Ted Peters.

CASE STUDY II

CHAOS THEORY
AND
DIVINE ACTION

DETERMINISTIC CHAOS AND QUANTUM CHAOLOGY

KARL YOUNG

I. INTRODUCTION

When asked by Napoleon about the place of God in Newton's mechanical model of the physical universe, the great eighteenth-century mathematician, Pierre Simone de Laplace, replied "We have no need of that hypothesis." Had Laplace been able to anticipate developments in nineteenth-century physics perhaps his response would have been far less sanguine. Buoyed by the tremendous success of Newton's mechanics, and its eighteenth- and nineteenth-century refinements to describe many of the most prominently observed regularities in the natural world, Laplace and his contemporaries were convinced that they had in hand a complete model of the workings of nature. The few anomalies that remained would no doubt be cleared up by clever scientists, but would not require the insight of a Newton.[1] As indicated by Laplace's reply to Napoleon, the theological implications of the then increasingly popular mechanistic view of nature were uninteresting at best. A deistic God or blind watchmaker seemed all that could be reconciled with this particular view of the physical universe. Plato's notion of a "celestial city of the stars" had helped to provide a philosophical foundation for both the Christian tradition and modern science. In accounting for the regular motions of the celestial city's wanderers, that is, the planets, mechanists felt they had eliminated the need for divine intervention as an explanation of anything.

The notion of Newtonian mechanics as a complete description of the physical universe, however, would come apart under pressure from a variety of directions, some, ironically, based on the work of Laplace. First there were problems reconciling Newton's theory with other important physical theories of the nineteenth century, primarily James Clerk Maxwell's theory of electromagnetism,[2] but there were also conflicts with thermodynamics. Maxwell's theory predicted that the speed of light, and all other electromagnetic waves, is constant and independent of the motion of any observer. If one were to accept the ideas of absolute time and space assumed in Newton's mechanics, this was a great paradox. Einstein eventually resolved the paradox with his Special Theory of Relativity, by shifting from the Newtonian notion of absolute time and space to that of an absolute and constant speed of light.

Thermodynamics, the physical theory of heat as developed by Rumford, Carnot, Clausius, and others in the eighteenth and nineteenth centuries, while based on no new laws of nature, was a tremendously successful phenomenological theory that described universal regularities in the behavior of macroscopic matter. The importance of the development of thermodynamics was clear, for as Herbert Callen puts it, the properties of macroscopic matter provide the interface between scientists and nature.[3] If a reductionist description of the physical universe with Newtonian mechanics at its core was to be successful, thermodynamics would have to be shown to be an epiphe-nomenal result of the laws of Newtonian mechanics. While there have been many bril-liant attempts at achieving this, the most notable being the introduction of the use of statistics in physics by Maxwell and Boltzmann, none has been wholly successful.

Perhaps the most devastating blow to the Newtonian view originated in the accep-tance of the atomic view of matter. The success of this view, for instance, in describing the chemical properties of matter, initially posed no challenges to Newtonian mechan-ics as the basis of physics. It only became apparent when trying to reconcile actual atomic models with observed properties, such as the optical emissions of heated gases, that Newtonian mechanics was inadequate as a fundamental theory. The theory that eventually replaced Newtonian mechanics in the description of atomic processes, quan-tum mechanics, was such a radical departure that physicists are still coming to grips with how to understand it as a complete description of microscopic reality.

But had none of these momentous developments—relativity, statistical physics, or quantum mechanics—occurred, the limitations of Newtonian mechanics as a descriptive theory would have no doubt been discovered. In fact these limitations, which we will gener-ically refer to as *chaos* and which are the subject of this paper, were first fully understood by the great French mathematician Henri Poincaré, now generally regarded as the father of chaos. His discoveries occurred in the context of trying to solve a problem of orbital motion, the domain of many of the great triumphs of Newtonian mechanics.[4] In the shadow of rela-tivity and quantum mechanics, Poincaré's discovery of chaos went virtually unnoticed by physicists for more than half a century. During that period however, mathematicians made great strides in understanding the nature of chaos, and engineers, for pragmatic reasons, became keenly aware of its appearance in mechanical and electrical systems.

While popular accounts have emphasized the complicated behavior uncovered by com-puter-aided studies of chaos, recalling its origins in a problem of Newtonian mechanics is useful when considering philosophical implications. Most importantly Newtonian mechanics is a deterministic theory, and the properties of chaotic systems are the result of the behavior of deterministic systems. (We will carefully define determinism below.) The unpredictable behavior of chaotic systems often necessitates a statistical descrip-tion.[5] The deterministic nature of these systems, however, implies a difference in kind between such descriptions and the statistical descriptions of quantum mechanical sys-tems. This has a direct bearing on any discussions of causality or the arrow of time that begin with physics as a basis.

As a way of illustrating this difference between the statistical treatment of classical deterministic and quantum systems, consider a crude analogy with the use of statistical analyses in a field like public health. When one finds a statistical correlation between occurrences of different types of events, such as smoking and lung cancer, one not only attributes some sense of reality to the correlations, but assumes that there must be some underlying causal relationship between the correlated events. This assumption is in no way affected by the fact that current circumstances may be too complicated for experiments directly to isolate the causal mechanism. This situation is analogous to the use of statistical descriptions for chaotic systems; there is a deterministic system underlying the observed behavior, but this behavior is so complicated that a statistical description is generally the only one available. The classic example of this sort of use of statistics is coin flipping; there, few would doubt that a causal relationship exists between the hand motions of the coin flipper and the subsequent deterministic flight of the coin. On the other hand, in the strange world of quantum mechanics, under its most widely accepted interpretation, statistical correlations do not imply underlying causal behavior. In fact, quantum mechanics explicitly excludes the notion of causal behavior underlying its statistical descriptions. This raises an issue which is perhaps the most fundamental I wish to discuss: while there is much debate as to whether the basic status of quantum uncertainty is epistemological or ontological, we will argue that the uncertainty associated with deterministic chaotic systems is most decidedly epistemological. I will have more to say about this below.

From a theological perspective, perhaps the most interesting property of chaotic systems is the intricate balance between apparent randomness and structure that is an essential part of any complete description of their behavior. I will here avoid the thorny issues alluded to above, and faced by quantum philosophers, as to the ontological status of the idea of randomness. I will focus on randomness as an epistemological element of our analysis of chaotic systems, which results from the incomplete knowledge any finite observer can have of their complicated behavior, as in the example of coin tossing. This leads to the need for statistical descriptions, as discussed above. Determinism plays an important role in being responsible for the intricate structures that are observed in the behavior of chaotic systems. It is important to keep in mind that this structure is generated by the nature of the system, and not externally imposed.

It might be argued that randomness could never be considered inherent in deterministic systems, in the way it is for quantum systems or externally influenced classical systems, being "only" a property of an observer's incomplete knowledge. This misses a basic point: it would truly take an infinite amount of knowledge to use the deterministic nature of the system completely to predict its future behavior. This is a situation that is unique to chaotic systems. This property, which we will discuss in more detail, is commonly referred to as sensitive dependence on initial conditions (SDIC), and is the essential signature of chaos.

Certain arguments of natural theology might be seen in a different light as a result of considering the above properties of chaotic systems. For example, as discussed by John Polkinghorne,[6] unquestioning belief in one of the cornerstones of natural theology, the argument from design was seriously undermined by Darwin's theory of evolution. There, randomness, combined with natural selection, stood to undercut the argument for the necessity of a designer. To the extent that Darwin's theory provided an adequate explanation of the complex process of the adaptation of living organisms to their environment through random mutation and natural selection, it seemed more economical than the invocation of a designer. Randomness in quantum mechanics deals an even more severe blow to the argument from design. There a designer is not only unnecessary, but impossible; to paraphrase Einstein, if quantum mechanics is correct, God must play dice to determine the behavior of the quantum mechanical world.[7] As indicated in the above discussion, the nature of randomness in chaos is of a wholly different and strictly epistemological character. There it expresses the notion of the application of limited resources in attempting to understand situations of great complexity. The notions of randomness combined with underlying determinism as in chaotic systems might lead to useful, but not absolutist, variations on the arguments of natural theology by postulating the existence of intricately designed systems whose properties can only be partially understood by finite observers. Given the current view of physicists, however, that the fundamental theory of the physical universe will be a relativistic quantum field theory, we will have to discuss in what sense the notions of randomness and determinism, as arrived at from the point of view of deterministic chaos, could ever be considered fundamental.

An important aspect of chaotic systems is that they are *dynamical* systems, that is, systems that evolve in time. The rich and intricate behavior we now think of as chaos is behavior that unfolds in time. For systems in equilibrium, that is whose behavior is unchanging, time is an irrelevant parameter. For systems that undergo simple periodic motion, time is only relevant in determining the phase of the motion—where in its cycle the system is at a given time. But for chaotic systems time is of the essence; the ideas of novelty and evolution become important in the study of chaotic systems. These ideas lead directly to some of the profound philosophical questions on the nature of time: Are the fundamental laws of physics reversible in time? Is the universe periodic in time? Do time and space have different ontological status? These questions in turn lead to important questions in theology, some of which form the basis of process theology, based on the work of A.N. Whitehead, which is concerned with the relationship of God to the unfolding of temporal processes.[8]

In the following sections, we will first discuss chaos in the setting of deterministic classical mechanics, where it was discovered by Poincaré. This section will in turn be divided into three subsections. The first will provide some examples and a heuristic overview of chaos in classical systems. The second subsection will discuss attempts to model previously hard to describe behavior, like fluid turbulence, as chaos. The final subsection will discuss the epistemologically important issue of how to recognize and categorize chaos in natural systems.

The final section will give a brief overview of current attempts to understand the relationship between quantum mechanics and chaos.

II. DETERMINISTIC CHAOS

What Is It?

Two things are necessary, although not sufficient, for the occurrence of chaotic behavior. These are determinism and nonlinearity. To see why these conditions are not sufficient to guarantee chaotic behavior, we need look no further than one of the problems that forms the bedrock of modern science, the study of two bodies interacting via the force of Newtonian gravity. This classic problem of mathematical physics, often referred to as the Kepler problem, is both deterministic and nonlinear. It is perhaps one of the supreme ironies of history that solutions of the Kepler problem can only exhibit regular, nonchaotic behavior. Had this apparent mathematical fluke combined with the apparent regularity in the gross motions of the planets not been the case, a strong argument can be made that science would never have gained the intellectual stronghold that it has in the twentieth century. We shall see that nonlinearity generally implies the mathematical insolubility of a problem. Had this been true for the Kepler problem, its stunning success in providing a basis for the description of the of the motions of the planets would not have been possible. Establishing the utility of mathematical physics, the prototypical modern science, would thus have been far more difficult than it was, and Laplace's bold reply to Napoleon's query regarding science and theology would most surely never have occurred. To discuss determinism, we must first discuss the notion of the state of a system.

Imagine that somebody asks the question "where on earth are you?" If you take them literally, it turns out that all you need to tell them to answer the question completely are two numbers. That is, if we think of the earth's surface as two dimensional, you simply need to give your coordinates, the longitude and latitude. These two numbers completely describe your "state of position." Generalizing from this example, we think of the state of a system as the set of numerical values necessary to answer completely some question we have about its behavior. In classical mechanics, a complete specification of a system's state is given by the positions and velocities of all the constituent particles of the system. In quantum mechanics, a complete specification is given by something called the wave function of the system, in this case an infinite set of numbers. Generally, for a given system this set of numerical quantities can represent any set that is considered necessary for its description—temperature, population size, anything that can be described numerically. Once we have decided on what constitutes a state of our system, we may then want to obtain a mathematical description of how the state will evolve in time, that is, given some initial state (a set of numbers), what states will we see in the future. This mathematical description is what we will refer to as the dynamics of the system. If the dynamics uniquely defines all future states, given the present state, we call the dynamics deterministic.

Assume that we have a set of deterministic equations as a description of the evolution of our system. If these are linear equations then, in the long run, the most complicated behavior that we can expect to see in our system is periodic, that is, regular behavior. We also might see the system come to a halt, that is, the state remain the same for all time, but periodic behavior is the most complicated we can expect. The important point is that we could never see chaos in such a system. For that we need nonlinearity.

Nonlinearity can perhaps be best described by mentioning that before the advent of the modern computer, nonlinear problems were the type that no mathematician in their right mind would attempt to solve. Mathematically, linear systems express relationships in terms of proportions. The development of methods to solve equations, expressed as proportions, began at least as far back as the time of the ancient Greeks, and the solution of such equations provides no mystery for the modern mathematician. Linearity in mathematics can thus almost be thought of as synonymous with solubility. Because of the few exceptions, like the Kepler problem, nonlinearity is not the exact logical complement of linearity in being synonymous with insolubility. One would be a fool, however, to bet on a general nonlinear problem being soluble in the standard mathematical sense.

To illustrate the above distinctions, we describe the difference between the way we think about the solutions of linear and those of nonlinear equations. When we try to solve an equation, we put some numbers in and get some numbers, which we call the solution, out. Consider the simple case of an equation for which we put in one number and get out another as the solution. Now consider two separate input numbers which would generally give two separate solutions. For a linear system, if we add the two numbers together and put that sum into our equation, the solution is always the sum of the two separate solutions. This is not the case for nonlinear systems, and it is this property which allows for the great instability associated with chaotic systems. A colleague once described a beautiful example of such behavior he noticed while hiking. He saw an old hollow log laying beside the road. Into one end of the log a slow steady trickle of water was flowing. Leaving the other end was not a steady trickle, but drops of various size. The log had performed a nonlinear transformation of the input just like a nonlinear equation acting on numerical input. In fact, reasonable mathematical descriptions of most natural systems are nonlinear, and it is a wonder that mathematical physics achieved as much as it did using primarily linear models.

As mentioned above, the implications of nonlinearity on the behavior of a deterministic system were first investigated in detail by Poincaré. In trying to solve one of the grand problems of classical dynamics, the problem of three bodies interacting via Newtonian gravitation, he discovered profoundly complicated types of behavior. He expressed this, while trying to obtain a visual representation of this mathematically intractable behavior. Poincaré went on to show that no simple generalization of the techniques that were then used to solve linear problems would work for solving non-linear ones. At the time people had hoped to solve nonlinear problems by starting with a similar, and solvable, linear problem, then making small mathematical perturbations from this problem to the nonlinear one. That is, it was hoped that the solution of the nonlinear problem could be found by solving a linear problem that was "similar enough" to the nonlinear one.

This was analogous to techniques that scientists of the late nineteenth century were using to try to determine the stability of the solar system, although in this case the "similar enough" problem, the Kepler problem, is nonlinear but solvable. They were try-ing to determine whether or not the wanderers of the celestial city would continue for all time to exhibit the regular motions that had provided the stable foundations for the birth of modern science, not to mention the physical stability for the development of life on earth. That the answer to such an important question seemed within reach at the time prompted the Swedish mathematician Gösta Mittag-Leffler to propose a prize for its discovery, to be awarded as part of the sixtieth anniversary celebration of the birth of King Oscar II. Poincaré won the prize, not for settling the issue but for show-ing in a manner that presaged much of twentieth-century mathematics, that current techniques were inadequate to the task. More specifically, he showed that for any sys-tem of orbiting bodies, if there were two or more of the bodies whose ratio of orbital periods was a rational number, a situation referred to as resonance, the then current techniques led to mathematical inconsistency, that is insolubility of a rather patholog-ical sort. As a result he was most likely the first to fully realize how radically different the mathematical tools needed for the study of nonlinear dynamical systems would have to be. Many consider the mathematical subjects of topology and its descendants, as well as ergodic theory to be a direct result of this realization.

The crucial phenomenon that Poincaré discovered in the context of celestial mechanics, and the signature of all chaotic systems, was the possibility for explosive instability, the property now referred to as sensitive dependence on initial conditions (SDIC). This property is a direct result of nonlinearity. That the additivity of causes does not lead to the additivity of effects, as in linear systems, allows for evolution from nearly identical states to extremely dissimilar ones. One of the most graphic examples of this phenomenon is the butterfly effect, first described by another of the great pio-neers in chaos, meteorologist Edward Lorenz.[9] His rediscovery of SDIC in computer sim-ulations of the earth's atmosphere was the seed from which the current explosion of research in chaotic dynamics grew.

Lorenz had developed an extremely simple dynamical model of the earth's atmos-phere, hoping to retain only the essential elements of global atmospheric circulation. He used a computer to evolve his model forward in time. When he inadvertently lost the results of a particular run, he attempted to recreate these results by starting the computer with an almost identical initial state. The simple fact that the initial states of the two runs were not exactly identical, to the precision obtainable on his computer, made scientific history, perhaps an impressive example of SDIC in itself. Lorenz's surprise that the new results seemed very different from his recollection of the previous results led to a detailed study of the phenomenon. It was eventually summarized metaphorically as the butterfly effect, which says that the flapping of a butterfly's wings, that is, slightly different initial conditions than if the butterfly had not flapped its wings, can effect eventual weather patterns halfway around the earth.

An important aspect of Lorenz's work, which was crucial to the further study of chaotic systems, was his use of a computer. Combined with the powerful mathematical tools developed by Poincaré and others, computers finally allowed for a systematic approach to the study of deterministic nonlinear systems. Far from a simple panacea, however, the study of nonlinear problems with computers has led to unique and profound epistemological questions. Before the advent of such studies, the relationship between theory and experiment in science, while never simple, was less complicated. The ability to use computers to study the mathematically intractable solutions of complex nonlinear models, and then compare these results to the behavior of natural systems, raises questions other than just the utility of the model. One must also be careful in establishing the fidelity of the computer simulation to the actual mathematical properties of the model. Can computer simulations of complicated mathematical models ever be considered fundamental knowledge? It seems that this is an important question to bear in mind when considering the implications of current research in nonlinear dynamics.

Where Is It?

As a case study in the types of scientific problem that researchers have used chaotic dynamics to try to solve, in this section we discuss the problem of fluid turbulence.

Turbulent fluids have been a source of fascination from antiquity. The erratic flooding of the Tigris-Euphrates Valley contributed to the dark and chimeric worldview of the ancient Mesopotamians,[10] as distinct from the orderly worldview of the Egyptians, who were used to the extremely regular flooding of the Nile Delta. Leonardo da Vinci's interest in the variety of whorls and tendrils observable in turbulent fluids led to his extensive and detailed phenomenological studies.

Despite the long fascination with the complicated behavior of turbulent fluids, the lack of a useful predictive mathematical model of fluid behavior has been one of the conspicuous facts of twentieth-century science. Independent of theoretical interest in turbulence, the solution of important practical problems, such as understanding the effects of atmospheric turbulence on manned flight, has generated tremendous research efforts in terms of funding and manpower. The primary source of the intractability of fluid turbulence problems lies in the inherent complexity of any reasonably accurate mathematical models of systems with as many strongly interacting components as a turbulent fluid. The best currently accepted mathematical model of fluids, a set of equations known as the Navier-Stokes equations, are nonlinear and hopelessly insoluble without the extreme sorts of simplification that rid the model of turbulence. This was the situation that led some to hope that the novel techniques of chaotic dynamics would be useful in a description of turbulence. While a description of fully developed turbulence is still elusive, some of the techniques introduced by chaoticists who work on such problems have created useful ways of modeling aspects of turbulent flow. To describe these developments, we must first discuss the importance of dissipation in fluid models.

Dissipation of energy is a ubiquitous phenomenon. It was a measure of Galileo's genius that he could abstract from the everyday world of dissipative systems, in which everything eventually comes to rest and Aristotle's theory of constant velocity free fall is eminently reasonable, to understand the true nature of gravitational acceleration. Dissipation in dynamical systems has an important consequence: if we think about a number of states that the system could be started in, there can be a vastly fewer number of final states that the system can end up in. The most extreme case is a system which comes to rest, the ideal state of an Aristotelian object, regardless of its initial state. For example, think of a child on a swing. No matter what height, that is, state at which the child and swing initially start, if no subsequent forces are applied, the child and swing will eventually come to rest. This state of rest is the final state. All of the initial energy of the child and swing is dissipated in the pivot point of the swing and the air. This is the simplest example of an attracting state, or attractor. This final attracting state constitutes a single point in the entire space of states. Geometrically a point is considered a dimensionless object. So, regardless of the dimension of the space of states we begin with, our description of the final state is zero-dimensional, a vast reduction of the description in any case. This reduction in dimension of the final description of a dissipative system is a critical property.

We can have more complicated attracting behavior in a dissipative system; for example, periodic behavior. Think again of the child on a swing. While the pivot point of the swing and the air dissipate energy, you can supply energy by "pumping" the child and swing. If you "pump" the child at the right frequency (which is essentially determined by the length of rope connecting the swing to its pivot point) the child and swing will continue to swing at the "pumping" frequency. As in the case without pumping, the final periodic behavior results regardless of the initial height of the child and swing. In dynamical systems theory, this type of final behavior is called a periodic attractor. If we have a system that can oscillate naturally at more than one frequency, the final behavior can consist of some combination of oscillations at these frequencies. This type of final behavior is referred to as a quasiperiodic attractor. Until the advent of chaos, quasiperiodic attractors were thought to be the most complicated type of attractor that a dissipative system could have. One of the great triumphs of dynamical systems theory was the discovery of what David Ruelle and Floris Takens dubbed "strange attractors."

These were sets of final states that initial states were attracted to in the same sense as point attractors or periodic attractors. But the behavior of the system on a strange attractor is not periodic but chaotic; it is fundamentally erratic, and exhibits SDIC. As turbulent fluids are dissipative, systems it was with strange attractors in mind that chaoticists Ruelle and Takens approached the problem of fluid turbulence.

In an attempt to start with a simpler problem than that of modeling a fully turbulent fluid, researchers decided to try to study the transition from smooth to turbulent flow, as can happen, for example, when you increase the flow rate through a garden hose: the so-called problem of weak turbulence. The physicist Lev Landau had developed a generally accepted phenomenological description of the onset of turbulence in terms of quasiperiodicity. He argued that as more energy was added to the fluid flow, for example by increasing the flow rate, more and more natural modes of oscillation of the fluid were excited. Under Landau's model, the complicated behavior of the turbulent fluid was due to the many different frequencies of oscillation that were excited.

In a classic paper, Ruelle and Takens[11] showed that the Landau route to turbulence is unlikely to occur in actual fluid systems. Rather than a slow mode-by-mode building up of turbulent behavior, they described a model that exhibits an abrupt transition from quasiperiodic behavior with a few excited modes to a strange attractor. Routes to turbulence resembling the Ruelle-Takens scenario, in various experiments on fluids, have established the plausibility of this description, though there is still significant doubt that strange attractors can provide a general enough framework for the description of fully developed fluid turbulence.

The notion of strange attractor is based on the time evolution of what are called low-dimensional models, which take little account of the effects that spatial structure can have on the evolution of the system. As such, it is currently believed that any complete theory of fully developed fluid turbulence will have to broaden current theories and explicitly take the spatially extended nature of fluids into account. The discovery of the rich variety of behaviors exhibited by even the simplest types of spatially extended models, called cellular automata, but not seen in low dimensional models, further underscores this point.

The importance of these developments lies not only in understanding fluid turbulence *per se,* but in noticing the generality of the epistemological questions addressed by studies of spatiotemporal chaos. Can a general theory be developed that describes the possible types of space-time evolution? What kind of balance between randomness and structure give rise to the types of behavior we actually observe?

How Do You Know?

One of the questions that distinguishes chaos as a science from chaos simply as beautiful mathematics, and underlies the epistemological focus of the discussion, is the difficult problem of how to determine whether or not a particular natural system is behaving chaotically. For example, prodigious research efforts were required in the recent identification of chaotic behavior in the previous prototype of regularity, the solar system.

Although many of the measures developed to quantify mathematical chaos are well defined, chaotic effects can be mimicked in natural systems in a number of ways, for instance, external perturbations. A nice example of this type of problem is the study of predators and prey in essentially isolated ecosystems. Often it is found that the populations of predators and prey vary erratically, that is, not periodically. Until recently this was generally attributed to external influences such as variations in weather patterns. It was discovered however, that in many cases the erratic variations could be attributed solely to the deterministic, and chaotic, interaction of the predator and prey species.[12]

To distinguish chaos from other effects experimentally is no small task. To further complicate the matter, the ideal systems which were used to develop the standard measures of chaos have very special mathematical properties which virtually no natural system is expected to have. While the situation of natural systems not being identical to ideal models is not uncommon in science, the explosive instabilities inherent in chaotic systems demand a more careful treatment of these differences. If this were not enough, even developing robust measures of chaos for general theoretical models is difficult. These problems have led many researchers, including this author, to try to develop a more inductive approach. Those involved in such approaches acknowledge the importance of rigorous mathematical measures of chaos in showing that systems that previously might have been expected to exhibit simple behavior can behave in very complicated ways due to strictly internal instabilities. There is an attempt, however, to go beyond the standard measures of chaos to develop more empirically based measures that is directly quantify degrees of randomness and structure, and that can be obtained from data. The approach is similar to statistical inference in choosing a particular model of the data. However, it uses the assumption of underlying determinism to make careful choices of a model. Before we describe this approach, however, we will briefly describe the standard measures of chaos.

As discussed above, Poincaré was the first to realize that radically different approaches would be necessary for studying systems that exhibited chaos. He realized that studying the evolution of a chaotic system from a particular initial state, was not particularly useful. Because of sensitive dependence on initial conditions (SDIC), starting from a close neighbor of that initial state, one could observe a completely different type of time evolution of the system. More useful in many cases might be a qualitative, global description of the time evolution from large sets of initial states. In his attempts to develop such a description, he invented, among other things, topological analysis and ergodic theory. Topology helped to determine the basic shape and structure of the set of all possible motions of the system, and ergodic theory helped to determine the statistical regularities that a chaotic system could exhibit.

To describe the uncertainties inherent in trying to observe and predict the behavior of a chaotic system, the notion of entropy was borrowed from thermodynamics, and modified.[13] I will refer to it as dynamical entropy in this context. The notion of dynamical entropy as used in describing chaos is directly related to the notion of information later developed by Claude Shannon in the context of communication theory.[14] Dynamical entropy in chaos represents a measure of surprise in obtaining a particular answer when trying to determine the state of the chaotic system. If one has any uncertainty about the state that a chaotic system begins in, then, as a result of SDIC, this uncertainty grows with time. Dynamical entropy measures the rate at which this uncertainty grows with time. As such, it is essentially a measure of the randomness an observer would perceive in trying to make measurements of the systems behavior. The connection with information theory helps to focus on the fundamentally epistemological nature of randomness in chaos. Dynamical entropy is a direct quantitative measure, *intrinsic to the chaotic system*, that describes the rate at which an *observer* loses information about the current state of the system.

Many researchers believe that the dynamical entropy of a chaotic system, and hence its randomness, is also what quantifies the "complexity" of its behavior. As will be discussed below, others believe that this characterization of the "complexity" of a chaotic system is incomplete, in that it ignores important structural elements of the system's behavior. In short it is not simply randomness that makes the behavior "complex," but a delicate balance between randomness and structure.

Given the surprising results that simple deterministic systems are capable of producing such apparently random behavior, it might seem reasonable to think of the "complexity" of a system's behavior as synonymous with its randomness. This analogy has been pushed to the extreme by researchers who link the erratic behavior of chaotic systems with the notion of algorithmic complexity proposed by Chaitin, Kolmogorov, and Solomonoff.[15] The idea of algorithmic complexity arose in the context of trying to determine exactly what it means to say that a string of numbers is random. To give an extremely oversimplified definition, the algorithmic complexity, as a number, is proportional to the length of the shortest algorithm, or set of rules, which could reproduce the given string of numbers.[16] It can be shown that for a chaotic system the algorithmic complexity is essentially the dynamical entropy described above. Therefore if one uses the algorithmic complexity as the measure of "complexity" in a chaotic system, randomness and "complexity" are indeed synonymous.

As opposed to this view, many, including this author,[17] have recently argued that it is not simply randomness that leads to the rich phenomenology of chaotic systems that is generally perceived as their "complexity." In fact it is randomness constrained by deterministic correlations that is critical for producing the structures we perceive as "complex." A simply analogy may suffice to fix this point. Think of the various sets of images provided by your favorite local television station. They perhaps run a test pattern immediately before their broadcast day begins. This pattern would generally be very regular but you would probably not think of it as very complex (or random, for that matter). On the other hand, when the broadcast day ends, the pattern of snow, corresponding to the random collisions of electrons with the screen, I would argue is also not very complex, although I perceive it as "very random," that is, unpredictable. The patterns consisting of broadcast images are far more complex than either of these cases (this might depend on the station) in the following sense. There is presumably some balance between pattern and randomness in the images (and hopefully in the sequence of images as well). If there were no randomness, at least as far as the viewer is concerned, the images would be about as exciting as a test pattern, and if there were no pattern, they would likely hold your attention as well as the postbroadcast snow. Here we see a delicate balance between randomness and structure.

Based on this intuitive notion of complexity, many researchers have developed quantitative "complexity" measures. It has recently been shown, that in analyzing a fairly typical set of chaotic systems, this type of "complexity" measure is distinct and complementary to measures of randomness like the dynamical entropy,[18] but essential in obtaining a more complete picture of the system's behavior.

III. QUANTUM CHAOLOGY

Finally we turn to a thorny issue indeed, the relationship between deterministic chaos and quantum mechanics.[19]

The strange title of this section stems from the ongoing debate as to whether the term quantum chaos is inherently oxymoronic. On the face of it, there would seem to be little common ground between classical, deterministic, chaotic and quantum descriptions of the world. As such, Michael Berry has suggested that to avoid possible contradictions the study of the relationships, if any, between chaos and quantum mechanics be dubbed quantum chaology.[20]

According to the prejudices of most present day physicists, if chaos is to say anything fundamental about the world, its relationship to quantum mechanics will have to be clearly understood. All current bets in physics are on a fundamental theory of the natural world being based essentially on relativity and quantum mechanics, although there remain significant theoretical problems understanding the relationship between general relativity and quantum mechanics. There are extreme long shots at overthrowing quantum mechanics as a fundamental theory; that is, there are loopholes in the current experimental results for retaining theories called stochastic hidden variable theories, but not many physicists take these possibilities seriously.

Chaos, however, has fundamentally changed the way that scientists in many fields, including physics, understand the behavior of the natural world. Experimental evidence of chaotic behavior abounds. Thus it seems that neither quantum mechanics nor deterministic chaos will soon be discarded as important epistemological elements of modern science. Any conflicts between their basic premises about the nature of the world must be addressed. On the face of it, the differences between the basic pictures of the universe they paint span a Kuhnian paradigm shift. But the problem seems deeper than just choosing one view or the other as a basis for the progress of Kuhnian normal science. "Normal science" seems to be progressing just fine in different directions with inconsistent paradigms in this case.

One might take the approach that, since classical mechanics provides a meaningful approximation to the behavior of the world on scales much larger than quarks, atoms, or molecules, it is somehow at this level that chaos could emerge as important in the description of the natural world. This approach, however, is fraught with paradox. First, a clear line between microscopic and macroscopic in terms of the need for a quantum description has yet to be established. More important in the present context, however, is that on the one hand, SDIC in chaotic systems is a property of the nonlinear evolution of well-defined mathematical states and has nothing to do with the scale of the system. On the other hand the existence of well defined states, in the sense of classical mechanics, is impossible in quantum mechanics. These are not research problems for the scientifically faint of heart; they are deep and fundamental problems.

So how does one go about trying to construct a consistent theory of chaos in an inherently quantum world? It might be instructive to look first at the basic properties of quantum mechanics, and see which of these might allow for chaos. First, quantum mechanics, like classical mechanics, is a deterministic theory. The difference occurs in what it is that evolves deterministically. In classical mechanics, a complete description of the state of a system is given in terms of the positions and velocities of all of its components. It is this state which evolves deterministically. So in principle, if we ever measure this state with infinite precision, and in a way that does not affect the future evolution of the system, we know all there is ever to know about the system. In quantum mechanics, a complete description of the state of a system is given in terms of an abstract quantity called the wave function. It is this quantity that evolves deterministically. The problems lie in asking the kinds of question that would have warmed the hearts of nineteenth-century physicists, such as "where is the system" or "how fast is it going." These are the questions that, for our classical system, are automatically answered by knowing the system's state. Not so in quantum mechanics; knowing the state of a quantum system completely in general neither tells us exactly where it is or how fast its going. In fact, if the system is in the very special state for which we know exactly where it is, it is a fundamental property of quantum mechanics, known as the Heisenberg uncertainty principle, that we can necessarily have absolutely no knowledge of how fast it is going, and vice versa.

Can we use the fact that both classical mechanics and quantum mechanics are deterministic theories to look for quantum chaos? Remember that the other necessary condition for a classical system to exhibit chaos was that it be a nonlinear system, which brings us to the second important property of quantum mechanics. It is inherently a linear theory. Linearity is such an important part of the structure of quantum mechanics that even trying to understand what a nonlinear extension of quantum mechanics would look like leads most physicists to profound states of confusion. So looking for chaos in terms of nonlinear deterministic evolution of quantum states seems currently to be an ill-formed problem.

The approach that current researchers actually take, an approach anticipated by Einstein in a comment made in a 1917 paper,[21] is to examine a version of quantum mechanics referred to as semiclassical. This version of quantum mechanics is based on acknowledging the great success of classical mechanics in the macroscopic domain. Any theory in physics that supersedes another is expected to agree with the old theory in overlapping domains of application. This principle is referred to as the correspondence principle.[22] One of the goals of semiclassical theory is to study the regime in which both classical mechanics as well as quantum mechanics should apply, and to establish a smooth transition between the two.

A quantum model of a system can always be obtained directly from a classical version of the system, although the quantum version of the system is always linear, regardless of whether the classical system is linear or nonlinear. The semiclassical approach to the study of chaos in quantum systems essentially amounts to studying and trying to classify the behavior of quantum systems whose classical counterpart is chaotic. This approach has indeed yielded some impressive correlations between classical chaos and the behavior of equivalent quantum systems. For example, there appears to be an important relationship between chaotic trajectories of the classical system, and the set of available energies for the quantum system. Also, some beautiful mathematical results have been obtained for abstract systems, for instance, the quantum analog of a billiard ball rolling on a curved surface.

This investigation of semiclassical systems has produced interesting results and appears to be the only fruitful avenue of research currently available in the study of "quantum chaology." Nonetheless, it is the author's view that the fundamental paradoxes regarding the relationship between quantum mechanics and classical chaos have yet to be addressed.

NOTES

1. It is perhaps ironic that after the tumultuous scientific upheavals of the twentieth century, some physicists are again pointing to a not too distant point in the future at which nature will finally be bereft of surprises. For example, Steven Wienberg recommends that we stoically accept that this will soon be the case, and predicts that physicists of the future will look wistfully back on the late twentieth century as that singular point in history when physicists were finally able to complete the reductionist program and obtain a complete description of the physical universe.

2. Maxwell's theory is what physicists now refer to as a field theory, and all field theories were presaged by Laplace's introduction of the notion of a gravitational potential.

3. H.B. Callen, *Thermodynamics and an Introduction to Thermostatics* (New York: John Wiley & Sons, 1985), p. 2.

4. H. Poincaré, *Les Méthodes Nouvelles de la Méchanique Celeste* (Gauthier-Villars, 1892); ET

NASA Translation TT F–450/452 (Springfield, VA: US Federal Clearinghouse, 1967).

5. Here again, Laplace was an early pioneer as one of the inventors of the theory of probability.

6. J. Polkinghorne, *One World: The Interaction of Science and Theology* (Princeton, NJ: Princeton University Press, 1986), ch. 5.

7. A caveat to the claim that God is a quantum gambler might be to claim that God is not concerned with the evolution of quantities like the position and momentum of objects that are of interest to human observers.

8. Alfred North Whitehead, *Process and Reality* (Boston: The Free Press, 1978).

9. E.N. Lorenz, "Deterministic Nonperiodic Flow," *Journal of Atmospheric Science* 20 (1963), p. 130.

10. Thorkild Jacobsen, "Enuma-Elish—The Babylonian Genesis," in *The Intellectual Adventure of Ancient Man* (Chicago: University of Chicago Press, 1946).

11. D. Ruelle and F. Takens, "On The Nature of Turbulence" *Communications in Mathematical Physics* 20 (1971), p. 167.

12. See, for example, R.M. May, "Simple Mathematical Models with Very Complicated Dynamics," *Nature* 261 (1967), p. 459.

13. For a helpful introduction, see H.G. Schuster, *Deterministic Chaos: An Introduction* (New York: VCH, 1988), ch. 5.

14. C.E. Shannon and W. Weaver, *The Mathematical Theory of Communication* (Champagne: University of Illinois Press, 1949).

15. See, for example, J. Ford, "What is Chaos, that we should be mindful of it," in P. Davies, ed., *The New Physics* (Cambridge: Cambridge University Press, 1989).

16. This is extremely vague, as this algorithm would presumably depend on the computer it was to run on and any number of other things. These issues are treated more carefully in the literature by inventing the notion of a universal computer, called a Turing machine. See, for example, J.E. Hopcroft and J.D. Ullman, *Introduction to Automata Theory, Languages, and Computation* (Redding, MA: Addison Wesley, 1979).

17. J.P. Crutchfield and K. Young, "Computation at the Onset of Chaos," in W.H. Zurek, ed., *Complexity, Entropy, and the Physics of Information* (Redding, MA: Addison-Wesley, 1990).

18. "Computation at the Onset of Chaos," p. 223.

19. For a helpful introduction to the topics treated in this section see M. Tabor, *Chaos and Integrability in Nonlinear Dynamics* (New York: John Wiley & Sons, 1989), ch. 6.

20. M.V. Berry, *Proceedings of the Royal Society of London*, A412 (1987), p. 183.

21. A. Einstein, "Zum Quantensatz von Sommerfeld und Epstein," *Verhandlungen Deutschen Physikalischen Gesellschaft*, 19 (1917), p. 82.

22. The simplistic expectation that a new theory must completely agree with the old theory in the appropriate domains is somewhat naïve. This is similar to the Popperian expectation that scientists will reject a powerful theory on the basis of a single piece of counterevidence. The correspondence principle, like the notion of falsification, however, has served as a powerful guiding principle.

CHAOS THEORY AND DIVINE ACTION

I. INTRODUCTION

JOHN POLKINGHORNE

Christian theology cannot evade the question of divine action. It speaks of God using the personal language of "Father" and not the impersonal language of "Force." However stretched and analogical such linguistic usage may be, it would hardly be appropriate if divine agency were so general and unfocused that God could ever be said to do anything in particular. Someone like Maurice Wiles,[1] who wishes to speak solely of God's one great act of holding the physical world in being and who, whilst acknowledging that act to be complex, does not want to speak of specific, identifiable acts of God within it, cannot repudiate the charge of deism. The motivation for this detached, single-action view of divine agency appears to be twofold.

One is a feeling that modern science leaves us with little choice. No longer is rain thought to be the opening of the heavenly water sluices. It just happens, as part of the complex interaction of the Earth's seas and atmosphere. Yet one feels an unease at so tight a drawing of the causal net of physical process, for will we not also find ourselves caught within it? Whilst there are those who have written books with titles like "Man the Machine," one cannot help suspecting that they dispensed their own scribblings from being merely the results of automatic writing. The foundational experience of human intentional agency is fundamental to a defence of rational discourse.[2] If the physical world can accommodate human action, it is not clear that it is not open to divine action also. This is a point to which we shall return.

The second reason for a detached, single-action account of divine agency is that, if God does nothing in particular, then God cannot be blamed for anything in particular either. To put it bluntly, such a God is off the hook of the Holocaust. Or, more accurately, the one deistic act is presented as the general answer to any specific problem of theodicy. The show goes on, under divine aegis but without divine endorsement or assistance. On reflection, this seems a Pyrrhic theological victory. The particular perplexities of theodicy are replaced by a single, all-embracing perplexity about why God should thus limit divine power simply to letting it all happen. Moreover, so detached and indifferent a deity can scarcely be the ground of hope. To speak bluntly once more, such a one is not the God who raised Jesus from the dead. Wiles acknowledges that Christian theology needs "to depict God as . . . victor in and through his involvement in the world's evil,"[3] but I do not find his account[4] adequate to the task. Of course, a stronger and more particular understanding of divine action will have to face the problems of theodicy that this entails and that, too, is a point to which we shall return. Meanwhile we note the necessary delicacy of the task for, as Keith Ward says, "It often seems that we can neither stand the thought of God acting often (since that would infringe our freedom), nor the thought of him acting rarely (since that makes him responsible for our suffering)."[5]

The classic account of divine action, going back in articulate form to Thomas Aquinas, is that God acts in and through the secondary causality of creation. As our knowledge of the nature of the order of that secondary causality has increased, so the concept of its being suffused with hidden divine causality has become more problematic. The idea must, surely, be more than a retrospective pious gloss put on what has actually occurred, for it must involve the discernment of what was actually present from God's side in what was happening. Yet a modern Thomist like Austin Farrer is determined not to allow any probing of the mystery. Speaking of divine agency, he says "as soon as we try to conceive it as action, we degrade it to the creaturely level and place it in the field of interacting causalities. The result can only be (if we take it literally) monstrosity and confusion."[6]

Farrer's concept of double agency seems in the end to be a fideistic assertion of what is claimed to be the case, as he resolutely eschews any attempt to conceive of the "causal joint" by which Creator and creation interact. Recourse to ineffable mystery may be forced upon us in our limited human attempts to explore the divine nature, but to make such an appeal must be a strategy of last, rather than first, resort.

II. TWO STRATEGIES

Two general conditions must surely apply to any adequate account of divine action. The first is that it must be continuous and not fitful, correctly referred to as "interaction" rather than "intervention." There can be nothing capricious or occasional in God's activity. of course, consistency is not the same as a monotonous uniformity. Divine action must always be perfectly appropriate to circumstance, and as circumstances change, so God's interaction will vary in ways that reflect this alteration. It may well be that there are times and situations which are particularly open to the play of divine activity, and that such activity is therein more clearly transparent than at other times or in other situations. One might draw an analogy with the operations of the laws of nature, which never vary in their character, but whose consequences, in particular circumstances, can take particularly striking or particularly perspicuous forms.

The second consideration is that divine action will always be contained within the grain of the created order. The laws of nature are not constraints externally imposed upon God; rather they are, in their regularity, expressions of the faithful will of the Creator. God is their ordainer and does not work against them, for that would be for God to work against God. God is free to act, yet we cannot give a satisfactory account of providential agency simply by saying that God brings about whatever it is that God wills, for the divine will is always self-consistent, and the last thing that the rational and faithful God can be is a capricious, celestial conjurer.

Human agency is also contained within the grain of the created order, and so the exploitation of some sort of analogy with our experience of intentional causality has been one strategy pursued by those who seek to understand divine action. The other broad strategy has been to appeal to the human experience of the activity of the divine spirit within the human psyche, and to make this the basis of an account of divine action generally.

Narrowly pursued, this latter line of thought might confine God's agency to the guiding and influencing of human beings and such other moral agents as there might be elsewhere in the universe. This leads someone like David Bartholomew to say that "the normal mode of his action is in the realm of the mind."[7] I think there are two fatal defects in this view. One is that it implies that the universe has been on automatic pilot for almost all of its fifteen billion year history before minds appeared on the scene. The other is that, if we believe that human beings are psychosomatic unities (as both scripture and modern science largely encourage us to do), then God cannot interact with our minds without also influencing the matter of our brains. And if we allow the latter, why should God not interact also with other aspects of the material creation?

One answer attempted to this last question is to believe that God interacts with all that happens in a way appropriately analogous to divine interaction with ourselves. This is the understanding of process theology,[8] which posits a divine presence in every event (each "actual occasion"), as the reservoir of past experience, the presenter of present possibility, and the persuader of future realization. Low-grade events (such as those comprising elementary particles or inanimate objects) are not thought of as involving conscious interaction with the divine, but they are held to involve some form of divinely influenced "selection" to realize one of a variety of potential options, so that David Griffin speaks of process theology's "pan-experiential" account of reality. This kind of nuancing of A.N. Whitehead's original and frankly panpsychic metaphysic is a move in the direction of credibility, which is also espoused by other writers who adopt a broadly process theological point of view.[9] Yet the picture painted remains one without obvious consonance with what we know about general physical process. This absence of anchorage in physical science is only one difficulty. More significant theologically is the confining of divine interaction to a purely persuasive role. In the end, true initiative lies with the event itself as it "selects" its own realization ("concrescence"). God's participation is as pleader rather than agent. Barbour is frank enough to say of process theology that it "does call into question the traditional expectation of an *absolute victory over evil*."[10] Christian theology must seek a more positive account of divine action.

The alternative strategy, of assimilating God's action in the world to our action in our bodies, has often been invoked in panentheistic accounts presented in such soft focus that all consideration of the causal joint is dissolved from scrutiny. If the discussion is sharpened up, it may take the form of talk of divine embodiment. The clearest account of this option is given by Grace Jantzen,[11] but it seems open to grave objection.[12] The universe no more looks like an organism than it looks like a machine. It has been and will be going through dramatic changes in the course of its history, from quark soup to present complexity to eventual decay or collapse. True embodiment implies for us that we are partly in thrall to the changes in our bodies; God cannot fittingly be supposed to be similarly affected by cosmic variations, so that embodiment language is highly problematic. And if the universe is of finite age, what then of divine eternity?

If we are to exploit the analogy between human and divine agency, it will have to be in a more subtle fashion. Necessarily, it will also have to be in a speculative fashion, for we possess only the most rudimentary and uncertain understanding of how it is that we ourselves can execute our intentional causality within the lawful physical world. Around 600 B.C., the pre-Socratic philosophers began to speculate whether the infinite variety of objects in the world might not arise from the diverse combinations of a small number of basic constituents. They were two and a half millennia too early to participate in the triumphs of elementary particle physics, but they had begun to push thought in a fruitful direction. We may well be at least two and a half millennia too early to talk with success about human agency (let alone, divine agency) but we must try to see if our thought can carry us in at least a moderately fruitful direction. I believe that the discoveries of chaotic dynamics may afford us useful aid in that bold enterprise.

III. CHAOS AND CONTEXTUALISM

Classical chaotic systems present us with the oxymoronic consequence of deterministic equations yielding the appearance of indeterminable behavior, because of their solutions' possessing such exquisite sensitivity to initial circumstance that their behavior is intrinsically unpredictable in detail. The central question is whether this reflects an inevitable ignorance on our part (an epistemological defect) or whether it is the clue to a deeper understanding of the nature of physical reality (an ontological insight).

Scientists are instinctive realists. They believe that what we can or cannot know is a reliable guide to what is actually the case. Their motto is "Epistemology models Ontology." Heisenberg discovered the uncertainly principle by considering what can be measured (what can be known). Very soon he and the great majority of physicists were interpreting it as a principle of indeterminancy (what is the case). This is not a forced move in quantum theory. Indeed, there is an alternative account given by David Bohm, with the same empirical consequences, which attributes uncertainty to our ignorance of the nature of certain determinate but "hidden" variables. Ultimately the decision between the two options is a metaphysical one.

In the case of chaos theory, I feel we face a corresponding metaphysical choice whose answer cannot be settled by present scientific knowledge alone. It calls for a metaphysical decision comparable to adherence to Heisenberg or to Bohm. Are chaotic systems merely unpredictable in detail or are they the sign of a true openness to the future? What are we concerned with, epistemology or ontology?

I shall commit myself to the second option. By "openness" I do not, of course, mean that the future arises in some whimsically random fashion. There are causal principles that bring it about, but their enumeration is not confined to the "bottom-up" description of the interchange of energy between the isolable constituent parts of a physical system. The causal net resulting from that bottom-up account is not drawn so tightly that it does not leave room for the operation of other forms of causality. We know that situations which differ only infinitesimally in their initial circumstances (and so, effectively, have the same energetic properties) will nevertheless (because of the exponential enhancement of those differences) display different behaviors as they explore the pattern of future possibility open to them. It is natural to consider these infinitesimal differences that determine what actually occurs as akin to "informational input," selecting a particular pattern of exploration of a strange attractor. Another consequence of recognizing the vulnerability of chaotic systems to small variation is the acknowledgment that they are intrinsically unisolable, in that the slightest change in their environment has large consequences for their subsequent behavior. That environment participates in the specification of future development. Therefore informational causality will have a holistic or "top-down" character to it. These considerations lead one to the following motivated *conjecture*:

> The physical world is subtle and supple in its constitution. It is open to causal influence by the exchange of energy between its constituent parts (as described by physics) and *also* to the operation of holistic pattern-forming agencies which can be thought of as "active information" (presently not described in detail).

The deterministic equations, from which classical chaos theory has been derived, are to be understood as *downward emergent approximations* to that more supple physical reality. They must arise from treating individual parts as if they were isolable from the environment. What role the microscopic indeterminism of quantum theory might play in the generation of openness to the future is not yet clear, both because of unresolved perplexities about the relation of chaos to the Schrödinger equation, and also because of the unsettled question of how microscopic and macroscopic relate to each other in the act of quantum measurement.

The difficulties of quantum chaology are discussed by Karl Young in his chapter. In my view the unresolved conflicts to which he draws our attention are to be resolved along the lines of the paradigm shift represented by my conjecture. Neither quantum physics nor classical deterministic dynamics is absolutely fundamental. The stance I am adopting is strongly antireductionist, affording no special status to my old subject of elementary particle physics, but regarding its beautiful insights as asymptotically simple approximations to a more integrated account of physical reality. A true Theory of Everything would be just that, not a description of bits and pieces. Of course, we are very far from the articulate attainment of such an understanding, but I am convinced that this is the direction in which to look if we are to begin to describe the world that we know contains intentional agents. The point of view presented could be called *contextualism*:[13] the behavior of constituents is not independent of the context in which they are set. It is, therefore, a form of strong anti-reductionism in which the emergence of new properties is not simply due increase in the complexity of organization of otherwise unmodified parts.[14]

The holistic agencies referred to in the conjecture might take at least three forms:

(1) There may be holistic laws of nature, presently unknown to us but in principle discoverable by science. The amazing drive for increasing complexity, discernible within fruitful cosmic and terrestrial history,[15] may well call for such an understanding.

(2) There may also be the first glimmer of an understanding of how it is that we ourselves act in the world; the way in which my mental intention to raise my arm (active information) results in the act of its raising (an energetic operation) through the interplay of top-down and bottom-up causalities. Of course, this picture is very crude indeed. Any real understanding of mind and brain will have to be much more sophisticated, in ways beyond our present power to conceive. But it is an attraction of the metaphysical conjecture presented here that it begins to describe a physical world of which we can properly conceive ourselves as inhabitants. That is a gain for *science.*

(3) It seems entirely conceivable that God also interacts with the creation through the input of active information into its open physical process. We glimpse, in a rudimentary way, what might lie behind theology's language of God's "guiding" and "drawing on" creation, language often associated with talk of the Spirit working immanently on the "inside" of creation.[16]

IV. CONTEXTUALISM AND DIVINE AGENCY

The concept of divine action through information input into a world made open to such agency through the dynamic flexibilities of chaotic systems is one which is already being explored.[17] The following consequences flow from such a picture:

(1) God's action will always be hidden. It will be contained within the cloudy unpredictabilities of what is going on. It may be discernible by faith, but it will not be exhibitable by experiment. It will more readily have the character of benign coincidence than of a naked act of power. It will be part of the complex nexus of occurrence from which it cannot be disentangled in some simplistic way that seeks to

assert that God did this but nature did that. All forms of agency intertwine in the inter-relating complexity and sensitivity of a chaotic world.

(2) Although much of the physical world is cloudy and unpredictable, there are also clockwork and predictable parts of what is going on. Their regularity will be to the believer signs of divine faithfulness. Long ago, Origen recognized that one should not pray for the cool of spring in the heat of summer (however tempting it might be to do so in his native Alexandria!). The succession of the seasons is a clockwork part of terrestrial experience, and the faithful God will not set that aside for the convenience of those who pray.

(3) The picture given is of an open future in which both human and divine agency play parts in its accomplishment. Christian theology has, at its best, striven to find a way between two unacceptably extreme pictures of God's relationship to the creation. One is that of the Cosmic Tyrant, who brings everything about by divine will alone. Such a God is the puppet master of the universe, pulling every cosmic string and keeping all within tight control. Such a God could not be the God of love, for the characteristic gift of love is the bestowal of freedom on the beloved.[18] In God's act of creation, God has allowed the other truly to be, in the degree of independence appropriate to each part of it. An evolutionary universe is to be understood theologically as one that is allowed by God, within certain limits, to make itself by exploring and realizing its own inherent fruitfulness.[19] This gift of creaturely freedom is costly, for it carries with it the precariousness inherent in the self-restriction of divine control. Something relevant to the mystery of suffering is contained within this insight. God wills neither the act of a murderer nor the incidence of a cancer, but God allows both to happen in a world which is permitted truly to be itself. But the God of love cannot be an indifferent spectator either.

The detached God of deism, who simply watches it all happen, is another extreme, unacceptable to Christian thought. We seek a middle way in which God interacts with the creation without over-ruling it. There are many perplexities in trying to understand in any detail what this could mean. We encounter the cosmic version of the theological conundrum of the relation of divine grace to human free will. All that we are attempting to do in the present discussion is to show that one can take with all seriousness all that science tells us about the workings of the world, and still believe in a God who has not left the divine nature so impotent that providence cannot act continuously and consistently with cosmic history. Every assertion of the possibility of divine action is a reassertion of the problems of theodicy, of apparent divine inaction at those moments when God's activity seems most called for. The only insight that we can offer for the understanding of that profound mystery has already been proffered: the intertwining of divine and creaturely agency in a creation that is both allowed to be itself and yet is not outside God's providentially interacting care.[20]

(4) It has sometimes been claimed that the view of God's action here advocated is a return to the discredited idea of a God of the Gaps. This is not so in the pejorative

sense implied by the criticism. God is not being invoked to explain that which is currently scientifically unexplained, but which is, in principle, scientifically explicable. A God used to plug such gaps of ignorance is a pseudodeity who will fade away with the advance of knowledge. Yet if there are indeed holistic causal principles (of any kind) at work in the world, there will have to be gaps in the bottom-up description that provide room for their operation. In this *intrinsic* sense, we are quite properly "people of the gaps" and God is quite properly a God of that kind of gap also. Many discussions of divine action refuse to grasp this nettle, taking refuge in so blurred or hidden an account of the causal joint as to fail as credible contributions to theological discussion in a scientific age.

(5) The picture given is that of a world of true becoming in which the dead hand of the Laplacean calculator is relaxed, and the future is not a mere rearrangement of what was already there in the past. Such a genuinely temporal world must be known in its temporality, not least by God, who knows things as they really are. If that is the case there must be, as the process theologians have suggested, a temporal pole in the divine nature alongside the eternal pole recognized by classical theology.[21] In such a world, even God does not know the future. That is no imperfection in the divine nature, for the unformed future is not yet there to be known. God possesses a current omniscience (knowledge of all that can now be known) but not a total omniscience (knowledge of all that will be knowable). The act of creation involves a voluntary limitation, not only of divine power in allowing the other to be, but also of divine knowledge in allowing the future to be open.[22]

(6) Petitionary prayer can be exercised with scientific integrity. In such prayer, we are not persuading God to do something which otherwise God would not have thought of, or that God would have neglected to perform without our importunity. Instead, we are offering our room for maneuver with respect to the open future to be taken by God and used to the greatest effect in collaboration with that room for manoeuvre which is reserved to the divine providential interaction. In more traditional language, we offer our wills to be aligned with the divine will. Just as laser light is effective because its coherence implies that all its constituent waves are in step and reinforce each other, without any mutual cancellations, so the coherence of divine and human wills in prayer can be genuinely instrumental in bringing about what would not have been possible if God and humanity were at cross-purposes. We see why corporate prayer is effective—not because there are more fists beating on the heavenly door, but because there are more wills to be aligned with the divine will.

V. CONCLUSION

Twentieth century science has seen the decay of a merely mechanical picture of the universe. Chaotic dynamics, together with quantum theory, has played its part in that development. Physics accordingly appears more hospitable, in its partial account of reality, to the accommodation of human agency within a world of subtle and supple process. That does not tell us more about human action (of which we have direct and foundational experience) but more about the nature of the world in which that action is realized. As we grope for an understanding of these matters, we seem also to discover a world which is open to divine agency within it. If the concept of top-down interaction through active information contains within it a glimmer of truth, we do not need to suppose that it exhausts all accounts that might be given of God's activity. At the heart of Christianity lies the belief in Christ's resurrection. No manner of exploitation of the cloudiness of chaotic physical process will bring it about that a man is raised from the dead to a gloriously transmuted and unending life. A different kind of act of God is here being claimed. This is not the place to speak of miracle[23] and of the eschatological restoration of a universe otherwise condemned to decay.[24] But all understandings of divine action will have about them the common feature that they are not irrational accounts of the whimsical acts of a celestial conjurer, but they are deeper manifestations of God's utter faithfulness and consistency, such as is also palely reflected in those regularities which scientists call the laws of nature.

NOTES

1. M.F. Wiles, *God's Action in the World* (London: SCM Press, 1986).
2. See, for example, ch. 2 of J. Macquarrie, *In Search of Humanity* (London: SCM Press, 1982).
3. *God's Action in the World,* p. 50.
4. See especially, *God's Action in the World*, ch. 7.
5. K. Ward, *Divine Action* (London: Collins, 1990), p. 2.
6. A. Farrer, *Faith and Speculation* (London: A.K.C. Black, 1967), p. 62.
7. D.J. Bartholomew, *God of Chance* (London: SCM Press, 1984), p. 143.
8. J.B. Cobb and D.R. Griffin, *Process Theology: An Introductory Exposition* (Philadelphia: Westminster Press, 1976).
9. I.G. Barbour, *Religion in an Age of Science* (San Francisco: Harper and Row, 1990), ch. 8; D.A. Pailin, *God and the Process of Reality* (London: Routledge, 1989).
10. *Religion in an Age of Science*, p. 264.
11. G. Jantzen, *God's World, God's Body* (London: Darton, Longman & Todd, 1984).
12. J.C. Polkinghorne, *Science and Providence* (London: SPCK, 1989), pp. 18–23.
13. Polkinghorne, *Science and Christian Belief* (London: SPCK, 1994), ch. 1.
14. See the discussion by A.R. Peacocke, *God and the New Biology* (London: Dent, 1986), ch. 1.
15. See P.C.W. Davies, *The Cosmic Blueprint* (London: Heinemann, 1987).
16. J.V. Taylor, *The Go-Between God* (London: SCM Press, 1972).
17. Polkinghorne, *Science and Providence*, ch. 2; *Reason and Reality* (London: SPCK, 1991), ch. 3; *Science and Christian Belief*, ch. 4; Peacocke, *Theology for a Scientific Age* (Oxford: Blackwell, 1990). The account of my views on p. 154 of the latter does not summarize them accurately.
18. See Polkinghorne, *Science and Creation* (London: SPCK, 1988), ch. 4.
19. See Peacocke, *Creation and the World of Science* (Oxford: Oxford University Press, 1974), chs. 2 and 3.

20. See *Science and Providence*, chs. 3 and 5.

21. See also Keith Ward, *Rational Theology and the Creativity of God* (Oxford: Blackwell, 1982).

22. See *Science and Providence*, ch. 7.

23. See *Science and Providence*, ch. 4.

24. See *Reason and Reality*, ch. 8; *Science and Christian Belief*, ch. 9.

CASE STUDY III

QUANTUM COMPLEMENTARITY AND CHRISTOLOGY

COMPLEMENTARITY

I. INTRODUCTION

EDWARD MACKINNON

Complementarity is a heady notion. It seems to signal some elevated perspective where contradictions can be tolerated, or even merged into a harmony that transcends common sense. Such overcoming of apparent contradictions has long been attempted, or at least signaled in various ways: Jung's Ouroboros symbolized by a snake swallowing its own tail; Zen contemplation of one hand clapping; Escher's paintings of hands drawing each other or of simultaneously ascending and descending stairs; the Penrose triangle, which looks right until one tries to trace the sides and finds one too many; Breton's surrealistic ideal of blending the real and the dream world into one seamless image; Magritte's picture of a pipe with the inscription, *"Ceci n'est pas une pipe"*; and even Dickens's observation, "It was the best of times; it was the worst of times": all use some sort of contradiction as a stepping stone to a higher truth.

Yet systematic thinkers have long realized that any toleration of contradictions effectively destroys the system that incorporates it. Aristotle counseled cutting off discussion with anyone who would not accept the principle of noncontradiction. In logic it is easy to show that any set of axioms that leads to a contradiction supplies a basis for deducing any conclusion whatsoever. The medieval slogan *"Ex falso sequitur quodlibet"* gave the reason: If anything and everything can be deduced from a set of axioms, then these axioms do not supply a basis for explaining anything.

This sets the general problematic I wish to survey. No systematic explanation in any field can be considered acceptable if it leads to contradictions. Yet attempts to pursue principles or problems to an ultimate resolution frequently lead to contradictions. If these are principles we are reluctant to reject or problems we feel constrained to pursue, then some way must be found for taming or tolerating these contradictions. Consistency is most easily achieved if the contradictions can be interpreted as apparent rather than real. Various strategies have been proposed to do this.

One such strategy stems from philosophical reflections on paradoxes. Consider the liar paradox, attributed to Eubulides the Megarian and promulgated in Paul's epistle to Titus 1:12:

The sentence in the box is false.

If it is true, then it is false. If it is false, then it is true. This typifies a family of paradoxes related to the foundations of logic and mathematics. Burali, Forti, Russell, Richard, Zermelo, Berry, Grelling, Skolem, Löwenheim, Moore, Hempel, and an anonymous prisoner all have paradoxes named in their honor, testifying to the labor logicians have expended on this. Most of these paradoxes are still subjects of dispute. These debates, however, center on syntactical and semantical issues.[1]

Niels Bohr introduced "complementarity" in the context of apparent contradictions that have an ontological significance, such as *the electron is a particle; the electron is a wave.* By 1926, the development of quantum physics seemed to entail attributing contradictory properties to aspects of the quantum domain. Though most interested physicists came to accept the basic features of the Copenhagen Interpretation, with Bohr as the presiding architect, most of them thought of Bohr's philosophical reflections on complementarity as something that goes beyond physics or the speculative tastes of most physicists. In recent years, many philosophers of science have developed detailed systematic interpretations of quantum mechanics (Bub, Redhead, Hughes, Healey, Krips, van Fraassen).[2] None of them incorporate Bohr's developed position on complementarity. Before this doctrine is extended to even more problematic domains, the immediate task is one of giving complementarity a philosophically acceptable interpretation. This is the goal of the present survey.

Bohr realized that his doctrine had some affinity to medieval theological discussions, though he never explored this. Others have noted that Bohr's epistemological position parallels Kant's on a deep structural level, though Bohr never cites and apparently was not directly influenced by Kant.[3] By bringing out some common elements in these diverse problematics, we can, I believe, both give "complementarity" a philosophically acceptable sense and also supply a basis for extending this to other domains.

II. COMPLEMENTARITY IN THEOLOGY

Discussions of the attributes of God presented medieval theologians with semantic problems that parallel the issues we have been considering. To see the parallels we should first consider the conceptual conflict which these theologians encountered. A Greek tradition, first articulated by Xenophanes and developed in Aristotle's Metaphysics, claimed that the one God, or the first mover, is a being with no composition of any sort, a pure timeless being whose existence and life are identical with his act of self-contemplation. A later overlay of neo-Platonic interpretations, coupled to efforts of Muhammedan theologians to combat any talk of attributes of Allah, led to an emphasis on the utter transcendence of God.

The Judaic tradition not only had a doctrine of God as creator, it also had sacred texts that spoke of God as an agent acting in history and responding to human actions. In the context we are considering, the distinctively Christian doctrine of God as triune is something of a conceptual embarrassment, and will be ignored. In keeping with the Jewish adage, "From Moses to Moses there is no one like unto Moses," I will focus on the treatment of this problem as presented in Moses Maimonides' *Guide for the Perplexed*. Since Thomas Aquinas subsequently taught the same doctrine, I also will consider his views.

The perplexed, for whom Maimonides was writing, were those experiencing conflicts between their religious beliefs and their philosophical studies. Some conflicts were easily handled. Philosophy taught that God is incorporeal. The Bible speaks of God's mouth, God's heart, God's hands, God's arms. Neither Maimonides nor other Talmudic scholars accepted the myth of a literal interpretation of scripture. Locutions attributing bodily parts or temporal extension to God were interpreted as anthropomorphic expressions that, properly understood, did not contradict Greek wisdom. For a Talmudic scholar such as Maimonides, such apparent contradictions were seen as routine challenges, not as a threat to the system.

Some conflicts between philosophy and tradition could not be dissolved in this way. If the Bible clearly taught that the world was created in time (at least Aquinas so interpreted it), while Aristotle held for the eternity of the world, then the orthodox believer should accept creation in time. Somewhere between such real contradictions, which required a choice, and superficial contradictions, which could be dissolved by a figurative interpretation of scripture, was a more nebulous territory involving apparently contradictory propositions, both of which seemed true. An example central to the Jewish tradition concerns God's revelation to Moses that he is: "the Lord, a God merciful and gracious, slow to anger, and abounding in steadfast love and faithfulness, keeping steadfast love for thousands, forgiving iniquities and transgressions and sin, but who will by no means clear the guilty, visiting the iniquity of the father upon the children and the children's children, to the third and fourth generation" (Exodus 34:6). How could anyone accept such a claim as true, while simultaneously denying that God has attributes?

The treatment of these conflicts depended on how the two basic sources of ultimate knowledge, the Bible and Aristotle's Metaphysics, were interpreted. Maimonides and Aquinas followed the same basic strategy. Aristotelian metaphysics was accepted as the highest form of human understanding; biblical revelation as the highest form of truth. So one accepts the truths taught by the Bible, but interprets them in a very Aristotelian fashion. The underlying assumption is that Moses, that is, the author of the Pentateuch, knew the *real* truth. Or, he understood in an Aristotelian mode. However, since he was speaking to simple, uneducated people, he used popular terminology. To understand what Moses *really* meant, one must recast his sayings in their proto-Aristotelian form.[4] Thus, Maimonides interpreted the narrative of Adam's fall as an allegory representing the relations that exist between sensation, the moral faculty, and the intellect.[5] When the Psalmist says God rides upon the arabot (or the clouds, Ps. 68:4), he really means that God rules the outermost sphere of the fixed stars.

The Torah speaks the language of man. Maimonides implemented this hermeneutical principle by a detailed analysis of how different types of terms get and change meaning, and their significance when applied to God. Since he was writing in Arabic, explaining Hebrew terms, and relating them to Greek philosophical terms, he was more acutely aware of the problems of language and meaning than most medieval philosophers. Here is the way he interpreted talk of God's attributes. Because God is the first cause, one, incorporeal, and free from emotion and limitation, any attribution directly or indirectly contradicting this is unacceptable. On this ground, four classes of attributes are ruled out: those which involve a definition; those involving a partial definition; those attributing a quality to God; and those attributing a relation to God.[6] These refer to accidents distinct from a being's essence, and therefore presuppose composition.

The same is not true about action terms. Thus we may describe a fire as bleaching, blackening, burning, boiling, hardening, and melting. This may seem to attribute different, and even incompatible, properties to fire. These, however, are all effects produced by the one action of heating. Similarly, attributing to God existence, life, wisdom, power, and differing effects does not entail separate powers or activities.

If we shift from a theological to an epistemological perspective, we can distinguish two different types of problems. The first concerns semantics; the second, knowledge of objective reality. "Socrates is wise"; "God is wise": both propositions have the same predicate and the same linguistic form. But, for Maimonides, they cannot have the same meaning. Wisdom is an attribute of Socrates. It cannot be an attribute of God; for God lacks attributes. Maimonides called such terms homonyms; Aquinas spoke of analogical predication. We should let Maimonides speak for himself: "In like manner, the terms Wisdom, Power, Will, and Life are applied to God and to other things by way of perfect homonymity, admitting of no comparison whatsoever . . . there is, in no way or sense, anything common to the attributes predicated of God and those used in reference to ourselves."[7]

Since this is a simpler version of the type of semantic problem that infects discussions of the reality of "theoretical entities," it is helpful to understand how radical an agnosticism Maimonides is professing. When he claims that predicates attributed both to God and to creatures function as perfect homonyms, he is claiming that "wise" in the pair of propositions, "God is wise" and "Socrates is wise," functions the same way "club" does in the pair of propositions, "The Ladies' Literary Society is a club" and "The murder weapon is a club." This semantics has a distinct bearing on the second problem, knowledge of theoretical entities. In the present context, "God" functions as the name of a theoretical entity. Maimonides was clear on the implication of his doctrine that terms applied to both God and creatures are perfect homonyms. There is no possibility of knowing the essence of God; all positive attributes are inadmissible, and negative attributes only serve to exclude human error.[8] Aquinas substituted "analogous" for "homonyms," a term that seemed less radical, but more in need of clarification. Yet he drew a similar conclusion: "We cannot grasp what God is, but only what he is not and how other things are related to him."[9]

This extreme position is partially conditioned by the fact that both Maimonides and Aquinas relied on the doctrine, taught in Aristotle's Treatise on Interpretation, that objects determine concepts, while concepts determine the meanings of terms. An essential difference in objects entails a corresponding difference in the meanings of terms predicated of them. If we drop this misleading semantics and rely on meaning as use, then this linguistic problem can be rephrased. The meaning of the terms used to attribute properties and activities to familiar objects is set by ordinary language usage, the language of man. What happens when we attempt to extend their usage to something, whether real or fictional, that is different in kind, not just degree, from any objects proper to our ordinary language framework? Then we bump our heads against the limits of language. We cannot abandon accepted meanings and their network of presuppositions, and still hope to say something meaningful. We cannot affirm these presuppositions and hope to say something true. Thus one is driven to rely on apparently contradictory statements such as: God exists without possessing the attribute of existence; God is wise without possessing the attribute of wisdom; and so on.[10]

Before passing to a new topic, we can reflect on the relation of this to the problem of complementarity. Maimonides and Aquinas faced contradictions that stemmed from their acceptance of two sources of truth, the Bible and Aristotle. The technique they employed was to eliminate any contradictions that could be dissolved through a reinterpretation of sources. This still left a residue of propositions of the form, "God is wise but lacks the virtue of wisdom." In affirming this, Maimonides was not affirming a contradiction. He was taming the sources of apparent contradictions by confining them to specific manageable propositions. The Aristotelian doctrine of virtues as habits presupposed a composition. Maimonides' tortured locutions deny such composition of God while claiming that he possesses the simple positive features proper to this virtue.

III. KANT, ANTINOMIES, AND PRESUPPOSITIONS

The rationalist ideal in philosophy eschewed even the appearance of contradictions. Logical deduction from clear and distinct ideas or intelligible principles should never engender a contradiction. Kant's philosophy developed more dialectically. His struggles with particular issues tended to take on a characteristic pattern. He might begin by defending one side of a disputed issue, only to defend the opposite side at a later stage in his own development. This is exhibited in the development of his position concerning rationalism versus empiricism; relative time and space versus absolute time and space; mechanistic explanation versus teleological explanation; metaphysics as the highest science versus metaphysics as the supreme delusion. Eventually he would try to find or develop a perspective in which the opposing positions could be interpreted as complementary aspects of a larger whole. This dialectical development meant that Kant continually wrestled with the problem of apparent contradictions, and began a systematic reflection on the role of reason in generating illusions and apparent contradictions. For Kant, an overall coherence is not something presumed or postulated. It is something a creative philosopher can achieve only through sustained effort.

Kant's most systematic treatment of the contradictions that reason is prone to generate is in the part of his *Critique of Pure Reason* labelled the "Transcendental Dialectic."[11] Here I will try to skim the formidable architectonic in which this is embedded, and bring out one idea pertinent to the present problem. A crucial distinction is the one Kant makes between objects in themselves (*Noumena*) and objects of knowledge (*Phenomena*). An object of knowledge is something we construct by imposing on the given of experience forms of sensibility, the schematism of the imagination, categories of understanding, and subsume under the transcendental unity of apperception. More simply, the objects we know and speak about are objects of knowledge embedded in a framework that we use to represent reality.

The contradictions that generate a doctrine of complementarity are those given in the three Paralogisms and in the Third Antinomy. Here again, I will try to extract the relevant ideas from the technical formulation. The key idea behind the paralogisms is that the application of systematic reasoning to our experience of ourselves leads to the conclusion that the soul is a substance that is simple, and that a person is essentially a soul. The point Kant makes here is that self-awareness is not a form of intuition. It is a condition of the possibility of any intuition. This self-awareness, accordingly, does not supply the basis for an object of knowledge. Categories such as "substance," "simple," and "person" apply to objects of knowledge. Kant is not denying the existence of some inner source of unity and consciousness. However, the noumenal soul, if there is such a thing, is not an object of knowledge. Any doctrine of substantial souls, or other sources of the unity of knowledge, concerns a representation of man, not noumenal souls as experienced through consciousness.

The third antinomy carries this one step further. The attempts to develop a science of physical reality led to an idea of causality which Kant developed as a detailed response to Hume's criticisms. Causality is necessary and universal in the sense that all changes of appearance fit into invariable sequences in accord with natural laws. More simply, determinism reigns. Yet our experience of ourselves as agents supports a different form of causality, freedom or spontaneity. The key point here is that actions are freely chosen by an agent, and are not necessitated by antecedent conditions. Allowing such freedom destroys the causal order. Kant's solution is that noumenal agents may be free, but we can never know the truth or falsity of such claims. Noumena are not objects of knowledge. This is not, as it might seem, a simple dismissal of freedom. The agent that acts is the real existent being, not the object of knowledge we construct to represent it. In ethics, accordingly, where we are concerned with setting guides for moral action, it is altogether reasonable to presume freedom.

This resolution led to a doctrine of complementary conceptual frameworks that was basic to Kant's work after the first Critique. Kant never used the term "complementarity." Yet, the idea clearly played a foundational role. His clearest expression of this was given in the preface to *The Metaphysical Foundations of Natural Science*. After distinguishing between "nature" in the formal sense, or the nature of some thing, and "nature" in the material sense, or the sum total of things insofar as they can be objects of our senses, Kant says of the latter:

> Nature taken in this signification of the word has two main parts according to the main distinction of our senses: the one contains the objects of the external sense, the other the objects of the internal sense. Therefore a twofold doctrine of nature is possible: a doctrine of body and a doctrine of soul. The first concerns extended nature, and the second, thinking nature.[12]

The term "complementarity" aptly applies to the two systems. In the *Foundations of the Metaphysics of Morals* (1785), *The Critique of Practical Reason* (1788), and the *Metaphysics of Morals* (1797), man is considered as an agent who must be represented as free and autonomous. Kant never attempts to prove man's freedom. Here he follows Rousseau's lead. Unless persons have free choice, there can be no ethics. The notion of free choice is implicit in the concept of a person as a moral agent. In *The Metaphysical Foundations of Natural Science* (1786) and in the *Opus Postumum*, all the motions of all observable bodies, not excluding human beings, are presumed as explainable through their determination by forces. Superficially Kant seems to be holding that a human is free and a human is not free. In Kant's critical perspective, these presuppositions are seen as complementary rather than contradictory.

IV. BOHR'S COMPLEMENTARITY

Bohr introduced the notion of *complementarity* in 1927. In subsequent publications and in interminable discussions with the young physicists at his institute and with anyone else who could be persuaded or coerced into listening, Bohr modified, refined, and extended this notion. From the mid-1930s on, he stressed the primacy of language in any analysis of concepts. We are, as he put it, suspended in language. For present purposes, I will begin with the linguistic orientation that characterized his mature thought, and try to explain the development of his doctrine of complementarity and its subsequent modifications. This linguistic orientation has a double significance. It relates complementarity to wider problems, and it helped to dissipate some contemporary confusion. In the last few years, the interpretation of quantum mechanics has become a growth industry in the philosophy of science. For technical reasons interpreting quantum mechanics has come to mean interpreting the mathematical formalism of quantum mechanics following the parallel between model theory and proof theory in mathematics. When the Copenhagen Interpretation is situated in this perspective, it seems confused and inadequate. The perspective misinterprets what Bohr was attempting. He was coping with a breakdown of the old Bohr-Sommerfeld model, a breakdown that, in retrospect, centered on language. From a tentative resolution of this breakdown he derived constraints for the acceptance and interpretation of the new quantum mechanics that replaced the older program. For this reason, we will consider the breakdown of the old theory as well as the interpretation of the new theory.[13] When Bohr presented his atomic theory in 1913 his goal was the traditional one of describing reality as it exists objectively. Yet reflections on his dissertation and on contemporary physics had already convinced him that certain aspects of physical reality could not be adequately described with classical concepts. For Bohr the term "classical concepts" gradually came to refer to a core of concepts derived from ordinary language and classical physics that played an indispensable role in describing reality. At this stage, he thought that the orbits of electrons could be described in mechanical concepts, and that radiation in free space could be described using Maxwell's laws. Bohr steadfastly rejected Einstein's light-quantum (or after 1926 photon) hypothesis. However he did not think that any fusion of these concepts supplied a basis for describing either the transition of electrons between orbits, or the production and absorption of radiation.

The Bohr theory blossomed into the Bohr-Sommerfeld program. Orbits became three dimensional. Quantum numbers served both to characterize atomic orbits and to systematize spectral lines. Spectroscopic analysis led to the introduction of the quantum numbers j, the inner quantum number, and m, the magnetic quantum number. The significance of these numbers for atomic structure was not clear. Around 1920, Bohr began to make a sharp distinction between descriptive elements and formal principles. The truth of descriptive elements depends on a correspondence between the descriptions given and the reality described. The significance of the formal principles comes from the role they play in theories. Bohr's explanation of the periodic table was the culminating achievement of the Bohr-Sommerfeld program. In this work Bohr interpreted atomic physics as resting on three formal principles and three descriptive props. The three formal principles are: Bohr's own *Correspondence Principle*, the basic tool for extending classical laws to the atomic domain; Ehrenfest's *Adiabatic Principle*, used to determine that orbits are stable; and the *Aufbauprinzip*, the stabilizing principle for quantum numbers which Bohr relied on in constructing electronic orbits by adding one more electron to get the next element in the periodic table. The three descriptive elements were: atomic electrons orbit the nucleus in elliptical paths; the azimuthal quantum number ($k = l + 1$ in contemporary notation) characterizes the degree of an orbit's eccentricity; and emission and absorption of radiation is due to orbital transitions of electrons.[13]

By 1923, the Bohr-Sommerfeld theory had encountered formidable difficulties in attempting to explain the splitting of spectral lines in weak magnetic or strong electrical fields, the helium atom, the hydrogen molecule, and some interaction effects now explained through electronic spin. To fit such complications, Landé, Heisenberg, Born, Pauli, and others had introduced ad hoc assumptions hardly compatible with the Bohr-Sommerfeld theory. Pauli was arguing for a rejection of the idea of electronic orbits and of the realistic significance Bohr had attached to at least the n and k quantum numbers. Bohr collaborated with Kramers and Slater in a paper (the BKS paper[15]) that reexamined the realistic significance previously accorded the descriptive elements in atomic physics. On the face of it, this paper was a peculiar prop for a last ditch defense of descriptive realism. It replaced electrons by fictitious virtual oscillators producing virtual fields that communicated in some unspecified way with other virtual fields. Effectively the strategy was similar to the one Kelvin had introduced, of determining the electrical field of a charge in front of a conducting plate by replacing the plate with a fictitious particle behind the plate. The tractable fiction produces the same fields as the real plate. The BKS paper retained the only descriptive prop Bohr still considered defensible, the wave description of electromagnetic radiation. He had been forced to abandon any realistic description of electronic orbits.

The BKS paper supplied a basis for extending the Correspondence Principle and for treating dispersion and the polarization of resonant fluorescent radiation, two problems that the Bohr-Sommerfeld theory had difficulty accommodating. Kramers and Heisenberg extended the treatment of dispersion, and Heisenberg used the virtual oscillator model to fabricate quantum mechanics.[16] The Compton Effect was the supreme obstacle. In deriving the formula that fitted his scattering results, Compton assumed that one light quantum interacts with one electron in a way that conserves energy and momentum. The BKS paper replaced photons with extended fields interacting with virtual oscillators so that momentum and energy conservation referred to statistical averages, not to individual processes. This statistical interpretation of the conservation laws was a consequence of the description of electromagnetic radiation as waves propagating in space-time. To this Einstein objected. Two groups set up difficult experiments to test the applicability of the conservation laws to the Compton Effect. Bothe and Geiger in Germany and Compton and Wilson in the U.S. found coincidences between X rays and scattered electrons too pronounced to be explained by statistical coincidences. The physics community generally interpreted this as a victory for Einstein over Bohr.

Bohr saw things differently. One theme continually recurs in his writing during the brief transitional period between the final failure of the Bohr-Sommerfeld theory and the formulation of a new quantum mechanics. The theme is that the framework of space-time descriptions breaks down for atomic events. He was encountering contradictions in the basic presuppositions grounding discourse about atomic states and particle events. Classical electromagnetism, which had set the limits for precision, presupposed that light is a wave. The only explanation of the Compton Effect that survived experimental refutation presupposed that light is composed of particles. Similarly, the presupposition that atomic electrons travel in elliptical orbits grounded the assignment of quantum numbers and the detailed treatment of the anomalous Zeeman Effect. The denial of this presupposition grounded the treatment of dispersion and resonant fluorescent radiation. There were other contradictions. One could put them in the form: atomic electrons travel in elliptical orbits; atomic electrons do not travel in elliptical orbits. However, this explicitness is a bit misleading. The contradictions really stemmed more from presuppositions implicit in discourse than from overt statement. Thus elliptical orbits were presupposed in the treatment of the periodic table, the anomalous Zeeman Effect, and perturbation theory. The treatment of dispersion and the polarization of resonant fluorescent radiation presupposed the virtual oscillator model with vibrating rather than rotating electrons.

The discussions that led to the Copenhagen Interpretation focused as much on experimental sources of information as they did on the new mathematical formalisms. The type of conceptual analysis this engendered may best be seen by considering two basic classical concepts, "particle" and "wave." To call anything a particle implies that its internal structure, if such there be, is irrelevant in the context. A particle has a space-time trajectory. It can impinge on a target, penetrate it, recoil from it, or be deflected by it. It can collide with another particle, or strike a photographic plate at a point. These interrelations are not determined by what electrons *really* are. They simply represent an unpacking of the cluster of conceptual entailments implicit in the ordinary usage of "particle." The classical concept, "wave," is at the nub of a different conceptual cluster. A wave has neither a precise location nor a proper trajectory. It propagates through vibrations in a medium. Waves do not collide, penetrate, or recoil. Waves are reflected, refracted, or absorbed. They may be diffracted by a target or interfere with each other. They cannot strike a photographic plate at a point, but can produce interference patterns on it. Here again, the cluster of conceptual entailments is not determined by what electrons really are or by the formalism of quantum mechanics. It is simply an unpacking of what is implicit in the ordinary usage of "wave" proper to classical physics.

The experimental sources of information about atomic systems and fundamental particles can be roughly divided into two types. The first is collision experiments. One hits a target with a projectile and then examines the behavior of the resulting fragments. The second type of information comes from the radiation that is emitted, absorbed, or modified by atomic or subatomic processes. In describing either type of experiment, and reporting and interpreting its results, one is forced to rely on either the "particle" or the "wave" conceptual cluster. Classical concepts remain indispensable. One of the two conceptual clusters can be adapted to any experimental situation. Neither fits every experimental situation.

When this conflict is reduced to a an explicit statement such as: "the electron is a wave and the electron is a particle," one seems to be countenancing explicit contradictions. Complementarity is an attempt to dissolve, rather than promulgate, contradictions. The language of classical physics is an extension of ordinary language that has incorporated new categorical and quantitative expressions and, by a painstaking historical process, fashioned these concepts into a coherent system for representing physical reality. This extended ordinary language (EOL) breaks down in the quantum domain. It is not possible to use this and give a coherent descriptive account of atomic states and particle processes. Here we bump our heads against the limits of language. Yet we cannot simply abandon this language. It supplies an indispensable basis for reporting and communicating information concerning experimental results. The doctrine of complementarity allows for limited mutually incompatible extensions of this EOL. Which extension is appropriate depends on the question we put to nature and the experimental setups that embody these questions. Thus one can use either the wave or the particle cluster to describe a particular experiment and interpret the results. One cannot use any fusion of these to describe reality as it exists objectively.

This was the core of Bohr's doctrine of complementarity. In atomic physics he extended the notion of complementarity to relations between space-time descriptions and causal accounts, and to the relation between classical and quantum physics. These three basic examples had slightly different features. Quantum physics and classical physics are scientific systems resting on mutually incompatible assumptions. Yet both are required to explain quantum phenomena. All the results of experiments, Bohr insisted, must be expressed in classical terms. Within any particular experimental report there is no role for complementarity. However, when one attempts to deduce results from a theory, then one must rely on quantum rather than classical physics. Thus, he spoke of classical and quantum physics as complementary frameworks. Within the framework of classical physics, one uses both space-time descriptions and causal accounts. These blend harmoniously. When one wants to extend this classical framework to describe experiments and report typical quantum phenomena, such as particles passing through slits, interfering with each other, and striking targets, then one must choose either a space-time description or a causal account. One cannot have both simultaneously. Wave-particle complementarity has a different conceptual status. In classical physics, "wave" and "particle" are, as indicated above, incompatible categories. In quantum physics one can apply either category to the same entities, for instance, electrons or photons. But both cannot be applied simultaneously. Thus "wave" and "particle" are complementary only in the quantum domain.

In the mid-thirties, Bohr's terminology took a more Kantian form. In his early writings on complementarity, he spoke about or reflected the idea of a *disturbance* theory of measurement. To measure the state of some system, we interact with the system and then record the results of the interaction. In classical physics, the interactions involved in measurement could be presumed to have a negligible effect. We do not change a stone or a slab of wood by measuring its weight, volume, or color. Heisenberg's idealized gamma ray microscope typifies the type of quantum measurement that played a prominent role in the discussions between Bohr and Heisenberg leading to the Copenhagen

Interpretation. An ideal measurement of the position of an electron would involve bouncing light off it, and then viewing the light in a microscope. However, long wavelength light would act on an electron in much the same way ocean waves act on a suspended cork. To measure the position of an electron, one would need light of very short wavelength, or X rays. Light waves (or photons) with such short wavelengths have high energy. In a collision with an electron such a photon would communicate energy and send the electron traveling in some arbitrary direction. There is, even in such an idealized experiment, no way to measure the position of an electron without simultaneously disturbing it. What is recorded is the result of the disturbing interaction.

In the mid-thirties, Bohr reexamined the conceptual problems involved in extending classical concepts to problematic domains and in the doctrine of complementarity. This was occasioned both by his sustained efforts to clarify the foundations of nuclear physics and quantum field theory, and also by his clash with Einstein on the Einstein-Podolsky-Rosen Paradox. As he reflected on disturbance accounts of measurement, he realized that such accounts implicitly presupposed that one could meaningfully speak of the position or state an electron had prior to measurement. This did not accord with his doctrine that reports of experimental results supply the only meaningful basis for speaking about properties of particles or states of systems. As a result, he began to use "phenomenon" to refer to the results of experiments, including the conditions that make particular experiments possible, and ceased to speak about measurements disturbing the system measured. He did not use the related term, "noumenon," to refer to things as they exist independent of our observations.

Bohr made a distinct effort to popularize the notion of complementarity so that it could be used in domains outside atomic physics. In popular lectures he used this notion to discuss domains that could be treated by clashing perspectives: detached versus participatory studies of cultures, the authority of the U.N. versus the sovereignty of individual states, and even the relation between religion and science. These were more in the way of suggestions than developed positions. The only extensions he developed in any detail were for empirical sciences, in which the experimental positing of questions affects the answer given in a way analogous to the phenomena originally treated by the disturbance account of quantum measurements. In biology, for example, any detailed attempt to determine the molecular composition of a living being would destroy its life. Hence, some form of vitalism is complementary to physicalistic accounts of living beings. Here Bohr was not suggesting or supporting any metaphysical doctrine of vitalism, but insisting that reductionistic accounts of living beings rested on a conceptual confusion which complementarity could clarify. Something similar arises in psychology from any attempt to describe the subject both as one having the experience of knowledge and as an object of investigation. Here again, there is a clear parallel with Kant's paralogisms, though this is never cited by Bohr. These extensions will not be developed here, since we are more concerned with conceptual extensions of the notion of complementarity than its application to empirical sciences.[17]

These linguistic reflections constrain the interpretation of mathematical formalism. But mathematical formulations supply the basis for extending and unifying the new quantum physics. Any detailed discussion of this mathematics is inappropriate in the present context. However, I will try to indicate how mathematical formalisms relate to the doctrine of complementarity. This in turn involves a split between the traditions operative within the community of quantum physicists and reinterpretations of quantum physics by philosophers, including physicists turned philosophers.

The new quantum physics developed along two competing lines. The first was the quantum mechanics of Heisenberg leading to the matrix mechanics of Heisenberg, Born, and Jordan. The second was Schrödinger's wave mechanics stemming from de Broglie's wave-particle duality. Bohr presided over the Copenhagen discussions that eventually lead to an interpretation harmonizing these approaches. Through Schrödinger participated briefly, he opted out and rejected the Copenhagen Interpretation fashioned by Bohr and Heisenberg with assistance from Pauli. Dirac developed a more general formalism that had the Schrödinger and Heisenberg formulations as special cases. As this came to function in the physics community, it incorporated a residue from Bohr's epistemological reflections. Quantum mechanics is geared to explaining observables. Observables are the results of actual and possible experiments expressed in a language that incorporates the basic features of complementarity, but without Bohr's reflections on language and concepts. The interpretative core of the formalism is the Ψ function (or state-vector). This is not interpreted as describing atomic states, but as supplying a basis for probabilities concerning the values of quantities characterizing the system. This has come to be called *the orthodox interpretation*.

John von Neumann, one of this century's leading mathematicians, found the Dirac formulation mathematically defective, and fashioned his own Hilbert space formulation of quantum mechanics.[18] Though von Neumann accepted the orthodox Copenhagen Interpretation, many philosophers who took the von Neumann formulation and subsequent refinements as foundational rejected the Copenhagen Interpretation. When this type of foundational approach is related to the currently fashionable semantic conception of theories, the interpretation of quantum mechanics is a three-step process. The first step is a relation between an abstract formulation of quantum mechanics and the family of models that can represent it. The second step is a relation between one of these models and some aspect of reality. In an antirealist interpretation (van Fraassen), this is essentially a relation between a model and phenomena. In a realist interpretation (Redhead, Hughes, Healey), this is a relation between a model and the reality underlying the phenomena. Neither approach incorporates reflections on the limits of language and complementarity.

The real testing ground between these approaches is the experimental refutation of Bell's theorem.[19] To oversimplify, Bell's theorem assumes that it is possible in principle to give some sort of hidden variable (or deterministic) account of the reality behind the phenomena quantum mechanics explains. From this assumption, Bell derived an inequality that contradicts orthodox quantum mechanics. All the unambiguous experimental tests have supported orthodox quantum mechanics over Bell. This has convinced even opponents of complementarity that it is not possible to give an account of the reality behind atomic phenomena that incorporates both space-time localization and causal determinism.

V. CONCLUSION

It must be admitted that what I have presented here is more an interpretation than a simple summary of the doctrine of complementarity. Many summaries give the impression that Bohr has a vested interest in conceptual confusion, and that the center of this confusion was a toleration of contradictions. Bohr's fundamental aim was to achieve the maximal consistency compatible with the incorporation of different types of information stemming from different sources. I have tried to interpret "complementarity" in a way that fulfills, rather than violates, this ideal. Also, I have attempted to give a central role to Bohr's later stress on the primacy of language in any analysis of conceptual problems. This relates more clearly to the issues treated in this book than a concentration on empirical science.

The three treatments summarized concern discourse about God, man, and quantum phenomena. Viewed from a linguistic perspective, they have one similar feature. When one attempts to infer conclusions about some domain of reality from two perspectives that presuppose different foundations, then one often encounters apparent contradictions. These apparent contradictions were seen as rooted in the presuppositions implicit in the language used. To get at the underlying conceptual issues we should first clarify the role of presuppositions.

Technically, a *semantic* presupposition has the form: X presupposes Y if Y must be true for X to be either true or false. Thus, "John's wife is ill" cannot be considered as being either true or false unless John has a wife. This may be extended from specific presuppositions to a conceptual core underlying our ordinary language and its extension to classical physics. Any discussion of a conceptual core in ordinary language involves a network of disputed issues. We can short-circuit the network by simply considering a minimal conceptual core found in commonsense realism; Aristotelian physics, essentially systematized commonsense realism; Strawson's descriptive metaphysics, an analytic systematization of the conceptual core presupposed in any use of language to refer to absent particulars; and in phenomenological analyses of the lived world and the I-world polarity. The ordinary language we use presupposes a world of objects with properties coexisting in a common space-time framework, and a sharp subject/object distinction. At issue here are not theoretical accounts of what physical bodies, space, and time really are, but the way they are implicitly represented in language. Any syntactic or semantic novelties introduced into ordinary language face a Darwinian struggle for survival. A condition for acceptance is that they must be compatible with a fundamental conceptual coherence. Elsewhere (MacKinnon, *Interpreting Quantum Physics: An Historical Perspective,* forthcoming) I will attempt to show by means of an historical analysis that the language of classical physics preserves the type of conceptual core Bohr presumed.

Ordinary language and its specialized extensions in different domains play an indispensable and irreducible role in describing reality and communicating information. What happens when we use such language to speak of some presumed reality that is not considered an object of experience within this space-time framework? The medieval theologians considered that God could not be considered an object with properties, and did not exist in space and time. Kant insisted that the subject of conscious experiences could not simultaneously be considered an object of experiential knowledge. Bohr developed the position that the framework of extended ordinary language has limits to its applicability. One cannot fashion any coherent extension of the language of classical physics that allows a coherent descriptive account of the quantum domain. The best one can do is to develop incompatible extensions that play a complementary role in describing reality and reporting experimental results.

One logical point should be noted. Both Kant in his treatment of the antinomies and Bohr in his slogan, *"Contraria sunt complementaria,"* treated the apparent contradictions generated by reason as contraries rather than contradictories. The significant difference between them is that contraries do not allow a valid inference from the falsity of one contrary (all men are wealthy) to the truth of the opposing contrary (no men are wealthy). Both can be false. The medieval theologians made a related conceptual point with their insistence on the primacy of the *via negativa*. Both suggest and support a moderate agnosticism concerning what can be said about postulated entities that do not fit into the ordinary framework of objects with properties coexisting in a shared space-time framework. We are much clearer on what these presumed entities are not than on what they are.

What if one wishes to speak about a being that is both God and man, that is atemporal and yet has a temporal existence, that is both creator of the world and an entity in the created world? The potential for clashes and seeming contradictions is manifest.[20] Whether an adaption of complementarity supplies a basis for mitigating or for dissolving such apparent contradictions is a task I leave to others.

NOTES

1. W.V.O. Quine, *The Ways of Paradox and Other Essays* (New York: Random House, 1966), pp. 1–23.
2. See, for example, R. Healey, *The Philosophy of Quantum Mechanics: An Interactive Interpretation* (Cambridge: Cambridge University Press, 1989); R. Hughes, *The Structure and Interpretation of Quantum Mechanics* (Cambridge: Harvard University Press, 1989); and B. van Fraassen, *Quantum Mechanics: An Empiricist View* (Oxford: Clarendon Press, 1991).
3. E. MacKinnon, *Scientific Explanation and Atomic Physics* (Chicago: University of Chicago

Press, 1982), pp. 370–376; J. Honner, *The Description of Nature: Niels Bohr and the Philosophy of Quantum Physics* (Oxford: Clarendon Press, 1987).

4. M. Maimonides, *The Guide for the Perplexed*, ET by S. Pines (Chicago: University of Chicago Press, 1963), Part I, ch. xxxiii; Thomas Aquinas, *Summa Theologiae* I, q. 68, a. 2.

5. *Guide*, Part I, chs. ii.

6. *Guide*, Part I, ch. lii.

7. *Guide*, Part I, ch. lvi.

8. *Guide*, ch. lviii.

9. *Summa Contra Gentiles*, Book 1, chs. 30, no. 4.

10. *Guide*, ch. lvii.

11. I. Kant, *Critique of Pure Reason* (London: Macmillan, 1961), pp. 297–484.

12. Kant, *The Metaphysical Foundations of Natural Science* (Indianapolis: Bobbs-Merrill, 1970), p. 3.

13. Much that has been written on Bohr's doctrine of complementarity is systematically misleading. Bohr's original presentation is in Bohr, *Atomic Theory and the Description of Nature* (Cambridge: Cambridge University Press, 1934). His clearest summary of his epistemological position is in his contribution to P. Schilpp, ed., *Albert Einstein: Philosopher-Scientist*, Library of Living Philosophers (New York: Tudor, 1949). I have summarized his development in my *Scientific Explanation and Atomic Physics*, chs. 4, 5, 8, and 10; and in my "Bohr on the Foundations of Quantum Theory," in A. French and P. Kennedy, eds., *Niels Bohr: A Centenary Volume* (Cambridge, MA: Harvard University Press, 1985); as well as in "Bohr and the Realism Debates," in H. Folse and J. Faye, eds., *Niels Bohr and Contemporary Philosophy*, Boston Studies in the Philosophy of Science, Vol. 153 (Dordrecht: Kluwer Academic Publishers, 1994). The best brief summary of his epistemology is in A. Petersen, *Quantum Physics and the Philosophical Tradition* (Cambridge, MA: MIT Press, 1968). H. Folse, *The Philosophy of Niels Bohr: The Framework of Complementarity* (Amsterdam: North Holland, 1985) includes a detailed summary and analysis of Bohr's doctrine of complementarity. These issues will be treated in much more detail in my forthcoming *Interpreting Quantum Mechanics: An Historical Perspective*.

14. These developments are treated in more detail in my *Scientific Explanation and Atomic Physics*, ch. 5; in M. Jammer, *The Conceptual Development of Quantum Mechanics*, 1st ed. (New York: McGraw-Hill, 1966), ch. 3; in J. Mehra and H. Rechenberg, *The Historical Development of Quantum Theory* (New York: Springer-Verlag, 1982), Vol. I, chs. 2 and 3; and in A. Pais, *Niels Bohr's Times, in Physics, Philosophy, and Polity* (Oxford: Clarendon Press, 1990), ch. 10.

15. L. Rosenfeld, ed., *Niels Bohr: Collected Works* (Amsterdam: North Holland, 1972), Vol. 5, Part I includes this paper and extensive background material.

16. MacKinnon, "Heisenberg, Models, and the Rise of Matrix Mechanics," *Historical Studies in the Physical Sciences* (1977), pp. 137–188.

17. A more detailed account of such extensions is given in *The Philosophy of Niels Bohr*, ch. 6.

18. J. von Neumann, *Mathematical Foundations of Quantum Mechanics*, trans. by R. Beyer (Princeton: Princeton University Press, 1955).

19. J. Bell, *Speakable and Unspeakable in Quantum Mechanics* (Cambridge: Cambridge University Press, 1987).

20. I have summarized some of the contradictions generated by the historical development of this doctrine in my *Truth and Expression: The 1968 Hecker Lectures* (New York: Newman Press, 1971).

BARTH, BOHR, AND DIALECTIC

JAMES E. LODER AND W. JIM NEIDHARDT

I. THE RELATIONAL LOGIC OF COMPLEMENTARITY AND CHRISTOLOGY

In 1986 a centennial celebration was held for both Karl Barth and for Niels Bohr. Although seemingly worlds apart, Barth and Bohr share more than a centennial year, and it will be the initial task of this essay to show why that is the case. In the main section following, it will be shown how the dialectic in the theology of Karl Barth may find common ground with Niels Bohr's concept of complementarity in postmodern physics. This is an unlikely convergence owing to Barth's famous *"Nein!"* rejecting natural theology and, indeed, any compatibility between theology and the natural or human sciences. However, we will argue that this dichotomy is superficial. Even Barth himself altered his position in his later years. Although this essay is not primarily historical, this historical note is important since it is evidence that our argument does not depart from the essential structure of Barth's position in order to make the case for a systematic connection between his dialectic and the philosophy of complementarity. On the scientific side, Bohr's view of complementarity will be viewed as an asymmetric bipolarity in contrast to the way it is most commonly construed. Thus, being faithful to Bohr's thought at a level deeper than usual will yield an unexpected compatibility with theology.

In the final section of this essay, it will be noted that both Bohr and Barth were indebted to Kierkegaard. Thus, the concept of a "qualitative dialectic" in Kierkegaard will be revealed as a root connection which may well lie behind the compatibility we find between Bohr and Barth; there is, in any case, a systematic and historic connection to Kierkegaard in both instances. The theological point of establishing such a connection is to show the christomorphic character of complementarity, which is explicit in Kierkegaard but only implicit in Barth's dialectic and Bohr's concept of complementarity. This discussion of the Kierkegaardian root should make it clear that, far from our establishing here a mere structural analogy, this essay will lend some substance and definiteness to the theological notion that all creation bears the mark of Christ's nature.

II. COMPLEMENTARITY: NIELS BOHR (1885–1962)

A fundamental definition of complementarity is: the logical relationship between two descriptions or sets of concepts applicable to a single phenomenon or object, which, though mutually exclusive, are nevertheless both necessary for a comprehensive description of the phenomenon or object under investigation. In physics the notion of complementarity was developed when it was recognized that a simple model did not adequately explain all the observations made on subatomic systems in varying experimental contexts. Specifically, in quantum physics it has been discovered that a *wave-particle duality* exists. Light, classically understood as waves of electromagnetic radiation, may have a corpuscular aspect, and electrons, classically thought of as particles, may have a wave aspect.

The idea of two different but complementary concepts to treat quantum phenomena was first proposed by Niels Bohr when he recognized that physical reality always reveals what can be known of its intrinsic structure by means of an interaction between objects of nature and the observer—through the observing apparatus chosen by the observer. Accordingly, he recognized that the wave and particle aspects of matter (or light) do not directly describe what a quantum object is; rather, they describe the nature of the relationship between the object and the experimental apparatus used to observe it. Furthermore, both wave and particle aspects of the observer-object relationship are required for comprehensive understanding, but both wave and particle aspects cannot simultaneously be observed due to the mutually exclusive character of their experimental, observational contexts.[1] Out of grappling with such problems arose Bohr's concept of complementarity. As his reflections on such problems matured, Bohr considered the interpretative framework of complementarity to be helpful in providing a unified understanding of phenomena encountered in the human sciences as well as the physical sciences.

Physicists commonly understand complementarity to be a form of perceptual circularity associated with bipolar sets of concepts intrinsic to a phenomenon or object (even though they often do not necessarily use the terminology of perceptual circular complementarity). As in the notion of figure-ground reversal in a perceptual gestalt, so in the observation of physical phenomena, as the knower-observer focuses on one concept in its observational context, simultaneous knowledge of the other concept in its observational context fades out; knowledge of the latter is then only possible indirectly, that is, in memory. For a comprehensive understanding of such complex situations, the observer as knower must engage in a dialectical circling back and forth between the two complementary, perceptual contexts. The dynamic nature of such dialectical circling is necessary if one is to be faithful to the dual yet unitary character of the bipolar reality structure being pointed to. The notion of complementarity as a perceptual, circular relationship is similar to C.F. von Weizsäcker's[2] efforts in both extending and modifying Bohr's complementarity interpretation of the wave-particle duality.

However, as Christopher Kaiser and others have suggested, complementarity in

Bohr's thought has a richer, more subtly complex structure than perceptual circularity. In particular, the sets of concepts referring to the same phenomenon or object do not necessarily exist on the same conceptual level. In such a case, their distinctiveness yet interrelatedness, together in a unitary whole, is preserved by a *differentiated* relationality maintained by the asymmetric character of the relations constituting the relationship between the two levels. This more subtle form of relationality we will call *asymmetric complementarity* or, alternatively, *strange loop relationality*.

A strange loop is a bipolar, asymmetric, relational pattern in which two distinct conceptual levels are bound together through a dynamic-asymmetric relationship. Such an interrelationality creates a complex yet unitary whole that is differential in character; that is, the asymmetric character of the relationship preserves the distinctiveness of each level. A striking and appropriate form for representing this relational pattern is the strange loop of a Möbius band. The asymmetric relations of the relationality are represented by directed line segments, that is, arrows, embedded in the Möbius band's one side. It is this one-sidedness, in contrast to an ordinary two-sided cylindrical band, that makes the Möbius band a singular mathematical structure representing a unique topological unity. Figure 1 is a schematic representation of strange loop relationality.[3]

Before considering in detail the way in which Barth's dialectical thought relates to asymmetric complementarity, it should be clear that the pattern which we are discussing is embedded in the relationality between the investigator and the phenomenon under investigation. In rigorous scientific methodology, we allow the object under investigation to determine the way we know and express our thoughts concerning the material. The same is true of rigorous theological investigation, where the nature of God must be allowed to direct the way in which God is to be known. Thus in both science and theology there are appropriate ways set by the object of inquiry whereby that object makes itself understood. However, to notice a pattern which is common to two different types of inquiry is not thereby to discover and extract an essential structure. The pattern we are discussing appears spontaneously in different contexts, but it remains embedded in the inquiry. Thus, the overall position developed in this essay is best characterized as epistemological realism, and the analogies developed around the above model are the outgrowth of carrying through that epistemological program in different contexts of inquiry. Although we are attempting to explicate unexpected commonalities which in themselves do not have a metaphysical or epistemological status, theology does make a claim about the ultimacy of the relationality described here. With this in mind, we turn to the dialectical pattern in Barth's thought which characterized his sustained and rigorous inquiry into the nature of God revealed in Jesus Christ.

III. DIALECTIC: KARL BARTH (1886–1968)

We will begin with a discussion of dialectic as it has appeared in the mainstream of western philosophical thought. This will allow us to place Barth's approach to dialectic

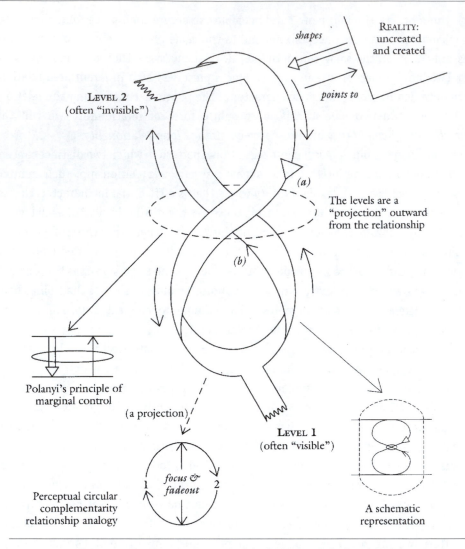

Figure 1: The Strange Loop Model of Bipolar-Relational Unity.

Relationality as unity-in-duality takes this shape in the model because it represents both coherence and openness. The model is open-ended partly because the organismic-environmental effect originating from both levels 2 and 1 of the a-b relationship is continuous. Also, within the loop, the duality is centered upon a moment in time, that is, the twist in the band, in and through which the underlying unity of the two sides of the duality is continuously being disclosed. Thus, the loop represents dynamic openness (continual development) in two respects: (1) openness in duality from both strata or poles of the relationship; (2) openness in unity through the twist, the moment in which the unity underlying the duality is manifested. (The 180-degree twist often corresponds to the moment of human imaginative insight, sometimes of theological proportion.) Although the loop is open in both respects, the relationality it represents is not dissolved; perhaps it is even sustained by this openness.

The two levels 1 and 2 and the two relations a and b of strange loop relationality, taken together as a holistic totality, constitute a generic pattern that is a mutually reciprocal (one pole implies the other), asymmetric, dynamic, bipolar-relational unity. In the use of our model to portray the relationality of spirit, the human spirit (theologically understood as properly functioning in conjunction with the Holy Spirit) binds together levels 1 and 2 to form an asymmetric relational unity by means of the strange loop. The broken circle symbolizes the binding relations a and b functioning together in continuous, dynamic unison.

in a context that will illuminate its distinctive characteristics. Dialectic is derived from the Greek word for discourse: *dialegein,* and it first achieves prominence in Plato. For Plato, the method for discovering essences is inextricably linked to the question and answer form of dialogue. Although his use of this notion went through several changes as his thought developed,[4] many of the key elements of modern dialectic were present. For example, the negative Socratic *"elenchus,"* or refutation in which a thesis is reduced to self-contradiction by being subjected to persistent questioning (*Phaedo*), the constructive alternative in which hypotheses are proposed and deductions are made from them in order to prove a thesis (*Meno*), the quest for the essence of a thing not just in the context of dialogue but in terms of objective reality itself, specifically the Idea of the Good (*Republic*), and the theory of negation to establish difference, for instance, proper use of "what is not" (*Sophist*). For Plato, the structure of discourse came to be mirrored in reality's own dialectical structure of Being and non-Being[5]; yet, as we will see, contrary to Hegel's assumption, Plato's rigorous preservation of careful distinction never permitted him to depart from the law of noncontradiction.

For Plato, dialectic was a way into reality, but for Aristotle, dialectic was not rigorous enough to establish or demonstrate first principles. Thus it was set in contrast to the deductive rigor of the syllogism. However, it should be noted that even the syllogism depended upon quick-wittedness to get the middle term. This bit of discontinuity at the core of syllogistic continuity was not a matter of rigor, but of insight. For Aristotle, dialectic was a systematic exploration of alternatives that had discovery value. To discover the first principles of a science, one must examine past opinions carefully and critically. This is not merely a sorting and eliminating, but an inductive intuition of first principles comes to mind through playing past opinions against each other and making fine distinctions of meaning. In this generative process, Aristotle came to recognize the synthetic function of dialectic.

As McKinney points out, just as there is an isomorphism between cognitional and real forms in Plato, there also exists an isomorphism in Aristotle's thought between intuition of first principles revealed by dialectic, and the objective forms and their relations constituting the extramental world. "Although both Plato and Aristotle assert a correspondence between the products of thought and the structures of reality, neither one recognizes a similar correspondence between cognitional *process qua process* and the unfolding of reality as a *process.*"[6]

If McKinney is correct, during the Medieval period dialectic was confined to disputation on the issue of faith and reason. No major insight regarding the nature of dialectic per se was forthcoming during this period.

Modern dialectic in Kant and Hegel set the proximate background for Barth's thought. Kant's dialectic takes the form of formulating antinomies or contradictions posed by carrying reason to its limits in an essentially dualistic view of reality, that is, a reality divided between phenomenal and noumenal realms. Hegel rejected Kant's effort to resolve the antinomies without resolving the basic dualism of his epistemology, and

set forth his own alternative. He rejected Kant because his way of dealing with contradictories yielded no synthesis.

Hegel introduced *process* into dialectic by ignoring the law of noncontradiction, saying in effect that every affirmation or positive object is both itself and not itself. This
made it possible for him to argue that dialectic is not only the process by which we
know, but also the process by which the Absolute Spirit actualizes itself in world history.
On this premise, Hegel built his triangulated view of all things in metaphysics, epistemology, ethics, and history. Thesis, antithesis, synthesis somewhat oversimplify his very
subtle dialectical system, but he clearly had a preference for thinking triadically. It can
be illustrated if one starts metaphysically with the *thesis*: Being. The *antithesis* appears
implicitly in the thesis as soon as one thinks it through: Nothing, and the synthesis
yields Becoming. In epistemology, as the knower's own consciousness posits any item as
object, that subject and its object become *thesis* and *antithesis*. This gives rise to the
synthesis in higher forms of consciousness, self-objectification. In historical terms,
Ancient Greece in the age of Pericles represents the *thesis*. The Sophists and Socrates
represented the negative force, *antithesis*. The *synthesis* shaped by the two previous
movements is represented by Plato, whose philosophy constructed an integrative resolution at a higher level of spiritual actualization than either of the first two.

It was Kierkegaard's critique of Hegel and his reinterpretation of dialectic which sets
the immediate context for our discussion of Barth's position. Kierkegaard's view of
logic and dialectic was fundamentally different from Hegel's on the critical issue of the
principle of noncontradiction. Kierkegaard reasserted the principles of classical
Aristotelian logic, and refuted Hegel's view on the fundamental grounds that what
Hegel described was an illusion of process, an attempt to capture existential humanity
in the unfolding of an idea. By contrast, he claimed the irreducible separation between
thought and being. He argued that these are perennial opposites for which there is no
synthesis. He said, in effect, that we think backward but we live forward. Thus, he
became an advocate of classical logic, on the one hand, and claimed the necessity for
one to choose for one's existence, on the other. One cannot dissolve either one into
the other. This is the "qualitative dialectic," as Kierkegaard called it, because the distinction between thought and being could not be resolved due to the qualitative opposition between them. The only alternative lay in the capacity of the existing individual
to hold these two in tension without collapsing the opposition in either direction. For
Kierkegaard, this ultimate, irresolvable bipolarity constitutes the fundamental human
condition, which is the basis of despair. Various efforts, "leaps" in one's existence, will
attempt to pull off a synthesis, but this dichotomy at the core of human existence
inevitably reinstates despair, "a disrelationship within the self," such that the choosing
self comes ultimately to the recognition that a human being is haunted by a relentless
sense of absurdity. It cannot hide from itself, any more than it can explain or repair its
own condition.

If we transpose this view of human existence into the theological context from which it came, we can recognize the deeper driving concern behind Kierkegaard's authorship. That is, it is only from the standpoint of this utter absurdity that one can begin to comprehend "the infinite qualitative difference" between God and humanity. As long as human nature remains naïvely well socialized, it cannot grasp the underlying absurdity of human existence. Note that this is not something that occurs because one has cancer, has gone to war, or is in a depressed state. This is a clearheaded, nonneurotic description of how it *is*. It is extremely difficult, however, for us to see it as it is, but it was Kierkegaard's task, as he conceived it, to disclose this infinite qualitative difference between God and humanity. Only when one recognizes oneself as being in this position can one begin to appreciate the power of the bipolar relational unity established for humanity in the nature of Christ, who, in the unity of his nature, was simultaneously fully God and fully human. This so-called hypostatic union, formulated at the council of Chalcedon in 451,[7] was succinctly focused for Kierkegaard as "The God-Man." When the paradoxical character of human nature encounters the reverse paradox in the God-Man, then what occurs is the Absolute Paradox, whereby one may allow the God-Man to bestow himself upon one's despairing existence. This is the "leap of faith" whereby the despairing condition is transformed in what Kierkegaard called the "happy passion of faith."

It should be quite clear that Kierkegaard is not here playing in the territory of anti-rationalistic fideism; it is just the opposite. Having pressed rational inquiry to its limits, he formulated the negative antithesis between thought and being, and described the inevitability of despair. This negative condition is placed against the Chalcedonian formula, which also represents rigorous rationality and vigorous dispute carried to their limits. Chalcedon, conceived as the theological version of complementarity, is the most rational statement that can be made about a reality that is fully as paradoxical as the nature of light. As Bohr said, Kierkegaard pressed every thought to its limit: this notion of the Absolute Paradox is not a fideist flight into absurdity; it is the most rigorous formulation of a necessarily nonrational situation that can be made.

However one may view Kierkegaard's dialectic, it is the immediate context for Barth's dialectical thought. To this we now turn with a view first toward description, then toward analysis of the dialectic in terms of its basic elements.

Barth's most powerful dialectical work in the Kierkegaardian tradition was the second edition of *The Epistle to the Romans*. Barthian commentators say the first edition was written under the influence of Platonic idealism, but the second was an attack upon liberalism similar to Kierkegaard's attack upon Christendom in its aesthetic and ethical modes of existence. However, Barth saw paradox as simple logical contradiction, and failed to see the extent to which the would-be believer's experience of contradiction was a function of transformation of existence into faith. This transformed person is portrayed in Kierkegaard's famous "Knight of Faith," who recognized the absurdity of existence, but from the standpoint of one for whom paradox was no longer necessary.

As a result of his view of paradox, in this second edition of Romans, Barth speaks freely of Christianity as paradoxical and absurd. The historical revelation of God in Christ is a "scandal" because it describes the positive relation between God and humanity as "an absolute paradox." Moreover, Christianity alleges that the paradox of faith is "unresolved and unresolvable." He characterizes the life of the believer as follows: "He is what he is not; he knows what he does not know, he does what he cannot do. . . ."[8] In answer to the question of whether he had a system, Barth said if he did it was limited to "what Kierkegaard called the 'infinite qualitative distinction' between time and eternity to my regarding this as possessing negative as well as positive significance."[9]

However, when Barth began in 1927 to write *Die Christliche Dogmatik* (*Christian Dogmatics*), he found he could not continue, and in 1930 shifted his ground on the basis of Anselm's rationality-of-faith. From this shift emerged his gigantic work *Die kirchliche Dogmatik* (*Church Dogmatics*). After 1930, Barth's references to Kierkegaard are highly ambivalent, as we will discuss in the following section. What we need to say here is that even after Barth shifted away from his explicit dependence upon Kierkegaard, his thought retained the dialectical quality which he described earlier as based upon the unresolvable infinite qualitative difference between time and eternity and upon the positive relationship between God and humanity as embodied in the nature of Jesus Christ described by the Chalcedonian council.

It remains for us to illustrate Barth's dialectical thought as it is retained in the *Church Dogmatics*. The following illustration shows how he understood the dialectic between the eternal and the temporal to be worked out and maintained by the Holy Spirit:

> The work of the Holy Spirit, however, is to bring and to hold together that which is different and therefore, as it would seem, necessarily and irresistibly disruptive in the relationship of Jesus Christ to His community, namely, the divine working, being, and action on the one side and the human on the other, the creative freedom and act on one side and the human on the other, the eternal reality and possibility on one side and the temporal on the other. His work is to bring and to hold them together, not to identify, intermingle nor confound them, not to change the one into the other nor to merge the one into the other, but to coordinate them, to make them parallel, to bring them into harmony and herefore to bind them into a true unity.[10]

If one were to see shades of Hegel's *Geist* here, it would not go very far, because there is no synthesis; the polarities are held together and apart in such a way as to preserve the infinite qualitative distinction between time and eternity, yet simultaneously their unity is preserved not by a synthesis but by the life of the Spirit.

This helps us to see the distinctly Christomorphic nature of Barth's dialectic based, like Kierkegaard's, on the nature of the God-Man. It is tempting to jump to the conclusion that this Barthian dialectic is simply a transposition of the logic of complementarity (not known as such by Barth) into theological context. This may be close to the correct conclusion, but it must be based on more solid premises than this apparent similarity. To pursue this further, we will examine a passage which appears at the outset of his *Church Dogmatics*.[11]

... All faith's unrest is, in fact, set aside in prayer, but its prayer is its profound unrest. And both as prayer and also as unrest it is expectation, expectation of its object. It lives by its object, at rest or in unrest, having found, seeking, finding again and seeking anew. But this object is the free God who is hidden from man because he is a sinner, who has, of course, put man in the new state of faith in which He can be known by him, but who in this very state—it is that of faith—wills to be sought and found anew and then anew again. For faith, He is and remains enclosed in objectivity, in the externality of the Word of God, in Jesus Christ. He must teach man to seek Him and He must show Himself to him in order that he may find Him. But it is by this external object that Christian faith lives [God, as free object controls humankind's search for him; humankind, in turn, is dependent upon the sustaining activity of God— asymmetric relationality].... "So ought Word and faith to stand splendidly together. For the one cannot exist without the other. Whoso has faith and not the Word believeth like Turks and Jews. They have the faith that God is gracious and merciful. But the promise is lacking, for God will not be gracious apart from Christ. Thus, whoso has the Word but not faith, there the Word accomplisheth naught. Thus Word and faith are given together in wedlock, and naught can cause them to part from one another" [quote from Luther].... Wobbermin wants to show from this that the relation between the Word of God and faith according to Luther is to be regarded as a relation of a "con- nexion" or "correlation," as a "circular" relation, a relation of "reciprocity" or "two- poled relation." ... I do not wish to contest these descriptions though they are too ambiguous for me to adopt. I would only say regarding Luther that he is simply stating that in a man's faith or erroneous faith or unbelief the decision is made what kind of a God he has, so that man always has the God he believes in. But this is not all the same thing as saying that faith is as it were the human counterpart of the Word of God, that the relation between the Word of God and faith is the symmetrical one of two part- ners, one superior and the other subordinate but still two partners, and that this rela- tion is just as basically grounded in faith as it is in the Word of God.... What makes Him the true God is that one believes in Him in true faith. And the fact that the faith in which the true God is believed in is true faith is not due in any way or in any sense to itself but to the fact *that the true God has revealed Himself to it, that is, it is due to the Word of God* [italics mine].... It should also be noted [referring to Luther's com- ments] ... that the emphasis of Luther's expositions lies throughout on the thought that without the Word there can be no faith. The dialectical supplement that without faith one cannot have the Word is simply added in both passages but not developed. In sum, when Luther speaks of the Word and faith he is saying, of course, that where there is no faith the Word cannot be, or cannot be fruitful, but he is saying primarily, and this is the point, that where faith is, it does not have its ground and its truth in itself as a human act of experience, but even though it is a human act and experience it has these things in its object, in Christ, or God's Word. In my view *terms like circular or reciprocal or correlative relation are very imprecise descriptions* of what Luther meant to say and did say in this matter. . . . [italics mine][12]

The first point to be made from this text is that Barth quite clearly argues that terms like "circular" or "reciprocal" or "correlative relation" are too imprecise to describe what Luther was saying or what he, Barth, would want to say. This approach is problematic because it waffles indeterminately between two affirmations, and there is no real principle of discrimination when one is saying first this, then that. In effect, "perceptual complementarity" is not sufficient to describe what is at stake in the theological matter under discussion.

Barth seems to be reiterating a classical Aristotelian objection to dialectic; namely, perceptual complementarity is too much a matter of opinion, or this principle against that, without any sense that the alternation among opposites is leading to any intuition of first principles or to the underlying reality about which these opinions are expressed. If one alternative is "superior and the other subordinate," this does not in itself change the situation, since the question is whether the interplay between the two does or does not lead to the discovery of that underlying reality. Strictly speaking, of course, Barth's position on this point is quite the opposite of the classical Aristotelian use of dialectic; Barth already knows by faith what he seeks to understand by means of the dialectic, and his intuition of that reality precedes, and does not derive from, the dialectic he employs.

Why then use the method of dialectic at all? The answer to this is what draws Barth closer to Bohr's view than one might at first expect; namely, the object he described is in itself inherently and irreducibly beyond the reach of reason as it has been understood in the ancient or in the the modern world. The phenomenon shows itself to be inherently and irreducibly bipolar. Reason, in the classical period, in the Enlightenment, or in the modern world, was eminently well suited for the nature of the reality as it was then understood, but the subatomic realm cannot possibly be described according to the same basic canons of reason, because its major premises are violated by the phenomenon. Such premises as the law of noncontradiction are literally defied by the phenomenon to be observed and described.

In quantum theory at the hands of Niels Bohr, reason is pressed to the limit but, in the end, one must attempt to allow the phenomenon to tell how it is to be known, even if it contradicts certain premises underlying "the right use of reason." Such a phenomenon might be left to some category such as anomaly or mystery, but scientists who are committed to attaining the deepest intellectual grasp possible upon the inner nature of reality must attempt to communicate what takes place *beyond* the limits of ordinary reason *within* the limits of reason as the modern world understands that. It is not surprising, therefore, that Bohr asserts the simultaneous truth of two contradictory concepts, and calls for a new kind of reason.

Much the same situation applies to Barth. By faith, he knows the reality of the nature of God revealed in Jesus Christ, Kierkegaard's "God-Man." The problem of explanation and accountability is like Bohr's: the phenomenon that is being investigated is itself inherently beyond the realm for which reason is ordinarily suited. Yet, as a rigorous-minded theologian, he has a dilemma: he must allow the phenomenon to say how it will be known, but he must communicate that to a realm of understanding for which only adherence to the familiar canons of reason count as adequate for establishing principles or demonstrating the truth of a proposition.

In the face of this same dilemma, the Chalcedonian Church Fathers described the hypostatic union, which is a bipolar-relational unity, and is the most carefully reasoned account of Christ's nature that could be given. The phenomenon in itself is inherently a bipolar relationality, yet unified and coherent. Indeed, the relationality *is* the unity, and the bipolarity persists precisely because the relationality is a real unity. This formulation endures because the relationality inherent in the conceptual formulation is isomorphic with the reality being described. If this isomorphism did not exist, then shifting from one opinion to the next is simply perspective taking; in which case, the method has been divorced from the reality it was designed to describe, and a dualism has set in. To this Barth soundly and rightly objects, because the reality of the object of faith will not yield its truth and coherence to a series of perspectives, especially if they are mutually exclusive in what they assert. On the other hand, it cannot yield up its coherence to Aristotelian logic, because that would be to reduce the phenomenon to the method for knowing it, which is both bad science and bad theology.

A further consideration in recognizing the nature of dialectic and its similarity to Bohr's philosophy of complementarity has to do with the role of the dialectician, or of the observer himself. In the study of quantum phenomena, the role of the observer is decisive; all that can be observed is observer-conditioned. Thus, the knower becomes an essential part of what can be know.

A similar situation occurs in the Barthian dialectic, but here the observer-phenomenon relationship is amplified by the nature of the object of the inquiry. That is, owing in part to Kierkegaard's influence, Barth's theological dialectic is intensely existential. That is, it is consistently and relentlessly derived from the passion of faith in relation to the Word of God. However, this is greatly intensified by the fact that, in this case, the phenomenon to be observed is irreducibly Subject. However objective one may become about the revelation of God in Christ, the nature of the object is distorted if it is not permitted to be and to remain the Subject who first knows the observer. The primacy of God's knowledge of us is what makes theological knowledge possible, and this condition intensifies the influence of the participant observer.

It is interesting to note that Bohr's passion to include the human factor became legendary among those who worked with him at the Bohr Institute in Copenhagen. A lecture which was perfectly clear at first writing would become increasingly obscure as he insisted on recognizing that the whole situation, not merely *what* was objectively stated, was essential to a grasp of the truth at stake. Most decisively, the whole situation necessarily included the human factor,[13] which Bohr understood in a way that reflected his avid reading of Kierkegaard and Paul Møller, the one distinguished Danish scholar whom Kierkegaard admired.

We must examine the connection between Bohr and Kierkegaard more thoroughly in a subsequent section, but we may simply note the analogies that pertain between Bohr's epistemology of complementarity and Barth's dialectical method:

(1) In both instances, classical forms of reason are pushed to the limits of their competence to explain the phenomenon in question. The law of non-contradiction is preserved assiduously in both cases so long as it pertains.

(2) In both instances the appropriate scientific premise that the phenomenon should be allowed to disclose how it can be known is carefully maintained. Reduction of the phenomenon to known forms of reason is avoided.

(3) In both instances, the phenomenon discloses itself as an irreducible bipolar relationality that imposes itself upon the knower as such. That is to say, from within the context of classical reason the phenomenon cannot be grasped in any way other than through some form of dialectic or complementarity.

(4) In both instances, the relationality between the two polarities in question is asymmetrical. This is owing to the unique nature of the phenomenon under observation.

(5) In both instances, the knowing situation requires that the influence of the observer become a part of what is known. Self-involving knowledge is the only form of knowing adequate to the respective knowing situations.

(6) The test for the truth of the observation resides in the power of the knower to communicate effectively in a new form of reason to the community of concerned scholars. Both Bohr and Barth relied upon the power of language to communicate the truth of their claims as a test of the validity of their positions.[14]

Of course there are obvious differences, but they are primarily due to different contexts of inquiry, and do not disqualify the epistemological principles outlined above. The point in stating these similarities is not to disembed the epistemology from the knowing situation, but to point out aspects of convergence in otherwise seemingly antithetical worlds of discourse. Thus, it seems at least plausible that the form of reason employed here by Karl Barth bears a close analogy to the form of reason employed by Niels Bohr in his philosophy of complementarity.

Yet it must now be asked whether this connection is not a fundamental violation of Barth's position. Would Barth himself be able to recognize or affirm the sort of epistemological convergence we have described? Would he not say *"Nein!"* again, and simply throw out the analogy as an attempt to reduce theological description to a by-product of the natural order and reason's investigation of it? These questions must be asked even if it is more the expression of a Barthian stereotype than of Barth's mature judgment. Basically we are saying, in agreement with T.F. Torrance, that Barth's view of natural theology must be reenvisioned, and then applied to the case at hand. Then it may be seen how this most rigorous of theological minds is in fundamental agreement with certain major tenets of contemporary science.

IV. BARTH AND THE NEW PHYSICS

In a very important but seldom-cited conversation between T.F. Torrance and Karl Barth,[15] the issue of natural theology emerged with a new and profoundly different turn from that which it assumed in Barth's famous debate with Brunner. As Torrance puts it, an analogy from the relation between geometry and physics made the case in such a way that Barth readily agreed to a theological approach to nature in which nature could have full voice. In effect, the natural theology to which Barth so strenuously objected was an attempt through extrinsic knowledge of nature to arrive at an accurate knowledge of God. In effect, one cannot "unscientifically" employ natural means for knowing God, and expect that those means will in any sense prove to be commensurate with the object of inquiry who must always remain Subject even while being the object of study. The natural order is not intrinsic to God's nature, so no intrinsic knowledge of God can be derived therefrom.

The analogy which Torrance employed with Barth said that natural theology is to theology proper what geometry is to physics. That is, as long as geometry is pursued as a detached and independent science, antecedent to physics, as it was in Newton's view of the universe, it cannot yield up knowledge of the physical universe. However, as this dualism between geometry and physics was overcome with the rise of four-dimensional geometry, geometry was pursued in indissoluble unity with physics as the subscience of its inner rational structure, and as an essential part of the empirical and theoretic interpretation of nature. Thus, the essential nature of geometry changes; instead of being an axiomatic deductive science, detached from actual knowledge of physical reality, it becomes a form of natural science, as Einstein puts it.[16] In relation to natural theology, the inner nature of God cannot be pursued extrinsically, abstractly and deductively, as if we could deduce from an analysis of the physical universe the nature of God. However, this does not mean that theology must reject the sciences. Rather, it means that scientific investigation of the natural or the human order must be brought within the body of positive theology, and pursued in indissoluble unity with it. The sciences must become *natural* to the fundamental subject matter of theology; they will provide the inner material logic that arises in our inquiry and understanding of God. According to Torrance, Barth responded so positively to this argument that he said he "must have been a blind hen" not to have seen it himself. Recall that Barth's famous *"Nein!"* was directed toward a natural theology that is *independent* of God's self-revelation in Jesus Christ. As this conversation shows, he was agreeable to a theology of nature seen as *dependent* upon God's redemptive self-revelation in Jesus Christ.

The question for us is whether or not what we have described here in relation to complementarity is in fundamental agreement with Barth's acceptance of natural science as a subspecialty of positive theology. In answer to this, if we do not lose sight of our earlier claim that what we are discussing in the strange loop model of relationality is descriptive of an epistemological realism, then we can lay claim to some agreement with Barth's theology of nature. That is, the logic of complementarity, as we have described and developed it, is not external to theology but supremely present in the nature of Jesus Christ, the core of Barth's theological thought. It is not being argued that this logic of the strange loop is a complete Christology, but it is arguable that no Christology could be complete without this relationality at its center. When the effort of reason to describe his nature comes up with the same pattern in its effort to describe sub-atomic phenomena, this is well within the theological claim that all creation "made through him" bears the mark of his nature. In Barth's own language, creation is the external basis of the covenant and the covenant is the internal basis of creation.

If one were to say that Bohr's philosophy of complementarity, taken in the abstract, explains the way to understand how God is revealed in Jesus Christ, and that is a way into the nature of God apart from the theological context which faith supplies, then the Barthian *"Nein!"* must be heard again.

"Faith seeking understanding" means that the character of scientific reason in the context of theology must take on a concern for ultimate meaning and purpose; scientific reason cannot rest content with merely describing what nature *does*. The human factor is an indispensable part of the knowing act, and of what can finally be known. Humanly we cannot not ask the questions of meaning and purpose. If good answers are not given, poor ones will spring up unexamined, and both science and theology will be impoverished thereby. This is not to lose sight of the necessity for scientific reason within theology's concern for meaning and purpose, to keep theological reflection upon creation as exact and as rigorous as possible.

V. BARTH, BOHR, AND KIERKEGAARD

Having pursued Barth's side of the issue at some length, we must now turn to Bohr, and to the cultural context within which Bohr's view of complementarity arose, specifically his connection to Kierkegaard. The question is put this way not to skew Bohr's agnosticism in the direction of theology, but it is to recognize that some of the most significant influences in Bohr's philosophy came from devout believers who shaped the culture of Copenhagen in his day. This is not to take anything away from Bohr's originality or his unique contributions to contemporary thought, but it is to acknowledge the obvious fact that no thinker emerges without bearing the marks of his context.[17]

For the purposes of this essay, we will focus on the significant contribution that

Kierkegaard made to Bohr's thought, since it is here that we find the historical connection between complementarity and dialectic. In Kierkegaard's "qualitative dialectic" we find a fundamental key to the analogy we have been drawing between Bohr and Barth.

In his early years, young Niels was a devout believer, but eventually he disavowed his inherited faith and his membership in the Danish Church. (Note in passing that, in a different sense, something similar could be said of Kierkegaard.) However, Bohr maintained a lifelong interest in religious and philosophical questions, which he frequently discussed with Professor Harald Høffding, the leading Kierkegaard interpreter of the late nineteenth century. It should be said that Høffding apparently read Kierkegaard with sufficient intensity to understand the claim Christianity makes upon a human life, and decided that he could never make such a commitment. In spite of this religious crisis, Høffding continued to write and lecture on Kierkegaard, and it must be assumed that Niels Bohr, who was Høffding's student and lifelong friend, heard a good deal of this. Bohr read Kierkegaard's *Stages Along Life's Way* enthusiastically, and commented to J. Rud Nielsen, when Nielsen asked him about Kierkegaard's influence, "He made a powerful impression on me when I wrote my dissertation in Funen, and I read his works night and day."[18] Bohr continued by saying he most appreciated Kierkegaard's thinking problems clear through "to their very limit," but there were things in Kierkegaard he, Bohr, could not accept.

It is possible that Kierkegaard—apart from influencing young Niels about what to think—was reinforcing in him a way to think, encouraging him to push reason to its intrinsic limits, to "think every thought whole," as Kierkegaard said. Leon Rosenfeld, who worked many years with Bohr, said in another context that it seemed as if Bohr "looked for and fastened with greatest energy upon a contradiction, heating it to its utmost before he could crystallize the pure metal out of the dispute."[19]

As to substantive connections, historians of science Gerald Holton and Max Jammer both cite connections between Kierkegaard's thought and Bohr's philosophy. Although these are disputed by David Favrholdt, they are too compelling to be ignored.

The first notion involves Kierkegaard's "qualitative dialectic," which holds thesis and antithesis in tension, allowing resolution in the opposition between thought and being to come only by human intention, as an act of choice. This bears a close similarity to Bohr's assertions that an explanation in quantum physics may entail not one but two equally valid conclusions, the one actually observed depending upon the choice of the human observer.

The second concept is Kierkegaard's accentuation of discontinuity in existence as a consequence of "the leap" of free choice by the existing subject. This concept is found and described by Bohr at the quantum level of physical existence, and designates quantum jumps leading to probabilistic causality. The leap here is not confined to subatomic particles, but extends, because of their behavior, to a leap in understanding from classical physics and its extension into relativity, to quantum theory—a radical new frame of intelligibility.

Third, the impossibility of excluding the subject from any so-called objective explanation is extensively developed by Kierkegaard. This, in turn, appears, as we have said above, in Bohr's thought at the point of observer-dependent description of quantum phenomena.

Even Favrholdt acknowledges that Bohr's reading of Kierkegaard may well have given him a higher tolerance for discontinuity than Einstein, and so allowed Bohr to formulate a theory of complementarity suitable to the uncertainties of quantum phenomena, which continued to distress Einstein for the later part of his life.

Returning now to the Barthian side of the discussion, Kierkegaard's influence on the early writings of Karl Barth has already been discussed. However, certain further observations should be made owing to the fact that, although Barth is largely responsible for the emergence of Kierkegaard's thought upon the European and American scene early in this century, the Kierkegaard who came to prominence through Barth is less than half of the full position of Kierkegaard. This is the "phantom Kierkegaard," to use Alistair McKinnon's phrase, but it is not the *real* Kierkegaard, whose faith included but transcended the absurd, the paradoxical, and the contradictions of reason. Kierkegaard writes:

> When the believer believes the absurd, the absurd is not the absurd—faith transforms it. . . . The passion of faith is the only thing capable of mastering the absurd. . . . In the category of the absurd, rightly understood, there is therefore absolutely nothing terrifying.[20]

As McKinnon points out, many similar quotes can be found in Kierkegaard's *Journals*, but they are neglected because of the widespread fascination with the phantom Kierkegaard. This aspect of Kierkegaard came to prominence partly through Barth and partly through the first German translation by Christoph Schrempf who, having lost his faith from reading Kierkegaard, translated his thought in a way that presented him as a thoroughgoing fideist and irrationalist. It seems that the ambivalence of the later Barth[21] toward Kierkegaard's writing is a response to his having accepted thoroughly the phantom Kierkegaard, and only later recognized that this was not the real Kierkegaard—or rather he recognized the reality which Kierkegaard also recognized through the transformative power of faith, and he (Barth) turned to Anselm. What should be noted is that this is not a move away from Kierkegaard, but it is a move from the pseudonymous works of the phantom to the positive faith of the real Kierkegaard, who wrote:

> What I usually express by saying that Christianity consists of paradox, philosophy in mediation, Leibniz expresses by distinguishing between what is above reason and what is against reason. Faith is above reason. By reason he understands, as he says many places, a linking together of truths (enchainment), a conclusion from causes. Faith therefore cannot be proved, demonstrated, comprehended, for the link which makes a linking together

possible is missing, and what else does this say than that it is a paradox. This, precisely, is the irregularity in the paradox, continuity is lacking, or at any rate it has continuity only in reverse, that is, at the beginning it does not manifest itself as continuity.[22]

This "continuity in reverse" is precisely what occurs when one comes into faith via the paradox. From this posture, everything then is "open to reason" in light of the transformation. The transformation of the observer now reveals that what was previously paradoxical is, rather, part of a profound continuity that includes the observer and the observed, the creation and the creator, the science of nature, of the human, and of God. Apart from this transformation, paradox will continue to be necessary, as the believer continues to move from this higher order of continuity to the world of disbelief, from which place that higher order will always appear to be a lesser form of knowledge or simply outright error.

McKinnon dramatizes the distinction between the two Kierkegaards, calling one "phantom" and the other "real," but what should not be lost in this distinction is that the real included as part of its reality the dialectic of the phantom. For instance, in Kierkegaard's commentaries on scripture, he frequently signs his own name because, we would argue, the dialectic of the pseudonymous works has been taken up in the higher order of continuity represented in the scriptural witness to the nature of Christ. Thus, the extraordinary claims of the real Kierkegaard, such as "love believes all things and is never deceived,"[23] are true to the scriptural concept of love, but they include a dialectical transformation of love. Thus, not only does the love of God revealed in Christ redefine all other forms of love, but this love can be appropriated by faith in a fully human way that has the capacity to establish one's personal integrity both in time and in eternity. Accordingly, Kierkegaard's striking claim does not mean one may not be deceived in this or that particular situation, but that such a love has the power to expose deception as a delusion about reality. Human integrity based on the love revealed in Christ will not finally be deceived, but will deceive deception into the truth. The pseudonymous works are not so much the works of a phantom as they are an emphasis on the human spirit at the expense of the Holy Spirit. When this priority is reversed, Kierkegaard can write directly from scripture into the deepest issues of human existence. But the dialectical relationality which characterizes the human spirit is now incorporated, not omitted or vanquished as a phantom.[24]

The point to be stressed here is not to make a contribution to Kierkegaard scholarship,[25] but to point out that rational explanation attempting to cross between two realms of discourse, one of which calls into question the axioms of reason itself, will eventually yield a form of understanding which is a bipolar-relational (often asymmetric) unity. Moreover, subsequent discourse between the two realms must continue to utilize some form of dialectic or complementarity which has the characteristics we described above. Clearly this epistemological situation is not confined to the subject matter at hand when one considers the fact that, at the same time Barth was reading

Kierkegaard in Basel and finding in his position some basis for the theological rejection of science, Bohr was reading Kierkegaard in Copenhagen and finding some basis for a radical reformulation of scientific theory. But all three, Kierkegaard, Barth, and Bohr, built continuities upon a common revision of reason which presupposes discontinuity of the type we have described as an asymmetric, bipolar relational unity: Kierkegaard in his nonpseudonymous works, Barth in his systematic theology, and Bohr in his philosophy of complementarity and its empirical implications for contemporary physics.

The theological point that should be made in conclusion is just this: the model we have set forth at the outset of this essay is not trying to set up a structure or capture an essence; it is a way of showing how seemingly widely divergent realms of discourse, as divergent as Niels Bohr and Karl Barth, can be mutually illuminated. If this is effective, we believe it is because it points to the ground of all truth revealed in the relational nature of Jesus Christ, which Kierkegaard insisted upon and communicated with such dialectical force.

NOTES

1. Heisenberg's "uncertainty principle" articulated here is to be understood within the more comprehensive concept of complementarity which is the cornerstone of Bohr's philosophy. This is described in MacKinnon's contribution to this volume.

2. C.F. von Weizsäcker. See discussion in Max Jammer, *The Philosophy of Quantum Mechanics* (New York: John Wiley & Sons, Inc., 1974). This text contains an excellent overview of the historical development of *complementarity* by Bohr and others, including C.F. von Weizsäcker's notion of circular complementarity (pp. 100–107).

3. For a more detailed discussion of this model, see James E. Loder and W. Jim Neidhardt, *The Knight's Move, The Relational Logic of the Spirit in Theology and Science* (Colorado Springs: Helmers & Howard, 1992).

4. Ronald H. McKinney, "The Origins of Modern Dialectics," pp. 179–190.

5. For a careful analysis of being and notbeing in Plato's thought, see G.E.L. Owen, "Plato on Not-Being," ch. 12 in Gregory Vlastos, ed., *Plato, I: Metaphysics and Epistemology, A Collection of Critical Essays* (New York: Doubleday and Co. Anchor Books, 1971), pp. 223 ff.

6. Ronald H. McKinney, "The Origins of Modern Dialectics," pp. 179–190.

7. This formulation, "Therefore, following the Holy Fathers, we all with one accord teach men to acknowledge one and the same Son, our Lord Jesus Christ, at once complete in Godhead and complete in manhood, truly God and truly man. . . ." is discussed at some length in *The Knight's Move*, ch. 5. If we are correct about this formulation's representing a forum of complementarity, then McKinney's position that no new form of dialectic appeared in the debates of the church fathers on faith versus reason would have to be revised.

8. References here are taken from Karl Barth, *The Epistle to the Romans*, trans. E.C. Hoskyns (London: Oxford University Press, 1933), pp. 94, 105, 108, 151–152, 276 ff.

9. *Romans*, p. 10.

10. Karl Barth, *Church Dogmatics* (Edinburgh: T. & T. Clark), IV/3, second half, p. 761.

11. *Church Dogmatics*, 1/1 (see especially the note on p. 9).

12. *Church Dogmatics*, 1/1, pp. 230–236.

13. *The Knight's Move*, p. 75.

14. Although this aspect of their respective positions has not been fully discussed here, it is perhaps the most self-evident similarity between them. For further discussion of this, see *The Knight's Move*, chs. 4 and 5.

15. T.F. Torrance, *Space, Time and Resurrection* (Edinbugh: The Handsel Press, 1976), pp. ix–xi.

16. T.F. Torrance, *Transformation and Convergence in the Frame of Knowledge* (Belfast: Christian Journals, Ltd., 1984), pp. 294–295.

17. Current debates taking place over the originality of Bohr's philosophy appear primarily in the papers of the *Danish Yearbook of Philosophy*. The primary disputants are David Favrholdt, professor of philosophy at Odense Universitet, and Jan Faye, currently at the Center for the Philosophy of Science in Pittsburgh. Favrholdt maintains that Bohr is minimally influenced by such figures as Kierkegaard, Hoffding and Møller, but Faye argues the opposed point of view. This is an argument that we find difficult to adjudicate from this side of the Atlantic. For a bibliography of this debate, see *The Knight's Move*, p. 68, fn. 7.

18. J. Rud Nielson, "Memories of Niels Bohr," *Physics Today* 16, No. 10: 27–28.

19. *The Knight's Move*, p. 67.

20. This is found in Kierkegaard's *Journals*. This translation is to be found in Cornelio Fabro, "Faith and Reason in Kierkegaard's Dialectic," in Howard A. Johnson and Niels Thulstrup, eds., *A Kierkegaard Critique* (New York: Harper, 1962), pp. 182ff.

21. Although Barth acknowledged the profound influence Kierkegaard had upon his thought, and stated that Kierkegaard's thought should be assimilated in the course of one's theological development, he insisted that one should not stop there. Yet, while Barth continued to refer to Kierkegaard, he completely omitted Kierkegaard from his historical work, *Protestant Theology in the Nineteenth Century: Its Background and History* (London: SCM, 1972).

22. Alexander Dru, ed. and trans. *The Journals of Søren Kierkegaard: A Selection* (London and New York: Oxford University Press, 1938), pp. 399–400.

23. Kierkegaard, *Works of Love*, trans. Howard Hong (New York: Harper & Row Torch Books, 1962), pp. 213 ff.

24. *The Knight's Move*, Sec. I.

25. This is what Alistair McKinnon has already done in his illuminating article, "Barth's Relation to Kierkegaard," in the *Canadian Journal of Theology*, vol. XIII (1967), No. 1, pp. 33 ff.

QUANTUM COMPLEMENTARITY AND CHRISTOLOGICAL DIALECTIC

CHRISTOPHER B. KAISER

Since the physicist Niels Bohr first proposed the concept of complementarity in 1927, there have been a number of attempts to apply the idea to the problems of Christian theology. As early as 1947, Bohr himself suggested an application to the apparent paradox of love and justice in God.[1] Bohr also made other tentative proposals and, on the occasion of his Gifford Lectures (Edinburgh, 1949), he challenged theologians to make more use of the idea of complementarity.[2]

At that time, one of the few theologians who had taken up the challenge was Gunter Howe, convenor of the original "Göttingen Circle" of scientists and theologians from 1948 to 1959.[3] Howe was probably the first to draw parallels between the ideas of quantum physics and theology of Karl Barth.[4] However, Howe's early ideas about complementarity were based primarily on the ideas of Werner Heisenberg and Carl Friedrich von Weizsäcker, not on the writings of Bohr. For example, he cited von Weizsäcker's notion of "circular complementarity" as a parallel to Barth's discussion of the veiling and unveiling of God, which also involves human beings in a "circle of knowledge."[5]

The possibility of applying the logic of complementarity to Christology was first explored by William H. Austin (1967) and Ian G. Barbour (1974). Both studies concluded that the parallels between quantum complementarity and the Chalcedonian teaching of the two "natures" of Christ were very limited.[6]

My own research on the topic, done while I was a doctoral student at Edinburgh (1971–1974), was based on a detailed study of the writings of Bohr, and my conclusions were more positive than those of Austin and Barbour.[7] The question has recently been reexamined by James E. Loder and W. Jim Neidhardt with similarly positive results (1992).[8] The paper Loder and Neidhardt have contributed to this volume is a good synopsis of their work. They follow Bohr's own ideas and interpret them in the context of other Danish thinkers such as Søren Kierkegaard and Paul Møller, both of whom had a significant influence on Bohr.

I shall respond to the paper by Loder and Neidhardt by making some comparisons with Edward MacKinnon's scientific and philosophical introduction, and then suggesting some directions for further research.

I. POINTS OF AGREEMENT BETWEEN THE TWO PAPERS

There are at least two major areas of agreement between the two papers. Both clearly defend complementarity against the charge of allowing logical contradictions, and both root the legitimate use of complementarity in the problems of human language.

The first major point of agreement is on what complementarity is not—it is not a license to irrationality. MacKinnon states emphatically that complementary statements are not contradictory statements. He thus agrees with Aristotle's teaching that the tolerance of logical contradictions would destroy any system of thought.[9]

MacKinnon goes on to explore medieval theology and the metaphysics of Immanuel Kant before turning to Bohr's ideas on this subject. Medieval Jewish and Christian theologians, Maimonides and Aquinas, realized that some Aristotelian ideas, such as the eternity of the world, were contradicted by Biblical revelation, while others were only apparently contradictory, and could therefore be accepted by believers. Thus medieval theologians could carefully construct statements about the attributes of God in which all contradictions were eliminated. An example is: "God is wise but lacks the virtue [or attribute] of wisdom."[10] Similarly, for Kant, the apparent antinomy between the mechanistic explanations used in physics and the human freedom presupposed by ethics could be resolved by clearly differentiating phenomenal and noumenal frames of reference.[11]

In Bohr's principle of complementarity, MacKinnon explains, quantum objects such as an electron can be described as both a particle and a wave. These two concepts are contraries rather than contradictories since, in any given experimental arrangement, only one of the contrary concepts, either wave or particle, will be appropriate. Complementarity is thus an attempt to resolve contradictions, not to promulgate them.[12] It is not so clear that MacKinnon's examples from medieval theology, Kant, and Bohr all have the very same logic, but the attempt to avoid outright contradictions is clear in all three cases.

Loder's and Neidhardt's stress on rationality is even more remarkable. After all, they are dealing not with metaphysicians, but with the likes of Søren Kierkegaard and Karl Barth—two theologians with a reputation for "leaps of faith" and "infinite qualitative differences." Nonetheless, our authors stress that both theologians moved beyond the idea of sheer contradiction to a higher view of rationality. Kierkegaard is described as pressing rational inquiry to its limits in order to do justice to complex realities such as the person of Christ. According to Loder and Neidhardt, this move was not antirationalistic fideism.[13] Barth may have verged on fideism in his early writings (prior to 1930),[14] but he moved beyond that stage under the influence of Anselm's rationality, and preserved the law of noncontradiction as assiduously as Niels Bohr did.[15] So Loder and Neidhardt agree with MacKinnon that complementarity is not a form of self-contradiction.

A second point of agreement in the two papers is the stress on the problems of human language. According to MacKinnon, such problems arise whenever human beings attempt to describe something that is qualitatively different from the objects of everyday experience. In order to speak at all about such things, one must use ordinary human language even though such language leads to apparently contradictory state-ments.[16] Similarly, in reporting the results of our experiments in quantum mechanics, we must use the language of classical physics (an extended version of ordinary human language), which is suitable to the behavior of the measuring instruments. Hence we must use terms such as "wave" and "particle" in order to communicate our experimen-tal findings, even though this leads to seemingly contradictory statements.[17]

Loder and Neidhardt place the emphasis on classical logic rather than on ordinary language, but their point is much the same. Barth and Bohr faced the same sort of problem: how within the limits of reason (as understood in Ancient Greece or Enlightenment Europe) to communicate things that are beyond the scope of ordinary reason. For Bohr, the new world to be described was the subatomic realm; for Barth, it was the nature of God as revealed in Jesus Christ. In fact, according to Loder and Neidhardt, the theologians at the Council of Chalcedon (451 A.D.) had faced the same sort of dilemma in trying to define the hypostatic union of two natures in Christ.[1] MacKinnon explicitly avoided treating such christological paradoxes, but our authors all agree that the invocation of complementarity is not an arbitrary move but a legiti-mate response to a real problem of communication.

II. DIFFERENCES BETWEEN THE TWO PAPERS

In spite of their agreement with MacKinnon on rationality and the limits of language, Loder and Neidhardt are stricter in what they allow under the rubric of complementar-ity. Of the three types of complementarity described by MacKinnon,[19] Loder and Neidhardt restrict themselves to one—the relationship between a quantum object as a wave and as a particle, two classical concepts which are mutually exclusive both in classical physics and in quantum theory.

In addition to the wave-particle type of complementarity, MacKinnon cites two oth-ers. One type is the relationship between two other classical modes of description: the location of events in space and time, and the explanation of processes in terms of causality. These two modes of description are compatible in classical physics (whereas wave and particle are not), but they turn out to be mutually exclusive in quantum the-ory, where they are closely related to the concepts of particle and wave.[20]

But the third type of complementarity described by MacKinnon is a relationship between quantum theory as a whole and the classical physics of which it is an exten-sion.[21] This third type is close to the "circular complementarity" of figure and ground that Loder and Neidhardt explicitly reject.[22] To my knowledge, the term "complemen-tarity" was never used by Bohr in this third sense.[23]

This difference in the breadth of definition of complementarity is related to several other differences between the two papers. MacKinnon's points of comparison with medieval theology and Kantian philosophy are more like the relationship of classical and quantum-mechanical frameworks than they are like the complementarity of wave and particle. Accordingly, MacKinnon's section on theology focuses on the relation between *two traditions*—the biblical-Jewish and the philosophical-Greek traditions—in describing God.[24] In contrast, Loder's and Neidhardt's theological focus is on the relation of *two concepts*, humanity and divinity, as applied to the person of Christ.[25] Furthermore, MacKinnon's philosophical position (evidently the same as the one he attributes to Bohr) is one that moves beyond the "descriptive realism" of classical physics and approaches the idealism of Kant.[26] In contrast, Loder's and Neidhardt's position is one of "epistemological realism."[27]

Finally, Loder's and Neidhardt's focus on the quantum complementarity of wave and particle allows them to stress an important feature that MacKinnon does not make explicit. The complementarity relationship is an asymmetric, one in that the concepts of wave and particle represent two levels of being and operation in the quantum object.[28] Thus, in Bohr's treatment of complementarity, the wave concept was required to explain the stability of the atom as a whole, a dynamic stability that could not be accounted for in terms of the properties of the constituent particles (space-time description).[29] Thus complementarity according to Loder and Neidhardt is a narrower, but also a more richly defined concept, than it is for MacKinnon.

III. DIRECTIONS FOR FUTURE RESEARCH

Each of the four points of comparison discussed above leads to a further question that would be worth considering for future research.

Loder's and Neidhardt's discussion of rationality in the work of Kierkegaard, Barth, and Bohr shows how all three moved beyond the point of outright contradiction to a sense of a higher order of unity. In the cases of the "real Kierkegaard" and the later Barth, it is stated that faith in the mystery of Jesus Christ, the God-Man, was the catalyst for such maturation.[30] But what was the catalyst for Bohr, who was not a believing Christian and who had not read the writings of the "real Kierkegaard"?[31]

In order to understand Bohr's insight, one could appeal to any number of currents in German philosophy from Kant's metaphysics to Schelling's *Naturphilosophie*, but there may also be a source closer to hand in the tradition of James Clerk Maxwell. Bohr worked with Maxwell's pupils at Cambridge and Manchester in 1911–1912 and later described himself as having come "under the spell of the great English physicists."[32] So his endless quest for "unity and harmony" could also reflect the deep faith in rationality held by the English school of Maxwell, a physicist who may himself have been influenced by the Chalcedonian tradition of Christology.[33] As current historical studies of scientists are paying more attention to their theological ideas, this sort of connection between modern science and theology would be worth exploring.[34]

A second area to consider is the relationship between the problems of language and the invocation of complementarity. Granted that both language and complementarity were concerns for Bohr, and perhaps also for Barth, is the relationship between the two a necessary one or only coincidental? Loder and Neidhardt suggest that it is a necessary one: for both Bohr and Barth, an object that is beyond the reach of classical (two-valued) logic shows itself to be bipolar.[35] Whenever rational explanation attempts to cross over to a radically new realm of discourse like quantum theory, they argue, it will lead to a bipolar (often asymmetric) unity.[36]

However, it is not patently clear that stretching the limits of language in this way must always lead to complementarity. The limits of language (and logic) are frequently strained in translating an idea from one language or culture to another. But bipolar unities do not emerge in every case. So what makes the treatment of quantum objects special in this sense?

Nor is it clear that description in terms of complementary modes can be legitimately invoked only when new problems of language arise. In biology, for example, the complementarity of mechanical and organismic modes of description discussed by Bohr (and mentioned in MacKinnon's paper) seems to be a fact of everyday life, not the result of straining language at some new frontier of science.[37]

In the case of Christology, it is true, linguistic difficulties arose from the fact that the two natures of Christ, human and divine, were often considered mutually exclusive in traditional Christian theology, which used the categories of Aristotelian logic. But were they really so exclusive in the Jewish thought that lay behind the New Testament?[38] In other words, are the paradoxes of Chalcedonian Christology universal for all worldviews and cultures? Or were they partly the result of the use of Aristotelian categories, particularly in the Antiochene school of theology, which influenced the Tome of Leo the Great and thereby the Definition of Chalcedon? If nothing else, the comparison between Christology and complementarity may lead us to ask significant questions of our received theology.

A third question has to do with the relationship between the frameworks of classical and quantum physics, which are used to describe the behavior of measuring instruments and quantum objects, respectively. As Loder and Neidhardt point out, this is a special case of the subject-object relationship.[39] Bohr also cited the classical problem of analysis and application. A measuring instrument is on the subject side of the relationship as long as it is applied as a measuring device. But as soon as it is analyzed in its own right, it becomes an object of observation and measurement.[40]

In other words, the subject-object boundary is variable, and it is objectively located in the empirical world (not somewhere between the mind and the body). Bohr drew an analogy to the use of a stick as a probe.[41] If the stick is held loosely, it can be explored as an object in the hand. But, if it is held firmly, it can be used to explore the environment.[42] For a nonseeing person, such a stick is effectively an extension of the body. It might be helpful to develop the implications of such an epistemology of embodiment and to relate them to issues of Christology and soteriology such as the doctrine of union with Christ.

Finally, Loder's and Neidhardt's observation that complementarity is an asymmetric relationship suggests the possibility of relating it to general systems theory as developed by Ludwig von Bertalanffy and others.[43] Bohr applied the concept of complementarity at a number of different levels besides that of quantum theory. For example, a living being is both a combination of atoms, and an organism; a human being is both body and mind. These bipolar structures can be embedded within one another to form a hierarchical system: a human being is both body and mind; a living body is both atoms and organism; atoms are both waves and particles. So, as Loder and Neidhardt point out, creation bears the mark of the God-Man who created it.[44] But the form of the God-Man may have been impressed on all of creation, not just on the bipolar objects of quantum physics.

NOTES

1. The first of Bohr's published references to the commplementarity of love and justice occurs in his "Atomic Physics and International Cooperation," *Proceedings of the American Philosophical Society* 91 (1947), pp. 137–138. Jerome Bruner has reported a conversation that occurred in 1943–1944, in which Bohr described the conflict between love and justice that he had experienced years earlier in trying to discipline one of his children. See the private communication in Gerald J. Holton, "The Roots of Complementarity," *Daedalus* 99 (1970), p. 1044.

2. Reported by John Baillie, *Our Sense of the Presence of God* (London: Oxford University Press, 1962), p. 217.

3. On the origin and history of the Gottingen conversations, see Harold Nebelsick, *Theology and Science in Mutual Modification* (New York: Oxford University Press, 1981), pp. 159–166.

4. Howe's first published discussion of Barth and the new physics can be found in "Vorbemerkungen zum Gesprach zwischen Theologie und Physik," *Evangelische Theologie* 1/2 (1947), pp. 64–92. For a fuller treatment, see his *Der Mensch und die Physik* (Wuppertal-Barmen: Jugendienst-Verlag, 1954); "Parallelen zwischen der Theologie Karl Barths und der heutigen Physik," in *Antwort: Karl Barth zum siebzigsten Geburtstag am 10. Mai 1956* (Zollikon-Zurich: Evangelischer Verlag, 1956), pp. 409–422, particularly p. 420, n. 19 on the complementarity of love and justice in Bohr; and "Zu den Ausserungen von Niels Bohr uber religose Fragen," *Kerygma und Dogma* 4 (1958), pp. 20–46, particularly pp. 34–39 on the complementarity of mercy and justice in Bohr and Barth. The three papers cited here have been republished posthumously in Howe, *Die Christenheit im Atomzeitalter* (Stuttgart: Ernst Klett Verlag, 1970).

5. *Der Mensch und die Physik*, p. 53; "Parallelen," pp. 421. Weizsäcker's idea of "circular complementarity" was formulated in his "Komplementaritat und Logik," *Die Naturwissenschaften* 42 (1955), pp. 521–526. I have contrasted it with Bohr's concept of complementarity in my doctoral thesis, "The Logic of Complementarity in Science and Theology" (University of Edinburgh, 1974), pp. 138–140. In this volume, see James E. Loder and W. Jim Neidhardt, "Barth, Bohr, and Dialectic," pp. 272-273, 278–280. The earliest of Bohr's published writings on religion cited by Howe is 1953. I infer that Howe's knowledge of Bohr's ideas was based on private communications, probably by Weizsäcker himself.

6. Austin, *Waves, Particles, and Paradoxes*, Rice University Studies 53 (Houston: Rice University Press, 1967), p. 86; Ian Barbour, *Myths, Models, and Paradigms* (London: SCM Press, 1974), pp. 151–155.

7. Kaiser, "Christology and Complementarity," *Religious Studies* 12 (1976), pp. 37–48. For my review of Austin's book, see *Scottish Journal of Theology* 25 (1972), pp. 94–95, where "trivial" is a typographical error for "rival."

8. Loder and Neidhardt, *The Knight's Move: The Relational Logic of the Spirit in Theology and Science* (Colorado Springs: Helmers & Howard, 1992), ch. 5. Another helpful discussion of christology and complementarity can be found in Russell Stannard, *Science and the Renewal of Belief* (London: SCM Press, 1982), pp. 157–166. K. Helmut Reich has done an interesting investigation of the matter with the aid of psychological research; Reich, "The Chalcedonian Definition: An Example of the Difficulties and the Usefulness of Thinking in Terms of Complementarity?" *Journal of Psychology and Theology* 18 (1990), pp. 148–57.

9. MacKinnon, "Complementarity," p.255.

10. MacKinnon, p. 259; see also p. 257.

11. MacKinnon, p. 261.

12. MacKinnon, pp. 263, 264, 268, 269.

13. Loder and Neidhardt, p. 277.

14. Loder and Neidhardt, p. 277.

15. Loder and Neidhardt, pp. 278, 280–281, 282.

16. MacKinnon, p. 259. MacKinnon does not discuss the possibility of developing a completely formal, context independent logic as advocated by Mario Bunge, "Analogy in Quantum Theory: From Insight to Nonsense," *British Journal for the Philosophy of Science* 18 (1967), pp. 265–86, esp. pp. 270–73, 280–82.

17. MacKinnon, p. 264. Note that the problem of language does not enter into MacKinnon's treatment of Kant's antinomies. Instead the antinomies are rooted in the forms of perception and the imperatives of action.

18. Loder and Neidhardt, pp. 280–281, 282f.

19. MacKinnon, p. 265.

20. In quantum theory, the experimental detection of a particle is usually its location at a point in space (e.g., on a photographic plate) at a particular time. A wave, on the other hand, is defined in terms of wavelength and frequency, which are related to the momentum and energy, the conservation of which is the basis of causality.

21. MacKinnon, p. 265.

22. Loder and Neidhardt, p. 272. Similarly, according to our authors, Barth rejected the idea of a circular relation between the human faith and the divine Word in our knowledge of God; see MS 14:2–16:1.

23. According to Bohr, the relationship between the classical and quantum frameworks was, rather, based on the "correspondence principle," according to which the results of quantum mechanics must agree with those of classical physics in the limiting case where the quantum of action (Planck's constant) is negligible; see Max Jammer, *The Conceptual Development of Quantum Mechanics* (New York: McGraw-Hill, 1966), pp. 109–118. MacKinnon makes the distinction himself in his *Scientific Explanation and Atomic Physics* (Chicago: University of Chicago Press, 1982), p. 271.

24. MacKinnon, pp. 256–259.

25. Loder and Neidhardt, pp. 276–277, 281, 284.

26. MacKinnon, pp. 262, 265–266; see also his *Scientific Explanation*, pp. 353–354, 365, 370–376. For arguments against the alleged similarities between Bohr and Kant, see Henry J. Folse, *The Philosophy of Niels Bohr: The Framework of Complementarity* (Amsterdam:

Elsevier/North Holland, 1985), pp. 49–53, 216–220; Dugald R. Murdoch, *Niels Bohr's Philosophy of Physics* (Cambridge: Cambridge University Press, 1987), pp. 102, 224–233.

27. Loder and Neidhardt, p. 273.

28. Loder and Neidhardt, pp. 271, 272, 282. This asymmetry is brought out clearly in their schematization of the "strange loop" in Figure 1. As the authors point out (Loder and Neidhardt, p. 273), the complementarity relationship is therefore also a dynamic. In other words, the history of a quantum object (or any bipolar entity) involves an alternation between the two poles of its existence; see also "Christology and Complementarity," p. 44.

29. Bohr, *Atomic Theory and the Description of Nature* (London: Cambridge University Press, 1934), pp. 23, 77–79; *Atomic Physics and Human Knowledge* (New York: Wiley, 1958), pp. 6–7, 19, 21, 99; *Essays 1958–1962 on Atomic Physics and Human Knowledge* (New York: Wiley Interscience, 1963), pp. 5, 11, 63.

30. Loder and Neidhardt, pp. 276-277, 278, 284, 286-287.

31. The evidence for Kierkegaard's influence on Bohr is reviewed by Loder and Neidhardt, pp. 285-286.

32. Bohr, "Maxwell and Modern Theoretical Physics," *Nature* 128 (1931), p. 691a.

33. The phrase "unity and harmony" is taken from Bohr's "Newton's Principles and Modern Atomic Physics," in The Royal Society of Great Britain's *Newton Centenary Celebrations* (Cambridge; Cambridge University Press, 1947), p. 57; see also Niels Blaedel, *Harmony and Unity: The Life of Niels Bohr* (Madison: Sciente Tech, 1988), p. 187. On Maxwell's theology in relation to his belief in a higher order of rationality, see Thomas F. Torrance, *Transformation and Convergence in the Frame of Knowledge* (Grand Rapids: Eerdmans, 1984), pp. 222–337; C. B. Kaiser, *Creation and the History of Science* (Grand Rapids: Eerdmans, 1991), pp. 293–300. Botond Gaal of the Reformed Theological Academy of the University of Debrecen, Hungary, has done further work, as yet unpublished, on this topic.

34. See Kaiser, *Creation*, pp. 301–307.

35. Loder and Neidhardt, p. 280.

36. Loder and Neidhardt, p. 287.

37. For example, Bohr, *Atomic Physics*, pp. 9–10, 20–21, 76, 92, 100–101; see also MacKinnon, p. 282.

38. See, for example, Karl Barth, *The Humanity of God* (Richmond: John Knox Press, 1960), pp. 37–65. Among recent Biblical studies, see D. Steenburg, "The Worship of Adam and Christ as the Image of God," *Journal for the Study of the New Testament* 39 (June 1990), pp. 95–109; Margaret Barker, *The Great Angel* (Louisville: Westminster/John Knox Press, 1992), pp. 37–38, 77–79, 115, 225, 228. Here I have reversed my former position on the biblical incompatibility of the human and the divine in "Christology and Complementarity," p. 41.

39. Loder and Neidhardt, pp. 272, 281, 282.

40. For example, Bohr, *Essays* p. 5.

41. Bohr, *Atomic Theory*, p. 99. On Bohr's use of the illustration in conversations, see Stefan Rozental, ed., *Niels Bohr: His Life and Work as Seen by His Friends and Colleagues* (Amsterdam: North Holland, 1967), pp. 93, 306.

42. Michael Polanyi uses a similar example, for example, in his *Personal Knowledge: Towards a Post-Critical Philosophy* (Chicago: University of Chicago Press, 1958), pp. 55–56.

43. For example, Von Bertalanffy, *General System Theory* (New York: George Braziller, 1969).

44. Loder and Neidhardt, p. 284; see also p. 288.

INFORMATION THEORY AND REVELATION

INFORMATION THEORY, BIOLOGY, AND CHRISTOLOGY

JOHN C. PUDDEFOOT

I. INFORMATION

Theology has an interest in any metaphor which threatens to limit and to distort the way we think of ourselves. In the "information age" it encounters a reductionist enterprise concerned to analyze all natural phenomena in terms of information processes, all living things in terms of the information content of their genetic material, with a growing interest in the information-theoretic aspects of intelligence and mind which some take to show that human beings are no more than information-processing machines. The impact of the concept of information on human self-understanding makes it a proper concern of theology.[1] As Joseph Weizenbaum has put it,

> [T]he computer is a powerful new metaphor for helping us to understand many aspects of the world, but ... it enslaves the mind that has no other metaphors and few other resources to call on.[2]

Failure adequately to distinguish the number of different ways in which the word "information" is used serves to sustain the ubiquity of the information metaphor and to tempt us to imagine that the mathematical theory of information covers all its aspects. This essay sets out to establish a vocabulary that will underline the distinctive uses of information, and in so doing, demonstrate the inadequacies of a solely mathematical approach. These distinctions may enable us to give an account of how significance can emerge from meaninglessness through *embodied* and *interactive information*, by which the world is able to progress.

Bits do not determine their own significance. 011010100100100 might be a code that opens a safe or an instruction telling a robot to move its arm. Only in the context of a complementary aspect of the system of which such a string of bits forms a part can it assume significance, can it have an interpretation, can it trigger the implementation of embodied know-how (the know-how in the robot's program, for example, that converts the string of bits into an action). This can be summarized in the dual principle: *nothing is self-interpreting* because *meaning is distributed over systems*.

The information content of a system such as a robot's program, and the information content of a communication, fulfill different but intimately related functions in all natural processes. Both can be measured mathematically using the fundamental unit of information theory, the bit. A two-state system (which need not be physically realized), that is, a system with two equally probable states, represents one bit of information. To put it another way, to ascertain which state the system is in at a particular time, we must acquire one bit of information.

If a receptor is conceived as a two-state device (although most naturally occurring systems are *not* two-state devices, being analogue rather than digital), it may either be "on" or "off," "high" or "low," and it is therefore possible to model the input to that receptor as a string of bits such as 0110 (low-high-high-low). Just as the string 011010100101 does not in itself mean anything, so the arrival of a string of bits or nerve pulses at a receptor on the boundary of a system, whether of an electronic or organic nature, is not sufficient to do anything (assume significance, effect a change) unless the receiving system "knows" what to make of it. The incident information must resonate with the information embodied in the system to produce some effect that may result in the system using its power to shape some other aspect of the world. This description invites the following fundamental threefold distinction between ways in which the word "information" is used:

Counting-information is mathematical information as defined by Claude Shannon in an epoch-making paper on communication theory written in 1948;[3] it has nothing directly to do with meaning: it relates solely to an arbitrary measure based upon the theory of probability.

Meaning-information is information in the colloquial sense of knowledge; it is completely different from Shannon's concept of information and largely language and culture-dependent.

Shaping-information denotes information as a noun describing the action of giving form to something. It is the oldest sense of the word, originating in the Latin verb *informoare*, further reflected in current usage in the German *informieren* and the French *informer*. In this sense we can speak of the "information" of a piece of Plasticine when it is given some specific form.

An incident pattern of counting-information will be recognized in two circumstances: when it is *familiar* (when it already *belongs* to the system upon which it falls); and when it *familiarizes* (when the system is sufficiently flexible to allow the incident information to induce new embodiment so that the incident information habituates itself and *comes* to belong). Without the second process (involving conditioning, programming, teaching, learning, selecting), the first is impossible (since the origins of

familiarity become unintelligible; the system cannot get started). So although familiarization seems the more remarkable (as has appeared again and again in the philosophical problem of how newness arises and can be appropriated and accommodated),
it is in fact the more basic. The world progresses through familiarization; the capacity
for familiarization is absolutely fundamental.

Two other uses of "information" may be mentioned in this context. J.J. Gibson has
shown the centrality of the capacity actively to make sense of incident information (to
look for patterns and to discern potentially significant patterns) for perception.[4] The
flux of sensations (affordances) carries information induced by its source to constitute
an information-stream (*informationstrom*, as C.F. von Weizsäcker calls it), a stream of
incident information upon which the receiving system acts by trying to construct possible patterns out of it.[5] Organisms with the ability actively to construct significant
order out of the information in an incident array possess selective advantage; the more
appropriate the order they construct, the greater that advantage. The roots of imagination lie in the structure of perception itself. Gibson's own words distinguish his use
of "information" from Shannon's very clearly:

> Shannon's conception of information applies to telephone hookups and radio broadcasting
> in elegant ways but not, I think, to the firsthand perception of being in-the-world, to
> what the baby gets when first it opens its eyes. The information for perception, unhappily,
> cannot be defined and measured as Claude Shannon's information can be.
>
> The information in ambient light, along with sound, odor, touches, and natural chem-
> icals, is inexhaustible. A perceiver can keep on noticing facts about the world she lives in
> to the end of her life without ever reaching a limit. There is no threshold for information
> comparable to a stimulus threshold. Information is not lost to the environment when
> gained by the individual; it is not conserved like energy.[6]

A flux of bits or pulses is meaningless unless it flows in the context of structures
which already embody the capacity to respond to it by recognizing the changes inherent in it as they present themselves at its receptors (on its boundaries) as either
already familiar or potentially significant. The essential process is:

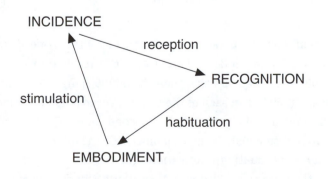

Behavioristic models stress stimulus and response rather than *recognition,* but an appropriate response is inconceivable unless the significance of the incident counting-information has already partly been assimilated and appreciated through prior embodiment. Our "responses"—automatic or otherwise—reflect recognitions made possible by the embodied information established by evolutionary achievement. Creatures which recognize and distinguish between beneficial and harmful incident information survive better; hence their genetic constitution reproduces to enable them to survive to embody better recognition patterns in succeeding generations.

The sophistication of currently embodied information governs the capacity of any system to recognize and respond appropriately to incident information. To fail to recognize a binary string as a code or to fail to recognize a predator may seriously impair the propensity of a system to survive and develop. In macroscopic terms, our capacity to know what is good for us may depend crucially upon the scope of the embodied information we can bring to bear upon the opportunities presented to us: Is what science tells us good for us? Is what a religion claims good for us? Can we recognize all significant order as significant?

To recognize order is to do more than to recognize regularity of pattern, for the notion of "pattern" presupposes a framework within which a pattern can be seen as such. Were we to be presented with one hundred digits from somewhere deep in the decimal expansion of π, we might easily regard them as random numbers exhibiting no pattern, but that would be because we lacked the embodied information needed to see them for what they are.

In each of the following diagrams, twenty black squares appear in a ten-by-ten grid:

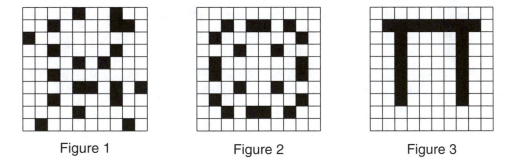

Figure 1   Figure 2   Figure 3

The *counting-information* of each diagram is exactly the same. If we do not know how many black and white squares there are in the ten-by-ten grid, the counting-information is 100 bits. If we know that there is a 20:80 split, the counting-information is $\log_2(^{100}C_{20})$ or about 69 bits in each of the figures. Yet to a human being, the third figure seems both ordered and significant, the second ordered but possibly not significant, and the first disordered. What is it about the third figure that gives it this additional quality to its counting-information? That the counting-information of these three patterns is the same shows that counting-information is inadequate to embrace or describe the differing *significances* of these figures. *Either* we need an additional mathematical technique that reflects the differences between the figures, *or* we must acknowledge that the differences are not reducible to mathematics. Knowing how many bits of counting-information a figure involves does not allow us to construct it; they are a measure of *ignorance,* not *knowledge.* An alien being might regard the first figure as the most significant if it happened to depict some symbol in its alphabet, if it had already embodied the necessary complementary information.

A distinction must be drawn between the *arbitrariness* of counting-information (arising out of the decision to count to base 2, for example) and the *inadequacy* of counting-information (arising from the need to add culture-relative components to the analysis of patterns). The alien, because he had counted to base 3, might arrive at a different measure of counting-information, but that would be no more significant than a difference between measuring temperature in Fahrenheit and Celsius. The inadequacy of counting-information to reflect differences in significance is not of this kind, because the counting-information of different figures, some significant and others not, can easily be identical. The alien—in Gibson's terms—has learned to search for familiar patterns in the ambient array (as if his brain tries out millions of possibilities, homing in on those that can be constructed from that array according to rules and memories that he has learned). To discern significant order is to *resonate* to a complementary aspect of oneself.[7]

When incident information fails to resonate with previously embodied information to generate meaning, we must make choices based upon what seems to be insufficient evidence. Familiar information produces predictable responses; unfamiliar incident information may be permitted to induce unfamiliar responses if it can overcome our inherent mistrust of the new.

Our response to the unfamiliar is nevertheless to try to make sense of it by actively constructing new accounts, stories, and theories by which to link it into our existing web of beliefs, and so explain, appropriate, absorb it, and consequently modify that web of beliefs. The basic Gibsonian process of striving to make sense of incident information is bipolar: such patterns as we can discern in the incident flux will tend to induce us to lock on to them, and so be changed by them, but visual perception becomes in this context a metaphor for *intellectual* perception and imagination, the guiding hand that enables us to reach new conceptualizations.

Potential information in the incident flux is counting-information which has not yet become meaning-information because it does not *belong,* because the reciprocal structures necessary to make sense of it do not yet exist and must therefore be induced in or constructed by the system or organism upon which it falls. (There is no more point in feeding a microchip a binary string that is not part of its instruction set than in presenting an eye with an ambient array outside the wavelength of visible light.) We facilitate such embodiment by theorizing, speculating, imagining, fantasizing, until we find a context of sufficient conceptual power to make sense of it, *or* until we exhaust our powers, *or* until we conclude that there is no meaning-information to be found, that the signal is pure noise, meaningless. The latter two options are difficult to distinguish, as the figures above and the example of the string of digits from the expansion of π demonstrate: how can I tell whether my failure to make sense of an incident array full of information arises from the inadequacy of my intellect or from the fact that the array is meaninglessness? And how can I tell whether the meaning I discern is made or found (imaginary or real)? As I shall remark in another context later, there are no criteria that will distinguish these possibilities.

One of the strongest reasons that can be given for belief in God is that, to make sense of the entirety of the world, we need to "jack up" our conceptual apparatus to higher and higher levels; we will be able to make sense of the largest amount of incident information impinging upon us if we embody the concept of God as a fundamental explanatory principle. The only alternative—an alternative we have used to good effect in the past in mathematics and science—is to restrict the range of diversity we will count as "real" or "important" by abstracting generality from particularity at every turn, by "hiding in the throng and calling numbers to our aid" as Pascal once put it, by refusing to allow, in other words, that individuality has any kind of ultimate significance.

Some theologians (Bowker, Peacocke, and Polkinghorne) have suggested that we can conceive of God's interaction with the world in terms of such an inflow of information. Again the scheme of embodiment and communication clarifies what may be involved in such a process. Just as incident information must belong to and be recognized by the system upon which it falls, so God's informing must be recognized by the universe. Several theological themes follow from this idea: concerning the disobedience of creatures whose minds are out of harmony with God and therefore neither recognize nor resonate with the incident information originating with God; concerning a *cosmic fall* as some degree of dislocation between the recognitional capacity of the universe and God's command; and concerning the sustenance of the universe by God as a dynamic (rather than mechanical, static, deterministic) process in which change and persistence are occasioned by the continual throughput of divine information in incidence and embodiment.

Dynamicists speak of the rate at which we need to add information to a system in order to continue to keep track of it (or keep it going) using the concept of *K-flow,* named after the great Russian dynamicist Kolmogorov.[8] The higher the value of K, the more information we need to keep track of the system. A completely predictable system implies $K = 0$, a very disorderly system involves K being very high (think of the size of Avogadro's number, the number of molecules of gas in one mole at normal temperature and pressure, 6×10^{23}). To monitor a simple device that switches every second between each of its two states in an unknown way (or one that cannot be known), we must acquire information at the rate of one bit per second (equivalently, we must ask one yes/no question per second). For such a system $K = 1$. Reliable machines have low K

numbers, but because they require attention and repair if they are to continue to function properly, their K numbers cannot be zero. The rate at which information is added to a system may also be regarded as the rate at which reordering needs to take place to compensate for the degeneration of what would otherwise be an isolated system.[9]

II. BIOLOGY

Most of us talk about "using" energy, yet we also know that the law of conservation of energy is fundamental. The energy organisms take in must eventually be released again, but an account of life given in terms of taking in so many kilojoules as food, and so on, and giving out so many kilojoules through heat, excreta, and so on, is scarcely very illuminating. As Schrödinger put it:

> For an adult organism the energy content is as stationary as the material content. Since, surely, any calorie is worth as much as any other calorie, one cannot see how a mere exchange could help.[10]

In other words, if we give out just as many kilojoules as we take in, how does this explain *anything*? What do we do with this energy? Are we obtaining something for nothing, and if so, what are we paying for when we pay our gas bills?

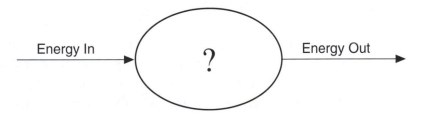

Usable energy has high quality and low entropy which organisms process to extract order. "High" and "low" are relative terms: to be usable, a source of energy must be *more* organized than the system using it; equivalently, its entropy must be lower than the state into which it is transformed in use. Just as a machine needs an inflow of information that can be measured in terms of K, so organisms need an inflow of information which they acquire from the (relatively) highly organized states of the things they eat.

To see the connection between counting-information and thermodynamics, suppose two regions of a tube are separated by a moveable frictionless piston as shown, and that the system is isolated (that is, undergoes no heat loss). The eight squares represent possible locations for six molecules of gas (the dark squares) which move in one dimension at random to fill adjacent empty squares or bump into one another or the piston.

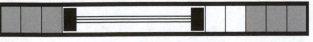

Collisions between the molecules of the left-hand region and the piston are more likely than collisions between the molecules of the right-hand region and the piston, *even if both sides are at the same temperature.* The left-hand side is in a state of *low entropy* (high organization) relative to the right. It will therefore engage in more collisions with the piston than the right until equilibrium is reached (in fact, of course, an oscillation will occur, but that is irrelevant to this discussion).

The total energy of the system (neglecting frictional forces in this idealized experiment) remains constant, but the entropy as measured by the Shannon formula[1] increases since the entropy of the original systems is (left plus right):

$$\log_2 {}^3C_3 + \log_2 {}^5C^3 = 0 + 3.321 = 3.321.$$

The left is zero because there is *no uncertainty* about the system: three molecules must fill exactly three squares; the right is 3.321 because there *is* uncertainty; the three molecules could be variously arranged. By contrast, the entropy of the final system is:

$$\log_2 {}^4C_3 + \log_2 {}^4C_3 = 2 + 2 = 4.$$

There are exactly four states each side of the piston can be in (think of the four possible positions of the white square), hence each side is a four-state system with two bits of information. Even if we begin from two unsaturated regions, similar results apply.

Having reached this state of maximum entropy, no further energy degradation can occur while the system remains closed, but if we interfere with the system by adjusting the piston so that it is again in the original position, effectively adding back the lost information—in this case of $4 - 3.321 = 0.679$ bits—the entire process can repeat. The system receives a net inflow of information.

Organisms also tend to degenerate, to become less ordered, and so to sustain their order they must constantly replace the degrading order with new order by eating. Extracting order from high quality energy generates heat, and that heat serves to maintain the organism at a temperature at which its metabolism works efficiently.

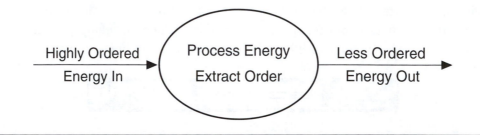

Like the piston system in the idealized example above, an organism denied access to (closed off from) its environment, in possession of a particular amount of energy (stored, say, as fat) can only gradually degenerate, because there is no source of new order once the reserves have been consumed. Brillouin came to the same conclusion in 1949:

> If there are some living cells in the enclosure, they will be able for some time to feed upon the reserves available, but sooner or later this will come to an end and death then becomes inevitable. . . .
>
> [T]he sentence to "death by confinement" is avoided by living in a world that is not a confined and closed system.[12]

But whereas the world is not confined and isolated, cosmology contends that the universe is, and concludes that it is destined for a "heat death" as the entropy of the universe rises. The "Maxwell demon" puzzle now takes on a more significant form: can intelligent life prolong the life span of the universe, perhaps indefinitely? In a more theological vein, is it possible to conceive of God's activity as the adding of information to the system (as we might add information to the pistons) in order to prevent the heat death from occurring?[13] There seems no reason to deny at least the *possibility* of the eternity of the universe, given a sufficient inflow of divine "reorganizing" information.

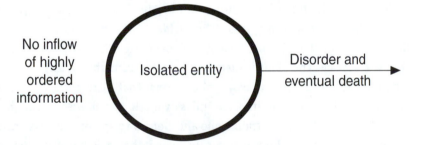

Organisms are engaged in "drinking orderliness from a suitable environment," as Schrödinger put it,[14] and for human beings that "drinking" involves both physical and intellectual feeding. But what is *intellectual* order?

Meaning-Information

I can trace my own interest in information to a seemingly abstruse question which first occurred to me when I was about twelve: what is it about *this* key that makes it open *this* lock? The obvious answer, which is as uninteresting now as it was then, is that the key is the right shape. But what exactly does this mean? It fits! Yes, of course, but what is it about this "fitting" that we need to grasp?

Part of the answer lies in the principle that *the meaning-information of any system is distributed throughout the system as a whole*. A key we find in the street, a random pattern of squares, or a random sequence of letters has been torn away from the complementary parts of the system which endows it with significance, and rendered not only useless but meaningless. It is nevertheless important to realize that we recognize a lockless key as a key or a pattern as a letter only because we already embody complementary aspects of the extended system of which they are a part, and that enables us to make sense of them.

Even to say this much, that information is distributed throughout a system, is to break the mold of reductionist biology and science. The key-lock analogy helps us to see that genetic material denied an environment such as a suitable cell in which to function and replicate cannot make an organism. The cell (or culture) in which it must reside if it is to replicate forms part of the complementary system necessary if the genetic material is to have significance; without the information distributed throughout the key-lock/gene-cell system, both are useless. The most obvious objection is "keys do not make their locks, but genes make their cells," but this is simply not so. Everything in a cell is or has been made by genes, but it has been made by the genes *in conjunction with the cell.* In the absence of a cell—including RNA, amino acids, and other essential components of protein synthesis—DNA is useless. Genes must inherit cells from parent organisms; cells must inherit genes from parent organisms. Organisms employ the gene-cell nexus to reproduce themselves. This contrasts with the view of Dawkins in *The Selfish Gene* that organisms are the means employed by genes to replicate themselves—a thesis that should strike us as odd.

If meaning is distributed over systems, are systems self-interpreting? In other words, once we have a complete system (the incident information and the embodied information that recognizes it), does that system generate self-sufficient significance? From within the system, the significance is generated through the differentiatedness of the parts, not their union; from outside the system, that differentiatedness is invisible and the system loses its significance unless we relocate it within a higher-order significance: the key and lock neutralize one another, so to speak, until we wish to use their relatedness to secure a house or a safe, when the lock becomes the receptor requiring the incident key to open it. A string of words or an object assumes significance not when absorbed by, but when "brought out of the background" from, a system; it individuates itself and in so doing defines its existence.

The essence of this differentiatedness is the *separation* through which actuality emerges from potentiality, rather as matter and antimatter separate to generate the possibility of the world according to some quantum cosmologies. Pure potentiality requires a transfinite number of bits; more bits, perhaps, than even God can contain? But actuality brings finitude from transfinitude (as do the decimal expansions of π and $\sqrt{2}$ in mathematics). The world that exists takes precedence over the worlds that might exist. Nobody can ever know all that might have been.

The conflict between potentialities is resolved by the passage of time which forces their resolution in actuality through separation. We regard certain patterns as significant to the exclusion of others. A signpost, a word, a familiar face, all impact upon our existing reservoir of embodied information and signification; their information resonates with our being to a greater or lesser extent and we move and change accordingly.

For someone sharing our acculturation, Figures 2 to 3 (p. 304) resonate with an extended system of actualized meaning-information, and Figure 1 does not.[15] This seems to be a firmer basis upon which to erect something like an evolutionary episte-mology by suggesting that just as genes must work in particular cells, so only organ-isms which have evolved in a particular environment can hope to understand it, for the *patterns* they see in it *will not appear as patterns otherwise*. Yet, unlike the highly spe-cific relationship between genes and cells, or machine-code and microchips, an alien who regarded Figure 1 as more significant than Figures 2 and 3 might nevertheless be able to discern in our artifacts the products of different organizational principles indicative of intelligent life capable of shaping its environment and of "seeing" the world quite differently. *Intellectual* order—at least for *homo sapiens*—arises from the dialectic of the separation of life from the world and the essential continuity between life and the world: we are part of the world, and our intellectual apparatus has been shaped by the evolutionary processes that form the embodied complement to the inci-dent information with which the world surrounds us. Our intellectual order is inescapably shaped by the need to adapt our imaginings to the structures which can be generated from the flux of the world's affordances.[16]

Theologically, the ambiguity, openness, and plasticity of the world supports the notion of God setting in motion a universe whose eventual significance may not and need not have been entirely foreseen, and which, as such, demands directive and redemptive shaping-information. This admittedly challenges traditional conceptions of divine omniscience and foreknowledge. But if the sense of the *imago dei* in humanity is reflected in the ever-changing circumstances of our living relationship with our envi-ronment, even God's creative activity may perhaps mean "more than he can ever know."[17] The concept of *K*-flow as a measure of the degeneration of the universe offers a way of thinking of God's directive and redemptive sustaining activity as God *inform-ing* the world. Even a cosmic fall can be conceived in terms of the failure of the uni-verse to embody the information necessary fully to recognize the incident divine input.

Shaping-Information

Organisms can extract significant order from the environment to sustain their bodies, and higher organisms can *impose* order upon the environment by exercising their minds. In both the physical sense (for example, in DNA and the synthesis of proteins) and in the mental sense (for example, in constructing nests) organisms display the long-term *achievements* of evolution as a knowledge-embodying process.[18] Thus Lorenz and Popper could regard life itself as a structural analogue of intellectual knowledge in their "evolutionary epistemology." More to the point, the *material* upon which we impose order and form and the *information-stream* upon which we impose order and form through recognition and familiarization *need no longer be regarded as distinct*.

The use of "to inform" to mean "to give form to" is particularly illuminating when extended beyond material shaping-information to its highest manifestation in language, and in particular to the way in which language users can *inform* not only matter but one another's minds. As I write these words, I employ the techniques of shaping-information embodied in my fingers, word processor, and printer to generate patterns of dots on a page whose counting-information could be calculated, in order to convey to the reader the meaning-information, in my head. The reader allows it to inform his brain and mind and through that shaping to convey meaning-information by drawing partly upon the *extended* system of meaning-information that is our common background as English speakers, and partly upon his own unique experience, stored in his memory. The process enables him to reconstruct aspects of my meaning, while ensuring that he will never interpret my written words quite as I intend.

If God acts upon the universe through the creative input of information, no better analogy exists for that action than the way words inform minds. To the extent that the analogy can be pursued, the rate at which God adds information to the world, both in order to keep track of it and in order to direct and redeem it, will be reflected in some concept analogous to the *K*-flow mentioned before.

Shaping-information can therefore be seen to take creative, directive, and sustaining forms. The first generates order (say, by making a machine); the second directs that order (by using the machine to some end); the third preserves and redeems that order (repairing the machine). This offers us a model for God's creative and sustaining activity in which the initially created universe receives a continual inflow of sustaining shaping-information rather as a helmsman constantly corrects the rudder to sustain a ship on course while the engineers struggle to maintain the ship in working order.

We can be sure that, with the emergence of species which have achieved levels of embodied knowledge sufficient to permit *decision,* there also arises the possibility of obedience and disobedience once it is possible to conceive what *ought* to happen. The world knows no future; the future is a feature of mind (not necessarily only of mind empowered with language). Language allows us to articulate our visions of possible futures, and although it is likely that higher animals are capable of conceiving of possible futures, in the absence of *some kind* of language (including, for example, art) they can scarcely communicate those visions to one another. Only a species capable of conceiving and articulating possible futures (a capacity dependent upon its ability to identify *potentially* significant order in an incident flux of stimulation) can issue commands or speak of obedience and disobedience.

III. APPENDIX: CHRISTOLOGICAL INTERPRETATION

The essay by Arthur Peacocke which follows was written before this chapter, and makes use of a number of the ideas presented here as they first appeared in my "Information and Creation." I was unable to agree with the christological perspective Peacocke advocated in the original version of his essay, and the editors of this volume invited me to present my own views of the christological implications of information theory as an appendix to my own chapter.[19]

The task of Christology is to give an account of the life and work of Jesus that does violence neither to human freedom, nor to the full humanity of Jesus reflected in genes, body, brain, and mind, nor to the full divinity of Jesus reflected in who He embodies, both in our understanding of Him and His understanding of himself. It is appropriate, therefore, to begin with some philosophical remarks on personal identity.

A *bivectorial ontology* [20] distinguishes the perspective of an individual as he gazes upon the world from inside looking out (FILO) from the way the world perceives that same individual from outside looking in (FOLI).[21]

Who is this? is a typical FOLI question; Who am I? is a typical FILO question. Sometimes we attempt, FOLI, to give an account of the self-understanding of a person FILO, in which case the appropriate question is: Who does this person believe himself to be? A more-or-less complete outside story must include accounts both of how the world sees a person, and of how the world understands the person to understand himself. Neither of these accounts has a privileged access to correctness, but each (correct or not) plays its part in governing the overall way in which a person is understood. In particular, any Christology must give an account *both* of who we understand Jesus to be *and* of who Jesus understands Himself to be.

After Jesus' ministry, death, and Resurrection, the church began to set out its answer to the question: Who is this? in ever greater detail, and the process continues to this day. For scientists, the question: Who is this? is intimately related to the question: How is this? and many of the christological problems in modern theology arise from the difficulty of reconciling the Jesus who has a full set of human genes with the Jesus who is the incarnate Word. The result is often a christology which reduces to an outside story, as in "functionalism."

To advance another interpretation of the person of Jesus convincingly we need to give an account of the relationship between His mind and brain, not physiologically but philosophically. Consider the following account of an experience FILO.

> Suppose that I am writing, as I am now.
>
> Things are occurring to me, and I write some of them down.
>
> There is a clear sense of temporal succession about this process: the idea comes first; the evaluation of the idea comes next; the decision to write it down (or not) follows.
>
> Something new occurs to me; some unforeseen idea pops into my head.
>
> Where has the new idea come from?
>
> A scientific rationalist says: from some transient configuration of my neurones and neurone-modules derived from a mixture of memory and external stimulation, that is, from a "bottom-up" process.

I have no quarrel with that as far as it goes, but I know that *words* (and other *Gestalten*) can *inform* my brain by inducing such configurations in it as are necessary for me to hear, or see, or smell, and so forth, so some external *informing* source may have been responsible for the configuration in my brain that produced the new idea.

Once this has been accepted, it becomes conceivable that some external stimulation could inform my brain and induce the appropriate configurations in it without me being consciously aware of any such stimulation (that is, I am not aware that I have heard, seen, felt, smelt or tasted anything at all). One can think of subliminal images, the effect of background music, the techniques of brainwashing, and countless examples from experimental psychology where stimulation is applied directly to the nervous system in a way that circumvents conscious awareness.

So a possible answer to: Where did it come from? is: from God who informed my brain, who "put the idea into my head."

The *information* of the world through the evolution of life and the universe, and the information of intellectual history, may all have been influenced by God's informing action in this way—we could never tell. We do not need special and different mechanisms by which to conceive and speak of divine action; the language of information will suffice.

Why did this idea occur to *me*? Because *feedforward* processes, in which we apply our lives to certain areas and not to others, prepare the ground for our own futures. A background in a Western scientific culture in conjunction with a life spent studying theology and mathematics will prepare the ground for certain kinds of ideas which will readily be *appreciated*. Without that prepared ground, an induced idea—an incident stream of information—would pass unnoticed (unrecognized). By engaging feedforward processes we effectively say: "let it be to me according to thy Word";[22] we make our minds places where certain kinds of ideas *belong*.

There remains the possibility that I will *suppress* the idea, refuse to take notice of it, act upon it, or write it down. My freedom enters into the process at a stage beyond that at which the brain has no option but to be configured in a certain fashion. This corresponds to the extraordinary difference between the universe as God's creation, which as such has no choice but to obey the creative command of his Word ("let there be light; and there was light"), and the human mind which, although based upon the material brain which has no choice but to obey God's command (or mine, conceived in a top-down, supervenient way, or the world's, conceived as a source of stimulation), can nevertheless choose to disobey.

Once temporal succession is introduced into the information-assessment-implementation process, we can conceive of the relationship in Jesus between divine information and free human response in terms of ideas which spring from divine and environmental information of Jesus' brain and from His brain's self-information, and present themselves to Him just as my ideas present themselves to me.

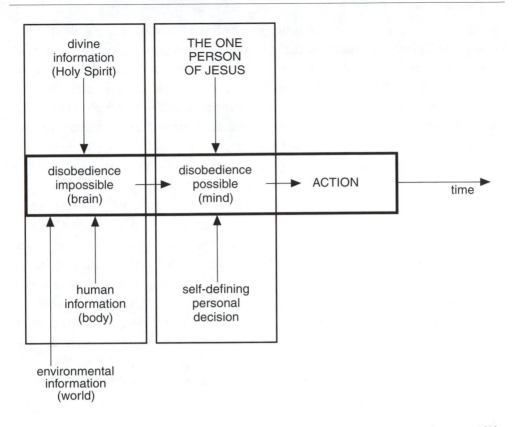

The process of information commences at the earliest possible moment in Jesus' life, and the person of Jesus makes self-defining choices by acting upon the "suggestions" that are induced in His brain by the process of divine information—"let it be to me according to thy Word." From the very first, whenever the "fallen," imperfect, "sinful" traits in the humanity of Jesus could assert themselves (which is to say continually), the person of Jesus redeems them by realizing in Himself the action which optimally embodies the will of God as manifested in the informing Word; that is, by so shaping the incident information-stream as to recreate it after the image in the mind of God. The sin inherent in human existence (which would lead each of us to obstruct the implementation of the divine suggestions that spring into our minds by imagining and therefore constructing lesser realities from the incident information-stream) is taken up into and engaged by the process of redemption in such a way that in the person of Jesus it never, in a sense, exists at all; the person of Jesus *realizes,* at every instant and on every step of His journey through life, the living embodiment and enactment of God's informing and self-revealing will. The tightrope that Jesus walks between full awareness of all the possibilities open to Him as to any human being, including disobedience, and realization of perfect obedience, is clear in the agony in Gethsemane: "Father, if thou art willing, remove this cup from me; nevertheless not my will, but thine, be done."[23] Nevertheless, the temptation to give the person of Jesus some extra powers as guarantors of His perfect obedience—the temptation, that is, to make his humanity more than human—is to be resisted. So is the temptation to make His obedience merely that of a human who happens by chance to find the path to obedience—and as such, to make Him less than divine. The ideas that appear in Jesus' mind do not carry labels saying "from God," "from the environment" or "from yourself." The choices made and the actions realized by Jesus are made as self-constituting decisions which, because He always chooses the way of God (unlike us), reinforce, construct, and condition Him in a way that further reduces any tendency to be tempted into disobedience.

The importance of this for Christology and for each of us can be seen from its connection with the dilemma Wentzel van Huyssteen discusses extensively in his *Theology and the Justification of Faith*: "How can a theologian be sure that his statements are in fact about God's Word, and not merely about a human expression of a supposedly divine Word?"[24] I would answer *emphatically* that the theologian cannot. That was Jesus' dilemma too. The search for a criterion of demarcation between these two possibilities denies the necessary ambiguities of the theological imperative that lead us into self-defining and self-realizing courses of action, without which we would lack any opportunity for personal definition. We would have become machines. Human beings, in other words, and *a fortiori* the person of Jesus, are defined by their responses to choices presented precisely as dilemmas admitting no solution by means of the application of impersonal criteria. Were van Huyssteen's search to succeed, we could obviate the need to make self-defining choices about our existence by using impersonal criteria. *There are no such criteria.*

Now the crucial (inside-story) question, which Jesus must ask of Himself as a human being, arises: Who am I? Unexpectedly, the very mind-body *monism*, understood in terms of the bivectorial ontology described above, that insists upon an integrated view of mind and brain in the process of nurture, and that leads us to understand that we are our bodies in their inside-looking-outness, resolves the question. Unswerving obedience of the person of Jesus to the informing Word transforms Him continuously into its embodiment. Jesus' humanity has no existence other than as the embodiment of the divine Word, and the embodiment of the divine Word in Jesus cannot be conceived otherwise than as manifested in that humanity. We find ourselves brought, by the most rigorous adherence to modern biological principles, to the doctrine of the *hypostatic union*—the union of divine and human natures in the one person of Jesus Christ. A biological argument brings us to a reaffirmation of the historic formulations of early Christianity, but interpreted in a modern sense.

All traces of fallen human nature are removed from and redeemed by Jesus, yet in such a way that human nature has not in the process been destroyed or pushed aside. This is essentially the doctrine found in Ephesians and Irenaeus, that Jesus, by living every stage of life, redeemed every stage of life. *A fortiori,* not only is Jesus the only human being whom we can know as God FOLI; the sheer indistinguishability of His own nature from the divine informing Word must mean that he is also the only God whom *He* can know (FILO). If Jesus is to be true to His own deepest self, He must know Himself to be the Incarnation of the Word, the Son of God, the Son of Man, the one spoken of by the Prophets, the one in whom all things are consummated, the one upon whom all things hang and through whom all things are to be accomplished.

Jesus' body had a beginning in time, but that which came to be embodied had no beginning in time. That which was manifested in Jesus had no beginning in time, but its manifestation in Him had a beginning in time. As Barth puts it:

> Jesus Christ, very God and very man, born and living and acting and suffering and con-
> quering in time, is as such the one eternal Word of God at the beginning of all things.[25]

Nevertheless Jesus might quite properly ask: How can I believe this of myself? and we might quite properly ask: How can He believe this of Himself? The account given here almost places too much emphasis upon the inside story, and runs the risk of making Jesus' self-understanding the very blasphemy of which He was accused. The outside story now restores the balance through the singular event of the Baptism of Jesus by John, reported in all the gospels in different ways. This is to be understood as the exter-nal (FOLI) ratification and confirmation by one greater even than Elijah—"among those born of women there has risen no one greater than John the Baptist"[26]—both that this man is who He believes Himself to be, and also that this man is recognized by God as the one in whom His purposes have been accomplished and will be fulfilled—"This is my beloved Son, with whom I am well pleased."[27] This Baptism is essential *for Jesus*.

It is with the baptism of Jesus by John that his ministry can begin, when he is "anointed with the Holy Spirit and with power."[28] The divine seal of approval has been given to the internal and the external understanding of who this man is. Thereafter both the inside and the outside stories answer the questions: Who is this? and Who am I? with one voice: Thou art the Christ, the Son of the living God.[29] Through the inform-ing action of the divine Word, Jesus' being and His inside-looking-outness *are* that of the Word of God who has become flesh in the fullest possible sense. The person of Jesus can no more tell His inside story in a way that distinguishes His own being from the Word than the Word can reveal Himself through Jesus in a way that is distinguishable from Jesus' being. The man whom we encounter in Jesus is *not* just a man through whom God reveals Himself, and whose words and actions are as such the mere vehicles for God's self-revelation; the man whom we encounter in Jesus *is* the very Word of God Incarnate, who knows and judges us, and who knows and judges Himself, as such. "The only God Jesus knows is the God Jesus is."[30]

NOTES

1. John Horgan's profile of Claude E. Shannon, *Scientific American* 262/1 (January 1990), p. 17, refers to an editorial of the *IEEE Transactions on Information Theory* in the early 1970s entitled "Information Theory, Photosynthesis and Religion," in which the incorpora-tion of information theory into a wide variety of disciplines is decried.

2. Joseph Weizenbaum, *Computer Power and Human Reason*, (San Francisco: Freeman, 1976), p. 277. For a discussion of this point in terms of linguistic metaphor, see my "Information and Creation" in *The Science and Theology of Information* (Geneva: Labor et Fides, 1992).

3. Reprinted in C.E. Shannon and W. Weaver, *The Mathematical Theory of Communication* (1949).

4. James J. Gibson, *The Ecological Approach to Visual Perception* (Boston: Houghton Mifflin, 1979).

5. Carl Friedrich von Weizsäcker, *Aufbau der Physik* (Munich: C. Hanser, 1985).

6. *The Ecological Approach to Visual Perception*, pp. 242–243.

7. For more details, see my "The Relationship of Natural Order to Divine Truth and Will," in *Theology and Science: Questions at the Interface*, Proceedings of the Otago Theological Foundation Conference, 1993 (Edinburgh: T&T Clark, 1994), ch. 1; and my "Resonance Realism," *Tradition and Discovery*, June 1994.

8. I owe this reference to Tito Arecchi's "Why Science is an Open System implying a Meta-Science," in *The Science and Theology of Information*.

9. For a discussion of the relation between information and thermodynamics, see H.S. Leff and A.F. Rex, *Maxwell's Demon* (Bristol: Adam Hilger, 1990), and Alvin Weinberg, "On the Relation between Information and Energy Systems," reprinted in *Maxwell's Demon*, pp. 116 ff.

10. Schrödinger, *What is Life?* (Cambridge: Cambridge University Press, 1967), p. 72.

11. The entropy may be regarded as the average amount of yes/no questions we would need to ask to ascertain the state of a system. Mathematically it is the *expectation* of a random variable denoting the number of bits of information in a system with a large number of possible states (which need not all be equally likely). A full discussion of the mathematical theory of entropy is not possible here. The simplified formulae given arise from the fact that the different states of the left system are equally probable (20 states each with probability 0.05), so that the more elaborate Shannon formula is unnecessary.

12. Brillouin, "Life, Thermodynamics and Cybernetics," in *Maxwell's Demon*, pp. 93, 97.

13. See John Barrow and Frank Tipler, *The Anthropic Cosmological Principle* (New York and London: Oxford University Press, 1986), ch. 10.

14. *What is Life?* p. 77.

15. I am frequently told, however, that Figure 1 looks like a little dog or a reindeer.

16. See Rom Harré, *Varieties of Realism* (Oxford: Blackwell, 1986).

17. See my "Complexity and Western Thought" in the first volume of the Yearbook of the European Society for the Study of Theology and Science, where the embryonic ideas relating to this point are set out.

18. This is a rough English translation of C.F. von Weizsäcker, "Erkenntnisförmigkeit der Evolution," *Aufbau,* p. 208. I am indebted to Christoph Wassermann for drawing my attention to the important notion of information-stream in Weizsäcker's work.

19. Other commitments forced me to complete my essay before the final version of Arthur Peacocke's chapter was available. It may be that, as a result of the friendly correspondence which ensued from our original disagreement, our views will seem less opposed in the final versions than was the case at the outset.

20. *The Science and Theology of Information*, proceedings of the Third European Conference on Science and Theology (Geneva: Labor et Fides, 1991), ch. 1. "Looking" is shorthand for the entire experiential apparatus.

21. For a similar distinction, see Donald Mackay, *Brains, Machines and Persons* (London: Harper Collins, 1980).

22. Luke 1:38.

23. Luke 22:42.

24. J. Wentzel van Huysteen, *Theology and the Justification of Faith* (Grand Rapids: Eerdman's, 1989), p. 89.

25. *Church Dogmatics*, IV: 1 p. 49. See also II: 2 pp. 104 ff, "Jesus Christ was in the beginning with God."

26. Matt. 11:11.

27. Matt. 3:17.

28. Acts 10:38

29. Matt. 16:16.

30. Rachel Puddefoot (aged eleven); personal communication.

THE INCARNATION OF THE INFORMING SELF-EXPRESSIVE WORD OF GOD

ARTHUR PEACOCKE

The conveying and receiving of information is so common an experience that we scarcely attend to it in ordinary life.[1] Yet a closer analysis, along the lines of the preceding essay by John Puddefoot, can offer a helpful way of penetrating the significance of familiar theological terms peculiar to Christianity. For example, the contemporary concept of "information" can shed important light on the possibility of a "natural" perspective on the traditional notion of revelation, thereby softening the distinction between revealed and natural theology and making the notion of God's "informing" more coherent.[2]

In biblical studies and systematic theology alike, "revelation" has, of course, been the focus of much attention in the twentieth century. Yet the discussions of christology, especially key concepts such as "Incarnation," have rarely been integrated into a contemporary scientific worldview. The consequence has been an artificial division between revealed and natural knowledge. This kind of disjunction between the "revealed" and the "natural" is not only increasingly suspect for theological reasons, it is a distraction from a more lively and compelling view of revelation that coheres with significant aspects of contemporary science. In particular, I believe that the concept of exchange of information offers a fresh perspective on and new ways of thinking about the intelligibility of the affirmation that Christ is the self-disclosure of God, the "Word made flesh." In my view it is capable of accommodating an interpretation of Chalcedonian insights, without compromising its core affirmations, by presenting christology along lines that regard the self-communication of God to humanity as an "informing" process.

First, we must recapitulate briefly the contemporary context for discussion of christology as well as some of its historical roots. There has been a continuous, and in recent years an increasingly intensive, study of the historical process whereby the "Jesus" who is uncovered by historical scholarship developed, during the first few centuries of the Christian Church, into the "Christ of faith." This is expressed in terms of that doctrine of the union of God with humanity which is known as that of the "Incarnation." This doctrine found its classical expression in the Definition of Chalcedon of 451 A.D.[3] These studies have generated keen debate both about the extent to which this classical christological formulation and its later developments and extensions can be properly inferred and extracted from the New Testament (by virtue both of its historical status and its own theological interpretations of Jesus), and about their validity today for expressing the significance of Jesus and His relation to God in a framework of thought totally different from the cultural milieu within which the Definition was propounded.[4]

I. THE JESUS OF HISTORY AND THE CHRIST OF FAITH

> *The Word of God, our Lord Jesus Christ who,*
> *of his boundless love, became what we are . . .* [5]

In relation to the role of the New Testament in the emergence of the "Christ of faith," there has been growing recognition that the understanding of Jesus in the New Testament is pluriform and diverse, and that the use of the concept of "Incarnation" to interpret the significance of the life, teaching, death, and resurrection of Jesus emerges only towards the end of its period (roughly that of the first century A.D.) in the Johannine writings, that is, the fourth gospel and the three epistles of John. Thus, in a widely respected study, J.D.G. Dunn asks "How did the doctrine of the Incarnation originate?" and he concludes:

> It did *not* emerge through the identification of Jesus with a divine individual or interme-
> diary being whose presence in heaven was already assumed. . . . It did *not* emerge from an
> identification of Jesus as Elijah or Enoch returned from heaven—exaltation to heaven was
> not taken necessarily to presuppose or imply a previous existence in heaven. . . . It did *not*
> emerge as an inevitable corollary to the conviction that Jesus had been raised from the
> dead or as part of the logic of calling Jesus the Son of God. . . . It did *not* emerge as a
> corollary to the conviction that Jesus had been divinely inspired by the eschatological
> Spirit, a concept of inspiration giving way imperceptibly to one of incarnation. . . . *The*
> *doctrine of the incarnation began to emerge when the exalted Christ was spoken of in*
> *terms drawn from the Wisdom*[6] *imagery of pre-Christian Judaism* . . . only in the post-
> Pauline period did a clear understanding of Christ as having pre-existed with God before
> his ministry on earth emerge, and *only in the Fourth Gospel can we speak of a doctrine of*
> *the incarnation.*[7]

Dunn further points out that:

> Initially at least Christ was not thought of as a divine being who had pre-existed with God
> but as *the climactic embodiment of God's power and purpose*—his life, death and resur-
> rection understood in terms of *God himself reaching out to men*. Christ was identified . . .
> with *God's* creative wisdom, *God's* redemptive purpose, *God's* revelatory word . . . *God's*
> *clearest self-expression, God's last word.*[8]

He argues that the use of "wisdom" and "word" imagery meant that these early formulations of the significance of Jesus were affirmations that

> *Christ showed them what God is like, the Christ-event defined God more clearly than any-thing else had ever done . . . Jesus had revealed God,* not the Son of God, not the "divine intermediary" Wisdom, but God. *As the Son of God he revealed God as Father. . . . As the Wisdom of God he revealed God as Creator-Redeemer. . . .* "Incarnation" means initially that God's love and power had been experienced in fullest measure in, through and as this man Jesus, that Christ had been experienced as God's self-expression, the Christ-event as the effective, re-creative power of God.[9]

A.E. Harvey stresses the constraint of their monotheism on the New Testament writers (and, I would add, also on *us*):

> The New Testament writers appear to have submitted to this constraint, and to have avoided using the word "god" or "divine" of Jesus . . . [they] are similarly insistent about the absolute oneness of God, and show no tendency to describe Jesus in terms of divinity.[10]

Harvey agrees with Dunn that the early application of Wisdom-language to Jesus precedes the doctrine of the Incarnation, and makes the further point that, although the language of "pre-existence" is applied to Jesus in the fourth gospel,[11] this does not in any case imply divinity. For "Wisdom's presence at the creation was a way of saying that no part of creation is an afterthought: it was all there from the beginning. So with Jesus."[12] Neither of these authors is especially radical in his handling of the New Testament data. The more conservative R.E. Brown also recognizes a development *into* the usage of calling Jesus God, even if he charts it differently from Dunn and Harvey.[13]

The widely acknowledged diversity of ideas, words, and images in first-century Christian writings concerning the nature of Jesus and His relation to God has been broadly interpreted in two ways, with many gradations in between.[14] It has been seen either as a "development," meaning "growth, from immaturity to maturity, of a single specimen from within itself"; or as an "evolution," meaning "the genesis of successive new species by mutations and natural selection along the way."[15] But we may well question if a sharp contrast between "development" and "evolution" can be maintained in the light of contemporary understandings of doctrinal history which take account of general philosophies of historical existence and interpretation ("hermeneutics").[16]

Clearly, the christological formulations in the New Testament impel us to acknowledge a diversity of interpretations, none of which should be suppressed even if, strictly speaking, they are not all compatible with each other.[17] New Testament scholars have uncovered a rich treasury of interpretations of Jesus' impact on His first disciples and their followers, and have clarified enormously both their relative independence as well as their interrelations. The New Testament vouchsafes not an intellectual synthesis, but a kaleidoscopic variety of poetic insights.

The synthesizing and systematizing activity of the Christian intellect was fully exercised in the following centuries, leading to the Chalcedonian Definition and subsequent elaborations. These ramifications cannot be entered into here, except to recognize that the interpretation of God and Jesus emerging from the Patristic era gained classical, even normative, status as it was enshrined in the church councils of the first five centuries. The "Fathers" undertook a task which is still incumbent upon us now in our own historical and cultural milieu.[18]

The problem today is to discern whether and how much the development or evolution of doctrine, especially that of the first five centuries A.D. concerning the relation of God and Jesus, can help us interpret and understand the same relation as we find it in the New Testament.[19] Inevitably those classical doctrinal formulations were closely integrated with the philosophy and theology of the prevailing Hellenistic culture (mainly neo-Platonic), and were expressed in terms such as "nature," "substance," and "person" in an ontological framework quite unlike our own—and certainly not that of a culture dominated by modern science. This is widely recognized and at least in Britain it has led to an intensive debate—begun over a decade ago with the publication of *The Myth of God Incarnate* (1977)—about how to formulate Jesus' relation to God and to the rest of humanity today.[20]

However, much of this intensive debate about how to formulate Jesus' relation to God and to the rest of humanity has been confused, in my view, by the absence of an intelligible and believable account of God's being and becoming, God's interaction with the world, God's communication with humanity, and the constitution of human beings. These must be considered in the light of what the sciences now tell us of the being and becoming of the natural, created world, including humanity.

This is the contemporary theological framework from which we must consider Jesus' significance for us today. J.D.G. Dunn summed up John's contribution in the New Testament to the beginnings of christology thus:

> John is wrestling with the problem of how to think of God and how to think of Christ in relation to God in the light of the clarification of the nature and character of God which the Christ-event afforded.[21]

Dunn urges *us* to follow John's model of conveying "the divine, revelatory, and saving significance of Christ" in language and conceptualities contemporary to us.[22]

To do this, we shall have to employ a theological framework that is viable, intelligible, and defensible in the light of the sciences. Is the concept of the "Incarnation" still credible in *this* framework? It may be the case finally that we shall find ourselves asking the question which D. Nineham poses in the penultimate paragraph of *The Myth of God Incarnate*:

Is it necessary to "believe in Jesus" in any sense beyond that which sees him as the main figure through whom God launched men into a relationship with himself so full and rich that, under the various understandings and formulations of it, it has been, and continues to be the salvation of a large proportion of the human race?[23]

Even if it transpires that more can be said than Nineham suggests, we shall have to accept that there is a certain indivisibility about the "Christ-event," as the New Testament scholars tend to denote the "things about Jesus." We have no option, in view of the once-for-all givenness of our historical sources, but to take as *our* starting point the whole complex of the life, teaching, death, and Resurrection-exaltation[24] of Jesus, *together with* its impact on His first-century followers that led to the formation of the first Christian community. This is indeed what is meant by the "Christ-event."

Generations of Christians have shared in the experiences of the early witnesses through the continuous life of the ensuing Christian community, as expressed in its liturgy, literature, visual arts, music, and architecture; in a nexus of transformed personal relationships; and through their direct apprehension of God through Christ, revered as the universalized human Jesus "raised" to the presence of God.[25] Thus, that arrow which was shot into history in the Christ-event lands squarely here today, and we ourselves are challenged to interpret it. Of course, "revelation" is relative to circumstances—that is, the meanings which God can express in creation and in human history are relative to the receptiveness and outlook, the hermeneutical horizons, of those to whom God is communicating. So, however strong a case may be made for a "high" ontological christology having its roots in the Christ-event, we cannot avoid asking whether we too can see what they saw in Him. Even if we were to accept that the New Testament represents a "development" of seeds of judgment and reflection on Jesus, rather than an "evolution" with mutations, we would still be bound to ask about Jesus: "What must the truth have been and be if that is how it looked to people who thought and wrote like that?"[26]

II. *HOW* COULD GOD COMMUNICATE THROUGH JESUS?

As we think of the Christ event from the perspective of the present scientific culture, one potentially valuable resource is the insight gained from information theory. At this point we must say a word more about "information." J.C. Puddefoot has carefully clarified the relation between the different usages of this term.[27] First, physicists, communication engineers, and neuroscientists use "information" which is related to the probability of one outcome among possible outcomes of a situation ("counting-information"). In this sense, it is connected with the notion of entropy. Second, there is the meaning, coming from the Latin root, which is "to give shape or form to" ("shaping-information"). Finally, there is the ordinary meaning of information as knowledge, or the imparting of knowledge ("meaning-information").

Puddefoot points out that information in the first sense must shape or give form to our minds, so "informing" us in the second sense, and thereby conveying information to us in the third sense. In the context of this essay, we will use "information" to represent this whole process, involving transition from the first to the third sense. Moreover, the end of the process can be not merely the acquisition of knowledge, for the possibility arises (though not the certainty) that when *persons* acquire knowledge, "meaning" is also disclosed. Puddefoot suggests that information is meaningless without minds, and he is correct to stress that, even with minds, information can remain meaningless.

The usage of information by physicists, communication engineers, and neuroscientists can be regarded as explicating the underlying processes which "inform" our mental experiences, giving us "knowledge." Hence, the language pertinent to information in the technical, scientific sense is one possible, but basic, description of the kind of conscious information we acquire, and such knowledge has the further potentiality of generating discernment of meaning.

We may characterize God's interaction with the world[28] as a holistic, top-down, continuing process of input of "information," conceived of broadly, whereby God's intentions and purposes are implemented in the shaping of particular events, or patterns of events, without any abrogation of the regularities discerned by the sciences in the natural order. Amongst the constituents of that world are human beings who are persons. These too can be "informed" by God through the nexus of events, which includes events in human-brains-in-human-bodies. When the receipt of such an "input" from God is conscious, it is properly called "religious experience." I have argued elsewhere that such an understanding of God's interaction with human beings can be regarded as revelatory, and as fully personal as that between human beings, in spite of the apparently abstract limitations of the terminology of "information input" and of computer science.[29]

How, in the light of this, might we then interpret the experience of God that was mediated to His disciples and to the New Testament church through Jesus? That is, how can we understand the Christ-event as God's self-communication and interaction with the world such that it is intelligible in the light of today's natural and human sciences? We need to explicate in these terms the conclusions of scholars about the understanding in New Testament times of Jesus the Christ. Note, for example, Dunn's conclusion that:

> Initially Christ was thought of . . . as the climactic embodiment of God's power and purpose . . . God himself reaching out to men . . . God's creative wisdom . . . God's revelatory word . . . God's clearest self-expression, God's last word.[30]

These descriptions of what Jesus the Christ was to those who encountered him and to the early church are all, in their various ways, about God *communicating* to humanity. In the broad sense in which we have been using the terms, they are about an "input of information." This process of "input of information" from God conforms with the actual content of human experience, as the conveying of "meaning" from God to humanity. I have argued that God can convey His meanings through events and patterns of events in the created world—those in question here are the life, teaching, death, and Resurrection of the human person, Jesus of Nazareth, as reported by these early witnesses. As the investigations of the New Testament show, they experienced in Jesus, in His very person and personal history, a communication *from God*, a revelation of God's meanings for humanity. So it is no wonder that, in the later stages of reflection in the New Testament period, John conflated the concept of divine Wisdom with that of the *Logos*, the "Word" of God, in order to say what he intended about the meaning of Jesus the Christ for the early witnesses and their immediate successors. The *locus classicus* of this exposition is, of course, the prologue to his gospel. John Macquarrie notes that the expression, "Word" or *Logos*, when applied to Jesus, not only carries undertones of the image of "Wisdom," it also conflates two other concepts: the Hebrew idea of the "word of the Lord" for the will of God expressed in utterance, especially to the prophets, and in creative activity; and that of *"logos"* in Hellenistic Judaism, especially in Philo—the Divine *Logos*, the creative principle of rationality operative in the universe, especially manifest in human reason, formed within the mind of God and projected into objectivity.[31]

Macquarrie has in fact attempted to interpret for our times the import of Word-*Logos* in the prologue to John's gospel by substituting "Meaning" for it. His paraphrase, now published in full, is worth quoting, for it succeeds in conveying in today's terms something of what it meant for its first readers (numbers refer to the paraphrased verses of John 1):

(1) Fundamental to everything is Meaning. It is closely connected with what we call "God," and indeed Meaning and God are virtually identical. (2) To say that God was in the beginning is to say that Meaning was in the beginning. (3) All things were made meaningful, and there was nothing made that was meaningless. (4) Life is the drive toward Meaning, and life has emerged into self-conscious humanity, as the (finite) bearer and recipient of Meaning. (5) And meaning shines out through the threat of absurdity, for absurdity has not overwhelmed it. (9) Every human being has a share in Meaning, whose true light was coming into the world. (10) Meaning was there in the world and embodying itself in the world, yet the world has not recognized the Meaning, (11) and even humanity, the bearer of Meaning, has rejected it. (12) But those who have received it and believed in it have been enabled to become the children of God. (13) And this has happened not in the natural course of evolution or through human striving, but through a gracious act of God. (14) For the Meaning has been incarnated in a human existent, in whom was grace and truth; and we have seen in him the glory toward which everything moves—the glory of God. (16) From him, whom we can acknowledge in personal terms as the Son of the Father, we have received abundance of grace. (17) Through Moses came the

command of the law, through Jesus Christ grace and truth. (18) God is a mystery, but the Son who has shared the Father's life has revealed him.[32]

The substitution of "Meaning" for Word-*Logos* helps to convey better the Gospel's affirmation of what happened in creation and in Jesus the Christ. For, as we have seen, conveying of meaning, in the ordinary sense, is implemented initially by an input of "information"—the constrained and selected elements among all possibilities that sufficiently delimit signals (that is, language and other means of human communication) so that they can convey meaning. As John Bowker has put it:

> How do we arrive at the sense of anything? How do we construct meaning on the basis of information which arrives at our receptor centres in the form of sensation, or which occurs in the internal process? The biological and neurological answer lies in the (initially latent) structured ability of the brain to code, store, and decode signals and represent (represent) them *as* information. This implies that "meaning" is constituted not by the quantitative amount of information, but by a qualitative selection (control into restriction), which enables meaning ... to transcend the mathematical base of its constituent elements; the way [in which "meaning" does this] ... does not mean that there is an automatic, radical disjunction between quantitative (in a semiotic sense) and qualitative information.[33]

The use of the concept of "information input" to refer to the way God induces effects in the world was, to the best of my knowledge, pioneered by Bowker. It also has been used by him to render intelligible the idea of God expressing Himself in and through the human being of Jesus:

> ... it is credibly and conceptually possible to regard Jesus as a wholly God-informed person, who retrieved the theistic inputs coded in the chemistry and electricity of brain-processes for the scan of every situation, and for every utterance, verbal and non-verbal ... the result would have been the incarnating (the embodying) of God in the only way in which it could possibly have occurred. No matter what God may be in himself, the realization of that potential resource of effect would have to be mediated into the process and continuity of life-construction through the brain-process interpreted through the codes available at any particular moment of acculturation. . . . There is no other way of being human, or indeed of being alive, because otherwise consciousness ceases. . . . That is as true of Jesus *de humanitate* as of any one else. But what seems to have shifted Jesus into a different degree of significance ... was the stability and the consistency with which his own life-construction was God-informed. . . .
>
> It is possible on this basis to talk about a wholly human figure, without loss or compromise, and to talk also, at exactly the same moment, of a wholly real presence of God so far as that nature (whatever it is in itself) can be mediated to and through the process of

the life-construction in the human case, through the process of brain behavior by which
any human being becomes an informed subject—but in this case, perhaps even uniquely,
a wholly God-informed subject.[34]

This illustrates how the notion of God communicating Himself through the complete
person of Jesus the Christ is consistent with all that we have been saying concerning
the nature of God's interaction with and self-communication to the world. It renders
such interaction intelligible in a way that seemed to be impossible for its critics in *The
Myth of God Incarnate*.

At this juncture in our enterprise, recognition that God has, in fact, communicated
God's own self to humanity in this way—that is, acceptance of the belief that God was
"incarnate" in Jesus—must be left to the judgment of the reader. That judgment has to
rest on the reader's assessment not only of its intrinsic intelligibility but also of its
moral and religious significance, of the Christ-event in the light of the New Testament
evidence, of whether or not the church teaching down the ages is to be regarded as
providentially guided, and of the experience of Christ as a living and active presence of
God in the church and in the world.

The present writer judges that these considerations are compelling, so—hoping the
reader is prepared to continue with him, at least provisionally, in this belief—we shall
proceed by exploring its implications and its relation to a more general theology for a
scientific age we have been developing. This belief in the Incarnation was founded on
the whole complex of what we have called the Christ-event, which I will now refer to as
"Jesus the Christ" to convey the personal and historical aspects intended. Those who
were actually involved historically in the interpretation of Jesus the Christ came to
believe that in the completely human person of Jesus, it was *God* whose self-expression
they experienced. In the following section, we pursue the question of what (according
to this Christian belief) God may actually be said to have communicated to humanity
about God's Self in and through Jesus the Christ.

III. GOD'S SELF-EXPRESSION IN JESUS THE CHRIST

Any communication of the nature of God's Self believed to have been transmitted in
and through Jesus the Christ will have to be related to those insights into what we are
able to discern of divine Being and Becoming from more general reflections on natural
being and becoming. Of course, we look not for proof, but for a consonance which
might consolidate the insights of such a "natural" theology. However, if Jesus the
Christ really is a self-communication *from* God and the self-expression *of* God in a
human person, as the church, in concord with the early witnesses, has affirmed, then
we can hope for much more. What were glimmers of light on a distant horizon might
become shafts of the Uncreated Light of the Creator's own Self. Hints and faint echoes
of the divine in nature might become, in Jesus Christ, a resonating word to humanity

from God's own Self, a manifest revelation of God. Jesus the Christ would then, indeed, be the very Word of God made human flesh, as the early church came to assert. What is only implicit and partially and imperfectly discerned of God in the created world would then be explicit and manifest in his person. We shall therefore need to reflect on what the early Christian community affirmed as their experience of God in Jesus the Christ, in the light of what we are able to discern[35] of divine Being and Becoming from natural being and becoming.

God as Continuous and Immanent Creator

From the continuity of the natural processes, we infer that God is continuously creating, as the immanent Creator, in and through the natural order. For the processes of the world exhibit an intelligible continuity, in which the potentialities of its constituents are unfolded in forms of an ever-increasing complexity and organization. These forms are properly described as "emergent," in that they manifest new features that are irreducible to the sciences which describe the simpler levels of organization out of which they have developed. One of the most striking aspects of natural becoming is that qualitatively new kinds of existence come into being. We witness in nature the seeming paradox of discontinuity generated by continuity. Hence belief in God as Creator involves the recognition that this is the character of the processes whereby God actually creates new forms, new entities, structures, and processes that emerge with new capabilities, requiring distinctive language on our part to distinguish them. God is present in and to this whole process.

This has important consequences for our understanding and expression of God's self-manifestation in the human person of Jesus. One might say that God "informs" the human personhood of Jesus such that God's self-expression occurs in and through Jesus' humanity. For when we reflect on the significance of what the early witnesses reported as their experience of Jesus the Christ, we find ourselves implicitly emphasizing both the *continuity* of Jesus with the rest of humanity, and so with the rest of nature within which *homo sapiens* evolved, and, at the same time, the *discontinuity* constituted by what is distinctive in his relation to God and what, through him (his teaching, life, death, and Resurrection), the early witnesses experienced of God.

This paradox is already present in that peak of christological reflection in the New Testament period that comes to expression in the Prologue to the gospel of John. For in that seminal text, the Word-*Logos*, which both is God and was with God in creating (vv. 1–3), and which becomes human "flesh" (v. 14), is the same "Word" that is all the time "in the world" (v. 10) and giving "light" (vv. 4–6) to humanity, even though unrecognized (v. 10). God had been and was already in the world, expressing God's meaning in and through God's creating, to use Macquarrie's interpretation. But this meaning was hidden and suppressed, and only in Jesus the Christ has it become manifest and explicit, so that its true "glory" (v. 14) has become apparent.

This encourages us to understand the "Incarnation" which occurred in Jesus as exemplifying that emergence-from-continuity which characterizes the whole process of God's creating. There both is continuity with all that preceded Him, yet in Him there has appeared a new mode of human existence which, by virtue of its openness to God, is a new revelation of both God and of humanity. Taking the clue from the Johannine Prologue, we could say that the manifestation of God which Jesus' contemporaries encountered in Him must have been an emanation from within creation, from deep within those events and processes which led to His life, teaching, death, and Resurrection. According to this understanding of God's creation and presence in the world, "Incarnation" is not God's "descent" into the world, wherein God is conceived as "above" (and so outside) it, as so many Christmas hymns would have us believe. Rather, it is the manifestation of the One who is already in the world, but not recognized or known. Thus, by virtue of His response and openness to God, the human person Jesus is to be seen as the locus, the icon, through whom God's nature and character are made open and explicit. Yet it must be kept in mind that God has never ceased to be continuously creating and bringing God's purpose to fruition in the order of energy-matter-space-time.

Because of this continuity between God's continuous creativity and the inherent creativity of the universe, it seems to me that we must see Jesus the Christ not as a unique invasion of the personhood of an individual human being by an utterly transcendent God, but rather as the distinctive manifestation of a possibility always inherently there for human beings by virtue of what God had created them to be and to become. Such a joint emphasis on continuity (corresponding to "immanence") as well as on emergence (corresponding to "Incarnation") is vital to any understanding of Jesus the Christ which is going to make what He *was* relevant to what we *might* be. For this interpretation of the "Incarnation" entails that what we have affirmed about Jesus is not, in principle, impossible for all humanity. Even if, as a matter of contingent historical fact, we think the "Incarnation" is only fully to be seen in Him, it is not excluded as a possibility for all humanity.

In proposing a strong sense of God's immanence in the world (largely suppressed in the West for the last three hundred years) as the context for thinking about the Incarnation, we must nevertheless recognize the transcendence of God. Admittedly, the sense of transcendence often has been so dominant that the very idea of Incarnation has seemed inconsistent, even nonsensical, in relation to talk about God. However, the fact is that the Jewish followers encountered in Jesus the Christ (especially in His Resurrection) a dimension of divine transcendence which, as devout monotheists, they had attributed to God alone.

But they also encountered Him as a complete human being, and so experienced an intensity of God's immanence in the world different from anything else in their experience or tradition. Thus it was that the fusion of these two aspects of their awareness— that it was *God* acting in and through Jesus the Christ—gave rise to the conviction that in Him something new had appeared in the world of immense significance for humanity. As *we* might say, a new emergent had appeared within created humanity. And thus it was, too, that they ransacked their cultural stock of available images and models (for example, "Christ," "Son of God," "Lord," "Wisdom," "*Logos*"), at first Hebraic and later Hellenistic, to give expression to this new, nonreducible, distinctive mode of being and becoming, instantiated in Jesus the Christ.

God as Personal, or "Supra-Personal," and Purposive

The operation of natural selection in biological organisms has an inbuilt tendency to favor increasing complexity, information-processing, and storageability, because of their survival value.[36] These are the foundations for sensitivity to pain, consciousness, and even self-consciousness, which also must be reckoned to have survival value. This process—albeit by the zigzag, random path carved out by the interplay of chance and law—reaches its maximum development so far in the emergence of the human-brain-in-the-human-body, which has that distinctive and emergent feature we call being a "person." One must also consider the "anthropic" features of the universe which allowed the emergence through evolution of human persons and so the appearance of *personal* agency.[37] This would seem to tentatively justify the description of the universe as a "personalizing universe," in the sense that "the whole is to be understood as a process making for personality and beyond."[38] Reflecting on what could constitute the "best explanation" of such a universe, I have concluded that God is (at least) personal or "suprapersonal." The awkward term "*supra*personal" signifies here that any extension of the language of human personhood inevitably, like all analogies based on created realities, must remain inadequate as a *description* of the nature of that ineffable, ultimate Reality which is God.

However tentative any use of personal language must be when applied to God, it remains the most consistent and the least misleading of any that might be inferred from our reflections on natural being and becoming. Furthermore, consideration of the emergence of the experience of transcendence-in-immanence that characterizes evolved human personhood, leads us to conjecture that:

> ... in humanity immanence might be able to display a transcendent dimension to a degree which would unveil, without distortion, the transcendent-Creator-who-is-immanent in a uniquely new emergent manner—that is, that in humanity (in a human being, or in human beings), the presence of God the Creator might be unveiled with a clarity, in a glory, not hitherto perceived.[39]

This leads one to ask: Might it not be possible for a human being so to reflect God, to be so wholly open to God, that God's presence was clearly unveiled to the rest of humanity in a new, emergent, and unexpected manner?

It was the affirmation of the early church, and continues to be the church's affirmation today, that in Jesus the Christ this has actually happened. That is, in Jesus the Christ, God's self-expression is such that it validates personal attributions to God, even though we recognize the inherent limitations of these attributions. For in Jesus the Christ, God has apparently taken the initiative to reveal His presence to humanity in and through a completely human *person*. The early disciples and subsequent members of the Christian church have no doubt that they encounter God in Jesus the Christ, and that His personhood conveys God's meanings to and for humanity.

Meanings that persons wish to communicate are conveyed through words. Thus, the concept of the Word-*Logos* of God, appropriated to understand the significance of Jesus the Christ, is essentially a personal one.[40] We have already had our understanding of the Prologue to St. John's gospel enriched by Macquarrie's substitution of "Meaning" for Word-*Logos*. The "Meaning" so communicated within the pages of the New Testament is principally about the significance of the personal relation to God as "Love," and of loving interpersonal relationships. Hence John Robinson's paraphrase of the Prologue, in which he substitutes the concept of the "personal" for Word-*Logos*, is particularly illuminating:

(1) The clue to the universe as personal was present from the beginning. It was found at the level of reality which we call God. Indeed, it was no other than God nor God than it. (2) At that depth of reality the element of the personal was there from the start. (3) Everything was drawn into existence through it, and there is nothing in the process that has come into being without it. (4) Life owes its emergence to it, and life lights the path to man. (5) It is that light which illumines the darkness of the sub-personal creation, and the darkness never succeeded in quenching it. . . .

(9) That light was the clue to reality—the light which comes to clarity in man. Even before that it was making its way in the universe. (10) It was already in the universe, and the whole process depended upon it, although it was not conscious of it. (11) It came to its own in the evolution of the personal; yet persons failed to grasp it. (12) But to those who did, who believed what it represented, it gave the potential of a fully personal relationship to God. (13) For these the meaning of life was seen to rest, not simply on its biological basis, nor on the impulses of nature or the drives of history, but on the reality of God. (14) And this divine personal principle found embodiment in a man and took habitation in our midst. We saw its full glory, in all its utterly gracious reality—the wonderful sight of a person living in uniquely normal relationship to God, as son to father.

(16) From this fullness of life we have all received, in gifts without measure. (17) It was law that governed the less than fully personal relationships even of man; the true gracious reality came to expression in Jesus Christ. (18) The ultimate reality of God no one has ever seen. But the one who has lived closest to it, in the unique relationship of son to father, he has laid it bare.[41]

In this perspective, the self-disclosure that God communicated to humanity in Jesus the Christ was an explicit revelation of the significance of personhood in the divine purposes. The Creator God in whom the world exists has all along been instantiating God's own personalness, and this has been expressed supremely in Jesus the Christ. Again we must note that this is being affirmed as the contingent historical reality, but this affirmation does not confine the incarnating of God the Word to Jesus alone, nor does it preclude the possibility of such language being the appropriate description of at least some other human beings—and perhaps, potentially at least, of all.

The distinctive feature of human beings *qua* persons is that they are potential carriers of values which they seek by purposive behavior to embody in their individual and social life. It was one of the well-attested features of the experience of Jesus the Christ that He not only inculcated values in His disciples through His teaching, but He also exemplified them in His life. Afterward they saw that this was especially the case in view of the circumstance of and reasons for the suffering and death inflicted on him.

We leave the content of these values for another essay.[42] Here we simply note that it is not just any kind of personhood, or personal life, that we see as the purpose of God to bring into existence. The acceptance of Jesus the Christ as the self-expression of God compels the recognition that it is the eliciting of persons embodying values which is the underlying purpose of the divine creative process. Persons can only be carriers of values if they are self-conscious and free, so that the "propensities" of the biological, evolutionary process have their ultimate limiting form in *this* person, Jesus the Christ. The "Incarnation" in Jesus the Christ may, then, properly be said to be the consummation of the creative and creating evolutionary process. It would follow that, if Jesus the Christ is the self-expression of God's meaning, then the evoking in the world of *this* kind of person, with *these* values, just is the purpose of God in creation.

God as Exploring in Creation Through its Open-Endedness

Recognizing that God as Creator acts through chance operating under the constraints of law, and that many of the processes of the world are open-ended (they are irreducibly unpredictable), combined with emphasis on the immanence of God in the creative and creating processes of the world, leads us to suggest that God the Creator is *exploring* in creation. The assertion that "God the Creator explores in creation" means that God improvisingly responds to and creates on the basis of eventualities which are irreducibly unpredictable in advance. The operation of human free will is, of course, a particularly notable and "unpredictable" feature of the world which demonstrates God's willingness to let it have this open-ended character. It is concomitantly a world in which God exercises providential guidance and influence.

Jesus exercises free will in such complete openness to God that His disciples come to designate Him as the "Christ" and their successors to develop an understanding of what was happening in Him as the "Incarnation" of God. That same Jesus risked everything on the faithfulness of God in the hazardous events of His times, and thereby united Himself with God in that painful process, in hope of bringing into existence

God's Reign, the "Kingdom of God." This means that, in the willing act of Jesus the Christ, the open-endedness of what is going on in the world fully and self-consciously united itself with the purposes of God for the still open future. In Jesus' oneness with God we see the openness of the creative process operative in a human person, fully united with the immanent activity of God. God is the source of the open future, and this openness is the medium of expressing God's intentions for humanity and the world. But is not this just that very close linkage between the advent of Jesus and the initiation of the Kingdom of God ("God's Reign") which is distinctive of Jesus' own teaching?

The historical evidence is indeed that Jesus *was* so open to God that He entrusted his whole future to God unequivocally to the point of abandoning, at His death, even His sense of God's presence to Himself.[43] The evidence attests that the historical Jesus staked all on God's future, and thereby made possible the Resurrection. In this manner, God further revealed Jesus as the Christ who would draw all humanity after Him into a full relation with God. This is why we may now see Jesus the Christ as a new departure point in the creative process, the beginning of a new possibility for human existence in which new potentialities of human life are actualized in those who are willing to share in Jesus' *human* and *open* response to God.

God as "Self-Limited" and as Vulnerable, Self-Emptying, Self-Giving, and Suffering Love

Elsewhere, I have attributed "self-limitation" to God with respect to God's power over all events and over knowledge of the future.[44] I arrived at this conclusion because of certain inherent yet created unpredictabilities in some systems of the natural world. These included, *inter alia,* the operations of the human-brain-in-the-human-body, and so of the deliberations of human free will. This led to the notion that God had allowed himself not to have power over and knowledge of the future states of such systems, because God wanted them to possesss a degree of autonomy that could develop into self-conscious, free human beings.

Now, if Jesus the Christ is the self-expression of God, this inevitably involves a self-limitation of God. For only some aspects of God's own nature are expressible in a human life. In particular, God's omnipotence and omniscience could not be expressed in the limits of the human person of Jesus, whose complete humanity certainly restricted His power and knowledge.

This "self-emptying" (*kenosis*) of God in Jesus the Christ has been much discussed since its revival in the nineteenth century to reinterpret the classical doctrine of the Incarnation.[45] It was predicated on a somewhat overcautious acceptance of the full humanity of Jesus, and was heavily dependent on the interpretation of certain key passages in St. Paul's writings as indicating the preexistence of "Jesus Christ" Himself, regarded as the God-Man.[46] There are many difficulties with this view, including exegetical ones, and there is considerable confusion about what and to whom the notion of "preexistence" refers. Suffice it to say, for our present purposes, that God (or the Word-*Logos* of God as a mode of God's being) and hence God's intentions and purposes, can be coherently conceived as pre-existent in relation to the human Jesus.[47]

Furthermore, on the interpretation of created natural being and becoming I have advanced elsewhere, God is all the time self-limiting in His immanent, creating presence in the world. Indeed, we must speak of the self-emptying (*kenosis*) and self-giving of God in creation. So the eventual self-expression of God in the restricted human personhood of Jesus can be seen as an explicit manifestation and revelation of that perennial (self-limiting, -emptying, -giving) relation of God to the created world, which was up until then only implicit and hidden. The only temporal *pre*existence implicit in this insight, relative to the Jesus who was in history, is that of *God*, whose transcendent Being is of such a kind that God creatively expresses God's Self in immanent Becoming in the world throughout created time. In any case, God always has ontological priority.

Because of the interplay of chance and law in the processes of creation, one can also infer that God may be regarded as "taking a risk" in creating, and therein making Himself and His purposes vulnerable to the inherent open-endedness of those processes. This vulnerability of God is accentuated also by the effects of human free will, an outcome of that inbuilt open-endedness. Such a suggestion can be only a conjecture, an attempt to make sense of certain features of natural processes that are also seen as created by God. But this suggestion is reinforced, indeed overtly revealed—that is, communicated by God—if God truly expressed God's Self in Jesus the Christ. For His path through life was preeminently one of vulnerability to the forces that swirled around Him, to which He eventually innocently succumbed in acute suffering and, from His human perception, in a tragic, abandoned death.

Because sacrificial, self-limiting, self-giving action on behalf of the good of others is, in human life, the hallmark of love, those who believe in Jesus the Christ as the self-expression of God have come to see His life as their ultimate warrant for asserting that God is essentially "Love," insofar as any one word can accurately refer to God's nature. Jesus' own teaching concerning God as "Abba," Father, and of the conditions for entering the "Kingdom of God," pointed to this too. But it was the person of Jesus, and what happened to Him, that early established this perception of God in the Christian community.

We see, therefore, that belief in Jesus the Christ as the self-expression of God is entirely consonant with the conception of God as self-limiting, vulnerable, self-emptying, and self-giving—that is, as supreme Love in creative action. On this understanding, Jesus the Christ is the definitive communication from God to humanity of the deep meaning of what God has been effecting in creation. And that is precisely what the Prologue to the fourth gospel says.

Furthermore, we have inferred even more tentatively from the character of the natural processes of creation that God has to be seen as suffering in, with, and under these self processes, with their costly, open-ended unfolding in time. If God was

present in and one with Jesus the Christ, then we have to conclude that *God* also suffered in and with Him in His passion and death. The God whom Jesus therefore obeyed
and expressed in his life and death is indeed a "crucified God," to use Jürgen
Moltmann's phrase, and the cry of dereliction can be seen as an expression of the
anguish also of God in creation. If Jesus is indeed the self-expression of God in a
human person, then the tragedy of His actual human life can be seen as a drawing back
of the curtain to unveil a God suffering in and with the sufferings of created humanity.
Moreover, this extends to all of creation, since humanity is an evolved part of it. The
suffering of God, which we could glimpse only tentatively in the processes of creation,
is in Jesus the Christ concentrated into a point of intensity and transparency which
reveals it to all who focus on Him.

In this contribution, for the most part I have been thinking about Jesus the Christ
in relation to how and what God was communicating through Him—in particular, what
God was expressing about God's own Self in and through His person and personal history. In this perspective, Jesus the Christ, by virtue of his openness to God as his
"Father" and Creator was able to express in a distinctive way the transcendence of the
Creator who is immanent in the world process. Thus His disciples and their followers
encountered in Him a presence of God which fused God's transcendence and immanence in a way that engendered the language of "Incarnation." However, when such
incarnational language becomes confined to assertions about Jesus' "nature" and
about what kind of "substance(s)" do or do not constitute Him, then it loses its force to
convey significant meaning to many today who are concerned not so much with what
Jesus was "in Himself," but rather with the dynamic nature of the relation between
God's immanent creative *activity* focused and unveiled in Him and the *processes* of
nature and of human history and experience, which are all "in God," and from which
God is never absent.

What the disciples and their followers experienced in Jesus the Christ, and the more
general notions of God's continuing relation to the world which were inferred from natural being and becoming, clearly render each other more intelligible, and mutually
enrich and enhance each other. In Him, we can say, general and special revelation of
God converge, coincide, and mutually reinforce each other.

NOTES

1. This essay was written while preparing *Theology for a Scientific Age: Being and Becoming—
   Natural, Divine and Human*, 2nd enlarged ed. (London: SCM, 1993; Minneapolis: Fortress,
   1993), hereafter *TSA*, and shares some material with ch. 14, "Divine Being Becoming
   Human." References to that and other sections of *TSA* are provided in this essay for readers
   interested in more detail.

2. *TSA*, ch. 11.

3. The Chalcedonian Definition established boundary conditions within which Christological
   reflection should proceed. It reads as follows:

Therefore, following the holy Fathers, we all with one accord teach men to acknowledge one and the same Son, our Lord Jesus Christ, at once complete in Godhead and complete in manhood, truly God and truly man, consisting also of a reasonable soul and body; of one substance (*homoousios*) with the Father as regards his Godhead, and at the same time of one substance with us as regards his manhood; like us in all respects, apart from sin; as regards his Godhead, begotten of the Father before all ages, but yet as regards his manhood begotten, for us men and for our salvation, of Mary the Virgin, the God-bearer (*Theotokos*); one and the same Christ, Son, Lord, Only-begotten, recognized in two natures, without confusion, without change, without division, without separation; the distinction of natures being in no way annulled by the union, but rather the characteristics of each nature being preserved and coming together to form one person and subsistence (*hypostasis*), not as parted or separated into two persons, but one and the same Son and Only-begotten God the Word, Lord Jesus Christ; even as the prophets from earliest times spoke of him, and our Lord Jesus Christ himself taught us, and the creed of the Fathers has handed down to us.

H. Bettenson, *Documents of the Christian Church* (London: Oxford University Press, 1956), p. 73.

4. For an accessible and readable account, see John Macquarrie, *Jesus Christ in Modern Thought* (London: SCM Press, 1990).

5. Irenaeus, *Adversus Haereses* translated by Dominic J. Unger (New York: Paulist Press, 1992), v. praef.

6. Wisdom was conceived of as "personification of divine action" in pre-Christian Judaism rather than as "a divine being in some sense independent of God," according to James D. G. Dunn, *Christology in the Making* (London: SCM Press, 1980), p. 262. Wisdom was especially conceived as being present at and in the divine action of creation.

7. *Christology in the Making*, pp. 258–259 (Dunn's emphasis).

8. *Christology in the Making*, p. 262 (Dunn's emphasis).

9. *Christology in the Making*, p. 262 (Dunn's emphasis).

10. A.E. Harvey, *Jesus and the Constraints of History* (London: Duckworth, 1982), p. 157.

11. Something which Dunn disputes; see *Christology in the Making*, pp. 38–45.

12. *Jesus and the Constraints of History*, p. 178.

13. See Raymond E. Brown, *Jesus God and Man* (London: Collier Macmillan, 1967), pp. 30–34.

14. For a brief discussion, see my *Creation and the World of Science* (Oxford: Clarendon Press, 1979), pp. 222–227.

15. C.F.D. Moule, *The Origin of Christology* (Cambridge: Cambridge University Press, 1977), p. 2.

16. See W.O. Chadwick, *From Bossuet to Newman: The Idea of Doctrinal Development* (Cambridge: Cambridge University, 1957); N. Lash, article on "Development, Doctrinal," in *New Dictionary of Christian Theology* (Philadelphia: Westminster Press, 1983) , pp. 155–156; M.F. Wiles, *The Remaking of Christian Doctrine* (London: SCM Press, 1974).

17. Dunn, *Christology*, pp. 266–267.

18. See James P. Mackay, "The task of systematic theology," in James D.G. Dunn and James P. Mackay *New Testament Theology in Dialogue* (London: SPCK, 1987), pp. 27–53.

19. See Wiles, *Remaking*, especially ch. 1.

20. J. Hick ed., *The Myth of God Incarnate* (London: SCM Press, 1977); M. Green ed., *The Truth of God Incarnate* (London: Hodder and Stoughton, 1977); A.E. Harvey ed., *God Incarnate:*

Story and Belief (London: SPCK, 1981)—and many other sequels. The debate was not confined to the English-speaking world, as witness the publication of, *inter alia*, W. Pannenberg's *Jesus—God and Man* (London: SCM Press, 1968—originally in German, 1964); and E. Schillebeeckx's *Jesus—An Experiment in Christology* (New York: Seabury Press, 1979) and *Christ—The Experience of Jesus as Lord* (New York: Seabury Press, 1980).

21. Dunn, *Christology*, p. 265 (emphasis omitted).

22. Dunn, *Christology*, p. 265 (emphasis omitted).

23. D. Nineham, in *The Myth of God Incarnate*, pp. 202–203.

24. Henceforth in this article we shall, for brevity, use the term "Resurrection" to denote *both* the "Resurrection" *and* the "exaltation" of Jesus the Christ.

25. See C.F.D. Moule's evidence that the individual Jesus of history turned out, after the Resurrection, to be one who transcended individuality—an unconfined, unrestricted, inclusive personality, the universal "Christ" to all humanity—in his *The Phenomenon of the New Testament* (London: SCM Press, 1967), ch. II; and *The Origin of Christology*, ch. 2.

26. This hermeneutical question is posed by Leonard Hodgson in *For Faith and Freedom* (Oxford: Oxford University Press, 1956), p. x.

27. See the preceding essay in this volume. Also see J.C. Puddefoot, "Information and Creation," in C. Wassermann, R. Kirby and B. Rordoff, eds., *The Science and Theology of Information* (University of Geneva: Editions Labor et Fides, 1991), pp. 7–25.

28. *TSA*, ch. 9.

29. *TSA*, ch. 9, section 4, p. 179; ch. 11, sections 2(a), 3(b), and 3(c).

30. Dunn, *Christology*, p. 262 (emphasis omitted).

31. Macquarrie, *Jesus Christ*, pp. 43–44, 108.

32. Macquarrie, *Jesus Christ*, pp. 106–107 (verse numbers added).

33. John Bowker, *The Sense of God* (Oxford: Clarendon Press, 1973), p. 95.

34. John Bowker, *The Religious Imagination and the Sense of God* (Oxford: Clarendon Press, 1978), pp. 187–188.

35. *TSA*, Part II, esp. ch. 8.

36. *TSA*, ch. 3, section 3(a).

37. *TSA*, ch. 4, section 3(a), and ch. 8, section 1(g).

38. See John A.T. Robinson, *Exploration into God* (London: SCM Press, 1967), pp. 83, 97.

39. *TSA*, ch. 10, p. 187.

40. See Adrian Thatcher, *Truly a Person, Truly God* (London: SPCK, 1990), for a recent investigation emphasizing the centrality of the concept of the person for any adequate understanding of the Incarnation. See also his "Christian Theism and the Concept of a Person," in Arthur Peacocke and Grant Gillett eds., *Persons and Personality* (Oxford: Blackwell, 1987), pp. 180–190.

41. Robinson, *Exploration*, pp. 98–99 (numbers refer to the verses of John 1).

42. *TSA*, ch. 15.

43. Mark 15: 34.

44. *TSA*, ch. 8, section 2(c).

45. For a useful recent discussion, see Macquarrie, *Jesus Christ*, pp. 245–250.

46. Phil. 2: 6–11, and 2 Cor. 8: 9.

47. See Macquarrie, *Jesus Christ*, pp. 388–392; and J.D.G. Dunn, *Christology*, esp. pp. 114–121.

MOLECULAR BIOLOGY AND HUMAN FREEDOM

THE MOLECULAR BIOLOGY OF TRANSCENDING THE GENE

R. DAVID COLE

I. INTRODUCTION

The rapid growth of biological knowledge in the last four or five decades has given new form to an old question: Are we self-directed, or are we predestined? This is a major concern when considering the nature of human beings. Our society is being bombarded with volley after volley of new biological information which increasingly defines human beings structurally and functionally in physico-chemical terms, and the rate at which this occurs will mount dramatically as the human genome is deciphered. The self-perception of individuals as beings with meaningful control over their own personality and destiny may be overwhelmed by the dazzling success of reductionist biology in describing human components and their molecular interactions. An impression might well be created that our nature and behavior are predetermined by our genes because they depend on our genes in essential ways.

I intend to reflect on some biological matters to explore how people might recognize ways in which they transcend genetic determinism to develop their lives within a broad range of predetermined potentials. Although the notion of determinism has faded somewhat in the physics community, it appears quite vividly among biologists, whose scale of operation is still well above that of the quantum world. While typical biologists probably do not think of life in terms of absolute genetic determinism, they would think of a determinism that incorporates the interplay of "chance and necessity" to produce organisms that are determined completely by the particular chances and necessities they encounter.[1] In this sense, chance and necessity are seen mainly in the evolution of genes by chance mutations screened through natural selection to enhance necessary functions. This idea is mainly applied statistically to populations of organisms rather than to individual organisms. In any case, individual organisms are not viewed as having any choice of the libertarian sort in their own development. Their genetic endowments merely respond in a deterministic way to immediate circumstances, thus producing the totality of their characteristics, i.e., their phenotypes. The concern of some biologists for determinism is manifested in the search for genes specific to particular behavioral characteristics, such as violence, alcoholism, homosexuality, or altruism. A casual reading of some scholars might lead one to believe that the total elucidation of the DNA structure of the human genome will give a complete definition of the human being. While I suppose that nearly everyone would agree that a full definition would require more than a knowledge of the nucleotide sequence of the total complement of human DNA (that is, the genome), disagreement might arise over the level of life at which the genetic information is perceived to be insufficient (though necessary) in the explanation of the human, or other organism. Moreover, there will surely be disagreement about what degree of freedom any biological system has in exploiting its toolbox of genes as it crafts its life.

Let us begin by recalling how the information contained in the genome flows out to determine the phenotype of the organism. The first order of information in the chainlike molecule, DNA, is the sequence of nucleotide bases which is *replicated* when a cell divides to form two progeny cells. Most of the life of the cell is spent between cell divisions, and during this time the nucleotide sequence of DNA is *transcribed* into a corresponding nucleotide sequence by the synthesis of chainlike molecules called RNA. Subsequently, the information in the sequence of bases in RNA is *translated* into a corresponding sequence of amino acids in the chainlike molecules of proteins, which make up the work force of the cell. It is estimated that in the human there are about a hundred thousand kinds of proteins which are directly essential in determining the phenotype of the human, that is, all its biological characteristics. Generally, no protein is an island unto itself, but instead the functions of all the proteins must be coordinated with others. Therefore, the genetic information underlying the structure of each protein must not only determine a particular structure that can perform such feats as the catalysis of a specific chemical reaction, but also play an active role in the determination of patterns of potential, specific interactions among proteins and between proteins and other cellular components. The patterns of potential interactions are occasionally simple, but more often they are vast networks indirectly linking large numbers of chemical processes. In any case, this second order of information, which specifies patterns of interaction, is inherent in the sequence of bases in DNA, just as is the first order, which specifies the primary structure and function of individual proteins.

A third level of information lies in the capability of the patterns of interaction to be modulated by forces external to the cell and beyond direct control by the gene. The interdependence of the many processes within a vast array of interactions endows these patterns with exquisite adaptability, while stabilizing their essential integrity. It is at this level, then, that the (actual) expression of (potential) genetic information becomes contingent, and I would like to reflect on the nature of some of the contingencies. Three situations will be addressed: adaptation of cells; differentiation and development of higher organisms; and memory and learning.

II. ADAPTATION OF CELLS

To survive in a dynamic world, cells must be designed to adapt to a wide range of environmental conditions. Most cells in higher organisms are internalized and pro-tected from the outside world, so that the environments to which they have adapted are relatively constant and their adaptive processes are obscured. Cellular adaptation is more obvious with bacteria and animal cells cultured in vitro, where the cell surface is exposed to the culture medium. When the composition of the medium or the tempera-ture of the culture is changed, the cells respond with functional changes to be better suited to their new circumstances. Many of these changes are metabolic ones that do not require changes in gene expression, but much of the adaptation requires repression of some genes and activation of others. A gene is not repressed by destroying it, nor by changing its base sequence, but rather by blocking the transcription of its nucleotide code, the first step in the synthesis of the corresponding protein. The gene continues its existence structurally, but does not express itself functionally; because its structure remains intact, the repressed gene can be reactivated by removal of the block. The mechanisms for gene repression and activation are in many cases sensitive to physical and chemical forces inside and outside the cell. In bacterial cells, a newly induced pat-tern of gene expression can be reversed readily by return to initial conditions. With cultured animal cells, however, there can be long-term adaptation when many steps of adaptation (changes in patterns of repressed and activated genes) are induced serially. The patterns in long-term adaptation tend to persist for several generations of new cells after restoration of initial conditions.[2] The inertia of the long-term adapted state of cultured animal cells is presumably due to the highly cooperative interactions in net-works of biochemical processes. In this sense, adapted animal cells demonstrate a degree of independence from their genes even in heritability. Of course, the genes define the kinds of adaptations that can be actualized, so that there is a particular, limited array of possibilities.

A form of adaptation that can be seen in higher organisms is the subject of endocrinology, the study of hormones. Hormones are secreted from cells in one part of the body for transport to target cells elsewhere. Receptor proteins on the surface of the target cells bind hormones to trigger functional changes within the cells. The endocrine system thus allows the organism to adapt to changes in circumstances. Parts of the endocrine system respond to changes in mental state. A well-known example is the stress response, in which stress induces the secretion of adrenaline and glucocor-ticosteroids, which increase blood flow, redistribute the blood, and cause other physi-ological changes, many of which can be construed as preparing a person for physical battle. Another example of the interplay between the brain and endocrinology is the group of hormones called endorphins, which are induced by physical or emotional trauma. Endorphins are natural painkilling hormones that alter the function of brain cells and that have most of the effects of opiates. There are, in fact, multiple inter-secting pathways between the brain and many hormones. Of course, it is clear that the sequence of bases in the genome specifies all the ways the organism can respond to these signals and adapt to changing circumstances, and so that nucleotide sequence is a necessary part of the description of the organism. It is also clear that the base sequence is not a sufficient explanation. The genome predetermines all the potential states of being and behavior for the organism, but it does not predetermine the organism to any one particular state.

III. DIFFERENTIATION AND DEVELOPMENT IN HIGHER ORGANISMS

The development of a higher organism such as the human being can be viewed as a series of adaptations forced on the cells of a population that grows by repeated doubling of cell numbers, starting with the single-celled, fertilized egg.[3] When the egg divides into two cells, and then each of those divide to make a total of four cells, each of the progeny cells receives a complete copy of the parental DNA, and the cells are identical in all observable characteristics (phenotype). After the first few divisions, however, cells are produced that differ in phenotype, even though all the cells continue to have identical complements of DNA. This process of differentiation thus generates different patterns of gene expression without changing the information stored in the nucleotide sequence of the DNA. Distinct populations of cells continue to arise, diverging in phenotype as development continues. When a human attains its adult form, the differentiation of its cells into many cell types will have resulted in different tissues and organs, for example, brain and lungs, each with distinct structure and function. It should be reemphasized that every cell contains the same genetic information, and that differentiation means the generation of different patterns of expression and repression of the genes. The majority of the hundred thousand or so genes in any human cell is repressed, with a different small subset of genes expressed in one cell type as compared to the subset expressed in another cell type. The combination of genes expressed in the brain is the basis for the structure and function of that organ, while the combination expressed in the lung enables the functions appropriate to that organ.

The mechanisms behind differentiation and development are not well understood, and their study is one of the most active in biological research today. It is generally agreed, however, that the differences arising in phenotype between progeny of a given cell generation are dependent on the location of the cells in different microenvironments.[4] The particular location of a cell within a colony of cells may fix it in an environment unlike the surroundings of another cell in the colony, and the two cells may adapt their phenotypes to their differing circumstances. In a colony of cells, the cells communicate with each other by physical contact and by the diffusion of chemicals from one to the other. During differentiation and development cells are adapting to a succession of environmental changes produced by changes in their neighboring cells and extracellular fluids. In the adaptation, the microenvironment dictates to the genetic system which genes will be expressed and which will be repressed. Each successive adaptation is superimposed on its predecessor, so that a terminally differentiated cell (for instance, in the adult) manifests the entire history of its cell line, and not merely its immediate state. Moreover, differentiation is essentially irreversible in animals, except in special cases such as cancer, where a very partial dedifferentiation occurs. This irreversibility may echo the long-term adaptation observed in animal cells cultured in vitro and, again, it may reflect the extremely high order of cooperativity in the vast networks of interactions of cellular processes.[5] In any case, the irreversibility means that the creature designed by the DNA has come to control the expression of its designer.

Is it fair to say that the creature escaped the predetermination decreed by the genetic information? In the absolute sense, an affirmative answer can be given, but it must be kept in mind that the entire system of genes was itself designed to permit and exploit the process of differentiation. Nonetheless, genetic predetermination is contingent—contingent on the normalcy of conditions during development. In abnormal situations, different adaptations result. For example, prenatal effects of teratogens and physical trauma can lead to birth defects. Thus, as the author of our biological destiny, DNA has been reduced to the role of coauthor, even if it might be the senior author.

IV. MEMORY AND LEARNING

One of the most active fronts in the advance of biological research these days is concerned with the operations of the brain. The functions of the brain are very numerous, of course, as it processes information regarding the senses, language, motor control, object shape and motion, and so on. I wish to focus on memory and learning. I am attracted to memory and learning because current observations and postulates suggest analogies with the kind of long-term cell adaptation we have just discussed, including a role for non-genetic factors, perhaps even a role for choices, as coauthors with DNA in the development of our personhood.[6]

A major kind of cell in the brain is the neuron, which possesses numerous long, thin extensions called neurites, and a thicker extension termed the axon. Every neuron is connected to many others by their neurites, and thus a vast network of interconnected cells is constructed. Each neuron receives, conducts, and transmits signals, passing signals from its axon to the neurite of another neuron. The junction at which the axon and the neurite intersect is called a synapse. Signal transmission across the intercellular gap in the synapse is accomplished by the release of chemicals called neurotransmitters from vesicles in the axon, the diffusion of the neurotransmitter across the gap, followed by its binding to receptors in the membrane of the neurite. The interaction of the neurotransmitter with the receptor activates ion conducting channels, altering the ion balance between the inside and the outside of the membrane of the neurite near the receptor. The modification of the first ion channels to be affected effects modification in their neighbors, and once the neighbors are modified, they cause the modification of the next neighbors in line, and so forth down the length of the neuron, so that a wave of ionic shifts is propagated along the neuron until the wave activates the neurotransmitter-containing vesicles at a synapse in the axon, and a signal is passed to a neurite in the next neuron. The signal thus transmitted is an electrical impulse, and the synapse is said to "fire" when transmission occurs there. It has been estimated that there are 10^{10} neurons in the human brain, and about 10^4 synapses per neuron. It is generally believed that memory and learning are achieved by functional and morphological changes in the networks of the synapses. An image or thought has been postulated to be the consolidation or coordination of synaptic firings from separate areas of the brain.[7] For example, in order for an image to be interpreted, the coordination may require the synaptic firings to be rhythmic, with particular frequencies, and to be in phase.

The neuronal networks with their vast arrays of synapses constitute the "hardwiring" of brain circuitry. Of course, there is genetic predetermination of the design of these circuits, as there is in all structures of the body, but our recognition that learning occurs reveals that there must be more to the story. Much current research is adducing evidence that, following the initial wiring of the brain, new synapses form so that new circuits intercalate among the existing ones. Experiments with mice have shown clearly that as brain development continues after birth, there is the addition of new, complex, neural circuits; presumably a similar process happens with the human, whose brain increases fourfold in weight between birth and maturity. Furthermore, rodents reared in complex and stimulating conditions have more synapses and neurites than control animals raised in simpler circumstances. A seminal observation in this aspect of neurobiology was that covering one eye in young, developing animals prevented the orderly organization of neurites and synapses that normally occurs between retinal neurons and their target brain cells.[8] In the case of the neurons for the eye that was not covered, normal organization took place during development. Combining these last two observations, we may infer that neuronal activity induces organization of synapses, and that changes in the structure of the neuronal network are associated with learning.

For some time, memory has been considered to include two systems, short-term memory and long-term memory. There is great activity currently in searching out mechanisms of short-term and long-term modifications of the neuronal system at various levels. Most studies on short-term memory are focused on the chemical modification of preformed enzymes, the proteins responsible for driving the many chemical reactions required for neuron function. Mechanisms for long-term structural changes are looked for in the modulation of protein synthesis, and there is recent evidence that the modulation of protein synthesis occurs by altering the pattern of gene expression.[9] That protein synthesis is involved was demonstrated when it was shown that the administration of inhibitors of protein synthesis in animals undergoing learning tests impaired their long-term memory. In addition to this, some very recent reports have indicated that electrical or pharmacological stimulation of nerve cells activates genes for certain transcription factors that direct the synthesis of the RNA which applies the genetic information to the protein synthesis machinery. Some of these genes, transcribed in response to neuronal activity, are the same as those concerned with differentiation and development in the brain.[10] This association lends some support to the postulate that learning mechanisms are similar to the somewhat better understood mechanisms of early development in the brain. The learning process seems to be specifying the formation of our intellectual apparatus beyond the particulars determined by our genes, though within the range predetermined by them.

V. SYNERGY AMONG GENES, CIRCUMSTANCES, AND THE SELF

I have tried to sketch in broad terms some of the major ways in which our genome determines who we are. We must stand in humility before the genome, recognizing how much of our heritage is derived from it—how much potential it gives us, and how rigidly it sets boundaries on our range of potentials. The boundaries that the genes set on our range of potentials might not be pleasing, but we do not have the power to change them. We might prefer to be taller in order to play better basketball, or to have bigger brains in order to store more megabytes of information, but we are forced to accept what our genetic endowment allows—no more. Moreover, our genes and the differentiated patterns of their expression and repression may well be more determinant than most of us had suspected. Probably as the picture of the human genome is drawn in finer and finer detail, we shall be amazed and sometimes annoyed to find that our nature and behavior are much more an expression of our genes than we would like. Nevertheless, as awed as we ought to be by the powerful effects of our genome in determining our personhood, it would be a mistake to perceive ourselves only as embodiments of genetic information. At the very least it is clear that we each have a unique personhood as an accumulation of one particular set of long-term adaptations, which imposes a specific pattern of gene expression and repression on the genome. That unique history written in each of us is a significant value in our personhood, though in large part it expresses our ancestry and the environment into which we were born, and over which we had little control. That ancestry and much of that history of circumstances could be viewed as "givens"—given by God.

While developing a picture of our predetermination by genes, I also tried to show that it was a range of potentials that was determined, and that there is an area of freedom within the boundaries set by our genomes. Within that area, we have some control over our destiny. A common and simple example is that we can exercise our bodies to build muscle and maintain good circulation, or we can choose a sedentary mode of life, with the resultant phenotype. We can choose to control weight through diet, or indulge our appetites at the expense of buying larger and larger clothes. Even with exercise and dieting, however, we cannot shape our bodies just anyway we please—our genome sets limits. Perhaps a more attractive example for most of us (pudgy) academics is that we can choose to teach our brains or not. It is gratifying to see a good example of intellectual discipline and its productivity, but it is plain that some intellects have great potential, while others are limited in productivity, regardless of discipline. As in the parable of the talents,[11] our genomes predetermine us with greater or lesser intellectual talents, but we have the responsibility for optimizing our minds within the range of potentials set by our genes. I tried to show earlier how that might be pictured mechanistically according to current biological ideas.

The notion that we can play an active role in the process of becoming who we are does not in itself require the action of such aspects of the human spirit as libertarian free will. Earlier it was pointed out how genetically based systems of cells develop and differentiate by a series of adaptations into a creature that exerts control over its creator, DNA; that process was not an exercise of free will. Nevertheless, it is intriguing to note how free will could synergize with genetic systems to maximize some potentialities and minimize others. Furthermore, synergy between the human mind and the genetic systems of the brain is more clearly seen, perhaps, in the learning process. In self transcendence the differentiated pattern of gene expression in brain and body would be the substrate on which the human spirit continually acts, affecting all subsequent action by modifying the substrate. Although relative magnitudes and priorities might be argued for body and spirit, focus on their respective autonomies or their arrangement in hierarchy leaves in the shadow a profound quality of the body-spirit relationship—creative synergy. Our personhood emerges from the multidimensional interplay of our genes and our history of circumstances, along with the present and past motivations of our spirit. Therefore, no matter how great the magnitude of genetic determinism, our sense of responsibility for who we are need not be overwhelmed. Indeed, the incorporation of our personal history into the fabric of our brains enhances the significance of a life of discipleship to whatever Lord/lord we serve.

NOTES

1. J. Monod, *Chance and Necessity* (London: Fontana Press, 1974).

2. H. Rubin, *American Journal of Physiology* 258 (1990), Lung & Cell Molecular Physiology 2, pp. L19–L24.

3. J.B. Gurdon, *Cell* 68 (1992), pp. 185–199.

4. I. Greenwald and G. M. Rubin, *Cell* 68 (1992), pp. 271–281.

5. H. Rubin, *American Journal of Physiology* 258 (1990), Lung & Cell Molecular Physiology 2, pp. L19–L24.

6. K.J. Skinner, *Chemical & Engineering News* 69 (1991), pp. 24–41.

7. S. R. Lockery and W. B. J. Kristan, *Journal of Neuroscience* 10 (1990), pp. 1811–1815; P. A. Getting, *Annual Review of Neuroscience* 12 (1989), pp. 184–204.

8. D.H. Hubel & T.N. Wiesel, *Journal of Neurophysiology* 28 (1965), p. 1041.

9. M. Sheng & M.E. Greenberg, *Neuron* 4 (1990), pp. 477–485.

10. C. J. Schatz, *Neuron* 5 (1990), pp. 745–756.

11. Matthew 25: 14–30.

THE THEOLOGY OF HUMAN AGENCY AND THE NEUROBIOLOGY OF LEARNING

W. MARK RICHARDSON

I. INTRODUCTION

Human free will has been a dominant theme in theological anthropology since the inception of Christianity. It is deeply embedded in biblical theism, with its stress on divine-human relations and moral community under God's sovereignty. Early Church Fathers, such as Origen, Irenaeus, Nemesius of Emesa, Augustine, and Gregory of Nyssa saw free will as an essential aspect of the dignity imputed to human beings by God, and as key to the articulation of several doctrinal themes. The picture of human agency in scripture is neither uniform nor systematic; Christian reflection not only has shaped, but has been shaped by, the philosophical frameworks of its host cultures.[1] Nevertheless, there are strong resemblances throughout times and cultures in Christian theistic conceptions of human agency.

In spite of the multiformity of theological reflection on free will, my assumption in this essay is that Christian theism today, even of a rather generic, noncontroversial sort, has a recognizable core understanding of human agency, and this core is inalienably wedded to what is frequently called commonsense psychology. Commonsense psychology (CSP) is the view that our ordinary understanding of human capacities of perception, rationality, intentionality, free will, and so forth, is essentially accurate and not basically deceptive about the reality of mind itself; that these capacities are necessary conditions of personal identity; and that they determine within limits the nature and course of human action. CSP fully recognizes the status of first person experience reports that arise from these phenomena. Since this experiential level cannot be exhaustively rendered in third person reports (for instance, the neuroscientific explanation of perception does not fully capture the "experience of seeing"), to rely strictly on the external level would compromise essential aspects of our self-understanding.

In contemporary philosophy, the theme of free will appears under other terms in investigations of complex human capacities, such as choiceful and intentional action in the face of alernative possibilities, discriminating value in one's environment, pursuing enduring purposes in the context of dynamic and changing circumstances, and holding multiple beliefs and desires in consciousness for the sake of deliberation. Much of this philosophical discussion of mind and agency is helpful in mediating the relation between the theological picture of free will and basic research programs in scientific fields such as neurobiology. However, on my assumption of a connection between a Christian theistic view of human agency and CSP, the theistic perspective is more congenial with some current theories of mind and agency than others. This implies that some classes of philosophy of mind today are *not* consonant with the commitments of Christian theism, as I understand them.

It is not within the scope of this paper to argue directly against such antagonistic philosophies, let alone to demonstrate that one philosophy of mind is better than its competitors. Rather, starting from a theological perspective, I wish to show that one theory of mind in particular—emergence—is consonant with the commitments of Christian theism (divine and human agents in relationship, and the moral and salvific aspects of this relationship), and that it also meets the conditions of intelligibility set forth in R. David Cole's essay on neurobiological learning theory. Emergence compromises neither theological nor neurobiological requirements for an adequate account of human agency, and appears to be a good philosophical candidate for mediating constructive links between theology and neurobiology.

In outline, then, I begin with certain core theological beliefs, then show that this core presupposes a commitment to CSP. Then I describe an emergent theory of mind, and show how it adequately accounts for the full force of the meaning of CSP concepts, whereas some of its competitors predict the demise of CSP. I then turn to Cole's essay on learning theory in neurobiology to see how an emergent theory of mind and agency might comprehend the general neurobiological picture that Cole presents. I conclude the essay with examples of ways that emergence is a helpful mediating link in making informative connections between neurobiology and theological constructions.

II. CORE THEOLOGICAL BELIEFS

There are differences from one community to the next about what constitutes Christian belief as it pertains to human agency, but I propose to focus on noncontroversial, broadly held Christian beliefs as uttered, prayed, and practiced. The aim is then, to detect the assumptions regarding human agency and free will underlying these core beliefs.

In Christian theology, the understanding of free will derives from the core belief that God (referred to in personal language) desires relationship with God's creatures. God's relationship with human beings is spoken of in varied terms, such as lordship, fellowship, communion, and using such models as kingdom, family, and friendship. It is dependent upon God's initiative, but awaits human consent, as it must be reciprocal to be enjoyed. The divine-human relationship is a moral relationship, involving promises, obligations, and goods to be pursued. The goal of discipleship based on the life and teaching of Jesus, and the meaning of his suffering and death, makes this moral dimension obvious.

God's will is made known in and through finite effects in the world, some of which carry special signficance for human destiny. Human response to God is realized through worship, and through moral action in the world. Since other human beings are believed to have infinite worth to God, to love and act justly toward them is to love and honor God. Likewise, to live in right relations with the world of other created things, living and nonliving, is to praise and honor God as source of all that is.

A further claim of personal theists is that divine relations with individual persons and with corporate humanity are in process: they develop, mature, and have a destiny. This destiny is sometimes characterized in terms of a future state in which God's presence is directly experienced, God's will is transparent, and the interaction between God and humanity explicitly embodies the fullness and diversity of divine love. With regard to free will, participating in this destiny is sometimes thought to be highly dependent upon the choice of our relations to God and God's community. Alternatively, in this ultimate destiny as Christian theists conceive it, God's goodness may be irresistible, placing a limitation on human freedom to choose or reject it. However, even in such an ultimate state, there might still be choices among an indefinite number of ways of *how* to enjoy the good that constitutes it, so that free will is not necessarily ruled out by encompassing divine love.

In the mainstream of Christian theism the above relational picture rests on the notion of the universe and its constituents as creation, and God as creator. Human existence essentially involves both the tension between creaturely finitude and limitation, and the power of self-determination within boundaries. This condition is thought to give rise to the possibility, and reality, of sin—the bias of the will that indicates, and further shapes, a path of alienation from God. Sin is located in the human response to finitude, not finitude itself. In response to sin, Christian theology affirms that the human agent is able to undergo a transformation and reorientation of character and destiny through faith in divine assistance of forgiveness and healing. For the baptized in a Christian community, through a life of prayer, worship, and guidance by God's spirit, the reoriented person is sustained and made whole.

Finally, social relationships are intrinsic to personal existence. The central metaphors of Christian biblical texts—ecclesia, body of Christ, kingdom of God, household of God—convey the social aspect of human agency. In effect, the person is definable only in the context of community-shaping factors.

In summary, therefore, Christian theism conceives of persons primarily as agents. It is an outlook of "doing" wherein, as Edward West states, "love, the chief virtue, is characterized as action taken as a result of conviction."[2] This practical bearing means also that the chief religious concern is embodied in the question: What must I do in response to God? and not the question, "How closely does God correspond to my (our) idea of God?" The model for the Christian, in answer to these questions, is the humanity of Jesus, whose consent to the will of God was complete, and whose life of self-giving actions was the form of this consent.

III. AGENCY CONCEPTS IMPLICIT IN THE THEOLOGICAL PICTURE

Now that we have a generic picture of Christian theism's core assumptions, insofar as its picture of agency is concerned, we must consider the basic philosophical commitments implicit in these assumptions. This will involve a discussion of the theist's presupposition of so-called *commonsense psychology*.

The finitude and conditioning of human freedom is derivable from countless sources but is clearly consistent with, indeed implicit in, the notion of creation in Christian theism. The classical biblical statement of this is found in the creation story: " . . . then the Lord God formed man from the dust of the ground, and breathed into his nostrils the breath of life; and the man became a living being."[3] This compressed portrait of human origins captures the complexity of the human condition, born of the material of the universe and having God's spirit or breath within. A serious grasp of finitude recognizes that human agency is constrained in rather formidable ways, including inherited biological characteristics; the natural and historical environment of one's life; the history of past actions that constitute one's preintentional cognitive, affective, and emotive background; and the influence of sociolinguistic features of human existence on the motivational structure of action. It is most likely that closer examination of the human being as biological organism will disclose even stricter constraints.

Nevertheless, the claim remains that human agency is *not determined*, but *conditioned*, by these forces. As John Macquarrie states, "Man's unique status in nature arises from the fact that in him the evolutionary process has for the first time become transparent to itself and capable to some extent of self-direction."[4] The theistic picture of the human person depends essentially on an emerging intentionality and unity of consciousness in the human agent as a whole. Unless the human agent exercises *some* degree of conscious self-determination over those things that condition his or her existence, then the picture we have of the human person would be radically altered, and Christian theism no longer recognizable.

What are some of the features of this self-determination that arises within the constraints of finite existence? One implication of the theology of divine and human agents in relationship is the reality of *personal unity* in finite creatures. This is far from being too obvious to mention, especially in view of the skeptical philosophical tradition emerging in the modern era from David Hume, continuing through the positivisms of the nineteenth and twentieth centuries, to the eliminative materialist philosophers of mind in the present. In spite of this skeptical tradition, personal unity can still be spoken of in terms of the human capacity to form *purposes*, the pursuits of which are character-shaping and constitutive of identity. Purposive action consists in the capacity to make valuations of other persons, things, and states of affairs in the world with which the agent interacts. These valuations form stable and enduring "goods," on the basis of which the agent makes choices among open alternatives.

However, since the outer environment and the inner biological context of agency are in constant flux, the pursuit of purposes requires the additional capacity of inventiveness or *novelty*. Human agents are able to discriminate meaning in the midst of an enormous range of factors and dynamic interactions that shape experience, and to act imaginatively (to adapt, adjust, revise) in order to pursue a long range purpose. Connecting novelty to the notion of purpose is what distinguishes novelty from capriciousness in behavior. Creativity in complex and changing conditions is what I mean by the capacity for novelty, and it is key to constancy of character.

We mentioned above that the personal theism of Christianity is a moral relationship because it is essentially human responsiveness to God's will. The tradition has supposed that the minimal condition of such moral agency is the capacity to *choose courses of action among open alternatives*, which, for the Christian theist, is the choice to consent to the will of God. Thus, we must speak of alternatives that are *bounded*, but also *open*, for there is an element of creativity involved in responding to God's will. This so-called "freedom of indifference" is meant to capture the intuition that human agents experience themselves as *acting* in the face of options, based on discriminations of meaning that are expressed in the *intentions* that represent the action. It also picks up the human experience of deliberating between alternative sets of beliefs and desires and, in a self-reflexive process, of judging and criticizing one's own judgments. Thus "freedom of indifference" is a necessary condition of moral agency, even if it is not the most robust claim to be made about free will, and it highlights a self-supervisory aspect of agency.

This touches on what Harry Frankfurt believes to be distinctly human about the will, namely, the ability to form "second order desires." Says Frankfurt:

> Besides wanting and choosing and being moved to do this or that, men may also want to have (or not to have) certain desires and motives. They are capable of wanting to be different in their preferences and purposes from what they are. . . . No animal other than man appears to have the capacity for reflective self-evaluation that is manifested in the formation of second-order desires.[5]

Frankfurt further refines this notion by asserting that an agent may not only want to have a certain desire, but also want the certain desire to be his or her will (the basis of action). He calls this "second order volition," and regards it as essential to free will and unique to human persons.

Frankfurt's philosophical point about second order desires and volitions seems to be fully consonant with the high view of human agency implied in the New Testament accounts of sin and the possibility of repentance and conversion. The reorientation or reprioritizing of the human will implicit in conversion suggests the ability *not only to make valuations* about oneself, other persons, things, and states of affairs, but also *to change these valuations*. This kind of personal resilience and flexibility is thought by Frankfurt to be quintessentially human.

It is also clear that the social aspect of human existence has deep implications for our understanding of agency and free will. The social reality of mind is a function of human linguistic capacities. The meaning imputed to an individual's behavior by the social context becomes part of the agent's own self-understanding, and shapes his or her future activity. It is also part of the background of action. It makes action intelligible in the context of one set of social conventions when it might not be so in another. Symbols convey the meaning that the social context imputes to our actions. In short, intentional action is shaped largely by a network of socially constructed meanings, which makes the social context an essential, constitutive factor in human identity.

In the various ways discussed in this section, therefore, the core beliefs of Christian theology make decisive theoretical commitments in the philosophy of mind and agency. These commitments are of a commonsense kind, and I shall treat them collectively as a partial definition of CSP. The outlook of Christian theism, with its conditioned yet free agents responding to a good ultimately named in personal terms, rests on the soundness of our basic intuitions about moral-intellectual capacities as conceptualized in CSP.

IV. EMERGENT THEORY AND PHILOSOPHIES OF MIND

CSP as described above is not a theory of mind; its concepts are based largely in first-person accounts of the experience of perception, representation, intention, and so on. In many quarters of present day philosophy of mind, this CSP perspective has received rather rough treatment. I believe this is due largely to the fact that the field is dominated by a monistic vision of the mind-brain relationship, coupled with a physicalistic ontology.

The broad class of theories of mind named eliminative materialism best exemplifies the antagonistic relation between CSP and current work in the field. Daniel Dennett and Patricia Churchland are prominent representatives of this position.[6] The eliminativists treat the whole network of mental concepts in ordinary language (CSP), including those discussed in the previous section, as naïve and unsophisticated *theory*, which must stand up to empirical testing and compete with other theories based more explicitly in scientific psychology. Churchland and Dennett view CSP as an acquired framework, and not protected from criticism by virtue of its basis in direct experience and introspection. First-person experiences of conscious states can, in fact, be quite misleading.

The eliminative materialist view adds that "folk psychology theory" (as they call CSP) is basically an antiquated picture of the mind held only by those who do not know enough neuroscience to get rid of it. They conjecture that a richer, more comprehensive theory of mind-brain based in neuroscientific categories will replace it. The kind of reduction eliminativists predict involves a radically new taxonomy of concepts or, as Churchland calls it, a new "categorial profile."[7] The basic idea is this: experimental psychology, which has until recently adopted the conceptual framework of folk psychology, will begin to coevolve with the neurosciences. In this symbiotic relation a gradual shift is predicted toward a more "scientific" conceptuality in psychology, causing our picture of human beings to be so altered that our present self-understanding will be unrecognizable. It is *the experimental psychology that will reduce to neurobiology, whereas folk psychology will not so much be reduced as eliminated*. Eliminativists believe that the correctness of this contention is an empirical issue that can be settled only by the success or failure of their program.

It is clear that this theory rests on a promissory note: an as-yet-incomplete neuroscience capable of explaining the phenomena of human representation and intentional action. However, by way of general evaluation, it would seem puzzling if a theologian were to accept the premises of this research program: that our ordinary view of ourselves (as rational, intentional beings who make valuations, discriminations, and choices, and form purposes) will someday be recast in forms that may render some of our most immediate and intuitive assumptions about conscious experience illusory. Given the relation between theological claims and philosophical implications that I have developed, acceptance of the eliminativist prediction would eviscerate our present network of theological beliefs.

It seems obvious that the theologian will find a more compatible relation with research programs other than eliminativism and its fully materialistic cousins. Yet it may also be the case that the theologian need not look outside the monistic framework to find theories congenial to CSP as described above. Monism is consistent with the idea that the created universe of matter-energy is capable over time, and with the proper influences, of producing forms of life in which the capacities for mentality, consciousness, and agency emerge. That is, a Christian understanding of creation as the continuous immanent action of God in the world is compatible with the view that mental capacities exist by virtue of the evolution of physical structures and processes of great complexity that make them possible. Most important is that the *belief in divine creation*, combined with *trust in the reality and efficacy of self-conscious experience*, makes some kind of monistic theories not only tolerable but advantageous to the theistic picture I have presented. In particular, there is a class of theories—*emergentism*—that shows a commitment both to the causal efficacy of the mental *and* to the natural basis of consciousness.[8]

Theories of emergence hold that capacities we call mental, found in sufficiently evolved biological systems, are effective forces that constrain underlying physical substrates without violating the lawlike processes at the physical level. These are nonreductive theories, in that they uphold a causal-explanatory role for intentional properties, while maintaining pressure to link these phenomena to bottom-up neurobiological processes. Stanford philosopher Fred Dretske, who takes a nonreductive stance toward mental properties, states bluntly that we speak of "believing this or desiring that" not as a heuristic device for predicting behavior, nor as a cover for our profound ignorance of the connections between neurobiology and behavior. Rather,

What we have to show is that what we think and know, what we desire and intend, the content of our psychological states and attitudes . . . [all of this] is actually the property of our
internal states that explains their distinctive causal efficacy, their effects on behavior.9

One emergent theorist, Arthur Peacocke, attempts to link emergence in mind-brain
theory to the larger picture of levels of complexity in nature. In an impressive overview
of theories in a number of sciences, he traces the continuities and discontinuities that
emerge through the evolutionary processes built into the universe. He offers an
intriguing map of the hierarchy of scientific and humanistic disciplines, each representing its respective methods which apply to its respective level of complexity of form
in matter-energy, and each representing a level of conceptual network and of explanation. The map illustrates continuities and novelties between levels in the natural world
and propensities toward complexity and higher levels of organization which cannot be
understood in terms of the principles at lower levels.

Peacocke cites Prigogine's work on the behavior of systems—the idea of "order
through fluctuation"—as potentially useful for explaining a number of natural phenomena that still puzzle us. It is a key factor in the emergence of new levels of complexity in matter-energy, the capacity of nature to bring into being "new forms entirely
by the operation of forces and manifestations of properties we already understand."10
According to Peacocke, this may be especially important when it comes to understanding the emergence and effectiveness of consciousness in human brains.

If the brain turns out to be analogous to a nonlinear, complex, dynamic system
then, as Peacocke asserts,

. . . we may have the physical correlate of the experience of consciousness, and so the
warrant for giving a "causal" account in mentalistic terms of successions of what we experience as mental states, including the operations of "free will."11

Mentality, according to this view, represents a "new regime" in states of the human
brain-as-a-whole. And this state of the brain-as-a-whole acts as a constraint on what
happens at the more specific level of the individual, constituent neurons. What happens at the lower level is "caused" by the state of the whole.

This top-down causation idea is highly significant for discussion of the mind-brain
relation. If this view were to hold, it would mean that, hypothetically, if we were to
reach a complete and accurate theory of neuroscience, it would corroborate (on the level
of processes and structures of the brain) the existence and effective force of the basic
mental features we refer to in ordinary language. Neurosciences (including observational reports and extentional explanations) would not replace or double for the mental, but,
would reveal and explain the processes and structures of the neural substrates that support the referents of mental terms we commonly use. In this sense, brain states could be
regarded as "aspects of the total action that expresses the intention of the agent."12

Peacocke's emergent vision of agency has critics, among both those who reject the causal effectiveness of the mental, and those who note that the problem of physical determinism still lingers in this approach. Among the latter, one complaint about the kind of picture Peacocke presents is that the physical paradigm for emergence is still a deterministic one. The new levels of order come about via a process of fluctuating states that are epistemically unpredictable. However, since the systems in principle do have precise initial conditions, and conform to deterministic laws, there is no real openness. This raises the question of whether or not free will rests on the "real" indeterministic openness of the future.[13]

Even if one answered affirmatively, and turned to implications drawn from quantum indeterminacy for support, there are problems of a different kind to be negotiated. We may believe that randomness or chance in the universe—in particular at microlevels of brain states—is somehow a condition of free decisive actions. Yet critical reflection will show that there is no clear or immediate connection between quantum effects in microstates of the brain, and intentional actions. Even if we skip the mediating details and go with the hunch that randomness is key to securing the notion of unpredictability of choice, it is contrary to another intuition, which is that free agents are *responsible* choosers. Moreover, randomness fits poorly with our understanding of the relation of free choice to the agent's history. Indeed, explanations of the giving-reasons variety usually include appeal to the agent's background of intentional actions, beliefs, and desires. In short, although I side with the view that a causally open universe is relevant to free will, the relation between randomness at the quantum level and free will is far from obvious.

In spite of this significant problem, it would appear that, at present, an emergent theory of mind-brain represents a live option as a research program, and one that is congenial with the beliefs and assumptions of the Christian theist. It indeed may be the best philosophical option for the Christian theist who wishes to find connections with the neurosciences.

With this conclusion, we now can turn to Cole's discussion of contemporary molecular biology. Cole is offering not a theory, but biological evidence that suggests certain generalizations, which he states clearly. The picture he presents can be interpreted variously, depending on one's metaphysical vision and philosophical commitments. Thus it is permissible—and the conclusion I have drawn about the fit of Christian theism with an emergent perspective means that it is also important—to place Cole's presentation of neurobiological learning theory within the framework of emergence in order to interpret it for our theological purposes.

V. BIOLOGY AND HUMAN AGENCY: COLE'S BIOLOGY OF PREDESTINATION

It is by no means easy to tackle the complex philosophical problem of relating the CSP presupposed by theology to the physiological and chemical substrate of all mental phenomena (the brain). The conceptual distance between "beliefs," "desires," "intentions," and "purposes," on the one hand, and "dendrites," "axons," "synapses," and "neural networks," on the other hand, is vast indeed. In fact, the two conceptual levels can not be related directly, even if we assume an immediate relation between mental states and the brain.[14]

Yet, as British philosophical theologian Austin Farrer has noted, there is a difference between looking for science to explain the mental in physical terms, complete with lawlike relations, and looking for science to make advances that help us understand how the brain's structures and processes make possible the higher functions of mind. This distinction can keep the philosopher from slipping into either reductionism, at one extreme, or complete linguistic dualism, on the other extreme.

With this caution in mind, this section is a distillation of the fundamental features of Cole's essay with the goal of finding coherent connections between neurobiology and other disciplines through the vehicle of emergent theory. If emergent theory, which we have adopted so far, can adequately interpret the conditions set forth in Cole's account of learning in neurobiology, then it may serve to mediate informative relations between neuroscientific evidence and theological constructions.

Cole's essay sets up the possibility for such interdisciplinary discussion on the topic of agency. He develops the theme of contingency and flexibility within determined boundaries in a general discussion of certain aspects of molecular biology. He also ventures outside his field to confront anew some perennial questions about human identity and agency based on developments in biology in recent years. He succeeds where few do in stating some of the key developments in his own science in clear but accurate terms for the nonspecialist. Of course, Cole is not attempting to establish univocal relations between biological statements and free will. His overview is for the most part well-informed analogies, perhaps prefigurations, of relations we might expect to obtain at the highest levels of brain organization, that would correlate with what we experience as freedom. He offers themes and patterns internal to biology which are illuminative because of their similarity to themes and patterns internal to our common sense psychology.

Cole treats three topics: the adaptation of cells, cellular differentiation and development in higher organisms, and memory and learning in neurobiological theory. In each case, we find inherited physical determinants (genetic code) realized in a biological system. The determinants set bounds on a range of potentials within which a number of contingent factors contribute to particular outcomes.

First, with regard to the basic idea of cell adaptation, Cole notes that cells have a fixed range of behavior-potential, but that *actual* functional expression of a given cell is dependent on adaptations to disturbances in the macro- and micro-environments of the cell, realized in molecular or chemical changes.

Second, Cole finds cell adaptation analogous to cell differentiation in higher organisms. The genetic code of each individual organism determines the range of cell functions and cell structures that are possible; however, factors in the micro-environment (for example, the placement of each cell in relation to the overall structure of a population of cells) play a crucial role in the actual structural and functional expression of each cell. So, whereas the information (one might loosely regard this as its potential) in each cell is the same, the actual functional and structural expression of each cell is dependent, again, on environmental factors.

Third, with regard to neurobiological learning theory—in which the relationship between biology and free will is most direct—each individual's genome determines the coded information that gets actualized in the kinds and numbers of neuronal cells and their connections in the early stages of life. This constitutes the inherited boundaries of potential for that individual's life. However, the brain is enormously complex and flexible, with a large number of feedback systems that modulate microenvironments. These modulations, combined with stimulations of particular kinds from the external environment, affect the quantity and kinds of neural networks that develop—again, within a range determined by the genome.

Learning theory, as Cole presents it, is not merely about how environmental contingencies lead to specific brain structures within a range of genetically determined possibilities. It also tells a fascinating story about how the direction of our attention *now* affects the destiny of our personhood *later*, shaping us in certain ways and not others. The brain grows (literally forming new neurites and neuronal connections) by virtue of (1) genetic predisposition, (2) environmental contingencies, and (3) the enigmatic element that Cole calls the human spirit (which the philosopher might call intentional action, and we might call "free will"). New growth, in turn, affects future potentials, and therefore the patterns and tendencies in the individual's behavior.

We might diagram the various " . . . changes in the structure of the neuronal network [that] are associated with learning"[15] in figure 1:

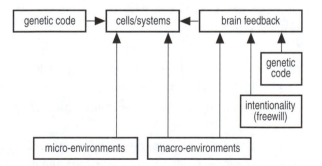

Figure 1: Influences on an Organism's Behavior

VI. INTERPRETING THE BIOLOGICAL PICTURE USING THEORY OF MIND

Cole's presentation of the restricting genetic determinants of human agency should have a properly sobering effect on philosophical and theological reflection. Nevertheless, his own account holds out for the influence of conscious, intentional action in human experience: "our genomes predetermine us with greater or lesser intellectual talents, but we have the *responsibility* for optimizing our minds within the range of potentials set by our genes."[16]

The eliminative theorists of mind, mentioned above, would be inclined to say that we ought to drop "intentionality" or "human spirit" from Cole's picture for the time being, and stick entirely with things we can empirically get our hands on. In other words, stick with neurobiological entities, and capacities such as plasticity toward which they point. What we will most likely discover, they conjecture, is that the cause of neural developments in particular directions bears little or no resemblance to personal descriptions in terms of *intentions, choices,* or *purposes.*

Emergent theorists, however, have a double strategy for explanation. On the one hand, they assume that we must credit mental experiences (perceiving, believing, knowing, doing) with the full force of what we experience them to be, and then seek to understand the physiological processes capable of giving rise to the richness of conscious life. On the other hand, they try to discern how the simpler physical properties, processes, and structures influence, and are influenced by, higher levels of organization in matter-energy.

The conjecture of the emergent theorist is that if, hypothetically, we were to have a complete theory of the brain, whereby we understood the causal connections at every level, *it would in principle still be no more valid to say that our choices were caused by certain brain events, than to say that our conscious intentions (realized in certain macro-structural levels of the brain) caused certain neural events to happen.* This conclusion seems to be supported by Cole when he says:

> In self-transcendence, the differentiated pattern of gene expression in brain and body would be the substrate on which the human spirit continually acts, affecting all subsequent action by modifying the substrate.[17]

This comment does not commit Cole to a specific theory of mind (in this essay he does not take up the problem of theories of mind), but it is quite compatible with the reciprocally bottom-up and top-down causality for which emergent theorists are looking.

It is important that, if this is an accurate rendering of Cole's account, then debates about human agency need not be radically changed from their traditional form. He brings into focus the neurobiological factors that fill in the details of the concepts of determinism and openness of which these debates have long spoken. Furthermore, if we embed the evidences and ideas that Cole presents within an emergent theory of mind-brain, then, I think we can account for all the factors he holds to be relevant in neurobiological learning theory, even if some of these factors are not fully understood in detail by neurobiologists.

VII. APPLICATIONS OF NEUROBIOLOGICAL EVIDENCES
TO THEOLOGICAL CONSTRUCTION

I have argued that an emergent theory takes both the experience of consciousness and bottom-up biological processes at face value, yet remains firmly monistic in its ontology of mind-brain. Within such a theory, we are justified in trying to make sense of some connections between the neurobiology of learning and a theology of human agency. Of course, some care is necessary in exploring such connections, because using models and evidence originating at one level to explain processes at another level is possible only in so far as it is illuminating within the concepts operative at the second level. For example, atomic principles constrain, but are not sufficient for, our understanding phenomena at the cellular level. This differs from assuming that a principle at one level is constituive and paradigmatic for our understanding at a higher level, which is essentially reductionistic. With this antireductionistic condition in place, I will comment briefly and unsytematically on four such connections.

Finitude and Genetic Determinants

Cole emphasizes the genetic *basis* of human life, and the considerable degree of genetic *determination.* He specifies biologically the finitude and creatureliness the theologian speaks about. It may be misleading in this context to use the theological term "pre*destination,*" even metaphorically, because, as Cole himself recognizes, voluntary action has a role to play in shaping destiny. Nevertheless, an individual's genome does "pre*dispose*" by setting strict limits on the range of possibilities for the individual's development. From what Cole tells us, it would appear that the general theological picture of freedom within constraints is not fundamentally altered by the biological evidence, even though biology may lead to specifications and revisions of discussions in both theological and philosophical contexts.

Emergence theory, used as the larger framework for interpreting Cole's presentation, illumines the meaning of finitude, a traditional theme in Christian theism. Theologians over the centuries have often treated finitude within the framework of spiritual freedom *over against* nature's limits. But in the emergent framework, or any monistic framework, to recognize genetically based constraints is to recognize the *finitude of human spirit*, consisting in limits of understanding, contradictions in actions, and obscured or weakened personal unity. Thus, theologians may discover that, by having improperly contextualized freedom, they have inadvertently confused the finite and infinite varieties of it.

Over the long run, the effects of a biologically grounded perspective on human finitude, combined with an emergent theory of mind-brain, may lead in the direction of revising the theological idea of *sin*.[18] The view that human beings emerge from natural processes—implying that the background of moral and spiritual life is partly biological—highly restricts interpretations of "the fall." But the notion of sin continues to have force in this framework so long as we distinguish the premoral biologically based propensities underlying human behavior from the meanings associated with this pre-moral background once it reaches consciousness and becomes a motivational influence on action. Choice must be a significant factor in at least some actions if the moral weight associated with sin and alienation from God is to make sense, as we saw in the earlier discussion of CSP. The role of biological determinants in the concept of sin is neither dominant nor excluded, therefore, but must be thought out with great care.

Implicit in the distinction between predispositional motivating forces (some genet-ically determined) and the human capacity for intentional action is an elevated con-ception of the status of human beings. This has enormous theological significance. As Reinhold Niebuhr states, consciousness of sin is simultaneously a consciousness of God and the possibility of relationship with God; thus it is ironic testimony to the biblical notion of the *imago dei* in humanity.

The Unity of Personhood

Cole tells us that brains, particularly the number of synapses and the pattern of the net-work they form, can change considerably with the application of certain kinds of stim-ulation. The *kinds* of stimulation received affect the *kinds* of change in structure the brain undergoes. The question that follows is: Who or what determines the kind of stim-ulation the organism will be introduced to? Given the wide range of sensations received at any given moment, what screens the various stimuli, suppressing some and focusing on others? If Jane's brain develops in a particular way that is conducive to mathemati-cal skills but is less developed in subtle hand-eye dexterity, what caused this to be the case for her?

These questions draw attention to what constitutes the unity of the human person, and the question of human intentionality. We generally assume that Jane—a person with certain purposes and interests—turned her attention toward certain tasks and away from others, and that this voluntary action, repeated often, stimulated certain physio-logical patterns in the brain. There are, of course, other contributing circumstances to her neurological development, such as internal environmental propensities (Jane is genetically endowed with a brain quite suited to developing analytic skills), and exter-nal environmental pressures (Jane's father, a theoretical physicist, loves to play math games with her in his spare time; enjoying his attention, she begins to prefer this activ-ity over playing volleyball with her big sister). But these nonintentional conditions, as component forces, do not completely overwhelm the person-as-a-whole, which is Jane, who *chooses* to be involved in certain activities and not others.

We can also apply the voluntaristic thesis to moral growth and emotional develop-ment. Through repeated kinds of behaviors, we reinforce patterns that are realized in physiological tracks in the agent-organism. Nearly a century ago, William James published an essay on habit in which he stated that "the phenomena of habit in living beings are due to the plasticity of the organic materials of which their bodies are composed."[19] He continued, in a more prescriptive vein, to tell his student-readers to "Seize the very first opportunity to act on every resolution you make, and on every emotional prompting you may experience, in the direction of the habits you aspire to gain."[20]

In the same chapter, James stated, "Sow an action and you reap a habit; sow a habit and you reap a character; sow a character and you reap a destiny." This is a poignant rendering of the personal moral one can draw from the physical facts, once the idea of physical substrates for every mental event has been fully absorbed, as it had been by James. The point is that choices about which tasks to do, which skills to learn, which knowledge to gain, have physical effects in the brain—the making of neural networks hitherto undeveloped. This intentional aspect of life is essential to what we experience as personal unity, and critical to a theological account of human agency.

Don MacKay, an interdisciplinary researcher in neurophysiology, experimental psychology, and communications theory, considered the human agent, for heuristic purposes, as a self-supervisory evaluating organism.[21] The physiological correlate of human agency is the conditional readiness of the organizing system of the organism to bring about goal-directed action in its field. With this in mind, he drew on the model of an information flow system. MacKay asserted that where we have systems that handle information, we have more than one causal level, and each complements the other. His most powerful example was that of a thermostat, an information flow system that is analogous to agency. Once a goal is established (keeping room temperature at 68 degrees) the system is set up to read information and respond.

Obviously, unlike a thermostat, a conscious agent sets its own goals whereby the current state of affairs of the organism in its environment is compared against a goal state, and new states also set up evaluations of the criteria for the goal state. There must be a function within the brain structure of goal setting and goal monitoring. MacKay conjectured that the human brain has a hierarchy of levels of self-supervising systems that monitor goals and change them, based on evaluations of the environment, and a hierarchy of organizing systems that determine actions required in order to keep the organism in line with its own goal state. These systems are enormously subtle, and capable of setting a wide range of behaviors in response to interaction of the person in his or her field. This supervisory function includes planning, representing, and evaluating—including the evaluation of the criteria for one's evaluating. Thus conscious agents evaluate ongoing states of affairs, revise goals on the basis of these states, and revise criteria of evaluation. The neurophysiological substrate for these phenomena, stated MacKay, is at the level of neural systems, not neurons. Conscious experience of intentional action on this model is due to no single part, but to an extremely complex and subtle feedback chain which essentially consists in the brain-as-a-whole.

The reason why this is an important picture for this discussion is that it helps us understand what determines the unity of consciousness by which one turns his or her attention one way and not another (a key factor in the learning theory that Cole has described). According to MacKay, the unity of agency (unity of consciousness) by which coherent and consistent neural developments are cultivated is constituted by the fact of there being one centralized organ for setting up goals. There is a unity of the evaluative process at the top level of the hierarchy of organizing and supervising systems in the brain.

This is one attempt (at the level of neurophysics and information theory) to address questions raised by Cole's neurobiological picture about how certain learning paths are selected, which in turn create certain neural developments. The model employed is suggestive of mechanisms that might account for the physical basis of the experience of personal unity. And, again, we take such unity to be an essential aspect of any Christian theistic account of human agency.

Transformation and Conversion of the Human Person

David Cole's paper is particularly challenging regarding the Christian perspective on conversion. One fascinating conclusion to be drawn from the biological evidence is that for God to affect change in the bias of the human will toward sin by forgiving and healing is no less a miracle than visible outward effects in the world. Reorientation of the will consists in physical change in the neural network: new directions of growth in neurites in the brain. Yet how are such changes brought about, except by the contingent factors already named: external stimuli, internal changes, intentionality (or personal spirit, as Cole calls it)? This poses a challenge to the theologian, for it is no longer possible for those who have rejected miracle in the conventional sense to talk glibly about God *inspiring* or *persuading* the human person. The world of the human spirit (that is, personal unity) is as natural as the outward features of the world, where interventionism is denied.

Let us first specify the theological conversion to mean *not* a radically new identity, so that the former character is unrecognizable in the latter—we must presuppose continuity of identity. Rather, conversion will be thought of as a radical change in the priorities of the human agent. Moreover, the newly claimed priorities are actualized over a process of time, and not all at once. MacKay, once again, furnished a model that may be suggestive for understanding the physiological mechanisms that underlie the change we associate with conversion so described.

In a discussion of random processes on the brain, MacKay pictured the mind as a pinball machine to illuminate this possibility for change. It should not be mistaken as a picture of free will. Rather, it is an analogy to shed light on the human capacity to change courses of action.

> A tiny difference in the ball's trajectory can make a difference in the angle of rebound which in turn might determine whether the ball stays in play. This process is random in

some sense, and yet has a certain amount of law-abidingness to it: a skill can get the ball roughly where you want it.[22]

Imagine next that the sloping surface of the pinball machine is grooved, and that these grooves can be deepened or filled in, according to what happens. (Notice the parallels to plasticity in neurobiology.) Successful balls deepen the grooves; unsuccessful balls send a signal causing grooves to be filled up. This is a "stochastic system," MacKay tells us, which combines discipline and spontaneity. He continues:

> . . . even a completely random shake-up (suppose you jolt the board) merely gives the system a chance to explore new paths. The paths are not necessarily chaotic, but they are paths that would not have been visited, had the exploration gone on without the random jolt.[23]

If we add that the system can detect, through feedback cycles, whether a random jolt was merely an error to be erased, or a change of course that gets reinforced by further moves, we have a picture that simulates (albeit crudely) the physical mechanisms of change in the brain.

Can pictures such as this lead to research programs that illumine the physical apparatus behind phenomena as experienced—in this case, the phenomenon of change in one's personal orientation? If so, we can apply to the theological context what we learn about the physical basis of change in the human agent, in order to see if it bears, even in subtle ways, on our conception of spiritual transformation.

Sanctification or Spiritual Formation

Perhaps the most interesting aspect of Cole's paper is the implications one might draw from plasticity of the brain for spiritual formation or sanctification: the forming of a life of holiness that is intellectually, practically, and emotionally integrated by virtue of alignment with God's will. I am not going to discuss the issue of God's coinhering action with the person, which is traditionally held to make such integration possible; nor am I going to discuss the role of community. Both are essential and interrelated aspects of the Christian life, which is not exhausted by autonomous actions, but is profoundly conditioned by a community whose corporate life is shaped by faith in God, worship, and action; it is a life guided by the spirit of God. Rather, I am interested in the relation of personal formation to biology, and this limits the scope of the discussion.

The empirical evidence for growth of neural connections and networks based on *what we do* calls to mind one of the deepest spiritual and moral intuitions of human beings, namely, that the purposes we pursue with persistence establish an enduring character and direction to our lives. Theologically we speak about this in terms of spiritual formation. Spiritual formation places stress on that aspect of agency expressed in the capacity to organize one's intentional actions around stable and enduring purposes. In Frankfurt's terms, we are free insofar as we have been able to make our second order desires our first-order volitions. This might be distinguished from the aspects of freedom we call novelty and choice.

Austin Farrer makes this distinction of aspects in noting the difference between the freedom of youth and the freedom of more mature persons. One might think that the more one's choices of action leave a background of past experience, formed desires, past resolutions, and habits, the less free one is in shaping the future. In fact it is the case that different aspects of free will surface at different stages of one's life. Farrer summarizes this point as follows:

> The freedom of youth is the freedom of choice [a kind of experimentation with the world whose goods are partially opaque to the partially formed judgment of youth; youthful choice] is rich in the ability to choose its own principal directions, but poor in the criteria of choice and in the power to attain fully specific objects. The prime of life is poorer in choice of principal direction [the tracks of habit and purposes formerly adopted are in place], but richer in choices which are fully specific and effective; there is less variety in the direction, but more detail in the *matter* of choice.[24]

If we consider the creativity of freedom to involve both choicefulness and innovative ways of meeting enduring purposes, then we can expect that the prominence of each characteristic varies with the phases of an agent's development. That is, as the background of mnemonic content and force becomes richer, and the criteria of judgment firmer, the agent more sharply specifies the potential good of present objects in his or her field of action. Freedom is expressed, in this case, in power and subtlety of discrimination. However, prior to the formation of a stable background, emphasis falls more on choicefulness, and less upon the strength of criteria by which one discriminates value in one's field.

It seems to me that Cole's comments on the long term adaptation of cells and pathways in the brain, based on repeated stimulations and outputs of the organism, have more than an analogical bearing on the topic of spiritual formation. The combination of the brain's stability, plus openness to change and growth, is a necessary condition for the development of the patterns of intentional action to which we impute spiritual meaning.

However, one can imagine moral-analogical applications. For example, a rather immediate insight is the relation between the importance of goal-directed behavior in the development of the brain, and the apocalyptic morality of Jesus—of being prepared, for the hour is at hand. *Now* is the time, because everything we do has an effect on our immediate and long-term destinies. Every new belief, every new valuation of our world on which we act, constitutes a physical change in the brain. As Don MacKay stated,

> There is . . . no knowing, no believing, no learning—or unlearning even—without physical change in the structure which embodies our state of conditional readiness to reckon

with the world ... our assumption [the brain scientists'] entails the fact that knowing and believing have physical costs.[25]

If this is true of the human organism, then the adaptibility of cells is not just analogous to the shaping of a way of life that the spiritual person talks about. The process of moral and spiritual growth and sustenance is consistent with physical fact.

I close this section with William James again, who is rhetorically quite powerful on this thesis (even if incomplete from the perspective of Christian theism):

> The physiological study of mental conditions is thus the most powerful ally of hortatory ethics. The hell to be endured hereafter, of which theology tells is no worse that the hell we make for ourselves in this world by habitually fashioning our characters in the wrong way ... we are spinning our own fates, good or evil, and never to be undone.[26]

The drunken Rip Van Winkle says it will not matter this time, but:

> down among his nerve cells and fibers the molecules are counting it, registering and storing it up to be used against him when the next temptation comes. Nothing we ever do is, in strict scientific literalness, wiped out.[27]

VIII. CONCLUSIONS

The object of this essay has not been to give a complete and robust account of the theology of human agency. Rather, I have attempted to show how, starting with even a minimal picture of a theology of human agency, certain philosophical commitments become evident; and these philosophical commitments inform one's selection of a theory of mind-brain among the live alternatives. Finally, the theory helps to specify the relation of the theology of agency to scientific data.

I have taken the position that some emergent theories of mind are useful—and I have offered a limited case that they are better than their competitors—in accounting both for the biological evidences of the kind that Cole presents, and for the assumptions about human agency that stand behind the core beliefs of Christian theists.

I have claimed that Cole's picture specifies the biological aspects of finitude without fundamentally changing the traditional issues associated with finite human agency. Once we embed the biological evidence he presents within a mind-brain theory of emergence, which acknowledges the full force of our commonsense psychology, the biological data can be illuminating because it offers analogies for, and specifies necessary conditions of, key features of our experience as human agents.

I have named a few areas at the intersection of biology and the theology of agency where I think there is room for much further research. It is critical to the future of theology, if it is going to interact with other intellectual domains, that it pursue interdisciplinary connections of this sort.

It is easy to underestimate the sophistication of the interior "language game" of theology—including its specialized semantics, its conceptual networking, and its historical nature—and thus to make oversimplified connections, assuming a kind of univocity between theology and sciences that does not exist. But the other extreme, equivocation, is just as dangerous. This problem occurs when theology privileges and isolates itself, while all along presupposing the truths of other domains but not accounting for them. My intention has been to offer an overview of one way between these two extremes, to show the possibility of critical interaction between assumptions we make theologically, and presuppositions of other spheres of human discourse.

NOTES

1. See Richard Norris, "Human Being," in Geoffrey Wainwright, ed., *Keeping the Faith* (Philadelphia: Fortress Press, 1988), p. 79.
2. Rev. Canon Edward West, *Outward Signs* (New York: Walker, 1990).
3. Genesis 2: 7.
4. John Macquarrie, *Principles of Christian Theology* (New York: Macmillan, 1971), p. 61.
5. Harry G. Frankfurt, "The Freedom of the Will and the Concept of a Person," *The Journal of Philosophy*, 68:1 (January, 1971), pp. 5–20.
6. See Patricia Smith Churchland, *Neurophilosophy: Toward a Unified Science of the Mind/Brain*, (Cambridge: MIT Press, 1986); and Daniel Dennett, *Consciousness Explained* (Boston: Little, Brown and Co., 1991).
7. *Neurophilosophy*, p. 312
8. See, for example, Arthur Peacocke, *Theology for a Scientific Age* (Minneapolis: Fortress Press, 1993); Donald MacKay, *Behind the Eye* (Oxford: Basil Blackwell, 1991); Fred Dretske, *Explaining Behavior: Reasons in a World of Causes* (Cambridge: MIT Press, 1988). For a more qualified commitment to emergentism, see John Searle, *The Rediscovery of the Mind* (Cambridge: MIT Press, 1992).
9. Dretske, "Reasons and Causes," in James E. Tomberlin ed., *Philosophy of Mind and Philosophy of Action* (Atascadero, CA: Ridgeview Publishing Co., 1989), p. 5.
10. *Theology for a Scientific Age*, p. 53.
11. *Theology for a Scientific Age*, p. 225.
12. *Theology for a Scientific Age*, p. 61.
13. Don MacKay, a neurophysicist and communication theorist, and advocate of emergentlike theories, believed that the deterministic structure of the physical sciences is irrelevant to what we mean by free will because determinism and free will are merely perspectives, and priority belongs to the perspective of the agent-subject. I find this thesis unhelpful, except that it underscores what is at stake is a commitment to one ontology or another: that is, one either accepts or rejects the causal force of the content of first person accounts of experience as part of one's ontology. See *Behind the Eye*, pp. 113–115.
14. Philosopher Donald Davidson, who has written much about this problem, believes that mental concepts and their relations cannot be described as being lawlike, and so argues that there can be no automatic extension of psychological and physical predicates from

description of private mental states to description of universal human psychology. This generalization problem means that "detailed knowledge of the physiology of the brain would not provide a short cut to a kind of interpretation required for the application of sophisticated psychological concepts." See Donald Davidson, "The Material Mind," in *Essays on Actions and Events* (Oxford: Clarendon, 1982), pp. 257–258.

15. R. David Cole, p. 348 in this volume.

16. Cole, p. 350 (emphasis added).

17. Cole, p. 350.

18. See *Theology for a Scientific Age*, esp. ch. 12.

19. William James, *Psychology: A Briefer Course* (New York: Fawcett, 1963; first published in 1892), p. 133.

20. *Psychology*, p. 142.

21. See MacKay, *Behind the Eye*.

22. *Behind the Eye*, p. 218.

23. *Behind the Eye*, p. 219.

24. Austin Farrer, *Finite and Infinite* (London: Dacre Press, 1943), p. 196.

25. *Behind the Eye*, p. 113.

26. *Psychology*, pp. 144–145.

27. *Psychology*, p. 145.

SOCIAL GENETICS AND RELIGIOUS ETHICS

MORALITY, RELIGION, AND HUMAN EVOLUTION

WILLIAM IRONS

I. INTRODUCTION

This paper presents a theory of the evolution of human morality by natural selection, and then expands the theory to formulate a parallel theory of religion. The theory of morality presented is a composite of ideas suggested by a number of theoreticians.[1] These theories and ideas, which I see as very similar at their core, all derive from the assumption that moral sentiments and the propensity to make moral judgments are a part of human nature, and that these sentiments and propensities derive ultimately from evolution driven by natural selection. They share, for the most part, two assumptions. The first assumption is that, in human evolution, natural selection has been sufficiently potent to create adaptation only at the individual level (and perhaps lower levels), not at the group level. This means that morality is seen as something that must have been advantageous for individuals in most ancestral populations. Group-level advantages favored by group selection are assumed not to have played a significant role in the evolution of morality. The second assumption is that morality is primarily a form of reciprocal altruism[2] and secondarily is a form of induced altruism (that is, altruism created by coercion or deception). The theory of religion presented here is my own, although I construct it in a direct logical way from earlier theories of morality, and base it on the same assumptions about individual-level selection, reciprocal altruism, and induced altruism.

For purposes of this paper, morality refers to the human propensity to judge certain forms of behavior as good and deserving of admiration, encouragement, and reward, and to judge other forms of behavior as bad, not to be imitated, and worthy of punishment. Morality also includes the systems of rules that particular societies develop to codify these judgments. These systems of rules are developed gradually over many generations, and represent the judgment of many individuals about exactly what sorts of behaviors are right, what sorts are wrong, and what rewards and punishments should accompany each form of behavior. Human beings have not only a propensity to judge various forms of behavior as morally right or wrong, but also a propensity to be sensitive to the judgments of their communities and to be strongly influenced by the particular rules of their own communities. This propensity to conformity is also a part of morality.

Clifford Geertz's definition of religion serves well for the discussion here. He defines religion as "a system of symbols which act to establish powerful, pervasive and long-lasting moods and motivations in men by formulating conceptions of a general order of existence and clothing these conceptions with an aura of factuality such that the moods and motivations seem uniquely realistic."[3] The theory presented here will emphasize the role of religion in creating, sustaining, and communicating motivations to behave in ways that are reciprocally altruistic, and thus serving to create large cooperative groups among unrelated individuals. It should also be noted that, while often the motivation is to behave in ways that are reciprocally altruistic, both religion and morality at times also entail induced altruism. Induced altruism, as explained above, is altruism based on coercion or deception, and involves one individual's gaining something at another's expense. Thus both morality and religion, in some of their manifestations, can be seen to have a dark side.

Much of this paper consists of explaining the various evolutionary theories of morality. A central element in this theory of morality is the idea that reciprocal altruism among human beings is facilitated by communicating one's commitments to behave in certain ways regardless of circumstances and, in doing so, influencing others to behave in a way favorable to one's own interests.[4] To some extent, communication of commitments may also play a role in facilitating induced altruism. I build on this idea about commitment by suggesting that religions serve to communicate commitments to other members of one's society. They communicate a commitment to follow certain rules, and to be loyal to certain groups, in a way that is deeply credible, and therefore effective at integrating individuals into a cooperative group.[5]

II. BASIC THEORY: HUMAN NATURE

Human beings are the products of evolution guided by natural selection, and their psychological characteristics are as much an end product of this evolutionary process as are their anatomical structures.[6] The human mind can be thought of as consisting of two parts: reasoning abilities, and passions.[7] Under the heading of the passions belong all of the feelings, sensations of pleasure and pain, emotions, and motivations which, one way or another, move us to action. Reasoning abilities allow us to understand reality, so that we can strive in effective ways to satisfy our passions. Since our reasoning abilities and passions are widely shared among members of our species, "human nature" is a useful label for them, so long as it is understood that there are differences of genetic and environmental origin among the individuals who share this nature.

Our passions are not in harmony with one another, and they do not influence us equally at all times. Rather, specific circumstances call specific feelings, emotions, or motivations to our consciousness. A hand accidentally placed on a hot stove creates pain and an irrepressible urge to remove the hand as quickly as possible. The smell of good food when we are hungry arouses the urge to eat. The sight of a shady spot by a cool stream when we are trudging down a long road under a scorching sun inspires the urge to sit quietly for a while in the cool shade. Each set of circumstances arouses a specific desire or urge which is temporarily thrust before our consciousness. When we are overwhelmed with one passion, we are temporarily unaware of other feelings and emotions that would move us to different actions in different circumstances.

Our past experience has a profound effect on our passions. A hungry Indian who smells a succulent curry dish will experience the urge to feast, but someone from Iowa who became sick after her only encounter with curry will react differently. Many of these differences in experience are associated with cultural differences. A hungry Baptist from Georgia is likely to think of pork chops as a very desirable meal, whereas a fundamentalist Moslem from Iran will see it as an abomination. One will react with a watering mouth, the other with disgust.

Our reasoning abilities are similarly specific to some degree. The way we reason about the nature of inanimate objects and the way we reason about conscious fellow human beings are different.[8] In trying to understand the nature of some novel inanimate object, we will be guided by a set of presumptions about the object, which are different from those we would apply when trying to understand the behavior of other human beings.

Both our passions and our reasoning abilities can be thought of as arranged in a hierarchy, with some being more general in scope than others.[9] Our most general reasoning ability is called to our consciousness when we make decisions that will affect our future in a very profound way. Whether to leave one community and take up permanent residence in another, distant community is one such choice that both we and our Paleolithic ancestors have pondered periodically. The choice may affect our future opportunities to satisfy a wide range of passions: hunger, the pursuit of mates, opportunities to gain in social status. As we ponder the choice, we think of how it will affect our ability to satisfy each of these passions.

We must then decide which is more important in the specific configuration of circumstances we face, or at least imagine we are facing. The contemplation of feelings and motivations in the light of the choice at hand is the condition that McShea refers to as calm passion,[10] the awareness and assessing of the importance of passions under nonurgent conditions. A person's age, gender, and other personal characteristics will influence the relative value assigned to each of the various passions. The decision will be based on how the conditions anticipated in each community will affect the satisfaction of the total array of passions over many years. In this process, the understanding of reality produced by reasoning is not an end in itself. Rather it is a servant of the many passions that the decision maker wishes to satisfy as fully as possible.

The steps through which our passions lead us over a life course are numerous, and we are not aware, most of the time, that they are leading toward reproduction. Each immediate goal—eating when hungry, acquiring status, respect, and affection as a community and family member, protecting ourselves from physical harm—is seen as an end in itself.

Natural selection has not favored a full understanding of the overall plan of the life course. Such a broad understanding would be too difficult to arrive at, and would be a distraction. It is better to see the satisfaction of each passion as a goal in itself and to pursue it undistracted by a knowledge of its place in a large life-course plan.

The larger plan constructed by evolution, for most individuals, consists of growing up, acquiring the skills needed to be an effective adult in the community we live in, acquiring a mate, bearing children, and nurturing them to adulthood. In moments of serious consideration of decisions that affect most aspects of our lives, we sometimes have a glimpse of this larger plan, but such a broad awareness of the total life course is only rarely perceived, and has relatively little influence on our actions.

III. MORAL SENTIMENTS AND THE COMMITMENT PROBLEM

Our moral judgments are specific cases of decisions guided by reason in the pursuit of certain passions.[11] Among contemporary evolutionary theoreticians, Robert Frank has been more explicit than any other about the role of moral sentiments.[12] He argues explicitly that human beings possess certain sentiments that aid them in doing what is best for the survival of their genes in a wide range of frequently recurring social situations. He describes these sentiments as solutions to the commitment problem, which he casts as an argument against the common assumption among economists that human behavior is driven by the maximization of personal gain.

One of the examples he uses to illustrate this is the desire for revenge. He recounts the destructive results for the Hatfields and McCoys of their long enduring feud.[13] He points out that a pure, *rational maximizer of personal advantage* among either the Hatfields or the McCoys would have recognized that vengeance would simply lead to more vengeance, and that the way to maximize personal advantage would have been to desist from seeking vengeance. This, however, is a retrospective view. Looking to the future, a commitment to take revenge no matter what the cost, can deter attack. If the neighbors of the McCoys know that the McCoys are committed to avenge any killing of a McCoy, no matter what the price, they will hesitate to kill McCoys.

Consider the situation of a hypothetical neighboring group, the Rational Maximizers, who lack this commitment, and instead are known to react to each situation in terms of maximizing their future personal advantages. Killing a Rational Maximizer poses less of a problem than killing a McCoy. Given this, the McCoys are safer among the Hatfields than the Rational Maximizers are. However, the McCoys achieve their greater safety by being committed to behave irrationally (that is, contrary to personal advantage) in certain situations.

There is an element of paradox in this commitment. By being committed to seek revenge at all costs, the result for the McCoys is that they are less likely to have reason to seek revenge than are the Rational Maximizers. When the commitment serves its purpose, it is never necessary to act on it. But the commitment must be believable to do its job. An emotional makeup that bypasses any thought of personal advantage in a situation of intergroup killing, and takes the form of an uncompromising commitment to take revenge does the job best, and this is what evolution has planted in us, according to Frank. As with most human passions, it is developmentally flexible.

Those of us who live comfortably in societies with police, courts, and prisons to punish killers can behave like Rational Maximizers without incurring great risks. However, where such law is absent, as in the Amazonian territory of the Yanomamo,[14] in the Appalachia of the recent past,[15] or throughout most of human evolution, a commitment to take revenge at all costs is the best ticket to personal safety, and that is what people in fact develop.

Frank argues that human nature contains a number of potentials for commitments of the sort illustrated by the Hatfields's and McCoys's commitment to revenge. Among others he discusses are scrupulous honesty, a scrupulous commitment to fairness in bargaining, love, and moral outrage. As with all human emotions, these are flexible. Most human beings have the capacity to develop these emotions, but whether we develop them or not depends on personal experience.

A person is likely to develop scrupulous honesty in response to growing up in a small community where honesty is highly valued, and where dishonesty is easily detected and severely punished through ridicule and ostracism. The person's honesty will be a deep emotional commitment of the sort that would leave the individual feeling guilty and remorseful if he were to behave dishonestly, whether caught or not. In fact, the anticipation of this guilt and remorse is what keeps the individual honest, not a continual calculation of the relative risks and benefits of particular dishonest acts at particular points in time. A similar individual growing up in a big city, where people frequently interact with individuals they never will see again, is less likely to develop the habit of scrupulous honesty in casual encounters with strangers. If he further finds that many people around him profit from dishonesty of one form or another and are generally admired for it, his chances of becoming scrupulously honest are even less.

Each of the potentials for developing particular moral sentiments evolved and became a part of human nature because, in one way or another, they solved a commitment problem among ancestral populations. Those who developed inflexible commitments to revenge in lawless environments were less frequent victims of violence. Those who never went back on a promise and were ever ready to help a friend were more frequently chosen as allies in environments where allies were crucial to survival.

An essential element in Frank's theory of commitment is the importance of the signaling and monitoring of commitments.[16] Commitments are of no value if they are not credibly communicated to others. *The signs of commitments are as important as the commitments themselves.* Further, a social world filled with communications about commitments is bound to give rise to false signals of commitment designed to deceive. Thus both signaling one's own commitments and monitoring those of other are a crucial part of human social life.

IV. PROXIMATE VERSUS ULTIMATE CAUSE: MORE THEORY

The picture of morality presented by Frank is cast in terms of what evolutionary biologists call *proximate mechanisms*. This means that the discussion focuses on actual psychological phenomena such as hunger, or a desire for revenge, or a commitment to honesty. The psychological phenomena are described as proximate because they carry out their functions over a short time period relative to the time needed for evolutionary change. They are called mechanisms to emphasize the fact that they display design. The design is created by natural selection "choosing"—from the variants introduced by mutation—those forms that best accomplish some goal. Sometimes the expression "proximate cause" is also used to describe the way in which proximate mechanisms create a particular adaptive effect.

An alternate way of thinking about evolution is that which is labeled *ultimate cause*. Ultimate cause refers to the creation of adaptations over many generations by natural selection. Ultimate cause theory is usually cast in terms of logically derived propositions about what sorts or traits natural selection will favor in general.

The numbers of eggs that birds lay in a breeding season can serve to illustrate the nature of ultimate cause thinking. Often members of an avian species have a typical clutch size, that is, a typical number of eggs that they lay at the beginning of a breeding season. The species' typical clutch size is usually optimal; that is, it produces on average the largest number of fledglings and is therefore the fittest trait, the trait most favored by natural selection.[17] Dawkins describes this optimal clutch size as the result of an optimal trade-off between bearing and rearing.[18] In order to reproduce, a bird must first bear offspring (lay eggs and incubate them till they hatch). Second, it must rear (feed and protect) its offspring until they are ready to live independently. There is an optimal balance between bearing and rearing, if we assume the goal is to produce as many surviving, mature offspring as possible. Natural selection favors genes that tend to move their bearers toward producing this optimal number. The general proposition that clutch sizes are optimal in terms of the trade-off between bearing and rearing is known as Lack's Rule, after its author, David Lack. The rule is deduced logically, and then evaluated against actual data on avian reproduction under a range of conditions, to see whether it successfully predicts what in reality happens.[19]

V. ALTRUISM AND SELFISHNESS

This same process of deriving logical propositions about what sorts of adaptations natural selection will produce, and then testing them through observation, has been applied to a wide range of questions. One of the issues that has been explored extensively is the conditions under which natural selection will favor altruistic behavior, and those under which it will favor selfish behavior. This is obviously a discussion relevant to morality. In this theoretical discussion among evolutionary biologists, the words "altruism" and "selfishness" are given meanings somewhat different from their every-day meanings. Altruistic behavior is defined as behavior that lowers the actor's fitness and raises the fitness of another organism (or organisms). Selfish behavior is defined as behavior that has the opposite effects; that is, it raises the actor's fitness and low-ers the fitness of another organism (or organisms).

Fitness also has a special technical meaning in this discussion. Fitness is a measure of the organism's success in bearing and rearing offspring. The issue is usually how successful an organism with a particular trait is at producing adult progeny, compared to organisms with alternate traits. The fitter trait is, by definition, the one favored by natural selection. This meaning of fitness is sometimes called Darwinian or *classical fit-ness*. *Inclusive fitness* is a distinct concept that measures an organism's effect on the reproduction of its genes both through bearing and rearing offspring and through help-ing relatives to bear and rear offspring. Throughout this discussion, fitness refers to classical, not inclusive, fitness.

Basically, evolutionary biologists have concluded that there are two situations in which natural selection at the individual level will favor altruism. One is when the ben-eficiary of the altruism is a genetic relative of the altruist,[20] and the other is when the beneficiary can be depended on to reciprocate acts of altruism.[21]

Between genetically related individuals, altruism is favored whenever the altruist reproduces more of its genes as a result of the altruism. This is the gist of Hamilton's 1964 classic theoretical paper on kin altruism.[22] When an individual altruistically aids a relative, its own fitness (the number of its surviving offspring) is lowered, but the rel-ative's fitness is raised. For most organisms, their offspring carry a higher portion of their genes than do most of their other relatives. Nieces and nephews carry one-quar-ter of one's genes; children, half. Thus, lowering the production of children to aid a sibling in producing nieces and nephews will be favored by natural selection only when the gain is more than twice the loss. Altruism is favored only when the cost to the altruist is less than the gain to the beneficiary.

Thus the expected adaptation in flexible organisms such as human beings is one of discriminate altruism. We should be willing to sacrifice for the benefit of relatives in some situations, but not others. Our willingness to sacrifice should be greatest for close relatives, and greatest when the costs to us are low and the benefits to the relatives high. There is empirical support for these theoretical expectations for both animals and human beings.[23]

However, kin altruism cannot explain human morality. Human morality often causes behaviors that are altruistic among unrelated individuals. The only way individual selection can favor these behaviors is through reciprocity. Thus the ultimate cause the-ories of reciprocity must serve as the basis of any ultimate cause theory of morality.[24] The primary difficulty limiting the establishment of reciprocal altruism is the possibil-ity of being cheated.[25] If individual A aids individual B in expectation of reciprocal aid, B can often gain the most by not reciprocating. Somehow arriving at a situation where reciprocation is probable is a necessary condition for the establishment of reciprocal altruism. Theoreticians have arrived at several conditions that make reciprocation more likely. These conditions are discussed below.

VI. GAME THEORY ANALYSES OF RECIPROCITY

Axelrod and Hamilton use game theory, and specifically the game of Prisoner's Dilemma, to elucidate the effect of probable future interaction on the probability of reciprocation.[26] Game theory is based on the assumption that the choices people make in playing games and in real life are parallel in many ways, and that we therefore can understand real life decisions by analyzing logically how players might strive to win hypothetical games. When used in evolutionary sciences, it is an ultimate cause type of analysis. It emphasizes the sorts of strategies natural selection will favor over many generations, and does not inquire about the psychological adaptations that, within the span of an individual's life, cause individuals actually to carry out these strategies.

Prisoner's Dilemma is a classical example of a game used by game theorists to analyze human decision making. In its original form, it was stated in terms of the choices facing two criminals who cooperated in committing a crime, a bank robbery, and were then arrested and offered the opportunity to turn state's evidence in return for a lighter sentence. The criminals agreed beforehand that if either one of them were caught, he would not give the authorities any information that might harm the other. The state's attorney has enough information to convict them of a minor offense, such as possession of an unregistered firearm, but not enough to convict them of the more serious crime of bank robbery.

The punishment for possession of an unregistered weapon is one year in jail. The punishment for bank robbery is ten years. The deal offered each criminal by the state's attorney is a suspended sentence, that is, zero years in jail, in return for turning state's evidence, with the consequence that his companion will spend ten years in jail. Each must, therefore, decide whether to stick to his agreement with his companion in crime, or turn state's evidence. The outcome for each depends on what his companion does, as well as what he does himself. If he turns state's evidence and his companion does the same they will each get five years in jail, a reduced sentence because of their willingness to cooperate. If he turns state's evidence and his companion does not, he will spend zero years in jail, and his companion will spend ten. If he sticks to the original agreement, and his companion does too, they will each get one year in jail, the punishment for the lesser offense of possessing an unregistered firearm. If he sticks to the original agreement and his companion turns state's evidence, he will spend ten years in jail. Thus, if he turns state's evidence, he will spend somewhere between zero and five years in jail. If he does not turn state's evidence, the range of outcomes is one to ten years. If there is no future interaction with his companion in crime to be considered, clearly the better choice is to break his agreement with his companion and provide evidence.

On the other hand if we look at the average outcome for the two criminals, the best choice is for both to stick to the original agreement. Then they each get one year in jail, a total of two years to be served by the two of them. If one gives evidence, one serves zero years and the other ten for an average of five between them. If they both give evidence, they each serve five years. Thus the average outcome for the group of two criminals is better if they stick to their agreement. Sticking to the agreement yields the best outcome for the pair as a whole, but from the point of view of each individual, giving evidence yields the best result. Thus, if one of the criminals places his own welfare above that of the group as a whole, he will give evidence.

There are many situations in real life that mimic this situation, where the outcome that is best for the group and that for a single individual, weighing only his own advantage are at odds. It is also clear that morality, as we usually conceive of it, often requires that an individual do what is best for the group. Consider the situation when a fire occurs in a crowded theater. The best outcome for the crowd as a whole is an orderly exit, but the individual advantage may be to break ranks.

Game theorists usually study the game of Prisoner's Dilemma as an abstract game in which outcomes, or payoffs, are expressed as points, where points are desireable. Diagram 1 is a payoff matrix for Prisoner's Dilemma in such an abstract form.

Diagram 1: Prisoner's Dilemma Payoff Table

Payoff (in points)	B cooperates	B defects
A cooperates	A: 4, B: 4	A: 0, B: 6
A defects	A: 6, B: 0	A: 2, B: 2

"Temptation" = 6 points; "Reward" = 4 points
"Punishment" = 2 points; "Sucker's Payoff" = 0 points

If a game such as Prisoner's Dilemma is played several times with the same players, the situation changes. This modified version of Prisoner's Dilemma is called Iterated Prisoner's Dilemma. If criminal A defects on the first move, criminal B is likely to defect in response on the second move. On the other hand, the response to cooperation on one move is likely to be cooperation by the other player on later moves.

Axelrod conducted two tournaments in which game theorists could submit strategies for playing Iterated Prisoner's Dilemma and the strategies would be assigned to hypothetical players, who would use their strategy in playing a series of games of Prisoner's Dilemma with other hypothetical individuals.[27] Considering all the built-in possibilities and rigorous controls, the most successful strategy was one named "Tit for Tat," submitted by a well-known psychologist, Anatol Rapoport. Tit for Tat is defined in terms of two rules: (1) on the first move with a new player, cooperate; and (2) on all subsequent plays with this player, do what he did on the previous move.

The general conclusion relevant to morality is that with repeated interaction between the same individuals, it is easier to establish reciprocity. Human beings evolved in small communities in which the same individuals interacted with each other repeatedly over their lifetimes. Thus conditions favoring a discriminate type of reciprocal altruism of the sort modeled by Tit for Tat were present during human evolution. However, later theoretical thinking has identified further conditions and strategies that can assist in the establishment of altruism.

VII. INDIRECT RECIPROCITY

In his 1987 book *The Biology of Moral Systems*, Alexander explored the consequences of what he labeled "indirect reciprocity." Indirect reciprocity, as Alexander conceived it, occurs when the individuals in a population observe the other members of the population interacting with each other. In very simple terms, the basis of indirect reciprocity is to be nice to those who are nice, and nasty to those who are nasty. Intuitively it does seem that human beings do have such a propensity, although it is hardly the only psychological propensity influencing choices to be nasty or nice.

One could model this type of interaction formally by expanding Iterated Prisoner's Dilemma to include this element of third-party observation. The new version of Tit for Tat, Indirect Tit for Tat, takes advantage of information gained by observing third-party interactions.[28] It consists of the following rules: (1) cooperate on the first move in playing with another player about whom you know nothing; (2) if you know the other player, either from having played with him before, or from having observed him playing with a third party, then use that information to decide how to play; specifically, defect if the other player has ever been seen to get the Temptation; otherwise cooperate. This second rule allows one to distinguish those who defect first from those who defect in retaliation.

This game, however, suggests some perverse possibilities. What if a player first defects with another player, but is not consistent, so that he tricks you into getting the Temptation the first time you play with him, and in the process ruins your reputation? This and other possibilities parallel familiar forms of human interaction, and responses can be seen as ways of protecting one's reputation in a complex set of interchanges where mistakes are possible.

However one chooses to think about potential reciprocity, Alexander's suggestion that indirect observation and reputation increase the ease of establishing cooperation seems correct. Of course, the use of indirect observation (observing people when they are interacting with third parties) opens up a number of other possibilities, such as deceitful manipulation of one's own and other's reputations, and counterstrategies of closer observation. These possibilities seem also to be things that really happen in human communities.

The implications of Alexander's suggestion may become clearer if we think about it in concrete terms similar to those used by Robert Frank. Frank discusses the case of two individuals, Smith and Jones, who can pool their talents to establish an excellent restaurant.[29] Smith is a talented cook, but he is awkward in dealing with customers and lacks good business judgment. Jones cannot boil water, but he is good with customers and has good business judgment. The two make a good pair. Each has talent the other lacks. Together they can run a business that neither can run alone. But cheating could make the venture less profitable. Jones, who will run the dining room and handle the cash register, could skim from the register without Smith knowing. Smith, who will run the kitchen, could take kickbacks from food suppliers. Neither will be in a position to monitor the behavior of the other. If both cheat, the venture will not be profitable. If only one cheats, the venture will be profitable only for the cheater. Each party to this potential venture will be more willing to enter into a joint arrangement if he knows the other to be scrupulously honest.

This is a clear example of a commitment problem in Frank's terms. In Alexander's terms, reputation is a crucial element. What if Smith and Jones have known each other all their lives? Neither has ever entered a joint business venture with the other, but both know third parties who have, and who vouch for the scrupulous honesty of the other. This element of communitywide reputation is, then, a resource each can use to open the door to a profitable business arrangement. In fact, any means by which one can convincingly demonstrate a commitment to honesty will be useful in persuading the other to enter the joint business venture.

What Frank calls commitment corresponds to what Alexander calls reputation and self-image.[30] He theorizes that we know that others will judge us and that we will come to have a reputation, and that we must manage that reputation. (Our conscious thought processes may not be framed in exactly these terms; nevertheless, we are aware of the advantages of maintaining a good reputation.) We deal with this situation by forming an image of the kind of person we wish to be, and then striving to become that person. Our self-image is, then, an internal guide to behavior. If our self-image is that of an honest person, then we behave honestly, even when we are not convinced that dishonest behavior will be detected. Frank drives home this view of self-image as a guide by discussing tipping on the road.[31] We tip while traveling alone in places we will never visit again because we reassure ourselves that we are the generous person that our self-image says we are. Alternately, he says that by tipping, we are buying self-respect or avoiding guilt.

Alexander's thinking runs along parallel channels, with one important exception.[32] Alexander emphasizes that, in the process of forming a self-image and letting it guide us, we may to some extent indulge in self-deception. For example, the man who returns wallets with money in them may be deceiving himself, and once the amount of money is large enough and his pressing need great enough, he may stop deceiving himself and keep the money.

It is also relevant that, despite the scrupulous honesty of many people, there is a small minority who make their living as confidence artists. These people live as parasites on the majority, who rely on certain signs of commitment to honesty. Frank includes in his *Passions within Reason*[33] an interesting analysis of the relative advantages and disadvantages of inflexible honesty versus opportunistic honesty (being honest only when there is danger of being caught).

VIII. COSTLY-TO-FAKE SIGNS OF COMMITMENT

Frank also explores what he calls the "costly-to-fake principle."[34] What if both Smith and Jones are members of a religious sect that demands strict honesty of its members and excommunicates any members who fail to meet this requirement? What if this religious sect also demands heavy contributions of money and observance of elaborate time-consuming rituals as a strict condition of its membership? Then each will have reason to trust the other, because their membership in this sect is a costly-to-fake sign of honesty. Someone who was not really honest would be unlikely to go to the trouble of all of the rituals, donations, and other strict observances just to persuade a business partner that he is honest. Costly-to-fake signs are very valuable as ways of communicating commitments, because they are believable.

There are other examples, such as fraternity hazing, Marine basic training, the subincision of young men among the Australian Aborigines, clitoridectomy and infibulation of women in the Sudanic region of Africa, and the former practice of binding women's feet in China.[35] These examples of costly signs of commitment imposed on individuals of low social status operate somewhat differently from voluntary costly signs. Voluntary costly signs are ways of proving one's commitment to others; the imposition of costly behaviors is a dominant individual's or group's way of communicating a demand for commitment to the subordinate individual.

In addition to costly-to-fake signs of commitment, a number of other forms of behavior can be interpreted as signs of commitment, even if less costly and hence less reliable.[36] Familiar examples include: wearing a white shirt and necktie along with a well-shined pair of shoes; displaying a flag on Memorial Day, giving to charities and displaying stickers on one's door attesting to the fact that one has given, and voicing agreement with general community standards of morality.

IX. PUNISHMENT AND MORALISTIC STRATEGIES

Boyd and Richerson recently suggested another basis for self-sacrificing moral behavior by exploring the significance of punishments as ways of establishing patterns of reciprocity.[37] They frame their discussion in terms of game theory, and specifically appeal to the idea of evolutionarily stable strategies. Briefly, an evolutionarily stable strategy is a strategy that cannot be improved on once the majority have adopted it. A very simple example is driving on one side of the road or another. The only advantageous thing to do is to imitate the majority. Tit for Tat, discussed above, comes close to being an evolutionarily stable strategy, although under certain circumstances it falls just short. Such a strategy is called a robust strategy. A robust strategy is successful under a wide range of circumstances, but not under every conceivable circumstance.

One can gain some insight into game theory by considering Frank's analysis of opportunistic honesty versus real honesty.[38] His analysis shows that once the majority are genuinely honest, monitoring the honesty of other people becomes a waste of time. Not monitoring becomes more advantageous than monitoring, and monitoring vanishes. Once monitoring vanishes, the advantages of opportunistic honesty go up, since the chances of getting caught go down. This is a case where imitating the majority is not the most profitable strategy. However, the situation can fluctuate. Once enough individuals become opportunistically honest, it pays to monitor again. The more opportunists there are, the more monitoring pays, and the less the advantages of opportunism. Eventually the situation stabalizes, with a certain portion of the population being opportunistic and a certain portion being genuinely honest, and with everyone monitoring.

Boyd and Richerson explore the consequence of allowing players in a hypothetical game to punish other players if they make certain choices; that is, to subtract points from the other players' scores immediately if they make the wrong choice.[39] Their finding was that something they call "moralistic strategies" can easily become evolutionarily stable, and can, in addition, establish the regular performance of costly acts in order to avoid punishment. A moralistic strategy consists of two parts, or two instructions for interacting with other individuals. The first instruction says that anyone who fails to perform some costly act should be punished. The second part says that any individual who fails to punish those who do not perform the act in question should also be punished. Again, the strategy invented here has a familiarity based on real-life situations.

Moralistic strategies are logically an extension of Alexander's idea of indirect reciprocity mediated by reputation. Alexander includes in his definition of indirect reciprocity both helping those observed to help others and punishing those observed to hurt others.[40] Boyd and Richerson add the ingenious (and intuitively familiar) instruction to reward and punish people according to how well they play the policing role itself.[41] Human beings do this especially when very sacred principles are believed to be involved, and the result can be a heavy demand for conformity.

One aspect of this demand for conformity noted by Boyd and Richerson is that moralistic strategies not only can establish the practice of reciprocity, they can establish the regular practice of any costly act.[42]

This could suggest that such costly customs as subincision and female circumcision need no explanation other than that they are maintained by moralistic strategies. However, I would suggest an alternate view.[43] Human beings are more imaginative and more flexible than the hypothetical maximizers who play game theorists' games. When faced with a costly behavior, they try to wriggle out of it, or at least to modify it in some way that decreases the cost. As a result, the required costly behavior will gradually be modified so as to become less costly.

Why, then, do costly customs continue? The answer is that, while they are costly to some low status individuals, at the same time they benefit certain high status individuals. These high status individuals are not interested in reducing the cost of punishing nonconformists; for them, the costs are worth paying. Australian elders use subincision and the other harassing elements of the initiation of young men as a way to control young men. In a society where older polygynous men monopolize the marriageable women, control of young men by old men is crucial (from the point of view of old men). Female circumcision is a way by which men control their wives, and military basic training is a way in which the military hierarchy controls its lowest status members.

X. RULES AS WAYS OF RESOLVING CONFLICTS OF INTEREST

Alexander suggests that moral rules serve as ways of resolving intragroup conflicts of interest without doing too much damage to the interests of either party.[44] With such a means of resolving conflicts of interest, some individuals would find group membership disadvantageous and would withdraw from the group. He further suggests that our intuitive sense of what is and what is not fair is an evolved capacity to identify rules that fail to do this, and motivate attempts to change them. Rules can also clarify expectations that people can act without harming one another (which side of the road to drive on is an example).

Moral sentiments by themselves play an important role in encouraging cooperative behavior, but, in addition, people often need explicit rules to clarify expectations, and to assist in monitoring others who may, on occasion, not be sufficiently motivated by moral sentiment alone. Frank's analysis of conditions favoring the coexistence of honesty and opportunism and Alexander's discussion of self-deception suggest that sentiments alone will not always create cooperative behavior. This is why most societies do not rely on sentiments and spontaneous rewards and punishments to maintain a pattern of cooperation but, rather, back these with rules.

Explicit verbal support of rules can also be a sign of commitment. It is true that tipping on the road will engender self-respect. At the same time, one can communicate one's generosity and adherence to principle by telling one's associates that they *should* tip on the road. Once a certain form of behavior becomes the requirement of some rule, one often looks bad if one does not state agreement with the rule. The result is that the rule gets regularly stated and passed down over the generations.

One final point concerning rules needs to be made. I think that Alexander is only partly right when he suggests that rules are ways of resolving conflicts of interest. For the most part, I think he is right. However, some rules are hard to interpret in this way. Take, for example, the Jewish and Moslem injunctions against eating pork. Such rules do not seem to resolve a conflict of interest. But they do make sense as hard-to-fake signs of commitment within particular communities.

XI. MORAL RELATIVISM

All human societies have social rules. In all societies, there is a belief that breaking these rules is wrong and following them is right. This is true although the extent of disapproval and approval involved may be very strong for some rules and very weak for others. Despite the universality of rules, however, the rules themselves vary a great deal among societies. In some cases, the exact rule is not as important as having a rule. Which side of the road the rules say one should drive on is unimportant, but clearly specifying one side *is* important. Which side is specified by a particular society is a matter of historic accident.

There is, however, a host of more interesting reasons for variation in rules among societies. The basic way of making a living in a society will certainly influence the society's rules. Hunting and gathering societies, for example, will have elaborate rules governing the division of the fruits of the hunt, whereas modern industrial societies have no need for such rules.

Take the case of a preliterate society such as the Yanomamo.[45] In this polygynyous society, there are not enough potential wives to satisfy every man's desire for at least one and maybe more wives. Much of the competition is played out through violence and threats of violence. The exchange of women in marriage is the strongest basis for political alliance among the Yanomamo, and allies are a necessity in their milieu of violence. Given this, it is not surprising that their most basic rules have to do with who can marry whom and who can arrange the marriage. Given the conflicts and alliances of Yanomamo society, elaborate and nuanced rules of this kind make sense.[46] However, in a modern industrial society like our own, the considerations underlying marriage and the ways of arranging marriage are completely different, and as a consequence, the rules involved are also different.

The particular moral sentiments encouraged by different societies also vary greatly among societies. Among the Yanomamo, the primary virtue for men is a commitment to defend kin in violent conflict. This willingness is often demonstrated by a number of signs, some of which may be hard to fake. A readiness to threaten violence when one's interests are threatened is one of these. In contrast, the greatest virtues in modern urban society include a willingness to get a difficult job done no matter what (usually for an employer). We cultivate hard to imitate signs of an ability and willingness to do this. Frank suggests that the importance of a college degree lies not in the knowledge gained, but rather in the fact that it is a hard-to-fake sign that a person will stick to the pursuit of a difficult goal over a number of years.[47]

As noted above, human beings do not inherit an inflexible set of moral sentiments. Rather they inherit the capacity to develop a range of sentiments; the circumstances they experience, especially those they experience while growing up, determine which sentiments they will actually develop. It is even more clear that human beings do not inherit belief in a particular set of rules; rather, as they mature, they develop a capacity to understand readily what rules are and how to use them to their own advantage. At the same time, while growing up they learn the rules of their own society and develop a set of actual sentiments which usually integrate well with the rules of their society.

The result is that what is considered reprehensible in one society may be admired in another. Individuals from different societies find it hard to agree on moral rules. This makes it hard to argue that there is such a thing as natural law, or natural rights. Since different societies arrive at very different rules and standards of morality, there is no way to argue that certain of these rules are natural and others, artificial. They are all natural, in the sense that they harness the human potential to develop moral sentiments and to learn, follow, and manipulate rules. They are all artificial, in the sense that specific rules have, over time, been invented by specific people, and that they reflect the experience of these particular people.

One can argue, as I would, that societies prefer moral codes and sentiments that entail as little as possible in the way of differences of power and of coercion. However, this is simply a preference. I can argue that people can be very happy and lead very satisfying lives in such societies. However, very privileged members of societies characterized by vast differences in power and opportunity are almost certain to disagree and devise arguments defending their privileged positions.

This view points in the direction of relativism, because of its incorporation of belief in the flexibility of human moral sentiments and judgments, and because of the openness of human beings to rules and practices set by tradition. It does not, however, argue that anything is possible. Human beings are capable of developing a range of moral sentiments depending on circumstances, but the range is probably not infinite. Many different human societies are possible, but not all imaginable ones are possible.

There is also another important way in which not everything is possible. There is an adaptive logic to the relationship between certain specific moral sentiments and the environments that evoke them. People develop a commitment to take revenge for a wrong to themselves or a relative in environments in which there is no law as we modern urban folks know it. It is in these environments that the commitment makes one safer. In environments where police, courts, prisons, and low crime rates make such a commitment unnecessary, it does not develop, or at least is not nearly as strong. The flexibility built into human nature is an adaptive flexibility. Within the range of conditions in which our ancestors evolved, we tend to develop sentiments that are adaptive responses to the environments we experience.

Human beings evolved to fit into ongoing social systems as they grow up. They have evolved psychological adaptations that lead them to understand and manipulate these ongoing systems to their own reproductive advantage. Sometimes this means conforming to the system they were born into. In other cases, it can mean subverting or transforming the system they were born into. However, human beings do not have to evolve adaptations for making cross-culturally valid moral judgments and, as a result, this is very difficult for them to do. As the world grows smaller, our inability to do this easily will become more and more of a problem.

XII. DIFFERENCES OF POWER

One of the reasons why societies vary in the nature of their rules can be found in the different distribution of power characteristic of different societies. As noted, Alexander suggested that rules are ways of resolving conflicts of interest. In the case of Smith and Jones, taken from Frank, we can imagine that their business venture might begin with the two drawing up a contract together that would be, in effect, a set of rules governing their interaction in running their jointly owned restaurant. Assuming both men were indeed scrupulously honest, and both were expected to put equal effort into the restaurant, the rules will probably not favor one partner at the expense of the other.

One test that has been suggested of the fairness of a society's rules comes from John Rawls.[48] A set of fair rules would be one that people would agree was fair if they could somehow study the rules before such people were placed in the society and before they knew what position they would occupy in that society. A person performing Rawls' evaluation of the Smith-Jones contract before he knew whether he were to be incarnated as either Smith on Jones would probably agree that the arrangement was fair; he would accept it as just, whether he should become Smith or Jones.

Of course, this is a contract between two men, not a society. Still, if the Smith-Jones restaurant should become a great success, grow into a national chain, and survive as a giant corporation for a hundred years, then it would be more like a society. New people hired by the chain would not negotiate a set of rules before accepting employment. They would think of the rules as something given, not something that they could renegotiate as they pleased. Still, if labor were scarce (which it often is not), and the chain had to compete for good employees with other chains, the rules governing employment might still pass Rawls's test.

However, what if jobs were scarce and unemployment widespread? Then the chain of Smith-Jones restaurants might decide to offer employment on tougher terms, and the company's rules might no longer pass Rawls's test. The rules of many societies are more like this. The rules have been made up, increment by increment, over many generations, but not all members of the society have participated equally in this process. In highly stratified societies, the extent of deviation from Rawls style of fairness can be extreme, reflecting the fact that one restricted class of people has made up the rules bit by bit over the generations. Often the moral sentiments that develop in these societies reflect a large degree of acceptance of the inequality that is built into the rules. The less privileged classes of such societies develop what Marxists would call false consciousness.

XIII. RELIGION AS A WAY OF COMMUNICATING COMMITMENT

Interpreting systems of religious belief as a way of communicating commitment is a logical extension of the theory of morality discussed above. Most religions are sufficiently elaborate to qualify as suitable environments for costly-to-fake communication of certain commitments. Often the commitment is one of loyalty to a particular community, as much as following certain rules of behavior. In interpreting religion in this way, we are very close to the Durkheimian view of religion.[49] According to Durkheim, religions affirm a person's place in society, and enhance feelings of community and of confidence.

The significance of commitment may make it clear why human beings, throughout most of their history, have not simply had moral codes which in a sense represent social compacts. Commitment to a particular way of life and to a community is much more believable if it is grounded in a strong belief that the moral code is somehow dictated by the basic nature of the universe, commanded by God, or in some other way seen as more than simply an agreement among people. This also suggests the importance of rituals and symbols which, to paraphrase Geertz, clothe the beliefs in a strong sense of factuality and make the motivations (the commitments to the community and its rules) seem realistic.

Such a view would suggest that each religion would tend to stress the particular commitments that are important to that particular society. Thus societies that stress unquestioning obedience to authority are likely to stress unquestioning obedience to divine authority. More democratic societies are likely to have a different emphasis, perhaps stressing not obedience to God, but rather love of God. Again, this is very close to the Durkheimian perspective that a religion's view of the supernatural world will mirror the structure of the society out of which it comes.

This view would also suggest that, as society changes, and the specific commitments that are most important change, religion should also change, so that it serves as a satisfactory vehicle for newly important commitments. However, religion need not always be seen as a lagging institution which changes in response to changes in the rest of society. In some cases, changes in religion may come first, and may serve as the means by which social commitments are changed and society is transformed. Thus changes in religion can be seen as a form of conversation or discourse among the members of a religious community in which they alter, in various ways, the commitments of the past.

Thinking of religion in this way may, on the surface, seem to move away from Malinowski's view, as functioning to allay anxieties—especially anxieties that people cannot deal with through what Malinowski labeled skill and knowledge.[50] Thus, in societies that lack effective medicine, religion is deeply concerned with curing illness. In all societies, death is a source of anxiety that cannot be completely allayed through action based on knowledge and skill; thus religion serves to reduce anxiety in face of death. Here, what religion is communicating does not seem to be commitments to behave in certain ways but, rather, an assurance that certain problems can be overcome.

However, it is possible to suggest ways that the anxiety-allaying function of religions can be seen as another aspect of the social commitment view of religion. One possible suggestion is that promising assistance in the face of anxiety provoking threats is a way of demonstrating commitment to help in whatever way possible. Thus, when we pray for the sick, we communicate to them and their families that we care and are ready to help when we can. The person who is ill, by partaking in or accepting the prayers, also communicates her willingness to accept the aid of others and her gratitude for the support. In a social world built on reciprocity, offering to accept aid may be as important as offering aid in the first place. Another interpretation, which is more Machiavellian, would be that religions are often means of manipulating people and that religious leaders can more easily manipulate people by promising aid in anxiety-provoking situations.[51]

XIV. WHAT IS RELIGION?

It is important to note that the definition Geertz gives to religion is a very broad one. Many systems of ideas, such as Marxism or capitalism, which are not ordinarily thought of as religions may in fact be systems of symbols that establish motivations and make them seem realistic. When a Marxist or secular-capitalist view of the world becomes a set of symbols that establish certain motivation, and when it is just an academic theory, may be hard to determine. Under this view, the same individual may take part in more than one religion.

I see this as posing no real problem for the theory, as it simply states that people have a propensity to fit into, and make use of, ongoing systems of symbols that function to establish certain motivations and to communicate these in credible ways so as to establish social systems built on indirect reciprocity. It does not predict that the systems of symbols will be intellectually coherent, have neat boundaries, or incorporate supernatural forces; only that they will create, to paraphrase Geertz, moods and motivations, and make them seem realistic.

XV. A FURTHER REFLECTION ON RELIGION AS COMMITMENT

Philip Hefner, in commenting on this paper, introduces Nowell-Smith's definition of morality[52] as a system that contains: (1) beliefs about human beings and the world; (2) beliefs about what is good; and (3) rules or "ought" statements built on these beliefs. Seeing in this way, we can gain some insight into why beliefs about the nature of the world can become sources of raging controversy. These statements are seen not just as matter-of-fact statements about something we cannot change; rather, they are seen as indirect (and sometimes direct) statements of a moral nature, statements about what others ought to do. Human beings have evolved in such a way as to take such statements very seriously, and to react to them in ways that are protective of their interests. Thus a new theory of human nature such as sociobiology is not seen by many as a set of hypotheses to test dispassionately. Rather, it is seen as a set of "ought" statements that may drastically change the nature of society and, as a consequence, many react strongly against it.[53]

Following Nowell-Smith, I would say that sociobiology provides only step 1 of his scheme.[54] While this view of human nature constrains what is possible in steps 2 and 3, it does not completely determine steps 2 and 3. If one is convinced that the central tenet of sociobiology is true—that human beings are bundles of inclusive, fitness-maximizing mechanisms, shaped by a history of natural selection—it is not immediately clear what one ought to do in response to this belief. Given this starting point, there are still choices to be negotiated among the members of a community.

A sociobiological view of human nature is compatible with a range of reactions to the belief, for example, that men are the most violence prone members of society. One reaction would be to encourage this violent predisposition, and direct it at external enemies. This reaction makes sense for a society that is continually threatened from the outside. Another reaction is to say that we must socialize young men in such a way as to discourage this tendency, even if this means socializing men differently from women. This latter decision makes better sense in a society that is part of an interdependent global community that cannot rely on war as a means of dispute resolution.

Pointing this out will probably not put hostile criticism of sociobiology to rest. If anything, it is likely to stir up critics. Yet, if the basic tenets of sociobiology come to be widely accepted because of the persuasiveness of supporting evidence, then it will be important to understand what sociobiology really does imply in the moral and even the religious sphere.

How important this is depends on how widely accepted sociobiology or behavioral ecology becomes in the future. It is always very hazardous to try to predict the future. However, if I were to guess, based on the trends of the last two decades, I would say that in another generation the basic tenet of evolutionary human science will be widely accepted among the better educated portion of the population. By this basic tenet, I mean the idea that human beings have a wide range of specific, evolved, psychological adaptations—including a number of moral sentiments—which maximized inclusive fitness in ancestral environments and which, in current environments, have a profound effect on behavior.

There is another point that needs to be made concerning the moral implications of sociobiology that, in a sense, belongs to all views of human nature in the modern and postmodern worlds. This is that sociobiology is not truth, but rather a theory to be evaluated. The interpretations of moral and religious views to which it leads are, in an important way different from those sponsored by traditional views of human nature. The idea in traditional Christian thinking, for example, that human beings are imperfect as a result of original sin was not a theory to be evaluated through research; it was taken as truth, and to question it was wrong. In the postmodern world, no view of human nature can have such a privileged position, whether sociobiology or some other theory of human nature. I would conclude, then, that the process outlined by Nowell-Smith of rethinking the basic steps of moral systems needs to be more explicit and more continuous.[55]

XVI. MEANS OF COOPERATING VERSUS GOALS

Most of the discussion above concerning commitments, indirect reciprocity, and moralistic strategies is concerned with strategies for establishing cooperation. That is, the discussion is concerned with means of preventing the separate, and potentially competing, interests of unrelated individuals from making cooperation unfruitful for some members of the group, and thus leading to the breakup of cooperative groups. This is the part of a theory of extensive reciprocity that has been hard for evolutionary biologists to explain without appeal to group selection.

There is, however, another question that needs to be answered. Why bother to cooperate at all? Why not simply live in small kin groups isolated from one another, as our ancestors, in all probability, did during prehuman stages of our evolution? This question is easier to answer. There are many things that groups of cooperating individuals can accomplish that single individuals cannot. Many fruitful forms of cooperation among unrelated or distantly related individuals can be found in the descriptions of the simpler societies that preserve more of the conditions of human evolution than modern urban societies.

However, Alexander suggests that there is one form of cooperation that has been especially important in the evolution of morality.[56] Human groups compete with one another often in very violent ways, and in this type of competition, the advantage to larger and better united groups was especially important. Thus, in Alexander's view, the primary advantage of indirect reciprocity was the creation of larger, more united groups for the purpose of warfare. There are other bodies of evidence that support Alexander's warfare hypothesis, including: (1) the evidence from several disciplines indicating a strong human propensity to identify with groups and enter into intergroup competition,[57] and (2) the anthropological evidence that warfare is endemic in prestate human societies.[58]

All this suggests that once a species evolves the means of overcoming the advantage of defecting for large nonkin groups, such groups will emerge, because there are numerous advantages of such groups, especially the advantage to be had by aggressive intergroup competition. It may be that the crucial step in human evolution that led to culture and elaborate sociality based on reciprocity was the development of strategies of indirect reciprocity, including moralistic strategies that allowed the formation of larger nonkin groups than had been possible in prehuman populations.

XVII. CONCLUSION

Behavioral ecologists and sociobiologists now have a coherent theory of the evolution of morality by individual selection. I suggest that this theory can easily be extended to form a theory of religion (as defined by Geertz). The advantage of morality is the ability to form larger and better-united groups for a wide range of purposes. Religion serves as a means of communicating the commitments that serve as the psychological mechanism for establishing indirect reciprocity. The end result is that human beings display a unique form of sociality in which they are able to form very large, intricately cooperating groups based on reciprocal altruism.

A concomitant of this unique form of sociality is the propensity to construct and maintain the elaborate systems of belief that we label religion. These systems of belief convey, in a deeply credible way, certain basic commitments that the members of society must share if they are to form large, cooperating groups of nonkin. These basic systems of beliefs are invested with very strong emotions, and they resolve, for believers, basic questions about the nature of the universe and human beings as part of that universe. They also resolve basic value questions about what is desirable, and provide, in effect, a set of rules or "ought" statements that believers can use to guide their lives.

NOTES

1. Richard D. Alexander, *The Biology of Moral Systems* (New York: Aldine De Gruyter, 1987); Robert Boyd and Peter J. Richerson, "Punishment Allows the Evolution of Cooperation (or Anything Else) in Sizable Groups," *Ethology and Sociobiology* 13 (1991), pp. 171–196; Robert H. Frank, *Passion within Reason: The Strategic Role of the Emotions* (New York: W.W. Norton and Company, 1988); William Irons, "How Did Morality Evolve?" *Zygon: Journal of Religion and Science* 26 (1991), pp. 49–89; Robert J. McShea, *Morality and Human Nature* (Philadelphia: Temple University Press, 1990); Michael Ruse, *Taking Darwin Seriously* (Boston: Blackwell, 1986); Ruse, "Evolutionary Ethics and the Search for Predecessors: Kant, Hume, and All the Way Back to Aristotle?" *Loccumer Protokolle* 78/89 (Rehburg-Loccum: Evangelische Akademie Loccum, 1990); Edward O. Wilson, *Sociobiology: The New Synthesis* (Cambridge: Harvard University Press, 1975); and *On Human Nature* (Cambridge: Harvard University Press, 1978).

2. Robert L. Trivers, "The Evolution of Reciprocal Altruism," *Quarterly Review of Biology* 46 (1971), pp. 35–57.

3. Clifford Geertz, "Religion as a Cultural System," in Michael Banton, ed., *Anthropological Approaches to the Study of Religion*, (London: Tavistock Press, 1966), p. 4.

4. Robert H. Frank argues that the altruism he discusses in *Passion within Reason* is contrary to what sociobiological theory predicts. Although his book is, in general, very insightful, I believe he is wrong on this point. The point of this paper and of several earlier sources is that extensive human propensities to be altruistic have evolved through reciprocal altruism. See, for example, Alexander, *The Biology of Moral Systems*; William Irons, "Why Lineage Exogamy?" in R.D. Alexander and D.W. Tinkle, eds., *Natural Selection and Social Behavior* (New York: Chiron Press, 1981), pp. 476–489; and Trivers, "The Evolution of Reciprocal Altruism." I see no way in which the arguments Frank makes about the commitment

problem and its solution are incompatible with sociobiology. On the contrary, in my opinion, they enhance sociobiological reasoning.

5. Readers who are not especially familiar with the theory of natural selection as it applies to behavior will do well to read Richard Dawkins, *The Selfish Gene*, 2nd ed. (Oxford: Oxford University Press, 1989) as a supplement to this essay. *The Selfish Gene* is an especially readable and accurate account of basic theory. However, it does not, for the most part, focus on human beings. There is no text of equal readability and comprehensiveness on the application of evolutionary theory to human social behavior. Those who are interested in becoming more familiar with the application of evolutionary theory to human behavior should consult some of the following sources: Richard D. Alexander, *Darwinism and Human Affairs* (Seattle: University of Washington Press, 1979); Napoleon A. Chagnon and William Irons, eds., *Evolutionary Biology and Human Social Behavior: An Anthropological Perspective* (North Scituate, MA: Duxbury Press, 1979); Laura Betzig, Monique Borgerhoff Mulder and Paul Turke, eds., *Human Reproductive Behaviour: A Darwinian Perspective* (Cambridge: Cambridge University Press, 1988); Eric A. Smith and Bruce Winterhalder, eds., *Evolutionary Ecology and Human Behavior* (Hawthorne: Aldine de Gruyter, 1992); Melvin Konner, *The Tangled Wing* (New York: Holt, Rinehart, and Winston, 1982); Lionel Tiger and Robin Fox, *The Imperial Animal* (New York: Holt, Rinehart and Winston, 1971); Mary Maxwell, ed., *The Sociobiological Imagination* (Albany: State University of New York Press, 1991); Charles Crawford, Martin Smith, and Dennis Krebs, eds., *Sociobiology and Psychology: Ideas, Issues and Applications* (Hilldale: Erlbaum, 1987); and Jerome Barkow, Leda Cosmides and John Tooby, eds., *The Adapted Mind; Evolutionary Psychology and the Generation of Culture* (Oxford: Oxford University Press, 1992). Those who are interested in an approach that emphasizes more the role of cultural evolution as a force interacting with biological evolution should consult Robert Boyd and Peter J. Richerson, *Culture and the Evolutionary Process* (Chicago: University of Chicago Press, 1985), or William H. Durham, *Coevolution: Genes, Culture and Human Diversity* (Stanford: Stanford University Press, 1991).

6. Charles Darwin, *The Expression of the Emotions in Man and Animals* (Chicago: University of Chicago Press, 1965; originally published 1872). See also Darwin, *On the Origin of Species: By Means of Natural Selection or the Preservation of Favored Races* (London: John Murray, 1858); and *The Descent of Man and Selection in Relation to Sex*, 2 vols. (London: John Murray, 1871).

7. McShea, *Morality and Human Nature*.

8. Cosmides and Tooby, "From Evolution to Behavior: Evolutionary Psychology as the Missing Link?" in J. Dupre, ed., *The Latest on the Best* (Cambridge: MIT Press, 1987), pp. 277–306; Cosmides and Tooby, "Cognitive Adaptations for Social Exchange," in Barkow, Cosmides and Tooby, eds., *The Adapted Mind*.

9. Kevin MacDonald, "An Ethological-Social Learning Theory of the Development of Altruism: Implications for Human Sociobiology," *Ethology and Sociobiology* 5 (1984), pp. 97–109.

10. McShea, *Morality and Human Nature*.

11. David Hume, *An Enquiry Concerning the Principles of Morals* (LaSalle: Open Court Publishing Co., 1930; originally published 1750); Wilson, *On Human Nature*; Ruse, *Taking Darwin Seriously*.

12. Frank, *Passion within Reason*.

13. Frank, *Passion within Reason*, pp. 1–2.

14. Napoleon A. Chagnon, *Yanomamo*, 4th ed. (New York: Holt, Rinehart and Winston, 1992).

15. Otis Rice, *The Hatfields and McCoys* (Lexington: University of Kentucky Press, 1982); Darrell C. Richardson, *Mountain Rising* (Oneida: Oneida Mountain Press, 1986), pp. 73–112.

16. Frank, *Passion within Reason*.

17. David Lack, *The Natural Regulation of Animal Numbers* (Oxford: Oxford University Press, 1954).

18. Richard Dawkins, *The Selfish Gene*, 2nd ed. (Oxford: Oxford University Press, 1989).

19. Lack, *The Natural Regulation of Animal Numbers*.

20. William D. Hamilton, "The Genetical Evolution of Social Behaviour" (I and II), *Journal of Theoretical Biology* 7 (1964), pp. 1–16, 17–52.

21. Trivers, "The Evolution of Reciprocal Altruism."

22. Hamilton, "The Genetical Evolution of Social Behaviour."

23. John Alcock, *Animal Behavior: An Evolutionary Approach*, 4th ed. (Sunderland, MA: Sinauer Associates, Inc., 1989); Monique Borgerhoff Mulder, "Human Behavioral Ecology: Studies in Foraging and Reproduction," in J.R. Krebs and N.B. Davies, eds., *Behavioral Ecology*, 3rd ed. (London: Blackwell Scientific Publications, 1991); Lee Cronk, "Human Behavioral Ecology," *Annual Reviews of Anthropology* 20 (1991), pp. 41–75; J. Patrick Gray, *Primate Sociobiology* (New Haven: HRAF Press, 1985); Irons, "How Did Morality Evolve?"

24. Trivers, "The Evolution of Reciprocal Altruism"; Robert Axelrod and William D. Hamilton, "The Evolution of Cooperation," *Science* 211 (1981), pp. 1390–1396; Robert Axelrod, *The Evolution of Cooperation* (New York: Basic Books, 1984).

25. Trivers, "The Evolution of Reciprocal Altruism."

26. Axelrod and Hamilton, "The Evolution of Cooperation."

27. Axelrod, *The Evolution of Cooperation*.

28. William Irons, "The Significance of Evolutionary Biology for Research on Human Altruism," *Loccumer Protokolle* (in press).

29. Frank, *Passion within Reason*, pp. 47–49.

30. Alexander, *The Biology of Moral Systems*.

31. Frank, *Passion within Reason*.

32. Alexander, *The Biology of Moral Systems*.

33. Frank, *Passion within Reason*.

34. Frank, *Passion within Reason*, pp. 99–102.

35. Subincision consists of cutting the underside of a penis open and letting it heal with the urethra open; something like circumcision but more drastic. Clitoridectomy consists of removing the clitoris, and infibulation consists of scarifying the vaginal opening so that it heals shut with a tube inserted for drainage. Clitoridectomy and infibulation are sometimes called female circumcision.

36. Irons, "How Did Morality Evolve?"

37. Boyd and Richerson, "Punishment Allows the Evolution of Cooperation."

38. Frank, *Passion within Reason*.

39. Boyd and Richerson, "Punishment Allows the Evolution of Cooperation."

40. Alexander, *The Biology of Moral Systems*, pp. 85–86.

41. Irons, "The Significance of Evolutionary Biology for Research on Human Altruism."

42. Boyd and Richerson, "Punishment Allows the Evolution of Cooperation."

43. Irons, "The Significance of Evolutionary Biology for Research on Human Altruism."

44. Alexander, *The Biology of Moral Systems*.

45. Chagnon, *Yanomamo*.

46. William Irons, "Why Lineage Exogamy?" in R.D. Alexander and D.W. Tinkle, eds., *Natural Selection and Social Behavior*, pp. 476–489.

47. Frank, *Passion within Reason*.

48. J. Rawls, *A Theory of Justice* (Cambridge: Harvard University Press, 1971).

49. Emile Durkheim, *Elementary Forms of the Religious Life*, trans. from the French by Joseph W. Swain (New York: Collier Books, 1961; originally published 1912).

50. Bronislaw Malinowski, *Magic, Science and Religion and Other Essays* (Garden City: Double-day, 1954).

51. Donald T. Campbell, "Comments on the Sociobiology of Ethics and Moralizing," *Behavioral Science* 24 (1979), pp. 37–45; Donald T. Campbell, "The Two Distinct Routes beyond Kin Selection to Ultra-Sociality: Implications for the Humanities and Social Sciences," in D.L. Bridgeman, ed., *The Nature of Prosocial Development: Interdisciplinary Theories and Strategies* (New York: Academic Press, 1983), pp. 11–41.

52. Patrick H. Nowell-Smith, "Religion and Morality," in *Encyclopedia of Philosophy* 7 (New York: Macmillan and the Free Press, 1967), p. 150.

53. See for example Philip Kitcher, *Vaulting Ambition: Sociobiology and the Quest for Human Nature* (Cambridge: MIT Press, 1985). In saying this, I do not mean to imply that criticisms by authors such as Kitcher are not well taken on scientific grounds, only that the vehe-mence of their opposition makes sense in terms of the theory presented here.

54. Nowell-Smith, "Religion and Morality."

55. Nowell-Smith, "Religion and Morality."

56. Alexander, *The Biology of Moral Systems*.

57. Reynolds, Vernon, Vincent Falger, and Ian Vine, eds., *The Sociobiology of Ethnocentrism: Evolutionary Dimensions of Xenophobia, Discrimination, Racism and Nationalism* (Athens: The University of Georgia Press, 1986).

58. Lawrence H. Keeley, *The Myth of the Nobel Savage* (Oxford: Oxford University Press, in press); Douglas Jones, "Rates of Killing in Prestate Societies in Relation to Group Size and Population Density," paper read at the Evolution and Human Behavior Conference, Ann Arbor, MI, April 8–10, 1988.

THEOLOGICAL PERSPECTIVES ON MORALITY AND HUMAN EVOLUTION

PHILIP HEFNER

William Irons's essay, "Morality, Religion, and Human Evolution," not only raises issues that in themselves are highly interesting, but it also provokes reflection that goes to the heart of religion and its relationship to the kind of scientific thought that the essay represents. In considering the details of Irons's presentation from a theological perspective, I find myself compelled to ask: What stands at the heart of the Christian vision of human life and what invitation to thought inheres in that vision? When I probe that invitation, as it has been elaborated by the tradition of disciplined, theological thinking, I come upon a train of concepts that seem quite appropriate to the struggle to comprehend the issues that Irons's essay raises for human living. I am compelled to work through some of that theological elaboration in order to get to the heart of his presentation. The reader should not mistake this as a digression that seeks to evade the burden of the anthropologist's concern. On the contrary, I aim to show that the thrust of theological elaboration allows us to enter fully into the anthropological domain. The theologian's concepts may also rearrange what the scientist offers us, and that rearrangement itself is offered as a proposal for discussion. The shape of the rearrangement and its inherent proposal will reveal at the same time both the content and the method of theologian's interaction with the scientist.

I. THE CENTRAL ISSUE POSED BY THE SCIENTIFIC ACCOUNT

It is utterly essential to get clarity on what central issue the scientist is posing, or else the theological discussion (as well as the philosophical and ethical discussions) will be beside the point. I understand the central issue posed by "Morality, Religion, and Human Evolution" to be carried by certain of the essay's basic terms: *altruism, cooperation,* and *commitment.* These terms point to concepts that pertain to *survival of the genes, self-interest,* and *fitness.* Each of these terms bears distinctive nuances of meaning bestowed upon them by the scientific peer group that has woven them together into the kind of investigation that Irons's article brings before us.

The central issue that is posed to us in these basic ideas can be phrased in this question: *What is the character of that behavior carried on in interaction with other individuals that best serves the continuation of the life of, first of all, the individual actor and, second, the group to which the individual belongs?* Morality becomes, in the scientific account, the system of behavior, winnowed by the relevant evolutionary processes that bears this character.

Each of the terms in the second group of three referred to above points to what serves life best, even though each has its own set of nuances. *Survival of the genes* accents the maintenance of the germline that specifies both the identity of the individual and also what the evolution of the human gene pool has supported. *Fitness* adds to our consideration the success of the individual's immediate progeny to survive, while *self-interest* suggests in a more diffuse way what the individual requires for well-being. The first three terms speak of the form of behavior that serves survival, fitness, and self-interest, and does so within the context of interpersonal existence. The nuances of each of these terms are illuminating and significant for our discussion. *Altruism* designates that aspect of interpersonal behavior in which the individual is faced with vulnerability and the prospect of losing something or endangering herself in the act of engagement with others. *Cooperation* brings to mind that interaction with others is a working-together, presumably to accomplish something or gain something that cannot be attained by individuals working alone. *Commitment* adds still another dimension: that in the engagement with other persons, the actor not only is made vulnerable and not only is caught up in teamwork, but also undertakes the investment of the actor's finite and nonrenewable personal resources, resources which, when taken all together, constitute the life of that individual.

We may collate these dimensions of meaning by restating the central focus brought by Irons's essay in these terms: *How are we to comprehend that our lives are served best by behaviors with other persons that render us personally vulnerable, that involve teamwork, and that turn out in the end to be the investment of our personal life-resources? Further, to be more specific, in order to serve our own lives best, what sort of vulnerability with others is to be sought, what type of working-together, and what kind of self-investment?*

Even though I have attempted to discern fairly and accurately what lies at the center of the scientific piece, the reader may feel that I have brought a perspective to my discernment that favors the introduction of theological and philosophical modes of reflection. Of course this is so, otherwise I would not be in a position to respond as a theologian. However, I aim to state the central issue in such a way that it is illuminating to both the scientist and the theologian—and also to persons who share neither of these specialized viewpoints. Put even more succinctly, the sociobiological thinking that William Irons has presented goes to the heart of a concern that presses upon all of us, even if in different ways, namely, that *life with others is a process of self-investment, and that the shape of that investment is such a significant matter that we label it "morality."*

II. THE LOGIC OF PUTTING THE QUESTIONS

Why does the argument involve these issues—fitness, self-interest, and altruism? And why are these issues unavoidably moral issues? It is in reflecting upon these questions that the place of religion and theology in this discussion becomes clearer. We turn first to the question of morality. Patrick Nowell-Smith has provided a standard definition of morality as refering to a system that contains: (1) beliefs about the nature of human beings in their world, (2) beliefs about what is good or desirable, and (3) rules laying down what ought or ought not to be done.[1] In his discussion, Irons follows this definition almost to the letter. It is instructive to observe how he does so. He articulates his beliefs about the nature of human beings in their world within a very specific set of ideas: natural selection in the form of the differential reproduction of individuals.[2]

Having staked out natural selection of human beings as his home territory, and moved therein to analysis of the mind's functioning within the dynamics of reason and passion, Irons's third step is to follow Robert Frank[3] in focusing upon "certain sentiments that aid them [human beings] to do what is best for the survival of their genes in a wide range of frequently recurring social situations."[4] The sentiments of interest here are those that can be termed "solutions to the commitment problem."[5] The "commitment problem" is explicitly set over against the argument that human behavior is oriented to the maximization of personal gain.

I consider two elements of this proposal to be of particular importance: that morality has to do with social situations in which commitment is at issue, and that behaviors are considered to be right or wrong, worthy of reward or punishment, on the basis of whether they serve the survival of the individual's genes.

Designating the moral situation as that in which the question of commitment emerges in social relationships goes hand in hand both with the focus of the scientific discussion upon altruism and selfishness and also with its use of game theory. Consequently, it does not surprise us that the research tradition in which Irons locates himself—Alexander,[6] Frank,[7] McShea,[8] Ruse,[9] E.O. Wilson[10]—is one in which investigation of the evolution of morality and of altruism are one and the same thing.[11] However it is defined, altruism is a concept that arises when commitment is at stake. Although I work with a modified definition for theological purposes, the scientific definition makes the point quite well. "Behavior that lowers the actor's fitness and raises the fitness of another organism"[12] speaks of considerations that would arise only in a particular kind of social relationship in which the actors must ask the questions: Is it wise for me to commit myself, to invest myself, in this social interaction, and if it is, what kind of commitment should I make, and how should I make it? Furthermore, the social situation in which these questions arise is most likely to be one in which an individual is in concrete interaction with one or more other individuals in such a way that a single act of investment, or a series of such actions, is asked for.

Note that I speak of *investment* as a synonym for *commitment*. The behavior entails loss or gain, survival or failure to survive. Here commitment blends into another key term, *self-interest*. The investment involves a person's nonrenewable resources—in the final analysis, the resources of nonrenewable genes. The interactions in this situation need not be direct; for example, today individuals often interact through representatives. Nor is the interaction necessarily on a one-to-one basis on both sides. The actor is always an individual, but the situation may, under some circumstances, be one in which the action is made with respect to a group (for example, an individual contemplating the size of a gift to a charitable organization). Irons's introduction of several levels of motivation accounts for this diversity. If reciprocity is at issue, the situation must be one to one, but if reputation and public image are the issue, the individual's interaction may be with an abstract or corporate entity.

Game theory is a viable means of obtaining data for studying the commitment problem, because its design is predicated on concrete instances of interaction. When one-to-one interactions are under consideration, as in the case of reciprocity, game theory is well suited for the observation. In cases where reputation is the motivation, game theory is only indirectly suitable (for example, since A knows that B gives large sums to charity, she behaves toward B under the assumption that B is a charitable person).

III. THE MOST INTERESTING ASSUMPTIONS

If we proceed still further in analyzing the structure of Irons's scientific discussion, we come upon several provocative assumptions. The first has to do with behaviors that put the individual at risk, the interactive behaviors with others in which self-investment puts individuals in positions of vulnerability. On occasion the sociobiological investigations have been interpreted as if such behaviors of risk could not be taken seriously unless they are shown by scientific analysis to be explainable in terms of natural selection in the form of differential reproduction of individuals. Coupled with the consensus that altruism can be explained by genetics only in terms of fitness theories and among kin, there has been some thought that altruism among nonkin is impossible, only an illusion.

In my mind, this is a serious misunderstanding of the sociobiological approach to altruism.[13] When, twenty years ago, Wilson brought altruism to the center of sociobiology's agenda on the very first page of his large book, *Sociobiology*, he made it clear that altruism does indeed exist, and that the very fact that it seems to contravene Darwinian theories of natural selection renders altruism "the central theoretical problem of sociobiology."[14] It could not be assigned a lesser place on the sociobiological agenda, precisely because it is an unavoidable reality, even though it "by definition reduces personal fitness."[15] In the same breath, Wilson asserted that such evolutionary maladaptiveness associated with altruism is more apparent than real, if we take genetic understandings of kinship and inclusive fitness into account.[16]

In the two decades since Wilson wrote, scientific thinking about altruism has become more complex, and Irons's essay is an example of the ongoing investigation that existed prior to Wilson and continues today. It is a mistake of interpretation to think that this scientific effort is aimed at clarifying whether or not altruism can occur in life that is governed by the principles that were described by Darwin, Mendel, and their followers. Rather, altruism is an acknowledged, if complex, actuality. The scientists, still believing that it is a central theoretical problem, continue to struggle with the questions of how it originally emerged and persists in biological systems.

The sociobiologists conduct their inquiries within rigorously defined constraints, however—constraints that they themselves articulate clearly. These constraints constitute the second interesting assumption that ought to be noted. Irons lays out these constraints at the outset: natural selection in the form of the differential reproduction of individuals,[17] and in this he follows in the train of his research tradition. The scientists will consider the acknowledgment of these constraints to be matter-of-fact, the most elementary requisite for genuine scientific thinking on the issues at hand, without which theorizing would be impossible, because theorizing, as Karl Popper asserted, depends on a clear statement of what a particular theory disallows, as well as what it must include.[18]

What seems matter-of-fact to the scientists must be commented upon, however, because it underscores that their investigations and theorizing concerning the evolution of morality and altruism rest on a prior understanding of certain basic features of the reality of the natural world. I speak of this as basic beliefs about *the way things (really) are.*[19] Perhaps the neo-Darwinian assumptions concerning natural selection that are in force in the work of the sociobiologists are comparable to the assumptions concerning the consistency of nature and natural laws that physicists (and biologists as well) depend upon.

There is more to be noted about these basic assumptions. Elsewhere I have spoken of the dimensions of *rightness*, *wrongness*, and *oughtness* that are intrinsic to morality as being grounded in a belief about the *way things really are* and in the innate drive to behave in ways that are commensurate with the *way things really are.*[20] Moral obligation is fundamentally rooted in the desire to act in ways that are in harmony with what really is; one's assumptions concerning the way things really are shape a determinative framework for understanding morality. As a consequence, when the sociobiologists approach morality under the assumptions of neo-Darwinian natural selection, they will inevitably be constrained to explain morality in terms of its role in fostering survival within the dynamics of natural selection of individuals, as Irons and his research tradition demonstrate so clearly.

The correlation with the way things really are gives the discussion of morality its seriousness and urgency. When morality is separated from what really is, it becomes tepid, trivial, and optional. The only authority of such a morality is located in some autonomy or heteronomy whose credibility is easily disputed. Moral systems that are rooted in the way things really are possess ontological credibility, provided that there is a deep conviction about the reality-pictures they carry with them. The explanatory power of the sociobiological theories of morality and its evolution derives from the clarity and specificity of explanation that is provided by the reality-picture that is conveyed by their neo-Darwinian constraints. The weaknesses of their theories are revealed precisely at the points where those assumptions concerning the nature of things are deemed to be insufficient to encompass the breadth of human moral experience or the seriousness of the human moral concern, or both. Note that the critical issue in this statement concerning the adequacy of sociobiological explanation of morality is not truth or falsity, but rather sufficiency and the ability to encompass the fullness of moral experience.

The point I have just made lays the foundation for the theological discussion that constitutes the chief contribution of this essay. Because moral behavior is essentially marked by an effort to conform actions to the way things really are, *the foundational assumptions of any attempt, from any discipline whatsoever, to understand morality will assume a profound metaphysical significance that might not be so telling in the investigation of other, nonmoral behaviors.* No approach to the study of moral behavior can avoid stepping onto this metaphysical level, even if it chooses to be silent about metaphysics altogether. The same may be true of all human behavior, but I choose here to deal only with moral behavior. Sociobiological investigation of moral behavior also faces the inevitability of metaphysics. In this essay, I attempt to show that this introduces a criterion of metaphysical adequacy into our discussion, even if the scientist neither intends nor desires to enter into such a discussion. The theological proposals that I make rest on the intrinsically metaphysical character of the phenomenon of morality. Research and study of morality inevitably share this metaphysical quality. The researchers may not share the metaphysical formulation of how things really are that grounds the phenomena of moral behavior they are observing, but they would not even be able to classify certain behaviors as pertinent to morality if they did not employ assumptions concerning what really is and what behavior attempts to conform to reality—either their own or those of the persons whose behavior they observe.[21] Without some such assumptions, they would not be able to distinguish between moral and nonmoral behaviors.

IV. WHERE RELIGION AND THEOLOGY ENTER

Theology is the religious community's ongoing effort to articulate the system of meanings that is embodied in the community's life—chiefly for its internal life, but also for the outside world. Throughout this essay, reference to theology will carry the weight that this definition implies. My discussion of religion and theology are restricted to Christianity.

We will not understand properly how theology carries on its conversation with the kind of scientific investigation that Irons has presented unless we recognize the determinative points of connection between the life and thought of the Christian community, and the phenomena that he focuses upon. These connections emerge at the point of the central issues that I have identified in his discussion: self-investing behaviors considered under the rubric of morality. The connections between Christian theology and the sociobiological theories of how morality has evolved occur at two levels.

At the level of behavior, Christianity encourages, even commands, self-investing behaviors, thus rendering the sociobiological theories relevant to and important for understanding the lives of Christians. At the level of meaning, Christian theology provides quite a different understanding of the way things really are, and, consequently, a significantly different framework within which the phenomena of self-investing, altruistic, behaviors are to be interpreted. This framework will not satisfy the scientists, insofar as it is not congenial as a conceptual structure in which scientific research can be carried out and theories constructed. On the other hand, the framework that is shaped by the Christian understanding of how things really are will result in significant redefinition and reinterpretation of some key concerns that the sociobiologists have expressed. At the outset, I termed this a theological rearrangement of what the sociobiologist offers, and I suggested that this rearrangement will itself constitute a proposal in conversation with the sociobiological theories of the evolution of morality. Now that the stage has been set for introducing this theological rearrangement, let us proceed directly to the matter.

V. HOW THINGS REALLY ARE: CONTRASTING FUNCTIONAL CONCEPTS OF GOD

The sociobiological proposal proceeds from neo-Darwinian assumptions about how things really are, and therefore consistently attempts to explain morality (self-investing behaviors) in terms of its role in fostering survival within the dynamics of natural selection of individuals. The Christian proposal does not necessarily take a position for or against the neo-Darwinian assumptions, although, since those assumptions appear to be conclusions drawn by a community of rational persons, it would be inclined to accept them. Christian theology argues, however, that a more expansive understanding of how things really are is called for. I will articulate the Christian proposal in two forms—in terms of the distinctive Christian metaphysical vocabulary and in functional terms. The formulation that is most congenial to traditional Christian rhetoric would be this: *God has created the world and human beings in it in such a way that God's will and blessing for human beings* are *actualized in lives that are devoted to the care and redemption of all that God has made.* In functional terms, Christian theology asserts that: *the nature of reality is such that the value and meaning of being human* are *most fully realized in self-investing behaviors that seek the most wholesome outcomes in the relevant situation in which the actors find themselves.*

The functional formulation renders references to God with the term "the nature of reality," which is equivalent to the earlier term, "the way things really are." It renders "God's will and blessing" with the term "the value and meaning of being human." These rhetorical equivalents should be noted seriously, because they clarify what the import of Christian God-talk is. God-talk refers to the way things really are in the most profound, most fundamental way.

Two terms in the functional formulation are strictly formal, which means that no specific content is assigned them. These terms are "the value and meaning of being human" and "most wholesome outcomes." The formal character of these terms does not render them unusable, however.

It is useful to contrast this theological proposal with a comparable casting of the sociobiological proposal, which would be as follows: *the nature of reality is such that the value and meaning of being human* are *most fully realized in self-investing behaviors that enhance the reproductive future (the inclusive fitness) of the actors*. This comparison is instructive, because it suggests where the grounding for oughtness and value lies. For the sociobiologist, the grounding is inclusive fitness within the processes of natural selection, while for the Christian theologian, the grounding is God's will in creation. These two concepts of grounding for moral behavior are asymmetrical except for those moral behaviors about which individuals are passionate, those that they consider to be essential to their identity as persons, those that they are willing to die for. When these very serious moral behaviors are considered, then it is clear that, *from a functional perspective*, the sociobiologist is ascribing a significance to inclusive fitness that correlates with that which the theologian ascribes to God. That is, when we view the discussion with an eye on what ideas of the nature of reality provide the foundation for defining morality, and, further, if we acknowledge that these ideas function as the idea of God does in Christian theology, then (and only then) we arrive at the provocative conclusion that inclusive fitness plays the conceptual role of God for the sociobiologist. In speaking of "God" in this context, I am not refering to an anthropomorphic image, nor to the theological content of various concepts of God. Rather, I refer only formally to the concept of God that serves as a Kantian regulative idea, and plays that role methodologically in the systems of thought employed by the theologian and the scientist. When we have once comprehended this conclusion, we are in a position to push more deeply into the proposals that theology generates for this discussion and the invitation to thought that inheres in those proposals.

VI. WHAT THE DIFFERENCE IN GOD-IDEAS AMOUNTS TO

Although there is more at issue here than the contrast of images that we have just observed, we should not overlook the provocation that this contrast offers. By associating the scientific assumptions with God, light is thrown on the significant role that inclusive fitness plays in the sociobiologist's system of thought concerning morality. On the other side, by translating the term "God" as it is used in theological discourse into talk about how things really are, we are able to see more clearly what is at stake in employing the otherwise empty formal concept of divinity.

The issue at stake in this segment of the conversation between sociobiology and theology, is not whether there is a God, or even whether what the theologian might call *ultimacy* is real. Rather, the issue revolves around concepts of the nature of reality, what really is. This is an issue which, as Immanuel Kant reminded us in his *Critique of Pure Reason*, the human mind is incapable of comprehending, and unable to provide a verifiable concept for consideration. However, as he asserted, ideas about what really is, whether they be cosmological, psychological, or theological,

> although they do not directly relate to, or determine, any object corresponding to them, none the less, as rules of the empirical employment of reason, lead us to systematic unity, under the presupposition of such an *object in the idea*; and that they thus contribute to the extension of empirical knowledge, without ever being in a position to run counter to it, we may conclude that it is a necessary maxim of reason to proceed always in accordance with such ideas . . . not as *constitutive* principles for the extension of our knowledge to more objects than experience can give, but as *regulative* principles of the systematic unity of the manifold of empirical knowledge in general, whereby this empirical knowledge is more adequately secured within its own limits and more effectively improved than would be possible in the absence of such ideas.[22]

Keeping in mind the qualifications that Kant described, we may say that what comes to light in the conversation at this point is the difference in functioning regulative ideas by which sociobiology and theology approach the question of the way things really are as a framework for understanding what grounds moral behaviors. Cautiously, keeping in mind what I have just said in the previous section about regulative ideas, one might say that the most significant difference that arises in the two perspectives occurs at this point, in their functioning ideas of God.

Theology does not challenge the validity of the theories of natural selection or inclusive fitness, nor does it challenge the solid scientific evidence that these theories are at present, our best ways of describing some of the basic dynamics of biological entities, including human beings. Theology does argue that a fuller regulative idea is required for understanding the nature of the reality to which human moral behavior seeks to conform. In other words, the discomfort is not with the concepts of selection and inclusive fitness as such, but rather with the strategy of permitting them to function as God-concepts in the effort to gain a *full* understanding of human moral behavior.

VII. WHAT IS AT STAKE IN THE CONTRASTING IDEAS OF GOD? INCLUSIVE FITNESS, BIOLOGY, AND CULTURE

In his book, *Biblical Faith: An Evolutionary Approach*,[23] Gerd Theissen makes the point that, since "all forms of life are attempts to find adequate structures for adapting" to what really is, "all life can be regarded as a hypothesis aimed at forming a better picture" of that reality.[24] In their study of human moral behavior, the sociobiologists are arguing, sometimes implicitly and often explicitly, that the best picture of reality is conveyed by some version of reality as designed on the principle of natural selection in the form of the differential reproduction of individuals. This is one of the hypotheses that forms the center of their research program. Quite naturally, hypotheses based on theories of selection raise the question of reality's design, but also the question of who or what has designed the program for selection.[25]

Theissen points to the emergence of culture within the continuum of biological evolution as setting the stage for a new situation with respect to the way selection is defined and exercises its authority.[26] He suggests that the emergence of culture and its evolution entail a fuller hypothesis in the course life's attempt to find adequate structures for adapting to the way things really are.

Here we are skirting the issue of reductionism. Wilson laid down a sophisticated and aggressive theory of reductionism in his "sandwich" view of the sciences. This theory pictures each discipline between two others, one above and one below. The discipline on the underside is obligated to play the role of "antidiscipline" to its neighbor above, in that it seeks to reformulate as much of that neighbor's discipline as possible in terms of its own laws. Contrariwise, it must resist the efforts that come from its own antidiscipline to reformulate its efforts. Wilson writes:

> It is easy to see why each discipline is also an antidiscipline. A tense creative interplay is inevitable because the devotees of adjacent levels of organization are committed to different methodologies when they focus on the upper level.[27]

Wilson understands that it is from this tense interplay that creativity and genuine knowledge emerge. After the dust settles, it becomes clearer just where the successes and the inadequacies of the antidiscipline lie. It is worth noting that he also recognizes the difficulty for meaningful interaction between disciplines that are more than two levels removed from one another—an observation that may be relevant to the present discussion.

Since sociobiologists are rooted more deeply in the biological disciplines than in any other, they are not predisposed to focus upon the elements in cultural evolution that are not susceptible to formulation in biological theories.[28] Theissen's breakthrough comes, not by rejecting the biologistic methodology of the sociobiologists, but rather by presenting a proposal that can integrate their work—in Wilson's own words, addressed originally to the social sciences, "absorb the relevant ideas of biology and go on to beggar them by comparison."[29] In offering its own proposal, theology adopts the methodology that Niels Bohr refers to in the maxim with which Wilson opens his 1977 discussion: "The opposite of a correct statement is a false statement. But the opposite of a profound truth may well be another profound truth."[30]

VIII. THEOLOGY'S PROPOSAL OF "ANOTHER PROFOUND TRUTH"

The phenomenon of culture lies at the interface of the social sciences with the bio-logical antidisciplines; the integration of which ("absorption" in Wilson's usage) has led to the epoch-making proposals of the sociobiologists. This position at the inter-face corresponds to the evolutionary history in which culture has emerged. Culture is here defined as learned patterns of human behavior, together with the symbol sys-tems that contextualize and interpret the behavior.[31] Since its emergence is corre-lated to the appearance of a creature with a highly complex and versatile central nervous system, as is found in *Homo sapiens*, culture must be considered to be a phenomenon within biological evolution. These conditions of emergence are the source of the long debate over whether biological theories are appropriate to the study of culture, whether there are distinctive theories governing culture, and if both of these are true, how to understand the relationship between the biological and the distinctively cultural. The classic nature-nurture debate is a variant of this controversy. Ralph Wendell Burhoe contributed to this issue in his theory of the rela-tion between genetic and cultural evolution. He asserts that the genotype coexists with a comparable culturetype within each individual. This coexistence is a kind of symbiosis between two organisms that have emerged and coadapted within the human organism.[32] His theory holds that while genetic evolution is capable of pro-ducing only kin altruism, following an argument comparable to that which Irons builds on, cultural evolution is able to elicit trans-kin altruism, chiefly carried by religious traditions.[33] Building on the work of Donald T. Campbell,[34] Burhoe insists that this trans-kin altruism not only is possible, but is essential for life at the cul-tural level.[35]

Theissen builds on the theories of Burhoe and Campbell in his insistence that life under the forms of culture offers a hypothesis that provides for human beings a dif-ferent and more adequate picture of what really is than biological evolution alone. Focusing upon the figure of Jesus in the New Testament, he interprets Jesus of Nazareth as a "protest against the principle of selection," in that the

> content of the proclamation of Jesus accords with the tendency which can be observed in the whole of cultural evolution, towards the diminution of selection, which in Biblical religion is accentuated so that it becomes a protest against the harshness of the princi-ple of selection in the belief that this is a way of doing justice to central reality [that is, the way things really are]. This central reality reveals itself in Jesus. . . . God no longer appears as a devastating power—in other words he is not the embodiment of the threat which proceeds from the pressure of selection; rather, God is described with the poetic image of the gracious father, a father who offers and makes possible life at the very point where human beings have offended against the basic conditions of reality. In Biblical terms, God offers the sinner life.[36]

Jesus' ethics embodies the alternative to selection. He praises eunuchs, as St. Paul encourages sexual celibacy; he calls for love of enemies; he insists that outsiders are as close to us as family members; he urges his followers to be servants rather than authoritarian. All these basic demands presuppose a basic trust that the ultimate reality not only allows a much greater range of variations in human conduct, but also permits human conduct which according to the laws of biological evolution would have no chance.[37] In conversation, Irons has aptly termed this the "upside-down quality of Christianity." Theissen and I, however, are arguing that this quality is a clue as to how things really are.

Against this background, Theissen calls Jesus a "mutation," who represents a new option for the future of cultural evolution. The New Testament formulates the basic demands of what really is as:

> ... a double commandment of love: love of God and love of the neighbor. Put another way, it is expressed as trust of the inner riches of reality and as the inner power to give of them. If cultural evolution represents a reduction of selection—i.e., an evolution of principles of evolution—a protest against the harshness of the pressure of selection through the deliberate action and thought of human beings can be recognized as an obligation which is "pre-programmed" into the structure of reality and which no one can escape who wants to accord with the ultimate reality.[38]

The suggestions merit discussion because Burhoe and Theissen are two of the few theologians who have dealt with these issues at length. Whether Theissen's rhetoric of rejecting selection is viable, or even the most adequate expression of his thinking, may be questioned. If selection is equivalent to death without the survival of the genome, one might think that Theissen has not so much eliminated it at the cultural level, or even at the level of Jesus, but rather "absorbed it and gone on" to another level of discussion. Neurobiologist Terrence Deacon speaks of the pressure of selection in terms of the challenge that an emergent in a biological system poses to the rest of the system to adapt in ways that take the most adequate account of the emergent, in service of the viability of the system. The challenge of the emergence of certain features in the brain organization of hominids relevant to language is a key example to which he points.[39] Such a concept of selection pressure puts the emphasis on the adaptation of a cybernetically functioning system, rather than on elimination of maladaptation, although the latter is not excluded. Theissen's suggestion could be interpreted as moving the force of selection processes from the elimination of persons through violence to that of developing societies that exercise selection in other ways.

Theology's attempt at another profound truth is identical with what we formulated earlier as the functional version of theology's assumptions concerning the way things really are: *the nature of reality* is *such that the value and meaning of being human is most fully realized in self-investing behaviors that seek the most wholesome outcomes in the relevant situation in which the actors find themselves.* For the purposes of this discussion, we may say that the doctrinal and sacramental system of Christian theology constitutes the attempt to construct a comprehensive context that will support this regulative idea of the nature of reality.

As the discussion of Theissen indicates, the point of contact with the sociobiological investigation is the theory of inclusive fitness as the regulative idea for understanding what really is. Since the way this theory must function *in the present context* (that is, the study of morality) is that of a regulative, rather than as a constitutive, idea, inclusive fitness is offered as a proposal, not a fact. Our earlier discussion should have made that clear. Irons is trying out this proposal, as if to say, "Let us assume that reality is designed along the lines of natural selection in the form of inclusive fitness, and, applying game theory, let us see whether this accounts for behaviors of altruism, cooperation, and self-investment within the context of human social interactions." Theology understands that it is highly important that science be able to reconcile the emergence of these moral behaviors and inclusive fitness. But when it comes to regulative ideas of what really is, theology counters with the proposal, "Let us rather assume that these three types of moral behavior (altruism, cooperation, and self-commitment) are of intrinsic worth, and that they are normative examples of what adaptation to reality requires, even if they do not result in the survival of the actor's genes." In other words, adaptation to reality includes more than the survival of the genes as such. Theology speaks of this "more."[40]

The theological proposal moves thought to the question of what it is that constitutes survival for human beings.[41] As an alternative to Theissen's rejection of selection, I would suggest that theology works with different notions of survival and selection—notions that may be more appropriate for the distinctiveness of culture over against biology.[42] Theologically, survival is defined by God and God's will. In functional terms, this translates into the survival of the creation as such, that is, the natural realm in its widest possible definition, because it is this realm that theology terms *God's creation.* Neuroscientist Roger Sperry offers such a wide definition when he speaks of nature as a

> vast interwoven evolving fabric . . . a tremendously complex concept that includes all the immutable and emergent forces of cosmic causation that control everything from high-energy subnuclear particles to galaxies, not forgetting the causal properties that govern brain function and behavior at individual, interpersonal, and social levels.[43]

Behaviors of self-investment are undertaken, within this scheme, not for the sake of the future of the individual actor's genome, but rather in behalf of the most wholesome survival of the created order as such. Since individuals cannot relate to the "created order as such," each of them serves the whole by relating to the specific situation or situations to which his or her behaviors are relevant. Furthermore, even though the material content of the formal category "most wholesome survival," is difficult to determine, even provisionally; all moral behaviors operate under a practical assumption of what that content is.

IX. THE THEOLOGICAL FRAMEWORK FOR THE PROFOUND TRUTH

Christian theology sketches a very large scenario (or ideology) within which self-investing behavior can find the support it requires. The theory of natural selection in the form of inclusive fitness provides strong support for the "profound truth" of the sociobiological proposal, because it is both a powerful engine of biological survival and also a persuasive argument to common sense. In contrast, the theological proposal is in many ways counterintuitive for common sense, because it exhorts self-investment under circumstances in which there may be no apparent gain, either to the individual actor or to the actor's progeny. Hence the need for a powerful structure of ideological support that describes what really is in terms that will support self-investing behaviors.[44] The scenario may be summarized in the following terms:

It begins with the affirmation that all that is, all of nature—cosmic and terrestrial—is grounded in a creator God whose character is marked by freedom, justice, faithfulness and reliability, and love. The traditional Christian doctrine of creation out of nothing expresses the conviction that there is no source or ground of nature other than this creator God, while the doctrine of continuing creation asserts that God continues as source to the natural world in every moment, and not only with respect to origins. God's presence as source and ground of nature is everywhere and always marked by freedom, faithfulness, justice, reliability, and love.

Human beings are part of this creation—one of the Biblical stories depicts them emerging on the sixth day, following a sequence that is generally evolutionary in its form (Gen. 1), while another pictures human beings as creatures of the earth into whom God has breathed the divine spirit (Gen. 2). This spirit is what makes the earth-creature genuinely human. The presence of God in the context of human identity is also affirmed in the single most important statement that Christian faith makes about human beings, that they are created in the image of God. There is no consensus in the Christian tradition as to precisely what constitutes the image of God, but when it is linked to the two creation doctrines it forms a strong statement about the purpose of human life, namely, that it is to instantiate God's will.

The scenario also speaks vividly of the dissonance that characterizes human existence. The dissonance is not presented as essential or normative nature, but rather as a disruption of that normative humanity, an intrusion that is imaged as a fall from the essential condition.[45] The dissonance is conveyed in the doctrines of fall and sin.

The figure of Jesus Christ is central to Christian faith. In Christ, on the one hand, and in union with him, the alienation and guilt that accompany sin are transmuted into reconciliation—oneness with self, others, nature, and God. On the other hand, Jesus is the model or paradigm of the form that normative human nature should take.

When Christians share in this reconciliation, and conform their lives to the life of Christ, they believe that they are actualizing what they were created to be. Since Jesus does hold this position as revealer of truth, reconciler, and model of normative human-ity, and since union with him is the centerpiece of Christian faith, normative human life takes the shape of the self-giving that God is said to have embodied in Jesus for the benefit of the whole creation and its people. This embodiment is so central to the system of meaning that the early centuries of theological development undergirded it with the heavy ontological machinery of the two-natures conceptuality.

The coherence of this Christian narrative is filled out in the conviction that human beings, together with the entire creation, are on a trajectory that is defined by God's will as embodied in Christ, and this trajectory will finally bring the fulfillment or con-summation of the created order, including human beings as part of that order.

The coherence of this narrative must be linked to the ritual of the Christian faith, which centers in Baptism and Holy Communion. These two rituals, together with innu-merable ancillary ones, reenact in symbolic form the behavior that is commensurate with the myth or narrative (which depicts the way things really are). The task of the believer is to translate this symbolic action into the actual behavior that takes place in everyday life. The rituals thus serve as a bridge or a sort of "interlude" between life as narrated in the myth, and the "arena of the social world where ethical decision making and character formation count."[46] Baptism is a ritual of regenerative cleansing, entrance into the covenant community with Christ, and incorporation into his life, death, and resurrection. Holy Communion is a ritual of community love and solidarity, remembrance of the pivotal events in Jesus' life, and incorporation into his action of self-giving for the world, both as recipients of Jesus' self-giving and as followers who extend his self-giving into our own worlds.

X. THE SALIENT RESOURCES IN THE FRAMEWORK

Since a full discussion of how this theological scenario of Christian faith provides resources for dealing with the issues that Irons raises is not possible here, a sketch is in order to show how the traditional thinking supports the "profound truth" that the-ology offers. Five elements of the scenario should be noted in particular for the resources they contain.

Creation Doctrines
Theissen's suggestions are permeated with the theme of trust—trust in the basic real-ity ("the way things really are") and trust in our own ability to embody trust in our lives. He writes:

> The pressure of selection means that resources are scarce and the weak have no chance. In view of this Jesus calls for trust in the Creator who cares for all his creatures...The basic

trust bound up with the metaphor of the father is ultimately trust that the central reality is "love," to which one should respond by loving one's fellows.[47]

Ralph Burhoe suggested a comparable view, grounding trust in God as the Lord of History, equivalent to a metaphysical rendering of natural selection, a God who takes up all of nature into a winnowing process for the Good.[48] Theissen's perspective is deeply influenced by his Lutheran heritage, while Burhoe's is Calvinist.

This emphasis on a regulative idea of nature as grounded in reality as trustworthy and trust-engendering is central to the Christian theological scenario and to the discussion with sociobiology. Obviously this is a difficult concept for scientists to entertain, because it seems to inject emotional, anthropomorphic considerations into our reflection upon nature. *This difficulty is so great and so important that it must, from the theological side, be raised to the highest priority for conversations between theology and science.*

Within the Christian framework of meaning, the doctrines of creation are foundational. The traditional "creation out of nothing" doctrine asserts that God alone is the source of all that is, and that, since God's creating work is intentional, the creation conforms to the character of the Creator—trustworthy, loving, just, and free. The equally traditional "continuing creation" doctrine maintains that God continues to be in this relationship to the creation. Together, as the initial notes of the primordial mythic score, these two doctrines establish the ground and necessity of both trustworthiness and trusting.

Human Beings Created in the Image of God

The traditional doctrine of their creation in the image of God binds human beings to the character and intentionality of God with ontological force. Despite their finitude and fallibility, which is underscored in the doctrines of the Fall, Original Sin, and Actual Sin, human beings cannot escape this fundamental truth about themselves: somehow, in ways that surpass their understanding, they are inseparably caught up in the ways and intentions of God, the ground of how things really are. Their existence finds its meaning in instantiating what is most consistent with this ground.

Jesus Christ

Jesus Christ is characterized as *Logos* (John. 1:1) and as that in which all things cohere (Col. 1: 15–20). In continuity with the way in which classical philosophers employed such terms, this way of talking about Christ ascribes to him the status of expressing in himself the meaning and intentionality of the way things really are. His life and work thus bring concretely into the realm of human history what was affirmed of all of nature in the creation doctrines. This status marks both what Jesus offers to his fellow human beings and also what he demands of them: trustworthiness and trusting by investing oneself in behaviors that aim at the well-being of the creation.

It is in this constellation of traditional affirmation and doctrine that the background assertions of trustworthiness and trusting concerning what really is are translated into the foreground of behaviors of altruism, cooperation, and self-commitment that intersect with the researches of the sociobiologists and anthropologists who follow in Irons's train. In this translation, we come upon the proposal that such behaviors are not engendered only by the requirements of natural selection in the form of inclusive fitness, but also by the nature of reality itself. Such behaviors are to be assessed not only for their impact (1) upon individual survival, but also (2) upon the total situation in which they occur, and (3) upon the final survival of the creation—survival here functioning as virtual synonym for redemption. When it is defined in this way, survival takes on meanings that amplify the use of the term in strictly scientific contexts.

The symbolic import of Jesus Christ underscores, in a normative fashion within the Christian theological scenario, that the reality system of nature in which we live is itself basically an ambience in which we truly belong, an ambience that has brought us into being and that enables us to fulfill the purposes for which we were created. Christ asserts that the central reality that undergirds all of concrete experience and to which we continually seek to adapt, is disposed toward us in a way that we interpret as graciousness and beneficent support.

Forgiveness of Sins and Justification by Grace

A major obstacle to human confidence in the trustworthiness of reality and the ontological grounding of the trusting on the part of human beings is a sense of the inadequacy of individuals' actions and the inability to conform themselves to the fundamental meaning of reality. Forgiveness of sins speaks of reality as accepting of and compassionate toward human inadequacy, thereby implying that the reality system can absorb error and evil intent without losing its integrity or momentum. The doctrine of forensic justification (that individuals are declared to be acceptable to God regardless of their behavior) asserts that fundamentally, as natural creatures, human beings are capable of being bearers of the basic meanings of reality; they are capable, as created, of bearing the image of God. These doctrines are not naïve refusals to acknowledge the sin and evil of human beings—both as individuals and as collectives—but, on the contrary, they assert the confidence that even their despicable sins cannot obliterate their created nature and its possibilities. The doctrine of forensic justification is especially powerful at this point, since it affirms unequivocally that God, as the ground of all reality, finds individuals to be suitable for life and acceptable to the ground of being *as they are*, in their actual existence. Furthermore, as Theissen explains, this doctrine gives hope and steadfastness to human beings in their state of unavoidable uncertainty as to whether the future will bear out the correctness or adequacy of their behaviors.[49]

The Trajectory of Fulfillment

Ralph Wendell Burhoe observed two central elements of traditional religion that most secular alternatives set aside.[50] He considers these omissions as irremediable flaws in the surrogate systems, because without them, adequate explanations or resources for human behavior cannot be provided. These two elements are belief in "a sovereign of evolving reality which created human beings and all other things and upon which human beings are utterly dependent," and "a definition of what it is about human beings and their lives that is of long-range importance ... some core element in human nature which transcends the death of the body."[51] Pierre Teilhard de Chardin gave a major portion of his attention to the far-distant future of evolution.[52] The physicist-cosmologist Frank Tipler follows Burhoe in ascribing major significance to this aspect of religious belief, a belief that he argues "is a testable physical theory for an omnipresent, omniscient, omnipotent God who will one day in the far future resurrect every single one of us to live forever in an abode which is in all essentials the Judeo-Christian Heaven."[53]

The theological proposal that responds to the sociobiologist rests for the most part on the assumption that, if reality is grounded in the meanings that the doctrines of creation and Christ assert, the determinative concept of survival must be larger than the inclusive fitness of the individual, or of even the community, the species, or the planet. Theological reflection upon the broad trajectory of future fulfillment is, of necessity, often marked by a high degree of speculation as to the specific characteristics of the trajectory. While this speculation is essential, the theological scenario does not necessarily stand or fall with the validity of those speculations, even those of Teilhard and Tipler.

XI. THE CHALLENGE OF THE ANTIDISCIPLINE: ANTHROPOLOGY AND THEOLOGY RESPONDING TO WILSON

The argument of this essay accepts (at least for heuristic purposes) Wilson's imagery of the disciplines related in sandwich fashion, with each discipline placed as the antidiscipline to those disciplines immediately above it, and each also confronted by an antidiscipline immediately below.[54] We also accept as a useful heuristic Wilson's injunction that the discipline above in each case is to absorb its antidiscipline and go on to beggar it by comparison. Richard Busse has pointed out to me that Wilson's concept of absorption and going on to beggar by comparison may be an example of what Hegel described in the dialectic of negation. Every phenomenon is accepted for what it is, "negated" (a metaphor for the work of the antidiscipline?) and then transformed or "sublated" (*aufgehoben*, in German) into a new synthesis that preserves the values of the original, but raises them to a new and fuller power.

If we may posit that sociobiological biology, represented by Wilson, is the antidiscipline to anthropology, then Irons's sociobiological anthropology (or, as he sometimes calls it, "human sociobiology") is to be assessed according to its success in absorbing and going on to beggar Wilson by comparison. Analogously, if we are permitted to suppose that Wilson s sociobiological biology and Irons s sociobiological anthropology are antidisciplines to this writer s (sociobiological?) theology, the argument of this essay stands under the criterion of whether it has absorbed and gone on to beggar both Wilson and Irons by comparison. Arrogance aside, it may nevertheless be instructive to conclude by commenting on both Irons and this essay in these terms.

Whether the biologist who pursues sociobiology would find Irons s argument satisfactory, this theologian cannot judge. I would call attention to the final sections of Irons s paper, in which he points to the larger implications of the reflections that his earlier sections have argued. His point is that cooperation (and altruism?) beyond kin is essential for building groups of large nonkin alliances; the stronger the group, the more advantageous for success in inevitable intergroup competition. Surely this is an important stage of absorption and going on beyond the sheer biological outcomes of the antidiscipline. This is particularly true in terms of the implication that Irons notes: that groups, in addition to individuals, have an intrinsic worth. When these groups are trans-kin (as Irons s argument assumes), genetic evolution (although it has the final word, so to speak) requires enhancement in order to move to the formation of nonkin groups, and this enhancement is cultural.

Consequently, Irons s proposed theory (building upon Alexander, Boyd and Richerson,[55] and Frank) beggars sociobiology by establishing the desirability, in evolutionary terms, of precisely that which genetic evolution as such cannot produce the cooperating nonkin group based on self-committing behaviors of altruism.

Irons seems to support Alexander s thesis that the adaptational value of nonkin groups is determined by their success in intergroup conflict. Building on this thesis, Ralph Burhoe and Solomon Katz suggest that intergroup conflict is presently maladaptive, drawing the conclusion that the entire global human community is one group, in which trans-kin altruism and cooperation must be enabled in their opinion through religion or its surrogate.[56]

If the theological proposal does truly constitute another profound truth set alongside the profound truths of Wilson and Irons, its truth lies in its insistence that trans-kin altruism, cooperation, and self-investing behaviors find their ground in the most fundamental character of reality. Natural selection in the form of inclusive fitness is a piece of this, but not the whole. The ongoing well-being of the entire created (natural) order is predicated on this basic law of nature, that in self-giving for the sake of the whole life is enhanced and the individual is fulfilled.

A kind of hierarchy may be glimpsed here. Wilson and his peers established that altruism, if it is practiced among kin, does not necessarily violate the calculus of natural selection in the form of inclusive fitness. Irons and his peers beggar this insight with the argument that altruism between nonkin also does not violate that calculus of the genes. The theological proposal that this essay advances rests on a further attempt at beggaring: that not only do altruism, cooperation, and self-investing behaviors not violate that calculus of the genes, but that they are both commensurate with and required by the fundamental character of the reality system in which human beings and all of nature exist, and which is far larger than genetic evolution, since it includes all that is encompassed in the concept of creation, which I cited earlier in Roger Sperry s terms.

Wilson s image of the interfacing of the disciplines suggests that that interface is also the border between that in the uppermost discipline which is successfully subjected to reductionism by the antidiscipline, and that which represents a breakthrough area because it resists reduction. Absorption involves accepting the reductionism, while beggaring, by comparison, refers to the breakthroughs by the uppermost discipline.

Theology s breakthrough (and that of philosophy, as well) would certainly include an aspect of moral behavior that genetic calculus as interpreted by game theory, by its very nature, leaves untouched. Game theory, by its very constitution, is applicable directly only to one-on-one interactions between individuals. It can refer to more individuals indirectly, as when one of the individuals represents a larger group, for example, in plea bargain negotiations between a prisoner and a district attorney. In such a case, the inclusive fitness criterion would apply only to the prisoner. If both individuals are representatives, then the genetic calculus is rendered of no effect. Even in the prisoner/district attorney example, the prisoner is not responding to an individual on the terms that are set forth in Irons s use of game theory.

Theology understands that morality comprehends more than the interactions between individuals. Morality at its most profound represents reflection on the meaning of one s life and a decision concerning just what investments of that life are most desirable or undesirable, good or bad. Paul Tillich (following Saint Paul and Martin Luther) speaks of the law that is embodied in our essential nature, the inner law of one s being. This inner law is the most effective expression of what makes for a good or bad investment of one s life.[57] In my scheme of thought, this law represents the way things really are. Disregard or disobedience of this law results in guilt, depression, and dread in the theological literature. The doctrines of forgiveness and justification speak of reality s capacity and intention to overcome these instances of disobedience. Much of morality occurs in the negotiation that the individual carries on with this law. Martyrdom, enlistment in enterprises that are known ahead of time to be lost causes, engagement in actions for social change that may well succeed, but that require the deaths of at least a few (the civil rights actions of Martin Luther King s movement in the 1960s or Gandhi s satyagraha movements) these are all examples of behavior that is just as much at the heart of morality as are the one-on-one interactions that Irons describes. Game theory does not have the capacity to deal with these examples on the criterion of inclusive fitness.

These examples of morality are especially appropriate to cultural evolution, because there is often an intention to make a witness to posterity, that is, to survive in the cultures of succeeding generations. Theologically, this type of survival is relevant to the criterion of serving the care and redemption of creation, or serving the well-being of the situation.

In its insistence that this area of morality must be included in comprehensive theory, theology is not repudiating the sociobiological theories as set forth by Irons. Rather, it is absorbing them as relevant to a certain domain of morality, but going on beyond them according to criteria that lie outside the domain of sociobiological anthropology in its role as antidiscipline to the disciplines located above it.

When theology introduces the criterion of survival in terms of care and redemption of creation, it is superordinating culture to genes, while at the same time maintaining the symbiosis of the two. In introducing this criterion, theology acknowledges that the most significant contribution of human beings to the creation, for both good and ill, is not their genes alone, but their culture (granting that genes have made their culture possible in the first place, and that culture without the genetic substrate is impossible). The moral implications of the Christian tradition are directed toward enabling human culture to share in God s fulfillment of the creation. In functional terms, this translates into a care and redemption of the natural order (which includes human culture) that both transcends human understanding, and also lies outside human control. The religious tradition insists, in other words, that morality is a venture of faith, as well as of reason. This may be close to Irons s reference to passion and reason in morality. In any case, Wilson, interpreted in a Hegelian vein, is correct: The truth lies in the genes, but in order for that truth to become actual in human affairs, it must be transformed into the genuinely human terms of culture and into the terms of nature understood in its largest frame as God s creation.

NOTES

1. Patrick H. Nowell-Smith, Religion and Morality, in *Encyclopedia of Philosophy* (New York: Macmillan and The Free Press, 1967), Vol. 7, p. 150.
2. Irons, Morality, Religion, and Human Evolution, p. 375.
3. Robert Frank, *Passion within Reason: The Strategic Role of the Emotions* (New York: W.W. Norton and Co., 1988).
4. Irons, 378.
5. Irons, p. 378.
6. Richard D. Alexander, *The Biology of Moral Systems* (New York: Aldine DeGruyter, 1987).
7. See Robert J. McShea, *Passion within Reason*.
8. See *Morality and Human Nature* (Philadelphia: Temple University Press, 1990).
9. Michael Ruse, *Taking Darwin Seriously* (Cambridge: Blackwell, 1986).
10. E.O. Wilson, *On Human Nature* (Cambridge: Harvard University Press, 1978).
11. Irons, p. 375.
12. Irons, p. 381.
13. Hefner, *The Human Factor* (Minneapolis: Fortress Press, 1993), p. 72.
14. Wilson, *Sociobiology: The New Synthesis* (Cambridge: Harvard University Press, 1975), p. 1.
15. *Sociobiology*, p. 1.
16. *On Human Nature*, pp. 1—2.

17. Irons, p. 375.

18. Karl Popper, *The Logic of Scientific Discovery* (London: Hutchinson, 1972), p. 86.

19. *The Human Factor*, pp. 33—35, 287.

20. *The Human Factor*, pp. 187—190.

21. This is one of the most important points at which Irons and I have encountered difficulties in mutual understanding, and one that we believe requires further reflection and conversation.

22. Immanuel Kant, *Critique of Pure Reason*, trans. Norman Kemp Smith, (London: Macmillan & Co. Ltd., 1958), pp. 550—551.

23. Gerd Theissen, *Biblical Faith: An Evolutionary Approach* (Minneapolis: Fortress Press, 1985).

24. *Biblical Faith*, pp. 111 f.

25. See John Tooby and Leda Cosmides, The Psychological Foundations of Culture, in Jerome Barkow, John Tooby, and Leda Cosmides, eds., *The Adapted Mind: Evolutionary Psychology and the Generation of Culture* (New York: Oxford University Press, 1992).

26. *Biblical Faith*, pp. 113 f.

27. Wilson, Biology and the Social Sciences, *Zygon: Journal of Religion and Science*, 25 (September 1990), p. 247; reprinted from *Daedalus*, 106 (Fall 1977), pp. 127—140.

28. Hefner, Entrusting the Life That Has Evolved: A Response to Michael Ruse s Ruse, *Zygon: Journal of Religion and Science* 29 (March 1994), pp. 71 f.

29. Biology and the Social Sciences, p. 260. Of course, it is clear that Irons does not work, as Wilson does, in biology, but rather in anthropology. Consequently, Irons is also attempting to follow Wilson s advice to absorb the relevant ideas of biology and move on. The appropriateness of my comments rests on Irons s explicit adoption of inclusive fitness as the bottom line regulative idea for his investigation; see Irons, p. 375.

30. Wilson, Biology and the Social Sciences, p. 245.

31. *The Human Factor*, pp. 145—156.

32. Ralph Wendell Burhoe, *Toward a Scientific Theology* (Belfast: Christian Journals Limited, 1981), chs. 6—7.

33. *Toward a Scientific Theology*, ch. 7.

34. Donald T. Campbell, The Conflict between Social and Biological Evolution and the Concept of Original Sin, *Zygon: Journal of Religion and Science* 10 (September 1975), pp. 234—249. See also On the Conflicts between Biological and Social Evolution and between Psychology and Moral Tradition, *Zygon* 11 (September 1976), pp. 167—208.

35. *Toward a Scientific Theology*, ch. 7.

36. *Biblical Faith*, pp. 112—113.

37. *Biblical Faith*, p. 115.

38. *Biblical Faith*, pp. 127—128.

39. Terrence Deacon, Brain-Language Coevolution, in John Hawkins and Murray Gell-Mann (eds.), *The Evolution of Human Languages* (Redwood City: Addison-Wesley Publishing Co., 1992). Rodney Holmes called my attention to Deacon s way of reshaping the concept of the pressure exerted by selection.

40. William James developed this concept of the more ; see *The Varieties of Religious Experience* (New York: Longmans, Green, and Co., 1908), ch. 20, esp. pp. 508—519.

41. Hefner, Survival as a Human Value, *Zygon: Journal of Religion and Science* 15 (June 1980), pp. 203—12.

42. These theological notions would incorporate the thinking of Deacon in Brain-Language Coevolution.

43. Roger Sperry, *Science and Moral Priority* (New York: Columbia University Press, 1983), p. 114.

44. Donald Campbell has reflected on the function of massive ideologies to undergird break-throughs into new forms of human behavior. See A Naturalistic Theory of Archaic Moral Orders, *Zygon: Journal of Religion and Science* 26 (March 1991), pp. 91–114.

45. See Langdon Gilkey, *Maker of Heaven and Earth: A Study of the Christian Doctrine of Creation* (Garden City: Doubleday, 1959), pp. 182 ff., 186 f.

46. Ronald Grimes, *Ritual Criticism* (New York: Oxford University Press, 1990), p. 164.

47. *Biblical Faith*, p. 127.

48. *Toward a Scientific Theology*, ch. 4. See also Hefner, To What Extent Can Science Replace Metaphysics? Reflecting with Ralph Wendell Burhoe on the Lord of History, *Zygon* 12 (March 1977), pp. 88–104.

49. *Biblical Faith*, pp. 171–174.

50. *Toward a Scientific Theology*, pp. 113–119.

51. *Toward a Scientific Theology*, p. 116.

52. Teilhard de Chardin, *The Phenomenon of Man*, 2nd ed. (New York: Harper and Row, 1965), esp. pp. 237–290. See also Philip Hefner, *The Promise of Teilhard* (Philadelphia and New York: J. B. Lipincott, 1970), chs. 3–4.

53. Frank J. Tipler, *The Physics of Immortality: Modern Cosmology, God, and the Resurrection of the Dead* (New York: Doubleday, 1994).

54. See Biology and the Social Sciences, p. 16. This maxim would have to allow for exceptions with respect to the bottommost and the topmost disciplines in the hierarchy. Is there any discipline above theology in this arrangement? Arthur Peacocke suggests not; see *Creation and the World of Science* (Oxford: Oxford University Press, 1979), p. 369.

55. Robert Boyd and Peter J. Richerson, *Culture and the Evolutionary Process* (Chicago: University of Chicago Press, 1985).

56. Ralph Wendell Burhoe and Solomon Katz, War, Peace and Religion s Biocultural Evolution, *Zygon: Journal of Religion and Science* 21 (December 1986), pp. 439–472.

57. Paul Tillich, *Morality and Beyond* (New York: Harper & Row, 1963), p. 34, and chs. 2–3. See also *Systematic Theology*, Vol. II (Chicago: University of Chicago Press, 1957), pp. 80 f., 119–122, 132.

REFLECTIONS ON THE DIALOGUE

PHILIP HEFNER AND WILLIAM IRONS

In the course of commenting through the means of electronic mail on each other s first drafts of the papers included in this volume, we developed a rather intense dialogue on some basic issues that we could not resolve to our satisfaction. Consequently, we offer this jointly authored statement not to argue once again the issues, nor to fashion a quick-fix solution to the issues, but rather to specify what an earnest and open-minded anthropologist and a theologian with the same attributes found to be the most interesting and most difficult nub of their conversation. Perhaps the scheme of Nowell-Smith s definition of morality (which both of us found helpful) focuses the issue most clearly. Nowell-Smith designated three elements of morality: (1) beliefs about the nature of human beings in their world; (2) beliefs about what is good or desirable; (3) rules laying down what ought or ought not to be done. One of the issues on which the two of us pursue variant lines of analysis is where science, specifically sociobiology, fits into this scheme. Irons understands that science provides only step 1 of this scheme, while it constrains, but does not determine, steps 2 and 3. Hefner suggests that reflection upon morality is distinctive in that the beliefs that qualify in step 1 serve intrinsically to shape our understanding of step 2, whether our discipline is science or theology. Hefner believes that this distinctive character of step 1 beliefs in the context of moral reflection means that step 1 beliefs function as concepts of the way things really are, which is the operational weight of a God-concept that is, that concept, conforming to which constitutes the definition of morality (this is the force of Kant s concept of a regulative idea). Irons allows that the interrelationship of steps 1, 2, and 3 is exceedingly intimate and complex, but bridles at the notion that scientific ideas could function as God-concepts. Indeed, he believes that such a suggestion clouds the true function of science. Hefner suggests that to deny the de facto function of certain scientific theories as God-concepts is to miss the profoundest moral implications of sociobiology, including its serious inability to take the measure of moral phenomena. Hefner does not intend this as a dismissal of sociobiology (as some critics seem to dismiss it), but rather as a necessary interpretational move if we are to recognize the profound relevance of sociobiology for religion and morality, as well as the limitations of such investigation. The limitations call, not for rejection of sociobiology, but rather, as Wilson challenges, the absorption and going beyond.

Irons does not reject Hefner s suggestions out of hand. He accepts the discipline/antidiscipline mode of relating sociobiology and theology. He even agrees that natural selection and inclusive fitness are just as central to sociobiology as God is to theology. However, he believes that sociobiology does not deal with the meaning of life and oughtness in the way theology does. Irons also insists that the affective qualities that are associated with the relationship between human beings and God are not applicable to sociobiology s use of natural selection.

Perhaps the point to which we have come is this: Irons recognizes more than before how intimately related sociobiology and religion are in their reflecting upon morality, but he is not yet clear about the nuances of that intimate relationship. Hefner is impressed with the genuinely theological import of the sociobiological reflections, but is not certain how to understand the significance of that import. Irons tends to think that Hefner is going too far in ascribing theological intent to sociobiology, while Hefner believes that Irons is fudging on the theological character of his assumptions. Irons and Hefner join in the conclusion that sociobiological reflection on moral behavior has a direct impact upon the myths and rituals by which all people conduct their lives, whether they are explicitly religious or not, and they agree that the nexus of myth-morality-sociobiology is a critical issue for further attention.

APPENDICES

The following suggestions for further reading are organized according to the various themes covered in the book. An additional section of recommendations has been added for several ethical issues with deep connections to both science and religion. As explained in the General Introduction, these ethical problems have deliberately not been thematized in this volume, in order to keep it relatively well focused. Users of the volume, however, are encouraged to use what has been covered here as a foundation for further investigation of the ethical problems for which an understanding of science and religion promises to be fruitful. Some of the important books in science and religion that do not easily fit into this classification are listed in a fifth section.

I. HISTORY OF THE RELATIONS BETWEEN SCIENCE AND THEOLOGY

1.1 Science and Theology in the Enlightenment

Brooke, John Hedley. *Science and Religion: Some Historical Perspectives*. Cambridge and New York: Cambridge University Press, 1991.

Buckley, Michael. *At the Origins of Modern Atheism*. New Haven: Yale University Press, 1987.

Dillenberger, John. *Protestant Thought and Natural Science*. Notre Dame: University of Notre Dame Press, 1960.

Funkenstein, Amos. *Theology and the Scientific Imagination from the Middle Ages to the Seventeenth Century*. Princeton: Princeton University Press, 1986.

Gascoigne, John. *Cambridge in the Age of the Enlightenment: Science, Religion and Politics from the Restoration to the French Revolution*. Cambridge and New York: Cambridge University Press, 1989.

Klaaren, Eugene. *Religious Origins of Modern Science*. Grand Rapids: Eerdmans, 1977.

Lindberg, David C. and Ronald L. Numbers, eds. *God and Nature: Historical Essays on the Encounter between Christianity and Science*. Berkeley: University of California Press, 1986.

Westfall, Richard S. *Science and Religion in Seventeenth-Century England*. Ann Arbor: University of Michigan Press, 1973.

1.2 Science and Theology in the Nineteenth Century

Chadwick, Owen. *The Secularization of the European Mind in the Nineteenth Century*. Cambridge and New York: Cambridge University Press, 1975.

Cosslett, Tess, ed. *Science and Religion in the Nineteenth Century*. Cambridge and New York: Cambridge University Press, 1984.

Draper, John William. *History of the Conflict between Religion and Science*. London and New York: Appleton, 1874.

Durant, John, ed. *Darwinism and Divinity*. Oxford and New York: Basil Blackwell, 1985.

Glick, Thomas F. *The Comparative Reception of Darwinism*. Austin: University of Texas Press, 1972.

Greene, John C. *The Death of Adam: Evolution and its Impact on Western Thought*. Ames: Iowa State University Press, 1961.

Gregory, Frederick. *Nature Lost? Natural Science and the German Theological Traditions of the Nineteenth Century*. Cambridge: Harvard University Press, 1992.

Hull, David L. *Darwin and His Critics*. Cambridge: Harvard University Press, 1973.

Kohn, David, ed. *The Darwinian Heritage*. Princeton, Princeton University Press, 1985.

Moore, James R. *The Post-Darwinian Controversies: A Study of the Protestant Struggle to Come to Terms with Darwin in Great Britain and America, 1870—1900*. Cambridge and New York: Cambridge University Press, 1979.

Roberts, Jon H. *Darwinism and the Divine in America*. Madison: University of Wisconsin Press, 1988.

White, Andrew Dickson. *A History of the Warfare of Science with Theology in Christendom*. London and New York: Appleton, 1896.

1.3 Science and Theology in the Contemporary Period

Peacocke, Arthur, ed. *The Sciences and Theology in the Twentieth Century*. Notre Dame: University of Notre Dame Press, 1981.

Polkinghorne, John. *Science and Christian Belief*. London: SPCK, 1994.

Powers, Jonathan. *Philosophy and the New Physics*. London and New York: Routledge, 1982.

Rolston, Holmes, III. *Science and Religion: A Critical Survey*. Philadelphia: Temple University Press, 1987.

Stanesby, Derek. *Science, Reason, and Religion*. London and New York: Routledge, 1988.

II. THE METHODS OF SCIENCE AND THEOLOGY

2.1 Ways of Relating Science and Theology

Appleyard, Bryan. *Understanding the Present: Science and the Soul of Modern Man*. New York: Doubleday, 1993.

Barbour, Ian G. *Myths, Models and Paradigms: A Comparative Study in Science and Religion*. New York: Harper & Row, 1974.

Drees, Willem B. *Religion, Science and Naturalism*. Cambridge and New York: Cambridge University Press, 1995.

Ferre, Frederick. *Hellfire and Lightning Rods: Liberating Science, Technology, and Religion*. Maryknoll: Orbis, 1993.

Gerhart, Mary and Allan M. Russell. *Metaphoric Process: The Creation of Scientific and Religious Understanding*. Fort Worth: Christian University Press, 1984.

Gilkey, Langdon. *Religion and the Scientific Future: Reflections on Myth, Science, and Theology*. New York: Harper & Row, 1970.

Harre, Rom. *Varieties of Realism*. Oxford and New York: Basil Blackwell, 1986.

McFague, Sallie. *Metaphorical Theology: Models of God in Religious Language*. London: SCM, 1983.

Polkinghorne, John. *One World: The Interaction of Science and Theology*. Princeton: Princeton University Press, 1986.

Santmire, Paul. *The Travail of Nature*. Philadelphia: Fortress, 1985.

Soskice, Janet. *Metaphor and Religious Language*. Oxford and New York: Oxford University Press, 1985.

Huysteen, J. Wentzel van. *Theology and the Justification of Faith*. Grand Rapids: Eerdmans, 1989.

2.2 Similarities and Differences between Science and Theology

Banner, Michael C. *The Justification of Science and the Rationality of Religious Belief*. Oxford and New York: Oxford University Press, 1990.

Clayton, Philip. *Explanation from Physics to Theology: An Essay in Rationality and Religion*. New Haven: Yale University Press, 1989.

Hesse, Mary B. *Models and Analogies in Science*. London: Sheed and Ward, 1963.

Kuhn, Thomas. *The Structure of Scientific Revolutions*. Chicago: University of Chicago Press, 1962.

Mascall, E.L. *Christian Theology and Natural Science: Some Questions in their Relations*. London: Archon Books, 1965.

McMullin, Ernan. *The Inference that Makes Science*. Milwaukee: Marquette University Press, 1992.

Midgley, Mary. *Evolution as a Religion: Strange Hopes and Stranger Fears*. Oxford and New York: Methuen, 1985.

Murphy, Nancey. *Theology in the Age of Scientific Reasoning*. Ithaca: Cornell University Press, 1990.

Polanyi, Michael. *Personal Knowledge*. New York: Harper & Row, 1964.

Pollard, William. *Transcendence and Providence*. Edinburgh: Scottish Academic Press, 1987.

Schoen, Edward L. *Religious Explanations: A Model from the Sciences*. Durham, Duke University Press, 1985.

Wildman, Wesley J. Similarities and Differences in the Practice of Theology and Science. *CTNS Bulletin* 14/3 (Fall, 1994).

Wolterstorff, Nicholas. *Reason Within the Bounds of Religion*. 2nd ed. Grand Rapids: Eerdmans, 1984.

Zygon 27/2 (June, 1992), pp. 221—234, for a set of reviews of majors works in theology and science; and 27/3 (September, 1992), for a set of responses to the reviews of the previous issue.

III. SUBSTANTIVE INTERACTIONS BETWEEN SCIENCE AND THEOLOGY

3.1 Cosmology and Creation

Barrow, John D. *The World Within the World*. Oxford and New York: Oxford University
    Press, 1990.

    . *The Origin of the Universe*. New York: HarperCollins, 1994.

    , and Frank J. Tipler. *The Anthropic Cosmological Principle*. Oxford and New York:
    Oxford University Press, 1986.

Davies, Paul. *The First Three Minutes: A Modern View of the Origin of the Universe*. 2nd
    ed. New York: Basic Books, 1993.

    . *The Last Three Minutes: Conjectures about the Ultimate Fate of the Universe*. New
    York: Basic Books, 1994.

    . *The Mind of God: The Scientific Basis for a Rational World*. New York: Simon &
    Schuster, 1992.

Drees, Willem B. *Beyond the Big Bang: Quantum Cosmologies and God*. La Salle: Open
    Court, 1990.

Dyson, Freeman J. *Infinite in All Directions*. San Francisco: Harper & Row, 1988.

Ellis, George. *Before the Beginning: Cosmology Explained*. London: Boyars/Bowerdean,
    1993.

Gilkey, Langdon. *Maker of Heaven and Earth: The Christian Doctrine of Creation in the
    Light of Modern Knowledge*. Garden City: Doubleday, 1959.

Harris, Errol. *Cosmos as Anthropos: A Philosohical Interpretation of the Anthropic
    Cosmological Principle*. New Jersey: Humanities Press, 1990.

Hawking, Stephen. *A Brief History of Time: From the Big Bang to Black Holes*. Toronto:
    Bantam Books, 1988.

Herrmann, Robert and John Marks Templeton. *Is God the Only Reality?* New York:
    Continuum, 1994.

Kaufmann, William J., III. *Relativity and Cosmology*. 2nd ed. New York: Harper & Row,
    1977.

Kitcher, Philip. *Abusing Science: The Case Against Creationism*. Cambridge: MIT Press,
    1982.

Margenau, Henry and Roy Abraham Varghese, eds. *Cosmos, Bios, Theos*. La Salle: Open
    Court, 1992.

May, Gerhard. *Creatio Ex Nihilo: The Doctrine of Creation out of Nothing in Early
    Christian Thought*, ET A.S. Worral. Edinburgh: T. & T. Clark, 1995.

Morris, Henry M., ed. (Institute for Creation Research). *Scientific Creationism*. 2nd ed. El
    Cajon: Master Books, 1985.

Peacocke, Arthur. *Creation and the World of Science*. Oxford and New York: Oxford
    University Press, 1979.

Peters, Ted. *Cosmos As Creation*. Nashville: Abingdon, 1989.

Polkinghorne, John. *Science and Creation: The Search for Understanding*. Boston: New
    Science Library, 1989.

Ruether, Rosemary. *Gaia and God*. San Francisco: HarperSanFrancisco, 1989.

Russell, Robert John, Nancey Murphy, and C.J. Isham, eds. *Quantum Cosmology and the*

Laws of Nature: Scientific Perspectives on Divine Action. Vatican City State: Vatican Observatory and Berkeley: Center for Theology and Natural Sciences, 1993.

Scientific American. *Cosmology + 1: Readings from Scientific American.* San Francisco: W.H. Freeman, 1977.

Tracy, David and Nicholas Lash, eds. *Cosmology and Theology*, Concilium 166 (6/1983). New York: Seabury, 1983.

Trefil, James S. *The Moment of Creation: Big Bang Physics from before the First Millisecond to the Present Universe.* New York: Scribner, 1983.

Van Til, Howard. *The Fourth Day.* Grand Rapids: Eerdmans, 1989.

, Robert E. Snow, John H. Stek, and Davis A. Young. *Portraits of Creation: Biblical and Scientific Perspectives on the World s Formation.* Grand Rapids: Eerdmans, 1990.

Weinberg, Steven. *The First Three Minutes: A Modern View of the Origin of the Universe.* 2nd ed. New York: Harper, 1993.

3.2 Chaos Theory and Divine Action

Abraham, Ralph H. and Christopher D. Shaw. *Dynamics: The Geometry of Behavior.* 2nd ed. Redwood City, CA: Addison-Wesley, 1992.

Bartholomew, D. J. *God of Chance.* London: SCM Press, 1984.

Crain, Steven Dale. *Divine Action and Indeterminism: On Models of Divine Action that Exploit the New Physics.* Notre Dame: University of Notre Dame, Dissertation, 1993.

Crutchfield, James P., J. Doyne Farmer, Norman H. Packard, and Robert S. Shaw. Chaos. *Scientific American* 255 (December, 1986), pp. 46—57.

Davies, Paul. *The Cosmic Blueprint: New Discoveries in Nature s Creative Ability to Order the Universe.* New York: Simon & Schuster, 1988.

, and John Gribbin. *The Matter Myth: Dramatic Discoveries the Challenge Our Understanding of Physical Reality.* New York: Simon & Schuster, 1992.

Devaney, Robert L. *An Introduction to Chaotic Dynamical Systems.* 2nd ed. Redwood City, CA: Addison-Wesley, 1989.

Ford, Joseph. How Random is a Coin Toss? *Physics Today* (April, 1983), pp. 40—47.

Gleick, James. *Chaos: Making a New Science.* New York: Penguin Books, 1987.

Gregersen, Niels Henrik. Providence in an Indeterministic World. *CTNS Bulletin* 14/1 (Winter, 1994).

Griffin, David R., ed. *The Reenchantment of Science: Postmodern Proposals.* Albany: State University of New York Press, 1989.

Hefner, Philip. God and Chaos: The Demiurge Versus the Ungrund. *Zygon* 19/4 (December, 1984), pp. 469—485.

Holte, John, ed. *Chaos: The New Science.* Nobel Conference XXVI. Lanham: University Press of America, 1993.

Horgan, John. In the Beginning. . . . *Scientific American* (February, 1991), pp. 117—125.

Houghton, John T. *Does God Play Dice?* Leicester: IVP, 1988.

Kadanoff, Leo P. Roads to Chaos. *Physics Today* (December, 1983), pp. 46—53.

Kellert, Stephen H. *In the Wake of Chaos: Unpredictable Order in Dynamical Systems.* Science and Its Conceptual Problems Series, David L. Hull, Gen. Ed. Chicago: University of Chicago Press, 1993.

Krohn, Wolfgang, Gunter Kuppers, and Helga Noworty, eds., *Selforganization: Portrait of a Scientific Revolution*, pp. 51—63. Dordrecht, The Hague, and Boston: Kluwer Academic Publishers, 1990.

Lewin, Roger. *Complexity: Life at the Edge of Chaos*. New York: MacMillan, 1992.

MacKay, Donald M. *Science, Chance and Providence*. Oxford and New York: Oxford University Press, 1978.

Peitgen, Heinz-Otto, Hartmut J rgens, and Dietmar Saupe. *Chaos and Fractals: New Frontiers of Science*. New York, Berlin and London: Springer-Verlag, 1992.

Polkinghorne, John. *Science and Providence: God s Interaction with the World*. Boston: Shambhala, 1989.

Prigogine, Ilya and Isabelle Stengers. *Order out of Chaos*. New York, Bantam Books, 1984.

Russell, Robert John, Nancey Murphy, and Arthur Peacocke, eds. *Chaos and Complexity*. Vatican City State: Vatican Observatory and Berkeley: Center for Theology and Natural Sciences, 1995.

Stewart, Ian. *Does God Play Dice?* Oxford and New York: Basil Blackwell, 1989.

Thomas, Owen. *God s Activity in the World: A Contemporary Problem*. Chico: Scholars Press, 1983.

Tracy, Thomas F. *God, Action, and Embodiment*. Grand Rapids: Eerdmans, 1984.

Ward, Keith. *Divine Action*. London: Harper Collins, 1990.

Wiles, Maurice F. *God s Action in the World*. London: SCM Press, 1986.

3.3 Quantum Complementarity and Christology

Austin, William H. *Waves, Particles, and Paradoxes*, Rice University Studies 53. Houston: Rice University Press, 1967.

Bell, J.S. *Speakable and Unspeakable in Quantum Mechanics*. Cambridge and New York: Cambridge University Press, 1987.

Bohr, Niels. *Atomic Theory and the Description of Nature*. Cambridge and New York: Cambridge University Press, 1934.

Bunge, Mario. Analogy in Quantum Theory: From Insight to Nonsense. *British Journal for the Philosophy of Science* 18 (1967), pp. 265—286.

Heisenberg, Werner. *Physics and Beyond: Encounters and Conversations*. New York: Harper & Row, 1971.

Herbert, Nick. *Quantum Reality: Beyond the New Physics*. Garden City: Doubleday, 1985.

Hofstadter, Douglas R. *Goedel, Escher, Bach: An Eternal Golden Braid*. New York: Vintage, 1980.

Jammer, Max. *The Philosophy of Quantum Mechanics*. New York: John Wiley & Sons, Inc., 1974.

Kaiser, Christopher. Christology and Complementarity. *Religious Studies* 12 (1976), pp. 37—48.

Loder, James E. and W. Jim Neidhardt. *The Knight s Move, The Relational Logic of the Spirit in Theology and Science*. Colorado Springs: Helmers & Howard, 1992.

Torrance, Thomas. *Transformation and Convergence in the Frame of Knowledge*. Grand Rapids: Eerdmans, 1984.

3.4 Information Theory and Special Revelation

Bowker, John. *The Religious Imagination and the Sense of God*. Oxford: Clarendon, 1978.
  . *The Sense of God: Sociological, Anthropological and Psychological Approaches to the Origin of the Sense of God*. Oxford: Clarendon, 1973.

Shannon, Claude E. and W. Weaver. *The Mathematical Theory of Information*. Urbana: University of Illinois Press, 1949.

Wassermann, C., R. Kirby, and B. Rordoff, eds. *The Science and Theology of Information*. European Conference on Science and Theology. Geneva: Labor et Fides, 1992.

Zurek, W. H., ed. *Complexity, Entropy, and the Physics of Information*. Redwood City, CA: Addison-Wesley, 1990.

3.5 Molecular Biology and Human Freedom

Birch, Charles and John B. Cobb, Jr. *The Liberation of Life: From the Cell to the Community*. Cambridge and New York: Cambridge University Press, 1981.

Churchland, Paul M. *Matter and Consciousness*. Cambridge: MIT Press, 1984.

Churchland, Patricia Smith. *Neurophilosophy: Toward a Unified Science of the Mind/Brain*. Cambridge: Massachusetts Institute of Technology, 1986.

Crick, Francis. *An Astonishing Hypothesis: The Scientific Search for the Soul*. New York: Scribner, 1994.

Davidson, Donald. *Essays on Actions and Events*. Oxford and New York: Oxford University Press, 1980.

Dennett, Daniel. *Consciousness Explained*. Boston: Little, Brown and Co., 1991.
  . *Elbow Room:Varieties of Freewill Worth Wanting*. Cambridge: MIT Press, 1984.

Eaves, Lindon. Exploring the Concept of Spirit as a Model for the God-World Relationship in an Age of Genetics. *Zygon* 27/3 (September, 1992), pp. 261—275.

Eccles, Sir John. *The Wonder of Being Human: Our Brain and Our Mind*. New York: The Free Press, 1984.

Farrer, Austin. *The Freedom of the Will*. London: Adam and Charles Black, 1958.

Hampshire, Stuart. *Thought and Action*. 2nd ed. Notre Dame: University of Notre Dame Press, 1983.
  . *Freedom of the Individual*. Princeton, Princeton University Press, 1975.

Humphrey, Nicholas. *A History of the Mind: Evolution and the Birth of Consciousness*. New York: Simon & Schuster, 1992.

Leakey, Richard E. *The Origin of Humankind*. New York: Basic Books, 1994.

MacKay, Donald M. *Behind the Eye*. Oxford and New York: Basil Blackwell, 1991.

Monod, Jacques. *Chance and Necessity*. New York: Random House, 1972.

Peacocke, Arthur. *God and the New Biology*. London: Dent, 1986.

Searle, John. *Minds, Brains and Science*. Cambridge: Harvard University Press, 1984.
  . *The Rediscovery of the Mind*. Cambridge: MIT Press, 1992.

Sperry, Roger. *Science and Moral Priority: Merging Mind, Brain, and Human Values*. New York: Columbia University Press, 1983.
  . Mind-brain Interaction: Mentalism, Yes; Dualism, No. *Neuroscience* 5, pp. 195—206.

Strawson, Peter. Freedom and Resentment. *Proceedings of the British Academy* 48 (1962), pp. 1—25.

Teilhard de Chardin, Pierre. *The Phenomenon of Man*. New York: Harper, 1959.

Wallace, Robert. *Biology: The World of Life*. 4th ed. Pacific Palisades: Goodyear Publishing, 1975.

3.6 Social Genetics and Religious Ethics

Alexander, Richard D. *The Biology of Moral Systems*. New York: Aldine De Gruyter, 1987.

Bannister, Robert C. *Social Darwinism: Science and Myth in Anglo-American Social Thought*. Philadelphia: Temple University Press, 1979.

Boyd, Robert and Peter J. Richerson. *Culture and the Evolutionary Process*. Chicago: University of Chicago Press, 1985.

Burhoe, Ralph Wendell. *Toward a Scientific Theology*. Belfast: Christian Journalism Limited, 1981.

, and Solomon Katz. War, Peace, and Religion s BioCultural Evolution. *Zygon* 21/4 (December, 1986), pp. 439—472.

Campbell, Donald. The Conflict Between Social and Biological Evolution and the Concept of Original Sin. *Zygon* 10/3 (September, 1975), pp. 234—249.

Dawkins, Richard. *The Selfish Gene*. 2nd ed. Oxford and New York: Oxford University Press, 1989.

Durham, William H. *Coevolution: Genes, Culture and Human Diversity*. Stanford: Stanford University Press, 1991.

Gans, Eric. *Science and Faith: The Anthropology of Revelation*. Savage: Rowan & Littlefield, 1990.

Hefner, Philip. *The Human Factor*. Minneapolis: Fortress, 1993.

Hofstadter, Richard. *Social Darwinism in American Thought*. 2nd ed. Boston: Beacon, 1955.

Irons, Willliam. How Did Morality Evolve? Zygon 26/1 (March, 1991): pp. 49—90.

Ruse, Michael. *Taking Darwin Seriously: A Naturalistic Approach to Philosophy*. Oxford and New York: Basil Blackwell, 1986.

Scientific American. *Recombinant DNA*. 2nd ed. New York: Scientific American Books, 1992.

Theissen, Gerd. *Biblical Faith: An Evolutionary Approach*. Minneapolis: Fortress, 1985.

Wilson, Edward O. *On Human Nature*. Cambridge: Harvard University Press, 1978.

. *Sociobiology: The New Synthesis*. Cambridge: Harvard University Press, 1975.

Zygon 19/2 (June, 1984), articles on sociobiology by Reiss, Singer, Rottschaefer and Martinsen, Peacocke, Baelz, and Hefner.

IV. ETHICAL ISSUES IN SCIENCE AND RELIGION

4.1 Environment and Ethics

Barbour, Ian G. *Ethics in an Age of Technology*. San Francisco: HarperSanFrancisco, 1993.

. *Technology, Environment, and Human Values*. New York: Praeger, 1980.

Cobb, John B., Jr. *Sustainability: Economics, Ecology, and Justice*. Maryknoll: Orbis, 1992.

Cooper, Barry. *Action Into Nature: An Essay on the Meaning of Technology*. Notre Dame: University of Notre Dame Press, 1991.

Daly, Herman E. and John B. Cobb, Jr. *For the Common Good: Redirecting the Economy Toward Community, the Environment, and a Sustainable Future*. Boston: Beacon, 1989.

Diamond, Irene; Gloria F. Orenstein, eds. *Reweaving the World: The Emergence of Ecofeminism*. San Francisco: Sierra Club Books, 1990.

Gore, Al. *Earth in the Balance: Ecology and the Human Spirit*. Boston: Houghton Mifflin, 1992.

Haught, John. *The Promise of Nature*. New York, Paulist: 1993.

Joranson, Philip N. and Ken Butigan, eds. *The Cry of the Environment*. Santa Fe: Bear and Co., 1984.

Nash, James. *Loving Nature: Ecological Integrity and Christian Responsibility*. Nashville: Abingdon, 1991.

Norgaard, Richard. *Development Betrayed: The End of Progress and a Co-evolutionary Revisioning of the Future*. London and New York: Routledge, 1994.

Oeschlaeger, Max. *Caring For Creation: An Ecumenical Approach to the Environmental Crisis*. New Haven: Yale University Press, 1994.

Primavesi, Anne. *From Apocalypse to Genesis*. Minneapolis: Fortress, 1991.

Rolston, Holmes, III. *Environmental Ethics: Duties to and in the Natural World*. Philadelphia: Temple University Press, 1988.

———. *Philosophy Gone Wild*. Buffalo: Prometheus, 1989.

Vandana, Shiva. *Staying Alive: Women, Ecology and Development*. Atlantic Highlands: Zed Books, 1989.

4.2 Genetics and Ethics

Bishop, J.A. and L.M. Cook, eds. *Genetic Consequences of Man Made Change*. London: Academic Press, 1981.

Bouma, Hessel, III, *et. al.*, eds. (Calvin Center for Christian Scholarship). *Christian Faith, Health, and Medical Practice*. Grand Rapids: Eerdmans, 1989.

Cole-Turner, Ron. *The New Genesis: Theology and the Genetic Revolution*. Louisville: Westminster/John Knox, 1993.

Harding, Sandra. *Whose Science? Whose Knowledge?* Cornell: Cornell University Press, 1991.

Kevles, Daniel K. *In the Name of Eugenics*. New York: Knopf, 1985.

Lammers, Stephen and Ted Peters. Genethics. *CTNS Bulletin* 11/4 (Fall, 1991).

Lammers, Stephen and Allen Verhey, eds. *On Moral Medicine: Theological Perspectives in Medical Ethics*. Grand Rapids: Eerdmans, 1987.

Longino, Helen. *Science as Social Knowledge: Values and Objectivity in Scientific Inquiry*. Princeton, Princeton University Press, 1990.

Mahoney, John. *Bioethics and Belief*. London: Sheed and Ward, 1984.

Meilaender, Gilbert C. *Body, Soul, and Bioethics*. Notre Dame: University of Notre Dame Press, 1991.

Reich, Warren Thomas, ed. *Encyclopedia of Bio-Ethics*. 2nd Edition. New York: Macmillan, 1995.

Shannon, Thomas. *Major Modern Biological Possibilities and Problems*. New York: Paulist, 1994.

Sherwin, Susan. *No Longer Patient: Feminist Ethics and Health Care*. Philadelphia: Temple University Press, 1992.

Shinn, Roger. *Forced Options*. Cleveland: Pilgrim Press, 1991.

Suzuki, David; Peter Knudtson. *Genethics*. Cambridge: Harvard University Press, 1990.

Weil, Vivian. *Biotechnology*. New Haven: Yale University Press, 1986.

Wheale, Peter R., and Ruth M. McNally. *Genetic Engineering: Catastrophe or Utopia*. Hemel Hampstead: Harvester, 1988.

V. OTHER BOOKS

Barbour, Ian G. *Issues in Science and Religion*. Englewood Cliffs: Prentice-Hall, 1966.

———. *Religion in an Age of Science*. San Francisco: HarperSanFrancisco, 1990.

Barr, James. *Biblical Faith and Natural Theology*. Oxford: Clarendon Press, 1993.

Birch, Charles. *A Purpose for Everything: Religion in a Postmodern Worldview*. Mystic: Twenty-Third Publications, 1990.

Burrell, David. *Freedom and Creation in Three Traditions*. Notre Dame: University of Notre Dame Press, 1993.

Collingwood, R.G. *The Idea of Nature*. London and New York: Oxford University Press, 1945.

Daly, Gabriel. *Creation and Redemption*. Wilmington: Michael Glazier, 1989.

Davies, Paul. *God and the New Physics*. New York: Penguin, 1984.

———, ed. *The New Physics*. Cambridge and New York: Cambridge University Press, 1989.

Glacken, Clarence J. *Traces on the Rhodean Shore: Nature and Culture in Western Thought from Ancient Times to the End of the Eighteenth Century*. Berkeley: University of California Press, 1967.

Hardy, Sir Alister Clavering. *The Spiritual Nature of Man: A Study of Contemporary Religious Experience*. Oxford: Clarendon Press, 1979.

Hendry, George. *The Theology of Nature*. Philadelphia: Westminster Press, 1980.

Laszlo, Ervin. *Evolution: The Grand Synthesis*. Boston: New Science Library, 1987.

Merchant, Carolyn. *The Death of Nature: Women, Ecology, and The Scientific Revolution*. New York: Harper & Row, 1980.

Nasr, Seyyed Hossein. *Man and Nature: The Spiritual Crisis in Modern Man*. London: Unwin Paperbacks, 1968.

Pannenberg, Wolfhart. *Toward a Theology of Nature: Essays on Science and Faith*. Philadelphia: Westminster/John Knox, 1993.

Peacocke, Arthur. *Theology for a Scientific Age: Being and Becoming Divine and Human*. 2nd ed. Minneapolis: Fortress, 1993.

Russell, Robert John, William R. Stoeger, and George V. Coyne, eds. *Physics, Philosophy and Theology: A Common Quest for Understanding*. Vatican City State: Vatican Observatory, 1988.

Toulmin, Stephen. *The Return to Cosmology: Postmodern Science and the Theology of Nature*. Berkeley, University of California Press, 1982.

APPENDIX B

CONTRIBUTORS

Ian G. Barbour: Winifred and Atherton Bean Professor of Science, Technology and Society, and Professor of Religion Emeritus, Carleton College, Minnesota.

John Hedley Brooke: Professor of the History of Science, The University of Lancaster.

Philip Clayton: Associate Professor of Philosophy, California State University, Sonoma.

R. David Cole: Professor Emeritus of Molecular and Cell Biology, The University of California at Berkeley.

Mary Gerhart: Professor of Religious Studies, Hobart and William Smith Colleges, Geneva, New York.

Philip Hefner: Professor of Systematic Theology, Lutheran School of Theology at Chicago; Co-Director of the Chicago Center for Religion and Science; Editor of *Zygon: Journal of Religion and Science.*

William Irons: Professor of Anthropology, Northwestern University, Illinois.

Christopher B. Kaiser: Professor of Historical and Systematic Theology, Western Theological Seminary, Michigan.

Steven Knapp: Professor of English and Dean of the School of Arts and Sciences, Johns Hopkins University, Maryland.

James E. Loder: Mary D. Synnott Professor of the Philosophy of Education, Princeton Theological Seminary.

Edward MacKinnon: Professor of Philosophy, California State University, Hayward.

Nancey Murphy: Associate Professor of Christian Philosophy, Fuller Theological Seminary, California.

W. Jim Neidhardt: the late Associate Professor of Physics, New Jersey Institute of Technology.

Arthur Peacocke: Director of the Ian Ramsey Centre, Oxford, and Warden Emeritus of the Society of Ordained Scientists.

John Polkinghorne: President, Queens College, Cambridge University; formerly Professor of Mathematical Physics, Cambridge University.

John C. Puddefoot: Head of Mathematics, Eton College, Windsor.

W. Mark Richardson: Assistant Professor of Philosophical Theology in Residence, the Graduate Theological Union, Berkeley.

Holmes Rolston, III: University Distinguished Professor of Philosophy, Colorado State University.

Allan Melvin Russell: Professor of Physics, Hobart and William Smith Colleges, Geneva, New York.

Robert John Russell: Professor of Theology and Science in Residence, the Graduate Theological Union, Berkeley; and Founder and Director of The Center for Theology and the Natural Sciences.

William R. Stoeger, SJ: Staff Astrophysicist, the Vatican Observatory, and Adjunct Professor of Astronomy, The University of Arizona, Tucson.

Claude Welch: Dean Emeritus and Professor of Historical Theology, the Graduate Theological Union, Berkeley.

Wesley J. Wildman: Assistant Professor of Theology, Boston University.

Nicholas Wolterstorff: Noah Porter Professor of Philosophical Theology, Yale University.

Karl Young: Scientist at the Stanford Linear Accelerator, California.

NAME INDEX